WHY CONTROL
YOUR
IMAGINATION?

WHY CONTROL YOUR IMAGINATION?

How Psychologists Can (Re)Discover Their Souls

Frederick Bauer

Author of *The Essence of Ethics*

iUniverse, Inc.
Bloomington

WHY CONTROL YOUR IMAGINATION?
How Psychologists Can (Re)Discover Their Souls

iUniverse books may be ordered through booksellers or by contacting:

iUniverse
1663 Liberty Drive
Bloomington, IN 47403
www.iuniverse.com
1-800-Authors (1-800-288-4677)

ISBN: 978-1-4759-0802-2 (sc)
ISBN: 978-1-4759-0803-9 (ebk)

Printed in the United States of America

iUniverse rev. date: 04/16/2012

To the Memory of William James

Who wanted science, but also religion

CONTENTS

CHAPTER FOUR: ALTRUISM WITHOUT A HOOK

Role Model: Saint Therese Martin

CHAPTER FIVE: THE PINNACLE

APPENDIX

DETAILED CONTENTS

CHAPTER FIVE: THE PINNACLE

APPENDIX: Further Footnote Weaving

PRELUDE

The focus. The focus of this book is on thought. On human knowledge. On understanding. On our ability to think, to know, and/or to understand. On all of those things. Collectively, they are what makes us humans different from any other creature on Planet Earth.

Radically different.

We can ask questions. More than that, we can understand questions. We can ask, "Does God exist?", a question no beliefless chimp or unthinking parrot can begin to understand.

If you are of the opinion that beasts can think and that we humans are only a bit more intelligent because our brains are only a bit more complex than the brains of Washoe the chimp or Koko the gorilla, then think of this book as an aid to better thinking, as an instruction for reflective self-knowledge, as a kind of food for thought, so that you can understand that you do something no other inhabitant of Planet Earth can do, understand.

Some history. The original draft of this book was written between 1992 and 1994. It was a follow-up to a much longer unpublished manuscript entitled *Will You Control Your Imagination?* That longer text's subject was human thought also, one facet of which we call "imagination." The title was an invitation to think about what really exists, in contrast to merely imagining what doesn't.

While planning this follow-up, I decided to highlight morality as well as thought, especially the connection between understanding and motivation. That's because understanding is at the core of motivation which is the essence of moral goodness. Being capable of understanding and of genuine morality and immorality makes us radically distinct from chimps, gorillas, bonobos, and every other creature on this planet, none of which are capable of either.

At no time in history, perhaps, has there been a greater need to understand the nature of thought and/or understanding and morality than the present. And who but those regarded as psychologists should be experts in such understanding? Yet, as the pages that follow will explain, today's 'scientific' psychologists deliberately blind themselves to the only evidence available for such expert understanding, namely, their own personal experience!

A comment that William James made near the end of his illustrious career must be the watchword for all that follows: "To know what the word 'illation' means one must once have sweated through some particular argument." An illation or argument is a piece of logical reasoning, and only people who are personally capable of reasoning from a premise or premises—i.e., a complete thought or thoughts—to a conclusion will ever know what reasoning is. Or thinking. Or understanding. Nevertheless, so-called 'scientific' or 'empirical' psychology during much of the twentieth-century was dominated by thinkers who thought they could train themselves to do the impossible, that is, to never appeal to their private, conscious experience. *Science, so the myth goes, must be based on facts that are objective and public. One's own psychological experience is subjective and private.*

That blunder will be critiqued in detail throughout the chapters of this book.

Learning the truth about experience, especially the experience of thinking and making moral decisions, should prompt a realization that certain obligations flow from it. This book will explain the connection between that knowledge and those obligations.

Perhaps "explain" is not the most appropriate word for what this book does. To repeat the above, it might be more accurate to describe it as a lengthy, meditative "reflection" on knowledge, obligations, and their connection.

Some comments. There are certain features of the text that call for comment.

For one thing, there is too much use of capital letters, boldface print, italicization, and scare quotes. Originally, there was also too much underlining. I have tried to remove all of the underlining and many of the other formatting devices. But to remove *all* the distracting features would have demanded too much time. For that, I must beg your forbearance.

Also, many citations from the writings of other authors appear without page numbers. Why? Because the full significance of such snippets can be gotten only by reading larger portions of the original texts.

Unfortunately, some of the originals are available only from from Abebooks, Amazon, or other on-line sources of out-of-print works. Nevertheless, many of those older works are more helpful than the writings of younger psychologists. The reason is simple. Before the twentieth century, what was called "psychology" was viewed as part of philosophy. Older psychologists were more informed about the original separation of psychology from philosophy and therefore about the philosophical controversies surrounding their theories. Consequently, whereas older works usually do make reference to those 'philosophical controversies,' today's psychologists rarely bother with them. Already in 1959, one of the older psychologists, Gordon Allport, referred to the difference:

> Picking up a recent number of the *Journal of Abnormal and Social Psychology*, I discover that the twenty-one articles written by American psychologists confine 90% of their references to publications of the past ten years, although most of the problems they investigate have gray beards. In the same issue of the *Journal*, three European authors locate 50% of their references prior to 1949. What this proves I don't know, except that European authors weren't born yesterday . . . A recent undergraduate said that all he knew about Thomas Hobbes was that he sank with the Leviathan when it hit an iceberg in 1912. ("The Open System in Personality," in H. Ruitenbeek, *Varieties of Personality Theory*.)

Here is a footnote to the preceding thought. Try to get in the habit of doing what the early 'scientific' psychologists did, namely, the habit of distinguishing the psychic from the physical. When William James composed his great masterpiece, *The Principles of Psychology*, he used what is described as a "dualist" framework. He assumed that all of his readers would know immediately what he meant by "brain." It is the most important part of what everyone thinks "your body" refers to. But when James describes thought, sensation, memory, etc., he is referring to something *distinct from*, something *more than*, what occurs in the body's brain. Once you fully appreciate the 'something' that is distinct from and more than the brain or anything else, you will also appreciate George Berkeley's claim that perhaps there is no dualism. But what that will mean in Berkeley's case is *not* that there may not be thought, sensation, the mind. "There is no dualism" will mean that there may not be any brain, body, or anything else that is physical or material.

And a 'Nota bene.' That previous 'footnote' should be regarded as almost the centerpiece of this book. Rene Descartes is, in one sense, the most important thinker in recent history. He certainly is the most revolutionary. That is because he inaugurated the process of using modern discoveries—nowadays collected under the umbrella name, "science"—to show how those modern discoveries prove the existence of God.

At the present time, however, there are many people who believe—mistakenly—that modern 'science' has exposed the real or 'true' nature of belief in God, namely, that it is nothing but prescientific superstition. An excellent, first-hand description of that type of mistaken thinking is given by Kenneth Miller in his *Finding Darwin's God*. Miller, a Catholic who teaches biology at Brown University, describes the 'godlessness' of smart, well-educated, sophisticated academics as 'pervasive.'

As for the soul, the empirical or scientific psychology pioneered by Wilhelm Wundt, William James, and others, was intended to be a science of conscious experience, period. Carl Jung commented, in *Modern Man in Search of a Soul*, that "it was left for the second half of the nineteenth century to develop a 'psychology without a soul'." Richard Watson, admiring author of a recent biography of Descartes, argued for the diametrical opposite of this book's subtitle. At the end of *Cogito, Ergo Sum*, Watson predicted:

> In the twenty-first century, this is how the last battle for the human soul will go. Materialists will discover more and more about how the brain works. Mentalists will never be able to show how an independent mind works. One day,

one hundred, two hundred years down the line, everyone will finally realize that the materialists have won and that the mentalists have lost this last battle for the human soul. When humankind finally faces the fact that the mind is the brain, that there is no independently existing mental soul to survive the death of the body, that none of us chirpy sparrows is immortal, when Descartes's ghost in the machine finally fades away and his animal machine is triumphant, then there will be a revolution in human thought the like of which none has gone before. (R. Watson, *Cogito, Ergo Sum*, p.327)

Were Descartes able to return and read that declaration, he would immediately sit down and write a book filled with *arguments* or illations similar to those you will find in the following chapters and pages . . . in order to show how *unscientific* are the claims of the academics and Watson.

OUTLINE

Chapter One, titled "I understand" (or "Intelligo" in Latin) should take precedence over Descartes' "I think." The connotation of "understand" makes it a more profound concept than mere "thinking." Chapter One is an exercise in 'consciousness raising.' QU: Consciousness of what? AN: Consciousness of that which is unique about us human beings: we understand. We think. We understand thoughts. And we are free. We are free to adopt different attitudes regarding the thoughts we understand: we can assent to them, or we can reject them, or we can suspend judgment on them. Above all we can switch from one of these attitudes to another regarding individual thoughts. That is, we can re-think our current beliefs. And we can understand what we're doing!

Chapter Two, titled "I see something, therefore I am" (or "Video, ergo sum" in Latin), draws the distinction between naive-realism and representationalism. It makes a case for the latter and thus against the former. Naive realism is the basic outlook of so-called 'scientific' psychologists, e.g., Burrhus Frederick Skinner. The contrast between naive-realism and modern representationalism is brought out by comparing Skinner to Carl Rogers. The chapter includes a discussion of theoretical constructs, also known as pragmatic or logical fictions.

Chapter Three, "Self-Interested Altruism," is about the nature of the human self, the self that is the desired beneficiary of self-interested decisions. Plato and, after him, Descartes and Berkeley, concluded that we humans are immaterial conscious beings or souls, living either with or without a material body. We selves or souls are moral—or immoral—agents capable of acting in our own interest or in the interests of others. Thinking and/or believing is the absolute prerequisite for morality, i.e., for morally right or wrong decisions, i.e., for the exercise of free will. For that reason, this chapter further explores the nature of thinking, and especially the moral obligation to seek and believe true thoughts. It ends with two related facts: each of us is a unique individual being, and all group concepts are fictions created by our imaginations.

Chapter Four, "Altruism Without a Hook," focuses on the concept of "motive." Having stressed the difference between one's self and all other selves, it is easy to understand the difference between self-interest and altruism: whose pleasures and pains are of concern, one's own or those of others? William James' pluralism reinforces this insight. The chapter ends with a thought-experiment regarding God's plan for us humans. A postscript ties the chapter focus with Christian morality.

Chapter Five weaves together the ideas related to the various facets of each of our selves, facets examined in the preceding chapters, and draws lessons from or related to each.

The Appendix can be called a variety of things. One reader suggests calling it "Chapter Six." But the concepts of both appendices and chapters are fictions. Things are what they are, regardless of what we call them. James composed more than one appendix, most likely for the reason this one is added here: he, like this author, always had more things to say, even if the 'more' was another way of saying what's already been said. Because the entire book can be considered "matter for reflection," the appendix too is more matter for reflection.

CHAPTER ONE

Intelligo

(I understand)

Does God exist? In the just-ended century, most people believed the answer is "Yes." In the same century, however, more people than in any earlier ones believed the answer is "No." Some of those believers were convinced they could prove that God exists. Other non-believing believers were convinced they could prove just the opposite.

Each of those believers had a name. We know some of them. We know, moreover, that some of them changed their mind. Without changing their name. Jean Paul Sartre grew up believing in God. He quit for good. Dorothy Day started by believing, sort of. Then she quit believing, sort of. Finally, she restarted and never quit. Simone Weil grew up believing there is no God. She later started believing there is and never stopped. One thing all three had in common was that "Does God exist?" became an explicit question for them only gradually, in the course of their learning. Once it did, though, their answer to it became fundamental to their understanding of everything else. To understanding the meaning of life. And the struggle between good and evil. And the meaning of death which, at first sight, brings to an end the time for struggling with the God-question as well as with good and evil and with the meaning of death.

As, at first sight, it will for each one of us. No matter what our name is. (You do understand?)

1

A Role Model: Socrates. Socrates, like William James, never stopped rethinking things. If Plato is to be believed, he was willing to rethink his belief in immortality in the waning hours of his life. His readiness to rethink such questions, coupled with his readiness to admit his ignorance—"I do not think I know what I don't know"—makes it easy for unwary minds to conclude that his mind was so open that it had never locked onto any firm convictions. But, besides his firm conviction that whoever lives without rethinking things is living a life unworthy of anyone mature enough to rethink, the actions of his life testified to an entire host of convictions. Foremost was his insistence that doing what we believe is wrong is worse than dying as a result of others' wrong-doing. His serenity in the hours before he voluntarily imbibed the hemlock came from that conviction. His mature-age shift from natural-science to moral-science issues showed his tacit realization that how well we relate to others here below is more important than how well we understand what's going on in the skies overhead. Behind everything, though, stood his firm commitment to thinking well. Especially about thinking. In this, he was Plato's model.

Chapter Preview. This opening chapter creates the framework for those that follow. It is about thinking. And rethinking. The intention is to open a path from your current way of looking at the world to alternative points of view. Or, if you have already learned about one or other alternative, to tell why it is important to learn the paths that connect all possible alternatives. The final aim is to lay out directions to the peak where it becomes clear that, whatever our viewpoint, we need imagery but also need to understand that understanding is something beyond experiencing imagery. The peak will be reached only when it becomes clear how the two needs converge while we understand the distinction between looking at images and understanding the thoughts that accompany the looking. After that, it will not be particularly difficult to rethink whatever was not rethought on the way to the pinnacle.

Or perhaps it is better to think of this opening chapter as a way to learn, first-hand, what James meant when he wrote, "To know what the word 'illation' means one must once have sweated through some particular argument." Once you have read what follows and then reread it to notice the reasoning you had to do while reading it, you will have a first-hand experience of what "illationS" in the very-plural plural sense means.

A. Meaning: The Problem.

Three Thinkers. "Cogito, ergo sum." I think, therefore I am. Surely one of the most famous statements of all time, by the most revolutionary thinker of all time. Its author, RENE DESCARTES (1596-1650), was a well-known mathematician and scientist. And a philosopher. According to many, the father of modern philosophy, because they think "I think" sums up modern philosophy's central concern. Descartes' statement comes from his *Discourse on Method*. Its full title, "Discourse on the Method of Rightly Conducting One's Reason and for Seeking Truth in the Sciences," is the key to Descartes' life. He wanted truth and wanted to know how to acquire it. By the time he wrote the *Discourse*, he felt confident he had discovered an error-free method for achieving it.

In view of what is to follow, it is also important to notice that his *Discourse* is more than a description of his method. It is also a brief account of his life. It tells of his formal education at one of Europe's best schools. It explains the dissatisfaction he felt at graduation-time when he realized he had learned a lot of facts but had become uncertain about the truth. His mini-autobiography records the turning point in his life, a memorable experience he had on November 10, 1619. Out of that experience grew his grand unified theory, outlined roughly in Part IV of the *Discourse* and later expanded into six *Meditations*. The foundation-stone of that theory, Descartes was convinced, was the single, impregnable certainty: "It is impossible for me to be mistaken when I assent to the thought expressed by 'I think, therefore I exist'."

Two and a half centuries after Descartes' death, WILLIAM JAMES (1842-1910) composed the masterpiece of modern psychology, *The Principles of Psychology*. James' masterpiece should be compared to Isaac Newton's *Mathematical Principles of Natural Philosophy*. In the same way that Newton's synthesis of the best discoveries in physics marked a climactic moment in the subsequent historical development of Descartes' philosophy of nature, James' synthesis of the best discoveries in psychology marked a climactic moment in the subsequent historical development of Descartes' philosophy of mind.

But neither of the developments of Descartes' theories went smoothly. For instance, where Descartes emphasized that there is only one method for achieving certain knowledge in any area, James felt that psychology as a "natural" science had a special 'introspective' method

3

that led him to reject half of the very belief that Descartes regarded as central. Empirical or scientific psychology, James tried to show, must begin by accepting, at least provisionally, that we, the thinkers of our thoughts, do not exist. In Chapter X of his *Principles* James summarized his objections against Descartes' view of the self, that is, against the thing that each of us uses the perpendicular pronoun, "I," for, and declared that psychologists do best to either ignore or to deny the alleged permanent self that is conscious or has consciousness. To readers for whom that seems too bizarre—it amounts to saying that, while consciousness certainly exists, there is no one who is conscious, i.e., there is thinking but no one to do the thinking—James recommended a verbal trick: simply call the latest thought "the thinker" and think of it as appropriating to itself all the thoughts that made up earlier portions of the stream of thought or of consciousness. Naturally, this will eliminate the common-sense meaning of "I think, therefore I am." As for the other half of Descartes central belief, thinking or consciousness, they were so brilliantly described in James' works that his phrase, "The Stream of Consciousness," has become as well known as Descartes' "Cogito."

The ink was barely dry on James' final works when JOHN WATSON (1878-1958) launched a crusade against consciousness. Descartes was absolutely certain that he, the thinker of his thoughts, was essentially a soul distinct from any and every physical body, i.e., merely an angel that has a body. Watson was equally certain that he was an animated organism, that is, an animal or a body that has no soul. James went out of his way to insist on his confidence in the reality of consciousness: "Every one agrees that we there [in our minds] discover states of consciousness. So far as I know, the existence of such states has never been doubted by any critic" (*Principles of Psychology*, vol. I, p.185; hereafter PP I:185). Watson pointed out what had become obvious by 1913: psychologists could no more agree with each other when they looked into their minds than philosophers could agree no matter where they looked.

According to Watson, psychology will achieve full status as a science only when consensus is reached, and consensus will be reached only when researchers admit that "consciousness" is a secular disguise for the religious "soul" and, in imitation of other natural sciences, focus on what can be seen: how people behave when we look at them.

Holding that psychologists should adopt the view that people are not conscious sounds too bizarre—it amounts to saying that it is possible to discover what makes people tick by pretending they are unconscious, feedback-equipped response-makers—so Watson employed his own verbal trick: simply double-name behavior or bodily responses and call it, now "behavior," now "consciousness." He couldn't have made his meaning clearer: "Speaking overtly or to ourselves (thinking) is just as objective a type of behavior as baseball," he wrote.

Three Revolutions: Put those three thinkers into the context of Western history and what do we see? In each case, we notice the same four things: a revolt, a liberation, a hope, and finally a defeat.

First, each inspired a revolution against the prevailing orthodoxy handed down from the past. Descartes' theories challenged the reigning "medieval scholasticism." James' *Principles* were presented as a revolt against both the atomistic sciences and the idealist monisms of the nineteenth century. Under Watson's leadership, American psychologists declared consciousness off-limits or non-existent much of his century.

At the same time, these revolts were (felt to be?) liberating. The bold new approaches rendered obsolete many of the controversies that preoccupied older thinkers. Descartes' astonishingly brief *Meditations*—perhaps one of the shortest books to have had such an enormous impact—walked away from mountains of detailed analyses of matter and form, of substantial change, of the psychological processes of abstraction, and dozens of other problems. But his new program was not without its own problems, and by the time James arrived on the scene, Spinoza, Leibniz, Locke, Berkeley, Hume, Kant, Hegel, and hundreds of other thinkers had created a vast new literature debating those new problems. James' *Principles* are exceptional because, rather than simply walk away from that new literature, he wrote 1400 pages summarizing its essentials and giving reasons for adopting his set of narrow guidelines for doing psychological research without bothering about "philosophical" debates. Watson, in outlining his new set of guidelines for doing psychological research, pointedly refers to the "literally hundreds of thousands of printed pages [which] have been published on the minute analysis of this intangible something called 'consciousness'"—the endless pages which proved to Watson that

James had steered psychology in the wrong direction—and then simply dismisses them as useless by-products of pre-scientific superstition.

Furthermore, each believed—or hoped—he had found the right path, the one that future generations would have to follow in order to reach the truth. Descartes wrote his *Discourse* in the vernacular French so that, by marshalling outside readers behind him, he could pressure establishment intellectuals to pay attention to his new program. Then he tried flattery, dedicating his *Meditations* to leading members of the academic world. A third work, *Principles of Philosophy*, was written as a classroom textbook to teach the true system to coming generations. James was hopeful that the new, scientific psychology was heading in a better direction, and the endless hours he put into the composition of his *Principles* testifies to that hope. When the two volume *Principles* turned out to be too lengthy to be used as a one-course textbook, he condensed it. The condensation's title? *Psychology: Briefer Course.* In the 1930 revision of *Behaviorism*, Watson looked back to his 1912 announcement of the new, "behaviorist," platform for psychology. That platform was born from frustration at seeing psychology bogged down in endless quarreling and from a conviction that the results of applying Pavlov's research method to non-human animals showed it to be a promising way to learn the laws governing human behavior, no more subject to dispute than the strictly objective methods used in medicine, chemistry, and physics. Try this new approach, he concluded, and you will find that your initial doubts gradually dissolve in a "perfectly satisfactory, natural science way." The key phrase for Watson was "natural science," and the key word he associated with it was "progress." All this hope for success seemed reasonable. Why else do writers try to spread the word about their findings?

Finally, each successive revolution failed to create the permanent consensus envisioned by its leader. So widespread is the rejection of Descartes' grand unified theory that the intellectuals who presently subscribe to it are, according to some commentators, "as obsolete as manual typewriters." James' contributions to the divorce of psychology from metaphysics have succeeded in one way, to be sure. So successful has been laboratory psychology's revolt against Descartes' program that it has gone on to achieve an independent niche in American universities, and thousands of psychology majors now graduate every year as learned doctors of psychology without knowing what Descartes' mind-body theory has to do, e.g., with stress problems, without bothering to learn what any "philosopher" ever wrote about anything. On the other hand, most also graduate without bothering to learn much of what James wrote about anything. After the behaviorist revolt, students started to be inaugurated into their psychology programs by studying mice, rats, pigeons, chimps, and so on, so that by learning how to study other animals they could learn the proper method for studying human animals. So successful was Watson's revolution that, by the mid-1900's, textbook after textbook defined psychology as "the scientific study of the behavior of organisms" rather than "the study of states of consciousness as such." But that revolution, too, has run its course and been superseded by the "cognitive revolution." Although the best-known of Watson's acolytes, B.F. Skinner (b.1904), was touted in the 1960's as "the most influential figure in modern psychology," he died in 1990 as "an embattled giant." In that same 1990, Harvard University published J. Bruner's *Acts of Meaning* in which he declared that "psychology, the science of the mind as William James once called it, has become fragmented as never before in its history." His verdict serves as a fitting epitaph to Watson's illusion that, by eliminating consciousness after James had already eliminated the personal soul, psychologists could finally achieve consensus and, thus, consensual validation of their theories.

What does it all mean? Three grand projects and three grand failures. Perhaps the lesson to be learned is that the recent notion that psychology has been converted into a science is an illusion the same way Descartes' hope of making philosophy scientific by the application of a new method was. Some of those who have devoted their lives to psychology have come to that conclusion. Others—keenly aware that today's gullible public puts as much faith in these secular "experts on the mind" as yesterday's put in priestly "experts on the soul"—return daily to their task with renewed urgency.

Rethinking. Pause a moment, step back from the discussion up to this point, and have a second look at what has been going on. By several times repeating the word "revolution," an attempt has been made to steer the reader toward the belief that something extremely important is being discussed. Is that true? In the final summary of human history, will these "revolutions" even be visible?

What does "revolution" actually mean? Mention that word or the word "revolt" to most people, even to well-educated people, and it is highly unlikely that the first thing that will come to mind for them will be thoughts about Descartes, James, or Watson! What is far more likely is that they will immediately think of a political revolution—or an attempt at one—of the type reported on by the 6 o'clock news, e.g., one of the recent revolutions in Eastern Europe. Or, depending upon the country they've grown up in, they're more likely to think of the October Revolution (1917), the French Revolution (1789), the American War of Independence (1776), etc. For most people, political revolutions are the only real or genuine revolutions. Revolutions that take place entirely in the mind would—in the minds of most people—be classified as "metaphorical in the extreme."

Even for thoughtful, well-read persons who regard revolutions in thought as far more interesting than history's record of political-allegiance realignments, it is more likely that the word "revolution" will conjure up Freud's theory of the unconscious, Darwin's theory of evolution, or Copernicus' heliocentric theory, than any of the three referred to above. Or that the title of T. Kuhn's revolution-causing *The Structure of Scientific Revolutions* (1962) will come to their mind, in which case the important revolutions are those that have occurred in biology, chemistry, physics, astronomy, or some other hard science, not the revolutions Kant discussed in the preface to the second edition (1787) of his *Critique of Pure Reason* (1781) or the one documented by B. Baar's *The Cognitive Revolution in Psychology* (1986).

So. What should we think? Were those really three revolutions? Three real revolutions?

Does it matter? Do they matter? And what do they have to do with the problem of meaning, anyway?

Three believers. "Thou art the man!" That statement is not as well-known in this secular age as "I think, therefore I am." But some people believe it should be the better known of the two. They complain that there is a huge gap in American education. The best students can graduate without realizing the important role played by religious ideas in the history of the United States. And without ever reading the Hebrew Bible, the book that has until recently been the source of most Americans' religious ideas. "Thou art the man!" comes from the Bible, specifically from what is called "The Second Book of Samuel." It comes at the end of the story of KING DAVID's adultery and participation in a murder. A courageous chaplain of his, Nathan, decided to confront him with the sinfulness of his royal actions. As a keen student of the human psyche, though, Nathan began his confrontation by setting the king up with a dark tale about a defenseless citizen cruelly robbed by a powerful neighbor. Then, after he had made the king angry enough to demand the criminal's name, Nathan uttered his blunt accusation: "Thou art the man!" David's next act is the exact opposite of the "Might makes right and does violence with high hand" philosophy. It is the act of a true believer: "I have sinned against the Lord." Not just against Uriah. Not merely against society or the body politic. But against God. If some of the Hebrew psalms come, as tradition says they do, from King David's quill, they provide us with a record of what subsequently went on in the depths of that ancient king's soul.

Many centuries later, in the same part of the world, another Jew named Saul set out on a mission to apprehend and bring to justice some of the increasing number of apostates from Jewish orthodoxy. It was a justice that could be as mild as an official rebuke or as extreme as a mob lynching. The story of how Saul went over to the side of those he'd previously regarded as sinful apostates is recorded in *The Acts of the Apostles*. It is a dramatic story of how a man's life was forever changed in a very short period. Again, we don't just have a third-person account of the event. Saul or—as he is usually named—PAUL wrote many *Epistles* which tell all about human sin and divine salvation and how he himself viewed his former life in that context.

In 1940, a learned journal devoted to the study of abnormal psychology published a reported paradigm shift in the thinking of HENRY MURRAY (b.1893). After several years spent in biology, medicine and surgery, and finally biochemical research, Murray turned to psychology. His life was changed forever when he spent a few days with Carl Jung in Zurich. Here are a few lines from his own account of the before and after:

> I can hardly think myself back to the myopia that once
> so seriously restricted my view of human nature, so natural
> has it become for me to receive impressions of wishes, dramas
> and assumptions that underlie the acts and talk of everyone

I meet. Instead of seeing merely a groomed American in a business suit, traveling to and from his office like a rat in a maze, a predatory ambulating apparatus of reflexes, habits, stereotypes, and slogans, a bundle of consistencies, conformities, and allegiances to this or that institution—a robot in other words—I visualize (just as I visualize the activity of his internal organs) a flow of powerful subjective life, conscious and unconscious; a whispering gallery in which voices echo from the distant past; a gulf stream of fantasies with floating memories of past events, currents of contending complexes, plots, and counterplots, hopeful intimations and ideals.

Murray was invited in 1927 to bring the Freudian revolution to the Harvard campus where Watson's revolution would achieve its apex during the tenure of B.F. Skinner.

Three conversions. Each of those three believers underwent a life-changing experience. Each of them turned from one something toward something different. What better word to capture what they underwent than the word "conversion"? Each of them became somewhat different from what they were before. The obvious conclusion? The preceding paragraphs have described three changes, turns, or conversions.

Rethinking. But are those life-changes really the same? Should they be given the same name, "conversion," if they are not the same? For instance, the word "conversion" is defined by one widely used dictionary as "a change from lack of faith to religious belief; adoption of a religion." That gives the term a religious meaning. The term was used quite fittingly by William James as the title for two lectures (IX and X) in *Varieties of Religious Experience*. Above, though, it would only fit the change undergone in the first century by Saul of Tarsus.

But using it to describe how King David came to his senses after allowing lustful passion to momentarily cloud his thinking reduces the idea of something grand to the idea of something trivial. Applying the concept to a purely secular change of mind, as in the case of Henry Murray, dilutes the word's meaning even further, so much further that it becomes almost meaningless. Converting what began as a powerful term for a perfectly clear and distinct thought into a term that can stand even for the conversion of a verb into a noun can indicate only one thing: a writer so careless in the use of words can only be a thinker careless in his thoughts. Did you notice the carelessness?

Noticing such carelessness in a writer is important for a careful reader. Careful thinking is needed for both activities, for both writing and for reading what is written. All of what is written. So, a careful reader will have noticed more than the sloppy use of "conversion."

And what about "believer"? For the average person, "believer" is a religious term the same way "conversion" is. Thus, while it may be appropriate to use "believer" for King David and Apostle Paul, why would anyone call Doctor Murray a believer?

Is the previous use of "believer" a misuse? A slip of the tongue at first, a slip only later noticed? Or was it a deliberate choice from the outset? A careful reader who noticed the same usage in the "QUESTION" at the beginning of this chapter may already have asked that question.

Words & Their MULTIPLE Meanings. So. What should we say? Has there been a misuse of words in what precedes? An attentive reader of a text such as this will begin making a list of questions that need to be answered before assenting to any of the major theses proposed in what follows. One of the most important of those questions will be this:

WHAT VIEW SHOULD GUIDE THIS AUTHOR'S CHOICE OF WORDS?

There are a variety of ways to answer that question. Here is one. The author can either subscribe to Immanuel Kant's rule for vocabulary use or else advocate the Humpty-Dumpty Rule. Which is the right choice between these two rules?

In his majestic *Critique of Pure Reason*, Immanuel Kant (1724-1804) stated one rule for deciding when a science was a genuine science. If later specialists are still using foundations that were laid much earlier, then the science is 'on its way' to completion. He uses this rule to explain why he regards *logic* as having been, from the time of Aristotle on, either a reliable science in its own right or, more properly, a reliable tool for all of the (other) sciences. He uses it to tell why he believes *mathematics* long ago reached the stage of a genuine science. What must have been most convincing to his readers, though, was his reference to the (then) recent case of *natural sciences* which, after thousands of years in the pseudo-scientific garb of astrology and alchemy, had become firmly established as the genuine sciences of physics, chemistry, and biology.

But not, alas, *metaphysics*. This "queen of the disciplines" is in an abysmal state. Rather than building on what earlier thinkers have achieved, each new generation of metaphysicians tries to begin all over again from the beginning. That, Kant announces, is about to change. Just as logic, mathematics, and the natural sciences became established only after a revolution transformed scattered fragments into properly unified systems, he has discovered how to revolutionize metaphysics so that it, too, can join the others on the highway of the sciences. Kant provided a handy snapshot of all this in the preface to the second edition of his masterpiece.

Kant's rule for vocabulary use follows from his view of science as something constructed with/from stable ideas. If later researchers are to add on to the body of knowledge already won through the efforts of earlier researchers, they must first understand the scientific ideas handed on from them. For that reason, it is important to use words with rigorous consistency.

> If there be only a single word the established meaning of which exactly agrees with a certain concept, then, since it is of great importance that this concept be distinguished from related concepts, it is advisable to economise in the use of the word and not to employ it, merely for the sake of variety, as a synonym for some other expression, but carefully to keep to its own proper meaning. Otherwise, it may easily happen that the expression ceasing to engage the attention in one specific sense, and being lost in the multitude of other words of very different meaning, the thought also is lost which it alone could have preserved.

Since that is a translation from Kant's German, a critical reader unable to read German will be reassured by inspecting other translations. Does the above say the same thing said—with different words!—below?

12

Whenever therefore there exists one single word only for a certain concept, which, in its received meaning, exactly covers that concept, and when it is of great consequence to keep that concept distinct from other related concepts, we ought not to be lavish in using it nor employ it, for the sake of variety only, as a synonym in the place of others, but carefully preserve its own peculiar meaning, as otherwise it may easily happen that the expression ceases to attract special attention, and hence that the thought, which that expression alone could have preserved, is lost with it.

The Humpty-Dumpty Rule comes from a writer of children's stories who clearly is interested only in entertaining his readers. (Really?!) His proper name was Charles Dodgson (1832-1898), at least when it wasn't Lewis Carroll (same dates), and he invented the H-D or Humpty Dumpty Rule for use in his nonsense piece known as *Through a Looking Glass.*

"When I use a word," Humpty Dumpty said, in rather a scornful tone, "it means just what I choose it to mean—neither more nor less."

"The question is," said Alice, "whether you can make words mean so many different things."

"The question is," said Humpty Dumpty, "which is to be master—that's all . . . Impenetrability! That's what *I* say!"

"Would you tell me, please," said Alice, "what that means?"

"Now you talk like a reasonable child," said Humpty Dumpty, looking very much pleased. "I meant by 'impenetrability' that we've had enough of that subject, and it would be just as well if you'd mention what you mean to do next, as I suppose you don't mean to stop here all the rest of your life."

"That's a great deal to make one word mean," Alice said in a thoughtful tone.

"When I make a word do a lot of work like that," said Humpty Dumpty, "I always pay it extra."

The key phrase in Dodgson's statement of the Humpty-Dumpty Rule of meaning is "Now you talk like a reasonable child." Getting in the habit of asking "Would you tell me what that means?"—or "What do YOU mean by that?"—is reasonable.

In fact, it is more than reasonable. It is indispensable. Misunderstanding is a major cause of human suffering, and a major cause of misunderstanding is a simple failure to notice the endless variations in humans' use of words. Ignorance about words and their ways is frequently behind our unjustified assumption that we know what someone else means when, in fact, we do not. It is matched by our frequently unjustified assumption that we know what *we* mean. We often are quite oblivious to the fact that, despite our protests to the contrary, our understanding of some matter at hand is not as clear and distinct as we claim it is. Our "meaning," or what we have in mind, is often ambiguous. We jumble quite distinct meanings together.

The importance of understanding what words mean seems obvious. How, for instance, can we know whether we should agree with someone else if we aren't clear on what they mean? How can we be certain we do agree with them until we're certain we are not wrongly assuming we understand them? How can we be certain others agree with us until we're certain we're not both mistaken in assuming they understand us? How can we get others to agree with us if they're too ignorant to realize that—protest as we may—they don't understand us? How can we not fail to win their agreement when we're too ignorant (or too stubborn) to realize that—protest as they may—we aren't clear in our own thinking because we're completely convinced that we are?

With an enviable measure of modesty and self-knowledge, Jerome Kagan, "one of the country's leading psychologists," recently wrote a book on a discovery he made while looking over works he had published years before. "Rereading those texts in later years," he confessed, "I realized, to my embarrassment, that I had assumed fixed meanings for ideas like maturation, memory, and continuity of mood and habit."

That realization led him to a further one. Empirical scientists can tailor their definitions to fit the tests they employ in doing research. The most famous—or infamous—example, of course, is the exasperated admission by experimenters unable to justify their definition of the I measured by IQ tests: "*I*ntelligence is defined as whatever it is that our tests measure and whatever our *Q*uotients are quotients of." Their

Humpty-Dumpty approach has encouraged more recent researchers to give two, four, even more definitionS of "intelligence."

The Humpty-Dumpty rule is tailor-made for using computers to do psychological research. A computer will use whatever term—or letter or number—to stand for whatever it is told to make it stand for, i.e., to mean whatever the researcher wants it to mean. Even better, researchers can combine the Humpty-Dumpty Rule and Kant's. Once given the researcher's "proper definition" rule, a computer will permit no deviation from the proper term. For instance, whoever wrote the program I'm using now designed it to be 100% unresponsive to even the slightest lapse in propriety.

Rethinking. Those latest paragraphs were supposed to be about "words and their meanings." However, they were not supposed to be about just any old words and meanings. The context had been specified by the question, "What view should guide this author's choice of words?" And the context for that question was the earlier use of specific words: "revolution," "conversion," "thinker," "believer," etc. Not one of these specific terms was discussed in those latest paragraphs. The paragraphs focused, instead, on rules about the use of words in general. Didn't they change the subject, therefore? The comments they contain apply, not to the text that constituted their immediate context, but to every page of every text ever written, since all such texts were created from words.

Or is that the point? By being about all texts and all words, those last paragraphs were also about the earlier pages and the words which make up their content. By being about an entire genus or class, they were also about the species or individuals. It doesn't make sense to ask about the propriety of any individual word unless we first get clear on the rules that determine the propriety of words in general. If we didn't know better from the last paragraph, we might be tempted to think it is not possible to follow Kant's "Same-concept, same-word" and Humpty's "Same-concept, any-word" rules at the same time. But it is. At least for limited stretches, such as a sentence, paragraph, section, or chapter. If the author notifies us of the switch, only our own laziness or lack of attention-skills are to blame if we ignore the switch. The conclusion is simple: the genus, "changing the subject," has two species, so that not everything that looks like "changing the subject" or concept really is.

This matter of using the same word when switching from discussing one thing to discussing a broader group of things that includes the first one involves deep-seated speech habits. And, at times, powerful emotions. In ancient, pre-sexist times, people used "men" for men exclusively or for the broader group that included women. Thus, "All men are mortal" was used for the broader group, but included the narrower one as well. Everyone understood this, it was a second-nature habit, people instantly switched from narrow to broad without a second thought. Now, in sexist times, we must pay attention to emotional sensitivities, and develop new second-nature habits. Propriety, in this context, requires "All humans are mortal," though—in this era of transition—sensitive writers follow Kant's rule here but others remain stuck with their old habits.

If we put aside our feelings, though, we can recognize a third rule for our use of words: We are free to adopt Kant's rule if, according to the Humpty rule, that's the rule we choose to adopt. Such close review reveals a fourth rule: Until we are certain it is possible to follow Kant's rule always and never have to switch meanings, we should never be caught off guard. We should always expect that the next old word may have a new meaning. All the more should we adopt that cautionary rule, if the author makes it clear s/he is deliberately following Humpty's rule.

Take the word "conversion." What you read earlier was only part of the truth. The dictionary that was cited lists two different senses—meanings?—for its first definition of "conversion," then adds six more definitions. That makes seven, perhaps eight, good definitions of that one word. Or seven meanings. Or senses. Dictionaries are a visible proof that the same word can have a switched meaning. Why? Because there are so many semantic law-breakers, so many people who use nonsexist, sexist, computer, think, and other old words for new meanings, dictionaries must continually add new uses to the old meanings . . . , so long as they are widely enough used, of course. Dictionaries could not possibly report every whimsical switch by every Humpty Dumpty. "Look it up" cannot serve, then, as an infallible guide to "What does that mean?" Since people do not always KNOW the dictionary and many do not KNOW they are switching meanings, critical readers, meaning careful thinkers, will always adopt the rule: Never assume Kant's "One word = one concept" rule is operating.

The major reason for this [non?]digression on rules is that the concept of rules has become absolutely central in the thinking of today's language experts, computer experts, and their hybrid counterparts, "artificial intelligence" (AI) experts who try to connect everyday language and computers. Learning to think about rules is now indispensable for anyone who wishes to discuss the proper and the improper use of language. Our first task is to understand words and their meanings. Trying to solve that difficult task while dealing with huge lists of rules might at first seem nearly impossible. It isn't. It just takes a lot of practice in Rethinking. It's not impossible, just tricky.

Here's how tricky. Some years ago, a meeting of Catholic bishops was called to decide what general rule all U.S. dioceses would adopt on a particular matter. After much debate, the rule that was adopted was that no general rule would be adopted. This allowed each diocese free to adopt its own. So, every diocese now follows the same rule: its own. Another time, someone objected to the statement that people are all the same. Each and every one of us is absolutely unique. No two persons have the same fingerprints. None have the identical DNA. And, once we descend to the details of memories and habits, differences in fingerprints and DNA pale by comparison. So we are all different, all unique. Which is precisely why we are all the same. All humans must be the same, otherwise there would be no point in calling us all by the same name, "human." By the same token, all unique persons must be the same, otherwise there would be no point in calling us all "unique."

Does that bit of reasoning violate any rule? Some logicians might say, "Yes, it must violate one of the rules of formal logic." But Bertrand Russell made a great stir when he pointed out a very tricky feature of logic's rules: we always have to make a personal decision when we do our calling, i.e., when we apply our terms. Are all women men, as was implied by "All men are mortal," or are all men women, as the logic texts on Lesbos might have claimed. Are humans animals, as evolutionists insist, or are humans humans and not animals, as Plato and Descartes would insist? Russell showed just how complicated the rules of logic are when he used the Humpty principle and gave logical arguments to show that "mathematics" and "logic" mean the same thing, not different things as Kant (like all of us before anyone tells us differently) believed. The fact that computers were doing that most rigorous type of logical reasoning called "mathematics" before the "everyday language" was introduced in

17

order to make them "user friendly," should give us something to think about before we scoff at Russell's claim. This mention of mathematics conjures up the name of Kurt Gödel who made an equally major stir when he proved logically and mathematically that no set of rules can get along without a Humpty Dumpty in charge to make certain necessary rule-decisions, even new axiom-choices, at crucial junctures. Is this the real problem facing AI experts, namely, that computers not only do not have any rational "homunculi" (midget-men) inside, they also don't have any Humpties inside to supply the kind of common sense that normal five-year olds possess? Computers are nothing but mazes of electron racetracks that can be mapped down to the last detail, with absolute precision, by the giant Humpties who design them. And who write the rules for operating them. Must they follow the dictionary? Which? Or are they free to use whatever rules "work"? Who makes the rules for deciding what works? The IRS and taxpayers often disagree over "owe" and have different notions about whose decision would work better.

Rethinking. Is there any deliberate design or plan to the last section? Or is it the product of a Freudian sort of free association, where surface subject-changing makes sense only if each subject is tracked down to a subterranean network of roots that unconsciously connect with every other subject? Or are they disconnected utterances, the way those of patients, whose diagnosis a century ago would have been "dementia praecox," were alleged to be disconnected? The paragraphs following "Words & Their Meaning" switched from the propriety of using just a few words to rules of propriety for all words, which—since the propriety of using those few words falls under the higher rules of propriety—was killing two birds with one stone. That gave way to talk about extra rules, which talk—a quick review will show how obvious it is—switched from rules to be adopted by speakers and writers to rules of interpretation to be adopted by listeners and readers. As if that were not enough, mention of those rules conjured up—by the rule empiricists call the "law of association"—the rules of church governance, the rules of logic, the rules of mathematics, and the rules used by computer experts. All of this raises the question: How many rules must a language-user master? Does it follow logically from the third last sentence that there are two entirely different sets of them, one for language users and another for language interpreters? Does each set have its own subsets, e.g., grammatical rules, pronunciation rules, spelling rules, punctuation rules, meaning or semantic rules, political rules, etc.?

Some idea of just how many rules confront us if and when we make a complete inventory of them can be got from a quick survey of the other experts who are thought to have something to contribute. Experts on literature, for instance. They are already consulted for the rules about text structure, e.g., about the rules for differentiating poetry from prose, drama from novels, truth from fiction, and so on. But, if they are experts on letters, and if all texts are made from words made from letters, the current outpouring of their literature on the rules for correct literary or textual criticism would need to be taken into account by everyone interested in language from which all literature is constructed. And what about the experts who legislate the rules for distinguishing history from sociology, those from anthropology and psychology, all of which are relevant to any critique of the cultural biases of culturo-historically conditioned literary critics? Who decides the rules separating those disciplines from the hard sciences or, as some people decree, from science *per se*, all of the preceding from philosophy and theology, etc.? The questions asked at the beginning of the previous paragraph can be seen to constantly reduplicate themselves: are the outpourings of these paragraphs deliberate, or the result of the psychological "law of association," or—if R.D. Laing is mistaken—purely random? Whoever reads the pages that follow must be committed to the difficult task of determining what rules are governing the composition of this text, i.e., for this author's choice of words (right down to the rule behind the increasingly short intervals between "Rethinking" sections), of determining which rules of interpretation are needed for that task, and finally of deciding which rules are proper and which are not.

Keen-eyed existentialists as well as Jacques Maritain regarded Thomas Aquinas with his sharp distinction between a thing's essence (answer to "WHAT is it?") and its existence (answer to "IS it?") as the greatest existentialist of all, will not have missed the most significant item in the preceding paragraph. They will have seized instantly on "(rules for differentiating) truth from fiction." Knowing the truth is understanding the way things really *ARE*. That requires knowing which things really *EXIST*. Fiction deals with what is unreal, with things that do not really exist. Things like ghosts and goblins, talking fawns and flying elephants, wonderlands and space-time continua. The expert on the rules for differentiating truth from fiction is the expert who presides over all the rest of the rules. The reason is clear. S/he must preside over evaluating all the other experts who lay claim to special expertise over, say, the rules of language, the rules of logic, the rules of mathematics, and so on, since such claims assume that rules are not merely useful fictions, but really exist. If they're real, s/he must know the real rules for separating real experts from artificial "experts" whose opinions are not really as expert as their artificial jargon makes them seem. S/he must possess something like the expertise the child in Hans Christian Andersen's "Naked Emperor" story possessed. That is, the ability to call a spade "a spade" and a naked emperor "a plain mortal wearing non-existent clothes."

The same fact-vs-fiction expert must serve as the expert on the rules for deciding which topics of inquiry should be assigned to which experts. [This section should be titled "Pre-conclusion."] That is, for making the rules that govern the entire structure of twentieth-century knowledge. This is an extremely emotion-laden, critical issue, for a reason that will be obvious to anyone who knows anything at all about cultural conditioning. The most glaring item in the contemporary landscape is the way we are steadily bombarded with the message "Knowledge is a pie to be sliced up."

The belief that knowledge is a pie that can be cut into separate pieces is the backbone of an uncounted number of widely held myths, e.g., "Science has nothing to say about religion" and "The opinion that creation-science is religion is not just an unscientific belief." Our entire education system is built on the *faith* that knowledge is really slice-able into neat, clear-cut classes, i.e., into various fields, specialties, branches, disciplines, pools, areas, bodies, interdisciplines, oceans (very large pools), concentrations, majors, minors, meadows (synonymous with "fields"), levels, and so on. How much of that jerrybuilt structure, already groaning beneath the weight of thousands upon thousands of theories, on top of which have been piled hundreds of methodological theories created solely to justify its manifold divisions and subdivisions and sub-subdivisions, that is, to justify the trunk's branching into branches, subbranches, sub-subbranches (Humpties feel free to mix metaphors), is fact and how much is fiction from imaginations already entangled in fictions?

The expert on truth vs error is the only one properly equipped to give true rather than false answers to that critical question. Unless that expert can be properly identified, those accustomed to being regarded as experts by "outsiders," meaning "laypeople," meaning "non-experts (vis-à-vis their garden)," may resist bold scrutiny from those same outsiders. All of us toil hard for our hoard of facts. Why should we welcome the possibility of learning that they are a pile of trivialities or a mountain of errors? Unless, of course, we are like Socrates and prefer truth. Then, we'll welcome the invitation to seriously rethink the pie/tree/pool of knowledge. Readers who decide it is largely fiction, though, will have to re-read, i.e., re-think, the original pages of this chapter with a new question in mind: How much truth remains if all references to mathematics, science, philosophy, psychology, religion, and so on, turn out to be references to mythical entities? If none of those things really exist as such, then what does?

Perhaps just people. [This paragraph should be labeled "Conclusions."] Each with vast stores of opinions best divided into two classes, the true ones and the false ones. Perhaps just people. Each charged with responsibility for becoming an expert on the fact-vs-fiction issue. Perhaps just people. Each with sole responsibility for her or his own decisions on the question, "Does what you're thinking about exist?" Perhaps just people. Each of whom has no legitimate right to claim s/he knows for certain what s/he is talking about if s/he declines to answer that question—"Does it exist?"—for certain. The properly existential question. Perhaps just people. Each of whom has a moral obligation to be honest and admit "I'm not sure" when that is the true answer. Perhaps just people. Each of whom is entitled to tell the truth and say "Yes, I'm sure, and I'll be happy to explain my reasons to you," when that is the true answer. Just people who, regardless of whether they are doing the explaining or listening to someone else doing it, must try to make certain they understand whatever gets said and admit it when they become uncertain they understand. To say "Non intelligo" when they don't.

So. What is the meaning of all of this? I mean it to present an introduction to the topic we can name "meaning," intend it to cast a wide enough net to engage each and every reader interested in the most fundamental inquiries of all. No computers will be caught in that net. Jose Benardete has noted that, unlike us who think "computer" is used properly of machines and only metaphorically of humans ("S/he's a regular computer," which is synonymous with "S/he's a real brain"), our ancestors would have been jarred if "computer" had been used to mean anything but humans. Here, the word is given its currently accepted meaning. No animals will be able to read or understand a single word on any of these pages. Nor will newborn humans. Or illiterate humans. But everyone else should be able to understand that these pages are designed to help readers wonder about meaning. I.e., that I designed them, mean and intend them, to do that.

B. Meaning: Our Tradition.

Rules? Among the uncounted sub-plans guiding the preceding pages' composition was an attempt to draw attention to the need for "Rethinking." What is obvious but very easy to overlook is how many years of looking-straight-ahead thinking we must do before we can begin rethinking. The word "rethink" carries "something you thought about before" on its back the same way "cogito" carries "I." There is thus a parallel between rethinking, rereading, and reexamining. No one can reread what they have not read, nor reexamine what they've not examined. We can all grasp the implication behind "You can never make a first impression twice" and the humor behind "If we always do things wrong the first time, why don't we just begin with the second?" Each of the above "Rethinking" sections followed paragraphs that simply said what they said without any prior announcement. That is, look-back-now paragraphs followed read-straight-ahead paragraphs. The read-straight-ahead paragraphs had to be written first, otherwise there would have been nothing to look backwards to. That is what is meant by saying and/or writing that we must first do a lot of just-thinking before we can do any Rethinking. Is it worth noting that a great deal of listening, speaking, and reading precedes the writing of the books we find in our libraries? That no writer is likely to write anything likely to end up in a library unless s/he has done a lot of thinking and rethinking before doing the writing that produces a library book?

If we combine those obvious facts of life we get the following. Each of the books in the library was authored by people who, unless they were radically different from us, had to do a lot of thinking, speaking, and reading before they wrote the words that transmit their thoughts to us. If we want to be good thinkers, then, we must notice that reading a book is a crossing of paths. Readers are at a particular point in their mad dash to learn as much as possible before they die, and the writer they're reading wrote each sentence at a particular moment in her or his dash. Like the twenty-year old who discovers how much his dad has learned in just the last three years, Saint Augustine learned later that his earlier scoffing at the Bible's silly ideas was the silly reaction of someone less learned than he was later on. Scholars today argue about the dates when Plato and Aristotle wrote their works, so that they can decide which of their opinions were youthful ones and which were later, closer-to-the-truth ones, but for a long time I regarded all of the latter's as truer than any of the elder's. This book is coming, one sentence at a time, from a "pen" being wielded during the summer of 1992, by an author sixty years out of the gate. You?

There's a lesson in this. When library books come from the pen of a writer who was influenced by an earlier writer and who, by adopting a path-setting error from the earlier one, took that path in a direction that led farther from the truth, then we who rely on the later writer may be getting farther from the truth than if we spent more time reading—critically—the earlier one. The present work comes from the pen of someone who did not study more recent theories on meaning until long after he had learned the mature theories of more ancient thinkers, from the pen of one who never paid much attention to language and the problem of meaning until he had already spent years taking both for granted. If the more ancient thinkers knew more of the truth than the more recent authors, theirs may be more reliable than recent works. If more recent thinkers have corrected flaws in older theories, theirs may be more critical on important issues than older theories. But, then, mine may combine the older flaws and the more recent errors. No reader (you) is excused from the task of rethinking.

In fact, there is more than one lesson in these obvious facts. First, there is a fifth rule worth remembering. When we go into a library, we must do what everyone with enough good common sense "instinctively" does, assume we can understand what we will read and, if we can't, examine to see if the fault is our own, as happens, e.g., when we can't read the language something is written in, don't have the background, or just don't have the brains. What the book says may not be true, but we won't know until we know what it says. Or what is meant by what it says. If we don't know whether what it says is true or not, we will admit it and then check out the evidence. We cannot check out the evidence, though, till we read what it says. And understand. Mindful of the fact that people who are determined to do so can read their stars, read tea leaves, read dead Mayan glyphs, we will hardly claim that what we're reading cannot be interpreted to mean anything. Everything can be given several meanings.

Second, there is a sixth rule that we must never forget. Our goal when we visit the library is *to learn the truth*. First and foremost, the truth about the author's meanings, i.e., what the author's thoughts were. Secondly, the truth about the things the author's thoughts are about. And certainly more than just the truth about rules. What should we think about someone who never read a single book about the stars, the atom, the big bang, or the brain, because s/he didn't have enough time to read all the books written recently about the genuine scientific method or about the rules for distinguishing science from pseudo-science? How advanced would a nation be whose libraries—and educational system—offered nothing but courses on how to properly differentiate academic disciplines and on the proper method for historians, the proper method for sociologists, the proper method for doing psychology, but none about ancient Greece, about various people's religions, about Plato's influence on Aristotle's logic, about Descartes' influence on James' psychology, about Watson's influence on the 20th-century psychologists, etc? Who goes to the library to learn nothing but the rules for correct spelling, pronunciation, punctuation, grammatical structure, semantic rules, rules for the syllogism, rules for proper narrative about narration as distinct from description, and so on? Most of all, though, how many go to libraries with the hope of learning nothing but lies and mistakes about any of those things? Or only mistakes about the rules for using language? Or only errors about the meaning of words? In other words, we must want the truth from the words whose meaning we understand.

Third, there is a seventh rule for anyone reading a book made up of words that are meant to explain the meaning of words. Since the only way to discover whether what it says is true is to consult the evidence for and against whatever it is that is meant by the words, the best way to discover the truth is to see whether what the book says about words' meanings can be applied to the words making up that book. If you wonder why there are so many references to you and to what you are doing right there right then (vis-à-vis June 1992), it is because I'll presume that what you are doing is reading words from this book. That is, you will not have to look any further than where you are for evidence. This will be something like riding a bicycle while reading a book on how to ride a bicycle. It will not teach you to do what you're doing, just try to draw your attention to various facets of it.

What is the reason for the preceding discussions about rules? Whoever is familiar with the most important responses to Descartes' revolution about how and what we can know will also understand why focusing on the truth that we expect from words (the last three paragraphs) rather than on endless lists of rules about their use is no small matter. There have been whole "schools" of philosophy whose cornerstone is a rule about books or the sentences in them. There is, for instance, the school whose rule David Hume enunciated in his *Enquiry Concerning Human Understanding*:

> When we run over libraries, persuaded of those principles, what havoc must we make? If we take in our hand any volume; of divinity or school metaphysics, for instance; let us ask, "Does it contain any abstract reasoning concerning quantity or number?" No. "Does it contain any experimental reasoning concerning matter of fact and existence?" No. Commit it then to the flames: for it can contain nothing but sophistry and illusion. (Vol. I, Bk. I, Pt. I, sec. vii)

More recently, various schools have been built around the rule that any talk of reality existing independently of human thought, either individually or in general, either this century's or that culture's, is simply unintelligible to us, meaning the same thing Hume meant by sophistry and illusion. Their members go by such names as idealists, positivists, pragmatists, historicists, relativists, and so on. Whoever catches on to the most important rhetorical device used by them will notice that they try to win every argument about basics by declaring that no one—you—is able to so much as propose an intelligible alternative to their own views. A debate with any of them is a non-debate. They turn every debate into a victory by default. Only *they*—they think—make sense.

The most famous school were the (Il)Logical Positivists who proposed the most sophisticated version of all rule-isms. They adopted a rule, constructed of words, that—in the version proposed by their *enfant terrible* representative, Sir Alfred J. Ayer—read:

> A sentence is factually significant [i.e., meaning-ful or sense-ible] to any given person, if and only if, he knows how to verify the proposition which it purports to express—that is, if he knows what observations would lead him, under certain conditions, to accept the proposition as being true.

According to Ayer, talk of God—for instance, "God exists" and "God does not exist"—is as literally meaning-less or non-sense-ical as "'Twas brillig, and the slithy toves did gyre and gimble in the wabe" (& "Nope!"), something children must understand, since they laugh when they hear it. Unless they laugh because they know—without being able to explain how—that it is literally nonsense because they know—without being able to recite a rule for it—how to recognize things that do make sense and, by comparing this to them, know—again without being able to put into words how—this does not measure up. The Illogical Positivists eventually did become more logical by realizing that their verification principle, as it was often called, was not verifiable and therefore not factually significant, i.e., was literally meaning-less or non-sense-ical. What bothered them most, however, was that when their rule, which was NOT meaningless even though it should have been according to itself, was applied, it turned out that physics was as meaningless as metaphysics. And theology.

The point of these last paragraphs is to warn that anyone who goes into a library or picks up a book to learn the truth would do well to summarize the foregoing into an eighth rule. There is no simple rule, such as that of the Illogical Positivists, that can be applied automatically to discover which pages of which books are nonsense and which are not. There is not even any simple rule for deciding what "nonsense" and "not" mean.

Therefore it is best to agree with Richard Rorty—second to none in his ability to read and understand the most abstract epistemological theories of all as well as in his ability to write accounts of his own theories about such theories—who reached the only true and now conclusively verified conclusion to be drawn from the history of theories of meaning based on simple-minded, *apriori* rules: "Everybody understands everybody else's meanings very well indeed." (*Philosophy and the Mirror of Nature*, p.88; His context must be kept in mind. He was not speaking, for instance, of students who often indeed do not understand their teachers' meanings very well.)

A bridge. This section of Chapter One is entitled "Meaning: Our Tradition." View the foregoing as a preface to it. View this as a bridge from that preface to the history that follows. The relevance of the preface to the history is this. Books do not fall from the sky, and this one is no exception. It will be one person's brief account of Western thinkers' theories about meaning. And, it will represent one person's time-out or pause from reading others' reports, taken to report what he judges to be their most significant contributions to the whole truth about meaning. Reading it will involve a second party, the reader. Readers do not read while they are asleep or actively engaged in such other incompatible activities as attentively answering a cross-examining lawyer before a packed courtroom, practicing transcendental mindlessness, deciding which should be the three top items on their list of "Things without which I cannot be happy," etc. What you will need most in order to understand meaning is to pay attention to what you're doing as you learn the meaning of the words that follow. To pay close attention, that is, to how you use your own eyes to see these lines of print, your own mind to interpret what you see, your own memory to recall what you've learned before that is pertinent to your interpreting, your own free will to decide which of the things you understand you'll believe, i.e., to decide which are the truth and which are fiction. You may have to visit the library for further research before deciding which parts of the history you'll believe. Will you have to visit the library, though, to learn what you'll be doing as you read on? When all you'll be doing in the library will be reading on? At what point in your dash to learn all you can will you decide it is you doing the dashing and getting closer to the finish line you are doing, you doing the reading—that is, the seeing, remembering, and interpreting—that you're doing, etc.? You needn't pause to reply. Though you may.

This History's Focus: Copy-Viewing. Or, "Knowledge as Looking-At Copies of What Is Known." This will be like the theory of evolution, the social contract theory, and that weird fantasy about Moses' monotheism: it will be a guess about events none of us alive observed. Someone, at some time, chanced to notice the difference between *what is observed* and *what is not*. That was the moment when scientific thinking about meaning began.

The difference between what is observed and what isn't is obvious to me any time I recall it. As I look around now, for instance, it is clear that there are many things that I can observe. They are the things that are right here right now. Among them, let's assume, are clothes, book-cases, stacks of papers, numerous items cluttering this desk, and so on. There is also an endless list of things that, for the simple reason that they are not right here right now, I am not observing. Yet I can think about them right here right now. Among them are the people I thought of earlier. James, Watson, and Murray, who died earlier, in the last century. Descartes, Paul, and David, who died long before it. Most obvious of all is the unobserved person I am thinking about right now, the person who, long ago, first took full note of the fact that s/he could think of things not observable right there right then. Who knows what that person was and was not observing? Perhaps s/he was inside a cave and noticed s/he was able to think about the sun, moon, stars, forests, and lakes outside the cave. Any reader who is not God—They alone see all things—should be able to notice the same distinction by contrasting what s/he can see as s/he looks around right now with what s/he cannot see but has been thinking about (while reading this) or can think about.

That starting-point relates to one of the most useful but dangerous classifications ever invented: empirical vs nonempirical. Relates only, however. It is not identical. It is similar but also different. In today's "professional" vocabulary, things that are observed are often described as experienced, and things that are experienced are often classified as "empirical." Unfortunately, though, "empirical" is broader than "observed," for its meaning—meaning, again!—usually includes things which, although they are not now observed, are things which were once observed or could have been observed or will be observed or would be observed by an observer in the right place at the right time, etc. Such looseness is bad enough. It is made even worse by the fact that most authors use "empirical" without giving any attention to the question: Who is supposed to be doing the observing? Authors who adopt the Humpty-Dumpty principle can use whatever words they choose for whatever thoughts they think, and we can follow their train of thoughts so long as they give us sufficient clues, e.g., by announcing it the way this paragraph announces that careful readers should note the difference between the starting-point in this historical reconstruction and today's popular empirical-vs-nonempirical distinction. Here, the focus is on facts, on what is actually happening, rather than on what did, might have, may, or will happen. Saying something is observed means someone is observing it somewhere right now. What is not being observed can only be known at this moment by something MORE, by some OTHER kind of knowing process. By thinking, for instance.

For the purposes of an easy step-by-step reconstruction of this history, we can imagine that the next question asked by our ancient ancestors would have been this: "How can we explain the fact that we can now think about—remember—things we have already observed but which we are not observing right now?" Some where at some time it occurred to some one to say "We can think of them because we carry pictures of them inside our heads." Our ancestors knew about things and their copies. Library books report that ancient peoples carved statues of people and things, painted pictures of them on cave walls, engraved images of them on pieces of stone, pottery, and metal. These physical copies, pictures, or images assisted our ancestors in remembering people and things they had experienced in the past, much the same way that photographs and videos assist us in remembering what we have experienced. The fact that we can see intangible images after looking at objects—the most vivid, perhaps, is the bright circular disk we continue to see for a few moments after we have looked at the sun—coupled with the further fact that we have no reason to doubt that our ancestors were like us in this, too, helps explain how it came about that someone, at some time, "put two and two together," i.e., connected the ideas of thinking about absent things while seeing portable outside reminders with thinking about unobserved things with only the inside pictures. Thus was born the theory that seeing inner picture-copies makes-possible thinking about things that aren't right here and right now.

Whoever goes into the library and begins reading up on ancient thinkers' theories about knowledge will begin to notice the frequency of comparisons between knowing and seeing. Consider the word "idea." It is the most famous word of all, so far as the theory of knowledge is concerned. This English word is descended from the Greek "eidos," which had descended from the word for seeing and which can be interpreted as shorthand for "something seen," a fact that helps to call our attention to an important detail we might otherwise overlook: the first account of non-observational knowing relates to our most noticed sense, sight. Our original idea of copies comes from things we observe by sight rather than from things we hear or feel or smell or taste. (Ever hear "Hearing is believing"?) Our favorite word for what we do to inside copies or images is "visualize."

Our idea of true knowing or thinking is also borrowed from seeing. When carvers, painters, and engravers create their works of art, they regularly situate themselves where they can directly observe—see—the original thing in order to make certain their copy is "close" to it. When the copy is finished, a direct inspection—a visual inspection, using one's eyes—will show the extent to which the copy is faithful to the original. Instant photography has brought copying to technological perfection for objects that are stationary. If the color is not right ("the picture is too light or too dark") or the lines are blurred, a better copy can be made on the spot. The predominant analogy for "truth" until recently has been what is called the correspondence theory: a true belief is one that corresponds to, matches, or fits the facts. Or represents them accurately. Which thought calls forth these further thoughts. This reconstruction explains why inner images and/or ideas are often called "representations" and why those who wish to draw attention to this constellation of images-&-ideas often give the name **"Representationalism"** to their theory. And when we discover from our library books that ancient thinkers often explained sight or vision with theories about "eidola," tiny copies thrown off by objects and flying through our eyes right into our head, lingering doubts about the accuracy of our reconstruction evaporate. The original explanation for thinking about things that are not right here right now was built on the experience of looking at things and seeing them. Thinking must involve "viewing" copies that are similar to or like them.

What about language and its meaning? The traditional theory is that the meaning of words is the thoughts they express. Words are our medium of communication. If, like animals, we never had any reason for communicating our thoughts about everything under the sun, we might get by with pointing at observable things in the immediate vicinity and with grunting or howling in response to sounds or other signs of nearby food or danger. But we can and do think of everything under the sun, and in order to communicate those thoughts, we use highly sophisticated languages or word-systems. One person makes known to another person what ideas, unobservable to the other, s/he is thinking about by producing hearable (audibly-observable) words for those unobservable thoughts or ideas. On this topic, the origin of language, we have nothing but our own guesses to help us reconstruct a plausible history of those long-since-dissipated first words. That is because recording devices had not yet been invented and because not one of the authors who wrote a book still in our library was alive when those first words were uttered.

But we do have books. That is because, eventually, written language was invented. People began to make seeable (visibly-observable) records of their internal, hidden ideas. And, although not one of them is a first-hand account by an actual eye-witness to the birth of written language, we do have samples of early writing, and it provides an indirect but direct confirmation of the fact that we almost "instinctively" compare thinking to seeing images. The earliest attempts to create a permanent record of thoughts or ideas took the form of tiny pictures. Pictographs. Hieroglyphics which are pictographs used for thoughts about sacred topics. The kind of glyphs that Mayan experts are trying to find the meaning of. Which is what we'd expect. If our thoughts of things that are not right here right now involve inner pictures of them, then what better way to record what's inside than in the form of tiny outside images or copies?

It is surprising we are not more surprised by the ingenuity behind today's form of written language. It couldn't be invented until people began paying attention to something we begin using without paying any attention to it at first: the uttered and heard sounds we refer to as spoken language. It required a gigantic shift, FROM making visual images of thought-about objects, TO making visual "images" of the heard sounds used as a means of communicating about invisible, unhearable thoughts about observable objects. Our lack of surprise testifies to the ease with which we can fail to notice things that are not just slightly obvious but "How could we have missed it?!" obvious.

Too-obvious-for-words obvious. But not actually obvious—just tacitly obvious, only taken-for-granted obvious—until our attention is drawn to them. But what's attention?

What's attention? Here, to what's obvious but not noticed? It's nothing less than the secret to all of this. Particularly for us who grow up with the habit of paying more attention to written words than to internalized images. It involves the central issue of similarity. There is absolutely no similarity between these ink marks that will be scanned by the eyes of readers and the sounds that their ears would hear if someone else were reading these words aloud. This is another of those "How could we have missed it?!" obvious facts that become so hard to notice till our attention is drawn to it. We English-users are fortunate, though, to have a language where the rules matching letters to sounds are notoriously unrule-y. By meditating hard on "reed," "read," "red," and "read," or on "rough," "through," and "trough," and similar cases, we can begin to crack our cement-hard habits and recognize the premier fact about written words (what we see) and their pronunciation (what we hear): UTTER DISSIMILARITY. Nor, of course, is there any similarity between the ink marks "cat," the sound that we call "the pronunciation of 'cat'," and the four-legged animal. On the other hand, every novice in these matters will recognize, as something quite obvious, the similarity between the inner image that the "word" will make her/him recall instantly—whether s/he sees "cat" or hears the sound called "the pronunciation of 'cat'"—and the four-legged animal. No wonder early writers wrote with pictures of things rather than with symbols for sounds.

Three of the most famous ancient Greek thinkers lived long after writing had been invented. All three could speak, understand, read, and—though we have nothing written by the first—write. The latter two's works are still unmatched introductions to the problem of meaning. Socrates (469-399BC) was a thinker for whom meaning became a running theme. Plato (427-347BC) built two of his most famous theories of all on Socrates' way of dealing with meaning. Aristotle (385-322BC) developed his account of knowledge largely in reaction to Plato's. More specifically, Socrates decided that the best way to anchor thoughts to words was by the technique of "definition." Plato came to believe that the most basic definitions pointed to things eyes could never see nor ears hear, things that our minds, therefore, must have observed first-hand in a former lifetime. Aristotle rejected such other-worldliness in favor of an "abstraction of this world's forms" theory. The stark contrast between Plato's and Aristotle's views set the pattern for subsequent debates.

We begin with Socrates. Twenty-five centuries ago already, the Greeks in Athens engaged in arguments about everything under the sun, arguments as sophisticated as any in recent times. They argued about the ultimate nature of matter as vigorously as contemporary physicists. They discussed the nature of the mind as much as any contemporary psychologists. They battled over the norms of justice, both individual and political, as vehemently as capitalists and socialists do. And they had the same problems with words and their meanings as intellectuals today have. So disunited and chaotic was the intellectual scene in ancient Athens that the ultra-liberal Sophists decided there was no single truth to things, that each person had separate perceptions and a separate truth. Socrates disagreed.

The first task, he decided, was to make a determined effort to keep words from changing meanings. He developed the good habit, when a key word was used as the fulcrum for an important debate, of looking for the word's definition. Before we can decide whether virtue is a thing that can be passed on from father to son, for example, we must decide what the thing called "virtue" is or—till the question of existence ("Is there any such thing as virtue?") comes up—what the word "virtue" *means*. Before we can decide whether justice is its own reward, we must pin down what it is we are talking about, what it is that "justice" *means*. If we are serious in our search for the truth, we can control our tendency to speak of *both* beasts and men as "beasts," of *both* dogs and women as "dogs," of *both* out-of-wedlock-borns and in-wedlock-borns as "bastards," by agreeing to give beast, dog, bastard—or I, think, exist, i.e., any key word—a fixed meaning and agreeing to stick with it. Or try.

Plato meditated long and hard on the fact that Socrates had built on. We can apply the same word with the same meaning to very different things because we encounter samenesses over and over again in our stream of experience. Look back to the things we observe as we move around during the day. We see this person named "John," that person named "Jane," this dog named "Tippy," that dog named "Trapper," etc. Regardless of how confused we might have been as young children calling every man "papa" and every four-legged animal "doggie," we eventually learn enough of things' different details to call them by their different proper names. Yet we call both Jane and John "human" and both Tippy and Trapper "dog." Things are both the same as other things and also different from them. With similar general names, different proper names. One general meaning or definition, many particular meanings or descriptions. Same and different. General and particular. One and many. Correlative oppositions. Others had noticed the same oppositions. Plato found a novel explanation.

Plato used the copy theory to explain the fact that we give to different things the same definition. At the major shrines in Greece, miniature copies of deities could be purchased with tiny likenesses of kings. The likenesses were called statues, the copies coins. Since copies are likenesses, either can be called either. Noticing that we call statues and the coin-images by the same name—e.g., Diana, Darias—because they are modeled after the same origin-al, Plato seized upon and began to explore the hypothesis that we give things that, to the senses, are radically different the same names, e.g., "same," "one," and "being," because they reflect the same model. He extended it to cases in which, paradoxically, we call the same things "different," "many," "not(-one)." Those are the hardest of the cases on which Plato tried out his hypothesis, but he began with Socrates' focus, on virtue. Just as we know a rose is a rose, we likewise know that virtue is virtue, and that changing a vice's name to "virtue" will not change any of the vice's features to those of a virtue. One of the questions raised by his theory of models that Plato asked was: Where did we learn about the models?

Until we have done sufficient rethinking, Plato's question doesn't seem so important. Most things, it seems, we learn by first-hand observation: we learn what roses are by looking, smelling, handling. Other things we learn from second-hand report: we learn about Santa Claus and God from our parents. We learn the names of everything from our parents, too, which explains why we all grow up speaking our parents' language. What made Plato famous were the alternative answers discovered after he had spent years rethinking such obvious-at-first but utterly-untenable "explanations." It had to do with not-observing.

Plato came to realize that our understanding goes far beyond what we sense. A small, nearly-scentless, frilly red rose and a large, perfumed, beautifully-petalled lavender one have little in common, but we are sure each measures up 100% to our idea of a rose. Though the behaviors are different, graciously putting a rose in the hand of a stranger who admires one's garden and patiently taking the insults cast at one's roses by a surly passerby both count as virtues (good), just as depositing a bomb in someone's car and taking the money from a poor widow's purse are vices (bad), regardless of what any sophist calls them.

How did we discover what makes two very different flowers 100% equal as roses, and a small, near-scentless, frilly red carnation not even so much as 1% a rose? More importantly, how do people from different 'cultures' learn the difference between "giving" and "good," between "taking" and "bad," so that they know which feature of behaviors is named "giving," which "taking," which "good," and which "bad"? Not by looking. Some of the things we know are things we could not have learned if we had only eyes. Nor will it do to say that we learn such things from our parents or from society. Think about it. Because, otherwise, French citizens would still have kings, American citizens would still have slaves, and the world would not have risen up against this century's Nazi citizens. Those are the things Plato thought and wrote about so clearly that the world would be a better place even today if every writer would model him.

That, however, is only the negative half—the 'not looking with our eyes' half—of Plato's theory. Which is confirmed by comparing humans and animals, both of which have bodies and senses. In contrast to animals that see but have no botanical, political, or ethical taxonomies about which they make claims and counterclaims, humans argue endlessly about them. So how do we learn to understand the meaning of "rose," "good," "bad," and so on? The positive side of Plato's theory, the one few people have ever regarded as wholly satisfactory, is that we learn them by a direct mental inspection. Or remember them. *From a previous existence*. From before we had this body and its five senses. So that, even if there were only one rose the way there is only one sun, we would be able to pick out the rose the way we pick out the sun, once we had gotten clear on what "rose" really means the way we get clear on what "sun" means. And, even if there were no perfectly virtuous and no perfectly vicious persons in the world, we would still understand the meaning of virtue and vice well enough to decide that no one measures up to the perfection of either. Just as, even though each lovely sunset, each child's smile, and each traditional song is truly beautiful, we do in fact know that none exhausts the full meaning of "total beauty itself."

The way to think of Plato's theory is to think that each reincarnated infant returns to this world with these standards for wise judgment locked within its soul. And that each will start recovering from its born-again amnesia with some jogging from the body's senses. Because those this-worldly things that jog our bodily senses are pale reflections of the other-worldly models. Models that can only be learned about and understood in our present, this-worldly life by our soul's intellect or reasoning part.

Senses and intellect. Observing and reasoning. Particulars and universals. Images and Ideas. Body and soul. Mortality and immortality. This world and a world beyond. Plato worked out the details of his vision in a series of question-and-answer dialogues designed for rethinking readers. For twenty centuries, his conclusion that the body's senses are suited for observing the world of bodies and the soul's intellect cut out for knowing an entirely different world of bodiless realities has formed the background for Western thinkers' theories about knowledge. Many, e.g., Augustine, who accepted the distinction between a heavenly Creator who cannot be seen and visible neighbors the Creator commands us to love if we want to get to heaven, found their insight into that distinction deepened by Plato's view of a dual reality, of a two-tiered universe. Others who disagreed with Plato's other-worldliness found in his writings a challenge to look for more sophisticated this-worldly explanations.

Aristotle was one of them. If, as some maintain, he originally accepted most of Plato's two-story world, he learned how to rethink everything by the time he composed the lecture notes we know as his "Works." He came to believe that body and soul are so interdependent that neither could exist without the other. In his later thinking, there is no possibility for a pre-existent soul to be importing memories as it climbs into a new taxi-body for another trip through this world. And when a person dies, the body—or rather the matter—is reorganized by a different form—the soul itself is only one of many kinds of form—to make some new unified whole—in this instance, a human corpse. His later-learned theory of human learning is dovetailed to fit this radically different view of the human learner. True, he continued to accept Plato's distinction between senses and intellect. So much so that he fixed on the intellect or reason as the major factor that makes us humans radically different from animals which are the things most

36

like us. But Aristotle came to think like a biologist more than anything else, and to his biologist's eye we humans are quite obviously animals. We are corporeal or three-dimensional, we are living organisms, we have senses. Because we are rational and not, like all other animals, irrational, we are essentially different from all other animals. Still, our senses are more than the mere memory-joggers Plato thought them to be, and human reason is intrinsically dependent upon the senses for everything it does.

According to Aristotle, the dependency of reason is easily explained. Our senses are the sole suppliers of raw data for our mind's operations. He attributed the newborn's apparent lack of stored-up information to the fact that the infant really does lack all information. He ascribed the infant's apparent acquisition of knowledge from its recently-begun sensory experience of the world to the fact that it really does acquire its knowledge from its sense experience. What was appearance for Plato was reality for his pupil. And, though Aristotle was forced to leave many of the details so vague that medieval authors disagreed radically about the correct interpretation of them, the rough outlines of his thinking are so clear and so clearly commonsensical that, once they have been thoroughly assimilated, it is next to impossible to shake loose from them. The senses collect information about different individuals belonging to various species of things. The information about these many individuals is passed inward and assembled by an internal junction-box called the "sensus communis." From this information gotten by experience and stored in memory, the intellect extracts what the individuals from each species have in common with the species' other individuals, and thus is born the general concept or idea in the mind. The experienced fact that when we utter a scientific generalization, e.g., "All dogs have senses," we have no clear picture of the exact details (color of eyes, shape of ears, specific height or weight, etc.) of the particular or individual animals, e.g., Timmy or Trapper, making up the dog-species, was used by Aristotle as evidence for his theory that general concept-forms are ex—or abs-tracted from particularizing matter. Following this abstraction process, the concepts which are marked by the nouns and verbs of the learner's language are joined into propositions designated by noun-verb sentences. Scientific reasoning, the model of which is the mathematical reasoning we find in Euclid's geometry, is carried out by an intellect which is most comfortable when dealing with vague generalizations. For Aristotle, then, we do not understand things we have never sensed. Rather, we understand what we have sensed, but only somewhat vaguely or abstractly, i.e., without all the rich details of sense-experience.

Connect the preceding to today's psychologists. Plato's and Aristotle's utterly contradictory attitudes on the relation of thinking to sensing, of theorizing to observation, became the central issue for the psychologists who carried on their inquiries for the next twenty two centuries. Until the last century's revolution toppled private thoughts and enthroned public language, those thinkers called "rationalists" championed *reason* as the final judge of the senses' witness have battled against the "empiricists" who counter that the *senses* must be the last court of appeal for determining matters of fact. Plato is the grandfather of all who insist that humans have a source of certainty superior to the senses. Aristotle is the ancestor of those who retort, *"Nihil in intellectu nisi prius in sensu,"* that is, there's nothing in the intellect that wasn't first in the senses.

Because Aristotle's theory is so much more congenial to common sense, our original, growing-up view of everything, his approach has usually been favored by a majority of those interested in human learning. That was true in the past. It remains true to this day.

Nevertheless, Aristotle's naive realism is hopelessly at odds with every last shred of up-to-date "scientific" research. Bertrand Russell captured that fact for all time with his classic formula:

> Naive realism leads to physics, and physics, if true, shows that naive realism is false. Therefore naive realism, if true, is false; therefore it is false.

Naïve realism is the two-sided, common-sense conviction that (i) mountains, birds, trees, and other three-dimensional things exist and that (ii) we know they exist because we can see and touch them. Until infants are born already ready to rethink naive realism, they'll continue learning it and spending years believing it before it provides them with enough knowledge to rethink it. Until our schools change, it is a safe bet that the vast majority of even the college-educated will go to their graves believing they can observe—see, hear, touch, etc.—graves, corpses, and living pallbearers carrying the latter to the former.

Still, the disagreements between Plato or Platonists and Aristotle or Aristotelians are not the focus of this highly selective narrative. For now, our focus must remain on the ancient idea that ideas are mental copies of outer realities. It is easy to overlook that fact because many of the combatants, when accused of believing in a copy theory, strongly deny that ideas are copies in any literal sense. They switch to other terms. "Sign" and "symbol" are two favorites. Medieval authors, after noting that words are purely arbitrary signs for concepts, and after noting that words are not at all like the concepts they (the words) are signs for and not at all like the objects the concepts are concepts of, went on to define concepts as a particular kind of signs, namely, formal signs.

Concepts are supposedly transparent signs whose entire being is to make other things—(wo)men, dogs, roses, virtue, vice, etc.—known. Concepts are so transparent that they cannot be discovered without a special effort. Even then, their presence is inferred, reasoned to indirectly, rather than directly inspected. On the other hand, all of the usual things called "signs" are things in their own right, things that must be recognized before they can serve as signs. Thus, we must see the clouds before we think of the rain they are a sign of, must see the road sign before we think of the nearby school crossing it is a sign of, must hear someone's words before we think of the thoughts they are a sign of. For this reason, concepts were often referred to as "formal signs" in contrast to other signs now designated as "instrumental."

But the adjective "formal"—an adjective derived from the noun "form"—is our tip-off sign that a "seen copy" model is behind this Medieval thinking. The fact is easy to notice once we train our mind's "eye" to look for it. Plato's famous theory of Ideas—a term, as explained earlier, is derived from a word for seeing or looking—referred to other-worldly Models for this-world realities, is also called his theory of Forms. A synonym for form is shape, "morphe" in Greek. Forms or shapes are the most prominent features of what we see. Aristotle built whole wings of his theory-mansion on this idea of forms, an idea borrowed by Plato from the geometer, Pythagoras. Form. Alias shape. Alias likeness. After all, geometers looks for similarity or congruence or proportionality in form or shape, not perfect exactness in size, color, and composition. And, so long as the facts which show that naive realism is hopelessly muddled had not yet been distilled into a sufficiently critical mass, the old viewed-copies model of knowledge dominated people's thinking.

But that mass of facts has been gathered. And it was Descartes who first drew their implications to the attention of the world. The physics of light show how our eyes' lenses operate on the same principles as the newly discovered telescope to create tiny images inside our eyes. His *Discourse* incorporated such "physics" facts into an inclusive picture of the human body as an intricate machine controlled by a skull-encased brain receiving input from the senses after they, in turn, have received input from the environment outside the skin-enclosed body. Descartes' conclusion is clear and unequivocal. The intellect has no direct contact with bodies outside its body. It has no direct contact with any body-organs, including sense-organs, outside its brain. In fact, according to Descartes, the mind has no direct contact with any part of the brain except the pineal gland. The first and sixth of his *Meditations* summarize his reasons for believing that, no matter how powerful our impression is that we see the bodies making up the world outside us, that impression is an illusion. His sixth Meditation analyses the experience of bodily pain to show that, no matter how irresistible is our sense of having direct contact with legs, arms, or other parts of our body, that sense is mistaken. By incorporating amputees' phantom-limb experiences and his theory of afferent nerves into his analysis, he shows that the mind feels pain only after a particular type of stimuli reaches the brain. These stimuli alone, even without the limb which is their normal source, will cause the soul to experience the same pain it once felt when the limb was there. The properly-fed brain alone is necessary.

The realization that, contrary to our growing-up conviction, we cannot look through our eyes to see whether our inside copies truly resemble what's outside forced on those willing to re-think matters a full recognition of the shakiness of easy assumptions about truth based on easy assumptions about true likenesses or representations. The most influential thinkers about thinking since Descartes' death in 1650 have been the ones who took it as definitively settled that our senses are not windows onto reality. Our sense that, from our secure place inside the fortress of our skull, we can directly inspect the world through the twin turrets we call our eyes is an illusion. Locke, Spinoza, Leibniz, Berkeley, Hume, Kant, Hegel, and Einstein took it as established that Descartes was right about that much at least. Modern physics and physiology, once they are taken seriously, lead inexorably and obviously to the conclusion that none of us has direct knowledge of anything outside our mind or, if "mind" is used as a synonym for "brain," outside our brain. *What we do have direct knowledge of are the private ideas and images inside our mind or brain.* This conclusion creates one gigantic problem: What assurance can we have that what's outside is like what's inside? If we cannot take a peek at what is outside, we cannot compare the inside and the outside in order to see how much or how little similarity there is. From the original question, "How can we think right here right now of things we are not observing?", we proceed to a new question: "How can we ever be certain that any of the things we think of are like outside things, none of which we are observing now, none of which we have ever observed in the past, and none of which we can ever hope to observe in the future?" Each of the thinkers listed above became famous in large part because of the novel answer he offered to solve the problem. Each took matters a bit farther than his predecessor.

Descartes began this modern rethinking with enormous confidence. He was convinced that there was no limit to what we can learn about a world we can never see, so long as we follow a method of rigorously logical deduction modeled after the procedures that mathematicians use to achieve complete certainty about their conclusions. After removing enough of the clutter from our thinking to recognize with perfect clarity and distinctness that all our doubts come from thinking and that, whenever we find ourselves thinking, we can be certain we who are doing the thinking must exist, we can further clarify our knowledge to realize how completely certain it is that we who have an idea of an infinitely perfect being must have been created by that same being, usually named "Deus" in Latin, "Dieu" in French, and "God" in English. Our irresistible tendency to believe there are physical bodies, even that we ourselves are intimately joined to one of them, is the final link in Descartes' chain of reasoning. For no all-perfect being would create us with that irresistible tendency unless bodies did exist, such deception being incompatible with the creator's perfection. Thinkers who followed him were not so confident. New questions were asked, raising new doubts. But that was only after Descartes died, filled with confidence that he had found the key to truth.

Descartes' greatest achievement was to pave the way for a renewed recognition that Plato's other-worldly concerns and this-worldly physics belong together. (Plato did, after all, write the *Timaeus*.) He showed that we need, not just a whole new way to understand knowledge, but a whole new way to approach physics. Spinoza (1632-1677) was the first to follow and, in imitation of Descartes, he began his system with an elaborate proof for the existence of an all-perfect being upon which he based his conviction that the mind's thoughts logically must parallel bodies' structures. After Locke (1632-1704), though agreeing with Descartes that we have intuitive certainty of our own existence and demonstrative proof for God's existence, switched to a Socratic emphasis on our *un*certainty about most other things, Leibniz (1646-1716) restored Descartes' basis for certainty: God's goodness. Berkeley (1685-1753) shocked the world by insisting he could prove with certainty that physics is about ideas in the minds, not never-sensed "bodies" outside. Hume (1711-76) seized on Berkeley's new insights to prove that, not only can we prove nothing at all about the thing we are used to calling our "self" or about an all-perfect being called "God," but that the causal-bridge to reality everyone was taking for granted is mental projection. Kant (1724-1804) tried to reinstate confidence in physics with his elaborate theory about the mind and the laws according to which it produces the "world" we experience. Hegel (1770-1831) crossed these strands of Western thought with Eastern thought and concluded that the "mind" creating the "world" and then learning about what it has created is not the puny human mind but the Mind of the World Spirit. Einstein (1879-1955), reverting to the pre-Hegelian common-sense notion that the minds we are concerned with are our individual human minds, de-rigidified Kant's view of our mind's structure and concluded—with great optimism—that we are free to create all sorts of concepts and test them against our stream of sensations to see which of them are most likely to be true.

Yet, for all their differences, it is possible for the keen-eyed inspector to detect the continuing influence of the "looking at a (possible) copy" model in Descartes' and his successors' theories about theorizing. In his third Meditation, Descartes handed on to those who would follow the traditional definitions of truth and error: truth is ours when our ideas match or conform to what is outside, whereas error consists in judging such similarity or conformity exists when it doesn't. Spinoza's sixth axiom is clear: "A true idea must correspond with its ideate or object." Berkeley, after asking the explosive question, "What can an idea be like except another idea?", answered that it is impossible to have an idea that is like a body and that, therefore, even if bodies did exist, ideas would be useless for knowing about them. Hume showed what follows once we notice that ideas cannot be like selves or gods either. Kant added a new twist by concluding that, given our mind's total lack of contact with outside realities, we should perhaps conclude that our concepts' primary function is to put form or shape into our inner sensations. What of Hegel, who joined Berkeley in denying unknown and unknowable realities distinct from private mental representations? We find at the very core of his system such old ideas as idea, concept, notion and form, and especially the most basic picture of all, i.e., of something—the phenomenon painstakingly described in his phenomenology—appearing, plus a subject to which/whom it appears. Finally, however vague his view of the relation between concepts and reality may have been, Einstein took over without question the simple picture of a mind surrounded by sense-experiences and concepts. Both looked at.

Locke was skipped in that last rundown. That is because he deserves special mention for re-drawing the ancient picture of the knower-as-looker, of only outside originals and inside copies. *Locke noticed inside originals.* Aristotle's common-sense model of the human learner was that of an outward-directed, wholly ignorant infant, born with a mind completely empty, who receives every last shred of raw-data/material through the five senses. Locke agreed with all of that, but added that the infant will eventually be able to look inward as well as outward. It can look forward at the ideas (effects) caused inside by those unseen causes lying out beyond them. But—once the unseen outside causes wake it up by creating sensory effects inside it—the mind can also look inward at its own, awakened (conscious) activities. Locke noticed, in other words, that Descartes and others were constantly talking about the mind's unsensed conscious activities, i.e., about sensing, remembering, thinking, etc. But no one can look into another's eyes and see, besides the eyes and its parts, the act of seeing. Or into another's ears and see the act of hearing. And who can see remembering or thinking? Or hear them? Or touch them?

But we all know what those activities are, for we have ideas of them. We even have names for those ideas. If ideas are copies of what is seen, and if we have ideas and names for inner activities that we have never seen by looking outwards, then *bending-back looking or reflection* must be recognized as an additional kind of looking. The mind gets its ideas from experiencing what emerges within it: the effects of outer stimuli, and the acts that are its responses to those effects. Locke used "sensation" and "reflection" as names for these two oppositely-directed experiencings or lookings.

Sensation and reflection. Parallel to extrospection (looking outward) and introspection (looking inward). Both contrasted, as forms of direct observation, to the thinking or reasoning that is possible once our mind acquires the raw-data (maybe-copies) it needs. In addition to these apparently simple correlatives, though, visitors to today's library must master a host of other English terms. Observation, intuition, attention, internalizing, projecting, interpreting, inferring, associating, induction, deduction, construction, analysis, synthesis, mastery, and so on. But it helps to keep in mind where it all began: copy-viewing.

Another bridge: William James. "Know Thyself." "The proper study of man is woman." Two formulas for one ought. Yet, in 2012, the system, i.e., that faceless entity otherwise known as the establishment, is the greatest obstacle standing in its way. Until recently, it was taken for granted that everybody could aim at understanding everything they had time to read up on for themselves. Not a single one of the rethinkers referred to above, whose works will remain as much part of the scientific canon as Galileo's or Newton's, felt that any part of the universe or reality was off-limits to the cutting edge of their minds. And, though the best thinkers continue to boldly mine others' lush meadows for nuggets with which to adorn their system-bouquets, timid thinkers are intimidated by the "Don't trespass on another's area of expertise" myth while the lazy are lulled into thinking they are excused from it.

This Myth of Distinct Disciplines has become an institutional epidemic whose most virulent form is the schizophrenic split between "philosophical" and "scientific" psychology, a form of mental illness—if Szasz was mistaken, it was here—that systematically stands in the way of putting everything together. Whoever believes the Greeks and Pope were right—we must know ourselves who want to know everything—then the idea that "philosophers" can ignore what the "scientists" are learning and vice-versa must be rejected. William James, the greatest "scientific" psychologist of all, refused to live with that split. His works, though they are presently an abandoned gold-mine, are marred only by two things. One was his failure to definitively adopt Descartes' crystal clear Cogito, that is, his failure to definitively adopt in theory what he more than clearly adopted in practice. He put more "flesh" onto the Cogito-skeleton than Descartes ever dreamed of doing and he never allowed it to wander off from the fringe of his thinking. The other was his failure to notice how trapped he was by the looking metaphor. Which is at the root of today's major mental illness.

> *Introspective Observation is what we have to rely on first and foremost and always.* The word introspection need hardly be defined—it means, of course, the looking into our minds and reporting what we there discover. *Everyone agrees that we there discover states of consciousness.* So far as I know, the existence of such states has never been doubted by any critic, however skeptical in other respects he may have been. That we have *cogitations* of some sort is the *inconcussum* in a world most of whose other facts have at some time tottered in the breath of philosophic doubt. (W. James, PP I:185)

A few decades later, John Watson blew on this *inconcussum* so successfully that "scientific" psychology metamorphosed into behaviorology. His attack was squarely aimed at the Achilles Heel of every wanna-be scientist who insists on EITHER consensus OR skepticism. Watson wrote:

> As a result of this major assumption that there is such a thing as consciousness and that we can analyse it by introspection, we find as many analyses as there are individual psychologists. There is no way of experimentally attacking and solving psychological problems and standardizing methods.
>
> In 1912 the objective psychologists or behaviorists . . . decided either to give up psychology or else to make it a natural science. They saw their brother scientists making progress in medicine, in chemistry, in physics. Every new

discovery in those fields was of prime importance . . . In his first efforts to get uniformity in subject matter and in methods the behaviorist began his own formulation of the problem of psychology by sweeping aside all medieval conceptions. He dropped from his scientific vocabulary all subjective terms such as sensation, perception, image, desire, purpose, and even thinking and emotion as they were subjectively defined.

The time has arrived for brushing away the cobwebs covering the entrance to James' brilliant legacy and re-joining inquiries that he, as much as anyone, helped to split asunder. And to do it by using his most important insights to correct his oversights. (The looking metaphor is ubiquitous.) First of all, the insight that *we do more than looking*. We do look. What we observe does exist. But to notice that obvious fact requires more than looking. Obviously. And to pick it out as a fact that is obvious requires more than looking. Obviously. Just as it takes more than looking to get over the myth that there are really distinct sciences, with established findings, about which there is a consensus. For those with eyes to read what's in our libraries, no myth has ever been easier to see through.

[In 1934] there is a bewildering Babel of tongues as to what logic is all about. The different schools, the traditional, the linguistic, the psychological, the epistemological, and the mathematical, speak different languages, and each regards the other as not really dealing with logic at all. (M. Cohen & E. Nagel, *An Introduction to Logic.*)

We know today [1980] that mathematics does not possess the qualities that in the past earned for it universal respect and admiration. Mathematics was regarded as the acme of exact reasoning, a body of truths in itself, and the truth about the design of nature. How man came to the realization that these values are false and just what our present understanding is constitutes the major themes [of what follows]. (M. Kline, *Mathematics: The Loss of Certainty*, 1980.)

A final thought and a note of caution; when we commissioned the interviews, several of our contributors (who shall remain nameless!) expressed the view that there is now [1986] no real doubt over how quantum theory should be interpreted. At the very least, we hope this book will show that there is little justification for such complacency. (P. Davies & J. Brown, *The Ghost in the Atom*, 1986.)

Those are three quotes from three twentieth-century authors concerning the three branches on the knowledge-tree that Kant, back in 1780, regarded as long-established, consensus sciences. Whoever is familiar with the controversies raging since T. Kuhn's 1962 *The Structure of Scientific Revolutions* will understand what is behind the bold proclamation contained in a speech to an audience at Moscow State University on 25 November, 1985, by the chairman of the company that publishes one of America's most prestigious scientific journals: "Scientists know nothing for certain." Which may have meant that scientists literally know nothing for certain, not even that they exist, or may have meant only that, though scientists think they know some things for certain, they do not agree on what those things are.

This brings us back to the ubiquitous problem of meaning. Watson, after rejecting James' claims about consciousness and introspection, took the precaution of warning those who might continue to side with James: "Let me hasten to add that if the behaviorist were to ask you what you mean by the subjective terms you have been in the habit of using he could soon make you tongue-tied with contradictions. He could even convince you that you do not know what you mean by them. You have been using them uncritically as a part of your social and literary traditions." James, years after his bold affirmation of consciousness as an *inconcussum*, wrote a 1904 essay entitled "Does 'Consciousness' Exist?" At the end of it, he concluded—in part—that thought, like consciousness, is a "careless name" for what is really part of the same "stuff" from which the rest of the world is made and that, if "consciousness" is used as the name for any other entity, "that entity is fictitious." If Descartes, like what's-his-name (you remember, the man in Washington Irving's story who fell asleep under the tree and didn't regain consciousness for a hundred years), woke up today, what would he think if he went into one of today's libraries and got caught up on his reading? Would he still feel confident he knew what "Cogito, ergo sum" meant?

If you've understood any of the preceding, then one thing at least is for sure. Even if you double up laughing at claims that logic, mathematics, physics, psychology, and philosophy do not exist but only people who speak and write to help others understand what they think, that their public verbal agreements can mask hidden disagreements and confusions as massive as those met with in theologians who pledge allegiance to the same scriptures and dogmatic formulae, you can be quite certain of this: you've understood. Something. Or some things. Or some thoughts. The only person who will ever discover that two *other* people disagree about something, whether about a fact or about the best choice of words to describe that fact, is a person who can understand both of those *other* persons. Even if those *other* persons use identical language to express utterly contradictory thoughts, only a person who can do more than look will get to the thoughts behind their words and realize that they are contradicting each other, i.e., get to the contradictory *meanings* of their words.

Go a step further. These pages are composed by a single writer to convey his thoughts about the contradictory beliefs of many *other* thinkers. If you have understood anything about those contradictory beliefs, it is because the single person you call "myself" can understand what you are reading. You may agree with some of the views expressed by this *other* person and disagree with others. Before you can do either, you have to understand them. So, if Descartes were a Rip Van Winkle, he should still say "Cogito, ergo sum." And, unless he got confused, he'd immediately add "*Intelligo* quod lego et quod dico." He would even have an explanation for the continued lack of consensus among "scientists." One of his most basic principles of all—one that was one of James', too—was that we have free-will. James took it one step further: our first wholly explicit decision should be to believe we are free to make such a first decision. Which decision is only an illusion if Descartes' Cogito is an illusion. The Cogito alone makes intelligible James' magnificent obsession with freedom. And with the varieties of individual human experience.

And what does "Cogito" mean? It means the same as "I am thinking." But we must understand what we are thinking about. "Intelligo" means "I understand." We must begin to be awestruck by the fact that we can understand.

C. THOUGHT: MORE! Not Less.

Thought. "THE!" Magic Carpet. On the wings of thought we can fly outwards in any direction, to the very edge of space. And beyond. Thoughts can carry us backward to the beginning of time. And beyond, all the way to eternity. They sweep us ahead into the future. Without end, amen. In thought we can descend to the dark despair of hell and in thought we can soar to the ecstasies of paradise. In thought, we can hover at any distance from earth's surface and take in at a single glance whatever that elevation's field of vision embraces. From a mile up, we could take in an entire village or town. From two hundred and fifty miles up, we might take in an entire continent. From two hundred and fifty thousand miles, we'd see the planet much the way the moon-walking astronauts did. From the edge of the solar system, our visual field would include our star and its retinue of orbiting planets. Or, if we choose, we can zoom back to one red blood cell navigating the ocean flowing through our arteries and veins in order to examine that cell's colossally intricate make-up: about 270 million hemoglobin molecules, each constructed of about 10,000 atoms. Or zoom in further to a single, nearly empty hydrogen atom's nucleus, whose lone occupant is an infinitesimal proton.

I trust that, as your eyes skimmed those tiny figures, your *thoughts* were taking you on a fantastic voyage from your armchair out to the edge of space, then back again to one of the infinitesimally small atoms in one single red blood cell making up a tiny fraction of the many pints of blood presently being cycled through your heart every sixty seconds. As they can take you back a few moments to when you first began reading this paragraph. Or to this morning when you woke and opened your eyes on a new day. Or to yesterday and the meal you ate in the evening. Or back to today, Sunday, June 21, 1992, the day I am (was, for you) sitting before a keyboard, typing these lines about the freedom your *thoughts* offer you, regardless of where your body is presently confined, regardless of how limited is your range of vision this very moment, that is, regardless of how little is and how much isn't observed by you right now.

Thoughts free us. But, in a sense, something else does, too, and those who believe the proper setting for psychological research is an animal laboratory too often overlook it. Build up to this next reflection slowly. There is a closet about ten feet from where I am seated. Here outside or there inside that closet, my thoughts can transport me to any place in the universe as instantly as they could take me aboveground if I woke in a coffin beneath six feet of earth the way miners trapped by an explosion regain consciousness beneath a mile of it. Whether I'm here outside or there inside the closet, I can roam in thought to the other rooms in the house, down the stairs, out to the street, across it, through the park, and so on. But what a difference there would be if I were in the closet and not out here. Why? A one-word question, with a one-word answer. What word?

Language. Words. Books. The thousands of words in the hundreds of books around the walls of this mini-library. Libraries are where most psychological research should be conducted, for it is there, where so little of the furniture of heaven and earth can be found, that so much human learning goes on. Routinely, prolifically, intensely. And all that library-learners need for their ongoing learning are rows upon rows of tiny figures just like these that your eyes are scanning. What can they learn in libraries where little else but tiny ciphers can be observed? All about anything in the universe, observed or not. Didn't William James—who forgot more than John Watson ever knew—notice what Watson, more intrigued by the animal laboratory, didn't: ". . . the truth remains that, after adolescence has begun, 'words, words, words,' must constitute a large part, and an always larger part as life advances, of what the human being has to learn." All I have ever known of the historical individual named John Watson I have learned from words. The triggers to any thoughts about John Watson or to any thoughts about my thoughts about John Watson you have had while looking at these pages have been words.

Words, words, words. My ability to explore other worlds would be vastly poorer this moment, if I were in the closet rather than out here. If I were, not so much locked into the closet, but locked away from these books. As it is, I can reach for books—about the first three minutes after the Big Bang, about the slow evolution of this planet and of the species that now populate its surface, about the remains of the Mayan words whose meaning is being painstakingly deciphered . . . about anything "in" those books—and their words conjure thoughts of details I'd never dream of without words but which come to me in profusion with them. Books containing nothing but tiny words. Rows and rows of them. But what worlds they open up. Not only real worlds, but worlds of imagination, and memory, and anticipation. Populated by things that never were and never will be, things that were but are no longer, and things that have never been but will be. Things never observed nor now observed. Things thought about.

That is the final frontier. The world of the non-existent. The world of the imaginary or, rather, the (merely) imagined. The world of the merely-thinkable, of the merely thought-about. The world Parmenides said could not be, could not be thought, and certainly could not be named or talked about. It is the final frontier, because it is the battleground where the greatest struggles of serious thinkers take place. Idealists like Berkeley and Hegel believed that those who believe in material bodies believe in fictions, because they decided bodies do not exist. Materialists like Watson believe that those who believe in non-material thoughts believe in fictions, because they've decided non-material thoughts do not exist. Others like James conclude that both idealists and materialists believe in fictions, since neither bodies nor thoughts but only islands of neither-one-nor-the-other experience exist. This is the final frontier. And, for those intent on truth rather than fiction, a truly lone-ly one. For, each skull-encapsulated brain or the taxi-driver using it must first ask: What else besides me can I be sure about? Is it possible I am only imagining my companions?

Re-view. Thoughts and language. Throughout this opening chapter, the aim has been to show that they go together but in a very *loose* sort of way. Yet not so loose that a determined reader cannot view and review the words in order to understand their meaning, i.e., understand the thoughts guiding their paper putting on. There are many bad errors we can make in trying to understand what goes on in libraries. One blundering error is becoming so obsessed with correct use, including the correct use, usage, employment, or dangling deployment prepositions of—people taught to hold everything in abeyance till the verb-caboose confirms or disconfirms their tentative image-construction show that *that's* all a matter of what James drew attention to, viz., culturo-linguistic or linguo-cultural *habit*—that we treat our ability to understand in spite of incorrections as trite or trivial. One that is even blunderinger is becoming obsessed with finding *rigid* rules coupling changes in thought with changes in language. But the blund'ringest of all is failing to notice the most important question of all: Do either thoughts or language really exist? Perhaps they are mere figments of my imagination. As critical thinkers intent on becoming confident we know what we're talking about, we must begin by getting clear on what there *IS* to talk about. We must examine the evidence for both thought and language. Are they both real? If not, which isn't? Which is a figment of imagination? Or are both unreal fictions? That is, are both unreal, therefore both real fictions?

We begin with thoughts. Is it possible that they are mere figments of my imagination? From Plato till the two W's—Watson and Wittgenstein—no one ever doubted thoughts, those things James too soon called *inconcussa*. Plato thought our thoughts can put us in touch with other worlds. Aristotle thought so much of thought that he thought the First Mover was only secondarily a mover and primarily a thinker. And Descartes thought that, regardless of whether there were any other worlds and any motionless mover-thinkers in them, he knew he could think, even about them. I may find it difficult to question a lifetime habit of thinking I've had thoughts and be open to saying that this organism can only *say* or *speak*, whether out loud or silently [sic], but anyone who is used to Descartes' doubting habit—pretend neither thinking I's nor speaking organisms exist!—will find this new wagon can be pulled by the old mare of doubt as easily as duck soup. (Humpties want their mixes noticed.)

If thoughts do not exist, then what are they? [Pretend that makes sense.] They would have to be figments of my imagination. At one time I thought a lot about Santa Claus, and I thought there was a Santa to think about, but that was an illusion, since no Santa Claus ever existed. Paranoids not only think a lot about FBI plots against them, but they also talk a lot about them, even though no such plots exist. Perhaps thoughts do not exist either. Perhaps they are simply figments of imagination.

The thing any scientifically-minded person does when questions about the existence of neutrinos, curved space, gravity waves, etc., arise is *examine the evidence*. The first kind of evidence we with the "Seeing is believing" disposition look for is something to look at. That is, observing or looking is the kind of evidence we feel most confident about. The earlier claim on an earlier page that we all know what remembering and thinking are because we have names for them does not prove that they exist. Such names as leprechaun, nonexistence, and Othello exist, but who thinks their real names make leprechauns, nonexistence, or Othello real? Anthropologists and sociologists train themselves to be mere reporters, not judgers. They don't automatically believe that what primitives say is evidence for what exists. We will someday drown in the endless words churned out by computers, but there are no thoughts guiding them. We need more evidence than the existence of the word "thought."

But who would say they have observed a thought? Plato explicitly tells us that no eye has seen nor ear heard an Idea. Are ideas and thoughts the same? Can they be sensed? In other words . . . Do either have a color? Do thoughts make sounds so as to be audible? Have I ever sniffed to detect the presence of a thought? Or licked my lips? Or reached out to touch one? Are they right who think we can see thoughts if we look inward? Each one must rely on her or his own mind's eye for this kind of looking, and most people are convinced "mind's eye" is a metaphor. Some who have taken introspection seriously claim they do find images, but no thoughts, and some historians believe the death of introspection as a reliable tool for psychology was caused by the (in) famous controversy about the possibility of "imageless thought," the outcome of which seems to have been that Wurzburgers in Germany could do what Ithacans in the U.S.A. could not. Images, too, have gone the way of thoughts, so powerful still are the ghosts of the two W's. That is, most non-introspecting psychologists deny that their would-be introspecting subjects see any images when they look inward because there are no images to see. Or thoughts.

On the other hand, perhaps the mistake is thinking that language exists. Perhaps the way a kiss is just a kiss, growls are merely growls, sounds nothing but sounds, and noises not anything except noises. Why believe indentations in tombstone marble are more than cemetery indentations? Or that slate-markings are more than chalk marks, ink marks not just ink marks, tiny figures against a dark-background oscilloscope screen anything but scattered glowings? Perhaps behaviorists had half the truth when they said that thinking is only talking. The whole truth is that talking is only the uttering of varied sounds by human mouths. Perhaps cognitive behaviorists would be half-right if they called THEIR 'introspective [sic]' raw data "products of verbal-behavior behaving." What's all-right is that their "written documents" are nice pieces of paper dirtied by shaped, arranged ink marks made by OTHER humans' hands. In that case, Herbert Terrace's claim that the gestures of chimps (to which we can add the squeals of whales, the squawks of parrots, and the stomping of horses named Hans) are merely instinctive and/or conditioned behaviors, period!, is true. If human language is not really language but only behavior and/or behavior's physical product, then animal language isn't really language either. And there's NO language, private or public.

How can anyone tell whether there is anything more than ink marks on this page? Ink marks with shapes and arrangements, to be certain, but nothing but shaped and arranged ink marks after all? For instance, is this> **b l i t** a word or only five ink marks? i, it will be noted, is two ink marks, a dot atop a pole. Is this> **p o d** three different ink marks, a circular ink mark flanked by another ink mark that is right-side up on the left and up-side down on the right (or is it up-side down on the left and right-side up on the right?), or one word that is both right-side up and up-side down at the same time? Is **69** a number, just two numbers, two different numbers, a number that is the same whether it is right-side up or up-side down, i.e., one number written twice in succession but right-side up on the left and up-side down on the right (or vice-versa? or is it impossible to tell until we're sure whether "the" number is a six or a nine?)? Oh, or is it . . . no, are they just two ink marks? In fact, which of the following is a word, which a letter, which a number, and which nothing but a shaped ink mark (or several?): one, I, i, 1, 001, unum, ein, un? Just look and see which look the same.

Many people, e.g., Thomas Kuhn, have been suggesting lately that astronomers do not see the same sky that our ancestors saw. Where we see a nearby star, ancients saw a sun, and where we see distant suns, they saw stars. The psychological switch is referred to as a gestalt-switch. It occcurs when there's a switch in the theories used for theory-laden perceiving. Perhaps the same psychological phenomenon is at work when people look at pieces of paper that have nothing but shaped, arranged ink marks on them and swear that they see an entire zoo-population: punctuation, vowels, consonants, morphemes, syllables, letters, words, articles, prepositions, nouns, pronouns, verbs, adjectives, adverbs, conjunctions, phrases, clauses, sentences, declaratives, interrogatives, imperatives, exclamations, compounds, protases, apodoses, hypotheticals, disjunctions, propositions, majors, minors, premises, statements, conclusions, raw data for the psychology of religion, verbal reports, and so on. Or maybe both our ancestors and we see the same sense-givens and impose different mental-theory interpretations on them, just as those who see a zoo on this page and those who don't do. Compare people watching what goes on in the night sky, people looking at a photo with streaks all over it, and people studying strips of paper with rows of squiggles running along them: perhaps our ancestors only had one "seeing" option because they knew only one interpretation-option, whereas we who have read astronomy books have several, just as layfolk have only one option ("Those are streaks") until they've learned what nuclear physicists think about, just as children can't see brain waves until they've learned to project as well as some neurologists do. Once we learn all the relevant theories of all lookers, we become free to "see" whatever we want by choosing whichever theory we want to apply, impose, project, interpret with. So, until we learn to "read" Mayan, we'll see indentations, the same way infants will see only the same boring little black marks a chimp, dolphin, or horse would until they—the children—learn to "read" the way no animal ever will. Granted, we see or observe something. But what?

And what are seeing and observing? Two different mental processes exercisable by one single mind? (Or, better, by one single person.) Names for two different concepts? Or eighteen ink marks? (Count them: s e e i n g a n d o b s e r v i n g) Sorry, I should have said twenty.* If you stick just to what you see or observe, which is the most obvious answer? Do the children watching the parade see better before their clear vision has been blurred by cultural accretions, i.e., by the sophisticated theories they learn in school? Or less well? Whoever does not acquire the habit of distinguishing names of realities (real mental processes) from names of concepts and both from names of names—the habit related to theories about supposition, reference, extension, and so on—will never learn to understand the question "Is what you call 'a name' anything but ink marks?" (*Did you count the dots?)

No decisions can be more crucial than these two. Do thoughts exist? Does language exist? Where should we apply that most dangerous of knives, Ockham's Razor? Which should be eliminated in the interests of simplicity and parsimony? Surely it would simplify the task of understanding everything by declaring that there is no cognition to understand. As for language and that zoo of distinctions and subdistinctions, would any schoolchild vote to keep them if they were offered a choice? Which simpler-ness will help us understand the truth about this world better? (Or does it all depend on what replaces what's eliminated?)

If these questions have answers, only those will understand them who learn to attend carefully and to notice well when they do so.

Understand. The first question to ask is not whether or not thoughts and language exist. The first question is: Do I understand the question(s)? How can I decide whether the answers to them are true or false unless I understand them? How can I look for evidence in support of them or against them unless I understand what the questions mean and what would count as evidence? How can I even understand the questions in this paragraph? Or rather, *do* I understand them? If Rorty is right, the premier fact is this: I not only understand the questions, but I also understand the contradictory answers proposed by people who understand each other but disagree, I also understand their claims and counterclaims regarding evidence, I also understand the reasoning they present to connect their evidence to their conclusions. I could do none of these things when I was a newborn infant. I couldn't even notice that I couldn't.

Attention. Conduct a ten-item experiment. First read through all of the sentences that follow, one at a time. As you finish each sentence, look up from the page and concentrate on doing what the sentence asks you to do. This is an experiment that anyone can conduct in the library whenever s/he wishes to. (After memorizing it.) Or, to count things differently, it will be many experiments—one per sentence—that anyone can conduct anytime.

1- Wiggle the toes in your right foot, feel those toes wiggle, then ask whether or not it's obvious that the wiggling feelings are down at the end of your right foot.
2- Do the same with the toes in your left foot.
3- Tighten the muscles in the calf of your right leg, feel the muscles tense, then ask whether it's not obvious that the tensing is part-way up your right leg.
4- Do the same with your left calf.
5- Tense your whole right hand, feel the tension, think if it's not obvious that the tension's at the end of your right arm.

56

6- Repeat that for your left hand.

7- Move your tongue around the inside of your mouth, notice all of the sensations that produces, notice where they are.

8- Flare your nostrils out and in, attend to the sensations, notice their location.

9- Alternate wiggling each ear, one at a time, then do the location-noticing.

10- Repeat the three steps for each part of your brain, one part at a time, beginning with the pineal gland. (Don't stop now till you reach the end of the next paragraph.)

That is an adaptation of an old trick. The old trick begins with a clear instruction that directs us to first read through an entire text without pausing, only to have the text begin with a counter-instruction to do something that requires pausing, which subjects do, only to be scolded at the end for not following the opening instruction to NOT pause until they had read through the entire text.

In this adaptation, the contradictory instructions are introduced immediately, in the same paragraph. "First read through all of the sentences that follow" does not explicitly add "without pausing." But which interpretation of "all of the sentences that follow" is most reasonable: All of those in the book? All of those in the instruction-paragraph? Or just the ten sentences that constitute the ten-item experiment? "One at a time" is added immediately, but that is ambiguous. It could easily mean pause after each one, but it could be (and was) added as a pure redundancy to the previous "First read through all of the sentences that follow." After all, how does any normal person read any sentences except one at a time?! The issuance of a counter-order follows immediately, though most of us probably won't pay attention to that: "As you finish each sentence, look up from the page and concentrate on what the sentence asks you to do." The trick was introduced here solely to draw attention to the present topics, viz., understanding, attention, and noticing.

Noticing. Literally, of course, attention does not exist, only people who are or arent' attending. Much the way thinking does not exist, only people who are or aren't thinking. Yet, so long as we are not taken in by our thing-making metaphors, using such nouns is not dangerous.

In most instances, such reifications are useful. In some cases, they are indispensable and unavoidable. Attention is just useful. (Reifications do not exist, either, only people who understand thoughts that are accompanied by imagery.) Our ability to attend and how our attending relates to our habits is usually not noticed, hence rarely appreciated. One writer who noticed and appreciated was William James, whose chapters on habit and attention are book-ends, so to speak, for his chapters on consciousness and the self. Those four chapters of his would make an excellent introduction to what follows.

People attend in different ways. There's the kind of attention that is not being deliberately controlled and there's the kind that is. When we see a bright flash of light (an explosion that lights up the night sky momentarily or a momentary brightening of the room when the camera's flash goes off) or hear a loud noise (a cherry bomb goes off or a peal of thunder reaches us) or detect a strong odor (the gas from the turned-on but unlit burner on the stove reaches us or the smoke from outside comes under the door), our attention normally is drawn automatically to the flash, the sound, the odor, or to what we believe is the flash's, sound's or odor's cause. If we are awake, that is. If we aren't, such strong stimuli will often wake us. When you carried out each of the above ten experiments by looking up from the page and doing what each one called for, you deliberately caused something to happen in some part of your body and consciously paid attention to what you felt as a result. Or noticed that you couldn't do the experiment: e.g., you don't know how to flare your nostrils or how to separately wiggle your ears. (And how about #10?!) If you can't cause the change, you won't feel the sensations that (don't) result from the change.

More experiments. To understand some of the implications of those ten experiments, see what you can notice by paying attention to the next ten.

a- Think back and ask, "Did I understand the instructions for those ten experiments?" Think back and ask, i.e., recall, try to remember, re-view, whether or not you were able to read right through them without having to get out your dictionary once and look up any words. If so, never forget that fact. It is a key to everything. What would you do without the thoughts that come to you so effortlessly and that you understand so clearly?

b- Next, look back at experiments 1-10. Recall whether you succeeded in all of them. Were there any you flunked?

c- Now review your present beliefs about other people. I think everyone can do the **Ready** first seven, but not everyone can do the last three. I can do the eighth, as well, but not the ninth or tenth. I believe I have met people who can do the ninth, but no one ever told me they could do the 10th. Do you believe, as I do, that everyone can do seven, that some can do as many as 1001, but that no one can do the last? (1001 = 9 in the binary system invented by Nature and revealed first to Leibniz.) Whose beliefs did you just think about? How many beliefs?

d- Try to remember your reactions to the items in the previous paragraph ("c"). Do you **Aim** agree with me that the item most people (most of the ones who read that paragraph, of course) would be surprised by would be "some can do as many as 1001"? And that the reason is that they are in the habit of thinking 1001 is a synonym for "one thousand and one" and haven't learned to be as quick with the binary code as they are with the decimal one? Were you surprised by 1001? Were there other things you were even more surprised by? For instance, the switching—in that paragraph "c"—from "tenth" to "10th" to simply "the last"? (In fact, did you even notice it until now when you read the sentence previous to this one?) Do you recall whether you balked at the claim that everyone can do the first seven experiments. I deliberately lied. I don't believe any infants or anyone totally paralyzed can do even one of them. Did you deliberate about whether or not you think everyone can do the first seven experiments? Did you ask "Can anyone without a highly developed language, e.g., infants and feral children, understand each instruction before carrying it out?" Have the above words helped you notice details about your thinking that you normally don't pay attention to or notice?

e- Has it occurred to you yet that the book you are reading may be instructions for one **Fire!** huge experiment made up of thousands of experiments such as these? And that you may have to reread it many times before it will become clear how all the pieces fit together? For instance, the reason the last experiment drew your attention to the [what do YOU think 1001 means?] switches from "tenth" to "10th" to "the last" was to draw your attention to what I regard as an obvious fact, namely, to the ease with which we can read right through things, get the general drift, and not even notice the shift in words or vocabulary. You may or may not have noticed, in the first of this new series of experiment-instructions, that I inserted some synonymous terms for "think back," namely, recall, try to remember, and re-view. Did you notice that the second of this new series of experiments began with "Next, look back," that its second sentence began with "recall," that the third set of instructions began with "Now review," and the last with "Try to remember"? Try to remember whether or not you noticed those details. Ask yourself whether, in the context of these pages, those various wordings generally meant the same thing? [Did you notice that the context-interrupting words in **bold letters,** inserted in three recent paragraphs, fitted together with each other to conjure a sub-context of their own? How many times can a person be interrupted—by sleep, meals, jobs, parties, etc.—and still put all the ideas from all the pages of this book together?] Since most people try to think as they speak, we are in the habit of tacitly including thinking whenever we are speaking of saying. And did you notice how this new set of experiments is being numbered with a, b, c, d, e, in contrast to the way the old set was lettered 1, 2, 3, 4, 5? (Even though both numbers and letters are really just fiction-concepts: notice how you can "impose" either concept or name on the ink-marks I, V, X, L, C, D, M.)

f- Distinctions—drawing lines—play a key role in any theory of knowledge. Some are extremely important. First, notice that we use the word "feel" in relation to two kinds of things, inside ones and outside ones. "What you feel" can refer to what you feel when you wiggle your toes while holding your bare feet in the air, what you feel when you tighten your calf muscles, tense your hands, roll your tongue around inside your mouth, flare your nostrils, wiggle your ears, and altar the various parts of your brain, or to what you feel when you rub your finger across this page, lean against a hot radiator, jump under a cold shower, step on a nail, etc. What we feel when we do our wiggling and tightening are inside. What we feel in the latter cases seems so much outside that we speak of "touching"—making contact with—them. Are there really two kinds of things to feel, though?

If so, they are *very* different things. The easiest way to begin noticing the difference is by noticing a correlated distinction between direct presence and physical presence. When I look at a page such as this, it is directly present. By saying that the page is directly present to me, I mean there is MORE than MERE physical presence. The pillow under my head is physically present even as I sleep. In the case of the book, it is physically present AND I am aware of it, whereas in the case of the pillow I am not aware of it. For something to be, not simply present physically but directly present, I must be aware of it. William James would say I have 'knowledge of acquaintance' with it.

The difference between the two classes of objects can now be made clear: their status changes differently. I may fall asleep, in which case the book will become physically present ONLY, or I may wake, in which case the pillow becomes directly present ALSO. In the case of the wiggling (having bare feet in the air avoids reference to feeling our socks, shoes, or the ground) and the tensing, the change in status is far more drastic: the feel(ing)s don't even exist when we're not feeling them. Such things-felt are not the kind of thing that can just plain exist, i.e., be physically present only. Ask most people if such "feelings" as muscle tenseness, tickles, aches, and other things we say we "feel" (which is why we call them feelings) can float around in the air, detached from muscles, feet, jaws, etc.

Can such minute details as these be understood by anyone? Of course. All of us grow up to unquestioningly take it for granted that the two sorts of feelings come from two different sources. The sensations we get when there is contact between our skin and outside objects come from those outside objects. What we feel in the second set of cases comes from inside our body. Simple!

g or 7- Once we notice the distinction between the things that are outside of our skin and those that are on the inside of it and begin to pay attention to it, we also begin to develop a habit of noticing when other people are not paying enough attention to it. For instance, suppose we ask which physical thing in our environment we touch and feel most often—would it be the ground under our feet, the air that blows across our face as a gentle breeze or through our hair as a strong wind or penetrates our skin as a freezing cold, the sunshine that we soak in at the beach, or the bed-sheets we spend 8-10 hours between each night, the clothing we wear 14-16 hours every day, etc.?—we will instantly reply "No, it's our own body!" Or we will, once we have acquired the habit of not forgetting that obvious fact. One of the things that made William James the greatest psychologist of all is that he seems to have noticed practically everything. He never forgot about the fact that the sensations that are least interrupted, most voluminous, and not at all escapable, the ones that we spend very few minutes of the day explicitly thinking about, are *our body-sensations*. The world we experience, James wrote, "comes at all times with our body as its center, center of vision, center of action, center of interest."

An excellent way to notice the kind of attention needed to notice something clearly enough that we can then attend to forming the habit of attending to it often enough to make it a habit, so that noticing others' lack of attention to it at critical points becomes habitual, is to begin noticing our body—or "body"—sensations. Tests one through ten above involved efforts to deliberately or "consciously" cause certain body-sensations that we can try to notice by deliberately, voluntarily, intentionally, or "consciously" paying attention to them. Now, we must begin noticing the body sensations that we do not ordinarily notice for the very simple reason that our attention is directed elsewhere, that is, because we are too preoccupied with other things to notice these. First, though, consider another distinction.

The distinction amounts to a combination of two earlier ones. The first is the distinction between observing and thinking. While observing some things, the furniture in our prehistoric cave, the bookcases lining the walls of our study, the lines of print on the open page of the book we are reading, we can think about entire worlds of other, not right here right now observed, things. The second is the distinction between having something directly present and paying attention to it. If we distinguish the things we observe into those we pay attentin to and those we don't, then we can test out the hypotheses that (1)everything we observe is something directly present to us and that (2)we cannot pay close attention to more than a very little of what is directly present to us. Are the hypotheses true?

Before getting to your body, think of this text. I assume that you noticed the o that was deliberately omitted from "attentin" in the last paragraph. But did you also correct the following "errata" earlier in the text: occcurs, arent', two f sections, and altar? If you did not know how to spell well and know the alphabet, would you even now regard those as "errors"? Did you notice that "Rip Van Winkle" was deliberately replaced a few paragraphs earlier by "what's his name" to suggest I couldn't remember it? Did "hundred years" distract you from your smooth train of thought? *How many infants, feral children, and animals, lacking the incredible "language skills" and vast amount of knowledge you possess, would notice those things.* Or notice the egregious blunder of asking, near the beginning of this paragraph, whether you noticed a missing o! Can anyone notice what doesn't exist?! (Can we not only think of things without observing them, but also notice things we are not observing?) That is the reverse side of observing things without noticing them. If you stop reading and look back at "attentin" in the previous paragraph, even stare at it and concentrate all your attention on it, will the rest of the page disappear? Will you stop seeing all the other things you are not attending to? Can you attend to each single thing you're seeing? That's the text.

Now your body. Earlier, the phrase "right here right now" was used a great deal. Where is "here and now"? We must not, as Hegel did, overlook the obvious. There isn't any "THE" here-and-now. Rather, whoever wonders where his or hers is will then-and-there find it where his or her body is. Normally. We can deal with out-of-body experiences later. I assume that, as you earlier read about looking at the earth from a few to a few hundred thousand miles in space, about roaming the corridors of time from early eternity to eons hence, you didn't find to your surprise that your body moved to those places. If someone asks, while you are inside a dark closet but thinking about the sun which is 93,000,000 miles distant, "Where are you?", you would expect them to understand you whether you answered "I'm in a closet" or "I'm millions of miles away." In the latter case, you would tacitly mean "from here," because otherwise "away" makes no sense, and you would mean you were millions of miles away in thought from where you were physically present. Bodily. The first meaning of "here" refers, not to bodies a few inches, a few miles, or a few light-years away, but to one's own body. One's body provides the anchor to here, the spatial half of the here-and-now from which our thoughts can set us free. The thesis here is that it provides evidence that we can attend to only a fraction of what we observe, of the things directly present.

Put the book down and stand up for thirty seconds. Do it . . . I'll wait . . . Too long? Ten seconds will be enough . . . Now, did you notice where your arms or your tongue were? Try it again and notice whether your arms were up over your head with only the very tips of your index fingers touching each other . . . You already know they weren't like that?! Were they straight out at your sides (try that for thirty minutes!)? Down at your side? Etc. Next, think back and ask yourself whether you really stood up or whether you actually got down and stretched out on the floor? Maybe you walked up the wall and stood upside down on the ceiling? (As a bonus question ask: "Did I get dizzy?" People who suffer from vertigo lose their normal 'sense of balance.') That's enough to give you the idea for what is meant by "the world we experience 'comes at all times with our body as its center . . .'" So unnoticed are these ever-present (during waking hours) body-sensations that, until recently, there was no special name for them. Recently, though, such terms as proprioception, somasthesia, interoceptive sense, kinesthesia, nisus, body-image, etc., have been introduced to refer to various components of the sensations which result from our routine (own-)body-observation. Unnoticed, unattended-to (own-)body-observing. But those unnoticed, unattended-to sensations can be noticed and attended-to. Their usually unnoticed, unattended-to status can be noticed and attended to, even though it cannot be observed. By the way, were you conscious while you did the experiments?

Conscious is not synonymous with *attended-to*. Not normally. Nor unconscious synonymous with unattended-to. We Humpty-Dumpties are perfectly free to change our normal speech habits. But, being unconscious of our doing so, i.e., not attending to the fact that we are doing so, is not just dangerous but disastrous. As a century of the Freud-spawned change has shown, with all kinds of 'experts' referring to unattended facets of experience as "unconscious"!

Whoever consciously begins paying attention to our common-sense understanding of things will eventually end up with an enormous collection of raw data on the subject. For examples . . . Arguers have an amazing capacity to walk from the post office back to their business offices while attending to the fine points of very abstract arguments. They seem quite conscious and quite able to see the sidewalk, the curb where it ends and they must step down to the street, the people they walk around, the cars they allow to pass, and so on. Blindfold them and they'll continue the argument, but begin tripping, bumping, getting run over, and so on, much the way blind (and not merely blind-folded) people who are not visually conscious of, i.e., who cannot see, things would. Too, people often do double-takes, seconds or hours after experiencing things while their attention is distracted, at which point they suddenly discover that what they saw and remembered had an important significance. Too, people can work in circumstances where a steady sound in the background becomes wholly unnoticed. Till it suddenly stops. Who wouldn't be startled if, while they are completely absorbed in a novel, the lights suddenly went out? Or if the earth and chair beneath them suddenly vaporized and the various pressures they felt suddenly ceased? The issue here, of course, is not whether you agree, but whether you understand the thesis being presented to you.

> h or 8- From the very outset of life, we acquire habits by the bushel without paying any attention to what is going on. Later, after we've learned enough, we can begin taking charge of our own habit-formation and habit-extinction (habit-changing) by dint of the things we are attentive enough to. Knowing about "birds of a feather," we become attentive to who it will be we'll associate with. Knowing that "repetition is the mother of learning," we'll be attentive to what messages are repeated in what we freely choose to read, listen to, and watch. (Books, radio, TV.) Wm.

James thought so highly of our power of voluntary attention that he came back to it, over and over again.

> . . . whether the attention come by grace of genius or by dint of will, the longer one does attend to a topic the more mastery of it one has. And the faculty of voluntarily bringing back a wandering attention, over and over again, is the very root of judgment, character, and will. No one is *compos sui* if he have it not. An education which should improve this faculty would be the education par excellence.

i or 9-   Orthodox behaviorists, i.e., those who followed John Watson's advice to ignore consciousness and to pay attention solely to the correlations between the (human or non-human) animal-organism's behavior and its environment, quite often developed the handicap-habit we name "tunnel vision" or "psychic blindness." That is what happened to John himself:

> He then who would introduce consciousness, either as an epiphenomenon or as an active force interjecting itself into the physical and chemical happenings of the body, does so because of spiritualistic and vitalistic leanings. The Behaviorist cannot find consciousness in the test tube of his science. He finds no evidence anywhere for a stream of consciousness, not even for one so convincing as that described by William James. He does, however, find convincing proof of an ever-widening stream of behavior.

When the details of twentieth-century "expert" thought are pared down enough to allow its most remarkable features to stand out, the most remarkable feature of that history will be the size of the parades that gathered behind two W's, i.e., those who believed they were specialists in philosophy and followed Wittgenstein and those who regarded themselves as experts in psychology and who followed Watson. These herdings will be remarkable for the way they confirmed the razor-sharp insight of William James into the relations between will, attention, and habit. Begin by deliberately—voluntarily, will-fully—attending to environmental changes and behavioral responses and carefully cultivate the habit of inattending everything commonfolk mean by "consciousness," and it will not be long until you wonder why you ever believed in consciousness at all. Habits, as James reminds us, do become "second nature." Thought habits are no exception.

> The great law of habit itself—that twenty experiences make us recall a thing better than one, that *long indulgence in error makes right thinking almost impossible*—seems to have no essential foundation in reason. The business of thought is with truth—the number of experiences ought to have nothing to do with her hold of it; and she ought by right to be able to hug it all the closer, after years spent out of its presence. The contrary arrangements seem quite fantastic and arbitrary, but nevertheless are part of the very bone and marrow of our minds. (PP I:552; *italics added.*)

Watson's and Wittgenstein's—and literally thousands of others'—view was argued for most cleverly in *The Concept of Mind*, by Gilbert Ryle (1900-76), when, at rare moments of candid clarity and distinctness, he announced his fundamental premise: we must erase the line—he treats it as purely imaginary—between what is inside us and what is outside us, between what is private and accessible only to us ("us" is shorthand for "to you OR to me OR to one of them") and what is public and accessible to everybody. The reason we still believe in private, invisible concepts and intangible minds, that is, in unobservable things distinct from the public, two-legged, upright-walking, observable organisms we call "persons" and their observable behavior, is—according to Ryle—a persistent myth about us having insides as well as outsides. There is no inside theater we should call our mind separate from what's public: our expressive face, our uttering vocal mechanisms, our gesturing arms, our body-language-speaking torso, and territory-claiming feet. Which means, of course, that Saint Augustine was the victim of delusion when he uttered his famous exclamation: "Late have I loved Thee, O Beauty so ancient and so new; late have I loved Thee. For behold, Thou wert within me, and I outside; and I sought Thee outside."

The issue is an important one. From the time that Plato first began building his scientific theories about unseen reality—the topic of chapter three of James' *Varieties*—on his analysis of thought, the most thorough of those willing to follow Xenophanes' trail-blazing example in rethinking their god-ology have also fastened on facts about human thought and its objects to reach their conclusions. A centuries-long dialogue has furnished our libraries with pointers to the final questions: How, from in here, can we prove anything at all about out there? How can we justify our irresistible belief in any unseen reality, physical bodies or nonbodily spirits? What should we think on such issues? Or don't we think? Do we do only public things?

But, if we are *wrong* in our belief that private thinking is something MORE than, something distinct from public speaking, then why DO we continue to think that, when we deliberately try to tell others what we believe, we are doing two separate things simultaneously: thinking AND speaking? Why DO we think innocent people and guilty people aren't both being honest when they both tell us right out loud that they are innocent? Why DO we have public warnings to put us on notice that con-artists are internally planning how to fleece us with their external smooth-talk? Why DO we upright-walking, bipedal animals—the only ones to do such a thing—continue to fear that, when we verbally behave, i.e., speak in order to tell others what we think, they may guess that we are thinking inside that what we hear ourselves telling them on the outside is a lie? Why do so many of us continue scribally behaving AS IF we think we can think as we write, even revise what we write because it doesn't capture our meaning-thought well enough? Or think we can do three things: think, mutter in a low voice to ourselves, and push a pen? Why haven't the combined efforts of some of last century's most famous thinkers [sic] and their minions been as powerless to stamp out this myth of minds as other minions have been powerless to wean the masses from their opium-dreams?

For anyone who has been able to understand the last nine noticing-tests, the answer couldn't be plainer. We need only remember what seems obvious if anything does: *What is hidden inside others is not directly present to me.* That does no more than repeat the bombshell—"just as I visualize the activity of his internal organs"—Murray tossed into his conversion-report cited earlier. In effect, he was warning his readers not to forget what every behaviorist knows about others: Unless we have Superman's X-ray vision, *we cannot see what is inside other people.* Their skin normally hides their insides, and clothes normally hide most of their skin. Whoever thinks about others' insides is normally—make allowance for surgeons, etc.—thinking about things that they are not observing. Therefore they are thinking about things they can only be thinking about. Or, Murray would say, visualizing. Or, others would say, inferring. Perhaps even remembering. Maybe, in Watson's and Ryle's versions, soundlessly muttering about. Only, NOT observing. Such not-observed but thought-about objects include others' beating hearts and red blood cells (we can see only the skin moving, hear only the thumps that come through the chest walls, feel the pulsing of the wrist-artery, etc.), others' peristalses (we can hear only the growls as air, etc., is squeezed through the intestines), and especially their brain and its inner processes. No need here for "more research." It is the only obvious truth needed to blast the lock off the door to the mind slammed shut by the pied pipers named W and their followers.

Today, those who reject Plato's and Descartes' science of the mind are quietly abandoning the behaviorists' denial of the private and scurrying to the private brain (which Murray alluded to). But why don't primitive peoples speak a lot about others' brain processes? For the same reason none of us do during our early years. We don't see them. We learn about them mostly from books which offer us lots of ink marks and many of those pictures worth a thousand words. The question we who want to get to the bottom of everything must get in the habit of asking is simply, "How many unseen things are there going on inside other people? ONLY blood circulation, digestion, respiration, etc.? Or is there *MORE*? Perhaps observing, visualizing, too? Maybe even some understanding, attending, and noticing? Thinking, too?" And the follow-up question, "Are all of those SIMPLY activities of inner organs? Or are they MORE?" And the next question after that, "How do I know? MERELY by some unobserved activities of inner organs inside me? Or is there MORE to all of this than meets anyone's eye? Are there things going on inside me that no one else observes, that not even I observe?" (Is there any understanding of this going on inside you? Can you watch it?)

The switches in that paragraph can be enlarged upon. Instead of just paying attention to the fact that what is hidden inside others is not directly present to us, we can start concentrating on what goes on inside us that *they* can't observe. Begin with your tongue. Can you feel your teeth with it right now? If your mouth is closed, can other people see your tongue? Your teeth? Those feeling-sensations? Did you just now pay attention to your mouth, your tongue, your teeth, your sensations, whether or not you can feel, what others can and cannot see when your mouth is closed? Did you check the evidence to find answers to those questions? Were you able to remember the questions while you checked the evidence? How could you tell which question that bit of evidence was related to? What did the evidence consist of? Right then and there? That is, was most of it memory? Ask: While you have been reading this paragraph, have other people been standing around, trying to get a look at your tongue, your teeth, your feeling-sensations? If not, then you were only remembering what you believe you've observed in the past. Perhaps your memory is playing tricks on you and you've forgotten what people are or what "people" means, forgotten what people would see if they looked when you had your mouth closed or what "looking" means, which parts of your body English-speaking people call mouth, tongue, and teeth, what such English'rs mean by sensation, thinking, etc.? How accurate is your memory? Are you sure you can still remember what "memory" means. Did you ever see memory or remembering? Or observe it? Could anyone look into your mouth, if it was open, and see or observe your memory or your remembering? If they put their ear very, very close to your utterly silent vocal cords, could they hear it? Can you ever be sure others remember what memory or remembering are long enough that they won't have forgotten by the time they have checked their evidence? Do seeing, observing, and looking mean the same thing? (Did you notice the switching around of those English terms?) Whom should you ask? Would you understand what they replied? See (by looking?) if you are still sure what understanding is. Or "understanding" means. Have you ever seen, observed, or looked at any of it? Perhaps Rorty is wrong and no one understands what anyone else says or writes. Because there is no such thing as understanding. And we can know that, because no one has ever observed any such thing. If atheists are right to believe God doesn't exist because no one has ever observed God, then by the same token no one understands that, because no one has ever observed any understanding. If Rorty is wrong, people only think they understand things, even such things as "God does NOT exist." That's what A.J. Ayer (1910-1989) proved in Chapter VI of his revolution-causing *Language, Truth, and Logic*. Or thought he had proved until, after convincing thousands of its readers that he had, he decided he hadn't. Much the same way he convinced the dying Somerset Maugham that immortality was impossible, before he, Ayer, had a Near-Death-Experience of his own and decided that just possibly it wasn't impossible.

No one familiar with the way parents grill their children when they suspect them of fibbing, the way defendants are cross-examined in court, or the way we try to "back others into a corner" in any argument, will fail to understand the purpose of those rapid-fire questions. They are an invitation to anyone caught in bad thought-habits to retrace the thoughts that took them into their cave and cues to help others notice what they must practice not forgetting lest they, too, wander into one. The technique of rapid-fire cross-examination can easily backfire. It may produce, not only the cognitive discomfort that indicates the presence of possible error, the fact of actual error, or the need for further learning, but resentment. The more fundamental the premises under attack, the more difficult it will be to face the possible need to rethink/review everything. The more public the facing, the more difficult it will be.

> A person who spends a great deal of his time hoarding facts is not likely to be happy at the prospect of seeing them converted into rubbish. He is more likely to want them bound and preserved, a memorial to his personal achievement. A scientist, for example, who thinks this way, and especially a psychologist who does so, depends upon his facts to furnish the ultimate proof of his proposition. With these shining nuggets of truth in his grasp it seems unnecessary for him to take responsibility for the conclusions he claims they thrust upon him. To suggest to him at this point that further human reconstruction can completely alter the appearance of the precious fragments . . . is to threaten his scientific conclusions, his philosophical position, and even his moral security.

This observation by the American psychologist, G.A. Kelly (1905-67), will serve as a preface to the major purpose behind this eighteenth experiment, viz., to draw attention to the fact that we have options. Once contradictory construals are proposed to us, we are free to assent to one and dissent from the other, free to believe instead that they only appear to be contradictory and to reject the claim that they really are, free to regard both of them as false and to feel certain that some other alternative is true, free to believe that both opposing claims need to be further analysed in order to extract the kernel of truth from each and leave the errors behind, free to practice what Wm. James called (selective) "INattention" even before H.S. Sullivan did and to avoid, repress, ignore, or shun the cognitive discomfort the issue causes in us, free to suspend all decisions on the claims until we have learned more, free to practice what James called "selective attention" by returning to an obligation, whether it's to an urgent job, a work of mercy, feeding the body, etc.

The major choice here is simple. What will you pay attention to?

> j or 10- Most times, choosing one option over another seems in retrospect to have been as trivial in its consequences as we thought beforehand it would be. I just crooked my right index finger, and all my evidence says only God and I will ever be sure about it. Let chaos theorists think their computer programs prove that a bat of a bat's wing will ripple to the edge of space. That is because their computers are not random as they appear but rigidly determined. Quantum physics argues against them as rigorously as it argued against Einstein's determinism. Readers may be affected by these ink marks (but not my finger-crooking), because readers will never know—certainly not without cross-examining me—whether or not I just lied. (I didn't crook it!) That is, they'll be thinkers, maybe believers, but not knowers. *IF* "knowers" is construed as excluding believers.

Descartes' program was not to eliminate belief. It was a program for sorting out what's certainly true from what may be true or may be false but we can't be absolutely sure about. Socrates' motto, "When I know I'm not sure, I don't say I am," coupled with "I cannot observe what is hidden inside others" and "I cannot observe—only think about—my brain, what any part of it is doing, whether it has parts, whether a cancerous tumor is now invading it, i.e., I have no direct, private-only evidence about such things," produces the conclusion that, like any juror, I cannot claim more than "moral certainty" about such things. I do not have to conclude, however, that I don't even know that I'm my own juror on these matters, don't even know whether I exist. Ask me which of all the universe's galaxies I live in. The Milky Way. Ask me which star-orbiting planet I live on. It's called "Earth" (in English). Which continent? North America. Which nation, state, city, street, house? I know. Which room in that house am I in now? I know. How do I know? I can see. Am I sure I see the room and what's in it? Certainly. Do I understand the thought I just assented to with such certainty? Certainly. Can it be mistaken? I'm now convinced it is. Am I certain I understood the thought I just said I'm certain is mistaken? Beyond any doubt whatever. (But I lie.) Am I the one doing the understanding of my belief-options? Who wants to know?

Deciding where my certainties begin can be a monumental, life-altering decision. Decisions of that nature are discussed by William James in the pivotal lectures of his greatest work of all, the one almost named *The Varieties of Human Experience*, the one he should have named that, the one in whose title he actually substituted "religious" for "human." That work's pivotal lectures bear the titles, "The Divided Self and the Process of Unification" and "Conversion." (Whoever may have wondered whether drawing attention to the complex modules or thought-packages labelled "thinkers," "revolutions," "believers," and "conversion" was done for a special purpose will now have their answer.) Earlier, Henry Murray's vivid depiction of his conversion was cited. Because he remembered, he knew that his description of the inner goings-on of humans would seem to neurologists and "objective" psychologists to be "absurd, archaic, tender-minded." But, he added, his description was "much closer to the actualities of inner life" than theirs. In a passage that reminds us of our need for Dostoevsky, he added:

> A personality is a full Congress of orators and pressure groups, of children, demagogues, communists, isolationists, war-mongers, mugwumps, grafters, log-rollers, lobbyists, Caesars and Christs, Machiavellis and Judases, Tories and Promethean revolutionists. And a psychologist who does not know this in himself, whose mind is locked away against the flux of images and feelings, should be encouraged to make friends, by being psychoanalyzed, with the various members of his household.

One of the most far-reaching decisions of all is whether we can study our own inner thoughts and feelings, as Murray decided to believe, or not. Whoever understands the options—understands them!—already has powerful evidence relevant to the answer.

j' or 10'- The reason that is such a far-reaching decision is because it involves, not simply an isolated detail, but the first step toward that whole other world of things that Plato, etc., began to discover. When Descartes sat down to provide over-the-shoulder-readers of his pseudo-diary with clues to the inner map of reality he had constructed, he did not offer his readers only that single nugget. He offered a well-rounded belief-system whose basics are as true today as they were at his death in 1650. All that is necessary is to eliminate his errors and incorporate the discoveries that have been made during the last three and a half centuries. That is as good a description of the aim here as any. **What follows is a 10-item SUMMARY** of a revised (Des)Cartesian belief-system, one that focuses on the question of meaning.

i- Our desire to make sense of everything can be satisfied in its essentials once we can answer three questions: What exists?, What does what-exists do?, and Why does it do it?

ii- It is convenient to classify What-exists? under four headings but to allow for the probability or possibility of a fifth. There are persons. There are three kinds of things that can be created and presented to them when they are conscious: complete thoughts, sense-data, and images (copies of sense-data). If Descartes is correct, there are also bodies, but if Berkeley is correct, there aren't. Having discovered no insurmountable objections to the existence of bodies, I continue to believe in them. It seems, however, that they are subatoms (subatomic particles), none larger than protons.

iii- These different existents do different acts. Subatoms, if they exist, can do only two things: stand still or move. Thoughts are understood by persons. Sense-data and images are directly present to persons who experience them. Unless it is kept in mind that these are not things done by thoughts, sense-data, and images, but things done by persons to them, it might be preferable to say that thoughts, sense-data, and images simply are, or are simply created and presented. Persons understand, are aware of, feel, attend to, notice, decide, etc. Persons do neither of the things bodies do, and they have no parts, hence persons have no moving parts.

iv- Clues to what I use "meaning" for have been presented throughout this chapter. So long as we assume that sounds, gestures, indentations, chalk marks, pencil marks, ink marks, etc., are more, i.e., are words, then the meanings of those words are the thoughts that their author means or intends the words to "convey" to others. When the others "receive" a thought other than that intended, then the meaning they "receive" is a misunderstanding of the other's meaning. "Meaning" can also be used in a variety of situations as part of the effort to "convey" other thoughts. The surrounding "words" will serve as extra clues that the "receiver" must take into account when guessing the author's meaning. Except when used as a synonym for "thought," meaning can be viewed as naming a reification. That is, the thoughts coming to you now are *real* things.

v- There are two major impediments to clear thinking, two major thinkers' blocks. At birth, we are all impeded by what may be called the *Infant-Thinker's Block* or—these are English synonyms—ignorance, lack of information, gaps in our knowledge, and so on. Since we later acquire errors along with our truths, our later impediments can be called the *Expert-Thinkers' Blocks* or—English synonyms—beliefs in things that do not exist, mistaken beliefs about things that do, and so on. A belief in what does not exist is belief in a fiction. Because the number of fictions we get in the habit of believing in during our gullible years is so large, we must cultivate the habit of submitting every belief in every thing to ruthless cross-examination. Especially every absolutely-basic belief.

vi- One of the major fictions used by Western thinkers in their efforts to understand human understanding is named "concept." **CONCEPTS DO NOT EXIST**. Images, which are directly present to us, are inspected (we have no eyes that literally look-backward or inward). The greatest thinkers who have reflected on thinking have noticed that there is MORE to human knowing than sensing and inspecting images of what we sense. From Plato on, the objects of this "more" have been called ideas, concepts, formal signs, intentions . . . and a host of other terms from other "languages." But thinking is not looking. The objects of thinking are not concepts or ideas that can be looked at. Not by any eye. Not by a body's-eye's looking, nor by a mind's-eye's looking. What we understand are **COMPLETE THOUGHTS**, the meanings of complete sentences. Thoughts are not copies of anything and also are not looked at, but understood. They are either true or false of reality, which to believe is our decision. This major revision must be combined with the next principle.

vii- It is essential to begin "seeing" the "words" making up "language" as just more sensed objects—sounds in the case of spoken "words," ink marks in the case of printed "words" such as your eyes are scanning right now—whose primary function is not to evoke thoughts directly, but rather to trigger off the recall of vast networks of associated imagery. *Sentences are not correlated with thoughts but with the image-networks* that are directly correlated with thoughts. The images that dominate all others are those best thought of as maps, diagrams, general scenarios, etc. The thesis that we do not understand by using concepts which are copies, but that, instead, we understand thoughts accompanied by, e.g., maps to which we add or from which we subtract items that are always "de-fined" within the context of or by relations to the other items in the map, is a major feature of this "new" theory of meaning. "Definitions" present a map or part of one.

viii- A major requirement for successful library use is acquiring an exquisite sensitivity to switches in writers' background imagery and the corresponding switches in their thoughts or meanings. We must not take the statement, "Normally, the sun rises and sets every twenty-four hours," used to introduce the polar exceptions, as indicating the writer has reverted to Ptolemy's cosmology. As Berkeley noted, we can *say* "The sun rose" while *knowing* the earth turned. That is, successful readers must map out the differences between loose (everyday) expressions, exaggeration, metaphor, appeals to emotion, etc.

ix- Finding answers for "Why?" leads eventually to the discovery of previously unknown existents (which adds new answers to "What exists?") and their doings (some existents are causes), to the discarding of fictions (which removes wrong answers to "What exists?"), to the discovery of previously unnoticed doings or the reduction of longer lists of doings to briefer lists, and most importantly to the analysis of humans' motives.

x- Whoever learns to correctly distinguish good reasons from bad ones will not find any good reason to doubt that there is no thought of which they can be more certain than they are of the thought expressed by "This is I thinking, and I exist."

Whoever reads that involved, ten-point reformulation of Descartes' Cogito can notice two things. It is typical of what we grow up to expect from "philosophers" who cannot say anything simply, and it is all about something that no normal person worries in the least about. Some would recommend that we waste none of the precious moments of already short lives on such far-fetched trivialities.

Yet, the last (x) is precisely one of the few issues William James could not solve satisfactorily. Rather, it is one he solved brilliantly in practice but could not commit himself to once he began to understand the mystery surrounding it. His first, 1890 masterwork, *The Principles of Psychology*, described various features of day-to-day experience. It is rich with glaring contradictions which he never satisfactorily overcame. Yet it is also rich with profound insights and with prose that introduces them to us with surprising ease, so that even when his treatment falls short or flies in the face of good sense in one place, we can expect to find a far better treatment somewhere else.

Twenty years later, James presented to the world *The Varieties of Religious Experience*, another report of his ongoing efforts to put masses of messy details into a satisfying order. This time, his attention focused on single individuals in order to discover some common threads beneath their no-two-alike lives. What his keen eye "abstracted" from the countless streams of experience he studied were nothing less than the major challenges everyone encounters in some way or other: confidence in one's own powers vs one's powerlessness in the face of biological compulsions, confidence about the seen vs doubts about the unseen, the desire for happiness vs the painful intrusion of evil, all of them adding up to the picture of pilgrims confronted in life with contradictions and contradictory choices.

If there is one theme that runs through James' thinking, from the *Principles* to *A Pluralistic Universe*, a series of lectures given in 1909, a short time before his death, it is the theme captured by the phrase "The Unity of Consciousness." Yet the climactic chapter of his *Varieties* is entitled "The Divided Self." James' is the perfect instance of a divided mind or self, torn between monism and pluralism, unable to find a theoretical unity broad enough to accommodate both comfortably. Rethinking, as his own life showed, is not guaranteed to bring everyone to a satisfying resolution. Nor—as our library resources show—does it bring any two persons to perfectly similar outcomes. Finally, even when it does bring people to somewhat similar conclusions, the paths they travel on the way to them can show remarkable diversity. James was a mystic intoxicated by diversity.

In view of my agreement with these themes so characteristic of and habitual with James, it makes sense to add a section to what has preceded in order to describe the path, so different, that took me from my earliest views to conclusions so close to his. It will concentrate on the common-sense theory that I learned first, then on how I learned one way of re-mapping things and my understanding of them, and finally on how I later revised that view, radically. These additional details should contribute toward further clarification of this "new" theory of meaning constructed from parts of older theories.

D. Common Sense:
the Starting-Point for All Rethinkings.

It is Sunday morning, June 28, 1992, well over half a century since I opened my eyes and took in my first glimpses of reality. Like every other normal person, I began life as a complete dummy, so unknowing that I had absolutely no idea at the time how dumb I was. Whatever else I may have had inside me by way of heart, lungs, partly-digested food, etc., I either had zero in the way of knowledge (Aristotle's preferred picture), or I had a highly-structured mind, though one as yet one devoid of data-input (the model advocated by Leibniz, Kant, and many moderns), or I had a mind filled with forgotten memories from previous lives' experience (Plato's reincarnationist image). I'd have drawn a blank on any question asked of me the same way that students often draw blanks on questions regardless of whether they never knew the answer because they never studied for it or did know it but couldn't remember it. [Did the switch from picture to model to image make any great difference above?]

The Shape of Our Common-sense Theory. In the same way that I could not read M. Adler's book, *How To Read A Book*, until I could already do it, I learned how to observe and think long before I learned to think about observing and thinking. Which is the point of the quip about the person who spoke prose for an entire lifetime before learning the difference between prose and poetry and noticing which one he was doing. Well before I would have understood the language they used to teach me that they existed and were giving me instructions in prose as to what I should and should not believe, I learned that some of the things in my world were people who spoke and thought, as distinct from books that don't make a peep and haven't a single thought, i.e., as distinct from texts that—*pace* literature teachers and even if they, books, existed—could not speak to one another.

Like other former newborns, I have learned much. As you have. It is to be expected that someone whose paid job and unpaid leisure have, for so many years, required so much reading, so much discussing, and so much arguing, will have accumulated an extensive familiarity with the varied contents of the books surrounding him right now. Whoever can follow the discussions of these pages has also acquired a large backlog of information.

But not everything we learn is true. Everyone old enough to know anything is already on the way toward being wrong about many things. Even by the age of five, the average learner has become quite familiar with the experience of being wrong—e.g., of wandering off in the supermarket, wrongly confident mom is right behind, of mistakenly going to get the toy that has been stolen—and can even, for relatively lengthy periods, play hide-and-seek, a game of hiding the truth from others, a game resting on the hope that others' beliefs about one's true location will remain in error. What's more, even by the age of five, the average learner has learned the difference between what George Washington and Pinnochio did, i.e., between honesty and lying. Combining those two premises makes it plausible that we ex-five year olds may have been led into some errors by others. When our "leaders" know the truth and lie, we are victims of propaganda. When they believe that the errors they teach us are true, we are victims of cultural myths. Either way, errors are errors, not truth. Myths are myths, not facts. Fictions are figments of imagination, not (true!) realities. Unless thoughts are.

This deduction is behind Descartes' Socratic re-examining in *Meditation One*:

> It is some years since I detected how many were the false beliefs that I had from my earliest youth admitted as true, and how doubtful was everything I had since constructed on this basis; and from that time I was convinced that I must once for all seriously undertake to rid myself of all the opinions which I had formerly accepted, and commence to build anew from the foundation, if I wanted to establish any firm and permanent structure in the sciences ...

In a century when "Science teaches" has replaced "The Bible says" as the most widely used sugar-coating for myth-pills, it is worth lingering a moment over the matter. When I believe something has been proven, but proven by someone else and not by me, my assent includes, not one, but two acts of faith. *At a minimum.* Faith in the particular "whatever," e.g., that the earth spins on its axis every 24 hours, and faith that someone proved it. Every "scientist" who believes something on the word of someone else—and "scientists" increasingly rely on others' say-so, which is why fraudulent claims are viewed as mortal sins—is making an act of faith as much as anyone who prefers Moses' or Paul's works to Einstein's or Bohr's. "Faith" is best understood here as "assent to a thought for which our evidence is less than conclusive."

We live at a time when dangerous cultural myths have been and are prefaced by "Science teaches." We should expect that Socrates, gadfly to those who long ago dreamed the Great Athenian Dream, would chide us if we followers of the Great American Dream don't ask whether "Are you better off than you were four years ago?" is better answered by checking to see how much after-tax income we have or by seeing whether we're trying harder to do for our country at least as much as we are trying to get our country to do for us. Or if, like the Athenians, we blindly assume that "Our way is best" means best in every respect, and best not just for us, but for everyone. Or if we never examine the song's lyric, "This land is our land," viz., yours and mine but not theirs. But those are matters of opinion. Science, we're told, deals with facts, facts that have been proven, facts which—because they have been proven—are agreed upon by the experts. Science has proven the earth is round, and allowing the Bible's flat-earth views to be taught in public schools would be counterproductive. Science has proven evolution, or at least produced such an overwhelming amount of evidence for it, that it is not merely blind prejudice when people continue to deny it but their desire to have a six-day-creation story taught as "science" is perverse. Science has now proven that "mind" and "brain" are just two names for the same thing (this disproves immortality), as *Newsweek* recently announced some philosopher-scientists have announced. No doubt many people will find the last three claims every bit as controversial as the preceding three issues, and they would be willing to listen to further debate on all six.

BUT when was the last time students were asked to ask, not whether science and scientists are fallible, but whether any such thing as science or a scientific method even exists?! When was the last time they were instructed to ask, "Has anyone ever *observed* science or the scientific method, or are we all just mutually reinforcing each others' faith in a myth?" Whoever wants 100% truth and 0% error must begin (re)examining everything they've taken on faith. Even a claim about which things can be proven (science's teaching) and which can only be taken on faith (religion's). Especially if that claim is believed solely on faith in the say-so of others, even though faith in the say-so of our flat-earth ancestors would clearly have been misplaced faith. Descartes' extreme method of trying to treat everything doubtful as if it is false, not just maybe false but actually false, was a clever device for carrying out a 100% reexamination.

There are three things, then, that we learners may, unless our attention is drawn to them, grossly underestimate. First, we grossly underestimate (i)how much even five-year olds already know, i.e., fail to notice how much information has come our way and stuck since we got out of diapers. We are blind to (ii)how much of our information is MIS-information, especially when, misinformed, we reinforce each others' errors. Finally, we rarely note (iii)how much we take on faith in the say-so of an often anonymous "they." Any final theory of knowledge, about what learning is and how we do it, must account for these three customary oversights, as well as incorporate into its own framework the three insights that remedy the all-too-frequent oversights. If learners' goal is to learn everything, then a theory of learning must be included. This is good logical deduction, Watson (not John) would be told. Good common sense.

The reason for beginning this final section of Chapter One that way is to emphasize that *learning theories are retrospective.* They are after-the-fact. No one investigates learning—going out to get raw data by observing (?!) learners and then coming back to the library to sit and compare their results with results reached by earlier students of learning—until they're old enough and already have done enough of the kinds of learning essential for such an investigation. Science about human-infants' learning is a particularly precarious reconstruction, since our memories of our own infancy are inaccessible and since infants currently doing the learning refuse to give interviews. We do have a name for the knowledge we graduate with on our fifth or sixth birthday and that we continually add to as we grow older. It's "basic common sense." Most today would thoroughly agree with A.N. Whitehead who wrote: "You may polish up common sense, you may contradict it in detail, you may surprise it. Yet ultimately your whole task is to satisfy it." (But it must never be assumed that any two people use "common sense" to label identical belief-bundles.)

Descartes nailed down a certainly true and truly certain common-sense belief. Others—James!—have since rejected it. Descartes took for granted other common-sense beliefs. Three of the most basic are that there is a difference between moral good and evil, that there is a difference between true and false beliefs, and that some things are causes and others are effects. (His arguments that God is the cause of our propensity to believe a physical world exists, and that God would be an immoral liar if that belief was false and not true, would otherwise have made no sense whatever.) But they, too, have been denied by many. People disagree in identifying common sense. Many lose touch with it.

This is essential to keep in mind with respect to retrospective theories, the most obvious of which is learning theory which is doubly retrospective. On a cosmic scale. When did Aristotle write the original logic text? Millennia after logically thinking humans began to inhabit this planet. When was Freud's theory of emotional development developed? More than two thousand years after Aristotle's logic and after even more thousands-of-years worth of people had developed emotionally. When were the stages of cognitive growth cognized by Piaget? Decades after Freud, two millenia after Aristotle, and thousands more years after Freud's and Aristotle's ancestors, had all passed successfully through the stages of cognitive growth. And on the individual scale. When do students typically study Aristotle's logic, Freud's pansexualism, Piaget's cognitive blossoming? Certainly no earlier than they typically study Augustine' theory of time. Which means, ordinarily, after being logical for years, after reaching puberty, after achieving the formal operations stage, and long after learning how to redescribe "The big hand points to twelve and the little hand points halfway between two and three" as "This clock's broken."

Why must we not lose touch with common sense? *Because its true parts are essential for correctly correcting its false ones.* We must rely on the true parts of our everyday common sense in order to understand that, although we can read a book on golf before going out to the links to play, no one can first read a book telling them how to read a book and then go and do it, just as we must rely on them to know that an apprentice-barber cannot skip the first three which are always disasters and begin with the fourth and to know that "haircuts" was tacitly or unspokenly referred to by "first three" and "fourth." Theories about logic and methodology, including the most famous of all, the "scientific," must be approached with extreme caution. They deal with the very basics of the learning needed to learn them and needed to assess the truth of what's learned, which means they can trap learners into becoming so obsessed by one insight that they develop a blindness against learning other essential truths. Theories about emotional growth must be approached with caution, for they will—when mistaken—develop into stunted, even demented caricatures of the human person, like those efforts to understand time that turn into grand explanations of why our everyday lives, measured by time-scales, are an illusion. There are, indeed, too many simple-minded "professional theories" that deserve the rebuke, "There are more things in heaven and earth, Horatio, than are dreamed of in your philosophy."

The above is a warning regarding this preface to my theory of learning, as well as a warning regarding this entire book from beginning to end. Notice that this preface goes far, far beyond my original, common-sense education. At the age of five or even fifteen, I could no more have selected, from the vast pool of beliefs I had already acquired, just the right ones to bundle together and label "original common sense" than I could have written this preface about it. The remainder of the book is a retrospective account of much radical adding-to, trimming-down, reorganizing-of, and polishing-up, carried on by one person over the course of more than half a century since his fifth birthday, vis-à-vis his original belief-kit. More specifically, what follows will report on some absolutely radical revisions of our original common sense, for that earliest set of Creators-endowed beliefs or convictions are about thirty percent errors or partial mistakes (much of naive realism), recognition of which is essential for acquiring the bare-outline truth about everything.

Sensations, Memory-Images, & Thoughts. What precedes was a preface for this section on "The Shape of Our Common Sense Theory."

Its chief point is that none of us begins by *reexamining* our everyday, common-sense beliefs. We begin by *acquiring* them. What follows now is a tentative reconstruction, in naive realist terms, of important features of that earliest learning.

Preparation for acquiring our beliefs begins when sensations begin. Probably while we are still in the womb, since sounds and vibrations and constraint-stimuli reach the fetus and, as we have no reason to doubt, Little-Albert-like reactions of startled anxiety, etc., are readily conceivable and the conditions often right for them. Certainly when we emerge from the womb and the beginning of a lifetime assault by the environment on our five separate senses produces that early unified-field-of-experience whose most famous name, "one [repeat, **ONE!**] great blooming, buzzing confusion," comes from William James, though without the brackets. Aristotle's analysis coincides here with James', though their further analyses differ. Both took note of something that all of us learn to take-for-granted while we're growing up: what we see comes in via our eyes, what we hear comes via ears, scents from the nose, sweet and bitter tastes originate with the tongue inside our mouth, and everything else is transported through the body's largest organ, that encapsulating membrane designed to keep inside guts safe from outside dangers, that Maginot Line we call our body's "skin."

But here, James followed Descartes by adding further to Aristotle's analysis. Where Aristotle stops his examination with the five peripheral sense organs, James continues his with the nerve-currents that have traveled all the way to the brain, which—James could thank Descartes for incorporating this modern finding into his psychology—is the only material thing that *immediately* affects what is sensuously experienced. What James wrote in 1890, Descartes would have approved:

> The fact that the brain is the one immediate bodily condition of the mental operations is indeed so universally admitted nowadays that I need spend no more time in illustrating it, but will simply postulate it and pass on. The whole remainder of the book will be more or less of a proof that the postulate was correct. (PP I:4)

Both Aristotle, 'the' philosopher of common sense, and James, a phenomenalist like Berkeley, Hume, and J.S. Mill, agree on the fact that, however unified the green color of the apple, the crunching sound as we bite into it, its tart flavor and cool feel may be as qualities of some object or substance on the yon side of our senses, and however much those qualities are broken up and fed inwards through five separate external or peripheral senses, everything gets reunited or recombined on the hither side of our senses. 'Experienced unity' is accounted for by Aristotle with his notion of a sensus-communis or integrating sense. James is content at first to simply emphasize the combined-FACT, the inner fact.

> That [one great blooming buzzing] Confusion is the baby's universe; and the universe of all of us is still to a great extent such a Confusion, potentially resolvable, and demanding to be resolved, but not yet actually resolved, into parts. (PBC, ch. II)

At the outset of his *Metaphysics*, Aristotle noted that sensation produces memory in human animals who, in this, are unlike those animals which act in the same old ways because of their inability to remember and thus learn from their experience. In a similar fashion, James emphasizes that, for us, each new unified-field-of-consciousness appropriates to itself our previous ones, but now as memories.

The most basic memory-factors are images of what we've sensed. We have visual memory-images of what we've seen, auditory memory-images of what we've heard, tactile memory-images of what we've felt, etc. But these memory-images begin to cluster in various ways. For instance, after enough memories of our sense-impressions have accumulated, we come to have, inside us, more than isolated experience-memories.

(i) Groups of them form *stable objects* or items, such as Mom, Dad, Fido, etc. They start to stand out from the simple flow of experience, their outlines at first hazy, like icebergs appearing and reappearing out of a fog, but later becoming more individually distinct. These become the original 'fixtures' in a kind of landscape model. James discusses this in the two chapters of his *Principles of Psychology* that follow his famous sections on the stream of thought and the self-selves. In his 1892 *Psychology: Briefer Course*, he summarized what he thought was most important in those chapters this way:

> So far as it [the "Confusion" or field of experience]
> is unanalyzed and unresolved we may be said to know it
> sensationally; but as fast as parts are distinguished in it and
> we become aware of their relations, our knowledge becomes
> perceptual or even conceptual . . . (PBC, ch. II)

Eventually, the memory-images coalesce further into (ii) an inner model or framework of the outer world. This *inner framework* can or, rather, must be described with a variety of analogies, lest our mental gaze become so fixated on one that we become blind to the important truths captured by alternative similes. The two most crucial aspects of it are those that correspond, respectively, to the two acts, looking and understanding. The *inner framework* can be described most graphically as an *inner model* of the outer environment. This picture corresponds to the unquestioned fact that we do much looking, both at originals and copies. Or, to use Hume's terms, at 'perceptions,' whether vivid 'impressions' or fainter 'idea'-copies that are similar to the vivid originals.

Correlative to the framework consisting of memory-images, we develop (iii) a set of intellectual or conceptual beliefs that fit together to constitute a set of logically interlocked propositions. We can understand thoughts about anything: about observed realities, about unobserved and unobservable realities, whether three-dimensional or non-three-dimensional, about models, about beliefs, about sets of beliefs, even thoughts about thoughts about those things.

Spatio-Temporal Inner Model. The notion of an *inner model* is easy to describe, at least so long as questions about details are held back until the main lines of the notion are put in place. As Kant noticed after he had reflected long and hard on Newton's theories of absolute space and time, this inner model has dimensions. First, *spatial*. The "permanent fixtures" that appear and reappear are deployed to their "proper places": sun, moon, stars, float overhead, whales, fish, and sea monsters, swim the depths below, while the leg'd, torso'd, arm'd, and head'd "I" takes up occupancy center-stage on earth. And *temporal*. Thoreau reports that even the Puri Indians, reported to have only one word for yesterday, today, and tomorrow, were also reported to understand the difference quite well, as translators guessed from the fact that the Puri pointed backward to make the word mean yesterday's past, overhead to mean "the passing day," and ahead for tomorrow's future. (A fact that is relevant to our critical assessment of Benjamin Whorf's guesses.) That is, we not only create a model of reality that resembles a once-for-all total snapshot, but "movies" constructible from 1001 snapshots.

This inner model allows us to situate—and thus refer to—every individual item we ever think about. It enables us to locate the item 'here' or 'there' in relation to other things, e.g., our body (which is usually thought of as 'here'). It also makes it possible to date an item's existence or one of its acts as 'now' or 'then' in relation to other items' existence or acts. (Mystery! How is it that we ever learn how to use "yesterday," "today," and "tomorrow" or "past," "present," and "future", as well as "in front of," "right there," and "behind"? Concepts so essential for *reference* and *denotation*?)

For example. That general description applies equally to all of us, but the proper details must be added to make it fit *individually*, for instance to fit myself. Like every normal learner, I experienced a new stream of sensations each time I woke. Memory-images of my sensations accumulated. I began by acquiring a very limited model of a very small area of outer reality, of the area, namely, that would be described as the house on Neptune, my two parents, visitors, especially relatives. The inner model began to expand. *Spatially.* First to include two more quasi-islands—the maternal homestead in Lakewood and the paternal homestead in Sharon—each connected to the Neptune hub by a highway corridor an hour or two of travel time in length. Then to include more details of the Neptune home's surroundings: parish church, corner candy store, bakery, grocery stores, playgrounds, and so on. *Time-wise.* Early on, an abstract schedule to predict the events of a single day, i.e., of the period from waking to bed-time and their unexperienced horizon, sleep. Going to the bathroom, breakfast, dinner, taking a nap, supper, washing, going to bed, were an early schedule's landmarks. Later, longer time-tables: a father's day-time absences for five days, both parents home on Saturday, church and often an outing on Sunday became the week's pattern, Christmas, Easter, birthday, Fourth of July, another Christmas, etc., became highlights of the winter, spring, summer, fall year.

Still later, this inner spatio-temporal, grand unified *model* of everything expanded to include distant galaxies all around, a molten-core'd earth below, a heart at the core of what is inside me, as a fixed cosmology, and a history that went back through 1900+ years to include events that took place before the birth of Christ, back to the creation of Adam and Eve and the first five and a half days' of creating that preceding theirs, which six days were gradually expanded into a fifteen-billion year history since the Big Bang, then to possible accordion-cycles of history. Etc.

Generalize. Now ZOOM OUT from my individual, particular history, to consider some general implications of the fact that all of us earth-dwellers construct "geographic-histories" that, however unique their details may be (e.g., how many other living persons began life at that house on Neptune, had parents from Lakewood and Sharon, etc.?), are yet similar enough that we can describe all five and a half billion of them as "earth-centered, naive-realist models." All of our known human ancestors were similar to us in this, as we can guess from those who have left writings behind. *The GENERAL IMPLICATIONS are several.*

First, this increasingly detailed inner model is an essential ingredient in all our future theory-laden perception. Our interpretations of sensory cues become so instant, reliable, and taken-for-granted that we get used to thinking we see what we don't see (because it's not there to be seen) but only think, i.e., don't observe but, while observing something else, mistakenly think we are observing and not only thinking about. A squeak in the dead of night? Visions of a tip-toeing intruder ALSO spring to mind. There are no prowlers within a fifty-mile radius? So what? A tiny streak in a photo that already has 1001 streaks? The Holy Grail for a nuclear physicist. Schroedinger is right and there are no particles? Irrelevant! Ribbons of squiggles along a strip of paper? Brain-waves? What?! What wild imaginations! The differences in our theories correlate with our disagreements about what—it seems—we so obviously see. If we can see words, why do those other persons insist that all they see are black ink-marks? Why do they insist they only hear a sound, even though it's obvious to us we hear a car? Or vice-versa.

This inner common-sense geography is also the foundation for language acquisition. A feral child, raised by speechless moon-howlers named Romulus and Rema or whatever, will doubtless construct inner models of their forest territory. Such learning will account for apparent acts of attention-paying, e.g., stopping in their tracks when they espy certain figures or perking up their ears when they hear certain sounds. But that will be the end of the road for a lone feral child. For the rest of us, the ADDITION of those EXTRA auditory stimuli we later call "words," create EXTRA memories attached as labels to the stable fixtures in our expanding inner geography: "mama," "daddy," etc. The constant addition of similar-but-different items becomes the deep well from which an awareness of general classes, each with its own name, will later seem to emerge.

All of that goes on at the same time that a single massive figure is taking shape center-stage, namely, that permanent item we will eventually learn to call "my self," that permanent item whose parts we will eventually—but only eventually—learn to separately name "toe," "nose," "mouth," and so on, that permanent item that remains with us (we'll think it IS us!), other items are coming and going. Among those others, the upright-walking, two-legged beings are notably different from other permanent items, which other items are noticeably different from each other as well as from the bipedal upright-walkers. The 2-leggeds play such a frequency of roles that the class to which they belong gets named first, by the same name we call mom or—according to Aristotle—dad. Eventually we learn to differentiate the class members and to call only one of them "mama" and only one of them "daddy," which makes it necessary to learn a new name for the whole class: "man," "people," "human race," etc. Which names or verbal cues we learn to associate with which items in our inner landscape will depend on which we hear regularly enough to forge the associative link. But whatever distinctive features we are prompted to add because of the distinctiveness of "our culture" are just that: added. To items in a similar mental geography.

Thirdly, this inner geography is the basis for all self-awareness. As William James noted, each of us early on begins drawing the most important "territorial line" through this "world" s/he'll ever draw. On this, the 'in' side, is me and mine. On that, the 'out' side lie all others, you as well as they. Those who have 'lost' their sense of self may later report on their strange experiences. "Mama brought me a gift—a little plush monkey . . . I said to myself 'I am I and he is he and there is no relationship between us,' however the confusion as to who was who was complete . . ." are lines from just such a report. This contrasts sharply with the normal child "in touch with reality" who knows exactly who is eating the candy bar and who only wishes s/he were. It is the basis for economic exchange as well as for understanding the injunction, "Love others as yourself."

Understanding "observed vs not-observed (but only thought-about)" is absolutely impossible to anyone without this mental geography, enough language to name the noticed classes, and an awareness of the distinction between oneself and objects (of one's knowledge). However, even before that express and expressly-named classification can be noticed, *there is no limit to the number of* **additions** *we can imagine,* i.e., add with the assistance of what Einstein and others call our "creative imagination." Once we have labeled (attached memory-tags to), catalogued (grouped tagged-individuals into tagged-classes), and cross-referenced (noted relations between) enough of the *sight*-related parts of our inner model of outer reality, we are in a position to begin adding items that are in*visible*. Feelings, for instance, cannot be seen, so—trust your imagination for now—we put extra little x's inside the skin of mom, dad, sis, everyone who looks like them, then inside wolves that howl, cats that meow, roosters that crow, etc., but not inside trees, or rocks. The x's (in English, we use "feeling" as the marker for the invisible extras rather than "x") remind us not to forget there's more than meets the eye: some things out there have invisible feelings inside. The same as ours. We add thoughts (similar to ours) to (other) people's insides, probably not to the insides of animals, and certainly not inside trees, or rocks. To this whole (world) picture we add un-normal people who have the power to become invisible or make other things invisible, ghosts that can do just the reverse, etc. (The rows upon rows of ink marks here will, it is hoped, be conjuring a rapid-fire string of scenarios right there right now, in the theatre of your mind, pictures about invisible imaginings or happenings on the insides of whatever other human learners you care to think about. Speed readers must slow down, pause, ruminate about each new point, so the pictures' details can "develop" and become less faint.)

Finally, by zeroing in on the ability of the beings we've named "humans" to **add** endlessly to their inner models, we can also add an ability inside them to **remove or delete** items from their model. When it finally dawned on Descartes that he could, if he willed, have freely decided to believe no never-observed bodies existed, his decision can be pictured as deciding whether or not to delete all of the body-taxis which "house" souls or minds, to delete the physical bodies constituting those soul-taxis' external environments, and to retain only the invisible souls and their conscious contents. His already-radical relabeling of bodies, i.e., *removing* "observable" from them and mentally pasting "not able to be observed but only inferred" in place of the original sticker, led to George Berkeley's revolutionary conversion—the effect of which was deciding to believe "physical bodies" is a label for mentally-grouped non-bodily colors, sounds, tastes, and so on. Berkeley *removed* physical bodies from his model.

Whoever has not forgotten this chapter's opening segments will observe (see?) that radical revisions in and of the inside map of outside reality are comparable to mind-quakes which are comparable to earth-quakes. Or to George-A-Kelly-type reconstruals, of the superordinate type, that threaten to "completely alter the appearance of the precious nuggets" of "fact" on which so much else hangs or de-pends.

Rethinking/remodelling Common Sense. Now ZOOM again to the place in your map where *you* are going to attach the invisible conclusions reached by the author of these ink marks at earlier moments in his history, in order to understand the revisions of the major features of the original inner model of the world—common sense—that I had already created by the age of five and have been taking everywhere with me as my means of interpreting those weeks-, months-, and years-long sequences of between-sleep streams of new conscious experiences that have preceded today, July 3, 1992. The rest of this chapter will attend especially to my gradual creation of additional "Thomistic" maps for that inner model, and then will attend to my 'higher' learning of radical alternatives, particularly as they relate to learning and to meaning.

This further narrative begins with my introduction, forty years ago in Pittsburgh, to the unifying theory of Saint Thomas Aquinas (1225-74). At the time all I knew was that St. Thomas' feast was celebrated each March 7, and that one reason he was a saint was because he chased away a naked woman sent to make him commit sin with her. But then I had an experience that remains *a model of "additional mental map-making"* whenever I think of it. In the space of an hour's class*, I heard of a mental diagram that showed how to organize certain of my thoughts in an extremely simple way. The contrast between the outline's clear simplicity and my previous state of mind made a lasting impression, even if the experience's details—day or month (I can reason to the year because I recall where I was living), seating arrangments, etc.—are seemingly forgotten. The lecture was on psychology. (*By the next morning, I had forgotten the beautiful outline and had to visit GF and ask for a quick review!)

Set the stage. Before I describe the map, diagram, outline, model, framework (are your eyes—body's or mind's—jarred by the semantic shifts?), make a mental note that it makes use of one of the most appealing of all the traditional myths: the myth that thinking involves **CONCEPTS**. Make a second mental note that it uses one of the most appealing of all the metaphors describing what concepts do vis-à-vis impressions: concepts **PUT ORDER INTO OUR EXPERIENCE**. Lastly, before I describe my Pittsburgh experience to you, let me set the stage for grasping the kind of "disorder" and "clutter" that is eliminated once order is introduced. At various times in this chapter, I have deliberately tried to pour onto one page so many closely-related questions so quickly that readers still at the stage I was at in my pre-Aquinas days will feel overwhelmed.

No need to look back, here is another sample. What is the definition of "walk"? Of "skip"? Of "step"? Now, define the differences between amble, ambulate, perambulate, pitter-patter along, pad along, saunter, shuffle, skip along, step, stroll, traipse, tread, walk, etc. (A good thesaurus will supply more.) It isn't necessary—though it wouldn't hurt—to work for a publisher on a dictionary-revision project to understand the degree to which someone can get confused about, bogged down in, swamped by, overwhelmed with [synonyms?] the endless nuances, shadings, connotations [ditto?] that Humpty Dumpties are capable of packing into their terms. *Can the clutter be simplified?* Notice the obvious fact that, so far as our common-sense view of everything is concerned, all of those are *essentially* the same, because they are all names for the way a human uses her or his two legs to move from one place to another. That is what they all "have in common" (important formula!). Their "individual differences" (another important formula) are nonessential or accidental. Attention to the former distracts from the latter.

Thomas Aquinas learned (in the classroom?, in the library?) how to conduct that kind of simplification on all psychological activities. (i)Seeing, looking, espying, observing, beholding, watching, witnessing, viewing, etc., are essentially acts performed by one of our knowledge-acquiring organs, our eyes. Hearing, listening, overhearing, hearkening, eavesdropping, etc., are essentially the same because they are performed with our ears. Such analysis yields the standard five-senses diagram: sight, hearing, smell, taste, touch. Experience assures us there is *MORE*. (ii)In addition to our *five (external) senses*, channels via which messages about color, sound, odor, taste, heat-cold-hard-soft are sent to the mind, we must **ALSO** have *four (internal) senses*: one to rejoin the messages (e.g., seen color, heard ticking, felt metalic coolness) into a complete inner image (e.g., of a Baby-Ben clock), one to record such complete images or phantasms, one to detect various invisible features such as desirability or dangerousness, and one for artistic purposes (e.g., to make collages from old pictures, e.g., to pluck the wings off a bird and attach them to a horse), as well as passions. Imagine that animals have senses, both external and internal, as well as the ability to feel desire, fear, anger, and other passions, and you have—so far as Aquinas was concerned—whatever basis there is for a psychology common to humans and animals. But experience teaches us there is even *MORE*: (iii)Humans are *ALSO* capable of forming abstract concepts, of organizing them into complete thoughts, of combining already-learned thoughts in order to learn new facts, therefore of scientific inquiry, *and* of making decisions on the basis of such knowledge. This means we have two MOREs that animals lack: reason or intellect and will. The total comes to five external and four internal senses, eleven passions, one intellect, and one will. In place of endless name-lists of human doings that could be compiled with the aid of a good dictionary and a thesaurus, we have "reduced them" or "boiled them down" to essentials by constructing a streamlined diagram inclusive of old and open to new nuanced, summary-descriptions—"names"—for human doings.

Within less than a decade, I had "internalized," not only this psychological model that is a key ingredient in Aquinas' "philosophy," but all of its other key ingredients. Like him, I did it through "words": spoken words (sounds) in the classroom, written words (ciphers) in the library. The same way, I presume, you are "internalizing" this scenario of how I "streamlined my thinking," of how I "put new-Thomist order into my thoughts," of how I "constructed a neo-Thomist conceptual framework on which to hang all the facts that I had learned and that constituted my detailed knowledge of the world." Calling it "new-or neo-Thomist" means that the conclusions I reached were more like the 1001-basic-principle packages adopted by the thousands of others who more recently adopted belief-frameworks similar to that of the old St. Thomas Aquinas than to the conclusions of thousands of other re-thinkers. So solidly based or grounded on common sense and so all-encompassing was this new system of mine, and so universally accepted by my classroom teachers and library authors, that I am not surprised now by my conviction then—one I vividly recall insisting on in early 1962—that any future radical improvement on Saint Thomas' philosophy was impossible.

From within my present framework I can also focus on something else I was doing, accumulating and classifying a hoard of other facts. I kept filing these other facts into three additional-to-philosophy, hermetically-sealed compartments labeled "theology," "empirical science," and "non-scientific, common-sense, human knowledge of particulars." Though, experientially or phenomenologically, that is, if I describe how matters *felt* to me, I was getting into the habit of dividing all of my beliefs or facts less into four compartments separated by thick walls than into several stories of a house divided by thick floors. The two upper stories were what I paid most attention to, and so complete was my confidence in Aquinas' distinction of *theology* vs *philosophy*, i.e., knowledge from divine revelation vs knowledge from unaided human reason, that I could barely bring myself to regard any doubts about the distinction as anything but a temptation to theological heresy. Most notable, in hindsight, is the fact that several years of practice made the sense of "a solid floor" between *nearest-heaven theology and next-levels-down of **philosophy, ***empirical science, and ***non-scientific common sense, almost palpably "there" in the middle of my head. (One's entire "felt-body" can get involved in such things!)

This "sense" of felt-body levels competes somewhat with another pillar of Aquinas' 'scientific' outlook, one he adopted from Aristotle and constantly re-worked in great detail: the **three levels of abstraction** thesis. Besides everyday-thinking common sense (almost entirely ignored), Aquinas, like Aristotle, held that there are special forms of intellectual knowledge—genuine science—that works with concepts abstracted from imagery. This yields an additional three-level distinction into a-(philosophical) physics which deals with matters closest to the material world known through the body's senses; b-mathematics, which uses less of the senses' raw material, occupies the next level; and finally—despite the usually overlooked distinction between judgments-of-separation abstraction and other types of abstraction used by physics and math—c-the scientific knowledge known as "Metaphysics." Part of this highest form of human science, metaphysics, was often called Natural Theology, to distinguish it from the Supernatural or Sacred Theology knowledge, located on the top floor, above the three natural-science or philosophy floors.

That additional, 'levels' framework 'put order into my knowledge' by providing a home for each and every classroom fact this convinced "Thomist" encountered. James once wrote that "Long indulgence in error makes right thinking almost impossible." How right his thinking was. The vise-grip that "Distinct Disciplines" framework exerted on my thinking became nearly invincible and safe from a revolution or conversion. Nearly.

But other, often incompatible 'classroom' facts kept accumulating and accumulating . . .

(Imagery's role continues.) Most of these 'other' accumulating facts were relegated to the area lower than the lowest of the 'philosophical' levels just mentioned, namely, to a floor even lower than the one philosophical physics was on. This lower floor was designated "empirical science." It included what are known as modern physics, modern chemistry, modern biology, etc. But these new sciences each had a counterpart in philosophy.

For instance, there are two sets of physics. *Today, the physics of Aristotle and Aquinas is often called "philosophy of nature" to remind learners to build a solid floor between the two, very different, philosophical and scientific disciplines of 'physics' and 'physics'.'* I can recall badgering a high-school physics teacher about the question: "Is TODAY's physics compatible with OUR (Thomists') physics?" And being reassured that it was. If "science" is defined as the knowledge of things through their *ultimate* causes, then it was clear that only our physics is genuine science. It is distinct from today's physics which, it was said, is constantly being revised, new doctrines replacing old ones, a physics which is merely pragmatic or technology-oriented and which relies so heavily on mathematics which is already an abstraction from concrete reality.

(This view of today's physics was the subject of a revolution-creating work by Thomas Kuhn, *The Structure of Scientific Revolutions*.)

One bottom line was this. Thomist physics is science, GENUINE science in the original sense of "science," and, so long as the outmoded illustrations borrowed from ancient physics are weeded out, it will remain "the unshaken, perennial truth" for eternity. All other physics (Galileo's, Newton's, Einstein's) and chemistry (Lavoisier's and Dalton's and Mendeleef's) and biology (Harvey's, Darwin's) and psychology (James' and Allport's and Kelly's and Rogers') are sub-scientific because infra-philosophical and, *a fortiori*, inferior to the Queen of the Sciences, Sacred Theology. The accumulating facts gained from courses in these subjects were relegated to a below-philosophy floor.

Is that all? Absolutely not! As already indicated, the bulk of human knowledge, our everyday, "common-sense" knowledge, occupies an even lower floor in the tower of learning. Everyday, "common-sense" knowledge is distinct from all *scientific* knowledge because its objects are the individuals, in all their particular individuality, with which we—individuals ourselves—must interact on a day-to-day basis. There is no hint of eternal, not even of half-century, permanence in this knowledge. What we learn about individual people, places, and things must be updated constantly, because these individuals change every day. We get information about changes only through our senses.

Which is why, from Plato—who, in the *Phaedo* which is his famous narration of Socrates' last day on earth, drew the contrast between the unchanging Ideas with which scientific or eternally certain knowledge deals and the ever-changing particulars with which the senses deal—onwards, scientific knowledge has always been regarded as superior (a Latinism for "higher") to plain, uneducated, inexpert, mere-layfolk knowledge. The latter, pre-scientific knowledge is only the raw "experience" from which the advancing intellect, now properly equipped with that organ(on), tool, or scientific method named "logic," could begin to extract the eternal truths of the various sciences. Fortunately, since I spent my days doing everyday living, it was guaranteed I would not lose touch entirely with that raw material. What's more, I spent my summers reading novels that helped to expand the amount of "flesh" I could throw over the bare-bones, abstract scaffolding of the scholastic philosophy I learned during the academic year.

Universals and universal concepts. For Thomists—for me at that time—the cornerstone of this theory about all theories or myths about distinct disciplines, the linchpin keeping this hindsight caboose attached to the learning process which gave "scientific" theories their start, the glue holding together the whole pigeon-holing apparatus, was that most useful of fictions: *the CONCEPT*. The idea of the idea. The key feature to keep in mind about concepts or ideas, the key that unlocks the secret to everything else, is something that everyone from Socrates and Plato, through Aristotle, right down to Descartes and Kant knew: *concepts are UNIVERSAL*. Our concepts abstract from the individual particulars. They furnish our intellect with generalized knowledge which is only indirectly related—by a kind of sidelong reference to the changing realities outside, a sidelong reference routed through our fallible senses (internal ones first and then external)—to actual, changing, real realities.

Most likely nothing will substitute for a full immersion in that most famous and important of all the medieval debates, that one, namely, which goes under the label "The Controversy Over Universals," as a means for acquiring a feel for the total ramifications of the distinction between particulars-senses-images vs universals-intellect-concepts. Some glimpse of the distinction is needed, though, in order to appreciate a few of those ramifications, and Plato's *Phaedo*, already mentioned, offers that glimpse. It is constructed on an elaborate diagram of the universe and humans' place in it. The distinction is between a world of unchanging Forms or Ideas as contrasted with a lower realm of impermanent particulars or individuals. We humans are similarly two-leveled; and, though our bodies are among the impermanent particulars or individuals accessible through our body's senses, our immortal souls put us in touch with the higher world of Essences. Our familiarity with those unchanging Forms, Ideas, or Essences is, in fact, Plato's strongest evidence that our soul is an immortal being, able to outlive our mortal body. That doctrine, passed on through Aristotle, became the cornerstone of Aquinas' 'proof' for the soul's immortality as well. And thus of my own confidence about immortality during my Thomist phase.

The ideal point of entry into the tradition of universals and universal concepts is through the propositions expressed by simple, declarative sentences which have different subjects but the same predicate. For instance: "Fifi is a dog," "Duffy is a dog," and "Trapper is a dog." In the course of my years, I've met—through my senses—dozens of dogs which were special because they belonged to relatives and friends. They're not here now, but I still remember what I saw, heard, smelled, and felt. When I think of some of them—Fifi, Duffy, and Trapper—I can visualize them vividly enough to feel confident I'd know instantly which was which if you put just three dogs in front of me and gave your word that these were not look-alikes but the actual originals. I am also absolutely sure that Fifi was a genuine dog, that Duffy was a true canine, and that Trapper was nothing other than a real hound. That is, that all three, however different in nonessentials they may have been, qualified a hundred percent as dogs, canines, or hounds, which three words mean or stand for exactly the same thing here, in this context, a fact which I know for certain because I am the one doing the meaning. None were just partially a dog, none was more a dog than the others, none was less a dog than the others. None were anything except dogs, i.e., none were cats, caterpillars, chimps, etc.

The three simple sentences, "Fifi is a dog," "Duffy is a dog," and "Trapper is a dog," are clues to the relevant aspects of my inner knowledge. The sentences' subjects take me to the details of the sensed differences between those three animals. The predicate "is a dog," on the other hand, captures the fact that I have a single general or universal concept that fits all dogs, regardless of any differences in their names, their ages, their height, their weight, etc. None of the dogs is present in this room, so I have no present SENSE knowledge of them. But I have two other kinds of knowledge: sense-memory-IMAGES and intellectual CONCEPTS. If I did not have BOTH images of particular dogs AND ALSO a universal concept applicable to all, how could I distinguish the particular dogs while at the same time recognizing that they all fit my one concept well enough to be called by the one general name of "dog"? Since I have both images and concepts of dogs which I did not have before I opened my eyes and first saw dogs, it seems perfectly logical to infer (because my earliest memories are incomplete) that, even as a child, I had sensations of the dogs directly, then got the images from the sensations and, finally, acquired the concept from the memory-images. All that is necessary to get concepts from imaged things is to attend to how they're alike and ignore how they differ, that is, to extract what is common from the differences. (A fatal "that is," if misunderstood!)

That ancient, then medieval distinction between sense-knowledge and intellect-knowledge, or between senses and intellect, became the common foundation for theories of knowledge. It hardened into the distinction between empiricism and association on the one hand versus rationalism and logic on the other. It also contributed to the myth that there is an intermediate realm, a kind of no-man's land that can be viewed as either separating senses and intellect or as joining the two: the world of imagination. Later on, Kant viewed this no-man's land as the mystery of mysteries so far as human knowing is concerned, the place where the marriage between phenomena and concepts is consummated.

A Revolution. Enough on the Thomist scaffold-building. The remainder of this first of five chapters will focus on its subsequent remodeling. Its high-point was a five-or-six day upheaval in early 1963. But the remodeling required many individual learnings that have only this in common: they led to my revision of certain basics of the traditional theory sketched above.

1. My attention was increasingly drawn to words. To the habit of "talking to oneself silently," which was not talking because it was unutterably silent. To the ambiguity of words, as a result of mulling over the old distinctions between univocity (same meanings), analogy (related meanings), and equivocity (unrelated meanings). To a rejection of Aquinas' notion that words are sounds PLUS a "virtus instrumentalis" [instrumental power], a rejection that resulted from writing a paper on the merely-analogous, therefore non-univocal sense of "instrument," a paper that examined Aquinas' idea that the priest's words give 'form' to ritual behaviors called "sacraments." So far as I recall, this was my first major step away from full agreement with Aquinas' thought.

2. My mental file labeled "images" gradually opened up. Originally, I accepted it as perfectly logical that every image was as definite as the sensed original it was an image of. Moreover, the only

images I was concerned with were the particular images accompanying universal concepts of sensed objects. If thinking (using universals) required an image for the agent intellect to operate on, any image of a particular sensation would do. My image of Fifi would serve as well as my image of Duffy or Trapper when I was thinking about the essential of 'dog-ness.' J. Maritain's *Creative Intuition in Art and Poetry* offered an expanded image of the human psyche's unhampered freedom to play with unimaginably complex imagery and showed where to insert it into Aquinas' outline. Later, this bec ame my bridge to the phenomenologists' discussions of our 'preconceptual knowledge of things.' One of Maritain's images stuck with me: ". . . before being formed and expressed in concepts and judgments, intellectual knowledge is at first a beginning of insight, still unformulated, a kind of many-eyed cloud which is born from the impact of the Illuminating Intellect on the world of images." That led me to think of my imagination as a pre-conceptual, multi-faceted, many-splendored cloud, from which lightning-bursts of intuition or insight could flash.

3. I developed a predisposition to what I encountered later on: Locke's notion of introspection or reflection. Besides long hours of silent chapel-meditation which fostered an awareness of the lively goings-on in the 'interior castle of my soul,' I began paying more attention to what was going on 'inside' when I was not in a chapel. I have no idea why, but I began occasionally to conduct an experiment while trying to get to sleep. I would try to put everything from my mind, then 'silently say' just one word to myself. "Dog," for instance, or "book," or "man." I began to notice that, when I interiorly pronounced a word, something like Maritain's 'cloud (of images)' and/or a 'world' of potential judgments—a dog has four legs, is alive, barks, etc., a book can be small, large, in any language, on any topic, etc., a man can be young or old, short or tall, etc.—would be sub-activated or put on alert. But, till the further 'words' that *completed a declarative sentence* were added, there was no truth or error, no possibility of 'correspondence to reality' or its lack.

"Images are indispensable to thinking" became "At least images OF 'WORDS' are essential to thinking."

4. From there it was a short step to becoming intensely aware of 'inner speech,' i.e., the inner images or copies of the heard sounds that constituted my earliest (outer) language. Confidence that the imagery called "inner speech" was the first thing specifically evoked by the written 'words' of whatever book or article I was reading solidified when I later encountered Helen Keller's reported experience:

> I recall her [Annie Sullivan's] repeated attempts to spell words—words which meant nothing—into my small hand. But at last, on April 5, 1887, about a month after her arrival, she reached my consciousness with the word 'water.'
>
> It happened at the well house, where I was holding a mug under the spout. Annie pumped water into it, and when the water gushed over onto my hand she kept spelling w-a-t-e-r into my other hand with her fingers. Suddenly I understood . . .
>
> To this day, I cannot "command the uses of my soul" or stir my mind to action without the memory of the quasi-electric touch of Teacher's fingers upon my palm.

5. My roller-coaster ride out over the abyss occurred in early 1963. I was rethinking two of Maritain's themes, namely, his notion that it is possible to experience 'an intuition of being,' (I felt confident that I had done so, more than six years earlier) and his reflections about 'judgements of existence,' i.e., acts whereby the intellect consults sense experience to know the individual existent through a subject-predicate proposition, e.g., "This thing is a page with words on it." At the same time that I was poring and re-poring over his analyses, I chanced to read A. Dondeyne's *Contemporary European Thought and Christian Faith.* His suggestion that Aquinas' 'natural light' of the mind—which Descartes so often invoked and which was another name for Plato's Sun, Aristotle's Illuminating Intellect, and Augustine's Inner Teacher—brought with it some minimum of 'content'

was a (camel's) back-breaking straw. The *"nihil in intellectu nisi prius in sensu"* [everything we know with our intellect comes somehow through our senses] rug was suddenly pulled from beneath the foundation of my 'philosophy.' The possibility that some of our knowledge does not originate with our senses, that some of our concepts have 'content' that originates elsewhere than in sense-deliverances, came to a mind 'prepared' to take note. Here is one of Dondeyne's phrases that reverberates for me to this very day:

> Descartes expressed his amazement that the scholastics claimed to demonstrate the existence of God, and at the same time held it as a maxim that there is nothing in the intellect which was not first in the senses, "where it is certain that the ideas of God or of the soul have never been."

As a good Thomist, I knew the official story about how we go from contact with sensible substances to inferential judgments about such non-sensed substances as souls and deities, so I was hardly disposed to accept Dondeyne's use of Descartes as a warrant for his own 'more' without some kind of permission from Aquinas' own words. For someone eager to find confirmation of a powerfully appealing new insight, nothing more was needed than returning to Thomas' *On the Truth* to verify a sentence Dondeyne culled from the beginning of Thomas' first 'corpus' in that work: "Being is what the intellect first conceives as best known; it is that in which all other conceptions are resolved *[Illud autem quod primo intellectus concipit quasi notissimum, et in quo omnes conceptiones resolvit, est ens]*." I'd never seen anything but very finite beingS, never sensed potentially-infinite BeinG. (Later rethinking showed that the Illogical Positivists were partly right: SOME hoary old theories are mountains of fiction constructed over unwarranted reifications.)

6. Many other things went into the dismantling of the old, new-Thomist scaffolding and the building of the present one which so radically reorganizes—without destroying—all of the information I had acquired during almost thirty previous years. One of the two other most memorable items was the

ferment in my thinking about sensation, brought to a head by reading Whitehead's *Introduction to Mathematics* which is recommended at the end of *What Is Science?*, an anthology edited by J.R. Newman. What was brought to a head was a realization that even the most concrete data of our senses do not, if ('modern') physics is to be believed, come from external bodies. An already-accumulated horde of fairly-firm convictions was waiting to be fetched up from the basement of my sciences-tower and led into my 'properly philosophical' chambers as equal rights participants in debates about 'essence' judgments vis-à-vis the physical world!, e.g., beliefs about colorless but light-reflecting bodies, colorless light able to cause different colors by virtue of its varying wave-lengths and wave-frequencies, retinal images whose outlines or shapes correlate far better with the contours of our experienced visual data than the shapes of the external light-reflecting bodies themselves, a brain into which all stimuli are funneled, etc.

7. But the most memorable 'straw' was Husserl's *Ideas*, as read by a student attending a course of lectures about Husserl and the question of 'meaning.' Unlike what it might have done, i.e., merely mired me more deeply in my belief in essences, thinking about meaning *liberated my imagination from the vice-grip of the CONCEPT fiction*. For a few weeks, I tried repeatedly to pay attention to or to 'catch sight of' what transpires within the mind's inner chambers when one passes from the state of NOT actually thinking (of anything specific) to thinking 'in words' of something specific. I would sit before the type-writer transcribing 'phenomenological descriptions' of what swims into view when some word, e.g., "man" or "book" or "dog," is internally pronounced, and then bringing to bear, without any restrictions, a lifetime accumulation of facts while doing so . . .

At some point, the gist of a note copied from somewhere—"The essence is not a word, not an image, not a concept, but rather more like the sense or the meaning"—returned from the fringe of my consciousness to center-stage. Suddenly it dawned on me that this in(tro)specting—directed, presumably, at one, sole, solitary, attended-to, essence-bearing 'object'—was actually being understood or interpreted by me in an incredibly-obviously-mistaken way. I was trying to study thought IN SLOW MOTION and thereby missing entirely what was obvious once I noticed the incredible number of nouns, adjectives, verbs, etc., that made up my description of what I supposed was a single object, all of which indicated HOW FAST THOUGHT IS. The description did not consist of the repetition of the same word, over and over. Granted, the same word did return over and over, but always amidst threads of CONTEXT-INDICATING-OTHER-WORDS and SENTENCES. The actual, i.e., *real* object before my inspecting mind was never just one thing. Not unless that one thing is renamed **"The MEANING of ALL the words."** Present to my inspection was not one thing like the word "dog," not one thing like an actual dog, not one thing like a dog-essence, not one thing like a concept signified by "dog," but the meaning of all the words that fly through my mind too fast for my fingers to transcribe them onto paper—and how could the associated imagery dredged up by the words (verbal images) be captured?!—and the meaning that, therefore, includes whatever meaning from earlier words on the page had provided context for the most immediately present word's meaning.

I understood, too, that meanings are not small original blobs that can be mixed into one larger one. Nor is a large meaning a big blob that can be sliced up into "the meaning of the first sentence on the page, the meaning of the second sentence, etc., and the meaning of THIS WORD in this sentence." We can only *imagine* or *pretend* that meaning can be sliced up so that we can 'talk about it' with our 'sentences,' just the way some say we *pretend* to slice up a partless deity in order to eff about the ineffable, put into words what cannot be put into words, and so on. ('Catching sight of,' 'having it dawn on me,' like 'attending' and 'noticing,' can't be put into words either. Nothing can, of course. There are no words.)

A new image, one that has anchored that moment of insight in my memory for three decades now, is of a many-splendored, multi-faceted cloud of meaning, floating just above the fast-flowing stream of imagery below. Inner speech, the flow of inner words, does—according to that image—just what the outer words on the page do, act as a fishing net dredging up memory-clusters of images faster, in vastly greater numbers, and with less predictability than any of us can possibly capture in our theories except with/in statistical laws. The key formula, from then until the spring of 1989 when a new picture finally swam into fully explicit view, was unvarying: **We must notice . . .**

the meaning of ALL the words!

8. Here was an extension of an insight that is basic to the way St. Thomas explains finite human efforts to understand the infinite, partless deity. According to him, we must use many distinct concepts, each of which reflects just one facet of God. We must believe God is good, intelligent, powerful, and just, even though God's goodness is not a thing distinct from God's intelligence, etc. The distinct, human concepts involved when we speak of God's goodness, intelligence, etc., are "entia rationis," beings-of-reason, created by our intellect, but beings that have 'some foundation' in reality.

Analogously (analogy is a favorite Thomistic idea), the thoughts that we understand are not made up from really distinct concepts, e.g., the subject-concept plus a predicate-concept. However, it is essential to pretend that, corresponding to the distinct words in the sentence, there are distinct parts to any thought that we can understand. (All of this is explained in detail in *William James on the Stream of Consciousness.*)

9. The last three decades can be described as the slow rethinking of the first three decades' worth of learning. A bare-bones summary of the results to date constitutes the ten theses that are part of experiment j' or 10'. The rest of the chapters in the book will expand on those theses.

Conclusion to Chapter One. Why control your imagination? Why notice and then be careful of the imagery around which you build your worldview or philosophy? Because, as James noted, "Long indulgence in error makes right thinking almost impossible."

James supplied the reason why Socrates' reminder that "A Person Living The Unexamined Life" cannot be "A Person Fully Alive." We are capable of more. It is summarized in what he wrote under the heading "habit": learners are habit-acquirers.

We are born with mere potential. Our earliest years are occupied by the unwitting acquisition of habits. Unwitting, not unconscious. Unwittingly acquired habits, that is, unselfconsciously and not deliberately acquired habits.

James also supplied the insight that underlies the assumption Socrates had in mind when he urged his listeners to lead the 'examined life': we can, by voluntary rethinking efforts, every one of which requires some attention, try to change our thought habits. James was also, like Socrates, concerned that we change our habits in the right, i.e., moral, as opposed to the wrong, i.e., vicious, direction. Whoever has not had any living conversation with Socrates or James, though, must rely on the words they've left behind to assist in learning what they concluded as a result of their lifelong learning. This chapter recommends that you pay very close attention to each everyone-else's ink marks in order to discover her or his inner geography, particularly what fixtures it includes and which it excludes. That "geography" will be your best guide to what answer an author gives to question one, namely, "What exists?", because that answer is the context for their invitations to the right examined life. Invitations to conversions, from one's presently habitual philosophy to another philosophy, i.e., to an inner revolution, can hardly be accepted unless they are first understood.

You do understand all of this, right?

CHAPTER TWO

Video Aliquid, Ergo Sum

(I see something, therefore I am)

A Role Model: Dorothy Day. To slake our thirst to know as God knows, we must learn to see everything at once, from an imagined perch high above the flow of time below. But, since the goings-on below are so many and so varied, we must learn to generalize. We must learn to search for the right mental patterns, templates that are definite enough to focus attention on some individuals rather than others, vague and loose enough to allow for the selected individuals' differences. Every good Ockhamist knows that generalizations are made for individuals and not vice-versa. Nor does any good Ockhamist ignore the differences in the ways we can view the same individuals or those temporal-duration-rivers (not streams!) of being and doing which we label "their lives."

Their lives. The focus for a good psychologist must be individual human lives, so radically different from vegetable and animal lives which are as devoid of understanding—of thoughts and decisions—as ours are of real, as opposed to merely apparent, biological features. Yet our inner, psychological life is—"by analogy"—made so much more intelligible by a sideways glance at the biological model of birth, stages of growth, and directedness to a fully mature, "actualized" form. All the great "religious" traditions offer blueprints to help their followers make sense of life's otherwise meaningless chaos. Great thinkers, from Plato to James, do, too. In fact, the lecture-titles of his monumental *Varieties of Religious Experience* form an outline of James' 'personality theory.' They tell which of the features of the typical human's life-pattern James judged to be central. But there are many ways of making sense of humans' lives, right down to focussing on specific features of human lives in general, even on specific features of specific "segments" of human lives in general, as Robert Coles shows in works with titles like that of his latest, viz., *The Spiritual Life of Children.* And so on.

Since generalizations' value comes from the service they render in enabling us to understand existing individuals, the pattern discerned will depend on the quality of the lives studied in the search for the best generalizations. (Compare Freud and Maslow.) William James' masterpiece is so rich because, after training to notice the tiniest details of human experience, he studied the gamut of richly varied lives in order to glean "the meaning of it all." Dorothy Day's autobiography, *The Long Loneliness*, which tells of an extraordinary, life-long, intellectual education as part of one lone person's quest for—and discovery of—a vision both modern and classical, more richly-faceted than Marx's, as cosmic as the Biblical writers', is like the "stuff" on which James' thesis was based. It is an education in itself.

Sex. Darwin and Freud, with their fundamentally biological construals of humans' lives, laid a theoretical foundation for viewing sex as the outstanding type of the only thing that makes humans' existence in an alien universe tolerable: pleasure. Like Augustine's, Dorothy Day's universe had room for infinite love as well. In the area of matters sexual, though, she rose above his sin-focused perspective. That is one reason, though not the usual one, why so many find in her life an inspiring witness to what life is all about, why her new "confessions" have so much to teach us. Tho the usual reason is best: she lived by her vision.

A. Lead-Up to the Door Closing

A warning. Chapter I was devoted to intellectual understanding. This chapter will deal with what at first seems easier to understand: seeing and other kinds of sensing. Be warned, though. Studying sensation in depth leads to conclusions that will initially seem simply preposterous.

For instance, Descartes, like Plato before him, claimed that your body—if you even have one—is not at all part of you. Naively, we think

Descartes' claim cannot possibly be true. In a century when language has replaced thought as the locus of meaning, it will surely sound bizarre to say that there is no such thing as language. Finally, all of us have been so brainwashed to believe there is a real difference between philosophy, physics, biology, psychology, and theology, that calling such a belief "a crude cultural myth" or "brainwashing" will seem almost ludicrous.

The pages that follow will argue for the truth of each of those views, perhaps not always with discernible modesty. I hope the risk is justified. To get things "said" effectively, the conclusions must be very forcefully, bluntly stated. These views weren't always my conclusions. I, too, once regarded them as unbelievable.

Initially we don't dream how many things are going on "right under our nose" at every single instant. How many people notice regularly that they are breathing? Or standing, sitting, walking, etc.? Or that they are receiving sensations galore relative to those things? Or that they are seeing a whole lot of things besides the very word, clause, sentence, they're taking in at any given moment? Or hearing whatever noises are reaching them while they're reading? Or that they're ready to respond instantly if someone yells "Fire!", or if they smell smoke, or if the seat under them begins to get hotter and hotter? Or just how many habits they are dependent upon as they read and the thoughts come to them so effortlessly? So much of what is going on at any moment for us comes under the heading of habit, habits that make it possible for us to do so many things we could not do as babies but can now do without paying attention to them because we are paying attention to other things, but how many of us are in the habit of noticing that? Which means that—in order to get out of the habit of overlooking them when they are critically important—we need to get in the habit of habitually noticing them. Since this book is being written for everyone who is old enough and curious enough and leisure'd enough to understand it, I have taken the risk of being more repetitious than necessary for some in order to be repetitious enough for the others.

The direct "I-Thou" form of address may also test the reader's patience. But you are probably the only reader within sight of you right now, so why write "the reader" rather than "you"? One of the most famous recipes for wisdom is "Know thyself," and part of that means getting in the habit of noticing that, because all of us similar enough to qualify as "human" must be suitably alike, learning about what a human being is will be learning about what you are. (And vice-versa.) In this era of "science," it is easy for us to become so "objective" that we contract the deadly disease of "habitual self-forgetfulness." Not the one synonymous with generosity but with impersonality. Kierkegaard and Tolstoy were both concerned to help us overcome this disease. It seems unrealistic to expect that most readers will be familiar with Kierkegaard or Tolstoy. However, reminding you that the human who is reading each new sentence here *is **you*** springs from a concern that this writer shares with K and T.

Appearance vs Reality. That's the name of the oldest and most famous of the snarls we run into in our pursuit of a grand unifying theory. It is customary to think that it began with the Greek Thales and philosophy, but that it has reached its climax with modern physics. Perhaps the distinction began even earlier, though, when what appears became a symbol for what does not appear.

> God said: "This shall be the symbol of the covenant which I am making with you and every living creature that is with you, to endless generations. I put my **RAINBOW** in the clouds, and it shall be a symbol of the covenant between **MYSELF** and the world."

The more we learn about what the most highly educated people in this century believe, the more obvious it is that there is not even one single question on which every expert agrees. We are easily seduced into thinking we have to study different societies and civilizations to understand that it is possible to 'see' this world in radically different ways. But we have only to pay close attention as we move from one college classroom to the next and from one textbook to the next to 'see' the world in radically different ways. Just think of the different ways people in our own 'culture' think of the spectrum called a rainbow. Do you think of it as God's trademark?

The appearances vs reality problem has never been as severe, however, as it is at this end of the 20th century. So acute, that the vast majority of us who live in societies where physics and medicine are most advanced have developed a form of schizophrenia. On the one hand we try very hard to cling to our growing-up, naive realism.

On the other hand, we take for granted all sorts of things that utterly contradict it. In the course of these pages, I have hinted at my own radical solution to the contradictions. It is now time to bring things to a head by discussing the two questions that every educated person must face if s/he wishes to integrate science and daily living. The first of them is the question Descartes raised: If physics and physiology are true, is there any way to be certain there is a physical world for physics and physiology to be true about? The other goes far beyond that, so far, in fact, that Descartes—to my knowledge—never once noticed it, even though it goes hand in hand with certainty about the physical world: Am I the only being in the universe? The answer "Yes I am" is called solipsism, and adherents of solipsism are called solipsists.

Solipsism is a problem for the same reason the existence of the physical world is a problem. By showing that the 'stars' we think we see are not really stars, modern physics and physiology show that the 'people' we see aren't people either. Fear of solipsism, therefore, has caused many thinkers a great deal of trouble. Martin Gardner, a long-time writer for the *Scientific American*, addressed the problem in *The Whys of a Philosophical Scrivener.* He began the first of his twenty-plus-chapters-report of his later-years conclusions with the reasons WHY—even though "there is no ironclad way to refute solipsism"—he has concluded that he is not the only being in existence. But the physicist, Percy Bridgman, decided that, in order to be exact in how he spoke, he should say "Only I am conscious." Most of today's psychologists dodge the issue. Many seem never to have thought about it. B.F. Skinner did, though, and he explains that he tried to explain to Bridgman why it wasn't such a big problem. (But B.F. Skinner didn't think even he himself was conscious!) William James, right into his last decade, was explaining his reasons why his radical empiricism wasn't a form of solipsism. Solipsism will be a big issue in the pages that follow.

Clearly I am not one, otherwise I would not be writing this book to explain for you what I believe. I would be reading more of what seem to be interesting things written by other people. True, I am certain beyond the shadow of a doubt that I have never seen another person and that, if I am right in believing others exist, none of them have seen me. But I am far more certain about the existence of other people than I am of physical bodies. Just as I am certain that, if any bodies do exist, the only ones are subatomic particles, infinitesimal in size. Such are the conclusions one should—I believe—arrive at who very carefully examines every last detail of what s/he is doing while s/he is reading—or seeming to read—any book. In this non-chapter, I will explain why neither books nor chapters exist, even though the discovery of those two facts begins with understanding what "This is a book" means. That is, understanding the thought that just came to you as—it seems—your eyes swept across that line of print.

The best way to grasp our Creators' Grandest Deception is to set the scene. Vividly. To create the right mindset. To my knowledge, what follows has never been surpassed. The 'right mindset' requires an ability to pretend there are two kinds of worlds. Or, perhaps better, one world and billions of different 'worlds.'

> There seems to be a single starting point for psychology, exactly as for all the other sciences: the world as we find it, naively and uncritically . . . In my case, which may be taken as representative of many others, that naive picture consists, at this moment, of a blue lake with dark forests around it, a big, gray rock, hard and cool, which I have chosen as a seat, a paper on which I write, a faint noise of the wind which hardly moves the trees, and a strong odor characteristic of boats and fishing. But there is more in this world; somehow I now behold, though it does not become fused with the blue lake of the present, another lake of a milder blue, at which I found myself some years ago, looking from its shore in Illinois. I am perfectly accustomed to beholding thousands of views of this kind which arise when I am alone. And there is still more in this world: for instance, my hand and my fingers as they lightly move across the paper. Now, when I stop writing and look around again, there also is a feeling of health and vigor. But in the next moment, I feel something like a dark pressure somewhere in my interior which tends to develop into a feeling of being hunted—I have promised to have this manuscript ready within a few months.
>
> Most people live permanently in a world such as this, which is for them *the* world, and hardly ever find serious problems in its fundamental properties.

Crowded streets may take the place of the lake, a cushion in a sedan that of my rock, some serious words of a business transaction may be remembered instead of Lake Michigan, and the dark pressures may have to do with tax-paying instead of my book-writing. All these are minor differences so long as one takes the world at its face value, as we all do except in hours in which science disturbs our natural attitude . . .

Centuries ago, various sciences, most of all physics and biology, began to destroy the simple confidence with which human beings tend to take this world as *the reality*. Though hundreds of millions still remain undisturbed, the scientist now finds it full of almost contradictory properties. Fortunately, he has been able to discover behind it another world, properties of which, quite different from those of the world of naive people, do not seem to be contradictory at all.

In that introduction to *Gestalt Psychology*, W. Kohler uses a bold metaphor: there are two radically different worlds. The one we grow up believing is THE world isn't. In fact, it cuts off our view of the REAL world. The real world is the one that scientists—especially in physics and biology—have discovered. It is important to adjust one detail, however. There is no "the simple confidence." There is only my confidence, yours, Kohler's, Descartes', etc. That is, each one of us begins life without any thoughts to feel confident about and then gains her or his confidence about the 'naive world' of stars, sun, moon, earth, people, books, hands to hold books with, eyes to see the pages with, a brain to receive the stimuli from hands and eyes, and a mind to understand the thoughts, and so on. The shock that comes can come to us learners only one at a time, in our own good time, though many go to their grave never having heard that they should have surrendered their simple confidence, while others go to their grave having declined the invitation to do so. That's my goal: to invite you. Your reply is up to you.

The purpose of using this long passage which Kohler used to introduce his gestalt theory of sense perception is to focus your attention on your common-sense view of your here-and-now, the same way Descartes did when he began his *Meditations* with a picture of *his* there-and-then (seated at his desk, pen in hand, making a record of his rethinking meditations), in order to invite his readers to take a look around at *their* here-and-now. Neither you now (your now) nor I now (July 22, 5:07pm) are sitting by the edge of the Lake Michigan he recalled when he penned that four-senses description. (Only taste was omitted.) But, even if you are, I am certain you are reading a book that has the line "you are reading a book" on the page you are or just finished reading.

For a moment, focus on what you see and feel and on how the two differ as well as on how they're similar. What you see disappears if you close your eyes, but what you feel won't. But, what you feel will disappear if you put the book down, regardless of whether your eyes are open or closed. You seem to see WITH your eyes (but it's the you who uses the eyes who does the seeing, not the eyes) and you seem to feel WITH your hands (but it's the you who uses your hands who does the feeling).

Now focus on the differences and similarities between what you sense and what others sense. Suppose you WERE sitting by the edge of Lake Michigan with W. Kohler. In that case, you would certainly take it for granted that you could see the same blue lake, dark forest, and gray rock, that you could feel your own hard, cool rock beneath you, that you could hear the wind and smell the boats and fish, even feel a tensing similar to his anxiety. But notice: there is a clear-cut line between what you know and what you guess. You would feel *certain* you sense the very same lake, forest, wind, and smell, and—though you now feel a rock only *like* his—you would feel certain you could exchange places and feel the very same rock he feels, just as he would then feel the one beneath you. On the other hand, you could never feel the very anxiety he feels, just anxiety of your own that's *like* his, so there is a measure of guessing, since we must take it "on faith" that what goes on inside others is *like* what goes on inside ourselves. A moment's further reflection reveals that you can never see Kohler's seeing nor his memories, cannot even see his hearing or smelling or thoughts. All those things go on inside his skin, just as yours go on inside you and thus cannot be seen by him. (Do you recall the very first time you ever wondered whether other people's pain, e.g., the pain of a stomach ache, was as bad as your own?)

Switching Between Two Models. Earlier pages have presented the notion that, though born without one, we begin very early to build up an inner model of our environment that helps to "put order into our experience." Once we have learned enough, we are capable of revising that model, either by adding new items or by deleting old ones.

But that picture, of a single model that can be revised, is not as suitable for understanding the essentials of human learning as another picture, equally easy to imagine, which shows each of us building up *one inner model* that we can label "the everyday common-sense model" and then, later, starting on *a second model* to serve as a rival to the first. Either picture can be used, neither is more than a model—that is, more than imagery—to assist in what's most important, understanding. But this second image of each learner eventually using two models—and having to switch from one to the other and back again—will be seen to offer advantages over the first image of each learner using only one map. Or model. The earliest or common-sense model will always be the foundation: we will always have to define the second in terms drawn from the first or common-sense model.

The most basic feature of our common-sense map is its boundaries. When we're born, we don't know anything, much less where we leave off and other people begin. Our likes and dislikes resemble, and

> [...] in my mind and your mind the rejected portions and the selected portions of the original world-stuff are to a great extent the same. The human race as a whole largely agrees as to what it shall notice and name, and what not. And among the noticed parts we select in much the same way for accentuation and preference or subordination and dislike. There is, however, one entirely extraordinary case in which no two [wo]men ever are known to choose alike. One great splitting of the universe into two halves is made by each of us; and for each of us almost all of the interest attaches to one of the halves; but we all draw the line of division between them in a different place. When I say that we call the two halves by the same names, and that those names are 'me' and 'not-me' respectively, it will at once be seen what I mean. The altogether unique kind of interest which each human mind finds in those parts of creation which it can call *me* or *mine* may be a moral riddle, but it is a fundamental psychological fact. (PP I:289)

This description by William James is as good as any for giving a sense of the most basic ingredient in what "ego-psychologists" have been insisting on for decades: the need for a clearly-established "sense of self" as the basis for psychological well-being.

But James does not say where—at what intersection of earth's latitude and longitude—that original line is located. Even though—common-sensically—it is utterly obvious: *our skin.* For everyone, what's inside our skin is us. What's outside is our neighborhood and the rest of the universe. Or, for those who prefer the word usually substituted when what is labeled "surroundings" in our common-sense map is transferred to our professional map, what's outside our skin is our "environment," a term that can be restricted to what's close or broadened to "society," "nation," "planet," and so on. For 'scientists' who think in mostly physical terms, the supposedly observed similarity between us and other skin-encapsulated beings, it has become common to replace "self" with "organism." Thus, the concept labeled "I and my neighborhood" is often relabeled "the organism and its environment." If clear thinking about details is impossible without clear thinking on the broad framework that allows us to keep different details clearly separated, e.g., the details about what YOU see as opposed to the details about what I see (there are ALWAYS discrepancies in those two sets of details), then this most fundamental of line-drawings is utterly crucial for clear thinking about everything. Or anything.

But no one muddied the common-sense waters worse than William James himself. In the very chapter that followed that line-drawing! That is, in the next chapter entitled "The Consciousness of Self," James distinguishes between the self as knower and the self as known. He begins with a description of the second, the self-as-known, and subdivides it into three selves or me's: the material me, the social me, and the spiritual me. Not one of which is the real self that is in charge of making the final decisions about where the line should be drawn!

The way to understand James is to learn a somewhat complicated distinction Immanuel Kant made famous regarding appearance vs reality. Kant said that all we know about nature is 'how nature appears to us.' Therefore we must distinguish nature as it appears from nature as it is in itself. Kant extended this to selves, by distinguishing our self as it appears to us from our self as it is in itself, that is, from our real self. The self as it appears consists of our beliefs, our memories, our sensory experience, and so on. Our real self is an invisible believer, rememberer, sense'r, that not even we have ever seen or directly experienced. Because our sensory experience of 'nature as it appears' is inside us, along with the rest of our 'stream of consciousness' (James' famous name for everything we experience) which includes our beliefs, memories, etc., it is convenient to divide what's inside into what SEEMS to be outside (but isn't), i.e., 'nature as it appears,' from what is also inside, i.e., our beliefs, memories, etc., which seem to be inside (and are inside). So, there's what is really outside, both nature as it is in itself and our self as it is in itself, and there's what is really inside, both (i)nature as it appears and (ii)our self as it appears. Because both 'i' and 'ii' are inside, Kant was in effect dividing what is inside into two things, an inside 'outside' (what seems to be nature) and an inside 'inside' (what seems to be inside).

James—adhering here to Kant's waffling division of the inner field of experience into an inner and an outer segment—treats such things as our physical possessions and others' opinions of us as part of the empirical self, the appearing self. "In its widest possible sense, however, a man's Self is all that he *can* call his, not only his body and his psychic powers, but his clothes and his house, his wife and his children, his ancestors and friends, his reputation and works, his lands and horses, and yacht and bank-account." (PP I:291)

This Kantian-Jamesian approach creates wholesale ambiguity, once anyone seriously incorporates it into his or her worldview. Whoever ignores the fact that other people, clothes, house, lands, horses, yacht, etc., *IF they really exist outside*, are part of the environment, and are therefore NOT part of the real self, has become seriously ill. Mentally. Theoretically. Even if such people function satisfactorily in real life by not allowing their silly professional model to interfere with their better common sense. James never did.

That is because he had acquired the modern schizophrenia I wrote of earlier. His later model, called "Pragmatism," is his effort to bridge the clash between his original common sense and his keen awareness of modern physics (his friend, C.S. Peirce, excelled in mathematics and physics) and modern biology (he had an M.D. from Harvard). Like all "empirical" psychologists from Wundt to Allport, James advised that for the purpose of doing "scientific psychology," the old purely philosophical (often called "metaphysical") controversies could be temporarily set aside. Therefore he declared that the real self could be ignored on the grounds that, if any such thing exists, it is NON-empirical—or transcendental or meta-empirical or metaphysical or *apriori* or, to get to what such term-users really want to say, uncertain—and therefore fit to be studied only by non-empirical believers, such as theologians [who, when being "professional," use "soul"] and philosophers [who prefer "mind"].

Many psychologists in Wundt's and James' day adopted the bad habit, the same habit those called "positivists" had, of profess-ing profess-ionally that there are two ego's, the empirical and the transcendental, theoretically preferring one and just ignoring or denying the other, but of then *actually* switching back and forth from one to the other in practice. James' more urgent reason for declaring the real self off-limits for empirical psychology was a desire to avoid becoming mired down in the idealist morass created by Hegel who convinced thousands of readers that they were really God. In fact, from Kant on, a great number of thinkers turned in the direction of Hegel's idea, one that eliminates any need to attend closely to one's *at-least-apparent* skin, because God—who is pure Geist [Ghost or Spirit]—has no skin. An idea that often led/leads to erasing any exact line between the self and the not-self. A practice unsympathetic readers, even former Neo-Thomists, find exasperating.

More clearly and in more detail. The above does not explain how the scientific ideas called physics and physiology were responsible for this schizophrenia. But the explanation is very easy. Look at this page in this book and at your hands. Look at it the way someone like Socrates, Plato, or Aristotle—who lived a long time ago in Athens, already famous for sophisticated science, but long before the super-sophisticated science made possible by the invention of the telescope and microscope—would look at it. It's easy. Look at it the way you would have during your first five years. Are your eyes out here on the page? Are they deep inside your head, hidden the way your brain is from the outside? Or are they on the borderline, transparent windows through which you can look out at this page in this book. When you close your eyes, your hands disappear from sight along with the book, so that your hands, too, are out here on the outside—at least outside your eyes. You keep your hands out of your eyes, too. They're far too large to fit inside your eyes, and the pain from trying to get them or anything inside your eyes would be excruciating. Suppose now that, after doing the first ten experiments of Chapter One, you developed a cramp in your hand. If you looked at the hand that had the cramp in it, it would *appear* or *seem* AS IF what you see (the hand) and what you feel (the pain in the hand) are in exactly the same location in the world outside your eyes. Open and close your eyes: other than the fact that you see when your eyes are open and stop seeing when your eyes are closed, do you notice anything at all except the muscle-tightening around your eyes?

Today, though, we know that there are extremely complex processes involved. Seeing involves light, which is why we stop seeing as soon as we close our eyes, i.e., pull down those 'shades' and cut the light off. Complex reasoning convinced Descartes that we never see anything FARTHER away than the tiny images which the light focused by the eyes' lenses create inside our eyes. Though light is invisible (if you can see any light bouncing from this page into your eyes, you are different from me), astronomers tell us that it must often travel so many billions of years from distant stars before it enters our eyes that some stars have burned out, are no longer shining, by the time we look up and see tiny pinpoints "in the sky." If that is correct, we see neither the stars nor our hand, but the *likenesses* of them inside our eyes. The "hand" we see isn't a hand, and—since we don't poke our hand into our eyes—what we see isn't what we feel, either.

Then the physiologists and neuroscientists come into the picture and, following Descartes, conclude that we do not EVEN see those images. The stimulated retinas must send nerve signals to our brain. Nor do we feel pain until the hand sends nerve signals to our brain. We are doubly mistaken: neither what we see nor what we feel is where it *seems* or *appears* to be. Every relevant scientific fact about the physics and physiology of seeing and feeling fits into the model Descartes created. Descartes, in a bold move, concluded that *the locus of seeing must be moved inwards FROM eyes TO brain or mind.* Once that is done, the outside world—and that includes every single one of the world's other billions of human inhabitants, if any exist (can anyone prove from these lines of print that I exist?)—is moved into the same category that everyone puts God into: that of the UNobservable, non-empirical, transcendental, thinkable-only, merely-inferrable, etc. That is the inexorably logical inference or conclusion for anyone who honestly and straightforwardly professes to accept as literally true the basics of modern physics and physiology. Still . . .

YOU DO SEE SOMETHING. BUT WHAT?!

What we see will now be named "what appears," or—for short—"the appearances." We broaden it to include the real things we feel, hear, smell, etc. These appearing realities make up the "naive world" that Kohler writes about, the things we MIS-take for the real world outside. The other world Kohler writes of is the world of stars, light, and hands that are somewhere behind or beyond or (fancy 'technical') transcendent-to the 'world' that is directly present to us. It is the world of galaxies too far away to be seen with the naked eye, of atoms too small to be seen by the naked eye, and so on. That the experts are on the right track—finally, in recent times, during this age of 'modern' science—is shown by the results it produces. Technological miracles—good (small-pox wiped out) and bad (Hiroshima)—boggle our minds as soon as we stop taking them for granted and begin learning their details.

More scene-setting. Descartes was astonished when he realized what Kohler later realized: the radically mistaken view we have of the world. Why, he asked, do we all grow up with such a mistaken view? He was convinced that God created our minds to know the truth, so he concluded that our errors are a result of not controlling our imaginations (his term was "free reasonings") carefully enough. Jumping to conclusions without good reason. He jumped to that half-truth explanation and died without discovering the true answer: God carefully planned and created our minds (us!) this way. For at least two very good reasons.

First, this great crossword puzzle we call "nature" is a cosmic brain-teaser designed by Cosmic Entertainers, the same Entertainers to whom Heraclitus referred when he wrote "Nature loves to hide," the Ones of whom the author of Proverbs said "The glory of God is to conceal a thing, but the glory of the king is to find it out"! Their intentions and/or motives in cleverly designing nature to both (i)seem quite obvious and yet (ii)to be so deceptive, thus affording a worthy challenge for our riddle-loving minds, so impressed Francis Bacon that, to start off his *Great Instauration*, he quoted Proverbs' author and then added ". . . as if, according to the innocent play of children, the Divine

121

Majesty took delight to hide his works, to the end to have them found out, and as if kings could not obtain a greater honour than to be God's playfellows in that game, considering the great commandment of wits and means, whereby nothing needeth to be hidden from them."

But, second, Descartes and James both put their finger on a fundamental fact about us humans, that we are free moral creatures. This fact relates to the Creators' other motive in their Grand Deception. They make it very, very hard to NOT-believe that the things we see and touch make up a world of bodies, especially the bodies of our conscious, human neighbors, because They want us to love our neighbors as much as we love ourselves. True, the evidence that They exist is greater by far than the evidence that (our neighbors') physical bodies do, but They give us the most complete, even frightening, latitude to believe what we will, right down to allowing us to believe, as so many have done, that They, Who furnish us directly with BOTH the text AND the alternative readings (including the atheistic), do not exist. They also provide us with the freedom to practice being open-minded or to repress invitations to rethink things. The more we choose to repress such invitations, the more They will "respect" our wishes.

Except—to repeat—for that most fundamental fact. As Fichte noted, those Creating Companions furnish us with the essentials for living the most important of our lives, the moral one. The one, repeat, that involves living with others like ourselves, the one that involves the obligation to love those others at least as much as we look out for ourselves. "Everyday common sense" is as good a name for those essentials as any. Throughout our lives, *They make certain we recall, and constantly return us to, these essentials.* Even ALL-IS-ONE, monist-idealist thinkers must interrupt their favorite musings in order to eat, answer the consequent call of nature, put their weary bones to bed for sleep, and each wake-up-time resume where they were before the [our ability to do so is astonishing; this and similar interruptions are inserted into the text to bring the fact to your attention/notice] interruption. "Modern science" challenges the belief that we eat, relieve ourselves, and have bones to put to bed. But no matter how muddled or confused we get—or how WELL we "see through" Nature's hoax or how OFTEN we see through it—and no matter what alternative, radically uncommon-sensical "philosophy" we adopt, we will be returned to "look-straight-ahead" thinking as soon as—it seems—a neighbor rings the doorbell, someone calls on the telephone, or nature calls. And, however much we may prefer aesthetics to ethics, our neighbors and the naive realism that creates the context for our dealings with them are never far from our attention. No one noticed the nearly irresistible power of common sense or naive realism better than Hume, who agreed with Descartes that we never experience anything but mental perceptions:

> The *intense* view of these manifold contradictions and imperfections in human reason has so wrought upon me, and heated my brain, that I am ready to reject all belief and reasoning, and can look upon no opinion even as more probable or likely than another. Where am I, or what? From what causes do I derive my existence, and to what condition shall I return? . . . I am confounded with all these questions, and begin to fancy myself in the most deplorable condition imaginable, environed with the deepest darkness, and utterly deprived of the use of every member and faculty.
>
> Most fortunately it happens, that since reason is incapable of dispelling these clouds, Nature herself suffices to that purpose, and cures me of this philosophical melancholy and delirium, either by relaxing this bent of mind or by some avocation, and lively impressions of my senses, which obliterate all these chimeras. I dine, I play a game of backgammon, I converse, and am merry with my friends; and when, after three or four hours of amusement, I would return to these speculations, they appear so cold, and strained, and ridiculous, that I cannot find in my heart to enter into them any further. (*Treatise of Human Nature*, Vol. I, Bk. I, Part IV, sec.7)

A thesis. Unless you're different from me, you DO see SOMEthing. Common-sensically, you see this part of this page of this book, as well as all the other things in your present field of vision. (All the things you stop seeing as soon as you close your eyes.) If naive realism were true, what you see would be something on the OUTside of your body. Your seeing, though, is not out here on this page but back where your eyes are. Whatever memories the words out here trigger are not out here with the words but are stored somewhere behind your eyes. Where your thoughts are. The revised thesis of this chapter will be that what you see is utterly private to you, on the inner side of your eyes. If you have eyes at all. What you see is in there, along with the memories and thoughts you are using to interpret what you see. *This thesis* embraces three crucial items: sensed data, memory-images, and thoughts. *Three things are coming to you*, i-an obvious six-channeled river of sensations, ii-a powerful flow of imagery, and iii-a steady succession of thoughts. All directly from our Creators. This thesis is a radical solution to the challenge posed by the findings of modern "science" which grow from common sense itself.

A few words to summarize what I have concluded are the basics of our everyday common-sense theory of the world will help to pinpoint my present revisions of it and make it easier to describe the remainder of this crucial "conversion" chapter.

First, the everyday semantics of "see" are straightforward. Without a second's hesitation, most of us see that there are at least three distinct senses to "seeing":

   i-   Seeing line-of-vision physical things with our eyes.
   ii- Visualizing, seeing or being aware of inner images OF things.
   iii- Understanding, e.g., seeing the difference between i and ii.

Secondly, there are two other things besides any of those three acts of see-ing: a see-r and something see-n. In your case, the see-r is YOU. Forget about what your eyes, ears, nose, tongue, and skin are doing, and concentrate on what YOU are doing. Perhaps your eyes, etc., are infallible. Or maybe they are constantly deceived. Then, too, perhaps God is infallible, or maybe God is not only a blind watchmaker but constantly making mistakes as a result of that blindness. God's infallibility won't help you if you are always wrong, and God's inability to get anything right won't hurt you if you're right about God always being wrong. Unless you get rid of your errors and replace them with truths, you will get it wrong and that should be your first worry, not what your senses or God are doing. What are YOU doing? Which YOU? The one who sees whatever YOU are seeing right now. The one that is inside your skin. (At least that is the way it will seem to you for most of the waking hours making up your life, because it will normally seem as if what you can look at and touch IS your skin.) This chapter's title, "Video aliquid, ergo sum" (translated "I see something, and that would not be true if I did not exist"), deliberately mimics Descartes' famous "Cogito, ergo sum" (translated: "I am thinking, and that would not be true if I did not exist"), and is intended to underscore the fact that the same you that sees is the same you that Descartes says thinks.

As for what is *see-n*, careful distinctions must be drawn. To begin with, it is imperative that we distinguish understanding from looking, that is, from seeing in the most usual sense of the term, imperative that we understand *that* what is understood cannot be looked at but only understood. The other two see-ings, though, ARE lookings, but controversy has raged about their objects from the beginning. Those disagreements, however, must not lead us to overlook something Descartes, preoccupied with thinking, underplayed, namely, the common-sense notion that seeing involves SOMEthing seeN. Seeing is evidence of something's existence. Something besides the seer. Besides "Video, ergo *EGO* sum" (I see, therefore *I* am), we can ALSO say "Video aliquid, ergo *ID* est" ("I see something, therefore *IT* exists").

You DO See SOMEthing.

Repeat. So far as common sense is concerned, there is no room for doubt. Every single person who grows up normally learns what "Peekaboo! Now you see me! Now you don't!" means. And learns it so well that they take it for granted for the rest of their life. The most that "society" can teach are the conventional "signs" or "names" used for clueing each other into whether we're seeing and what we're seeing. No one literally teaches anyone else to see. What the blind suffer from is not a learning deficit but a handicap. Which is obvious when we stop and take note of how well some of them have learned how to TALK about seeing, colors, etc.! Our Creators-given common sense is in no doubt whatever on the principle that when any seeing is done, there is both a see-er and a see-n. Every cross-examining attorney launches his or her attack from that vantage point: no one is a reliable eye-witness who did not see anything! However, cross-examining attorneys also reinforce the Creators' trick by always stopping far too short in trying to shake the witness' answers to "*EXACTLY* what did you see?"

But what DO you see?

The answer is so astonishing that I would laugh at anyone who proposed it—if I had not, by a thousand-fold rethinking of a vast range of facts and the issues connected with those facts—decided that all the other theories are impossible and that this one must be true, however implausible and astonishing and preposterous it seems at first. A large number of thinkers have decided it is not just astonishing but impossible and have filled the library with truly impossible solutions: we appear to be seeing but it's only our eyes responding to certain stimuli, we think we're seeing but it's really only our brain doing some information-processing, we seem to see but are really only thinking we see, we do see but not colors since we only see bluely, redly, greenly, and so on. Once we come to understand the morass that the "appearances vs reality" and the "observing vs thinking" controversies have created, as well as the absolutely radical conversion—so radical it amounts to an intellectual revolution—necessary to resolve them, it is understandable why so many resisters, each recognizing that OTHERS' alternatives are non-solutions, have tried to invent something new, anything new, of THEIR OWN, in order to avoid accepting the truth. The truth requires a radical gestalt-shift vis-à-vis everyday common sense.

Return to Kohler. If we think that each of us sees what appears to her or him to be "THE world," then we can call that our 'original text.' Many have, in fact, referred to what we experience as "the book of nature." There are contradictory interpretations of that book, however. That is, there are contradictory 'readings.' Once we learn what they are, we are free to select the 'reading' that makes most sense to us. We may have to overcome long-standing habits, though, just to become used to other options. We can compare our situation to people who grow up using different temperature scales. Some grow up using a thermometer with the Fahrenheit-scale numbering, others become used to the Centigrade-scale numbering. When they go outdoors, they *feel* the same weather; when they visually check the measure of the weather's kinetic energy, they *see* the same column of mercury. But they have different ways of *thinking* and *talking* about the supposed realities: the kinetic energy of the air molecules and the eye-level of the mercury-column. In their respective languages, "one degree" means different things.

Whoever lacks an appreciation for the power of semantic habits should take some time thinking hard about why English-speakers resist the adoption of the Centigrade and Metric Scales.

The shifts here are far more radical and complex. They involve one's views of the nature of the one doing the action (if there is a doer), of the nature of the action (if there is any), and of the nature of the object (if there is any). They radically affect one's views of just about everything else. Most of all, they affect one's semantics, e.g., the meanings of such words as "I" and "see" and "thing." The result is that people can appear to be speaking the same language even though entire sentences and paragraphs can mean really different things.

The remainder of this second chapter will be a *meditation* on the fact that such radical revisions of one's original common sense involve individual conversions and revolutions. That is, it will reconfirm the *learning-theory* presented in Chapter One. It will offer examples of conversions from naive realism. Section "B" will concentrate on B.F. Skinner's revision of his original common sense. In terms of Kohler's description, Skinner decided only the 'outer world' is psychologically important; therefore he spent his life working on a model to eliminate the world of immediate experience. Section "C" will contrast his view with that of Carl Rogers, who—when pressed for an answer—insisted that we experience and can know only the world of appearances, the other side of which is that we cannot have any certainty about the world out there which the scientists tell us they are making discoveries about. The reason for this section's title, "Lead-up to the Door-Closing" is to help notice what happened to 'scientific' psychology during the twentieth century. What happened can be dramatized by focusing on the basic disagreement between thinkers whose mindset resembled Skinner's and those whose mindset resembled Rogers', a disagreement that led to damaging professional and cultural repression in the twentieth century. The final section will explain in what sense solipsism is an issue that must be faced squarely by anyone willing to grapple with the implications of contemporary physics and physiology.

Postscript. One of the most important factors in this 'new but old' theory of meaning is the theory of inner maps. Had not the researches of R. Shepard, M. Levine, and others on 'cognitive mapping' come to my attention, it is doubtful that I would have come to notice this essential feature of our experience. Its importance, already emphasized in earlier sections, should become even more obvious as various issues are discussed below.

B. Behaviorism:
Stay On The OUT Side Of The Line.

If Kohler is right—and he is!—that EVERY science begins with the naive realist component of original common sense (the two other components being the truth-error sense and the right-wrong sense), then it is obvious that we must start with what seems to be obvious: what we see is on the OTHER or OUT! side of our eyes. Watson's instinct was absolutely right. To be scientific, psychology canNOT begin by looking inward. Understanding what looking INwards means demands that we understand what looking OUTwards means. Further reflection reveals that it is not even possible to look inward literally. Taken literally, it would mean either that our eyes could swivel in their sockets and look inwards at the brain that is ordinarily behind them, or else that we have a second pair of eyes besides the ones we use to look outward with. The only true or real looking is looking outward, and, when that fact is recognized, it becomes clear that we must begin with material bodies. "Material bodies" is simply short-hand for "sun, moon, rocks, lakes, fish, pigeons, people, etc."

Aristotle, Aquinas, and any others who believe the senses are the font of all human knowing, will be in agreement. They certainly accepted the view that the things we see—sun, moon, stars, earth, and so on—are material bodies, three-dimensional things, which are also tangible, hearable, smellable, and tastable. Whoever agrees that Aristotle and Aquinas, not Plato or Augustine, are the philosophers closest to common sense should have no difficulty in understanding why today's scientific or empirical psychology which rests on naive realism is materialistic and why the standard definition of the subjects studied by scientific psychologists, when the link with biology is explicitly alluded to, is "organism."

This obvious point is one of cardinal importance. Those who believe there are more things in this world than are dreamed of in materialists' philosophies—particularly those who claim to rely on the same original source of knowledge, i.e., the same raw material that materialists claim to rely on, because they know (by classic post-hoc, propter-hoc reasoning) that, inasmuch as they did not begin knowing until *after* they began seeing the world, therefore their seeing the world must have *caused* their knowing—must ask why they believe anything but material things exist. Do anti-materialists who believe in more than physical bodies believe their senses are different and take in more than physical bodies? Do they, for instance, believe that the people around them have souls or minds or thoughts or feelings? Then, if so, have they seen them? If not, what gave them the idea or concept OF those *MORE'S*? Those more-than-physical-bodies?

> **RULE**: Whoever intends to give an exact description
> of what s/he sees or visually observes must be as exact as any
> physiologist or neurologist, must resist all Walt-Disney-like
> **PROJECTION** or anthropomorphism.

John Watson's standard-bearer, Burrhus Frederic Skinner (1904-90), once offered an extremely clear illustration of this rule. He described an experiment in which an experimenter trained a pigeon to emit a chain of behaviors describable as "turn[ing] around in a clockwise direction." Then he transcribed his un-Skinner-conditioned-students' emitted describing-behavior:

> Students who had watched the demonstration were asked
> to write an account of what they had seen. Their responses
> included the following: (1) The organism was conditioned to
> *expect* reinforcement for the right kind of behavior. (2) The
> pigeon walked around, *hoping* that something would bring the
> food back again. (3) The pigeon [NOTA BENE!] *observed*
> that a certain behavior seemed to produce a particular result.
> (4) The pigeon *felt* that food would be given it because of its
> action; and (5) the bird came to *associate* his action with the
> click of the food-dispenser.

Such projections contrast markedly with Skinner's eye-witness account, one worthy of a student of Pavlov and Watson and every expert witness who refrains from guessing about what goes on, *unseen*, inside the organism and who sticks to what is *seen*:

(1) The organism was reinforced *when* it emitted a given kind of behavior.

(2) The pigeon walked around *until* the food container again appeared.

(3) [NOTA BENE!] A certain behavior *produced* a particular result.

(4) Food was given to the pigeon *when* it acted in a given way; and

(5) the click of the food-dispenser *was temporally related* to the bird's action.

This initial description contains all of Skinner's philosophy in its germ-state. He began by rejecting James' introspection and embracing Watson's LOOK AT ORGANISMS INTERACTING WITH THEIR ENVIRONMENT model. Do "psychology" in the natural-science mode, which means do what physicists, chemists, and biologists do. Galileo created his revolution by looking through the telescope and seeing what was in the sky. Lavoisier did experiments and looked at the results. Biologists do not learn by introspection. When he was in graduate school, Skinner proposed writing a thesis that would be little more than showing how the above kind of behavior-descriptions could be used to make RE-definitions of mental or "consciousness" terms perfectly concrete and unmistakable. Though he came to realize that things were not quite as simple as they seemed, he never swerved from that early-chosen, teleological course of action.

Skinner's instinct was infallible: he saw clearly that there can be very loose, common-sense descriptions of what we see and there can be the kind that everyone swears to give when they take the witness stand and attempt to be *precise* about what they saw. It is our deeply-ingrained habits of (common-sense-)theory-laden 'perceiving'—i.e., seeing and thinking simultaneously—that make taking this step so difficult. The demands of morality require that we have some 'sense' of what other people feel in order for us to have some idea what it is they would have us do. That is, if "Do unto others what you would have them do unto you" is the supreme moral imperative, we have to know what we would have others do for us when we feel this way or that—leave us alone if we have a headache, be company if we are in top-notch form—and then be able to tell whether this or that particular 'other' at this moment has a headache or is in top-notch form. This is obvious.

Those who have learned to think of animals as if they are slightly inferior humans—and perhaps been further educated, i.e., *habituated*, to do so by watching many Walt Disney films—will naturally, when they come into Skinner's classroom, have to spend time *re-habituating* themselves, so they see pigeons as robots with 'information-processing' brains whose level of miniaturization and complexity dwarf those of a Cray-3, etc., i.e., acquire the rigorous habit of regarding each animal as an 'it' rather than as a 's/he.' Though the hour-by-hour demands of moral concern induce us to constantly re-entangle the double-helix strands of common sense, one of which suggests direct access to others' outsides (facial expressions, speech, and behavior), the other of which instantly infers, i.e., guesses! what's on their insides (feelings, thoughts, desires), the demands of scientific accuracy require that we unzip the tightly-knit coils. (N.B. The importance of being on guard against anthropomorphism is brought to mind by the title Dawkins gave to one of his books, *The Selfish Gene*. As he himself warns, in the first pages of Chapter 1: "It is important to realize that the above definitions of altruism and selfishness are *behavioral*, not subjective.")

It is very difficult to focus on what we do see by straining to see what we don't see, but we must try. That is, each of us who aspires to construct a *second* inner model that improves and corrects everyday common-sense theory, a second one based on fact rather than old habit or wishful thinking, must make the effort to be as cool, objective, and dispassionate as Pavlov, Watson, and Skinner are supposed to have been. Even if, during 'off-duty' hours, we lapse back into the easy, casual use of everyday, fuzzy-common-sense.

WE DO SEE SOMETHING. BUT WHAT?

Once we begin taking physics and physiology seriously, we tend to become tongue-tied when answering that question. Berkeley, long ago, underlined the difficulty that Kohler nicely captures with the words ". . . so long as one takes the world at its face value, as we all do *EXCEPT IN HOURS* in which science disturbs our natural attitude." Berkeley's solution was: "We ought to 'think with the learned, and speak with the vulgar.'" But Berkeley failed to take into account what is obvious: except when we're thinking about atoms and inside-the-eye images and nerves and brains, we inattentively revert to *thinking* with the vulgar, as well as speaking with them.

Matters are clarified once we realize we are simply switching back and forth between RIVAL theories when we "put into words" our TWO contradictory habits of theory-laden perception, the everyday one and our professional one, the common-sense phrase and the more accurate one. For instance, astronomers reply "5:34am" if you ask "What time did the sun rise this morning?", the physicist won't laugh if you complain "The air is stuffy in here," the chemist will do what you expect her to do when you ask for the salt, the obstetrician may keep a straight face as he tells the proud new dad "The stork arrived at 10:18," and so on. Such common-sense and/or metaphorical utterances are easy for someone with sufficient education to translate. That is, the (pre-relativity) astronomer knows the sun never rises, though the earth turns, the physicist knows "air" is not on Mendeleef's Table of Elements, the chemist knows it's really sodium chloride she's passing, both obstetrician and dad know that storks are not allowed into the delivery room, etc. Each one knows that, if called upon to defend her or his literal, improved version, s/he can do so—in 1992—at great length: the library holds the results of all of modern science to call upon. But . . .

But for those experts who are idealists, all such "scientific" theories are ultimately subalternated to a superordinate "metaphysical" system in which not even suns, earths, atomic elements, molecules, storks, or newborn bodies exist REALLY. And, by the same token, experts who are materialists will ultimately subordinate all descriptions of theories, perception, expectations, knowing, and so on, to a system in which everything that REALLY exists is matter. Etc. From which further facts Daniel N. Robinson drew the obvious conclusion:

> The concept of wisdom is perforce dependent upon a prior metaphysical commitment, taking metaphysics to be composed of ontological and epistemological elements. To regard one as *wise*, after all, is to ascribe a deeper understanding of reality, but this assumes that a more or

less settled (ontological) position has been reached on the question of what is *real*. And this very position can be reached only after taking a stand (epistemologically) on the question of how one can know anything.

What we need today are not more unscientific theories, that is, not the apriori idealisms and not the fuzzy dualism of everyday common sense and not the Thomist defense of naive realism, theories that can be found in thousands of books already occupying the library's shelves. *We need science that out-sciences* the materialists, mathematically exact certainties that can pinpoint their errors and provide a better explanation for the sensory evidence people mistakenly believe "science" alone relies on and correctly explains. What we need to do is to step into the lion's den and ask materialists what THEY think THEY see. We must expect that their initial, unguarded answer will be: physical bodies. That is because the opening answer, if the later theories allegedly constructed upon observation are to be sound, should be couched in terms of normal, everyday, theory-laden perception or naive-realist common sense. That is, we see skies, lakes, rocks, desks, books, pages, rose upon rose of print, etc. And RAINBOWS.

B.F. Skinner is a worthy opponent. Like Einstein who for a time was regarded as the greatest living physicist but, at the end, was viewed as fighting a rearguard action against further progress, Skinner was long regarded by many as this century's greatest psychologist until behaviorism was overtaken by the cognitive revolution. In defending his views, he did what all defenders of science and the scientific method do: *he pointed to results*. A few weeks ago, my parents and I were comparing our respective watches. My mother's is hand-wound, my father's is self-winding, mine kept almost unbelievably accurate time for three years, minus twelve hours, with a single $1.00 three-year battery. Yet, though each watch is such a marvel of human ingenuity that the watch was used by Wm. Paley as the starting-point for his proof that the universe is the product of even greater science or knowledge, mine was both the most advanced and the least expensive, much the way that today's "personal" or desk-top computers are both more powerful yet far less expensive than earlier models. Whoever turns a blind eye to the science that is the knowledge whose "fruit" is a world-ful of technological miracles—putting humans on the moon, unlocking the energy inside the tiny atom, etc.—can scarcely expect a hearing from those who understand why the common-sense adage of the Master Parable Teller, "By their fruits ye shall know them," was such a favorite of pragmatists like James. What more powerful evidence is there than "It works!" That was Skinner's claim: behaviorism works.

Those paragraphs are relevant to understanding Skinner. He is a materialist, he believes as Watson did that psychology must rely on the same type of observation all science relies on, and his philosophy is that the best theory is not the one that is truest but the one that works best. They also help explain his attitude toward two of behaviorism's recent rivals, brain-science psychology and cognitive 'science.' To him, cognitive 'science' was akin to Freudian fiction, if not to Creation 'Science.' It is a regression to discredited notions about what is truly going on inside the organism. He tried, without much success, to dispel the popular, almost perverse misconception that he was stupid enough to think the human organism is an empty black-box. He knew that organisms are full of things that are important for understanding people's behavior. "A great deal goes on inside the skin, and physiology will eventually tell us more about it. It will explain why behavior is indeed related to the antecedent events of which it can be shown to be a function" are words from perhaps the most controversial of all his works, *Beyond Freedom and Dignity*. What is going on inside is not "consciousness," but just what all scientists now understand is going on: the types of physiological and neurological processes that even William James used in his *Principles* in order to convert "philosophical" psychology into "scientific" or empirical psychology. The key word in Skinner's protest is "eventually." He never dismissed brain-science as myth the way he dismissed cognitivists' interest in introspection, consciousness, inner imagery and models. His point is that FOR THE FORESEEABLE FUTURE we will not be able to predict interactions between organism and environment on the basis of neurology with anything close to the success with which research directed to documenting correlational patterns between observable behavior and observable environmental variables does. Though they differ in what they infer to be going on, UNSEEN, inside organisms, both brain-psychology and cognitive "science" bypass what is observable in favor of what must be inferred. And inferred from precisely what behaviorists observe and study!

"THE" Scientific Viewpoint. Skinner adopted what thousands of his professional colleagues would describe as "the" scientific viewpoint. That is, the one and only overall unified theory that is fully consonant with all of the latest research in physics, chemistry, and biology. It is supported by evidence that must be accounted for in some way. If not by this materialist theory, then by some other equally powerful theory that can even account for whatever is true in the materialist theory. "Educated" persons ignorant of it are ignorant.

The journey from the old "world" of appearances to the new world of reality began twenty-five centuries ago. Thales started the ball rolling. Look around, we can still hear him saying. You think things are all really different. And we do. We think the sun is large and bright, stars are very tiny and dim. Flesh is soft and moist, rocks are dry and hard. Wax fresh from the honeycomb is whitish, firm, sticky, cool, sweet, still smelling of flowers, makes a tapping sound if tapped; the same wax, when heated, is transluscent, loses the smell of flowers, is liquid, makes a splashing sound, doesn't keep your finger stuck to it, and warm. Water can appear under various guises: driven white snow, crystal clear ice, plumes of steam from a Yellowstone geyser, sweat from the outsides of the carton of cold milk dripping into the spreading puddle on the table, beams stretching from sun-filled breaks in the drifting-cloud sky down toward earth, invisible humidity in oppressive summer air, death for someone trapped in the sinking Titanic, and so on. "But," Thales said, "that—'How different!'—is only how things appear." In reality, things are, as in the last case with the water, *appearing* to be different and being *really* the same H2O. The journey was half-completed when Locke wrote the following:

> Had we senses acute enough to discern the minute particles of bodies, and the real constitution on which their sensible qualities depend, I doubt not but they would produce quite different ideas in us, and that which is now the yellow color of gold would then disappear, and instead of it we should see an admirable texture of parts of a certain size and figure. This microscopes plainly discover to us: for, what to our naked eyes produces a certain color is, by thus augmenting the acuteness of our senses, discovered to be quite a different thing; and the thus altering, as it were, the

proportion of the bulk of the minute parts of a colored object to our usual sight, produces different ideas from what it did before. Thus sand, or pounded glass, which is opaque and white to the naked eye, is pellucid in a microscope; and a hair seen this way loses its former color, and is in a great measure pellucid, with a mixture of some bright sparkling colors, such as appear from the refraction of diamonds and other pellucid bodies. Blood to the naked eye appears all red; but by a good microscope, wherein its lesser parts appear, shows only some few globules of red, swimming in a pellucid liquor; and how these red globules would appear, if glasses could be found that yet could magnify them one thousand or ten thousand times more, is uncertain. (*Essay* I, XXIII, 11.)

The journey from the appearances of nature to its reality is being completed, late in this century, even as these words are being written. (Recalling the preface, you will update that to mean "The journey was being completed, late in the twentieth century, even as these words were being written.") We are now accustomed to the idea that the ink we see on the paper is really made up of atoms with one kind of molecular structure, the paper is really made up of atoms with a different kind of molecular structure, in fact everything in the universe is presently made up of atoms which are all made up of protons, neutrons, and electrons, which particles are really mass that can be converted into energy—which, in the original three seconds, were in an entirely unique state—which can be reconverted into mass. Accustomed even to the idea that, by building just one last particle-accelerator, we will finally have reached the absolute bottom-line particles. Thales' idea that things are not what they appear has become second-nature habit to those who have even a rudimentary, science-appreciation-course acquaintance with the essentials that permeate the contemporary intellectual milieu. Though for some, the essentials are still only a fringe, they should be for everyone close to the forefront of their consciousness.

This modern-science account of the reality beneath things' sensible appearances accounts for Skinner's view that there is no more inside the organism than what physiologists and neurologists will discover. There simply is nothing else TO discover inside humans than what biochemists with their test-tube assays, biophysicists with their x-ray diffraction photographs, and laser-surgeons with their direct, fiber-optics inspections will discover. Most certainly there is nothing that psychologists can learn by trying to peek at their own insides! Does anyone seriously believe Wilder Penfield, the famous Canadian neurosurgeon, could have done his famous studies on the brain by locking himself in a closet and doing some concentrated introspection? Skinner's attack on cognitive so-called-science—"a great hoax and a fraud"—is reminiscent of the attack of many scientists on what they call the tendency to supplement science with myths about gap-filling gods. Granted, there are many gaps in psychology, but the overwhelming bet is that they will be filled with more science, not with regressive myths about some consciousness stuff.

Brief reminders of certain other fundamentals of "the" current scientific model of the universe will help greatly in understanding Skinner's no-nonsense mindset. Even in grasping how he rectified an error in John Watson's professional model. The best way to grasp Watson's and his mindset is to begin with Ryle's attack on Descartes:

> The legend we have all been told and sold runs like this. A person consists of two theatres, one bodily and one non-bodily. In his theatre A go on the incidents which we can explore by eye and instrument. But a person also incorporates a second theatre, Theatre B. Here there go on incidents which are totally unlike, though synchronized with those that go on in Theatre A. These Theatre B episodes are changes, not in bits of flesh, but of something called "consciousness," which occupies no space. Only the proprietor of Theatre B has first-hand knowledge of what goes on in it. It is a secret theatre. The experimentalist tries to open its doors, but it has no doors. He tries to peep through its windows, but it has no windows. He is foiled . . . No, what prevents us from examining Theatre B is not that it has no doors or windows, but that there is no such theatre. (*The Concept of Mind.*)

But Watson's and Ryle's views fail to do justice to the major innovation by Descartes vis-à-vis Plato: his recognition of the central importance of the central nervous system, the focus of which is the brain. Skinner plugged that gap in their thinking. He recognized that, besides interacting with the environment outside itself, the organism also responds to various "internal signals"—food and drink deficits, tooth decay, intruding objects (nails, arrows, spears), etc.—and that the parts of the body which are between skin and brain can be viewed as an intermediate environment. This became Skinner's version of introspection.

> We respond to our own body with three nervous systems, two of which are particularly concerned with internal features. The so-called interoceptive system carries stimulation from organs like the bladder and alimentary tract, from glands and their ducts, and from blood vessels. It is primarily important for the internal economy of the organism. The so-called proprioceptive systems carries stimulation from the muscles, joints, and tendons of the skeletal frame and from other organs involved in the maintenance of posture and the execution of movement. We use the verb "feel" in describing our contact with these two kinds of stimulation. A third nervous system, the exteroceptive, is primarily concerned with seeing, hearing, tasting, smelling, and feeling things in the world around us, but it also plays an important part in observing our own body ...
>
> Introspection has had to use whatever systems were available, and they happened to be systems which made contact only with those parts of the body that played a role in its internal and external economy. All that a person comes to know about himself with their help are just more stimuli and responses. He does not make contact with that vast nervous system that mediates his behavior. He does not because he has no nerves going to the right places ... We can never know through introspection what the physiologist will eventually discover with his special instruments.

It is worth inserting a note here that one reason William James' writings are often difficult to interpret correctly is that he often wrote in a materialistic-sounding style. For instance, in 1904, two decades after his *Principles* and a bare six years before his death, he wrote "Does Consciousness Exist?" to explain why, despite his earlier insistence, he had decided that consciousness does not literally exist. In it he confessed:

> [. . .] I greatly grieve that to many it will sound materialistic. I can not help that, however, for I, too, have my intuitions and I must obey them. Let the case be what it may in others, I am as confident as I am of anything that, in myself, the stream of thinking (which I recognize emphatically as a phenomenon) is only a careless name for what, when scrutinized, reveals itself to consist chiefly of the stream of my breathing. The 'I think' which Kant said must be able to accompany all my objects, is the 'I breathe' which actually does accompany them. There are other internal facts besides breathing (intracephalic muscular adjustments, etc., of which I have said a word in my larger Psychology), and these increase the assets of 'consciousness,' so far as the latter is subject to immediate perception; but breath, which was ever the original of 'spirit,' breath moving outwards, between the glottis and the nostrils, is, I am persuaded, the essence out of which philosophers have constructed the entity known to them as consciousness. (A note: James was a phenomenalist who didn't really believe in what most people call "matter.")

With that in mind, consider the question, "What about inside toothaches?" The answer requires a careful distinction. Even common-sensically, we distinguish between what is *private in fact* and what is *private in every way*. Hitler's diaries remained private in fact, much as many of William James' letters remain private in fact. That simply means "the public" had no easy, ready access to them. But any member of the public guided to the right location and supplied with sufficient light would be as capable of seeing the diaries and letters as Hitler himself. This means that what is private in fact can also be called "public in principle." What goes on inside organisms, physically, is therefore private in fact, so long as nobody looks—has anyone ever seen your brain?—but public in principle, and that means that Penfield (and Hippocrates, Descartes, Broca, Wernicke, Jackson, Sherrington, Eccles, and so on) could see even the most private parts of your brain,

139

so long as everything getting in the way (scalp, etc.) was removed, they were nearby, had enough light, etc.

If, though, any brain has a mind or soul inside it, as Descartes claimed, THAT would be private in principle, completely UNpublic in both fact and principle, and its thoughts—as Ryle mentions—would be accessible only to its possessor. Skinner agreed with Watson and Ryle: those who believe they can look into a *brain* and discover non-physical thoughts, images, a will, etc.—i.e., into a brain which sends out no afferent neurons to self-monitor its own operations—are as deluded as those who thought 'Hitler's diaries' were genuine.

Anti-teleology. The most persistent habit to overcome, because it is at the center of our common-sense-theory-laden perception, is *anthropomorphism*, the habit of "seeing" human characteristics where there are none. That Skinner was supersensitive to this trap is the positive lesson to be learned from the contrast cited earlier between the unSkinner'd students' naive attributions vis-à-vis the pigeons and Skinner's hard-nosed, anti-Walt-Disney approach. Fierce resistance to that habit of naive attributions was his great passion.

One form of anthropomorphism strenuously resisted by "scientific" psychologists as a kind of mental projection or bad-theory-laden perception is what they label "the illusion of *teleological* thinking." "Telos" is the Greek word for goal, something aimed at. If there is any aiming, of course, there must be an aimer, and the aimers we know first-hand are ourselves. Each of us knows there are some things we do deliberately: e.g., leaving indeliberate misspellings, such as Pinnochio, in place; or else deliberately omitting a second c for the same reason that "rows" is often misspelled on purpose; mentioning both possibilities to make readers wonder whether the error was unintentional or not; not mentioning the incorrect addition of a second n so as to prolong the suspense, etc. Those who try to interpret apparent errors in ancient texts of the Bible but who have no access to original manuscripts, only to much later copies which do not match other later copies, must use their wits to guess which was more likely the author's intention, that is, the author's intended "original reading."

There is, of course, no more crucial element than intention in matters of human morality. Whether someone *accidentally* killed someone else or did it *deliberately* but tried to make it appear accidental makes all the difference between an accident and a teleological crime. A classic passage late in Plato's *Phaedo* discusses the relation between conscious plans and virtuous behavior. Socrates emphasizes that the behavior that brought him to prison was distinct from his deliberately chosen refusal to flee: "By the dog, I think these sinews and bones could long ago have been in Megara or among the Boetians, taken there by my belief as to the best course, if I had not thought it more right and honourable to endure whatever penalty the city ordered rather than escape and run away." A passage from Aristotle's later *Physics* shows the ancient Athenians were quite as conscious of the difference as we are. And just as aware of its implications for human origins as Darwin was:

> Why should not nature work, not for the sake of something, nor because it is better so, but just as the sky rains, not to make the corn grow, but of necessity? What is drawn up must cool, and what has been cooled must become water and descend, the result of this being that the corn grows. Similarly if a man's crop is spoiled on the threshing floor, the rain did not fall for the sake of this—in order that the crop might be spoiled—but that result just followed. Why then should it not be the same with the parts in nature, e.g., that our teeth should come up *of necessity*—the front teeth sharp, fitting for tearing, the molars broad and useful for grinding down the food—since they did not arise for this end, but it was merely a coincident result; and so with all other parts in which we suppose that there is a purpose? Wherever then all the parts came about just what they would have been if they had come to be for an end, such things survived, being organized spontaneously in a fitting way; whereas those which grew otherwise perished and continue to perish, as Empedocles says his 'man-faced ox-progeny' did. (*Physics*, II, 8)

Aristotle goes on to reject the evolutionists' reading of the book of nature, but in doing so he showed he was as confused as most of us are before we have had time to sort everything out. Instead of recognizing that, if there is ANY purpose or teleology present in "nature," then Paley is right in insisting that there is a deliberate, i.e., human-like, free, intelligent agent, at work, Aristotle hopelessly muddled the issue by replacing the "for a purpose vs without any planning or aiming" contrast with the "necessary/*DETERMINISTIC* vs chance/spontaneous" one. A free, intelligent human like Willie Hoppe can deliberately beat his grandmother in billiards *every* single time or deliberately lose to her on occasion, and even if he tells us the reason he sometimes loses is because he chooses to, we must guess whether or not he's telling the truth. When nature acts *always* the same way or only with a statistical measure of probability, we must still guess why. That is, whether Newton's laws of inertia and gravity are "obeyed" *without exception* or are, for divine purposes, broken on those occasions designated as "miraculous" is irrelevant to the question: Is the source of those laws an intelligent Creative Three-Member Community or not? The brute fact remains that no other intelligent answer has ever been forthcoming for any laws of nature than an intelligent Source, so atheists must simply conclude that regularities in nature are *brute facts*, laws which cannot be explained, facts that have no cause.

Skinner adopted *determinism* in relation to human behavior, just as Baruch Spinoza (1632-77) and Sigmund Freud (1856-1939) did. Thomas Huxley (1825-95), "Darwin's Bulldog," captured their *determinist*, "automatons" view best:

> [. . .] to the best of my judgment, the argumentation which applies to brutes holds equally good of men; and, therefore, that all states of consciousness in us, as in them, are immediately caused by molecular changes of the brain-substance. It seems to me that in men, as in brutes, there is no proof that any state of consciousness is the cause of change in the motion of the matter of the organism. If these positions are well based, it follows that our mental conditions are simply the symbols in consciousness of the changes which take place automatically in the organism; and that, to take an extreme illustration, the feeling we call volition is not the cause of a voluntary act, but the symbol of that state of the brain which is the immediate cause of that act. We are conscious automata, endowed with free will in the only intelligible sense of that much-abused term—inasmuch as in many respects we are able to do as we like—but none the less parts of the great series of causes and effects which,

in unbroken continuity, composes that which is, and has been, and shall be—the sum of existence.

The only difference between Huxley's picture of a universe-machine, in which we are mere cogs, and Skinner's is that Huxley is explicitly an *epiphenomenalist* and Skinner is not. Huxley regards thoughts, feelings, and other conscious states as non-material but useless byproducts of the brain's functioning, as dependent on the brain as the sound of a train-whistle is dependent on the train. So, while Huxley has the brain control the body *and* produce useless states of consciousness the way steam turns the wheels *and* makes sounds come from the whistle, Skinner has the non-self-monitored brain directing the body, period. Humans and animals are thus 100% unconscious in Skinner's picture; for him, 'consciousness' is no more than a second—or double-name for physi(ologi)cal behaviors already possessing other non-consciousness names. *Saying* we are "conscious" is, for Skinner, like saying our watch or car has "died" on us, the missile "sought out" its target, a silent vinyl disk has all the "sounds" of a Beethoven symphony stored on it, a pocket calculator "remembers" what's in its "memory," etc.

Huxley's and Skinner's "Universe as a Machine" view continues the modern rejection of the older "Nature does nothing in vain" or "Everything is goal-oriented" **PHYSICS**. Bacon and Descartes pioneered the effort to set aside too-often-absurd guesses about *why* God does certain things until we first make certain we know *what* God is doing in nature. They aimed to thoroughly root out the anthropomorphism so blatant in Aristotle's physics, with its claim that inanimate bodies have "appetites," that they "desire" to head back for their "natural habitat" (determined by the natural appetite peculiar to the predominant air-earth-water-fire element in their makeup) when they are violently removed from it and feel "delight and satisfaction" when they are home in it. Aristotle's division of bodies' motions into natural vs violent was based on his picture of an ideal, onion-layered cosmos with earth at the center, quintessential fire in the heavens, and water, air, and terrestrial fire in between. Newton's universalization of Galileo's inertia—"All bodies remain at rest or continue moving straight the way they are moving unless acted on by an outside agent"—was the final victory in the moderns' long campaign to replace Aristotle's early-science model with more powerful and simpler generalizations.

BIOLOGISTS were the next to follow Descartes in eliminating the common-sense teleology so basic in Aristotle's and all the Greeks' view of plants, animals, and humans. The obvious difference between living and dead things is that the living ones move by themselves. A dog that moves itself by panting, wagging its tail, walking over to us, standing with paws on our chest to lick our face, and so on, is alive, whereas the dog, though its color, shape, weight, size, smell, and other *appearances* are the same in the afternoon as they were when we went to work in the morning, must be dead if it does not move at all on its own, i.e., if it does not jump to bite us when we kick it but only moves the same way a C.O.D. package with roughly the same size, weight, etc., would move, i.e., BE moved, if we kicked it. To account for the difference, the Greeks postulated an invisible mover and called it soul or breath. Thales is reported to have thought that (self-moving) magnets had souls and everyone thought people, animals, even plants (no one has to go out to the garden each night and attach new molecules in just the right places) had souls. But no more. What biology text ever mentions souls?

The revolution in biology is critical for understanding Skinner. So critical that a further word or two about the significance of recent discoveries will not be superfluous. First came the portentous day when urea was artificially constructed in the lab, thereby reducing the 'natural' classification of organic vs inorganic chemistry to the status of 'arbitrary' or 'conventional.' Then, in 1953, came perhaps the most momentous discovery in human history, viz., Crick and Watson's unravelling of nature's most complex double-helix, the DNA molecule. Biology became 'natural history' for which bio-chemistry and bio-physics supply the scenario-details. The way to think of any 'living organism' now is to liken it to an internal-combustion engine, occasionally taking on fresh fuel and emptying spent fuel. Though there are still many who believe an adequate biology requires the introduction of a soul, élan vital, enteleche, or other 'life principle,' history seems to be against them. No one has presented the case better than the eminent biologist, Theodore Dobzhansky's second chapter, "On Gods of the Gaps":

> The hypothesis of mechanism has triumphed everywhere, if you wish, by default; whatever biological process has been successfully analysed has proved to represent

patterns, usually exceedingly complex ones, of chemical and physical components. It is this remarkable complexity, not the presence of some peculiar vital forces, that constitutes the core problem of biology. As to the mechanism/vitalism contest, it has been pretty nearly a dead issue in biology for about half a century.

The death of the soul as a force shepherding the living organism toward mature adulthood made way for the replacement of purposeful design by evolutionists' unplanned coincidence. Mendel's study of peas' mathematically predictable but purposeless variations, the study of genetic alterations which produce mutants more often doomed by their weird mis-inheritance of normal features than advantaged by it but whose mutant nature on rare occasions becomes a new-species "normality" reproduced—like their old-species parents—"always or for the most part," the current wave of research into genetic (re-) engineering designed to repair the "mistakes" of nature, and so on, are all factors that support Descartes' theory of the mechanistic, non-living nature of "living" organisms. Common-sense appearances must, for the open-minded, always yield to empirically-verified realities.

Finally, **PSYCHOLOGY**. The true significance of the initially-groping, trial-and-error, fits-and-starts efforts throughout the nineteenth and twentieth century to establish a 'scientific' psychology should be viewed as a determination to extend the borders of non-teleological, scientific, materialistic mechanism to the workings of the so-called "mind." Aren't the organisms studied by psychologists the very same organisms whose functions the biologist turns to bio-chemistry and bio-physics, not to souls, to explain? What *apriori* reason is there for thinking that the triumph of scientific fact over pre-scientific myth will not be repeated here? William James, recognized even by John Watson as "the most brilliant psychologist the world has ever known," lay the groundwork in *Principles of Psychology* when he deliberately used his famous Chapter II on **HABIT** as a transition from sections on the brain to those on consciousness. He begins:

> When we look at living creatures from an outward point of view, one of the first things that strike us is that they are bundles of habits. In wild animals, the usual round

of daily behavior seems a necessity implanted at birth; in animals domesticated, and especially in man, it seems, to a great extent, to be the result of education. The habits to which there is an innate tendency are called instincts; some of those due to education would by most persons be called acts of reason. It thus appears that habit covers a very large part of life, and that one engaged in studying the objective manifestations of mind is bound at the very outset to define clearly just what its limits are. (PP I:104)

Coached as he was by C.S. Peirce who had written ". . . the whole function of thought is to produce habits of action" after he had already written "The essence of belief is the establishment of a habit, and different beliefs are distinguished by the different modes of action to which they give rise," and who had shown how to connect the "chance/spontaneity" beloved of Darwin and evolutionists with the spontaneous evolution of new laws of nature in an essay whose key is the phrase "I make use of chance chiefly to make room for a principle of generalization, or tendency to form habits, which I hold has produced all regularities," it is not surprising that James, with his ever-present awareness of the farthest implications of everything, even minute details, should immediately add to the above-cited passage:

> The moment one tries to define what habit is, one is led to the fundamental properties of matter. The laws of Nature are nothing but the immutable habits which the different elementary sorts of matter follow in their actions and reactions upon one another. (PP I:104)

What are the laws of nature? Routines, regularities, patterns. What do behaviorists, often named "learning theorists," focus on? Routines, regularities, patterns in organisms' behavior, "laws" that correlate those behaviors with environmental factors, on the one hand, and with the histories of the organisms' prior interactions, on the other. For anyone whose learning history is of the right kind, the name of Ivan Pavlov (1849-1936) will come to mind as "automatically" at this juncture as English-language habits rather than those of Sanscrit or Mayan spring into action to guide my fingertips while I write and your inner-speech pronunciation while you read, as automatically as the word "habit" will come to mind for those whose learning history extends to James and Skinner, as automatically as the phrase "psychology's supreme law" will come to mind for those who have learned about the law of habit formation. Laws of nature are habits learned by matter, instincts are habits acquired by species, "learning" is the name of habits acquired by individuals. Whoever studies Skinner's writings will find in that sentence a thumbnail sketch that nicely encapsulates the geography of his scientific model of reality:

> According to Skinner, "laws of nature" are **HABITS** ingrained in matter, "instincts" are **HABITS** acquired by species, and "learning" is the name for **HABITS** acquired by individuals.

The more we look, the more regularities, uniformities, seemingly exceptionless patterns begin to take shape behind what initially appeared not a little chaotic. To see it, we need only rise to the right elevation and survey the "same old" terrain from an unfamiliar vantage point. Lest the full significance of the shift from chaos to cosmos be missed, reconsider the importance of the first Great Mechanist Synthesis known as Newton's physics. Begin with a question: If a meteor from outer space landed on a city inhabited almost exclusively by Christians—Lisbon, perhaps?—or on the single Christian church in a Moslem city on a Sunday morning, killing thousands or hundreds of worshipping Christians, how would the various newspaper headlines read? "God sends heavy cross to people of Lisbon"?, "Allah purges infidel Christians?", or simply "Freak accident! Meteor destroys city [or church]"? Think a moment before you read on.

"Mechanist determinism" is the name we can give to the thesis of Pierre La Place (1749-1827), enunciated as his conclusion after the application of Newton's laws to the workings of nature. From La Place's point of view, Allah would not be involved and nothing is a freak accident. To understand why, all that is needed is to change the name of "meteor" to "body," realize that the city and/or church are bodies located on the surface of the great body called "earth," zoom far enough away to watch those bodies, as neither swerves even a centimeter from the path decreed by Newton's laws of inertia and gravitation, and predict the moment that their vectors will intersect . . . , with the same inexorable precision Voyager II was rocket-blasted aloft on a trajectory that took it to meet—12 years and 4.43 billion miles later—the planet Neptune on August 24, 1989. Well, almost. Voyager II was off course by 21 miles. La Place was so impressed two centuries ago that he exclaimed: If there were a SuperIntelligence that knew the exact location, mass, and velocity of every single atom-body in the universe, that Being could predict every last detail of the universe's future down to the last second in time!

The change in vantage point is stunning. What it means is that "chance," "freak accident," etc., are names, not for events as they occur in reality, but for our lack of advance notice. In plain English, when we call something "luck"—good or bad—we are simply confessing our ignorance beforehand of something that has been "in the cards" for centuries already. Since we are not God, and since we do not know every bat of every bat's wings or every flutter of every butterfly's, we're bound to be taken by surprise regularly. Sigmund Freud's assertion that there isn't a slip of the tongue or snatch of a dream without its pre-determining antecedents and Skinner's science are from the same philosophy, though Skinner's reinterpretation of Freud shows he was even more ruthless in rejecting subtly-disguised teleologies. The facts that served as Skinner's paradigms were: the mindlessness of the Sphex Wasp's pre-programmed, egg-laying routine, the coordinated behavior patterns proverbially named "a chicken running around with its head cut off," the experiments with decerebrated frogs Huxley described, the predictable but useless drooling of Pavlov's dogs, the criminal's hand reaching toward the tickled spot on his chest an hour after he has been decapitated, the little boy's understanding-less switch from reaching for white, furry objects to cringing at the sight of them, etc. (You remember, his name was Albert.) And . . .

And the regularities in human **LANGUAGE**-use. This is the most challenging step into the mindset of B.F. Skinner. Aristotle said we humans are unique by virtue of reason. Descartes said we can always tell the difference between a mindless body-machine (animal) and a mind-guided body-machine (human) by its use of language. B.F. Skinner combined reason and language by deciding that—to use his own words—"The history of human thought is what people have said and done." Since animals—think of parrots—say and do, "animals think" has whatever sense "humans think" has, a redundancy since humans are animals. Humans are just slightly or else unbelievably more complex than pigeons, but still animals, just as rats are rats but *also* animals, chimps are chimps but animals *as well*, dolphins dolphins *and* animals, etc.

Skinner's views on language—and therefore on thought—have been severely criticized. Nevertheless, the apparent superiority of his position is almost too obvious for anyone with an eye trained to resist presupposition-laden perceiving and to "Just LOOK!" at what can be observed. What is observed is this. Children raised in English-speaking families do not grow up speaking Chinese, nor vice-versa. Children raised by parents who speak American rather than British English do not grow up speaking British English. Children brought up by northern rather than southern Americans do not speak with a Texan drawl. The reason: language-behavior is the result of environmental shaping. What could be more obvious? Anyone who carefully examines the grammar books used in courses on the French, Chinese, German, and Arabic languages will see things that are patently different. Whoever is familiar with history knows that every **HABIT**-shaped feature of every language has observably changed, i.e., evolved: pronunciation, alphabets, semantics, spelling, punctuation, declensions, tenses, etc.

Language—and therefore thought—is not an isolated phenomenon. It is one of the many things, mostly **HABITS**, we verbally telescope into what we call "culture." No one ever captured this truth better than James with his remark that **HABIT** is the "flywheel of society." These notions are the foundation of anthropology, sociology, etc. And psychology. For instance, some psychologists have seen the origin of schizophrenia in the cognitive dissonance created by inconsistent verbal signals from parents. One family psychologist testified to the fruitfulness of these principles in his practice: "Somewhere around 300 [families treated] you begin to understand that people aren't what they're traditionally thought to be. That is, you begin to believe that people do what they do because of what *other* people do, and not because of individual choice or free will." Etc.

Compare this approach with that of Noam Chomsky, for instance. The unobserved nature of what the latter calls "language" is in plain view. When J.J. Katz drew out its implications in a book, he gave it the quite appropriate title, *The Underlying Reality of Language*. He titled chapter one, "On Appearance and Reality." Its very first lines recall the tradition begun by Thales:

> Science and philosophy sometimes attempt to show that things are not what they seem to be on the basis of direct experience.

But something must appear, and Skinner focuses on that rather than the alleged "underlying reality." The only *empirical* reality anyone can call "language" are sounds from lips, gestures from hands, ink marks from pens; more specifically, the sounds recorded during Chomsky's lectures, the gestures preserved on video-tapes of them, the ink marks in his books. His attempt to put his own shoes on the Skinnerians was apparent when he wrote of them that they mistakenly regard language . . .

> [. . .] as an externalized object—a collection of behaviors, of actions, of sounds, of sounds paired with meanings, or whatever—and regarded a grammar as a collection of statements about the language, which is the real object of study . . . [That concept of] "language" as an external object is derivative and in fact has no very clear or definite meaning.

Whoever takes the more common-sensical approach is bound to think that it is rather Chomsky's view of language which has no very clear or definite meaning—weigh the significance of his claim that language is "really there in your brain and mine"!—and to conclude that he is more of a philosopher than an empirical scientist. After all, hardly anyone thinks of brain activities rather than spoken sounds or written ink marks when they think of language. (Chomsky, of course, focuses mostly on grammar.)

But the full sophistication of Skinner's philosophy cannot be grasped until we appreciate how he improved on Watson's presentation by incorporating into his writings recent advances in our understanding of the role of fiction in all the sciences. Those living late in the twentieth century are fortunate in having libraries supplied with an abundance of help in cutting through the deceptions of language, especially help in noticing how extensively we use names for which there are no exact counterparts in nature. The most overwhelmingly important of them are **GROUP-NAMES**, such as species, races, civilizations, histories, galaxies, solar systems, etc. **AND LANGUAGE.**

THE GROUP AS A BEHAVING UNIT

It is common to speak of families, clans, nations, races, and other groups as if they were individuals. Such concepts as "the group mind," "the instinct of the herd," and "national character" have been invented to support this practice. It is always an individual who behaves, however. The problem presented by the larger group is to explain why many individuals behave *together*.

[. . .] if we are able to account for the behavior of people in groups without using any new term or presupposing any new process or principle, we shall have revealed a promising simplicity in the data. This does not mean that the social sciences will then inevitably state their generalizations in terms of individual behavior, since another level of description may also be valid and may well be more convenient.

This passage from Skinner's book, *Science and Human Behavior*, expresses an idea that is fundamental to the book which you are reading right now. It means that, in order to do justice to the sophistication of Skinner's professional theory, we must learn the skills of "**LANGUAGE ANALYSIS.**" This ties in with the earlier claim that "Humans and animals are thus 100% unconscious in Skinner's picture," that "for him 'consciousness' is no more than a second—or double-name for physi(ologi)cal behaviors already possessing other non-consciousness names." Saying that "Italy declared war" is simply shorthand for various deeds by individual Italians too numerous to mention in detail. It does NOT mean that the observable individuals with names of their own did what they did AND some never-observed group-al person called Italy did something **MORE**, viz., the "declaring."

Whoever wants to, of course, is free to believe that the universe is full of such unobservable ghosts as plants' souls, people's minds, and nations, but the only things anyone will ever see will be the cabbage's

151

body, the person's clothing topped by a visible head, and the individual Italian people, landscapes, buildings, etc. Gilbert Ryle's ideas about "category mistakes" should be connected here. He points out the error we'd commit if, after someone had shown us all the buildings on campus, all the administrators, staff, faculty, and students, we complained that we still hadn't seen "the college," an error similar to that made by someone watching all the floats, all the bands, and all the marchers march by and then asking how long it will be until the parade arrives. As for language . . .

A major reason why this analysis of group NAMES is fundamental to the book which you are reading right now has to do with the fact that Skinner's notion—that *words are the sounds we hear, the ink marks we see,* etc.—is our original common-sense notion. "Language" is verbal shorthand, a group name, referring to all "words" or—more literally—all the sounds, ink marks, gestures, called "words." Their sheer numbers are overwhelming. Add up the individual words one person uses in a single day. To get the full impact of the totals, try pretending for a day that you are a Trappist: do not utter a single word. Imagine how different the world would be if no one ever said a word, if movies were all silent, if TVs made no more sounds than a radio that's turned off, if all the world's radios were turned off, etc. Then mentally add up all the words on each page of each individual newspaper bought and sold, each page of each magazine, copy of a book, student notebook and computer screen, etc. "Language" sums them all up in a single cue! But there is literally no such thinG as language, just as there is no family, clan, nation, etc. Because it is so crucial to make sure one's spade-calling is noticed, notice:

Literally no such thinG as language. We can *say* "Language does exist" IF that is only convenient shorthand for saying uncounted mountains of spoken soundS, ink markS, gestureS, etc., exist. But there is no "essence" that all those ink marks, sounds, gestures have INSIDE, that we extract and then "mean." Which brings us back to the problem of meaning.

Reading Skinner, like reading any psychologist, requires intimate knowledge of the inner geography that dictates his choice of words. That means it is essential to know which names he uses habitually for things that exist and which as shorthand for things with more precise names. The problem goes to the core of all modern 'science,' and psychology is no exception. Those who have been trying to point out the mythical nature or fictional status of consciousness (including its un-, sub-, and pre—status as well as its actually-conscious varieties), the mythical status of MI's (mental illnesses), IQ's (intelligence quotients), LD's (learning disabilities), etc., do a service if their badgering forces us to look past our verbal shorthand and mental devices—also called *entia rationis* (beings of reason), theoretical constructs, models, paradigms, logical fictions, logical constructs, etc.—in order to notice the realities to which they refer. So, although Skinner routinely refers to persons, self-control, thinking, and the like, we misread him if we do not first learn his mental geography and then 'translate' his verbal behavior appropriately.

If there is still a missing link in anyone's picture of Skinner's map of human automata and language, G. Weissman's essay "Gertrude Stein at the Beach" may supply it. Stein did some "undergraduate research on automatic writing" under a famous psychologist named William James who realized its implications. Weissmann reports that Stein and a collaborator, using themselves as subjects, "were able to show that with a little practice they could regularly produce automatic writing as they took dictation while reading another text: 'The word is written or half-written before the subject knows anything about it, or perhaps he never knows anything about it . . .'" Weissman learned of that research through a 1955 essay, "Has Gertrude Stein a Secret?" Its famous author was another psychologist named B.F. Skinner.

Conclusion. This section—"Stay on the Out Side of the Line" dividing the organism's outside from its inside, or the environment from conscious experience—has traced the natural path that leads from naive realism to materialism. This half-common-sensical and half-anti-common-sensical reading of experience is widely adopted at the present time. Its great weakness is its naivete and lack of real, as opposed to apparent, sophistication. Especially its utterly unsatisfactory answer to the question: What do behaviorists, who claim to base their science on what is observed, actually see? Skinner's final, professional solution was to REALLY eliminate observing or seeing. Doing that is the only way a psychologist can stay outside the line. These are emotionally-charged issues. As many readers will probably be able to verify as they read on.

An Interlude. One designed to shock you, you old fart. Why is it that, although you can pick your nose and you can pick your friends, you cannot pick your friend's _____? It is time to recall the distinction between what is observed and what is thought about. If you look back at the pages of section "B" whose title was "Stay on the Out Side of the Line," is it not true that, in terms of your original common-sense map of the world, you have seen nothing different from what an illiterate nomad from old Arabia, an illiterate peasant from ancient China, an illiterate aborigine from recent'r New Guinea would see, if this book were handed to them to examine? If you were blind, would you be able to answer the question, "What color is the paper used for the pages of this book?" Could you name the color of the ink used in printing the "text" onto the paper? Or tell which way you turned the pages as you read? Or tell how much of the time you spent thinking about or rehearsing those answers?

If you weren't thinking of those things, you old phahhrrdt, what were you thinking about? If you closed your eyes now, would you be able to answer the question, "Did anything in what you have read so far in this 'Interlude' strike you?" Or "Did anything strike you twice?" Is it fair to say that it was not so much the spelling, two different spellings, as the sound of the word that created the felt effect? Or was it the whole inner "world" of memories and associations, related chiefly to your body and others' bodies—chiefly in connection with the action of the friendly bacteria that contribute to the final extraction of fuel from the raw material the body normally takes aboard three times a day—and which, if you were brought up in Arabia, China, or New Guinea would have remained safely tucked away in memory even if you "heard" the sound that instantly comes to mind when you see F-A-R-T? But again, if you weren't thinking about what your eyes were scanning while you "read" the previous section, what WERE you thinking about? If the distinction between the two processes of seeing and thinking is already clear, forgive the indelicacy introduced here. In matters of etiquette, it is not always easy to know just how far to go without stepping over the line. (Were your eyes arrested in the last sentence by how FAR To go?)

I recall a friend of my mother's complaining that *Kristin Lavransdatter* was a dirty book. Do you think an illiterate aborigine, examining any book, would say "Oh, filthy!" What does it mean to say "words" are "dirty"? Or thoughts? Unless it is the link they have with functions of our body that we have acquired/learned strong feelings toward? Yet, if we were simply animals and had no language or "culture" of any kind, how many of these feelings would we have? A young woman once wrote a letter (to Ann Landers?) asking for advice about how to tell her boyfriend that he should be helping her to defray the expense of the birth-control pills she was using. She and her boyfriend 'had' sex, they just didn't feel comfortable talking about it. Anyway, the answer to the question at the beginning of this interlude was "pocket." If you thought the answer was something else, it was probably because I forgot to add that I meant "What would Dorothy Day say is the missing word?" She put stealing ahead of the body and feeling shame about it. Timewise, anyhow. Why I think that is because of what she wrote in *The Long Loneliness*.

> Very early we had a sense of right and wrong, good and evil. My conscience was very active . . . Morality lay in the realm of property and sex. Violence, murder, all had to do with our relations with one another over property. Sex was a deeper matter, and in some obscure way had a connection with the supernatural law and God Himself. Sex and religion! It was immodest to talk of either. People were uncomfortable and embarrassed in talking about God.
>
> Modesty at first had to do with our bodies. We used to dress around the big kitchen range down at Bath Beach and if anyone came in, the grocer, the laundry boy, we would *back out of* the room to hide our nakedness. We did not know why and whatever obscure sense of shame we had may have been connected with that part of our anatomy which was seriously smacked for punishment . . .
>
> We did not learn shame as children until we learned about sex. The dark fascination of this knowledge, incomplete, legendary and instinctive, struck deep into our inmost parts. A shuddering pleasure accompanied the contemplation of it, a pleasure which we knew was *evil*, but did not know why.
>
> Later we were confused in our adolescence, as to why such a consciousness linked up in some obscure way with beauty and love, could be evil.

When we're babies, we all do things without shame that, later on, we may cringe to remember. If we did them publically, that is. Would YOU volunteer if you were among students invited to show the rest of the class your preferred way of picking your nose, even if you felt certain the number of them who do it in private would be statistically significant of something that Edwards could have worked into his SD (Social Desirability) scale. Anyway, babies growing into children fart shamelessly while filling their diapers and get red-faced while doing so, not—as adult onlookers do—from embarrassment, but from squeezing the way dogs do while crouching at the end of the leash. (In connection with the thesis about words conjuring imagery, ask whether you know what you'd see if any of these descriptions were instantiated; then look again to see if you see any babies, dogs, etc., on the page.) Very few people develop the kind of ego-strength that would allow them to put into a letter (then into their autobiography!) what Bertrand Russell did:

> With regard to *The Meaning of Science*, I have an abstract of it and have done some 10,000 words. I am afraid I could not do the sort of conclusion that you suggest. I do not believe that science *per se* is an adequate source of happiness, nor do I think that my own scientific outlook has contributed very greatly to my own happiness, which I attribute to defecating twice a day with unfailing regularity. Science in itself appears to me neutral, that is to say, it increases men's power whether for good or for evil. An appreciation of the ends of life is something that must be superadded to science if it is to bring happiness. I do not wish, in any case, to discuss individual happiness, but only the kind of society to which science is apt to give rise.

You may be wondering what the point of all this is. Before I say what it is, examine your reaction to the 6-15-92 *Newsweek*, p.17, report that a male Philippino named Carlo is due to deliver a baby next month. (It's now July 31.) Or to the claim that it will never happen, because no one has ever had a baby, not even Mary who is prayed to as God's mother. The reason is simple. No one has a body with sex organs to have babies with. That's what G. Berkeley believed, Wm. James agreed with Berkeley, and I certainly agree with Wm. James. On this. In ninety percent of what he wrote, Descartes implies that it is what he believes, too, though he fudged the other ten percent of the time.

Consider another question. What struck you most about the above lines from Dorothy Day's pen? Did it remind you of the final paragraph about her from the opening page of this second chapter? (Why is it first rather than onest, and second rather than twost?) That she had a remarkably healthy attitude toward sex? Folks from her generation are frequently made fun of because of their hang-ups about sex. (Yet celibates do seem to be safest from the most talked-about plague in recent times.) When, at the age of fifty-five, she wrote about her common-law marriage and the birth of her daughter, she titled the chapter "Man is Meant for Happiness," and she later told Robert Coles that "God put us here to go through this kind of mental gymnastics, and He certainly put us here to enjoy our sexual lives." Dorothy Day was celibate when she did the writing and telling just referred to. Catherine de Hueck told of an old custom in Poland according to which newlyweds, after their first lovemaking, get on their knees to thank God for the beautiful gift of sex, and told of it at the time of her celibate marriage with an old Chicago newspaperman named Eddie Doherty. Puberty and the sensations it brings with it challenge every learner who experiences them for the first time. But those aren't always the earliest feelings we must struggle to make sense of. What struck me when I reread portions of D. Day's story (to reconfirm my sense that she had none of Saint Augustine's notorious attitude toward sex), was her underlined memory of backing out of the room.

Our bodies. Are there any of us who do not understand what patients mean when they describe a hospital stay as losing their dignity and feeling reduced to being just a slab of meat? Whoever is raised in a family where the teachings of the *Baltimore Catechism* served as the standard interpretation of the Ten Commandments should remember struggling to sort out issues that had such names as age of reason, desire, serious matter, sufficient knowledge, full consent of the will, thought, word, deed, and so on. And may remember their own sigh of relief when they finally found a truly-basic, light-shedding principle, such as that enunciated by Rev. John Thomas, SJ, who wrote an essay arguing that the greatest error principled people make in relation to sex is projecting the badness of sinful decisions (of the will) onto the marvelously constructed organs used for procreation. Those who are embarrassed by their bodies forget that the Blessed Virgin had a vagina and her son had a penis. Those are a few of the flood of thoughts that can come back to someone after almost sixty years of doing what Dorothy Day said God put us here for, namely, "to go through this kind of mental gymnastics."

What is the point of this interlude? Partly to focus attention on the kind of data—human experience is so enormously rich with such details—that get at the radical difference between Skinner's and Rogers' understanding of humans. Whatever you have *felt* as your eyes scanned the above lines of print, which *seem* to be on the OUTside, has been felt back in there, on the IN-side. Is it any wonder that Skinner, whose organism-model was the pea-brained pigeon, should have slighted all the things that contribute most to the drama of human lives? If ever a philosophy resembled a shrivelled nut by comparison with the things of heaven and earth, it is his "science." Is it any wonder why Carl Rogers, who did his research on people who, unlike rats and pigeons, had deep emotions and even deeper thoughts, had a far better *theoretical* understanding of humans than Skinner? (The qualification must be noted. All theoreticians, Skinner included, revert to their tacit or un-professional understanding when they're off-duty. What's more, it is their pre-professional knowledge that guides much of their on-duty theorizing.)

All of the above is secondary in the context of this chapter, however. The question here is one which goes to the core of all scientific and—if there is any distinction—unscientific thinking. How much of our believing, i.e., our choice of which theories we **understand** we will **assent to**, is determined by something beyond evidence and clear thinking? David Hume is the source of a well-known saying: "Reason is, and ought only to be the slave of the passions." Unless we have passions, how can that be true? If Hume was right, though, what passion did Skinner follow when he denied that passions influence our decisions and behavior? If Skinner was wrong, what passion drove him to his absurd denial that passions are psychologically relevant? Most of all, though, why do YOU believe what you do on such issues? Or on what is the true answer to this crucial question: What DO you see-observe?

C. Stay On YOUR Side Of The Line.

Procrustean though Skinner's system is, its inner coherence is impressive. The number of psychologists who pay mere lip-service to cognitivism and continue working with his philosophy testifies to that. By the end of his life, Skinner could have said of his grand unifying theory what J.P. Sartre said about his atheism: "[It] is a cruel and long-range affair; I think I've carried it through." No one was better able to put a finger on just how frightfully consistent he was than CARL ROGERS (1902-87) during the debates the two of them had. Rogers always contended that Skinner had stayed too exclusively on the OUT-side of the line between self and not-self, that he had locked himself *professional-theory-wise* away from any theoretical recognition of what makes humans different from inanimate, unconscious machines. Skinner agreed more than once with Rogers' account of the reason Skinner engaged in the verbal and scribal behavior so habitual for him:

> After hearing his [Skinner's] comments, I directed these remarks to him. I said, "From what I understood Dr. Skinner to say, it is his understanding that though he might have thought he chose to come to this meeting, might have thought he had a purpose in giving this speech, such thoughts are really illusory. He actually made certain marks on paper and emitted certain sounds here simply because his genetic makeup and his past environment had operantly conditioned his behavior in such a way that it was rewarding to make these sounds, and that he as a person doesn't enter into this. In fact, if I got his thinking correctly from his strictly scientific point of view, he as a person perhaps does not exist." I thought I would draw him out on the subjective side of why he was there, but to my amazement he said he wouldn't go into the question of whether he had any choice in the matter, and added: "I do accept your characterization of my own presence here."

In the epilogue to his three-volume autobiography, Skinner—who later repeated his conviction that "Human thought is human behavior"—reconfirmed Rogers' ability to "get inside" him: "If I am right about human behavior, I have written the autobiography of a nonperson."

A Clear Contrast. Gordon Allport made many astute comments on the verbal and scribal behavior of his colleagues. One of the most astute was this: "Except for a common loyalty to their profession, psychologists often seem to agree on little else." Disagreements became so sharp in 1988 that many dissenters broke away from the American Psychological Association to form the American Psychological Society.

In fact, whoever wishes to operationally define the meaning of "disagree" need not go beyond that section in the library marked "psychology." Whoever wishes to do some empirical research in order to see whether the difference between 'scientific' psychology and unscientific philosophy belongs in the null class (i.e., the class which holds all those non-entities called "not a real difference" and is empty since the only real and genuine differences go into other bins) or in a non-null class can compare what s/he finds in the psychology section with what s/he finds in the philosophy section. Of course, Skinner's works may be found in both sections, for—although most psychologists want them in their section—Skinner did say his behaviorism was not the science of behavior but the philosophy of that science.

Where, then, should Carl Rogers' writings go? Here is Rogers' description of his starting point:

> Man lives essentially in his own personal and subjective world, and even his most objective functioning, in science, mathematics, and the like, is the result of subjective purpose and subjective choice. In relation to research and theory, for example, it is my subjective perception that the machinery of science as we know it—operational definitions, experimental method, mathematical proof—is the best way of avoiding self-deception. But I cannot escape the fact that this is the way it appears to me, and that had I lived two centuries ago, or if I were to live two centuries in the future, some other pathway to truth might seem equally or more valid. To put it more briefly, it appears to me that though there may be such a thing as objective truth, I can never know it; all I can know

160

is that some statements appear to me subjectively to have the qualifications of objective truth. Thus there is no such thing as Scientific Knowledge; there are only individual perceptions of what appears to each person to be such knowledge.

When he repeated this opinion to an interviewer ten years later, the latter said: "You appear to be agreeing with Immanuel Kant who suggested that there is no reality except in terms of man's perception of it." To which Rogers replied:

Yes, I am. I have tried stating that sometimes and find that it always leads to fruitless arguments, so I don't say so very often. But, as you suggest, it really fits in with my response to your earlier comment. None of us knows for sure what constitutes objective reality and we live our whole lives in the reality as perceived.

To which Skinner's basic attitude was always the same. Rogers is unscientific and going at things all the wrong way.

The techniques available to such a science [the behavioral] give an empirical theory of knowledge certain advantages over theories derived from philosophy and logic. The problem of privacy may be approached in a fresh direction by starting with behavior rather than with immediate experience. The strategy is certainly no more arbitrary or circular than the earlier practice, and it has a surprising result. Instead of concluding that man can know only his subjective experiences—that he is bound forever to his private world and that the external world is only a construct—a behavioral theory of knowledge suggests that it is the private world which, if not entirely unknowable, is at least not likely to be known well.

Their utter disagreement is highly educational, very instructive, for learners. At least for those who refuse to draw from the fact of so many disagreements the self-canceling conclusion of the skeptics, viz., "The only thing I am sure of is that it is impossible to be sure of anything."

It is highly educational for those who are courageous enough to plod on in the quest for certain wisdom. The lesson to be learned by serious learners is that half of the truth-finding process is error-elimination. When there are radically different answers, the decisions are often easier than when the answers are only slightly different. In the case of Skinner vs Rogers on "What do I see?", the radical nature of the contrast makes it easy to eliminate Skinner's view as the obviously absurd one.

Counting what we've classified. Just how many worlds are there? Giordano Bruno was burned at the stake in 1600 for holding the wrong answer to that question (and sundry other errors). Would the same thing happen to Kohler who speaks of another world behind this one, and to Rogers who suggests each of us has a whole world of our own, if they were transported back in time to the Rome that almost did to Galileo a few years later what it did to Bruno? The scientist, devoted to the empirical method, will surely consult the evidence offered by *experience*.

The trouble with this admirable approach turns out to be two-fold. We first must define "world" in order to know which experience is relevant to making a decision about how many worlds there are: did Bruno, Kohler, and Rogers mean the same thing by "world"? Then we have to define "experience" in order to know what to consult. And that is when we discover the brazenness of those who argue that the reason psychology is distinct from philosophy is because it is *empirical*, based on *observation*. (Ever study to see what the philosophers claim to have found out about seeing? Ever meet a laboratory psychologist who could prove, before going into the lab to do empirical research on seeing, which philosopher was right?) The disagreements among 'scientific' psychologists when they try to become scientific about the meaning of "see" and "observe" and "experience" are every bit as numerous as among the non-empirical philosophers. i.e., the disagreements are as profound among those on one side of the "Leipzig Wall," reputed to have been erected in 1879, as on the other. Take Skinner and Rogers.

Skinner's theory about seeing and what is seen is a strong candidate for the most palpably unscientific theory ever proposed. About seeing itself. By his behavioral defining, "pigeons see red" *means*, e.g., "on a great number of tries, pigeons peck the disk the experimentalist labels 'red' a certain percentage of the time" (whether one chooses the 5% or the 10% chance that the result is due to chance is arbitrary), regardless of whether they have any subjective seeing-experience or not, regardless of whether the experimentalist can be sure it's red (he admitted he couldn't answer Bridgman's worry). According to his theory, any robot that can pick out "red" cans (they're the ones the pigeon picks out) from all the others passing by on a moving assembly-belt fully qualifies as "able to see red" in Skinner's sense of the term. (One philosopher who didn't keep up on Bridgman's change of heart—or talk—on operational definitions changed his mind [talk?] from an initial denial that computers can, e.g., "feel" pain: "I now believe that it is possible so to construct a super-computer as to make it wholly unreasonable to deny that it had feelings." All it has to do is "utter" them in print at the approved [by whom?] time, etc.) If Skinner had been right, newspaper writers could remove the hesitant quote-marks from such headlines as The Brain May 'See' What Eyes Cannot (1-15-91 *N.Y. Times*, p. C1) whenever the following article is a report to show that brain-guided organisms respond discriminatively to distinct neural inputs. According to Skinner's definition, a blind person who uses a cane to successfully cross a roomful of furniture without knocking any of it over has "seen" the furniture with as much certainty as the pigeon or computer "sees" anything. Finally, a clever UNblind person could select red items from a pile with sufficient inconsistency to qualify as "color-blind" by the operationalist's operational definition. The only reason the absurdity of Skinner's and operationalists' operational-definitions of "see" are not seen by more people is that their defenders hastily reintroduce—by the Humpty-Dumpty device—their pre-professional common-sense meanings into their verbal behavior and thereby confuse the unwary.

On one occasion, however, the semantic-switching Skinner mystified even a linguistic-analyst philosopher with the comment that "The heart of the behavioristic position on conscious [visual] experience may be summed up in this way: seeing does not imply something seen." Or observed. That means that, according to Skinner, the very heart of behaviorism, proposed to us as **THE MODEL** of what objective, scientific psychology should be, is this proposition:

MAYBE YOU DON'T SEE ANYTHING.

What Skinner meant is simple. A man who rushes up to greet the cousin he sees getting off the bus will clearly not be seeing the cousin when the 'cousin' he sees turns out to be a total stranger, and Lady Macbeth didn't even see that much. Which means that Skinner, like perhaps a majority of today's scientists, rejects the common-sense theory about visual experience taught to us by our Creators, which is summed up thus: "Whenever you see, there's something seen." Skinner thereby threw away the one key that can (dis-)solve the Great Entertainers' Great Deception.

Seeing, our premier sense, can elicit a vast range of emotions. People whose attention is on something else may barely notice they're picking their nose, but feel an instant shock-wave pass through them if they turn and realize that someone was watching them. (Of course, just to see the shock in their youngers, some elders belch or fart as they did decades earlier.) Except for children—chronologically or mentally—everyone's breath is taken away by their first naked-eye view of the Grand Canyon or Niagara Falls. (Of course, many elders don't, because they're afraid the youngers don't have enough sense of humor.) Some people pray best if they have images or ikons to look at, while others find it blasphemous to even suggest that God is something corporeal, able to be seen with bodily eyes. (Some writers are considerate of readers who feel uncomfortable at the sight of such words and avoid them.) It has been reported that some couples who have sex with each other only undress while under the covers, and not even entirely at that. (Some people refrain from visiting photography exhibits because they see what kind of message it will send out, which is the very reason others give for going to see the photographs.) But what does see mean? Ask empirical psychologists to give you an operational definition.

Of operational definition. That is, not an operational def'n for "see"—those are simple (simply see the paragraphs above)—but an oper'l or beh'l def'n of oper'l def'n. Here is P. Bridgman's UNoperational definition of it in *The Logic of Modern Physics*:

> In general, we mean by any concept nothing more than a set of operations: *the concept is synonymous with the corresponding set of operations.* If the concept is physical, as of length, the operations are actual physical operations, namely, those by which length is measured; or if the concept is mental, as of mathematical continuity, the operations are

mental operations, namely those by which we determine whether a given aggregate of magnitudes is continuous.

When Bridgman later rethought matters, he took a view that some view as a recantation. Some, because there is a conspiracy of silence about what he wrote in *The Way Things Are*. For instance:

> In the years that followed [the earlier work], the importance of the individual became increasingly obvious to me, even in science which is sometimes actually defined in social, public, terms. My reason for insisting on the importance of the role of the individual in science was that "proof", without which no science is possible, is entirely an affair of the individual and is therefore private, with the result that any creative science is of necessity private rather than public.

Skinner sensed that Bridgman's new emphasis was bound to lead to difficulties. "Bridgman's physical operationism could not save him from an extreme solipsism within science itself. Though he insisted that he was not a solipsist, he was never able to reconcile seemingly public physical knowledge with the private world of the scientist." And this *was* a problem for Bridgman.

> It became increasingly evident, however, that use of the conventional, impersonal, third person language of society makes it exceedingly difficult to express what is perhaps the most important characteristic of my own personal experience, the operational dichotomy between my own immediate experience and that of others, for example, the dichotomy between my pain and your pain. I came to see that this operational dichotomy could be kept in view by the adoption of a relatively minor [sic] conventional restriction in the use of language. . . . with this new convention, it is only I that am conscious, and I must not say that you are conscious.

Skinner's solution was an equally "minor" semantic switch, by which he defined what he'd meant by "public physical knowledge."

> I spent many an hour trying to explain to him how one might deal with the question of whether the green he sees is not the red I see, and so on, and he went to his grave not knowing the answer and very much worried about it. I think he was on the wrong tack. I don't think science is the experience of scientists at all. It is a corpus of procedures and practices. I should hate to think that physics is in any sense what goes on in the mind of a physicist. It is what physicists have done and what they can do. It is a series of marks that belong to conventional languages which permit other people to do things, including to talk about them . . .

"Knowledge," including "science," *means* for Skinner the behaviors people have emitted, including the sounds they have uttered and the marks they've stuffed libraries with. And what is the "experience" used to verify the "knowledge"? The same operations? (Skinner never did give a sensible definition of the difference between operations and behavior, i.e., one that would make anyone not already biased in favor of his "Stay outside yourself!" mindset renounce the common-sense identification of the two.)

Does Rogers do any better? How, for instance, does he define "experience"? He offers two different definitions.

> *Experience* (noun). This term is used to include all that is going on within the envelope of the organism at any given moment which is potentially available to awareness . . . It does not include such events as neuron disharges or changes in blood sugar, because these are not directly available to awareness. It is thus a psychological, not a physiological definition . . . Synonyms are "experiential field," or the term "phenomenal field" . . .
>
> *Experience* (verb). To experience means simply to receive in the organism the impact of the sensory or physiological events which are happening at the moment.

Semantics! Skinner tells us that science is not something inside the physicist. That means it's outside. What's outside? Well, if it's an astronomer, the astronomer's peering-through-a-telescope-behavior, a public operation "observed" by someone (else), perhaps by a behaviorist psychologist studying astronomy (as opposed to studying the stars, since the astronomer is doing that). Both—when they begin uttering or inscribing—"know" something, but the knowledge is the uttering or inscribing, the sound-waves or ink-marks, out in Ryle's Theater A. Nothing private here! Only a society of X-raying Super(wo)men able to read each other's brains would think brain-behavior was public and call some of it "seeing."

So, what is the observing that Skinner gathers his evidence with? Akin to pigeons' pecking? UNconscious nerve-system events, like the astronomer's? Unconscious, inaccessible, unverified verifications? No wonder Bridgman lost his patience, even before he went to his grave frustrated:

> I thought I could understand the behaviorist position and that I could talk his language when I wanted to. On the other hand, I argued that there was no inconsistency in my position which would prevent the behaviorist, by the exercise of good will, from talking my language, although he might have reservations about whether it was a sufficiently profitable language. But under the stimulus of repeated conversations and the needs of detailed exposition, my position hardened somewhat and became less liberal. For, although I continued to think that I could talk the behaviorist's language if I wanted to, it became evident that the behaviorists were not capable of talking my language. It seems to me that in consequence they almost of necessity lose part of the picture.

Semantics! Rogers tells us he includes "all that is going on within the envelope of the organism that is accessible to awareness." But, if the brain's neuron disharges are not available to awareness, why not? And can we be forgiven if we wonder why Rogers continues using the word "organism" rather than "mind" or "soul"? Unless it is because of that universal feature of experience known as "peer pressure"? Academic freedom does not extend to peers?

Plato, twenty-four centuries ago, decided how to deal with such contradictions: nail the perpetrators if and when the issues are monumental enough to demand nothing less. Here is the rule he enunciated. In what context? In a discussion of seeing, etc.

> To use words and phrases in an easy-going way without scrutinising them too curiously is not, in general, a mark of ill-breeding; on the contrary there is something low-bred in being too precise. But sometimes there is no help for it, and this is a case in which I must take exception to the form of your answer. Consider: is it more correct to say that we see and hear *with* our eyes and ears or *through* them? (*Sophist*)

The correct answer is, "Neither." Sometimes the truth is more drastic than we realize at first. QU: Will the sun rise tomorrow or will it fail to come up for the first time in history? AN: Neither; there has yet to be a first time. QU: Does it stay stationary in the center of the universe or does it do at least some moving? AN: Neither, since—literally speaking—there is no sun. QU: What do I see when I watch a beautiful sunset? AN: What do you see when you watch a beautiful rainbow?

We thus find ourselves back where Socrates began: asking people to define their most basic terms and discovering that they aren't very clear, though only outsiders seem able to notice that. Each one seems to feel the problem is the other person's. We must get the parties to provide us with better definitions so we can decide who is right and who is wrong by checking the evidence.

WRONG!

The solution is not simply definitions. We must look beyond isolated definitions to complete models. All that definitions, cues attached through habits of association to parts of an inner model, do is help us situate, say, part X or Y of the definer's model in relation to its other parts. They are our clues to how the other person is classifying things. Follow-up questions, such as "OK, then what do you mean by Z?", are sometimes a request for some further information. Other times, they are efforts to force into the open a glaring contradiction in the other's systematic view of things. The more models a person learns beyond that starter-kit called "common sense" that every normal person is furnished with by age five, e.g., the revisions made by Descartes, James, Watson, etc., the greater the number of different "definitions" s/he can give of anything. Anyone who is limited to a single meaning of "see" hasn't even begun to discover the rules of the language game Wittgenstein wrote a lot about but never understood.

First, we must become explicitly aware of our common-sense theory of everything, especially its basic, **PORPHYRIAN** classifications. Porphyry (232-c.300) noticed that we can mentally divide most of the things we believe in by the age of five or six in many, many different ways. We can first divide everything into those that are things in their own right and those that are parasites. Men, women, children, belong to the first group, their weight, height, skin—and hair-color, etc., belong to the second. Grinning cats, red apples, and green leaves belong to the first group, the grin (lip-shape), the red and green color, belong to the second. Or we can divide all the independent things into those that are three-dimensional (animal, vegetable, and mineral ones) and those that are completely dimensionless (pure spirits like God, souls, and so on). We can, if we wish, take the three-dimensional group and break it down into living ones (animals and vegetables) and non-living ones (minerals), subdivide the living into those with senses (animals) and those that are alive but not conscious (vegetables). If we stick with pre-animal-rights tradition, then the animals subdivide into those that have reason (human animals) and those that don't (irrational animals). Those mental classifications govern ninety-nine percent of how we live. When people say "Killing is wrong," they don't mean we can't pick flowers and put them to work adorning our table, can't slaughter pigs and eat pork, etc. But pacificists raise doubts about killing in battle, and others condemn condemning murderers to death. But who, because some experts claim it can "think," thinks twice about disposing of an old computer without a burial service?

Note that each *correlative* in that mental diagram is defined in relation to another. *In the end, all defining becomes circular.* For instance, it is a mistake to think that we can define "finite" by itself. It's simply half of a mental diagram invented to help keep things clear, a map with half its area on the one (e.g., right) hand and half on the other hand. On one side we mentally situate the things that are not infinite, i.e., that are finite, and on the other we put the things that are infinite, i.e., the ones that are not finite. Geometers who define "straight" all by itself waste their time: it means the opposite of "curved" or "not-straight." Who but Riemann would call lines on a doorknob "straight"? Now, add large vs small, these words (revolution, conversion, thinker, etc.) vs those, words vs not-words, male vs female, and so on.

But, though everybody *understands* the classifications of Porphyry, not everyone remains loyal to them. Conversions occur. When someone shows us that what we think is a purely biological process can be duplicated in a laboratory test-tube with chemicals off the shelf, we begin to wonder whether we have been applying our mental classification "living vs non-living" the right way. Some decide that Descartes was right—there are only non-conscious robot-bodies and conscious minds, but not conscious bodies (e.g., animals)—and others refuse to convert away from Porphyry to Descartes. Some decide that Skinner was right and reclassify "complex living organisms" by mentally moving them over to the "non-living, unconscious automaton" bin; others refuse to convert. Some, like Rogers, partly overlook what they've done. Rogers understood what was involved, though:

> Each current in psychology has its own implicit philosophy of man. Though not often stated explicitly, these philosophies exert their influence in many significant and subtle ways. For the behaviorist, man is a machine, a complicated but nonetheless understandable machine, which we can learn to manipulate with greater and greater skill until it thinks the thoughts, moves in the directions, and behaves in the ways selected for him. For the Freudian, man is an irrational being, in the grip of his past and of the product of that past, his unconscious.

Rogers at least took two steps toward the truth by rejecting both behaviorist and psychoanalytic determinism. His Socratic open-mindedness was like G.A. Kelly's: he could spot absurdity. What did Kelly think? "One does not have to be a psychologist to treat another person as an automaton, though training in 'experimental psychology' may help. Conversely, treating him that way does not make one into a scientist."

170

Skinner's and Rogers' views are not my primary concern. Nor are my views your primary concern. I have done my best to understand the core of their philosophies and, while incorporating what is valuable, I use what is foolish to illustrate what is foolish. My views of what a person is are my concern, not yours. Yours is yours. After you have understood. Do you believe you can understand thoughts? Even thoughts about others' thoughts about what YOU are—you're a machine, you're an animal, you're neither but rather a being with access to all of reality—and free to decide which of those thoughts or theories about you is the true one? Are you unable to weigh the evidence to decide what you will believe you are? That is, are you a machine programmed to say what your "genetic inheritance" and "social environment" pull your strings to make you say OR are you a free agent, able to consider the options and weigh the evidence and choose what "makes the most sense," regardless of adverse passions such as vanity, weariness at the prospect of rethinking things you've long regarded as closed issues for you, fear, etc.? Skinner and Rogers had their turn to choose. And died. Now it's your turn.

The disagreement I have focused most on, however, relates to the *evidence* used to decide which is the true answer to what you are. Have you ever seen the colors of a rainbow? Heard the evening symphony of sounds from the woods? Breathed in the fragrance of a rose? Given in to the temptation to scratch your poison-ivy rash? Had a headache? Climbed, dead-tired, into bed after a long day of unusually heavy manual work and felt just so, oh, so good . . . , no more work, just warmth and comfort and rest and sleeeeep? When you strip away the semantic switchery, the re-defining, Skinner *says*(verbally behaves): "No, you have never really been awake, peppy OR weary, only moved in ways others can 'describe'." Rogers *believes*: Have you ever done anything but be consciously aware of such things, whether they're physically real or not?

A thought-experiment. N. Chomsky put his finger on the ultimate absurity of Skinner's behaviorism, the thesis that our verbal behaviors are NOTHING BUT mindless, automatic, feedback-controlled talking and/or writing. He also put his finger on the ultimate psychological reason why it is so difficult to recognize that the "external" behaviors, sounds, ink marks, are NOTHING BUT those things: familiarity. "Phenomena can be so familiar that we really do not see them at all."

Those who grow up by the seashore come to not notice the ocean sounds. One way to begin really noticing what is going on is by 'making it strange.' A thought experiment can help.

Pretend the year is 3992. Imagine that the English language is as dead as ancient Mayan is today. Finally, imagine that you are an archaeologist in charge of translating the only extant works of English, a set of ancient books found in a leaden container in a cave near the Great Salt Lake in what was once Utah. Since you DO know English and CAN read this easily, pretending it is foreign or strange language can be done if you have to read it from right to left.

Help, can experiment thought a. 'Strange it making' by is on going is what noticing really begin to way one. Sdnuos naeco eht eciton ton ot emoc erohsaes eht yb pu worg ohw esoht, makes it much harder.

Making things strange is even easier if you simply turn the book upside down and read from the pages' bottoms upwards. For example, pick five pages, read them as usual, and time yourself. Then, pick five other pages, read them upside down, and time yourself. The time difference will give you some measure of how much pure familiarity is contributing to what you are doing to or with whatever these things are that you're seeing. (Leonardo da Vinci was a switch-reader and writer, but not an upside-downer.)

The importance of finding the truth about what reading involves should be obvious. William James remarked on the extent to which our learning relies on "words, words, words." On first-hand observation of sounds and ink marks, as opposed to first-hand observation of the things themselves we think about when we "listen" and "read." How much of the world's history, how much of the universe's geography, how much about exotic animals, how much about Descartes, James, Watson, King David, Apostle Paul, and Dr. Murray would you have learned in the course of your lifetime without "words, words, words"? Without printed words. Without reading? What IS this reading you're doing? How well do you understand what you are doing RIGHT NOW? Where are these thoughts coming from? Where have all your other reading-thoughts come from? How are the seens and the thoughts related? One cognitivist confessed:

> What else has cognitive psychology discovered? Well,
> we have found out how recalcitrant the cognitive activities of

everyday life are to experimental study. For example, the fact that we understand so little about reading after years of study is very impressive to me.

The method. No one can read enough to conduct this experiment who can only look. At what's out here. Or at what's in there. James was wrong. He couldn't literally look in, i.e., introspect. But he was also right. The only way to have any inkling of what psychology is all about is to open the door to what is inside, in the sense that it's not out here. The reason James was such a magnificent student of what was NOT-OUTside, i.e., of what was INside in the very sense of NOT-outside his own skin, is not that he used a special inward type of looking. What he excelled at was in *noticing*, in learning tradition by heart so as to construct the best "professional" map or inner model possible for the various things he *noticed* (see the chapter headings of his early masterworks: e.g., habit, stream of consciousness, self-as-known vs self-as-knower, *attention*, and so on, not one of which things has ever been filmed or touched), in paying the closest attention to "see" if he'd missed anything that others had noticed, etc. The task isn't literally looking in. It's attending. No one ever did it better than William James, no one. And no one ever beat him at noticing, not ever.

D. Why Aren't YOU A Solipsist?

One reality? It's August 4, 1992. Not by the Persian calendar, of course. It's Tuesday. Not in some Pacific islands, though. It's 6:57am. But only in one twenty-fourth of the world's locations. What is the truth? Is it really 1992? The books tell us that the exact date of Christ's birth is unknown, though 1992 implies that it took place two thousand minus seven and a half years ago. They also tell us the universe is anywhere between ten and twenty billion years old but, even if they did know the exact number of years, who would want to write out, say, 15,872,745,136 S.B. (Since the Beginning)? How interesting. The physicists write books about the first three seconds of the universe's existence, but they're not sure whether it was ten or twenty billion years ago. Some exactness! Come to think of it, what does it mean when they say it may have begun ten billion years ago? A year is 365 days, the day is measured by how long it takes the earth to spin once on its axis, but the earth has only existed about 4.5 billion years. What clock do they go by? One that keeps Newton's absolute time? No wonder Kant said we know nothing about real time out there, only about the steady rate with which the present experience flows past only to be replaced by the next moment's experience, upon a horizontal picture of which we can "impose" our choice of invented *custom*ary measurements. [DO I PROJECT, not merely language-measures, but time-measures as well? PS Scientists have, in 2012, concluded that the universe began 13.7 billion years ago.]

And what is real about people? I just woke a few minutes ago. I've decided I dream an average amount, but usually I pay no attention to dreams and rarely remember them. Not this morning. What a dream. The first day of classes, running to the secretary's office in my bathrobe to get the class list so I'd know which classroom to go to, reaching my apartment—at school!—to get dressed, only to find most of the clothes I'd left in the closet gone. Thank heavens there was a pair of trousers and a long-bodied, short-sleeved yellow shirt to put on. Only, next thing I know, I'm screaming at the secretary for sending my clothes to the dry-cleaners during my summer absence and not bothering to make sure they all came back in time.

Weird! Weird, because there is no one at school more efficient than our secretary, and I don't have an apartment or any clothes there. Nor were that 'office' or 'my apartment' places I'd ever before seen, though those facts didn't even occur to me till now. Come to think of it, that yellow shirt isn't in my wardrobe, either. But which secretary is the real one? The one from my dreams? I recognized her alright, there's not the slightest doubt in my mind that it was she. Or the real one I've dealt with so often that I have a yards-long memory-file on her (which is why I'm sure she'd never do anything so careless)? And why didn't I instantly know, in my dream, that it wasn't her real office or a real apartment of mine? Even though now that I'm awake, I know where things in this house, the surrounding neighborhood, the city, the campus, are? So well that, without looking out (the shades are pulled), I know the direction, even the distance, of many of those landmarks. [DO I PROJECT space-measures, too?]

Is my reality the same as everyone else's? The very first thing I must do with regard to Kohler's two-worlds is highlight what some might think is a 'minor' detail—opinions about what's major and what's minor are so often radically different—but is really so important that it is difficult to think of anything being more important. It's a detail in Kohler's description. "Centuries ago, various sciences, most of all physics and biology, began to destroy the simple confidence with which most human beings tend to take this world . . ." "**THIS** worl**D**"?

What worl**D**? Are there really only two, THIS one and the ONE behind IT? Isn't he overlooking what everyone who wants to avoid massive confusion, the confusion which Kant created by skating back and forth over it all the time, had better keep fixed firmly in her or his mind, namely, that—if recent estimates of the world's population are correct—there are five and a half billion this-world**S**? One for each person. All distinct from the one real world behind **THEM**?

Rogers, too, made that obvious slip. He said: "Man lives essentially in his own personal and subjective world"? Surely he knew there were MANY (wo)men? We know it's mere rhetoric, but a singular flourish too easily becomes a singular fact. We must begin noticing how many people say "We cannot know objective reality" and then ignore the glaring assumptions they are making: that there is someone listening, that it's someone whose identity they know, that it's someone who they think understands their thoughts, that it's someone whose thoughts about THEIR thoughts they understand, etc. Not once did Rogers voice any doubts to Richard Evans that Richard really existed, that he could understand what Evans meant about Kant's suggestion, etc. Did he ever really doubt that, when he heard some Skinner-sounds ("I do accept your characterization of my own presence here"), he (Rogers) was right to interpret them as verifying the objective accuracy of his thoughts about Skinner's thoughts about himself. Who is this man who "lives in his own personal and subjective worl**D**"?

Rogers' view makes sense of Kohler's picture only if I count correctly and draw my lines correctly. To my inner picture of our planet surrounded by the other planets which, together with our local star, make up part of the Milky Way Galaxy somewhere inside a universe whose farthest galaxies are traveling outward into endless empty space, I add 5.5 billion humans (i.e., I add markers for them) who are this planet's inhabitants. Each one of us has an outer skin which encloses all the physiological organs diagrammed in the books. Each of us 5.5 billion has her or his own skin, her or his own inner organs. There may not be enough food to go around, but there are enough regularly-hungry mouths to do so. The chief organs in the world are our 5.5 billion brains. William James' basic principle in his *Principles* is that each person's brain is the one "immediate bodily *condition of*" that individual's states of consciousness. I count: 5.5 billion brains, plus 5.5 billion-1 "personal and subjective world**S**," ALL over there, on the "out" side of my skin, in *that* world. [DO I PROJECT others and my thoughts of others' experience, too?]

That's the mental picture—spanning absolute time and absolute space—that I draw when I imagine myself taking a God's-eye view of things. Of course, the picture is only to assist the understanding. My thoughts are the thing, not literally an eye. No eagle-eyed eagles have ever done astrology, let alone astronomy, whereas even coke-bottle-eyeglasses-wearing people who can think can do either or both. Galileo must have been thinking about that when he exclaimed how much he admired Aristarchus and Copernicus for using their reason "to commit such a rape on their senses." Perhaps it is God sharing this God's-eye view with me?

But wait, I commit a **MAJOR BLUNDER** if I stop there. I can't make the same mistake Descartes, Spinoza, and so many since have. I cannot deny colors, sounds, etc., nor can I leave them out there. They're what I do NOT "project." MINE are what I am directly and certainly aware of. They are so much of MY evidence, as YOURS are yours. Try to get along without what you see. Put the book aside and see how well you can follow my reasoning then. Close your eyes to see how uninterruptedly the thoughts now coming to you continue coming. Turn out the lights and/or climb under the covers and blic izzle flerp blitiri scindapsus pirots kerulize elactically (Mayan for "and notice whether you still notice just the same surprises at just the same moments.") What IS this seeing you're doing? What ARE you seeing, etc.? [DO WE ONLY INTERPRET? If we sense nothing, there's nothing to interpret.]

Repeat. For all the most famous physicists from Galileo on, the "real" world that Kohler said science is learning about, the one that includes my brain, is utterly devoid of color. Bodies are all dark and colorless, silent and noiseless, odorless, painless and pleasureless. When Locke wrote about the remarkable changes we SEE in the colors when we (think we're) looking through a microscope, he got close to what old Democritus and not-so-old Newton almost saw. The totality of sense-evidence points to one two-sided conclusion: the colors are not out there, but in here. As surely as the tickles *caused* by feathers and pains *caused* by needles are *effects* "in here," not out in their causes. Every one of the 5.5 billion brains are colorless, odorless, painless. That means that I must attach to each of them a "private world" of utterly real colors, sounds, odors, tastes, weariness, and ambition, to go with the private thoughts. If I keep my picture straight, each human has a brain to which s/he has no access, and a "world" of sensed-appearances, imagery, and thoughts, to which s/he has it. 5.5 billion persons. 5.5 billion private "worlds." 5.5 billion sets of beliefs, everyday and professional ones.

When I "look around," I must keep reminding myself that blue-sky, sunset-sky, rainbow'd-sky colors are not part of the the world outside my skin, though they are *indispensable clues to it*. They're not on the other side of my eyes (which I've never seen and which may not even exist, if Berkeley's right), and certainly no part of my very dark, very silent brain. (It, after all, is encased in a skull that shuts out all light and floats in a fluid that muffles the vibrations.) I still remember the most terrifying aspect of this when it hit me in Rome in January, 1963: *those aren't other people I see*, either. The people, like the books, trees, sun, stars, are part of the one real world out "behind" these body-appearances that I cannot climb over or peek around. If I can't peek at books, pages, sentences, then I can't peek at the authors who've written them. The pre-Skinner'd students were wrong. They saw none of the things Skinner said they didn't. He was wrong, too. No one has ever seen a pigeon or students or their own hand putting ink marks on paper. These reflections help make sense of cognitivist "writings." E.g . . .

> The perception of reality is best understood as a constructive process by which the brain builds useful models of the world. All of us possess useful internal models of what a room looks like, or how tall or small a person may actually be. We can spend a lifetime, and most of us do, without encountering a situation where our perceptual model of rooms and people are thrown into conflict. But such conflict situations can be constructed with rather haunting philosophical implications.

Morton Hunt, in that report on the cognitive revolution titled *The Universe WITHIN*, wrote that many of these thinkers think it's no longer relevant to wonder how good is the match between my inner model and outer reality. They won't say. The inner world "is a selection and transformation into neural impulses, a *processed* version, of what is outside." How silly.

> We never see, hear, touch, etc., things in the physical world, only effects p**roduced in our mind by never-seen causes or a never-seen Cause.**

I'm now in the habit of always, ALWAYS correcting such brain-centered reports that regularly overlook what's obvious: I am NOT an unconscious brain, processing colorless, soundless, 'encoded' information arriving from my afferent neurons set into motion by retinas, cochleas, etc., stimulated by the outside-my-brain environment, but a person wide awake to colors, sounds, and the like. Even though my *private, non-physical MODEL* must include an increasingly-detailed MODEL of a never-observed, colorless, painless, etc., brain whose processes parallel or correlate with various experienced features in my experienced, non-physical "world."

The *spaciousness* of this inner world that seemed for years to BE the world to me—and which STILL seems that way almost all the time—is what took me the longest time to get used to. Like Descartes, I was used to the whole tradition that says only physical things have any dimensions, whereas all spiritual or immaterial things are dimensionless. I suppose the fact that the old tradition seemed so persuasive is what delayed the recognition by Kant that it just ain't so.

However, the spaciousness I *EXPERIENCE* is a feature of the *non-physical* phenomena I am directly aware of. The most obvious dimensions in my experience are provided by the colors I see: they are spread out into an immaterial, total visual 'field.' Exactly the way, commonsensically, it seems that the colored paints are spread out on the canvas, the colored images or movie-colors are spread out on the movie-screen, the colored phosphors are spread out on the TV screen, and so on. The *third*-dimension may be an illusion if not one of the points of the TVF (*T*otal *V*isual *F*ield) is literally anywhere except flush up against me, but the *two* dimensions are not just thought-about.

(Descartes, Spinoza, Leibniz, Fichte, etc., all had problems with this dimensional extension, especially Descartes who made it the essence of matter.) But this spaciousness is not just visual. Sensed sounds, etc., also seem to be 'in space.'

For instance, as I thought harder about the reports of phantom-limb experiences—which Descartes himself made much of—and began to notice so many spatial *metaphors* about 'levels' of knowledge, 'inner' space, 'on the one hand,' and 'on the other,' I've come to understand why I sided so strongly against Plato and Descartes at first. It is because they often say that the person, I myself, have no body, am not a body, that I am an immaterial (which meant unextended) being, essentially a thinking being. My thinking is up here in my head, behind my eyes. As a result, it seemed Plato and Descartes had to be thinking that I end at my neck and all those things I feel down below my neck are not part of me. Yet, if someone kicks my leg down there, or if a nail goes through my foot down there, or if I feel a stomach ache down there, those things are happening to ME. I FEEL them. Only when I (mentally) took those felt pains out of my flesh and re-mapped them in my 'virtual reality' or my 'phenomenal field of experience' did I realize what was really going on. The cleverest part of the Great Entertainers' Deception is to make us feel as if we ARE bodies, even though all those 'body sensations'—muscle tensing, tickles, anxiety, etc.—are immaterial, spread-out given-to-me's, what are called "sense-data."

The confirmations that what I grew up thinking was my body isn't, are endless. Not merely amputees' reports and my own 'hip-pain' that is caused by nerve-pinching in my sacroiliac. Not just all of the facts learned by neurologists. Not just the spectacular report of his non-physical 'limb sensations' by the gifted reporter, O. Sacks, in *A Leg to Stand On*. But the abundance of memories or body-*images*—all of them in exactly the same 'place' as the original sensations!—of the pain of the anti-tetanus serum injected into the nail-wound in the sole of my right foot, an image I can still almost 'feel' down there, of the pain in my right knee that took a moment or two to 'develop' after I fell and my knee hit the concrete pavement, of the toothache I remember being right 'there' in my jaw, etc. And the most stunning of all: even though we see the exact same 'page of print' whether it's upside down or right side up, the activation of stored-up memories is radically altered. (Do the experiment: turn this book upside down and see how much slower your reading becomes. Kant might have used this rather than the pair of gloves as evidence that experienced 'space' is in us. What's 6 except an upside down 9 and vice-versa?)

"Think Movie!" The way I've found best for making myself understood here is to begin with the experience which most of the people I try to explain this to have, fortunately, had a lot of: *movie-going*. Intellectually, we KNOW there are no people up on the screen, no mummy able to come down into the aisles and kill me, no cars or planes about to crash, no ships going down. Just the rapid-fire projections, 24 per second, of 35mm colored "slides" onto the screen. To which are added the air-molecule vibrations created by the woofers and tweeters of the loud-speaker system. *But pictures and sounds are all my creative mind needs*: I "create" people, places, things, events by an entirely unintentional, un-pre-planned, very-difficult-to-resist process. I can remember having to repeat over and over to myself "There's not really a mummy coming to get you" when I was younger, otherwise I had to leave the theater. Or seem to do so. Seeing how Berkeley, who did not believe there were any real physical bodies behind the sense-givens ("ideas" is his name) in the mind, could write so much about "nature" becomes easy: just as the story of Snow White and the Seven Dwarfs is entirely a creation of the mind—except for the "moving" pictures and sounds—so is nature. The most important thing to remember is to not forget the "body":

> [...] the same warning applies to the relation between my organism as a physical system and my body as a perceptual fact. My body is the outcome of certain processes in my physical organism, processes which start in the eye, muscles, skin and so forth, exactly as the chair before me is the final product of other processes in the same physical organism. If the chair is seen "before me," the "me" of this phrase means my body as an experience, of course, not my organism as an object of the physical world. Even psychologists do not always seem to be entirely clear about this point. (W. Kohler, *Gestalt Psychology*)

These words, also from Kohler, will make no sense unless we notice how carefully he distinguishes between "my organism" and "my body."

(Psychologists not only redefine words, e.g., "ego," "mind," and "self," to mean radically different things, they even give "organism" radically different meanings. Just like "philosophers" do.) Using one name, "body," for two things—a biological entity and a 'perceptual fact'—is bound to create confusion. I grew up believing that the physical body that didn't stop existing when I fell asleep and stopped feeling it AND the thing I felt once again when I woke were one and the same physical reality. I now know that, even if a physical organism exists, I don't feel it and what I DO feel isn't it. I now use two names—body and, usually, body-image—to make sure which thing or set of things I am thinking about. James warned against using the existence of names as proof for realities. He ALSO warned that

> . . . the *lack* of a word quite as often leads to the opposite error. We are then prone to suppose that no entity can be there; and so we come to overlook phenomena whose existence would be patent to us all, had we only grown up to hear it familiarly recognized in speech. It is hard to focus our attention on the nameless, and so there results a certain vacuousness in the descriptive parts of most psychologies. (PP I:195)

It is not enough, though, to double SOME names when we double the items in our professional map. We must also extend it with consistency. Would Kohler use "the chair" to mean both the thing ten feet from his eyes and brain AND the thing that "*is the final product of other processes in the same physical organism*"? Of course not.

For the same reason, using distinct terms helps counteract any and every effort to point to James' emphasis on habits in order to make it seem that he agrees with behaviorists. We must learn to distinguish UNexperienced "physical" habits—all postulated modifications of postulated bodies—from both the **SENSATIONS** we experience and their image-residue, i.e., conscious **MEMORIES** and **EXPECTANCIES**, and sometimes give them different names like that. In a decapitated chicken-automaton running around the barnyard we find coordinated muscular movements, but no accompanying sensed data, memories, or expectancies. James so firmly emphasized the conscious nature of these memory-expectancies that he referred to them as "unattended-to sensations." As newborn infants, we have no expectations of anything, but the older we get, the more streams of sensations we have experienced, and the more often we have experienced *similar sensations in similar patterns*, the greater will be our *repertoire* of activatable-scenario-memories. A sample of what he has to say will be sufficiently suggestive.

> We all of us have a definite routine manner of performing certain daily offices connected with the toilet, with the opening and shutting of familiar cup-boards, and the like. Our lower centres know the order of these movements, and show their knowledge by their 'surprise' if the objects are altered so as to oblige the movement to be made in a different way. But our higher thought-centres know hardly anything about the matter. Few men can tell off-hand which sock, shoe, or trousers-leg they put on first. They must first mentally rehearse the act; and even that is often insufficient—the act must be performed. So of the questions, Which valve of my double door opens first? Which way does my door swing? etc. I cannot tell the answer; yet my hand never makes a mistake. No one can describe the order in which he brushes his hair or teeth; yet it is likely that the order in which he brushes his hair is a pretty fixed one in all of us.
>
> . . . these immediate antecedents of each movement of the chain are at any rate accompanied by consciousness of some kind. They are sensations to which we are usually inattentive, but which immediately call our attention if they go wrong. (PP: ch. IV)

These *unattended-to given-to-awareness's* provide our 'sense' of the smooth, usual flow of experience—our sense of what-to-expect next—and thus play a powerful, normally unnoticed role in our lives. These scenario-memories are instantly sub-activated by incoming sensations, even become attention-callers for us when what comes next isn't what's expected next.

This undertow of imagery plays a large part in our normal confidence about what we've experienced vs what we've dreamed. In my dreams, one person is likely to simply 'become' someone else, one location or building slowly transforms into a totally new one, or—to sum it up—the 'laws of nature' are violated more violently than they are by miracles. When I wake—when the vividly sensed 'givens' start coming to me again—I am able to think-about, reflect-upon, my dreams, i.e., to compare them with what I am used to, with what I *expect as a matter of course or HABIT*, and to recognize how bizarre, unusual, and unexpected the dream-sequences were. What I call "nature"—i.e., sun, moon, stars, plant life, animal life, and humans' arms, legs, torsos, heads, and brains—can be thought of as 'virtual reality,' by analogy with the recent technology of the same name. This 'nature-AS-IT-APPEARS-to-me' is 'my personal movie.' It is complete—I am not blind or deaf or anosmic—with three-dimensional technicolor, quadraphonic sound, smell-avision, taste-avision, and feel-avision. These incoming sense impressions constitute a 'likenesses-text'—as rows of tiny dark figures against a light background, **PARTS OF THE SAME VISUAL FIELDS**, constitute a 'language-text'—and the more theories I learn (Plato's, Aristotle's, Descartes', etc.), the more 'readings' I have at my disposal when I come to decide what interpretation to give to ANY parts of my life-movie/text.

Two questions inevitably pose themselves to anyone brought up to think the way Aristotle and Aquinas did. One question relates to the nature of color, sound, odor, taste, and heat, the other to the nature of their cause. But only after first becoming re-convinced that such things really exist. As things. As such.

What kind of reality are colors, etc.? Now that I've learned some of the history of these matters, I realize how fortunate I was to be introduced to Aristotle's firm 'excavation,' explicitation, or analysis of the tacit basic premises or 'first principles' of everyday common sense.

At first, the question, "You see something, but what is it?", seems adequately answered by "stars, sun, moon, forests, butterflies, etc." And apples.

Having been raised in this latest century when our English language has more words than we know what to do with, though, I didn't hesitate for an instant when I was introduced to the more exact answers which Aristotle and Aquinas worked with. Seeing is different from hearing, which is why "blind" and "deaf" do not mean the same thing. We don't see the taste of the apple, we taste it. We don't hear the color, we see it. Five senses, five special objects: the apple's eyes & color, ears & crunching sound, tongue & taste, nose & odor, skin & temperature. But, as Aristotle noted, we can both see the apple's shape as well as feel it, so some senses (e.g., sight and touch) have a few features in common: shape, size, location, etc.

Historically, as the theory that everything in the universe is made of nearly empty atoms whose components, the protons, neutrons, and electrons, are all colorless, odorless, tasteless, etc., became confirmed by more and more evidence, more and more of those who were fixated on the material-object answer simply denied the existence of color, sound, odor, etc. Some use the facts showing that rainbows have no color to argue that our belief in color is an illusion. I, too, nearly succumbed to the blunder of eliminating colors, sounds, odors, and so on—the things I experience!—from my inner model of reality, i.e., of *what really exists.*

I was saved at the last moment because I was familiar with a problem Aquinas wrote about. If, during the mass and eucharist—one of the seven sacramental rites of the Church—the bread is really changed into Christ's body and the wine is miraculously converted into his blood, then why does it appear that the bread and wine keep right on existing and why don't the body and blood show up? Aquinas called upon the Aristotle-noticed common-sense distinction between things in their own right ("substance" is handy short-hand) and their quasi-parasites (usually called "qualities," "qualia," or "accidents"), and declared that our senses only reach as far as the qualities or outer appearances but not to the essential, inside substance. So, at the same time that the substance-change occurs, the color, taste, smell, etc., of the former bread and wine are miraculously conserved in being. Revelation-informed believers' minds can know what real things are there: not merely new substances of flesh and blood, but the old accidents of bread and wine, which accidents, because they are now miraculously made to exist without a substance to inhere in, might as well be classified as "very short-lived substances that exist only while they are perceived!" In fact, only our everyday, headstrong, common-sense habits explain the fact that we ever think we see the never-appearing bread and wine rather than shaped colors or colored shapes that constitute only part of our total visual field.

The details are available in dozens of library texts. The bottom line in all this? The most exact answer to "What do I see when it seems I'm looking at an apple or a rose or a thermometer?" is (part of) a field of **COLORS.** Common-sensically, of course, it seems that it's all the one, same apple, that I see, touch, taste, hear, and (maybe) smell, so in a way all the senses have the 'thing itself,' i.e., the possessor of the sensible features, as their common 'object.' It was left to Berkeley to say it: the groups of color, taste, feel, etc., are things-in-themselves that exist only while they are perceived.

What kind of realities are images and thoughts? Substance-vs-attribute is a loose correlation-classification (which is space?, time?) invented by our minds—*or proposed by God*—to help us put order into our understanding of whatever-is. We don't extract the ideas one by one, first the idea of substance by examining a lot of them and then the idea of "quality" by inspecting lots of them. The question isn't "Which things did the ideas *come from*?", but "What things—if any—do they *apply to*?" The astonishing fact is that all colors, sounds, odors, etc., are things in their own right. They're not parasites of anything. They are presented to, ob-ject-ed at ("thrown at") us. The fact that they don't exist for more than an instant in so many cases is irrelevant. The same thing is true of many allegedly real nuclear particles. [IS IT ALL PROJECTING when I accept as true any guess about out-there?]

This view begins to make more and more sense, once its initial weirdness wears off. It also helps make sense of other things. Take images—e.g., those bright INNER after-images of the sun—which Aristotle and Aquinas believed in: the efforts to squeeze them under attributes (*I'm* bright, etc.?) Procrustes'es them, and makes it more difficult to recognize them for what they are.

David Hume, the thinker who confessed to finding himself over-whelmed by all the problems raised when he took a closer look at such details, said one thing was easy for him. We have a blind and powerful instinct to think we see physical things themselves: tables, houses, trees. "But," he wrote, "this universal and primary opinion of all men is soon destroyed by the slightest philosophy." One of his favorite methods for recognizing this 'destruction' was this: "When we press one eye with a finger, we immediately perceive all the objects to become double, and one half of them to be removed from their natural place." (Chapter XX of James' *Principles* is a magnificent discussion

185

of such issues.) Parts of *what we see* clearly move and change, the *distant bodies* do not. If our senses are infallible, we have to believe that the VISIBLY moving, changing seen-objects are distinct from the unmoving, unchanging bodies. (School children put their two index fingers together, pointing at each other at eye level, stare off into the distance, and see a small "hot-dog" floating, suspended in the middle.)

William James. William James appears to contradict himself more, perhaps, than any thinker on record. IF HE IS QUOTED OUT OF CONTEXT. He could put the 'flesh of experience' onto the bare bones of any and every abstraction imaginable, and—in the course of his many writings—did. If Cicero said there's not one absurdity that hasn't been taken seriously by some philosopher, then we can say that there's no other philosopher who could so instantly make any absurdity begin to sound reasonable. But, though—for a variety of reasons—he resisted to the end the one gestalt that would have allowed all the pieces to fall into their true shape, he was like Socrates and Rogers: he rejected what he knew to be absurdities: monist idealism on the one side and atomist materialism on the other.

True, he finally decided consciousness was a reification, but he merely replaced it with "experience." He did it for reasons, moreover, that are worthy of the title "ontological" or "metaphysical." True, he did as he promised and tried—between the four covers of his *Principles of Psychology*—to be an epiphenomalist, holding that the brain causes ephemeral effects called, for short, "the stream of consciousness." But his ultimate repudiation of such materialism was never made clearer than when he wrote:

> But the 'entire brain' is not a physical fact at all. It is nothing but our name for the way in which a billion of molecules arranged in certain positions may affect our sense ... Their aggregation into a 'brain' is a fiction of popular speech. Such a figment cannot serve as the objectively real counterpart to any psychic state whatever. (PP I:)

To underline this passage, he rescued it from near oblivion in Ch.6 of *The Principles of Psychology* and enthroned it at the center of the *Briefer Course's* epilogue. He never swerved from that view. In the next chapters, more of what this greatest of modern thinkers had to say will be presented and its supreme importance highlighted.

More than one author has repeated Carl Jung's protest against the dogmatic materialism of contemporary thinking. One writer is quoted as making the point that, "if the concreteness of reality is but a holographic illusion [or, we may add, virtual reality], it would no longer be true to say the brain produces consciousness. Rather, it is consciousness that creates the appearance of the brain—as well as the body and everything else around us we interpret as physical." This is not really a new theory. The Biblical tradition has always been that both our flesh and the spirit breathed into it have come from a pre-existent Creating Spirit (a conscious being) Who continues to hover over all of Their creation(s).

This confronts me with novel alternatives, though. I experience only one tiny parcel of that great creation: the steady stream of sensed-data, image-data, and thought-data that are my own private 'world.' (If you're out there, the same is true for you.) Can I be confident that any of my *thoughts* about what is out-there, NOT observed by me, are true? Yes! My thoughts about other people. What is my best evidence for them? My sensed-data? 'Of' what, though? Naive empiricists say, "Don't think, LOOK!" At what, though? At a picture worth a thousand words? That is, at LIKEnesses 'of' their bodies? Or at UNlike sounds and marks? I never met James. Which of his DISsimilar photos is like the REAL James? On the other hand, speaking common-sensically, I've read James' words. Which gives me a truer understanding of James, the pictures or the words?

As for you: have you met me? Can you understand anything of 'my mind'? If these pages 'represent' the real thoughts of some real other person, i.e., if they are not merely figments of your own overheated brain or illusions perpetrated on an unsuspecting you by the Creators, then you have thoughts which are true thoughts about something in the world beyond your own private 'world.'

Wm. James, in his *Varieties* lectures on "The Divided Self" and "Conversion," draws attention to what is obvious: radical conversions in a person's old habits do not normally happen overnight. Plato made up a story about a prisoner escaping from a dimly lit cave, and its major lesson is that "Seeing the (sun-)light" at first blinds the new learner. Our belief-system is unimaginably more complex than most of us ever dream—everything you've thought about since beginning this book has been first of all part of YOUR inner, private 'reality,' EVERYTHING! (they're first of all *your* thoughts *about* Descartes', etc.'s, thoughts)—and reorganizing all of its parts is a long project. We're fortunate to live at a time when our libraries are well-stocked with helpful catalysts, just so long as we lay our hands on the right ones or at least do not succumb to the errors of the wrong ones.

Dorothy Day was a bold, inquisitive seeker. She thought and re-thought the world's problems—power, poverty, pleasure, pain—during a long journey of more than eighty years. If ever anyone proved with her life what James went to considerable lengths to clarify in his *Variety of Religious Experience* lectures on "The Value of Saintliness," it was she. What sustained her in her long, lonely life of service? Asked once "Is God very real to you?", James answered: "Dimly real; not as an earthly friend." In a note about one of his visits with Dorothy, Robert Coles told of her very different answer: "I believed in Jesus Christ—that He is *real*, that He is the Son of God, that He came here, that He entered history, that He is still here with us, all the time . . ."

CHAPTER THREE

Self-Interested Altruism

A Role Model. She was a typical semite. An overage adolescent, fussed over by adoring parents. A near-psychotic anorexic, with a libido so fiercely repressed that, predictably enough, it eventually erupted in an orgy of sublimated delusions. She was an overwrought intellectual, one who came to think so highly of "her thoughts" that she would probably have given her very life to insure that they would live on. She was so anti-social that she not only refused to join the one social crusade accepted by her generation as scientifically inevitable, but refused to join the antiquated "accursed thing" to which her finally-awakened passions inclined her. She was a colossal mess.

Simone Weil was her name, and those are a few of the hasty generalizations we're likely to impose on her after hearing only a little about her, if that little is carefully selected from her whole history. Other more adequate impositions are "a saint for our time," "a true mystic," "a model for intellectuals," "a social-cultural analyst," "a moral critic," even "an individualist with a passion for community." Robert Coles, as he did for Dorothy Day (and—as he and Jane H.C.—did for other, mostly unknown giants in their own right), has written a guide to the most remarkable facets of this many-splendored person. Person, not woman. "Woman," like "man," names either a null-class or useful shorthand. As a person who learned what persons are for and then lived by that learning, she was an eminent success.

The last is the point. What are persons for? What is a person or human being? No questions are more important. And Simone can serve

189

as a model for those who are willing to indulge only one passion, the passion for truth, in their quest for the best answers to life's questions. No questions are more controversial, since it seems to so many that recent science has disproven pre-scientific views. In *Modern Man In Search of a Soul*, Carl Jung included a provocative essay horribly titled, "The Basic Postulates of Analytical Psychology." In it, he offered one intellectual's God's-eye view of the transition from the Gothic to the Modern Age. As he viewed the last four centuries, they symbolized for him a growing revolt against the Gothic Age's "exclusively vertical perspective" that has left us with the Modern Age's overly "horizontal perspective." As someone interested in the psyche, Jung was particularly concerned about today's vision of "man" as a biological organism without a soul. "Today the psyche does not build itself a body, but on the contrary matter, by chemical action, produces the psyche." Jung cautioned against such materialism with this declaration:

> The conflict of the material and spiritual aspects of life only shows that the psychic is in the last resort an incomprehensible something. Without a doubt psychic happenings constitute our only immediate experience. All that I experience is psychic. Even physical pain is a psychic event that belongs to my experience. My sense impressions—for all that they force upon me a world of impenetrable objects occupying space—are psychic images, and these alone are my immediate experience, for they alone are the immediate objects of my consciousness. (Chapter 9)

What a revolution would be accomplished if enough individuals underwent the profound conversion from naive realism needed to grasp Jung's—and Rogers' and James' and Descartes'—concluding premise, namely, that each of us gets to experience an entire "subjective world" of her or his own, the other side of which is that none of us gets to *directly* experience anything BUT our entirely private stream of consciousness. It would change the course of history . . . **IF** a reliably scientific understanding of the world behind and beyond were to accompany it. Especially a scientific understanding of persons.

Why especially persons? Because the universe may not contain anything but persons and their streams of consciousness. As for material *bodies*, we now have a magnificent theoretical apparatus to cover every last essential aspect of them, even if—contrary to what Descartes thought—we have no absolute certainty that there are any real bodies which that theoretical apparatus matches on a one-to-one basis. What we need next is a scientific model for *persons* that has room for the reasons why the physics-and-physiology fictions are necessary or, when not necessary, at least useful. We need a scientific understanding of persons.

The first scientific conclusion was alluded to above: there are no males or females. That is because human bodies as such do not exist. All of us, naive realists in our earliest years, grow up viewing persons as bodies or at least as having bodies. But physiology helps us learn that blood and brain are not single substances; the billions of red and white blood cells are separate swimmers, and the billions of neurons remain at neuro-transmitter-length from each other. These lessons are reinforced by modern physics which confirms the view that nothing larger than protons make up any part of this planet's bodies. This makes it necessary to review the view that persons are asexual beings able to be temporarily incarnated as either male or female, depending upon which model of flesh-taxi they've 'drawn' for their current lonely journey. Even now our traditional ideas of gender as identified with the body and its organs are routinely challenged. Many people take seriously the question, "Should we take seriously the claim by some women that they are men trapped in a woman's body or, more usually, the claim by some men that they are women trapped inside a man's body, i.e., take it seriously enough to approve their application for transexual surgery?" As noted earlier, the 6-15-92 *Newsweek* reported on the due-month (this one) of Carlo, a pregnant hermaphrodite legally registered as a male. More than our forebears ever were, we are called on to rethink all the distinctions we habitually make between persons, distinctions such as Jew and gentile, slave and free, and . . . male and female.

Another scientific conclusion vis-à-vis people follows from this: there are no people of color. Even if bodies of some kind or other do exist, color is not one of their features. Color exists only in those non-physical regions known as total visual fields. Nor, therefore, are there any people of this or that race. For, if the merely-apparent bodies begot from egg

191

and seed are, at most, person-taxis, then persons come, not from some family tree, trunk, vine, or root, but rather, like the sense-data, imagery, and thoughts given to us after our creation, directly from the Creators' hands.

A third important truth about us is that what we sense will, at least for now, continue to SEEM like physical bodies. It is important not to misunderstand the discovery that naive realism is an illusion. The full range of connotations behind the word "human body" will retain their importance for daily living. All of us can count for now on relatively consistent sense-data OF "bodies," our own and others'. For instance, our apparent-body's genitalia will be male or female. Or hermaphroditic. There will continue to be the appearances of apparent-gene correlations between apparent procreators' and apparent procreateds' apparent bodies, even the phenomena behind talk about pre-dispositions to such things as baldness, freckles, diabetes, etc.

Persons are thinkers. Most important of all scientific truths about persons, though, is the one Descartes made the bulwark of his thinking: each of us is a thinker. And each of us must learn to see clearly that s/he must do her or his own thinking. No one else can think for us. Not any more than they can see or hear for us, pay attention for us, remember for us, enjoy for us, suffer our pain, or decide what to believe for us. Kant's "Dare to think for yourself!" is a fine but dangerous piece of rhetoric. *No one has ever done anything else.* Anyone who lets someone else think for them or who unthinkingly thinks the same as someone else on *this* matter should dare to think for herself or himself. (Such rhetoric is useful, so long as we're not taken in by it.)

We need the truth. We need honest open-mindedness in our search for it. Simone Weil recognized our need for it: "The need of truth is more sacred than any other need," she wrote. And when she was challenged to rethink her refusal of Christian baptism, the public rite of "joining the church" (both she and Dorothy Day confessed that the prospect of baptism struck them as a betrayal of those who remained "outside"), she took it to heart:

> You said: "Be very careful, because if you should pass over something important through your own fault it would be a pity."

> That made me see intellectual honesty in a new light. Till then I had only thought of it as opposed to faith; your words made me think that perhaps, without my knowing it, there were in me obstacles to the faith, impure obstacles, such as prejudices, habits. I felt that after having said to myself for so many years simply: "Perhaps all that is not true," I ought, without ceasing to say it—I still take care to say it very often now—to join it to the opposite formula, namely: "Perhaps all that is true," and to make them alternate.

"Make them alternate." Perhaps she WAS nothing but an evolutionary degenerate as Hitler thought all Jews were. (Perhaps Hitler and those who believed that were the neurological degenerates.) Perhaps she would have been a typical JAP* if she'd been brought up in America. (Perhaps there are no more "typical JAPs" than there are typical Wasps or Japs.) Perhaps she was simply a mentally ill—or personality-disorder'd or abnormally-brain-wired or genetically-maldisposed—anorexic. (Perhaps those who believe in such fictions are the mentally ill.) Perhaps all her "ideas" were automatic products of an id warring with a socially-imprinted superego that co-produced the illusion that she could arrive at conclusions on the basis of evidence, the way Freud said some critics' ideas of him were. (*JAP, acronym for Jewish American Princess, is an ethnic slur or stereotype; "Jap" can also be an abbreviation for "Japanese.")

Maybe her fear of one-sided thinking is just the kind of fear that is the beginning of wisdom, the wisdom that might—had it been more widespread—have prevented so many millions from becoming slaves of the one-sided thinking that such names as "Hitler" and "Freud," "Adam Smith" and "Karl Marx" will someday stand for, enslaved thinkers whose slavishness has caused victims more pain and unhappiness in this one century than the antiquated 'accursed thing' to which Simone was passionately drawn caused in earlier centuries.

A. What Is Thinking? vs Where Put Mine?

We Need Better Thinking About Thinking. From Plato (or was it Socrates?) who focused on the soul as the knower of Forms, through

Aristotle who identified intellectual reasoning as the human soul's superiority over animal souls, to Descartes who said his thinking was his very essence, thinking has appealed to Western thinkers through the centuries as one of the keys for those who accept the challenge, "Know thyself."

A remarkable feature of our thinking is that, once we are old enough and while we are healthy enough, we can to some extent think what we want. Or, at the very least, our thinking seems to be less subject to outside forces. Put candy in my mouth, I'll get a sweet taste, put an anchovie in my mouth and I may gag. Hold a burning candle to my hand, I'll pull back almost irresistibly, but let me scratch my poison-ivy rash and the pleasure will be just sooo gooood I'll have a hard time pulling away.

Of course, there are differences in who starts the automatic chain of events. I may be able to not-start the chain of events: I could leave the candy in the dish, pull the anchovie off the pizza, keep my hand away from lit candles and rashes. But if a 280-pound behemoth who plays tackle for a professional football club decides the candy or anchovie goes into my mouth or that my hand goes above the flame or over and over the rash, the only thing I'll be able to control will be my mouth, and what I say may make things even worse. I didn't know these things when I was born. Thinking them now is easy. I have learned thousands of things like this, and those thousands of things guide my decisions about what I put into my mouth, what I do with my hands, and so on. But I am not doing any of those things right now. Only thinking of them.

But feelings can interfere with thinking about thinking. David Hume once wrote that "Reason is, and ought only to be the slave of the passions." The cautious thinker will naturally wonder what passion Hume had enslaved his reason to when he chose to keep his hand from changing what it had written: a passion for truth or a passion to justify his despair of ever finding it?

More reasonable people than Hume distinguish reasoning from rationalizing, honestly weighing the reasons for and against some conclusion from simply looking for an excuse to do what we want to do, being objective from being biased, and so on. In other words, people with a passion for truth have found many ways to express what seems clear, namely, that different passions can motivate us in deciding what to think and we can choose which passion we will TRY to follow. We can even think that, if Hume had been more careful when he reread what his pen had put on the sheet of paper, he'd have re-written what he knew as well as we: "Reason isn't always, but it should be, slave to a passion for truth above all." Particularly when we are trying to reason carefully to discover the true purpose of human reason. And what kind of beings we are who use it to do so much thinking.

In fact, what we think influences our passions. If we think Freud is right, that human civilization is possible only if libidinous passion is dammed up rather than allowed to spill out behind every bush, but that too much damming up will create neurosis or worse, we will call our think-tanks together to design educational programs and advertising campaigns to get the people to think that. We may think anger, like steam building up in a boiler, will explode unless we let off steam, and that will impel us to publish books to get people to think the same way*. But, if we reflect on past experience and discover how often we were furious with someone until we learned to our embarrassment that the reason why our anger began to well up inside us was a misunderstanding, a mistake in our thinking, we will advise angry people to review the thinking that causes them to become angry. Believing we can conquer an addiction makes us take steps to overcome it, which taken-steps often lead to liberation from the torture of constant craving or passion. A mother, terror-stricken when the child who wandered off along the water's edge cannot be found anywhere on the beach, cries for joy when told the child has been found, an instant switch in mood caused, not by any external change in the facts, but by thoughts. (*If we agree with Freud who was a determinist like Skinner, we will realize that, IF his conclusions were true, his theories were libidinously motivated and that, like Skinner, he—Freud—was unable to dispassionately adjust his conclusions to fit the evidence. James highlighted this latter hypothesis in his *Varieties*, Lecture I.)

Thinking about thinking is difficult, however. As anyone can understand who realizes that fiction—false thinking—arouses passion as easily as true thinking does. What if the reported "child-finding" turns out to be false? The first switch will be followed by a second. Othello killed the one he loved because of passion aroused by false thinking. Romeo killed himself because he, too, got fooled. In fact, people who go to see Shakespeare's plays can emerge a while later, drenched by a whole repertoire of passions even though they know that Othello, Romeo, Juliet, etc., are fictitious characters and that no one was dying up there on stage. Then, too, there are those fictitious reasons called self-deceptions. Confronted with so much error or bad thinking, it is no wonder some people become overwhelmed by the challenge to seek the truth, especially the truth about thinking.

Encouragement comes from noticing something that is obvious: the average person already manages a life that calls for extremely complicated thinking. Even about thinking. It might not be too far off to say that about a third of our common-sense beliefs hinge around thoughts. We know our thoughts are invisible to others and that the consequences of this can be GOOD or BAD. If we're LYING—whether from fear of what will happen to us if we tell the truth or from fear of causing pain to someone else (or in the hope of sparing them the pain?!)—it seems good. If we're TELLING THE TRUTH—whether in the hope of saving ourselves an unjust imprisonment or even capital punishment or in the hope of sparing others the pain they'll suffer if they do not believe our first-ever GENUINE cry of "Wolf! Wolf!"—it's bad. Trying to help others believe what is true is called "being honest," except when it's called "gossip," "slander," "backbiting," "tactless," etc. Trying to make them believe what is false is called "lying"—even if what we tell them turns out to be the truth that we falsely believe is false (Sartre wrote a novelette, "The Wall," based on this)—except when it's called "being tactful," "good business," "campaigning," "advertising," etc. What mature person does not understand this complex web of thoughts about thinking? And about the difference between truth and error?

And that our passions complicate matters? Particularly because our ethics and our values are intimately bound up with thinking. Our common-sense beliefs about thinking—they can be called "the basics of EPISTEMOLOGY"—converge with that third of our beliefs which can be called "the basics of ETHICS." (The remaining third make up our "naive realist" beliefs.) There is really only one absolute rule in ethics, and it can be stated quite simply: "Do good and avoid evil." That is vague, and another way of stating it sounds more definite: "Love your neighbor as yourself." It can also be formulated as "Do unto others what you would have them do unto you (if you were smart)." "Love and do what you will." Or "Be a lover." If we are smart, we will want others to tell us the truth rather than lie, which means that to do unto them we must want to tell them the truth. Except when they are playing poker, when they want to see the movie, read the novel's ending, or do the crossword puzzle *for themselves*, or when their spirits are already so low that one more piece of bad news may be more than their current supply of courage can handle.

Of course, the converging is commutative, so that all of us will want to know—if we're smart—whether it is true that all of the commandments really are summed up in the one-word categorical imperative, "Love!" And we'll want to know what is the true way to do that in particular situations where deciding what's really best is extremely complicated. For instance, suppose there is a public-servant politician who does not believe in allowing men to pay women for sex, regardless of how hot they are, who is even naive enough to think such men should just donate the money, then take a cold shower. Should he adopt *Saint Thomas Aquinas'* principle that voting to pass a law allowing restricted prostitution may produce the most good and/or the least harm for all of the individuals who will be affected, or should he vote his conscience? Or does "voting his conscience" (i.e., he is not a john but a politician*) mean he should vote to pass the law if he believes it will do more good than harm? Then again, he may be wrong, and it may do more harm than good. And what should a politician's conscience tell him to do when he believes that voting for what he thinks will be best for all concerned will result in his not getting enough reelection votes so he can continue voting for good laws? Does anyone think a woman should follow different rules if she is elected to replace the male who voted his conscience about prostitution? (*Most five-year olds can tell the difference between mom *saying* "You can have a cookie" and mom *eating* the cookie herself. Why do so many former five-year olds forget that?)

The time is ripe for better thinking about thought. Many who think of themselves as 'philosophers' and 'psychologists' have recognized the shortcomings of the linguistic turn and radical behaviorism. Thus we have a swelling revolt against 'analytic' philosophers whose crude materialism has produced a bias fully the match of any crude idealist's and in favor of those mind-openings described by B. Baars' *The Cognitive Revolution in Psychology*. The time has come to resume the scientific study of thinking that those 'movements' interrupted.

The time is ripe, too, because many of those who assist people suffering from emotional pain and distress recognize the links between thoughts, feelings, and life. They practice what they call "cognitive therapy." The more educated people become, the more likely it is that they'll turn for help to 'secular' counselors, e.g., to clinical psychologists, psychiatrists, and psychoanalysts, rather than to 'religious' advisors, such as gurus, rabbis, monks, nuns, shamans, and so on. The reason is not difficult. The knowledge we call "science" has not only made deep inroads into what is regarded as "religious teaching"—popes nowadays have accepted Copernicus' view, have reinstated Galileo, even allow that Lyell's geology may have been more accurate than *Genesis'* author's—but scientific knowledge has also created technology which has radically altered our world. No wonder most people regard 'secular' psychological science as more reliable than advice taken on faith. So clients' thinking about where they'll find the best thinking takes them to the 'secular' therapists, and secular therapists report that, in many instances, helping clients replace bad thinking patterns with better ones is sufficient to restore their clients' emotional equilibrium, a combination that shows the power of thinking.

Most of all, the time is ripe because, unless we learn how to think of better ways to live together, more and more are bound to die together. If death is not the end of humans' enjoyments, that might not be altogether bad, but most who believe in a life beyond are enjoying life now and have no wish to hasten matters. That thought, however, is an unpardonable levity for anyone who is unable to shut out an awareness of the horrific pain, misery, and despair suffered by the innocent caught in the many cross-fires between people who think armed conflict is the only way to put an end to undeserved pain, misery, and despair caused, not by their own poor thinking, but by others' injustice towards them (caused, no doubt they would agree, by others' bad thinking). To the extent that the increasing cross-fires ARE the result more of bad thinking than of bad will, they can be brought to an end by better thinking. We must learn how to think better than today's 'social thinkers' and see how many wars come from bad thinking.

Still, the task of thinking well about the connection between our thinking and our living poses an enormous challenge. Many, even Plato himself, have argued that no one does evil knowingly, as if everyone who knew what's good would do what's good. That raises the problem of equivocation. What does "knowing" mean in this context? And what does "good" mean? In his *Nichomachean Ethics*, Aristotle offered his rules for finding happiness, which is—according to him—the really common good-thing being sought by people's apparently different pursuits of such "goods" as wealth, pleasure, power, fame, wisdom, and so on. And what does "ethics" mean? Kant challenged the use of happiness as a yardstick for the good life by insisting that "moral science" is not about how to *be* happy but about how to *deserve* to be happy. Not at all the same thought. E.g., many people *have* a great deal of money who most would agree have done nothing to *deserve* it.

Unexamined classifications get in the way. Morality: how important is it for cognitive therapists—or any psyche-therapists—to think well about it? Some people think that morality is the same as religion, but then some think therapy has the same goal as religion. Carl Jung is frequently cited as one who believed that, of his over-thirty-five clients, "all have been people whose problem in the last resort was that of finding a religious outlook on life." Jung is often thought of as a psychoanalyst, but his claim is hardly what one would expect of Freud, who is also classified as a psychoanalyst. But, then, O.H. Mowrer is often classified as a behaviorist, yet, unlike Watson who complained that James' belief in consciousness was a disguised form of religion, Mowrer openly advocated views about the connection between sin, guilt, and psychological distress, all of which are reminiscent of what people use the labels "morality" and "religion" for. So much for labels. Perhaps we should just put the labels aside and look at the realities. Except it's not looking, but thinking we need.

And what about science? One of the problems everyone who wants to think well about thinking must confront today is: "What should I think about science?" Many people think scientific thinking is the best kind of thinking. We have the technology to prove it, they think. Others believe science and technology pose more of a threat than a blessing. At least in pre-nuclear days, humans were no match for hurricanes, earthquakes, volcanic eruptions, etc., so far as their ability to cause destruction was concerned. Some believe that, even if science cannot offer us all the answers, it at least offers us the only ones we can count on. Others claim that the glitter of scientific knowledge blinds us to other, equally certain kinds of knowledge. A trip to the library will convince anyone who has not already made up her or his mind that there is no consensus whatever about the nature of scientific knowledge or its alleged method.

For rethinkers in quest of certain truth, the view that should be of most concern is the conclusion by some that those who wait for science to provide them with answers are the real "waiting-for-Godot"-ers. According to them, there is no truth, certainly not certain truth, not from any source. According to them, 'science' is simply one more myth pursued by gullible humans seeking the impossible. No one stated this (regarded as true?) thesis any more dramatically than F. Nietzsche:

TRUTH AND FALSITY IN AN ULTRAMORAL SENSE

In some remote corner of the universe, effused into innumerable solar systems, there was once a star upon which clever animals invented cognition. It was the haughtiest, most mendacious moment in the history of this world, but yet only a moment. After Nature had taken breath awhile, the star congealed and the clever animals had to die.—Someone might write a fable after this style, and yet he would not have illustrated sufficiently, how wretched, shadowlike, transitory, purposeless, and fanciful the human intellect appears in Nature. There were eternities during which that intellect did not exist, and when it has once more passed away, there will be nothing to show that it has existed. For this intellect is not concerned with any further mission transcending the sphere of human life. No, it is purely human and none but its owner and procreator regards it so pathetically as to suppose that the world revolves around it. If, however, we and the gnat could understand each other, we should learn that even the gnat swims through the air with the same pathos, and feels within itself the flying center of the world . . . So the very proudest man, the philosopher, imagines he sees from all sides the eyes of the universe telescopically directed upon his actions and thoughts.

Albert Camus wrote a sequel to this passage, entitled *The Myth of Sisyphus*, which opens with the startling assertion: "There is but one truly serious philosophical problem, and that is suicide." Camus built his sequel on a lengthy analysis of the human condition which he labels "absurd," and his conclusion is that "the absurd is the confrontation between this irrational and wild longing for clarity whose call echoes in the human heart" and the fact that "the world is not reasonable." Camus, long before the project for the SSC—the Waxahachie Superconducting Super-Collider—was devised, pointed out that the whole notion of a tiny solar-system atom is poetry, so that those who are willing to spend billions on the SCC ($8.25 B is the most recent figure as reported by the 7-7-92 *N.Y. Times**) are deluded fools. Our desire to get to the bottom of things is, according to Nietzsche, Camus, and even many physicists themselves, already doomed to eternal frustration. (*This USA project was cancelled, succeeded by the Large Hadron Collider in Europe.)

Still, there IS all that technology. Ask the survivors of the buzz-bombs that fell on London during World War II whether modern rocket weaponry is a myth. Hiroshima and Nagasaki are facts. Ask how many educated people disagree with the modern popes who believe now that Galileo was right and his Aristotelian critics wrong. Ask how many believe the TV's they watch every night for instant news from around the globe are just imaginary. Ask the skeptics whether they intend to consult pipe-smoking shamans when they next fall ill or whether they will put their trust in the doctors of modern medicine. If it's all myth, let's ask Nietzsche why he trusted the history of the Greeks so much that he based his *Geneology of Morals* on it? Or ask Camus if he knew why so many physicists prefer Rutherford's model of the atom over that of Leukippus or Democritus, or why, after all, he believes there ever was a Leukippus or Democritus he never met. Ask those who think the atom is a myth whether they also believe the money for the Waxahachie Waste would have been wasted anyway, because no values are better than any other. Let's ask all skeptics what logic they follow, what evidence they have, what good reasons they offer, for their refusal to agree with Einstein who said that the challenge is not to surrender our belief that the universe is intelligible, but to find a suitable explanation for the miraculous fact that it is. Why they do not agree with Whitehead who believed, like every advocate of freedom of speech, that "a clash of doctrines is not a disaster but an opportunity."

To sort matters out on 'science,' we need to keep touch with our everyday common sense and to realize that our usual thinking about 'science' is directly related to our thinking about the physical world. After all, the 'technology' we refer to is always relative to sensible things: telescopes and microscopes to see things too small because they are too far or too small, recorders to preserve sounds, loudspeakers to reproduce what has been preserved, medicine that heals bodies and bombs that harm them, and so on. Until we get our thinking clear about the physical world, we will not be able to keep our thinking clear about the technology supposed to demonstrate the superiority of 'science.' Nor will we be able to get clear on our thinking about thinking, whether we call it "scientific" or anything else.

Faced with the difficulty of thinking well about thinking, Hume recommended that we put less emphasis on thinking and stick to living and to doing what comes naturally. But 'doing what comes naturally' for humans is so different from what people *think* it is for the birds and bees that it is 90% or more thinking. Isn't the very fact that we can understand and compare the preceding thoughts—and tell that they contradict each other—evidence that we carry within us a standard of harmony which these thoughts clearly do not measure up to? We are not actually useless passions confronting a senseless world, but free-thinkers face-to-face with a cornucopia of belief-options. Once begun, we can't quit. E. Fromm opens Chapter Two of *The Art of Loving* with this:

> Any theory of love must begin with a theory of woman, of human existence . . . While we find love, or rather, the equivalent of love, in animals, their attachments are mainly a part of their instinctual equipment; only remnants of this instinctual equipment can be seen operating in woman. What is essential in the existence of woman is the fact that she has emerged from the animal kingdom, from instinctive adaptation, that she has transcended nature—although she never leaves it; she is a part of it—and yet once torn away from nature, she cannot return to it; once thrown out of paradise—a state of original oneness with nature—cherubim with flaming swords block her way, if she should try to return. Woman can only go forward by developing her reason, by finding a new harmony, a human one, instead of the prehuman harmony which is irretrievably lost . . .

Woman is gifted with reason; he is *life being aware of itself* . . . [This is a 1990's up-date, with Fromm's "man" replaced by "woman."]

Return then to our need to think well. Each of us can reinforce Fromm's poetry with a few moments' worth of personal reflection on one obvious truth: each of us thinkers has a unique thinking career, and that career comprises a variety of stages. How many of us older folk envy one-year olds whose senses may be keener than ours but who understand nothing? How many of us look forward to senility when we will no longer understand what's really going on? How many, if our doctor held out the chance of living—but only like a vegetable—for many more years, if we'll consent to surgery for a brain tumor, would reply "Go for it!"? Even sex, they say, is 90% "in the mind." The fact that Fromm's poetry captures is that *human* life is largely *thought* life. Lived with passion.

Whoever comes to understand such matters will understand that trying to think well is not a luxury. It is a fundamental obligation for anyone who wishes to be a human fully alive. The need to try and think well is perfectly obvious even in our everyday lives. For instance . . .

(1) **Trials.** Every juror is supposed to listen to two complete theories—even, like S. Weil, think that each one MAY BE TRUE—and then, on the basis of what they have learned inside the courtroom (a safe distance from the crime, both in terms of space and time) AND all the good sense and experience they bring into the court-room (stored away in their memory) from their past life, make a decision about something they will never OBSERVE. Whoever is familiar with these things knows how, in many instances, the prosecutor can create a case that looks so airtight that any juror would be inclined to think "Guilty as hell!" Then Perry Mason takes over, shoots holes in the prosecutor's case, and eventually does the state's job for it: gets the real killer to make a voluntary confession after confronted with evidence dug up by Paul Drake. The point is clear. In *many* cases, there are good reasons for deciding one way and good reasons for deciding the other way. When there are thousands of reasons (facts or alleged facts) that are known

and thousands or millions that are unknown—did JFK's killer act alone?—there will always be jurors who decide one way, jurors who decide the other way, some spectators who lean one or other way but are glad they don't have to decide, and the people, jurors or spectators, who say "I really can't make up my mind at all." Did you learn this from studying philosophy or 'scientific' psychology?

(2) **Debates** about the BEST laws. For citizens living in a free-press democracy, the greatest temptation is to think the laws are deliberately made to favor 'the other guys' by legislators who have been bought or are biased. Those who are in the habit of thinking that way in the case of ANY vote they dislike are simply confirming the fact that their own thinking is simple-minded. Being a good citizen—one who, not having the time or task to make the laws, but only the task of following them—requires above all a habit of recognizing how complex our world is and how much greater intelligence than ever before is required to make laws that will allow not just millions but billions to live in harmony. If we reflect on the lawyers involved in trials, and even more if we can reflect on our own experience as debaters, it helps keep things in perspective. The interesting thing about debates is that, much the way the prosecutor hired to marshall as many facts as possible to prove the defendant guilty tends to believe in that guilt and the defense attorney hired to line up as many arguments as possible to prove the defendant innocent often comes to believe in that innocence, those who have had some debating experience know how easy it is for debaters to become wholly convinced their side of the argument is obviously right, even if 'their side' is the opinion they initially opposed. Why? Partly (largely?) because they begin selectively attending to facts favorable to their imposed conclusion and selectively inattending to the unfavorable ones. By going to the library to read up more on their side, the only-slightly-informed find the facts on both sides are so many and so complex that each side can mount a persuasive 'case.' Even on 'scientific' issues. 'Scientists,' they learn, do not agree on the most *basic* 'scientific' issues. Einstein and Bohr, for instance! The absolutely best work

on their basic, fundamental disagreement is Manjit Kumar's *Quantum: Einstein and Bohr and the Great Debate About the Nature of Reality*.

(3) It is August 20, 1992, and here in the USA we have just finished the two conventions. After the first, polls showed that the audience was swayed by what they heard for that side. Once the second convention got under way, polls showed that voters are exactly like jurors and debate audiences.

We're *so* fortunate to have the media, however, for they take *such* great care to weigh the issues at length, to educate the voters, to make certain the public is not swayed by clever one-liners or carefully-staged media-events. That is because we live in a society where freedom of speech guarantees we are allowed to hear 'truly' serious and wise presentations of the extraordinarily complex issues—these things affect not just the 250 million of us but the 5.5 billion of the rest of the planet's inhabitants—in order that we can be well-informed when we go to the polls. This is what makes democracies so much better than, say, countries where the media are dominated by the desire to stay in business, where they pander to viewers' grosser appetites in order to win ratings wars to get contracts from sponsors of products that the people genuinely need because they are good for the consumer and not just for investors' portfolios, etc. Thank heavens for true freedom of speech!

What the world needs today is better thinking, and it must begin with better thinking about thinking. Which means noticing what is obvious from hard thinking about trials, debates, campaigns, and MOST OF ALL! about the *freedom of speech*. After all, the best argument of all for freedom of speech is that it should make good thinking easier by providing unlimited access to all the facts. Like most good things, free speech is often perverted by the ignorant and the corrupt, with the result that some would like to outlaw it. Cautious thinkers who want the whole truth will always—when confronted with a true fact like the fact that freedom of speech can be easily abused—think, "That's true, but . . ." The buts here are superabundant, as you can "induct" from a few samples. Few people want to outlaw cars because 47-50 thousand people die in them each year (we need cars more than we need apples with alar on them). Few want to outlaw alcohol, though the CDC in

Atlanta said in 1990 that 105,095 deaths occured in 1987 that were traceable to alcohol (the tobacco companies would have challenged any figures on how many deaths were caused by second-hand cigarette smoking). Who is there who says celibacy should be mandatory because, as our well-balanced news sources prove each day, numerous problems—ranging from social! diseases (which range from herpes to AIDS) to child abuse and friendly rape—are caused by lust for the pleasures of sex? Most people in 1992 appear willing to take risks on cars, alcohol, and sex, even though they can be abused like freedom of speech can. The solution is not less freedom of speech, but more responsible listening and reading. We have an obligation to think well, i.e., learn both sides, be objective in weighing the evidence, and be courageous but prudent in defending what we finally decide is the truth. If so much of our thinking is affected by words—prosecutors', defense attorneys', debaters', candidates'—we should be keeping a careful eye on how well ANY AND ALL word users do the thinking that lies behind their words. And if—as seems obvious—the thinking any one of us has the most control over is our own, then that is where our efforts to think well must begin. How many of us monitor our thoughts well?

Another way to view the same thoughts is this. If democracy is the wave of the future, and if freedom of speech is the rule for successful democracy, it means that what the world needs more is not just love, but better thinking. About the difficulties involved in living with other people who often believe we are wrong, people who in our opinion are mistaken. About the difficulty any of us find when we think the other party is not just wrong, but stupid, selfishly motivated, and/or even dangerous to society. If we want others to listen to our side of the story when we explain why they are wrong, then we must learn to think hard about how we think about others and about what is said by them. And should be insistent that our childen—the people upon whom we will rely as we get older and they take all the political, economic, and social power away from us—learn how to think as well as we do. Especially about their responsibility to think well, so they'll be more likely to make wise decisions when situations arise that are brand new, global-scale ones.

Where are your thoughts? If thinking is important, then what is the best way to begin thinking well about thinking itself? The title for this section is "What Is Thinking? vs Where Put Mine?" Most often, we *think* the best way to start thinking well about something is to ask "What is X?" And our tendency is to think that "What is X?" questions are requests for a definition. We normally do not think twice about that thought and all that it implies. But it's a BAD HABIT to think like that.

First, it is too easy to get in the habit of not noticing the difference between "What is an X?" and "Does any X exist?" Once we get an idea to go with the word that "X" stands for, we who learned so easily to believe in Santa Claus and bogywomen will tend to think that there is a reality that the idea is an idea about. Unless we get in the habit of asking "What would an X be IF any X's exist?", we will tend to lengthen our list of "What exists" when we ask "What is space-time?", "What is society?", etc. And dictionaries are utterly useless on such important issues. My dictionary has a definition for "bogyman" as well as for "God," yet it has no "Not for Adults or Atheists" across the front of it.

Another reason to avoid the BAD HABIT of being content with "What is X?" is that it too easily leads us to overlook the complexity of the relations between words and ideas. We can even come to think that this or that word has only one GENUINE definition. No one is more prone to this error than academics who get in the habit of using this or that word 'professionally' to mean *only* this and *not* that. This makes them/us prone to being deaf to the meanings of others who use words in a way different from ours. Especially if we are not in the habit of attending to different background-beliefs, so that we do not realize, e.g., that when James uses "tree" and "quad" he uses them to mean what George Berkeley meant and not what John Watson did.

In our everyday conversation, of course, we all show a stunning ability to combine accuracy and flexibility. We need go no farther than the skill that a five—and six-year old shows when s/he uses "I" and "you" to mean or refer to just the opposite person that the person s/he is conversing with uses them to mean or refer to. Examples abound. Who doesn't understand the thought expressed by "You can kill a bat with a bat" or "Can't you see the difference between seeing someone and visualizing them?" or "Do you think animals can think?" (Except, of course, the billions who cannot speak English, etc.) Every smart atheist except the Illogical Positivists (according to whom not even the word "God" really existed if "word" is defined as "something with a meaning") should begin a definition of "God" with the words "a concept that many other-than-me people believe matches some reality which is . . ." No theists define God as a concept. But every smart theist can understand what a smart atheist means by "God is only a concept." Everyone who is wise will get in the habit of asking, not "What is X?", but "What do YOU mean by X in that context?" or "What does s/he mean by X in that context?", etc. And, above all, "What do I usually mean by X in such contexts?"

Did you notice that *none* of the preceding has offered what looks like an Oxford-Dictionary definition of thinking or thoughts? It has been straight-ahead exposition. Yet, unless my intention failed, unless what I meant to happen didn't, you read and understood the thoughts that came to you without running for the dictionary to look up "thinking" or "thought." Without taking a course on rules for meaning, too. Have you ever noticed that no one teaches babies a language by handing them a dictionary? Did you ever wonder why not? Did you ever notice that the only people who learn a new language with the aid of a dictionary are people who already know one language, i.e., their old language's words whose meanings are, presumably, the same as the meanings of the words of the new language? Did you ever wonder why? Did you ever wonder whether bilingual people are capitalists when they speak English and communists when they switch to Russian? Did you ever wonder why not?

Did you ever hear of "the Linguistic Turn"? That is a general name for the theories of people who sowed much confusion because they—like behaviorists—have turned everyone's attention *away from* in-side where meanings, that is, thoughts, can be found *to* sounds and ink marks called "language." P.S. Still, we library-users who do not reject the possibility of an 'experimentum crucis' (a crucial experiment) that convinces ready-minded Pasteurs which theories to eliminate, owe them a debt of gratitude for making available to us the voluminous outcomes of their failed experiment to reduce thought to word-use. We also owe them for valuable work-books to help us *notice* the evidence Chomsky used to persuade everyone except Skinner and behaviorists that Skinner's view of human thought was as idiotic as Watson's, namely, our endlessly creative flow of novel, never-before-experienced-by-us word-combinations we call "complete sentences," except when we use such substitutes as "responses," "statements," "judgments," "proposals," "propositions," "views," "notions," "concepts," "constructs," "theses," "facts," "claims," "analyses," "denials," "disclosures," "disclaimers," "truths," "dogmas," "null hypotheses," "dogmas," "guesses," "dogmas," etc.

Hence, we must ask not for definitions, we must look for models. Or, rather, we must look beyond definitions to the models and the belief-systems they serve. 'Words' do not connect directly to thoughts but only 'through' imagery to thoughts. The imagery, particularly the imagery that is part of our grand frameworks or mental maps is too easily overlooked. Once we have, in place, our original common-sense picture of our world, whether of a parochial one or of a speeding-outwards-galaxies one, we get in the habit of 'marking' its contents with those cues and clues we name "names." The things we label "people's thoughts" are put somewhere inside them and 'marked off' from other things—sense-data and imagery—which are given their own labels. That is the idea behind the replacement of "What is thinking?" by "WHERE DO I PUT **MY** THINKING?"

This realization will help each person to get in the HABIT of attending to her or his OWN thoughts or to her or his OWN meanings. Me to mine, you to yours. YOUR thoughts. They are the only ones you have direct access to. Thinking about others' thoughts requires a thought of your own to do it. They are coming to you continually. There is no distance between them and you. It is almost as if your "world" of direct experience is permeated with them. Which, in a sense, it is. Your beliefs constitute your interpretation of reality, which is why some thinkers say your belief-decisions "constitute" reality. YOUR reality.

Which is why those with different models have different (subjective) "worlds." Chapters One and Two were designed to deal with the twin facts that others are often using such radically different 'profess-ional' models of the universe as the materialist's, the idealist's, the dualist's, etc., and that all of us who develop different 'profession-al' models revert back to our naive-realist model most of our waking hours. To think well about thinking requires that we get into the HABIT of being on-our-toes-alert to the possibility that what looks like a familiar word is a clue to an unfamiliar thought and to trace the meaning of every word back to that original, common-sense view of things.

Interlude. It is fitting that the final step in solving the great riddle of nature should consist in noticing one of the most obvious clues: the entire array of realities we collect beneath the umbrella term "language"

209

are, one and all, things that are NOT language *as such* at all but which ARE other (kinds of) things. Dissolving this Last of the Great Myths is the *aqua regia* for dissolving the myth embraced by so many 'experts' today, the myth that science is social. The 'collective-enterprise' nature of advanced knowledge is a classic case of appearance vs reality, and not till the illusory appearance is overcome will the overcomer advance to true knowledge of the reality. Still, so powerful are the twin illusions that sounds and ink marks have ghosts of meaning lurking inside them and that we get knowledge from others via those sounds and ink marks, that even Simone Weil was taken in. Once, when she was searching for 'symbols' to explain why she felt God wanted her to wait yet a while longer before accepting baptism, she latched onto this fantasy:

> By one of those laws of nature, which God himself respects, since he has willed them from all eternity, there are two languages that are quite distinct although made up of the same words; there is the collective language and there is the individual one.

Adopting this proposal was not one of her best decisions. But at least it allowed her to defend her conviction that, though the collective body called "church" might be using a 'collective language' as a "guardian of dogma," she had to be a guardian of the 'individual language' she used for the thoughts God had given her as an individual. She believed firmly in intelligence and refused to surrender her insights. "The world needs saints who have genius," she wrote in 5-26-42 letter, though she then added:

> If no one consents to take any notice of the thoughts that, though I cannot explain why, have settled in so inadequate a being as myself, they will be buried with me ... Happily God can quite easily send not only the same thoughts, supposing they are good, but a great many much better ones to somebody who is unblemished and capable of serving him.

The link between the myth that language as such exists and the myth that science has a more than *apparent* social dimension is apparent as soon as we probe deeply into the question: "Do I learn from others by ESP or do I learn from them via LANGUAGE?" Who is there who would answer "By ESP"? Yet "Via language" can't be correct unless there is such a thing as language as such. There isn't. The question is a trap. It assumes what is not true, namely, that language as such exists.

Many controversies have raged over pseudo-problems arising from the myth of language. Thinkers in this century argued at length over a contrast similar to that made by Simone: Which is more authoritative, the FORMulas or FORMal terminology used by 'scientific communities' and 'churches' to propose supposedly-PERMANENT truths or the INformal expressions of individuals' ORDINARY expressions of passing thoughts? They have also argued over the question, "Is all language a social product or could someone have a private, one-person language?" In each case, the true answer is "Neither."

Just as a kiss is just a kiss, utterly distinct from what is going on in the kissers' souls, sounds are just sounds. The myths that either the touching of moist lips or the sounds they utter are MORE are on a par with other confusion-sowing myths. Worst, of course, is the fantasy that such word-dispensers as sacred scribes and popes, parents and teachers, physicists and chemists, poets and novelists, therapists and spiritual directors, etc., perform quite distinct roles. Nonsense! They are, one and all, never more than *outside* environmental catalysts for the learning going on *inside* the learners.

Why is obvious. Just as those naively regarded as their audiences use the same kind of ears to hear "words" with, the same kind of eyes to read "words" with, the same kind of minds to interpret "words" with, the dispensers of "words" use the same kind of neurons to carry the same kind of signals to the same kind of muscles, the same kind of vocal apparatus to make the same kind of heard sounds, and the same kind of hands to make the same kind of seen ciphers. The better thinking required here is the kind that tackles the hard questions about thoughts and 'words' raised in Chapter One. The first thing that successful rethinking will eliminate will be the myth that words *as such* exist. ("As such" means "as distinct from everything else.")

Nevertheless, God has made it appear AS IF we learn FROM words. And it is essential to find the right place for that major AS-IF in our overall view of everything. James did. At age fifty, he made the following induction and passed it on—in 'words'—to teachers who mostly taught with 'words':

211

In all these later studies, verbal material is the vehicle by which the mind thinks. The abstract conceptions of physics and sociology may, it is true, be embodied in visual or other images of phenomena, but they need not be so; and the truth remains that, after adolescence has begun, "words, words, words," must constitute a large part, and an always larger part as life advances, of what the human being has to learn. This is so even in the natural sciences, so far as these are causal and rational, and not merely confined to description [sic]. So I go back to what I said awhile ago apropos of verbal memorizing. The more accurately words are learned, the better; if only the teacher make sure that what they signify is also understood. (From Talk 13 of *Talks to Teachers*.)

Take a few minutes to review your memories of your past. Think how different your life would be if there had been none of these things called "words." Imagine everyone not only Trappist-wordless but statue-gestureless as well. Imagining that will help you learn that all your learning has been strictly first-hand. You began life in a crib, not knowing how to interpret those EXTRA sounds the speakers were making, only hearing them along with such NATURE'al sounds as sucking lips, ringing telephones, soft footfalls, snapping light-switches, squeaking door-hinges, and so on, i.e., other sounds you also had to learn how to interpret.

The miracle is that those EXTRA sounds were eventually accompanied by more and more distinct thoughts. Later on, without being taught how to learn anything, you learned about your immediate world and learned enough English—or French or German or Chinese, etc.—to talk about it. And to seemingly learn even more about that world by means of others' words. At least that was the case with me. The learning I did consisted of the thoughts that came with those non-word 'words' or sounds that I had to hear with the same ears I heard any other sounds, sounds I had to interpret the same way I had to interpret all other sounds, namely, via the thoughts that came to me.

But they aren't all true thoughts. Like everyone else, I had to decide which of the thoughts and/or interpretations that came to me were true and which were false. Why? Because as many nutty thoughts came 'via' the words or via the 'words' as sensible ones. James asked:

"Who can count all the silly fancies, the grotesque suppositions, the utterly irrelevant reflections he makes in the course of a day?" To which we must add that, besides the 'silly fancies,' etc., that saunter into our minds all by themselves, there are the ones that come to us as we listen to friends rant and rave, watch TV talk-shows, scan the rags at the supermarket check-out, sit in college classrooms, and so on.

The task of the re-thinker anxious to solve nature's riddle is to continue sifting through the stream of thoughts that come his or her way in order to choose those which will fit together into a grand unified theory of everything. The way Newton, for instance, sifted through the thoughts that seemingly came from books on Ptolemy's and Copernicus' cosmologies, Descartes' theories, Kepler's mixed bags, Aristotle's and Galileo's physics, in order to assemble a cosmic, absolute-space geography with a linear, absolute-time history. The way you must sift through the further thoughts will now come your way. Apparently via the non-word 'words' that follow.

B. Scientific Proof That You Have No Body.

James' revolt against monist idealism. It is not well-enough known that Wm. James' *The Principles of Psychology* is a thought-experiment far more important and broad in scope than any of Einstein's. He wrote it toward the latter end of the nineteenth century when most, or at least a large number, of the academics in charge of teaching 'psychology' in colleges and universities in the United States embraced some version or other of Hegel's monistic idealism. One way to vaguely generalize about those academics is to say they embraced the theory that, not only is 'physical reality' something non-physical (Berkeley held this), but individual human persons are REALLY anonymous cells in some larger Only Truly Real Being (Berkeley didn't hold this). Such teachings drive a psychological wedge BETWEEN our 'unthinking,' day-to-day life where our families, friends, and circumstances have a paramount importance for us, like those of Phineas Gage or Broca's aphasics had for them, AND 'higher' thoughts about a universe in which our roles are so insignificant that we could be replaced without the universe ever feeling the difference.

James was passionately convinced of the importance of our individual everyday lives. Hence he began *The Principles* with a preface in which he wrote:

> I have kept close to the point of view of natural science throughout the book. Every natural science assumes certain data uncritically, and declines to challenge the elements between which its own 'laws' obtain, and from which its own deductions are carried on. Psychology, the science of finite individual minds, assumes as its data (i)*thoughts* and *feelings*, and (2)*a physical world* in time and space with which they coexist and which (3)*they know*. (PP I:v-vi)

A mature science must end, tho, by becoming critical about its uncritical 'data.' Hence, when James sat down to write the *Principles'* abridgement known as *Psychology: Briefer Course*, he emphasized the fragile underpinnings of his 'science.' On page one of the *Briefer Course's* first chapter, he wrote:

> Psychology is to be treated as a natural science in this book . . . We have a lot of beginnings of knowledge made in different places, and kept separate from each other merely for practical convenience' sake, until with later growth they may run into one body of Truth. These provisional beginnings of learning we call "the Sciences" in the plural. In order not to be unwieldy, every such science has to stick to its own arbitrarily-selected problems, and to ignore all others. Every science thus accepts certain data unquestioningly, leaving it to the other parts of Philosophy to scrutinize their significance and truth. All the natural sciences, for example, in spite of the fact that farther reflection leads to Idealism, assume that a world of matter exists altogether independently of the perceiving mind. Mechanical Science assumes this matter to have "mass" and to exert "force," defining these terms merely phenomenally, and not troubling itself about certain unintelligibilities which they present on nearer reflection. Motion similarly . . .

Unfortunately, the success of physicists and physiologists in discovering models that make it possible to 'put order' into the world of sensed phenomena has been so spectacular that students are now taught the models without being taught that the models, if true, utterly undermine our growing-up, naive-realist ideas about our experience of the world. As a result, the majority haven't a clue to what James meant by "idealism" or why anyone so intelligent as he was would refer to the physical world as something 'assumed.' This means that, as a result, *the majority of today's graduates are poorly educated.*

This poor education explains why such vast numbers of today's college graduates read James' and others' theories about the dependence of consciousness on the brain so uncritically, that is, AS IF he believed the thoughts common-sensically evoked by his words are literally true. Though he did not believe in the literal existence of brains any more than Berkeley or Kant did, he adopted its existence as a central AS-IF premise for his natural-science psychology.

> The fact that the brain is the one immediate bodily condition of the mental operations is indeed so universally admitted nowadays that I need spend no more time in illustrating it, but will simply postulate it and pass on. The whole remainder of the book will be more or less of a proof that the postulate was correct. (PP I:4)

But only correct 'pragmatically,' that is, in the sense that the belief will 'work' well enough to fit a vast range of our experiences, so long as we do not do that "nearer reflection" that "leads to Idealism." This means that, despite the current progress in mapping out the correlation between experience and the merely-apparent, merely-assumed, merely-phenomenal brain, there can be no mature psychology which does not come to grips with the fact that it is a deception. Which does not come to grips, that is, with the facts that show why naive realism—the view that there are enduring physical bodies AND THAT WE CAN SEE AND FEEL THEM—is an illusion.

Naive realism will normally seem to be self-evidently true. That is, to NOT be an illusion. No matter how often we run through the evidence which reveals that Kohler is right and that this "world" is not 'the' world. The moment we let our attention lapse is the moment our disbelief is re-suspended, the vast push of a lifetime's worth of acquired habits takes over again, and our old naive-realist thoughts regain the upper hand. It takes strenuous effort—we must almost force ourselves at first—to pretend that Kohler may just be right. Even though Einstein came to regard the task as a "relatively simple" one. At least that's what he wrote in a comment about Bertrand Russell:

> The overcoming of naive realism has been relatively simple. In his introduction to his volume, *An Inquiry Into Meaning and Truth*, Russell has characterised this process in a marvelously concise fashion:
>
> "We all start from 'naive realism,' i.e., the doctrine that things are what they seem. We think that grass is green, that stones are hard, and that snow is cold. But physics assures us that the greenness of grass, the hardness of stones, and the coldness of snow are not the greenness, hardness, and coldness that we know in our experience, but something very different. The observer, when he seems to himself to be observing a stone, is really, if physics is to be believed, observing the effects of the stone upon himself. Thus science seems to be at war with itself; when it most means to be objective, it finds itself plunged into subjectivity against its will. Naive realism leads to physics, and physics, if true, shows that naive realism is false. Therefore naive realism, if true, is false; therefore it is false."
>
> Apart from their masterful formulation these lines say something which had never previously occurred to me. For, superficially considered, the mode of thought in Berkeley and Hume seems to stand in contrast to the mode of thought in the natural sciences. However, Russell's just cited remark uncovers a connection.

The best way to understand how modern physics and physiology connect with Berkeley and Hume is to take note of Russell's "We all start from 'naive realism,'" that is, from the situation so graphically described by Kohler. Recall your inner model of the world out here.

On the continents of this planet there presently live some five and a half billion two-legged, upright-walking humans like yourself. We communicate with each other in a variety of ways that, at first, we pay no particular attention to. Once we do take a closer look, however, we discover that all except those who are blind and deaf must rely on two things that permeate our atmosphere: *air* and *light*. They are the keys to prying apart the two halves of Kohler's picture of every human's situation: the experience of a "world" that is private and an unexperienced, hypothesized world behind it.

First, *air* is needed for the most common form of communication. It serves as the carrier of the *sounds* speakers make and listeners hear. Even the ancients recognized that sounds do not travel instantly. It takes a certain amount of time for the air to carry vibrations from a speaker's vocal chords to a listener's ears so that, by the time one sound has covered the distance, a new sound is on its way. Even after the source of the journeying sounds has stopped vibrating, the air will carry the continually weakening sounds outwards. That is why, in an area enclosed by sound-reflecting walls, echoing sounds will reverberate even after the vocal chords have fallen silent. Most of us fail to notice the tell-tale time-lapses between what we see and what we hear—e.g., the burst of color from a July-fourth rocket and the exploding sound, the contact of the bat with the baseball and the delayed crack of the bat, or the flash of lightning and the rumble of distant thunder—to be alert to them. The time-lapses are *experienced facts* that fit conveniently into the physics-text's thesis that sound-waves take roughly a second to travel every thousand feet of distance that separate the listener's eardrums from the arriving sound-waves' cause. When there is no carrier to conduct the waves from the source to the ear, as is the case in bell-jar or outer-space vacuums, the listener will hear nothing. The unequivocal conclusions are simple. We do not hear the *causes* of the sounds we hear, and all of the sounds are *effects* that, *at the moment we hear them*, are flush up against us. So much for the first of our alleged 'distance' senses, hearing. Perhaps overcoming its deceptions is, after all, relatively simple.

At least in comparison with the deceptive nature of what we see. Sight, the other misnamed 'distance' sense, poses the greatest challenge for those committed to the examined life of a rethinker. We rely almost entirely on facts connected with *what we SEE* in order to discover that

217

we cannot FEEL anything distant like the stars, that we cannot TASTE the apple even though it is an inch away from our mouth, that we do not SMELL the cigarette smoke until it is puffed across the table and reaches our nostrils, and that the rocket's HEARD burst trails its red glare the way the crack of the bat follows its meeting with the ball. This makes it all the more difficult to accede to the fact that *what we SEE* are NOT stars, apples, smoke, rockets, bats, balls, or anything that is not just as flush up against us as the other sensed phenomena are. So powerful is the illusion that we see separate birds, planes, even people dressed as Superman at Halloween time, rather than a TVF* or a single visual spread of colors, the illusion that those separate 'things' we see moving towards or away from us are only colors occupying more or less of our total visual field, and the illusion that the colors we see only seem to change, rather than actually changing . . . so powerful are these illusions that it is easy to only seem to adjust our theories to experience, i.e., to the empirical evidence, rather than to actually do so. The dodges—invoking the word "seem" over and over, designating the experiences "illusions," etc.—that have been proposed to escape the truth are enormously varied and often rather persuasive at first. But anything less than absolute exactness here becomes a severe handicap on learning the whole truth about everything else. (*For Total Visual Field)

That is why the theory that there exists an utterly invisible, intangible entity named "light" becomes so useful as a key for rethinking. The question, "Is light's or color's existence more certain?", becomes pivotal. For anyone who has never heard of *light*, that "stuff" alleged to travel at the unbelievable speed of 186,000 miles per second (more than seven times around the equator in the second it takes sound to travel a fifth of a mile), the idea that things do not have colors—e.g., that roses aren't red, the sky is never blue, snow isn't white, and rainbows are colorless—seems preposterous. That is because we all start with the naive realism that Kohler rightly describes as containing countless internal contradictions. Yet Einstein, in this century, put seeing on a par with hearing when he laid down as the basis for his theory of relativity the finite speed of light, a postulate which leads to the conclusion that we can no more see what is distant than we can hear what is distant, and a postulate that has led many to also conclude that it is light rather than color that we see.

Even our everyday talk has by now become hopelessly inconsistent and contradictory. For instance, when we were learning how to use our crayons, each of which had one and only one color, we discovered that certain ones could be used together to make additional colors. If we wanted to make black, we could mix all the colors together. If we wanted to have white snow appear in our picture, we left the area blank, that is, we didn't put any color there. And, if we ran out of green, we could use blue and yellow crayons instead. Later, in physics class, it was explained to us that we had it just backwards: white is the presence of *all* the colors and black is the *absence* of all color. Yet, when we go to the store to buy a shirt and ask which colors the shirts come in, we'd laugh if the clerk told us "We have some with all the colors, some with no color, and some that absorb all the light except the blue and yellow frequencies" rather than "We have shirts in white, black, and green." (In fact, if we asked for "a shirt with all the colors," we'd expect a Hawaian shirt.) We prefer movies in color rather than in black and white (and all shades of gray), but surely "black and white movies" are merely a species under the genus "movies in color." Calling black "no color, only the total absence of color" seems, common-sensically, to be nonsense that is just the reverse of John Cage's calling 4'33—in which the performer makes no sounds—"a musical composition" or Ryle's calling the keeping of one's vocal chords from moving "*talking* silently." And this sample of semantic problems comes from the sound-making habits of 'English' speakers only. D.E. Brown's *Human Universals* explores some of the difficulties confronted by anthropologists who study other peoples' usage. How can we decide, from what people SAY they see, what they DO see? Or whether they see color at all?

There is only one way to sort all of the apparent confusion out, and that is by using Ockham's Razor with utter precision in order to create an overall model that has just enough items to fit the phenomena. We need a model that we can use to answer all of the following connected questions: WHAT do I see?, WHERE IS what I see?, What CAUSES the things I see, What is SEEING?, WHO is doing this seeing?, WHAT KIND OF BEING must I be in order to do it as well as everything else *I* do?, and so on. Why the first-person, perpendicular pronoun? Because the only phenomena anyone can have first-hand certainty about are those s/he personally experiences. The top requirement for a suitable model is that it fit all of one's own experience. In this case, all of one's own experience of colored things or things' colors.

"We all start from naive realism." Because I never would have had it revealed to me that my early naive-realist package of beliefs had to be replaced by a better set of beliefs except by virtue of "words, words, words," it is convenient to link this revolution in my thinking with words about the 'words' you are reading. Note what you see and hold. Attend to its features: one color for the letters, another color surrounding them, the two colors clearly patterned in relation to each other. We have labels for each of the colors and dozens upon dozens of "language" labels to use in thinking about the patterns.

Color. Aristotle spoke for every naive, unsophisticated naive-realist when he wrote that "each sense has one kind of object which it discerns and never errs about." Hearing has sounds and sight has colors. But twenty three centuries ago, he and his contemporaries were well aware of certain problems.

Start with this piece of paper. Hold it under a red lamp, it'll turn red, just as it will turn blue, green, yellow, etc., under a blue, green, yellow, etc., lamp. Much the same way that the white movie-screen gives way to the colors projected onto it. Much the way the same area of the sky that takes on sunset-colors to one person and blue for another, the way the white cloud turns gray when it settles on us down in the valley or we climb into it along a high-mountain trail, the way a colorless diamond flashes all the colors of the rainbow when it is placed in the sunlight, and so on. What color ARE these things, really? Are the colors really IN the things? The long history of efforts by determined researchers to find a single, coherent model to accommodate ALL of the facts has left us with libraries so stuffed with word-clues to those efforts that the only thing each one of us needs to do is to select the right from the wrong pieces of the puzzle and assemble them correctly. It is easiest to discuss the puzzle's sections separately: e.g., the nature of naive-realism's 3-D bodies vis-à-vis color, the nature of light vis-à-vis color, speculation about light itself, the role of eyes and brain, and lastly the nature of color.

When we go to the library, we discover that many/most of those who write about light and color have decided that, EVEN IF the apple that fell next to Newton's head was round, was larger than either of his eyes but smaller than his head, weighed more than eyes but less than heads (i.e., has more and less mass that increases and decreases the gravitational pull), STILL it possessed no taste, smell, odor, warmth, coolness, as such. **AND NO COLOR.** Galileo, Descartes, Newton, Locke, and most physicists agree that the apple really has in it only those qualities that can be measured mathematically, i.e., shape, size, weight, motion, and that it does not have the features that cannot be measured that way. The paper in your hands, like the ink printed onto it and your hands holding it, has no color. **IF COLOR DOES EXIST** (the crucial decision), it is, like pain and tickles, an *effect* that is caused by colorless objects, the way pain is caused by needles that have no pain and tickles by feathers that don't laugh. Here's Galileo's opinion, one that had already been proposed by Plato's contemporary, Democritus:

> [. . .] that it [a piece of matter or corporeal substance] must be white or red, bitter or sweet, sounding or mute, of a pleasant or unpleasant odour, I do not perceive my mind forced to acknowledge it necessarily accompanied by such conditions; so if the senses were not the escorts, perhaps the reason or the imagination by itself would never have arrived at them. Hence I think that these tastes, odours, colours, etc., on the side of the object in which they seem to exist, are nothing else than mere names, but hold their residence solely in the sensitive body; so that if the animal were removed, every such quality would be abolished and annihilated.

Light. Light has never been seen or felt, but for centuries its existence has been postulated by careful thinkers, making it one of the oldest and most important theoretical constructs ever invented. And even though there is still utter disagreement over its real nature, certain things have become clear about it. If it exists, that is. Isaac Newton—who was born the year Galileo died—was most curious about light and did careful research with prisms that convinced him light is as colorless as apples. Different rays of light cause the 'animal' or sensitive body to have different visual sensations the way one body, a hammer, causes a different kind of pain from that caused by, say, a decayed tooth, but light as such has no color. He warned:

If at any time I speak of light and rays as coloured or endued with colours, I would be understood to speak not philosophically and properly, but grossly, and according to such conceptions as vulgar people in seeing all these experiments would be apt to frame. For the rays to speak properly are not coloured. In them there is nothing else than a certain power and disposition to stir up a sensation of this or that colour. For as sound in a bell or musical string or other sounding body, is nothing but a trembling motion, and in the air nothing but that motion propagated from the object, and in the sensorium 'tis a sense of that motion under the form of sound; so colours in the object are nothing but a disposition to reflect this or that sort of rays more copiously than the rest . . .

Later experiments eventually led to the hypothesis that particles of light—or waves of ether, as a rival hypothesis claimed—differ in mathematically measurable ways:

In Newton's day the vibratory nature of light was unknown. Red light differed from green light [sic], but this qualitative difference manifested itself as an irreducible fact for which it was impossible to account. Under the circumstances, if the observer were to rush towards a red light or move away from it, it was quite impossible for science to anticipate what effects would arise. As soon, however, as Fresnel discovered the vibratory nature of light, red light was found to differ from green light owing to its slower rate of vibration; prevision then became attainable. It was possible to anticipate that were we to approach a red lamp with sufficient speed it would appear green, that with greater speed it would also cease to appear visible. This was the celebrated Doppler-Fizeau effect, which astronomical observations soon succeeded in detecting; it is thanks to this effect that we are able to determine the radial speed of approach or of recession of the stars.

These comments from page 389 of A. d'Abro's *The Evolution of Scientific Thought* about astronomers' reliance on spectra are well explained and, above all, illustrated in *Stars*, a volume in the Time-Life Books series designated "Voyage Through the Universe."

From the time of Descartes on, close attention was being paid to what happens to light once it reaches the seer. Even before Newton, Descartes wrote a work entitled *Optics*, in which he described the role of the eyes' lenses in focusing light from various points in the environment to congruent points in the rear portion of the eye. He likewise speculated about the role of the nerves in carrying effects from inside the eye to the brain. In fact, Descartes left us a rough sketch of the various steps in the cause-effect-cause-effect chain, and later researchers have simply filled in more and more of the details. To most, it now seems clear that the final visual sensations depend on—change that! to "are correlated with"—the frequencies of the light when it is originally radiated, the atomic constitution of the various bodies which partly absorb and partly reflect it, the wavelengths of the reflected light, the pattern of light after it has passed through the eyes' lenses, the normal vs abnormal constitution of the optic portion of the seer's central nervous system, and so on.

Most of us surrender only grudgingly to the onslaught against our life-long, naive-realist thought-habits. Almost everyone finally modifies that "mass" of old opinions in some way, but—as James noted in *Pragmatism*'s second lecture—each of us "saves as much of it as he can, for in this matter of belief we are all extreme conservatives." For many years, my retreat was akin to this:

> Only the objects touching the sense organs, however, are immediately perceived through external sensation. What is immediately seen is just the object that touches the retina, what is immediately felt is the inner surface of the skin in contact with the nerve ends, what is heard immediately is only the sound within the ear, and so on. These are all objects really distinct from the knowing subject. (J. Owens, *An Elementary Christian Metaphysics*, 1963, pp.219-20.)

To this day, I cannot explain why that compromise did not satisfy me for good. It was woven tightly into an intricate grand unifying theory that had taken years to construct, one that required many years more to reconstruct. But, in late January of 1963, it suddenly came to me how wrong that compromise was. Word-wise, the compromise seemed precise. But it was built on a systematic vagueness involving what can be called "the jazz about 'as[-if]'." I came to realize that I no longer thought of color as color. I adopted the widely-used formula, "We interpret light as color." Once that systematic vagueness or equivocation was exposed to me for what it was, I began to recognize that it was a dodge. A defense mechanism against calling a spade "a spade." The question everyone today must ask themselves is:

WHAT DOES "INTERPRET X AS" MEAN?

In my case, it represented a semantic subterfuge as innocent looking as that lurking in the following, *very informative* passage (half-truths are often valuable) copied from *The Incredible Machine*, published in 1986 by the editors of *National Geographic Magazine*:

> If you say that something is green—a palm leaf, for instance—a member of the Jale tribe of New Guinea will disagree, even though his eyes are the same as yours. He will describe the leaf only in degrees of light or dark—whiteness or blackness. His language has no specific word for the color green. On the other hand, the Maori of New Zealand have scores of words for red, and use color words to describe stages of plant growth and cloud formations.
>
> The failure to label colors as we've been taught to do in our linguistic shorthand has nothing to do with so-called color blindness, which means simply that the retina is deficient in certain color receptors. It's not that the "color-blind" person can't *see* the color, because there isn't any color to see. There is no red to the rose, no yellow to the bumblebee, no green to the bean. It's all in your head. (Page 316.)

"There isn't any color to see." If so, then WHAT's "all in your head"? Whoever gets in the habit of thinking and saying what I did, namely, that bodies have no color but only light-absorbing and light-reflecting properties, that light has no color but only wave-lengths and wave-frequencies, and that we see only the "things" on our retinas, i.e., patterns of colorless light, which we "interpret AS color," has fallen into *the habit of denying the existence of color as such*. In literal terms, this means that "there isn't any color to see." That becomes clear once we ask: Is the "thing," the pattern of colorless light on the retina," the color we are visually aware of? Or is it merely something our eye, our brain, our mind, or we *interpret AS color*? That is, **AS IF** it is color, though it **IS NOT**! If bodies as such are colorless, if light-absorbing and light-reflecting properties only modify colorless light, and if there is nothing in the colorless eyes except the pattern of colorless light called "the retinal image," then color does not exist in the physical world. The pitch dark brain, inside the fortress called "the skull," has no color and does not give off phosphorescent glows that are looked at by some ghostly being inhabiting it. Nor, of course, is there any sound, any odor, any taste, heat or cold, any pain or tickles. Just colorless, odorless, tasteless, heatless, coldless, painless, etc., bodies, colorless light, noiseless movements of air molecules, and so on.

What came to me was that Aristotle had been right all along about seeing color, but also that I was no longer in agreement that the color is outside of me. When I looked at a page of print such as it must seem to you this is, it was easy for me to get in the habit of ignoring what I saw—the shaped and arranged *black* of the ink surrounded by the *white* of the paper, the *flesh-color* of my hands, etc.—and to merely THINK my way from the unseen overhead bulb radiating invisible light that travels invisibly to the unseen page and thence to my eyes, where it passes through invisible lenses, strikes invisible retinas, stimulates invisible nerve-impulses that journey invisibly through invisible optic nerves to an invisible brain where SOMETHING (what? my brain?, my mind?, me?) interprets THEM (what? unseen nerve-impulses?) as if THEY? ARE! color, though they are not. All of THEM are things I canNOT SEE but can only THINK about. My compromise converted theory-laden perception into perceptionless theorizing. Much the same way all idealists except Berkeley convert what is seen into what is thought.

My conversion away from that dodge was *in part* a return to a robust naive realism, but only in part, at least in the sense that I reaffirmed *my early confidence in the existence of the colors I saw, the sounds I heard, the pains and tickles I felt, and so on.* Bertrand Russell reported an experience that bore some resemblance to mine. He had, for a time, converted from his naive realism to idealism. Until he experienced a reconversion.

> I felt it, in fact, as a great liberation, as if I had escaped from a hot-house on to a wind-swept headland. I hated the stuffiness involved in supposing that space and time were only in my mind. I liked the starry heavens even better than the moral law, and could not bear Kant's view that the one I liked best was only a subjective figment. In the first exuberance of liberation, I became a naive realist and rejoiced in the thought that grass is really green, in spite of the adverse opinion of all philosophers from Locke onwards. I have not been able to retain this pleasing faith in its pristine vigour, but I have never again shut myself up in a subjective prison.

This temporary reconversion to naive realism by Russell, who later on accused John Watson—the same whose battle cry was "Let's be scientific!"—of being scientifically naive, took place at the end of the nineteenth century and before the explosion of nuclear physics in the one just now ending. The results have confirmed a thousandfold the claims of Galileo, Descartes, Newton, Locke, etc., that there is no resemblance whatever between three-dimensional, physical bodies and the non-physical phenomena we experience.

That is abstract, and it is important not to leave these issues disconnected from concrete experience. Since so much of your first-hand evidence for your conclusions will consist, as mine did, of apparently seeing what are apparently rows and rose of words, words, words—or of "words, words, words"—like these, found in books, it is time for every rethinker to ask: What ARE this "book" and these "words" I'm "reading"?

Common-sensically, the book, if it exists, consists of ink, printed onto paper made from cloth or wood-pulp, some binding materials, and two covers. As Locke suspected we'd learn if we had powerful enough microscopes and as Leibniz predicted we'd learn if we could make ourselves tiny enough, we've learned that what we think of AS paper and ink is neither. Under a microscope, this solid-looking paper turns into individual strands of fiber, and they—under a more powerful microscope—turn into still other things. So what's REALLY here in front of you?

The quickest way to get to the difference is to notice what most physicists believe until they begin to understand why Bohr sat on the fence with his Hegelian Both/And-ism that Einstein was right not to accept. What follow are "words" for the only *consistent* picture that has ever been proposed for whatever bodies may exist out here. Only the really bold thinkers are willing to accept it. Arthur Eddington was one of the boldest, which is why he was made the target of considerable mockery by the less bold. Here is what he wrote in *The Nature of the Physical World*:

THE DOWNFALL OF CLASSICAL PHYSICS

The Structure of the Atom. Between 1905 and 1908 Einstein and Minkowski introduced fundamental changes in our ideas of time and space. In 1911 Rutherford introduced the greatest change in our idea of matter since the time of Democritus. The reception of these two changes was curiously different. The new ideas of space and time were regarded on all sides as revolutionary; they were received with the greatest enthusiasm by some and the keenest opposition by others. The new idea of matter underwent the ordinary experience of scientific discovery; it gradually proved its worth, and when the evidence became overwhelmingly convincing it quietly supplanted previous theories. No great shock was felt. And yet when I hear to-day protests against the Bolshevism of modern science and regrets for the old-established order, I am inclined to think that Rutherford, not Einstein, is the real villain of the piece. When we compare the universe as it is now supposed to be with the universe as we had ordinarily preconceived it, the most arresting change is not the rearrangement of space and time by Einstein BUT THE DISSOLUTION OF ALL THAT WE REGARD AS MOST SOLID INTO TINY SPECKS FLOATING IN THE VOID. That gives more an abrupt jar to those who think things are more or less what they seem. The revelation by modern physics of the void within the atom is more disturbing than the revelation by astronomy of the immense void of interstellar space.

The atom is as porous as the solar system. (CAPITALS ADDED)

Rutherford described the experiment that revealed the silent, outer-space-like void inside the atom with graphic imagery. It consisted of bombarding thin gold foil with helium nuclei.

> It was almost as incredible as if you fired a 15-inch shell at a piece of tissue paper and it came back and hit you . . . When I made my calculations I saw that it was impossible to get anything of that order of magnitude unless you took a system in which the greater part of the mass of the atom was concentrated in a minute nucleus. It was then that I had the idea of an atom with a minute massive center carrying a charge.

Over and over, physicists out here—outside your stream of experience—vie with each other to dramatize the near-hollow atom. **BUT NOTE WELL!** Like Rutherford, they perform their experiments in their naive-realist mindset, and like him they normally describe the results in naive-realist terms. But their 'experienced worlds,' like yours right now, are fluffed up out of soft to glaring colors, melodious to grating sounds, fragrant to stinking odors, PLUS a sense of orientation (steady-on-our-feet-ness to wobbly dizziness), body-position-feelings (hunched over a microscope, writing at a desk, etc.), that only SEEM solid. An effort must be made to keep the Kohler-described 'world'-vs-world model in mind while, it seems, your eyes scan these rows and rose of black figures against a white background and thoughts about what's REALLY out here come to you. To situate what's in there, begin with your naive realist model, fill the space between you and the page with fast-moving (186,000 mps) light, come inside through your eyes, follow the slow-moving impulses through your optic nerves to your brain, and finally enter the 'world' made of stereopticon colors (these!), wrap-around sounds, and body-feelings, a kind of closed-off balloonful of sense-data near the unseen, gnat-like a-toms out here that you think-together under "my brain."

The space in the atom outside the nucleus is enormous compared with the size of the nucleus, or with the much smaller size of an electron. In the atom of hydrogen the single electron is near the outer rim of the atom. If its nucleus were enlarged to the size of a baseball, its electron would be a speck about eight city blocks away. Actually, of course, this atomic distance is small. The diameter of a hydrogen atom is nearly 1/200,000,000 of an inch; in other words, 200,000,000 hydrogen atoms could be placed one next the other in an inch. Relative to the nucleus or to the electron, however, the atomic space is prodigious. (Selig Hecht, *Explaining the Atom.*)

From that day in 1911, when Rutherford described the inside of the atom, our whole idea of matter has been changed. The atom, formerly likened to a solid billiard ball, has become a transparent sphere of emptiness, thinly populated with electrons. The substance of the atom has shrunk to a core of unbelievable smallness; enlarged a thousand million times, an atom would be about the size of a football, but its nucleus would still be hardly visible—a mere speck of dust at the center. (Otto R. Frisch, *Atomic Physics Today.*)

The new atomic model was definitely planetary. The surprising thing of the planetary model was how small the nucleus appeared. If the golf ball-sized atom was once again inflated, this time to the size of a modern sports arena or football stadium, the nucleus of the atom would be the size of a grain of rice. (Fred A. Wolf, *Taking the Quantum Leap.*)

Our mental pictures are drawn from our visual perception of the world around us. But the world as perceived by the eye is itself exposed as an illusion when scrutinized on the microscopic scale. A bar of gold, though it looks solid, is composed almost entirely of empty space: The nucleus of each of its atoms is so small that if one atom were enlarged a million billion times, until its outer electron shell was as big as greater Los Angeles, its nucleus would still be only about the size of a compact car parked downtown. (The electron shells would be zones of insubstantial heat lightning, each a mile thick, separated by many miles of space.) (Timothy Ferris, *Coming of Age in the Milky Way.*)

Now how do we know this is true if we can't see it? What proof have we that matter is made up of these quintillions of infinitesimal particles? Robert Millikan, one of the world's most noted physicists, said, 'We can count the exact number of molecules in any given volume with more certainty than we can count the population of a city or a state.' . . .

An atom is the smallest part of an element that can exist either alone or in combination with other particles. There are more atoms of hydrogen in a pail of water than there are drops of water in all the oceans of the world combined. So small is the diameter of an atom that half a million atoms piled, one on top of another, would not even equal the thickness of this page! The volume of the average atom is about 1.56 X 10 of a cubic inch, which means that there are approximately fifteen-thousand-six-hundred-billion-million-million atoms to a cubic inch. Of course, such a number is totally incomprehensible, yet in spite of its inconceivable minuteness, the atom is mostly empty space! Its entire mass is packed into its nucleus which, believe it or not, is one trillionth the size of the atom itself. This is very fortunate. If the atom were all nucleus without any space in it, a glass of water would weigh as much as a two-ton truck and you would weigh as much as half a dozen locomotives . . .

Because they are so incredibly close to the nucleus these electrons make approximately 10,000,000,000,000,000 revolutions around it every second . . . (Jerome S. Meyer, *The ABC of Physics.*)

In every single drop of sea water, there are fifty billion atoms of gold. One would have to distill two thousands tons of such water to get one single gram of gold . . .

If we magnify the atom to the size of a football, the nucleus would be but a speck in its center and the electron, still invisible, would be revolving around its surface. Similarly, if we picture the atom as large as New York's Empire State Building, the electron, the size of a marble, would be spinning around the building seven million times every millionth of a second. There is relatively more empty space in the atom than between the planets in the solar system. (Bernard Jaffe, *Crucibles: The Story of Chemistry*.)

At any point, we can switch back to our common-sense mindset in order to check on what James wrote, viz., that much of our learning comes from words, words, words. Have you done all the experiments that convinced Lavoisier that Priestley was wrong about phlogiston or only read about them? Done all of Dalton's experiments to see if exact weighing indicates matter is added or taken away from bodies in exact steps, one whole step—for one whole particle—at a time, never just in half-steps or third-steps, etc., or just read about them? Done the thousands of eye-wearying experiments R. Millikan did on 58 oil-drops over a 60-day period to determine the mass of an electron, or just read about them? I've just read about them. But the library is filled with personal testimonies of presumably honest researchers of direct observations of their visual data, plus cues and clues to the subsequent thinking exercised by thousands to build up what D.L. Anderson's *The Discovery of the Electron* refers to as "the whole web of modern experimental and theoretical physics."

The same Eddington provided a vivid picture of the modern form of schizophrenia most have developed, R.D. Laing-wise, to handle what drives us naive realists crazy when we first come upon them, namely, the massive number of facts which show that our naive-realist system is *internally incoherent*. We develop two contradictory views of all bodies.

I have settled down to the task of writing these lectures and have drawn up my chairs to my two tables. Two tables! Yes; there are duplicates of every object about me—two tables, two chairs, two pens.

This is not a very profound beginning to a course which ought to reach transcendent levels of scientific philosophy. But we cannot touch bedrock immediately; we must scratch a bit at the surface of things first. And whenever I begin to scratch the first thing I strike is—my two tables.

One of them has been familiar to me from earliest years. It is a commonplace object of that environment which I call the world. How shall I describe it? It has extension; it is comparatively permanent; it is coloured; above all it is *substantial*. By substantial I do not merely mean that it does not collapse when I lean upon it; I mean that it is constituted of "substance" and by that word I am trying to convey to you some conception of its intrinsic nature. It is a *thing*; not like space, which is a mere negation; nor like time, which is—Heaven knows what! But that will not help you to my meaning because it is the distinctive characteristic of a "thing" to have this substantiality, and I do not think substantiality can be described better than by saying that it is the kind of nature exemplified by an ordinary table. And so we go round in circles. After all if you are a plain common-sense man, not too much worried with scientific scruples, you will be confident that you understand the nature of an ordinary table. I have even heard of plain men who had the idea that they could better understand the mystery of their own nature if scientists would discover a way of explaining it in terms of the easily comprehensible nature of a table.

Table No.2 is my scientific table. It is a more recent acquaintance and I do not feel so familiar with it. It does not belong to the world previously mentioned—that world which spontaneously appears around me when I open my eyes, though how much of it is objective and how much subjective I do not here consider. It is part of a world which in more devious ways has forced itself on my attention. My scientific table is mostly emptiness. Sparsely scattered in that emptiness are numerous electric charges rushing about with great speed; but their combined bulk amounts to less that a billionth of the bulk of the table itself.

Whoever wants to incorporate into their second or "professional" theory ALL the facts must work to get the habit of switching with knowledgeable ease from the "solid" view of bodies to the "zillion gnats" view Eddington describes in these opening words from *The Nature of the Physical World*. Common sense assures us that, had Newton shirked

232

the work needed to become knowledgeable about Ptolemy, Copernicus, etc., he would have had no Pasteur-readiness enabling him to pounce on the brainstorms that came his way, no ability to trace out their implications, no success in weeding out the wrong ones so as to emerge with the final Total-Space, Evenly-Flowing-Time framework within which to locate the bodies that exist and to describe their doings with his exquisitely precise large-scale "laws" (descriptions of what they've done that serve as predictions of what they'll continue to do). To climb onto his or any other researcher's shoulders, we must work to learn their thought-habits.

Words, learning, meanings. The above analyses must be applied to reading, i.e., to whatever the complex goings-on are that you are presently engaged in. You must learn to analyse "looking across and down rose and rose of words," both commonsensically and more accurately. That is, to translate the naive-realist description into true-fact understanding. For instance, it is difficult to imagine anything better to explain why "The **DEFINITION** Approach" cannot work. We ask "How does Eddington define 'table'?" His answer? "Two ways!" It will require ever-cautious reading to know when is which. This lesson is one each of us must learn for our self, because—no matter how many *other* people have learned it (millions) or how long ago it was known (Aristotle pointed out that, once we begin defining one word with two others that need two more apiece to define, it balloons into an impossible situation, so that we have to invoke such alternatives as intuition of Forms or of First Principles or of Universals or an active Cosmic Mind's assistance)—it won't make us former-infants smart. Nor unaware professors with their Ph.D.'s right. We must look behind others' words for their world-models and their most-basic-beliefs systems. A meaning is always someone's thought. The meanings of any speaker/writer putting out words are the thoughts s/he has at the moment of putting them out, just as the meanings the audient/reader understands are the thoughts that accompany the "words" s/he senses.

Whoever re-reads any of the preceding pages of this or earlier chapters will now understand that there have been constant shifts away from the naive-realist third of common sense to various other models—therefore constant semantic-switches in meanings—and back again to the naive-realist model which, at present, remains our "lingua franca," our Esperanto, our "common tongue," needed to deny that there are any tongues, either the ones we imagine ourselves to taste with or the ones we imagine ourselves able to communicate with. What you see here as you continue "reading" will SEEM like paper with inked figures on it. It's not.

Con-ceptualizing the above. Whoever invented "concept" was, we can guess, struck by the fact that A WHOLE LOT OF THOUGHTS (or thought-about "things") can be "captured together" WITH A SINGLE THOUGHT. Others, too, noticed our ability to think-together many things at once, and—for variety's sake—re-captured their insights with new concepts: synthesize, integrate, interrelate, relate, correlate, pull together, etc. What concept will help us conceptualize the above? "**A CORNUCOPIA OF READINGS.**" Each of the authors referred to here is/was a lone individual who experienced a personalized life-movie, a private "world." Each learned ways to create a professional map-plus-theory to replace, during on-duty *thinking*, the original common-sense map-theory that s/he continued to use for off-duty *thinking*. Each later "writer" had more options because there were more books in the library than when the "writers" of earlier books visited it. We, in our turn, can use any of the aboves' books to learn how they *read the text* of experience. Then to will which reading shall be ours.

For instance, to choose how we'll answer "AM I or HAVE I a body?" Descartes asked that and decided he had one that was one with him. Now we know there's no suitable body to have OR to be.

Conclusions re the body. And brain. When we put together the facts about which we can be certain from direct experience and rely on brute logic to draw the conclusion, this is the conclusion. If bodies—and bars of gold, drops of water, tables, etc.—exist, they are not what we sense. Therefore, their existence can only be inferred. But the experiences upon which modern physics is based prove that no bodies, bars of gold, etc., exist. Nothing larger than subatomic particles exist 'out there' where we think the bodies, bars, etc., are. Imagining that many separate subatomic particles ever 'make up' one thing is a clear example of 'not controlling the imagination.' This applies especially to our idea of the brain. Imagining, as materialists do, that a billion separated, unconscious neurons are a unified brain that produces consciousness is like imagining that eleven unconscious football players stretched out in a line constitute one conscious team.

Interlude. The gravest DANGER in mis-thinking about thinking is that, since it is a central piece of evidence for deciding the true answer to "What is a person?", an error about thinking and thoughts may lead us to mis-think, as Hume did, the purpose of our existence. Hume concluded that our thinking is different only in degree from what animals can do, hence he concluded that we are animals. True, we'd be unique ones, just as lions and mice are. But, like them, we'd be animals nonetheless. Most people are convinced that animals are not immortal; hence, if "person" means only "more complex animal," then neither are we, which means we have only a certain amount of time for completing whatever plans we plan to complete. But, if we have no bodies, it means we should begin thinking about what we expect to be doing after the brief sundown referred to as "our death."

There is no question about the fact that people think very differently about people. In the early 1970's, *Psychology Today* published a series of interviews by Sam Keen, later published as *Voices and Visions*. One interviewee *thought* "We do not *have* bodies, we *are* our bodies." Roberto Assagioli *thought* the opposite:

> Often a crisis in life deprives a person of the function or role with which he has identified: an athlete's body is maimed, a lover's beloved departs with a wandering poet, a dedicated worker must retire. Then the process of disidentification is forced on one and a solution can only come by a process of death and rebirth in which the person enters into a broader identity . . . [This process] involves practicing awareness and affirming: I *have* a body, but I *am not* my body. I *have* emotions, but I *am not* my emotions. I *have* a job, but I *am not* my job . . . , etc.

Passions run high on this question. Our very lives and values are at stake. Which explains why the Greeks' "Know thyself!"—advice about thinking ("Know!") and what to think about ("Thy self!")—is such wise advice. In the words of Sir Conan Doyle, or was it Sherlock Holmes?, we must be ready to discover that, after eliminating the impossible, the initially implausible is what's true. At first the truths about our bodies which, thanks to the hard efforts of so many curious (re)searchers, are now available to us, seem just *too astonishing* to be possible. Only a love of truth, whether for our own or others' sake, will sustain us in attending to thousands of DETAILS in order to gain confidence that they fit these rather than those GENERAL principles.

Attention. Simone Weil learned well the virtue William James called the education *par excellence*: improvement in one's power of attention. She wrote "Reflections on the Right Use of School Studies With a View to the Love of God." It is about alertness, about attentiveness, i.e., the Pasteur-like preparedness of the kind that animals, lacking the theories needed for ANY theory-laden perceiving, are utterly incapable of. In it she describes that "waiting for whatever may come" alertness that makes "Waiting for God" an apt title for her brief autobiography. But in *Waiting for God*, she allows us to see that she also valued the more narrowly-focussed, "muscular concentration" type of attention.

> Last summer, doing Greek with T____, I went through the Our Father word for word in Greek. We promised each other to learn it by heart. . . . some weeks later, as I was turning over the pages of the Gospel, I said to myself that since I had promised to do this thing and it was good, I ought to do it. I did it. The infinite sweetness of the Greek text so took hold of me that for several days I could not stop myself from saying it over all the time. A week afterward I began the vine harvest. I recited the *Our Father* in Greek every day before work, and I repeated it very often in the vineyard.
>
> Since that time I have made a practice of saying it through once each morning with absolute attention. If during the recitation my attention wanders or goes to sleep, in the minutest degree, I begin again until I have once succeeded in going through it with absolutely pure attention.

We need both. Attention to doggedly study, say, the jots and tittles of what a Freud or Skinner have to say, lest we mis-understand what they really meant by what they really said. Then attention to the jots and tittles of what James and Rogers have to say, lest the same. It takes close attention to notice whose theories are best attuned to ALL of the evidence, attentiveness to make us open to critical, mind-changing evidence. Whether to an ugly fact that slays a theory we find so beautiful or to a beautiful fact that vindicates a view we've always considered ugly.

C. Be Practical, But Do It Wisely!

Fictions. Most names do not stand for real things, only for 'things' that exist in our imagination. That is one of the chief lessons of physics. The things we think of as the universe's furniture—stars, planets, trees, chairs, books, hands, etc.—exist only in our imaginations. That coin has another side. Until the learner has ideas for real things, s/he will have no use for their names. Thus, only recently have we had such names as "protons," "neutrons," "electrons," and "photons." Still, even after we have understood such facts, the thinking we do in our day-to-day lives will continue to revert back to our naive-realist model and related fictions. Recognizing that fact is the first step in being practical. Or pragmatic. And doing so wisely.

There is a good reason why James was attracted to "pragmatism" as a name for his thinking. He wanted to prove that good thinking should make a difference. James wanted us to ask "What concrete difference will an idea's being true make in any one's actual life?" His pragmatist theory grew out of his desire to recognize and pay tribute to the value of the day-to-day thinking of ordinary folk who, though they have little leisure for highly technical, abstract theorizing, do an awful lot of thinking. But the thinking that he did about the relative values of day-to-day, common-sense theorizing and highly technical, 'expert' thinking was no ordinary thinking. He had mastered the basics of all the theories about thinking to be found in the library, he had gathered what he regarded as the best ideas from each theory, and he had woven them into a highly original tapestry of his own.

Consequently, James' works are difficult to understand well. On the surface, his words suggest thoughts that seem perfectly clear and down-to-earth. But the surface appearances are deceptive, a fact that becomes instantly clear as soon as we ask a simple question about the basic premise of his natural-science psychology: "What did he think the brain is?" His answer: "A fiction of popular speech." What he meant will become clear only when we recognize that James lived on the borderland between two radically incompatible mindsets: the naive-realist one which regards the biology-lab's pickle-jar'd brains as visible and tangible realities and the phenomenalist one which translates "lab," "jar," and "brain" into things on a par with the color-image-and-sound "things" experienced by a movie-goer. *His own theories were radical in the extreme.* They were as Uncommon-sensical as those of Berkeley, recently accused of having a "power to believe in the incredible" that is "one of the wonders of the philosophical world." It was that uncommon sophistication in James' habitual thinking that made him open to thoughts that less-sophisticated critics criticized him for.

What a revolution would occur if the dogmatic materialism so fervently believed in by so many were replaced by James' wiser pragmatism. In an 1898 lecture, he invited his audients to do just what Plato invited readers of his *Republic*, Bk. VII, to do:

> Suppose, for example, that the whole universe of material things—the furniture of earth and choir of heaven—should turn out to be a mere surface-veil of phenomena, hiding and keeping back the world of genuine realities . . . ("Human Immortality.")

Having posed that supposition, James went on to his favorite topic: experience. Imagine a world in which conscious experience is the prime reality. The amount of it may be enormously greater than we imagine, even constantly increasing: "When one man wakes up, or one is born, another does not have to go to sleep, or die, in order to keep the consciousness of the universe in constant quantity." That said, he turned his audients' thoughts to spiritual reality: "There seems no formal limit to the positive increase of being in spiritual respects." The final sentence in this lecture was a response to those who thought he was too open-minded: letting them dictate what is possible (or IMpossible) "would be letting blindness lay down the law to sight."

How can we imitate James' wise pragmatism? First, of course, by leaving the illusory safety of our naive realism in order to begin dreaming of all the unseen things in heaven and earth that Horatio didn't. And then by learning how to fit 100% of the ninety-five percent of all our thinking, viz., 100% of our off-duty naive-realist thinking, into the five percent of our on-duty professional thinking, that is, by learning how the entire range of our naive-realist experience can be REunderstood within the framework of really true thoughts, lest our final theory leave out even some of the things Horatio HAD dreamt of. Wise pragmatism can succeed only one way: by using *OCKHAM'S RAZOR* to expose reifications and/or shorthand for what they are in order to work our way to certainty about what we're not dreaming of.

Concepts (again), but Useful!, Often Indispensable. Paradoxically, the best way to apply Ockham's Razor is by using a fiction. The useful fiction in question is the one that held my imagination captive for many years. It goes by the name of "concept." The basic thinking behind "concepts" was explained in Chapter One. Its inspiration was the recognition that the things that seem best at helping us remember unseen things are seen things that resemble or are similar to the unseen ones. It is a short step from believing that we have mental replicas of previously experienced things—images of books, ideas of print on pages, concepts of words such as "words," generalized universals of all words in general—to believing we can have concepts of things that no longer exist, don't yet exist, and won't ever exist: e.g., the Garden of Eden (or was it the Big Bang?), the Final Paradise (or will it be the Next Great Collapse?), and nothingness. By reflecting on such thoughts, we can begin a very useful classification of *that very useful fiction, "concepts."*

That initial classification is into two categories: concepts of realities and concepts of fictions. Only the first can be likenesses, for "likeness" names a relation, and there can be such a relation only if BOTH the concept/likeness AND the reality exist. We can have thoughts *that* some reality DID exist. In fact, an enormous amount of our thinking is about what's past. But if something no longer exists, i.e., if it has perished, there is no longer any IT, only a thought *that* it existed but no longer does so. An enormous amount of our thinking is about the future and involves much thinking about what does not yet exist, even about future states of things that exist now but in their present state. And if something does not yet exist, then there is not yet any IT, only a present thought *that* it will exist. After getting comfortable with the thought *that* we can think of non-existent (non)things as easily as we think about reality (here, a substitute 'definition' for "reality" is "whatever exists, period!"), we can begin our own mathematical measuring of concepts: (i) some are one-to-one, or one-concept-one-reality type, and (ii) others are one-to-none, or one-concept-no-reality type.

Ockham's Razor is a dangerous instrument. It is, of course, only a metaphor for particular acts of believing. Or, from another point of view, for particular acts of disbelieving. Beginning with our present mindful of concepts, we decide which we will believe do not represent anything real, that is, decide which things we will disbelieve in. This tool is dangerous in the wrong minds; too many throw out the babies with the bathwater. This has been the story behind much "psychology as a natural science" in this century. Many otherwise successful rethinkers came to discover that the arguments for concepts are faulty, decided concepts do not exist, lost confidence about images, then decided to translate all talk about consciousness to talk about brain processes or—even safer, they think—to external behaviors. While the Razor shaved well enough, it was simply applied to the wrong things. With disastrous results.

A Rule: Our Words (talk) must be made to fit our Thought.

But, to prepare ourselves to apply the Razor well, we need two more categories of possible concept-reality relations. A third class is (iii) the one-to-many, one-concept-many-realities category. James was a master at using these useful concepts without losing sight of the plural particulars they were used for. "Shorthand" is a good name for this one-to-many type. I have decided that "human race," "animal species," "scientific psychology," etc., are names for concepts that would belong to the one-to-many type if concepts existed. (I now use "fiction" to label my thoughts about them.) The fourth is the many-to-one, many-concepts-one-reality pigeonhole as essential to Newtonians as it was to the medieval schoolmen: for instance, the former use two separate concepts named "momentum" and "deceleration" for a baseball's single trajectory and many concepts named "mass," "size," and "charge" for a particle, much as the latter used concepts of distinct perfections to understand God and concepts of distinct 'metaphysical grades' to conceive a single essence.

Today's naive-science 'psychology,' like so much 'philosophy,' is in desperate need of trimming. The Ockham-Razoring psychologist has a task that's a simple one to describe, a gigantic one to carry out. S/he must run through all the things s/he can think of by looking at all the names s/he uses, then decide which are names for what does not exist at all, which are names for concepts that match realities on a one-unified-concept-for-one-single-reality basis, which name ideas useful in thinking-together many single realities, and which are for viewing a single existent from different angles. The most important part of the task is shaving off just the right things. Sadly, today's naive-science psychology is full of fictions that, if and when anyone bothers to "reduce" them at all, get reduced in the wrong direction, i.e., in the direction of THOUGHTS about animal organisms rather than in the direction of thoughts about PERSONS and their EXPERIENCES. James' example is important because he normally went in the right direction.

Starting Point for 'Scientific' Psychology. The place to begin is where James began: with persons and their lives. Their whole lives. *The detailed stories of their whole lives.* Because this claim will be the core of much that follows, it will not hurt to highlight it:

Focus on the detailed stories of people's whole lives.

To understand anyone at whatever is the 'present' moment, learn the detailed story of that individual person's growth and development. That is the only basis on which to make an informed guess about where s/he'll go next*.

This means that it is risky to begin with his *Principles of Psychology* or textbooks titled *General Introduction to Psychology*. These inevitably suggest an atmosphere more akin to the auto repair-shop rather than the open road. They foster the illusion that experience can be disassembled into sensation, memory, cognition, emotion, etc., the way cars can be broken down into pistons, carburetors, wheels, and other parts. James didn't personally succumb to this pitfall because he kept life, the open road, in sight the whole time he composed his 'parts' manual. Not till we glimpse the broader vistas of James' overall mindscape can we understand the role of the reified "parts." Such integral wisdom as his is no easy achievement, but we may not survive unless more of us acquire something like it. (*This is where the stories told and talked about by the Coles' books are helpful. They are notably superior to, say, Freud's "case histories.")

In this context, consider, say, what Thomas Szasz campaigned against over a period of decades: *The Myth of Mental Illness.* As an eye-opening introduction to that myth, probably nothing can rival the sense of history available from the appendix to K. Menninger et al's *The Vital Balance.* Nor is there any better way to undersand Szasz's perhaps-extreme point of view than to study Francis Bacon's Idols of the Mind, especially those he called "The Idols of the Marketplace." Bacon warns there of the too-often unnoticed influence of names.

For instance, a study of *The Vital Balance*'s opening three chapters will show how, once a name is introduced by someone, the still-naïve learner assumes it names a reality. The current result? There are now armies of foot-soldiers churning out reams of "research-papers" on every illness, disorder, and syndrome imaginable, even though not one of them is a real entity any more than an IQ is. A close study of the (personal!) STORIES behind the successive editings of the *Diagnostic and Statistical Manual* and the *Behavioral Assessment: A Practical Handbook* must become the matrix for courses entitled "Abnormal Psychology." The utility of one-to-many fictions as forms of verbal and mental shorthand is undeniable (see the 1909 proposal James made for an "American Psychopathological Society"). But till learners discover that an agoraphobic, for instance, is no more a person with a disease than kindergartners suffer from kindergartenitis and seniors from senioritis, *those learners' mental thinking will be diseased.* (Study "Shared Psychotic Disorder" in the DSM; it has a much, much greater incidence than most people recognize.) Unless they acquire a sound grasp of what humans are and what humans should aim for as a framework for understanding everything from so-called precocious madness to adjustment disorders, they will be prone to the serious mental illness known as "tunnel vision."

James' treatment of the emotions is instructive here. Without an appreciation for the full scope of his thinking, it would be possible to read only his *Principles*' or *Briefer Course*'s chapter entitled "Emotion" and fail to appreciate the massive importance of emotion in our lives. It would also be possible to read it and fail to appreciate that, brief as it is, it shows James' exceptional ability to notice everything and to offer wise guidelines to students aspiring to learn what he'd learned.

First and foremost, he kept in mind the fact that what he was describing were indescribable things we all FEEL, directly and immediately: "As inner mental conditions, emotions are quite indescribable. Description, moreover, would be superfluous, for the reader already knows how they feel." With respect to someone who never felt an emotion, it would be as futile to try and help them understand what a feeling is as it would be to help someone born blind to understand what a color is (or someone with the usual form of color-blindness to understand how different red is from green).

Secondly, he wanted to emphasize his conviction that concrete emotions are "innumerable," hence he underlined the following assertion: "[From this] we can see why there is no limit to the number of possible different emotions which may exist, and why the emotions of different individuals may vary indefinitely."

At the same time, he valued efforts to find an abstract CONCEPTUAL framework to help the learner learn the mental and verbal shorthand needed to control this mass of data, which is why he had worked to become familiar with efforts of thinkers from Descartes onwards to catalogue and classify the indefinite variety of particular feelings.

Yet, at the end, he rebelled against the illusion that the abstract catalogues are anything but handmaids to help grasp the real things, the full range and mix of coarse-to-subtle sentiments that pass and re-pass every day, usually unattended to, in the bosoms of billions of un-average individuals*: "And not only is it [the text-book treatment] tedious, but you feel that its subdivisions are to a great extent either fictitious or unimportant, and that its pretences to accuracy are a sham." (*It is relevant to note that he inserted a note relevant to that mass of the most important kind of evidence psychologists need: *people's stories*. A little beyond the "tedious" complaint, he remarked: "As emotions are described in novels, they interest us, for we are made to share them. We have grown acquainted with the concrete objects and emergencies which call them forth, and any knowing touch of introspection which may grace the page meets with a quick and feeling response.")

The focus of this chapter is thinking. The thinking we do when we classify people's living problems, the thinking we do when we choose the name "mental illnesses" rather than "living problems," the thinking we do when we classify people's emotions, the same thinking activity required when we wish to integrate our classifications of living problems and the emotional problems that are so much a part of many living problems that we often call the latter "emotional problems" rather than "mental illnesses," the same thinking activity required when we wish to resist the emotions, feelings, passions, and so on, that often make us stubbornly cling to old ways of thinking rather than make ourselves open to the possibility that there are *better* ones, and so on. James, in fact, inserted into his discussion of emotion this comment: "In short, *any* [thinking] classification of the emotions is seen to be as true and as 'natural' as any other, if it only serves some purpose." His pragmatism focused on purposes. His aim was to use concrete experience to measure aims alias purposes to find the *best* one or ones.

The focus is also on the learning process, especially the process of learning to think well about thinking. Even this learning theme is woven into James' chapter on emotion, for he describes the emotion he feels AT THAT POINT IN HIS LIFE (over forty!) whenever he thinks about reading any more abstract descriptions of emotions. We must learn to go beyond them:

> But, as far as "scientific psychology" of the emotions goes, I may have been surfeited by too much reading of classic works on the subject, but I had as lief read verbal descriptions of the shapes of the rocks on a New Hampshire farm as toil through them again. They give one nowhere a central point of view, or a deductive or generative principle. They distinguish and refine and specify *in infinitum* without ever getting on to another logical level. Whereas the beauty of all truly scientific work is to get to ever deeper levels. Is there no way out from this level of individual description in the case of the emotions? (PP II: chapter XXV)

Aiming for the "deeper levels" in order to find "a central point of view." The trouble is that, when he wrote this paragraph, James already had two broader mindsets with two different central points of view, and he was already in the habit of switching from one to the other with ease. It is crucial to distinguish them. There is the central point of

244

view he used for his AS-IF or PSEUDO-SCIENCE psychology, the one he donned most of the time he spent between the two covers of *The Principles*. In his psychology-as-a-natural-science's chapter on the emotions, his "way out" was downwards, through hypothesized bodily conditions—"Emotion follows upon the bodily expression in the coarser emotions at least" is the next section's title—and backwards in time via a discussion of Darwin's and Spencer's theories about evolution. But . . .

There is also the broader, more genuine "central point of view" he relied on the rest of the time. Most of the time, that is. Outside the covers of his natural-science texts, he was composing "The Sentiment of Rationality" (1879), "Reflex Action and Theism" (1881), and "The Dilemma of Determinism" (1884), lecture-essays that argue for a view that goes far beyond the agnostics' and atheists' Darwinian perspective. It formed the matrix for his second masterpiece, *The Varieties of Religious Experience*, that dealt with the role that the belief in a god or gods plays in most humans' lives. It is noteworthy, as well, that in *Pragmatism's* third lecture (1906-07) James refused to close the door even on the most traditional theists' thinking:

> Theologians have by this time stretched their minds so as to embrace the darwinian facts . . . So the aim of God is not merely, let us say, to make men and to save them, but rather to get this done through the sole agency of nature's vast machinery. Without nature's stupendous laws and counter-forces, man's creation and perfection, we might suppose, would be too insipid achievements for God to have proposed them.

And in this "going-beyond," he appealed to emotion, alias "sentiment," to ascend to a lofty, moral-universe 'metaphysics.' The feelings he relied on for evidence in this second "way" to a broader viewpoint that would include ALL individuals' individual emotions were the ones that accompany thoughts about the purpose of human life and the nature of the universe as a whole: thoughts about amoral killing vs regrettable crime, about the world ending with no trace that humans ever lived vs an eternity in which human greatness would be forever preserved.

In brief, James' broader outlook built heavily on emotions that only learners capable of thoughts can experience: human learners. Human learners' thoughts. Increasingly complex thoughts, that is, ever-later thoughts which, if learning well is taking place, appropriate the lessons of earlier thoughts. Thoughts. These became James' first and last concern. And no one wrote more brilliantly about one of the most important of all aspects of individuals' thoughts than James. That aspect is simply this: a thought's many-faceted unity.

A pivotal chapter in his *Principles* is named "The Stream of Thought." When he abridged it, he gave it the better-known title, "The Stream of Consciousness." It was when he sat down to 'put into words' his convictions about thought, alias consciousness, alias experience, that he expressed his most firmly-held conviction of all. Overlook his changing taste regarding the best name for what his attention was focused on, for what no mere name could ever capture. Notice only that he refers in his 1890 *Principles* to the present, ever-new, effervescing, conscious thought (e.g., yours now) as "the *inconcussum* [unshaken thing] in a world most of whose other facts have at some time tottered in the breath of philosophic doubt" and that, almost twenty years later, one of his last essays expressed the view that "the perceptual flux is the authentic stuff of each of our biographies, and yields a perfect effervescence of novelty all the time."

If you (now) think about it sympathetically, it will be clear that James' overall view overlapped considerably with that of Descartes. The differences between them are important, but the agreements are even more so. Descartes uses his first meditation to show that the thinker has sure contact only with what is inside his own mind or soul. Recall that, according to James, the only *inconcussum* in the world is "that we have cogitations of some sort." Both also felt a compelling drive to discover what lay beyond his subject'ive experience. With a personal, well-thought-out system. One that was true. Thirdly . . .

. . . both rejected the brain as the real I.

'Scientific' Theory of Thought. For the remainder of this section, numbered "C" and titled "Be Pragmatic, But Do It Wisely!", I will gather together some of James' best thoughts on thought. In the same way that Descartes made the "I think" insight the cornerstone of his thinking, James made the "unity of conscious thought/experience" the cornerstone of his. The following passages show him to have been one of the best thinkers of all time, perhaps THE best, concerning the difficult question "One? or Many?", when that question is asked with respect to the most important thinG?! or thingS?! of all: your field of experience (for you), mine (for me), and theirs (for them). In doing so, he made use of one of our most commonsensical ideas, the idea of a single thing. That idea, brought to the fore by Parmenides, wrestled with by Plato, and built upon by Aristotle, played a central role in the thinking of the medieval schoolmen who so profoundly influenced Descartes. Alias "identity," *oneness*—as opposed to similarity (similarity is impossible unless there are at least two, that is, more than one thing, to compare for similarity versus difference)—was a key weapon in Hume's attack on traditional theories. And Hume's attack on the unity of a person's experience was the chief target of James' attack when he defended its unity-in-plurality.

Begin with what James had to say about meaning vis-à-vis words:

> In popular parlance the word object is commonly taken without reference to the act of knowledge, and treated as synonymous with individual subject of existence. Thus if anyone ask what is the mind's object when you say 'Columbus discovered America in 1492,' most people will reply, 'Columbus,' or 'America,' or, at most, 'the disovery of America.' They will name a substantive kernel or nucleus of the consciousness, and say the thought is 'about' that,—as indeed it is,—and they will call that your thought's object.' Really that is only the grammatical subject, of your sentence. It is at most your 'fractional object;' or you may call it the 'topic' of your thought, or the 'subject of your discourse.' But the *Object* of your thought is really its entire content or deliverance, neither more nor less. It is a vicious use of speech to take out a substantive kernel from its content and call that its object; and it is an equally vicious use of speech to add a substantive kernel not articulately included in its content, and to call that its 'object.' Yet either one of these two sins we commit, whenever we content ourselves with saying that a given thought is simply 'about' a certain topic, or that that

topic is its 'object.' The object of my thought in the previous sentence, for example, is strictly speaking neither Columbus, nor America, nor its discovery. It is nothing short of the entire sentence, 'Columbus-discovered-America-in-1492.' And if we wish to speak of it substantively, we must make a substantive of it by writing it out thus with hyphens between all its words . . . , with every word fringed and the whole sentence bathed in that original halo of obscure relations, which, like an horizon, then spread about its meaning. (*Principles*, I, pp.275-76; a few pages later, he discusses this 'meaning of the complete sentence' in relation to M.V. Eggar's views about the "words" that are "spoken" in silence, namely, inner speech.)

The attending required as a prerequisite for noticing these details AND SO MANY OTHERS that James noticed and never quit attending to, takes effort. But this was the kind of effort he came to view as the intersection where morality and long indulgence in error meet. Even before it was foreseen that "Golgi or Cajal?" would be the pivotal question for determining whether or not "Our brains, Our selves" is the height of wisdom or of folly*, James made the idea behind the question a pivotal issue in his professional thinking. It has to do with correct counting. (*Long indulgence in error is fully compatible with being moral. An honest mistake is no more immoral than a broken bone or a cancerous tumor would be if they existed. Badly mistaken thinkers are often heroically faithful to their conscience, while brilliantly correct thinkers are as capable of violating theirs and afterwards rationalizing those violations as anyone.)

01 23 45 97 86 10

Call that "Picture One." Then examine it closely to find the answers to these Socratic questions. How many things do you see in that picture? One 12-item thing? Two 6-item things? Six 2-item things? Is there a picture? Are there two pictures just called "one"? And so on. Is it more certain that you understand the questions or more certain that you know which answers are the true ones? Or are the questions actually answers, but posed, not as definitely true thoughts, but as possibly true options offered for you to choose from? Are you more certain that whatever you see consists of things that either are colored or are colors that adjoin each other, or more certain that literally colored things or colors do not exist? Are you more certain that, whatever idea you apply to what you see, you see something or some things, or more certain that perhaps you do not see anything? Are you more certain that you see what you see or that what you feel is identical with what you see? Are you more certain that you exist or that electrons orbiting around almost unimaginably tiny atomic nuclei exist? Are you more certain that you exist, or that whoever dreamed up this series of questions exists?

Try now to remember what went on while you "read" the preceding paragraph. Try to remember as clearly as you can while you try to answer these further questions. How many things did you see in the paragraph? That is, did you count the things you saw while the thoughts about the picture (or whatever it should be called, that is, if any "it" exists) were coming to you? Did you wonder what your brain was doing while you were seeing (scanning whatever you saw) and thinking (understanding whatever you thought)? Did you wonder whether you were looking at colorless atoms with particular light-absorbing and light-reflecting molecular arrangements while you were "reading" that paragraph about the picture, pictures, or pictured item or items? Try now to take all of the questions asked about that paragraph in this paragraph, redirect them to this paragraph, then answer them about your "reading" of this paragraph. Then narrow them down to your "reading" of this sentence, to your "reading" of this word and now this word, to your seeing of the first letter of "the" and the second letter of "the" and the third letter of "the" in the next "the": *the* first word of this phrase, etc.

When you finish that experiment, count the thoughts you had.

There is only one way to avoid becoming lost in mazes when we confront such questions and that is to return to the point at which the puzzles begin: that total complex of thoughts that are conveniently referred to as one's original common-sense theory of everything, the cluster of beliefs we fall back on as soon as—in Hume's description—we put our wondering aside and settle down (it seems) to a game of backgammon or to lunch, the set of unquestioned convictions that settle upon us as soon as we relax our efforts to get beyond sensed appearances to unsensed realities. The question, "How many things do you see?", builds on an inner model of reality which includes an earth on whose surface you are situated, three-dimensional things like books, a body with two arms and two hands to hold the book and turn its pages with, two eyes to scan the rows upon rows of print on its pages with, an area inside the body where stomach aches are felt and an area inside the body's head where thoughts and memories of all these things are located, etc. The opening chapters have outlined, briefly, the reasoning that has led so many—especially since Galileo—to conclude that the spread-out colors we see, the quadraphonic sounds we hear, the tickles and pains we feel, etc., *are real things in their own right*, distinct from physical, three-dimensional bodies, that the fainter "copies" of them *are also things in their own right*, distinct from external bodies, etc. From Plato on, the theory grew that, **IN ADDITION TO** whatever else is inside, private, and non-physical (mapped out as entities distinct from the bodies constituting the *presumably*-observable landscape), there are utterly unextended, purely intelligible, hence not-observable-at-all entities whose further qualifications have been disputed and whose names—in English—are ideas, notions, concepts, propositions made from concepts, and so on. Here is where the present thesis grafts onto that picture.

A HUGE QUALIFICATION is needed, though. The way to picture these "in-addition-to's," these "besides," these "more's," these "extras" is to call them "thought" which, *in relation to "language,"* is best thought of the way James came to think of each thought, viz., as "the total meaning of the current complete sentence being put forth (by a speaker or writer) or being taken in (by a listener or reader)." We can, and do!, pretend that total thoughts have parts—this is where ideas, notions, etc., tie in—but that is pretending. Literally, thoughts have no parts. Therefore, when you 'analyse,' do *not* begin with isolated words. *Start* with whole sentences. Notice that any 'verbal report' of your analysis of whole sentences *will be whole sentences*. Whole sentences. Complete thoughts. Here are two of James' warnings:

> I know there are readers whom nothing can convince that the thought of a complex object has not as many parts as are discriminated in the object itself. Well, then, let the word part pass. Only observe that these parts are not the separate

'ideas' of traditional psychology. No one of them can live out of that particular thought, any more than my head can live off of my particular shoulders . . . . Dismiss the thought and out go its parts. (PP I:279, note*)

I use the common phraseology here for mere convenience' sake. The reader who has made himself acquainted with Chapter IX will always understand, when he hears of many ideas simultaneously present to the mind and acting upon each other, that what is really meant is a mind with one idea before it, of many objects, purposes, reasons, motives related to each other, some in a harmonious and some in an antagonistic way. With this caution I shall not hesitate from time to time to fall into the popular Lockian speech, erroneous though I believe it to be. (PP II:528, note*)

Keep in mind, also, that the most basic principle for understanding any PART of this entire Big Picture Theory is: **NOTHING CAN BE UNDERSTOOD IN ISOLATION FROM A TOTAL THEORY**. The total theory we all rely on at the beginning of our 'higher learning' is our complex common-sense worldview! The only further principle that accounts for all the evidence that seems to be accumulated in our libraries is: Each of us has a variety of basic total theories to choose from when we search for the adequate "reading" of our total-experience text. In particular, each of us has several alternatives to choose from when trying to understand WHAT WE SEE in the case of "Picture One." Our theories or interpretations are, therefore, not abstracted from, not extracted from, not caused by, what we sense. Our theories or interpretations—whence they come is a separate issue—are by us imposed on, projected onto, applied to, chosen as true of, our experience. They also are *freely* chosen by us when we attempt to discover *through them* whatever exists that we do NOT experience. By the time we are old enough to wonder "How *many* do I see?", we already have an incredible versatility in using the notions of I, we, one, none, many, etc.

Oneness is an indispensable everyday notion, as indispensable as my notion that I am one person and that each other person is one more than me. Just as all of us develop an absolutely keen appreciation for the difference between conscious and intelligent THOU's and wholly unconscious IT's, regardless of how we finally decide to explain our understanding of the difference or where we will impose/project it, so all of us have an absolutely keen appreciation for the difference between ONE and both NOT-ONE's, i.e., between ONE, ZERO (not even one), and MORE-THAN-ONE (or many, i.e., many ones), regardless of how many problems we have handling such dynamite in our later "nearer reflections." Regardless of how many humans exist, i.e., whether I am one of five billion ones or am the only one, I am certain I understand *that* it makes all the difference in the world whether I have to share my candy bar because it is the only ONE around or whether the two of us can each have a whole candy bar because there are TWO of them. Even "layfolk" can grasp these essentials of every abstruse metaphysics, as is shown by the fact that they can read and understand *Newsweek* which informed all of us last April about the claim by "scientists" that they had "stumbled upon the biggest and oldest creature on earth: *Armillaria bulbosa*, a fungus that covers at least 30 acres along the Michigan-Wisconsin border, weighs more than 22,000 pounds, began growing at least 1,500 years ago and produces small honey mushrooms" (4-13-92, p.62) and the metaphysical essay thrown in as a remarkable bonus (the way stores sometimes give us two ounces of peanut butter FREE, which is only a problem for people who can't find the line between the ounces they've paid for and the ones that are free: are they near the top, below what they eat first, or lower, on top of the two they eat last?) at the end of *Time* magazine's report (same date, same page number):

> But what is meant by an "individual"? A patch of grass that spreads from a single seed may be considered an individual organism. The same is true with fungi, which, incidentally, are now looked upon as a kingdom separate from plants and animals. [What about human kingdoms such as England? And—though we now know the king of fungi—who's the king of plants and animals?] Complicating matters is the fact that pieces of the *A. bulbosa* may have broken off over the milleniums. If so, do the pieces count as one organism or many? There's no agreed upon answer, says Clive Brasier, a British botanist. [A botanist can't study animals but only plants, so what does he know about fungi

which aren't plants?] Insisting on a yes or no, he says, "gets to be a Guinness Book of Records kind of question." [Do two Mohicans constitute a nation? A race? A group? A pair? That's crucial for deciding when the Mohicans actually became extinct. Was it when the second last died—one member does not a tribe make—but then which of the last two was 'THE' last MohicaN*?]

(*The bracketed comments are clearly my own.)

Of course, all of this is to focus on the challenge which modern nuclear physics presents to our naive realist notions of bodies. The faint-hearted use verbal dodges to skirt the problems. "It seems," "it appears," and "we think," are examples. We say that, though the piece of paper REALLY is not solid, I always THOUGHT it was, or we switch and say that, though it APPEARS to be many under a microscope, it REALLY is one continuous solid. We decide what to believe, then we smother evidence for the opposition with a blanket of dodges. The paper is really a WHOLE "made of" many PARTS. The components are the MATTER, but they are "unified" by the FORM. It is ACTUALLY one but POTENTIALLY many. If potential wears thin, previously unnoticed "VIRTUAL things" are discovered. If the most natural interpretation of sub-atomic physics research is accepted and we admit that, behind what appears to be the paper but is really part of a whole visual field of patterned colors extending from periphery to periphery, there are really trillions of tiny, whole protons, neutrons, and electrons (or whatever those tiny bodies are, if any exist) AND NO SINGLE, LARGE BODY, then by the same reasoning we must admit that, behind what appear to be hands, feet, legs, torso, and face-reflection but are really parts of single visual fields, there are really trillions of tiny, whole protons, neutrons, and electrons AND NO SINGLE, HUMAN BODY. Even if bodies exist, which cannot be proven, there are no bodies in the universe large enough to match our concept of a human body. Unless we resort to various verbal subterfuges, this is the inexorable conclusion we human researchers must draw with respect to ourselves. (*The reason we can handle written "interruptions" or incorporate new insights that come to us from nowhere is that, until we become senile, we carry with us wherever we go two relatively stable models of the world—our common-sense one and our personally-chosen revision of it—which we use in our theory-laden interpretations, and it is THOSE that we deal with directly or immediately. "Visible" words can instantly take us to part of an inner "world," and we can add a new detail we did not know before—e.g., Galileo died and Newton was born in 1642—or erase an old detail—e.g., the colors we see are not part of the physical world—or we can decide to adopt an entirely new framework for all of our beliefs about everything, e.g., believe all our thoughts about physical bodies are fictions the same way our beliefs, while reading *Alice in Wonderland*, are about purely imaginary beings doing purely imaginary things. To get an uninterrupted version of the *Time's* writer's thoughts is easy: we underline just his/her text, or cross out the bracketed additions, or check the original in, it will seem, the library.)

Though William James said that THE method of psychology as a naive science is introspection or "looking inwards," he himself constantly made use of the correct method. It IS something different from "looking outward" or extrospection. But the something different is *ATTENDING, NOTICING, AND UNDERSTANDING.* Which are noticed only by attending to the fact *that* we understand what we do not and can not look at by outward or inward looking, by extro—or introspection. The pages of this chapter are written to emphasize that, even when you think you are looking outward and making direct visual contact with real physical pages outside your skin, you are directly aware of visual sense-data that are flush up against YOU. Being directly aware and understanding what it is that you are directly aware of are separate processes exercised by one you. Trying to notice and attending, as matters of choice, result from understanding.

William James grew up in a family headed by Henry, Sr., whose thinking was permeated with one particular version of oneness, the one which so many western thinkers in the nineteenth century embraced: the version according to which all the things which appear to be so many and so varied are really various appearances of a single reality. This version of oneness was, throughout James' lifetime, battling against another version, that of the atomists. The atomists chose to believe that naive-realist ones, e.g., human bodies, puddles of water, piles of mud, etc., are only *apparent* ones, and that instead of being whole ones or single things as they appear to our senses to be, they are *really* trillions of tinier ones or single things. When James finally chose his own version of the ultimate ones, onenesses, or unities in the world, he put first on his list what Carl Rogers focussed on: the unified fields of experience each one of the world's millions of inhabitants are presently aware of. Millions of momentary, unified consciousnesses or experiences or "thoughts" which flow rapidly into the next moment's, each of which incorporates its precursors as integral parts of itself, so rapidly that together it and its precursors seem like a single continuous stream. Except in multiple-personality, amnesic, senile, dream, etc., cases.

Throughout his lifetime, he contrasted his view of each moment's consciousness as unified to Hume's view that there are only *many* perceptions "bundled together" but with each perception as distinct from every other as one atom is from every other atom. Here is Hume's view, expressed in one of the most famous and influential passages ever written by someone obsessed with the looking-at-copies model of thinking and understanding:

> For my part, when I enter most intimately into what I call *myself*, I always stumble on some particular perception or other, of heat or cold, light or shade, love or hatred, pain or pleasure. I never can catch *myself* at any time without a perception, and never can observe anything but the perception. When my perceptions are removed for any time, as by sound sleep, so long am I insensible of *myself*, and may truly be said not to exist . . .
>
> But setting aside [those who see differently], I may venture to affirm of the rest of mankind, that they are nothing but a bundle or collection of perceptions, which succeed each other with an inconceivable rapidity, and are in a perpetual flux and movement . . . The mind is a kind of theatre, where several perceptions successively make their appearance; pass, repass, glide away, and mingle in an infinite variety of postures and situations. There is properly no *simplicity* in it at one time, nor *identity* in different, whatever natural propension we may have to imagine that simplicity and identity. The comparison of the theatre must not mislead us. They are the successive perceptions only, that constitute the mind; nor have we the most distant notion of the place where these scenes are represented, or of the materials of which it is composed. (Flew, p.190)

James disagreed, not re what's not seen, but re what is:

> The world of experience consists at all times of two parts,
> an objective and a subjective part, of which the former may be
> incalculably more extensive than the latter, and yet the latter
> can never be omitted or suppressed. The objective part is the
> sum total of whatsoever at any given time we may be thinking
> of, the subjective part is the inner 'state' in which the thinking
> comes to pass. What we think of may be enormous,—the
> cosmic times and spaces, for example,—whereas the inner
> state may be the most fugitive and paltry activity of mind.
> Yet the cosmic objects, so far as the experience yields them,
> are but ideal pictures of something whose existence we do
> not inwardly possess but only point at outwardly, while the
> inner state is our very experience itself; its reality and our
> experience are one. A conscious field *plus* its object as felt or
> thought of *plus* an attitude towards the object *plus* the sense
> of a self to whom the attitude belongs—such a concrete bit
> of personal experience may be a small bit, but it is a solid bit
> so long as it lasts; not hollow, not a mere abstract element
> of experience, such as the 'object' is when taken all alone. It
> is a *full* fact, even though it be an insignificant fact; it is of
> the *kind* to which all realities whatsoever must belong; the
> motor currents of the world run through the like of it; it
> is on the line connecting real events with real events. That
> unsharable feeling which each one of us has of the pinch of
> his individual destiny as he privately feels it rolling out on
> fortune's wheel may be disparaged for its egotism, may be
> sneered at as unscientific, but it is the one thing that fills
> up the measure of our concrete actuality, and any would-be
> existent that should lack such a feeling, or its analogue, would
> be a piece of reality only half made up.

This stunning passage occurs almost dead-center in his twentieth
and final *Varieties* lecture, and should be read aloud after its preceding
description of the "objective" viewpoint has been read aloud. The unity,
the seeming oneness of our total experience at each moment, like any
one of the "senses" that is another "plus," is not a thing that can be seen

or looked at. Hume, the looker with one of the most acute "senses" of oneness in history, saw it couldn't come from any observed impression, and concluded that therefore the unity was unreal, an illusion, and that the disconnected atoms of perception were all that was certain. (The unity is from the complete thought, essentially distinct from colors, sounds, imagery, etc., which ARE distinct, a fact James tended to deny.) James—in his moment of profound insight—wasn't bothered by the fact that he could not see, look at, or observe the unity. But he NOTICED it, could ATTEND to it, could UNDERSTAND (the thought) *that* the unity was no illusion. Even if, in fact, he chose the wrong explanation for it, James continued to emphasize the **UNITY OF (the field of) CONSCIOUSNESS** from the time of his *Principles* till his final lectures on *A Pluralistic Universe*.

> Take a sentence of a dozen words, and take twelve men and tell to each one word. Then stand the men in a row or jam them into a bunch, and let each think of his word as intently as he will; nowhere will there be a consciousness of the whole sentence. We talk of the 'spirit of the age,' and the 'sentiment of the people,' and in various ways we hypostatize 'public opinion.' But we know this to be symbolic speech, and never dream that the spirit, opinion, sentiment, etc., constitute a consciousness other than, and additional to, that of the several individuals whom the words 'age,' 'people,' or 'public' denote. The private minds do not agglomerate into a higher compound mind. This has always been the invincible contention of the spiritualists against the associationists in Psychology,—a contention which we shall take up at greater length in Chapter X. (PP I:160)

That passage from *The Principles*' sixth chapter is the basis for its tenth chapter's conclusion about naive psychology's "I", viz., that the knower is a *Thought*!

> This me is an empirical aggregate of things objectively known. The I which knows them cannot itself be an aggregate, neither for psychological purposes need it be considered an unchanging metaphysical entity like the Soul, or a principle

257

like the pure Ego, viewed as 'out of time.' It is a *Thought*, at each moment different from that of the last moment, but *appropriative* of the latter, together with all that the latter called its own. All the experiential facts find their place in this description, unecumbered by any hypothesis save that of the existence of passing thoughts or states of mind. The same brain may subserve many conscious selves, either alternate or coexisting; but by what modifications of its action, or whether ultra-cerebral conditions may intervene, are questions that cannot now be answered. (PP I:400-01)

In a footnote to the 12-men experiment, he cited an observation from Franz Brentano that recalls Plato's *Theatetus*: "Someone might say that although it is true that neither a blind man nor a deaf man by himself can compare sounds with colors, yet since one hears and the other sees they might do so both together . . . But whether they are apart or close together makes no difference; not even if they permanently keep house together; no, not if they were Siamese twins, or more than Siamese twins, and were inseparably grown together, would it make the assumption any more possible. Only when sound and color are represented in the same reality is it thinkable that they should be compared." How central this **UNITY OF ONE'S FIELD OF EXPERIENCE** remained in James' thinking is clearly stated in 1908's *Pluralistic Universe*:

In the year 1890 I published a work on psychology in which it became my duty to discuss the value of a certain explanation of our higher mental states that had come into favor among the more biologically inclined psychologists. Suggested partly by the analogy of chemical compounds, this opinion was that complex mental states are resultants of the self-compounding of simpler ones . . .

I found myself obliged, in discussing the mind-dust theory, to urge this last alternative view. The so-called mental compounds are simply psychic reactions of a higher type. The form itself of them, I said, is something new. We can't say that awareness of the alphabet as such is nothing more than twenty-six awarenesses, each of a separate letter;

for those are twenty-six distinct awarenesses, of single letters *without* others, while their so-called sum is one awareness, of every letter *with* its comrades. There is thus something new in the collective consciousness. It knows the same letters, indeed, but it knows them in this novel way. It is safer, I said (for I fought shy of admitting a self or soul or other agent of combination), to treat the consciousness of the alphabet as a twenty-seventh fact, the substitute and not the sum of the twenty-six simpler consciousnesses, and to say that while under certain physiological conditions they alone are produced, other more complex physiological conditions result in its production instead. Do not talk, therefore, I said, of the higher states *consisting* of the simpler, or *being* the same with them; talk rather of their *knowing the same things.* They are different mental facts . . .

[After offering a lucid survey of the paradoxes that beset each alternative solution, James continued:] Sincerely, and patiently as I could, I struggled with the problem for years, covering hundreds of sheets of paper with notes and memoranda and discussions with myself over the difficulty. How can many consciousnesses [each one a single lifetime's momentary, present "thought"] be at the same time one consciousness? How can one and the same identical fact experience itself so diversely? The struggle was vain; I found myself in an *impasse.* I saw that I must either foreswear that 'psychology without a soul' to which my whole psychological and kantian education had committed me,—I must, in short, bring back distinct spiritual agents to know the mental states, now singly and now in combination, in a word bring back scholasticism and common sense—or else I must squarely confess the solution of the problem impossible, and then either give up my intellectualistic logic, the logic of identity, and adopt some higher (or lower) form of rationality, or, finally, face the fact that life is logically irrational. (Chapter V)

Compare that with today's most popular theory*, which is that "the mind" is simply synonymous with "the brain" and that both refer to the three-pound organ each of us who thinks of our physical body as something real thinks is a thing inside our body's head, an organ kept utterly in the dark by a thick skull, cushioned against sharp noises by the fluid it swims in. This view is summed up in the recent naive-science slogan, "Our Brains, Our Selves," a far more exact slogan than "Our Bodies, Our Selves." But only physiologically, **THOUGH NOT EXPERIENTIALLY**: when we "look inwards," it FEELS like *our* feet down there, *our* shoulders up here, *our* glottis at neck-level, all parts of *us* but **NEVER** excitations in our brain! (*As Hunt noted, many try to soften the simple identification by claiming that the brain is what is, the mind is what the brain does.)

Then, like Hume and James, recognize the naivete of naive realism by recognizing that no one ever experiences his or her brain. Hume even ignored his own brain, for he—like Descartes—believed no one ever senses their arms, legs, etc., either! He went out of his way to say that "the least philosophy" (a term by which he, like Newton with *The Mathematical Principles of Natural Philosophy*, meant what we today call "science") refutes naive realism. As for James, he never bothered to note that no introspector is ever tempted to say "Wow, there's my brain!" In fact, unlike today's materialists, James kept in mind that modern physics and chemistry overwhelmingly show that "the brain" names a pragmatic fiction:

> The second difficulty [with the biologists' version of the relation between "mind" and brain] is deeper still. *The 'entire brain-process' is not a physical fact at all*. It is the appearance to an onlooking mind of a multitude of physical facts. 'Entire brain' is nothing but our name for the way in which a million of molecules arranged in certain positions may affect our sense. On the principles of the corpuscular or mechanical philosophy, the only realities are the separate molecules, or at most the cells. Their aggregation into a 'brain' is a fiction of popular speech. Such a fiction cannot serve as the objectively real counterpart to any psychic state whatever. Only a genuinely physical fact can so serve. But the molecular fact is the only genuine physical fact—whereupon we seem, if we are to have an elementary psycho-physical law at all, thrust right back upon something like the mind-stuff theory, for

the molecular fact, being an element of the 'brain,' would seem naturally to correspond not to the total thoughts, but to elements in the thought.

What shall we do? Many would find relief at this point in celebrating the mystery of the Unknowable and the 'awe' which we should feel . . . Others would rejoice that the finite and separatist view of things with which we started had at last developed its contradictions, and was about to lead us dialectically upwards . . . (PP I:178)

In *The Briefer Course*, James moved this passage from Chapter VI of *The Principles* (where the "12 Men" passage is found) to the epilogue where he argues that naive-science psychology is no science, but a very inadequate basis for true understanding. Unless we keep these explicit qualifications in mind, the naive-realist language of James is as misleading as the passage cited earlier, in Chapter Two, section B, was. In the opinion of Gordon Allport, James would often be "so filled with enthusiasm for the idea he is momentarily expounding that he forgets to make appropriate qualifications." In fact, when he abridged his *Principles* even further and presented them in a lecture-series entitled *Talks to Teachers*, he once again made his position clear:

I have been accused of holding up before you, in the course of these talks, a mechanical and even a materialistic view of the mind. I have called it an organism and a machine. I have spoken of its reaction on the environment as the essential thing about it; and I have referred this, either openly or implicitly, to the construction of the nervous system. I have, in consequence, received notes from some of you, begging me to be more explicit on this point; and to let you know frankly whether I am a complete materialist or not.

Now in these lectures I wish to be strictly practical and useful, and to keep free from all speculative complications. Nevertheless, I do not wish to leave any ambiguity about my own position; and I will therefore say, in order to avoid all misunderstanding, that in no sense do I count myself a materialist. I cannot see how such a thing as our consciousness can possibly be *produced* by a nervous machinery, though I can perfectly well see how, if 'ideas' do accompany the workings of the machinery, the *order* of the ideas might very well follow exactly the *order* of the machine's operations . . . (Chapter XV)

But wait. Did he retract his claim that a unified brain is a fiction of popular speech? What did he really believe, this phenomenalist who in his famous 1906 lectures entitled *Pragmatism* said that the famous denier of matter, Bishop Berkeley, "doesn't deny matter, then; he simply tells us what it consists of. It is a true name for just so much in the way of sensations"?!

His "confession" in Lecture V of *A Pluralistic Universe* confirms that his mind oscillated from a common-sense brain-mind interactionist dualism to a more radical rejection of matter in favor of "pure experience." Even his latter vision hovered between two possibilities. One is a picture of us being surrounded by a "mother sea" or ocean of experience, so that the "thought" that is us is either a drop or a small ripple in that ocean. Then he shies away from that picture which suggests pantheism and views humans as something like floating islands of consciousness, a universe-ful of them, each one a separate pool or field of pure experience. Thus each of us, from the center of the moment's particular field that is OUR empirical self, is free to hypothesize about the nature of the "objective" world beyond, including those other floating-galaxy selves.

In terms of the unifying theory presented *in this present work*, however, our internal, early common-sense theory, the one which we fall back on for daily, practical living, includes certain very clear *thoughts*: thoughts about outside things such as the age-old sun, moon, stars—plus other people, other people's thoughts and feelings. But those things out there, if they exist (and are not just my thoughts about them) are radically separate from my recent thoughts *about* them IN HERE, but also a thought in here of a real self, I myself!, out there. My real self is not a thought, and it existed long before I had any thoughts or notions *about* it.

As my learning advanced, I now find myself in possession of *alternative* beliefs. About my BODY: a single, continuous body with arms, legs, brain, etc., vs quintillians of gnat-like particles. About my SELF: a drop in an ocean of godness, a cell in a social organism, a psycho-physical organism, an immaterial soul, and so on. Based on new things I learn in here, I constantly revise my common-sense theory, including the idea of my brain, in order to obtain a model of reality out there that is more adequate to predicting the 'phenomena' I call "my future experience." That James saw matters the same way is clear from an early (1877) book-review:

> . . . brain physiologists would still be groping in Cimmerian darkness without the torch [of introspection] which psychology proper puts into their hands. The entire recent growth of their science may, in fact, be said to be a mere hypothetical schematization in material terms of the laws which introspection long ago laid bare . . . But whereas we directly see their [mental] process of combination in the mind, we only guess in the brain what it *may* be from fancied analogies with the mental phenomena. (Cited by G.E. Myers, *William James: His Life and Thoughts*, pp.8-9.)

"The brain" is a "mere hypothetical schematization"!

Why must we insist on getting clear about the brain? The answer is simple. Since Descartes died in 1650, his view that our brain is our sole link to the rest of the vast physical universe has been confirmed a thousand-fold by psycho-physics or, to be more exact, by hypothetical psycho-neurology. The one organ in our body whose relation to "the mind" was never fully recognized by Plato, Aristotle, Augustine, Aquinas, turns out to be the most essential ONE.

But is there any ONE thing referred to by "brain"? No! And, let us add, whoever cannot think straight about her or his alleged brain will not be able to think straight about the rest of their body.

As it turns out, James' 'fiction' view has been verified extensively in the century after his death. There used to be two alternative views of the brain, however, the one-continuous-whole-organ view championed by Camillo Golgi versus the billions-of-disconnected-neurons one championed by Ramon y Cajal.

> We now know that Cajal was correct. With increasingly sophisticated stains that would have appealed to Cajal the artist, brain scientists over the ensuing fifty years have demonstrated that neurons in reality are separate cells that

communicate with each other but are never in direct physical contact. This rules out the view that nerve impulses travel through the brain like water through a system of pipes . . .

Communication between neurons is achieved when an electrical potential is generated in one cell and travels along its axon at a constant rate and coded sequence. The code can be compared to the letters of the alphabet—not quite the message, but the elements from which the message will be composed. You can also think of it as Morse Code, with the signals transmitted unchanged from the sender to the receiver. Along the greatest distances, usually the length of the axon, the process is purely electrical. But when the signal reaches the end of the axon, it is ready for transfer to the next neuron, and the most important aspect of nerve communication, a chemical process, is ready to take place . . . Special chemicals called neurotransmitters are released. These cross the synaptic cleft . . .

Obviously, at some point our model of the brain as a city breaks down. There is certainly no proof that individual neurons possess even a rudimentary form of consciousness. (Richard Restak, *The Brain: The Last Frontier*, 1979.)

This fact of *disconnected* neurons fits with the earlier fact of *disconnected* nuclei and electrons, which fit together with the other fact of *independent* body cells (e.g., the trillions of red blood corpuscles floating through arteries and veins) and all of them constitute massive evidence against your never-experienced brain's unity.

Conduct a thought-experiment. Take 15 billion people, have them lie down in such a way that none is in direct physical contact with any of the others, have each take a powerful sleeping-pill that guarantees they will fall asleep. Do you think it makes sense to believe that some sort of "collective conscious mind" emerges like a ghost from those unconscious persons? In his valuable "Neurology and the Soul" review of current brain-models for the 11-22-90 *N.Y. Review*, Oliver Sacks reports being asked "Why do all you neurologists go mystical?", meaning "Why do so many—e.g., Sherrington, Adrian, Penfield, Eccles, and others—resist the identification of mind and brain?" The best answer of all is simply that all the evidence points at one conclusion: James was right to say that brains, as such, do not exist.

James' thinking about 'unified brains' is crucial. John Watson, the pied-piper, turned the clock back for his naive-psychology followers when he chose, ostrich-like, to be SO pragmatic and to avoid SO many speculative complications, that he decided to pretend that not even when people wake up are they really conscious. Skinner perfected that view of Watson, the view which James, beginning with Chapter V of *The Principles*, had dissected with razor-sharp logic before Watson ever began his behaviorist revolution. James possessed what—if Angela was right—Hemingway regarded as the most essential gift of a good writer: "a built-in shock-proof shit-detector."

We must, however, respect the MOST BASIC "natural law" decreed by the Creators: we cannot escape spending the bulk of our waking lives thinking with our original, naive-realist mindset. It will normally SEEM that we directly rub elbows with other people WHOM WE CAN SEE (at least their faces and the clothes hiding their skin which hides their insides where THEIR fields of experience are hidden). We must now work out a suitable PRAGMATIST enlargment of it to include the PSYCHO-NEUROLOGICAL fact that it will always SEEM as if what people experience is correlated with what goes on inside their cranium, whether it is the effect of a small dose (it seems) of chemicals like LSD, some low-voltage current applied via an electrode implanted deep (it seems) in the amygdala, or a select set of stimuli created by light reflecting from a page of print with a paragraph "made up" of (it seems) sentences like the ones your eyes (it seems) are scanning right now.

The one who put the finishing touches on Kant's AS-IF'ism was a physicist who, like James, knew something of Kant: Albert Einstein. Though he, too, was unable to settle on the truth which practically stares us in the face, he was able to apply the Hemingway Principle to Bohr's Hegelian Both-And'ism. Though Bohr's quantum theory "works," it cannot possibly be the truth. Here is how he, a physicist familiar with the fictions of geometers who pretend a line one inch long has the same number of points as a line one light-year long, namely, an infinite number of them, broadened Kant's constructivism:

I am convinced that even much more is to be asserted:
the concepts which arise in our thought and in our linguistic
expressions are all—when viewed logically—the free
creations of thought which cannot inductively be gained
from sense experiences . . . Thus, for example, the series
of integers is obviously an invention of the human mind,
a self-created tool which simplifies the ordering of certain
sensory experiences.

Or was it the more recent psychologist, George A. Kelly, who
put the best final touches on Kant with the theory he named, in an
"unpublished manuscript" which J.C. Mancuso published in his 1970
anthology, *Readings for A Cognitive Theory of Personality*, "Constructive
Alternativism." Kelly's approach—incorporating as it does discussions
of all the science-traditions of theory-generation, basic postulates,
premises and conclusions, experimental procedures, and, especially!,
freely-chosen interpretive selecting—is broad enough to embrace the
ultimate, verifiable fact of inquirers' experience: *we have total-system,
alternative-readings options.*

Verify this for yourself right now. Look back at Picture One. Do
not stop at the easy questions, such as "Are the 6 and 9 in the wrong
order or are they simply upside-down?", "Are those 12 numbers or
simply visible symbols for invisible numbers?", "Are the O's letters or
numbers?", "Are I I or O O one symbol written twice or two symbols
exactly alike?", or even the question raised by Einstein's opinion, "Are
ALL such concepts, numbers included, obvious inventions of the
human mind?" Begin with the decisive question: Is there REALLY
something I see or NOT? Next, imitate Hume's test by crossing your
eyes and noting the "doubling" of what you see. (That, he said, takes
care of naive realism.)

On the assumption that you—like me—do see SOMEthing or some
thingS, review your basic lading-theory options for the earlier "Picture
One." Here are a few suggestions: (i)I see markings made of dried black
ink carefully spread on white paper, (ii)I *SIMULTANEOUSLY* see 12
symbols for invisible entities (either numbers or letters), (iii)I see zillions
of atoms too tiny to see with the naked eye unless they are all bunched
together like this, (iv)I see colors which are qualities or properties but
not the substances or underlying realities they are the qualities of, (v)I

see a total visual field best described as shaped colors or colored patterns which—if I uncork the process called "free association"—will "evoke" a nearly endless list of "concepts" which I can apply to or project onto or read into what I see, (vi)It's not I who see, but only the society of neurons inside my cranium and I just follow what they tell me, (vii)I don't exist and, even if I did, I couldn't understand these impractical and unpragmatic and meaningless and unverifiable metaphysical thoughts. Finish with: What's this *I*?!

What conclusion can be drawn about *I*? I begin with what Kohler, like Hume and James before him, concluded: the experienced "world" I deal with is a complex of here-and-now sense-data, imagery, and thoughts. Like Hume but unlike James, I recognize that the sense contents—color fields, sounds, odors, body data—are entities distinct from each other. Unlike Hume and like Plato, etc., I understand *that* the thoughts I understand are radically distinct from look-at-ables, that is, from both the vivid sensed things and the faint images or quasi-copies of original sensed things. Like James, I understand *that* there is a feature of my total experience that is best described as "the unity of my present total, directly-experienced reality," but that there are many ways to describe it. Above all, like James I understand *that* verifying all of these things requires a process analogous to creating an extraordinarily-complex inner model with features to match—in general—all of the seemingly infinite things Kant often described as things-in-themselves, but above all the acts which I include in my model and call "attending," "noticing," and "understanding." Whatever is the agent behind the attending, noticing, and understanding is one and the same agent that does the looking, observing, or being directly aware of the observables or look-at-ables, and is what I label or call I, me, or my self, what I used to call Ronald but now use a legal alias for. I have control over which of the teeming thoughts proposed to me I'll believe.

If you are like me, you will find the above "fits" you as well. Among the thoughts you can entertain when you look back at Picture One will—when you've finished this sentence—be one cued by "I can add to the possibilities listed under the 'Picture' the fact *that* those resemble the things some other person was directly aware of when these pages (or whatever it is I see) were being written." That can be added to your free choices.

You, whoever you are (if you even exist), will also notice—if your experience is like mine—that, as soon as you let your attention lapse from the challenge to think with unusually obstinate clarity and consistency, you will "fall right back into" the unique set of everyday belief-habits you've built up during the years between your birth and your today.

James' pragmatism is easily readjusted to this model of two-switchable-models/theories. It is not for the dull, the lazy, the faint-hearted, or the biased. It is based on a clear Berkeleyan, Humean, Kantian recognition that I live within a "world" whose parts can be "fished up" with those EXTRA sense-data or image-copies of them I call "language" and "inner speech," respectively. When James drew attention to the power of words, words, words, he had in mind the power that rows upon rows of the tiny things you're "scanning" can exert on minds of readers like you, viz., the power of "evoking" THOUGHTS.

Interlude. Re solipsism. "No man or woman is an island." The idea reverberates through my soul. But a wide-awakened recognition of the Creators' Great Deception confronts me with the fact that there is no way I can prove it. If there are other thinking and feeling free-agents out there, they are entirely beyond the reach of my direct experience. Deciding who they are and which of them I adjoin to make up something more than an island is a decision I must take full responsibility for. Recognizing that the phrase "No person is an island" is poetry also forces me to make an unusually obstinate effort to think clearly and consistently before deciding what true meaning(s) I should project onto it. Deciding whether I belong with others—whether called philosophers, theologians, physicists, biologists, anthropologists, historians, etc.—in a "scientific community" who are experts on particular issues or in a "political community" who follow the same rules vis-à-vis some of their goals or in a "religious community" who hold relatively similar beliefs about the context for scientific and political pursuits is a decision I cannot surrender to others because it is entirely my responsibility to decide which others actually exist.

Simone Weil, from an atheistic background, became convinced that God was the most important Person she related to. Discerning and then obeying God's will became her dominant pursuit. Discerning and then accepting the truth was, she decided, the first item in God's will for her. Avoiding any passion that would lure her from the truth was, she also decided, part of that obligation.

> The obstacles of an intellectual order, which until lately stopped me on the threshold of the Church, might if necessary be considered as eliminated, since you do not refuse to accept me just as I am. Yet there are still obstacles.
>
> After thoroughly considering everything, I think this is what they come to. What frightens me is the Church as a social structure. Not only on account of its blemishes, but from the very fact that it is something social. It is not that I am of a very individualistic temperament. I am afraid for the opposite reason. I am aware of very strong gregarious tendencies in myself. My natural disposition is to be very easily influenced, too much influenced, and above all by anything collective. I know that if at this moment I had before me a group of twenty young Germans singing Nazi songs in chorus, a part of my soul would instantly become Nazi. That is a very great weakness, but that is how I am. I think that it is useless to fight directly against natural weaknesses. One has to force oneself to act as though one did not have them in circumstances where a duty makes it imperative; and in the ordinary course of life one has to know these weaknesses, prudently take them into account, and strive to turn them to good purpose; for they are all capable of being put to some good purpose . . .
>
> . . . It follows from this [she quotes the devil's claim to own power and to be able to give it to any who would bow to him] that the social is irremediably the domain of the devil. The flesh impels us to say *me* and the devil impels us to say *us*; or else to say like the dictators *I* with plural signification. And, in conformity with his particular mission, the devil manufactures a false imitation of what is divine, an *ersatz* divinity.

"The flesh impels us . . ." Thinking of my self as an individual *me* is important. But it's not really the flesh, and it does not compel.

True, swimming against the powerful flow of life-long common-sense habits in order to recognize the falseness of naive realism demands great effort.

Still, *constant review of the experienced facts* that fit no other conclusion than that the peach-colored disk pausing at the horizon is no sun eight light-minutes or ninety-three million miles distant and the white points are not stars billions of light-year miles away (some already "burnt-out"), convinces me as well that what appears to be another's face when, it seems, I gaze into eyes that return my gaze, is not. If there are no other bodies than colorless subatomic bodies flitting about in solitary isolation, thousands of particle-lengths from their nearest neighbors, all hidden from me by a curtain of visual-field colors, then there is no sun or stars, no faces or eyes. I accept the conclusion that the inhabitants of my Kohlerian "world" are not flesh-and-blood others, but only "possible others." It is entirely my call to decide whether or not I believe these "virtual-reality people" inhabiting my inner, utterly private, field-of-experience "world" are matched by real persons out in some real world beyond. Real persons who are not fleshy or bodied. As I am not, despite that "flesh."

Besides individual humans, I also have thoughts about groups. Here, too, it is entirely up to me to decide whether to believe there are any such things as human collectives or groups, e.g., Church, State, Party, etc. These are what Simone Weil—if the individual I imagine really existed—devoted much of her time to thinking and, it seemed, to writing about. During a period when totalitarian thinking was at its height, she never put the needs of mythical collectives ahead of individuals. While she would readily have agreed with the insight that inspired the climax of the classic movie, *Casablanca*, namely, the insight that the needs of millions add up to far more needs than the needs of just three, she would have added that no one of those other millions weighs more, in itself, than any one of the three.

Clear-headed thinking on such basic issues is the only thing that will defuse the passions that fuel so much endless fighting and killing, whether in neighborhood or parochial worlds or in our all-continents global world. Such thinking requires attention to the endless details that constitute "the truth, the whole truth, and nothing but the truth." But attention, over the course of time, works miracles. Those who have studied anger, for instance, have drawn attention to what happens when we have a choice of whether to direct our attention at the deed that provokes our ire or at the anger that, like so many feelings, seems centered in our midriff. Not until we learn that passion is not unconsciously generated like steam in a boiler but remains unignited until we entertain the right—OR WRONG!—thoughts, can we catch up with Simone's insights.

D. Individual Selves vs Group Fictions

Fictions. This third chapter has, to an extent, concentrated on the subject of mental fictions. The fictions most difficult to unmask are the naive-realist ones: to analyse the apples and oranges of our immediate sense experience into non-physical sensed-givens and thoughts on the one hand and, possibly, colorless atoms on the other requires as much hard thinking as the Catholics' analysis of transubstantiated "bread" and "wine" into flesh and blood requires strong faith. But analysing the theoretical fictions of the modern "sciences" often requires an equal amount of mental elbow-grease. Einstein issued this warning:

> If you want to find out anything from the theoretical physicists about the methods they use, I advise you to stick closely to one principle: don't listen to their words, fix your attention on their deeds. To him who is an explorer in this field, the products of his imagination appear so necessary and natural that he regards them, and would like to have them regarded by others, not as creations of thought but as given realities.

In the preceding section, I referred to "mental illness" as one such fiction. R.L. Spitzer, in his introduction to DSM-III (third edition of the *Diagnostic and Statistical Manual*), noted that the Manual's first edition "reflected the influence of Adolf Meyer's psychobiological view," that the second edition avoided terms implying "a particular theoretical framework for understanding nonorganic mental disorders," and that the third edition would make "no assumption that each mental disorder is a discrete entity with sharp boundaries (discontinuity) between it and other mental disorders, as well as between it and No Mental Disorder."

In this latter case, the "it" cannot be a real entity! So, "Mental disorders: None?, One?, or Many?"

Has anyone ever seen a mental disorder? If someone who wanted to have a look at the Grand Canyon asked for directions, we might produce a map. But where should we direct someone desiring to have a look at a mental disorder? To a psychiatric ward? And what will s/he see there? Is it so hard to believe that, even without questioning our naive realism, s/he will see, not mental disorders, but persons who supposedly have or suffer from one?

What's more, if physical illnesses are not visible as such, but only the symptoms supposedly caused by the unseen microbes, etc., the same is even more obvious in the case of mental illness. Imagine that the disorder is paranoia. Whoever has met real paranoids knows that they may at first appear quite normal. It is only when they turn their unseen attention to some unseen conspiracy that we decide is an unreal product of an unseen imagination and they begin to "express" their unseen suspicions . . . , it is only then that we begin to suspect there is something wrong. Which of all the words they speak will we use to convict them of carrying inside themselves an infection by that terribly disruptive "illness," paranoia? In *Personality*, a panorama on personality-theorizing, R. Lazarus reminded his readers of the enormous abstractions involved here:

> It took one pair of psychologists 435 pages of a book to record in some detail the activities of a seven-year-old boy during *one day* of his life, and not even completely at that. Considering the multitude of events, imagine the task of documenting through observation the whole life span of an individual, or even important experiences over so limited a time period as one year! (Second edition, page 156.)

Finally, are paranoids to be found only in psychiatric wards? Or is the world full of them? For instance, are whites in the U.S.A. paranoid in their fear of what will happen to property values if blacks move into their neighborhoods? Are blacks in the U.S.A. paranoid in thinking that drugs are funneled into their neighborhoods by whites who are determined to keep them "in their (inferior) place"? Are those who live beneath the poverty-line paranoid in thinking that the government is under the control of the wealthy? Are the wealthy paranoid in thinking those below the poverty-line are lazy parasites? Are Americans paranoid in thinking the Japanese are engaged in a massive conspiracy to destroy U.S. industry by unfair trade practices? Are the Japanese paranoid in thinking the Americans are paranoid?

Is it any wonder, then, that those who have noticed that paranoia is not a thing like a pimple but a subset of beliefs whose deadly tentacles may spread insidiously throughout the other ninety-nine percent of a person's belief-habits, plus an array of emotional attitudes and reaction-tendencies that sit atop that subset of beliefs, protest against the naivete of thinking that mental illnesses are real 'its,' similar to physical illnesses and curable with pills? Is it any wonder that still others object to so many of the current naive-science psychologies built on the myth that humans are conditioned super-rats or super-primates?

The most dangerous 'mental illnesses' of our times are beliefs in mythical entities, which beliefs block the rethinking efforts needed to understand the true facts. Most dangerous of all are today's pseudo-scientific reductionisms, with their deep-seated delusions about 'objectivity' and 'the scientific method.' So prevalent are they, that their victims call it "introspection" when a psychologist-of-religion reads (*other*) people's 'religious writings' or a chronometer-toting researcher asks someone *else* to speak into a tape-recorder while trying to solve a problem. Or are these assertions the paranoid ravings of a hostile critic?

The Ease of Fiction-Creating. Inserting words—e.g., nothingness, vacuum, space, time, Santa Claus, bogeyman—into our vocabulary can entice us into believing in realities where there are none. Inserting extra words or phrases—e.g., paranoia, schizophrenia, mental illness—into our vocabulary can entice us into thinking there is one rare kind of thing rather than many things, e.g., half-truths, distorted attitudes, and destructive habits which are by no means the exclusive property of 'abnormal' people. So, while time-saving is a good reason for verbal shorthand, e.g., for "submarine" rather than "a means of transportation which carries people from one port to another while submerged beneath the ocean's surface," an ability to re-translate terms into more common ones is crucial, because the old ones 'spell out the (accompanying) picture's details.' Recalling what is really going on in our use of 'words' is imperative at this point.

As there is no such thing as language, there are no such things as sentences, nor such things as names. What we mis-take for written sentences are parts of our private sense-data the same way that, at the movies, the subtitles are part of the pictures flashed onto the screen and the spoken words are part of the vibrations emitted from the loudspeakers. There are two things happening when we sense such EXTRA, 'language' sense-data: they spark imagery, and the imagery's calling-up is accompanied by the calling-forth of thoughts. In other words, words are not directly related to thoughts. They are first complex-imagery evokers, and it is the evoked imagery that evokes the thoughts.

How obvious! Notice the switch in imagery from "It's on the desk" to "It's in the desk." From "Indian Ocean Talks" in a headline to "Indian Ocean Talks!" in a joke about it\them. From "When we abstract from things' differences and attend only to how one is similar to others" to "When we abstract the essence things have in common from their accidental differences," from "When we look away from" to "When we pick out," from "I exist" to "I have existence," from "I am a body" to "I have a body," from "I am a car" to "I have a car," and so on. (You understand all of this?)

Understanding these matters helps to understand that, instead of explaining certain behaviors of certain people by mentally lumping them into a package and labeling them "paranoia," we have merely used a verbal shortcut to mentally isolate certain behaviors of one person and put them, along with what we regard as similar behaviors of other persons, into a larger, vaguer, more general mental pigeonhole. Naming them by mentally including them with others does not explain any of them.

Only those who still labor under the illusion that a name matches an "essence" and that "essences" are causes which explain the essence-owners' behaviors should think otherwise, though many people with still-unnamed 'symptoms' become nearly ecstatic when they're handed a name ("Now at least people will know 'it' isn't just my imagination" or "I am not alone in this") and others too sophisticated to believe in essences still do think otherwise (when pressed, they usually confess "It is still not clear what exactly paranoia is" or "It is still not clear why paranoia should cause such behavior" or "Much more research is needed before we can explain these matters"). Till we've demythologized language, Last of the Great Myths, we are too prone to worship idols of the mind better described as "theoretical fictions mis-taken for realities." (Modern logic and set theory have made obvious the mental-group-picturing behind "special-naming.")

Most critical of these fictions are those we use for people. Since there are only individuals, and since all generalized thoughts apply to reality only if they help to understand what real individuals do/did at some here/there location at some now/then moment, it is important to understand that what we know through a generalization is no more than whatever nitty-gritty particulars we can recognize once we're asked "What do you mean by that?" (Stolen from Wm. James, the ultimate Ockhamist, who rethought Kant's "Concepts without content are empty" into his own more accurate "No one sees farther into a generalization than his own knowledge of details extends.") We need generalizations, without them no one can handle the masses of information required by even ill-informed citizens for living in the late twentieth-century, but no one can become an objective (unbiased) citizen who is well-informed, but not well-informed about generalizations, theoretical fictions, and the dangers of being ill-informed about them. We need the simplest general framework, the simplest second-level generalizations, and so on, plus comprehensive files on the concrete, particular individuals that we connect with EVERY generalization we use. If this is abstract . . . then nitty-gritty particulars will "clarify" what I have in mind. When we label someone a "psychiatrist," we select one feature of that person and lump her or him with whomever else that label reminds us of—usually persons we think of as specialists dealing with 'mental illnesses'—and when the average person sees "paranoid" by itself, s/he will, if s/he 'speaks English,' most likely think of certain people with a certain type of thinking disorder. When we label someone a "politician seeking office," attention is focused on certain features of the total-picture of that person and, if our listeners are average citizens in 1992, they will not be surprised if the person we've labeled "politician" says the other candidate is "appealing to voters' paranoid fears about . . ."

The thing to notice about such uses of words or labels, which evoke unnoticed mental groupings, is that they select certain features of infinitely complex persons, focus attention on those, and—unless we are constantly on our guard—draw attention away from all else about those complex persons, including all the ways each of them differs from every other, and even the ways each individual today may differ from what s/he was in the past. It makes a great difference which items are selectively attended to. Rabble-rousers, whether their name is Adolf Hitler or some other, are dangerous, whereas charismatic leaders, whether their name is Winston Churchill or some other, are at times desperately needed.

Group thinking. Our mental grouping and regrouping is, we grow up believing, matched by physical behaviors. The atomists' view of the physical world is that tiny bodies, listed on Mendeleev's table, are constantly recycled into ever-new combinations. If we think of the world population—we mentally group and regroup the same 5.5 billion humans—as remaining steady for, say, a week, we may notice a somewhat similar situation. As every Martian spy hovering overhead in invisible UFOs can testify, humans group and regroup constantly. Watch one person for a period of time and s/he will be seen gathering with certain people in the morning of the first day of the week, with other people in the afternoon, with others each Monday, Tuesday, Wednesday, Thursday and Friday from early morning till noon and early afternoon till five, with others each of those days from noon till one, with others on one or other weekday evening, and so on. The question of paramount importance for those whose 'expert' thinking tends to end at the group-level will be: Is s/he a church-goer (Sunday services), a musician (Sunday afternoon rehearsals for Thursday evening concerts), a sports fan (Sunday at the football stadium, the basketball arena, the baseball park), a blue collar worker (eight to five job five days a week), a restaurant patron (mid-day), a union officer (Monday evening meetings), etc.?

We fail to notice to what degree the group-'sciences,' e.g., sociology, social psychology, (normal) abnormal psychology, anthropology, economics, political science, political philosophy, etc., capitalize on groupings that are mental only. Watch how the 'experts' classify and re-classify each of the above-mentioned individuals: as an American, a consumer, a democrat, an employee, a heterosexual, an incipient alcoholic, a nuclear-family member, an offspring, a parent, a relative, a religious person, a sibling, a slightly borderline personality, a stockholder-hence-partial-owner-of-several-large-corporations,   a television viewer, an upright citizen, etc. Then watch how they write and speak as if the groups are real entities, with properties of their own, as they try to explain the cause(s) of, e.g., inner-city poverty, juvenile delinquency, homosexuality, cannibalism, corporate greed, revolutions, good government, etc.

Human groups are fictions. They are concepts of things that do not exist as such. They are of great use in helping us think simultaneously of individual persons too numerous to think of individually. But every instance of converting an adjective describing a human to a noun is a thing-ification or re(s)-ification, since the only adequate mental category for a person is "person." Such reifications—e.g., "musician" instead of "person who does what we call 'playing a musical instrument'," "parent" instead of "a person who has done what we call 'begetting a child' or does what we call 'raising a child'," etc.—are dangerous once we get in the habit of thinking about them in abstraction from the totality of the complex persons who are the concrete realities the abstract thoughts should be thoughts about. The lesson is a universal or general one. Especially in the 1990's when so many millions of the world's five and a half billion inhabitants simplify their thinking with the principle that "if you've know one, you know them all," e.g., all white honkies, all black niggers, all power-hungry males, all castrating females, all delinquent juveniles, all unconcerned adults, all psychologists, all philosophers, all . . .

Psychologists' Selective Inattention. In order to understand William James, I had to learn this lesson, that we must rivet our attention on the principle that each person, like every other person re those things that make each a person rather than a chimp or a bee, is a unique blend of memories, beliefs, habits, attitudes, potentials, and so on. It is the essence of his thought. Perhaps his greatest essay was "On a Certain Blindness in Human Beings," about which he wrote:

> I wish I were able to make the second [essay], 'On a Certain Blindness in Human Beings,' more impressive. It is more than the mere piece of sentimentalism which it may seem to some readers. It connects itself with a definite view of the world and of our moral relations to the same. Those who have done me the honor of reading my volume of philosophic essays will recognize that I mean the pluralistic

277

or individualist philosophy . . . The practical consequence of such a philosophy is the well-known democratic respect for the sacredness of individuality—is, at any rate, the outward tolerance of whatever is not itself intolerant.

In the essay itself, which is little more than James' selection of passages from other authors which testify that those others had also noticed the blindness all of us are so prone to, he offered an introductory description of our typical blindness:

Take our dogs and ourselves, connected as we are by a tie more intimate than most ties in this world; and yet, outside of that tie of friendly fondness, how insensible, each of us, to all that makes life significant for the other!—we to the rapture of bones under hedges, or smells of trees and lampposts, they to the delights of literature and art. As you sit reading the most moving romance you ever fell upon, what sort of a judge is your fox-terrier of your behavior? With all his good will toward you, the nature of your conduct is absolutely excluded from his comprehension. To sit there like a senseless statue, when you might be taking him to walk and throwing sticks for him to catch! What queer disease is this that comes over you every day, of holding things and staring at them like that for hours together, paralyzed of motion and vacant of conscious life?

How serendipitous that James, before Watson ruled thought out of court for 'scientific' psychology, chose the most unnoticed of a psychologist's behaviors in discussing "human blindness." What, after all, are they doing when they read Freud, Skinner, reports on drug research, literature on the behavior of Pavlov's dogs, of the Yerkes chimps, of Lilly's dolphins, and other "words, words, words" that supply the facts they must take on faith because they have no time to conduct all the research personally? Serendipitous, too, that James, in the same pre-Watson preface to his lecture on the worst kind of human blindness, wrote: "There is no point of view absolutely public and universal. Private and incommunicable perceptions always remain over, and the worst of it is that those who look for them from the outside never know where"!

Why draw attention to these *unpleasant* facts about those plain humans we squeeze into our narrow mental category labelled "psychologist"? Because they are often looked up to as the experts on what makes humans tick, as members of a priesthood in charge of secular salvation. Because, as inheritors of Watsonian blindness, they often fail to achieve the Socratic self-knowledge evident in U. Neisser's answer to B. Baars' question, "How would you summarize the situation in psychology today compared with the way things were in the '40s and '50s?", that was cited on an earlier page:

> Well, we have found out how recalcitrant the cognitive activities of everyday life are to experimental study. For example, the fact that we understand so little about reading after years of study is very impressive to me.

Today's 'scientific' psychological literature, naive-science in inspiration, is straitjacketed or book-ended between two materialist models: we humans are what our inherited genes make us, we are what society makes us, or we are a combination, a product of biological nature and social nurture. So powerful is the evolutionist dogma—as naïve-realist as the creation-science myth—that it is rare that anyone focuses all of today's physics and physiology, as well as all of the traditional literature William James was so intimately conversant with, on the obvious question: What IS going on while I sit here reading these rose, wrose, and more roes of 'print'? What a revolution would occur if we recovered the wisdom available for more than a century in the 'writings' of James, the physiologist and physician of whom Watson's words, "the most brilliant psychologist the world has ever known," still ring true, of whose rich and varied thinking Gordon Allport wrote, somewhat prematurely: "Now that we have recovered from the irreverent shocks administered by Freud, Pavlov, Watson, we begin to perceive that the psychological insights of James have the steadiness of a polar star."

Each of us must choose, all alone, what 'reading' we will give to our life 'text.' Once I learn—is it from ink marks, letters, rows upon rows of words, tiny letter-shaped colors standing out from light-background color in a non-physical visual field, or some unseen author of the "words, words, words" in my Kohler-ian 'world'?—how many 'other minds' regard naive realism as false, the choice of what I will believe is my choice. This 'sense world' with its 'starry heavens above' is not a matter of thin, bloodless thought, as Descartes often suggests. It looks and feels as thick and solid as Eddington's common-sense 'table.' The pleasures of 'eating ice cream' and 'wrapping my arms around loved-ones' are not fleeting-dream fantasies that evaporate upon awakening, but wide-awake experiences that can often be repeated in detail, almost at will. Watching a marching band, even one made up of the twenty 'Nazis' that Simone Weil, if she existed, referred to, seems as real as 'this phrase and now this one' you are reading do right now. But which of the many alternative 'readings' I choose to impose on this field-of-experience 'text' is utterly my own private decision. In "What is Enlightenment," Kant dares his readers to *"Sapere Aude!"* Dare think for yourselves! Only those who dare to turn from or repress an uncomfortable thought will imagine they ever really do anything else.

Moreover, what we selectively turn our attention away from is not thereby wiped from memory. Unremembered is not synonymous with unconscious. The person who persists in using "We," as in "We thought" and "We know," does not thereby become different from a single conscious agent who is either in good faith error or bad faith denial. Every act of selective attention has, as its other-side-of-the-coin, a volume of selective inattention.

Better thinking than ever is demanded by our times. Vicious abstraction is rampant. Even those who reject Hegel's idealism—that our separate reality is an illusion and that we are really interchangeable and replaceable "parts" of a single Reality—are, often enough, victims of "collectivist thinking." Many who think of themselves as "scientists" think of science as a collective process, think of scientific progress as a centuries-long enterprise, yet every single person who learns enough to believe that begins—if they are like me—to learn everything they know on the day of their birth and not one of them learns a single thing, whether about the course of the stars or about others' discoveries about the stars, except what s/he learns, it seems, by using her or his own eyes to see stars or to read words about the stars or to read words about those others who discovered new facts about the stars. Try, if you can, to think of one thing you did not learn on your own, either first-hand or, it may seem, second-hand through first-hand scanning of and interpretation of "words, words, words" such as these. All the thinking in the universe—I've decided—is conducted by solitary individuals prone to lapsing into self-forgetful, impersonal, collective, personal-understanding, personal-deciding.

We need, each one of us, to memorize and live by the lesson so nicely captured by the 'words' of the historian, Carl Becker:

> "In the year 49 B.C. Caesar crossed the Rubicon." A familiar fact this is, known to all, and obviously of some importance since it is mentioned in every history of the great Caesar. But is this fact as simple as it sounds? Has it the clear, persistent outline which we commonly attribute to simple historical facts? When we say that Caesar crossed the Rubicon we do not of course mean that Caesar crossed it alone, but with his army. The Rubicon is a small river, and I don't know how long it took Caesar's army to cross it; but the crossing must surely have been accompanied by many acts and many words and many thoughts of many men. That is to say, a thousand and one lesser "facts" went to make up the one simple fact that Caesar crossed the Rubicon; and if we had someone, say James Joyce, to know and relate all these facts, it would no doubt require a book of 794 pages to present this one fact that Caesar crossed the Rubicon. Thus the simple fact turns out to be not a simple fact at all. It is the statement that is simple—a simple generalization of a thousand and one facts.

What kind of better-analysed thinking is needed? Clear-eyed and honest acknowledgement by each of us as to "What do I control and what do I not control?" I do not have absolute control over what thoughts come to me, but whatever is the source of my thoughts—and my images and sensed-givens—presents me with the option of believing my brain, which I have never observed or experienced, is their source, and with the option of believing that "my-brain" at most is fiction-shorthand for sub-atom-sized bodies and their incredibly intricate, quantum-formula'd dances.

My thoughts' source has not stopped there, however. More than anything, it or they impress upon me in the most forcible way imaginable a conviction that other humans like myself exist and are, at least indirectly, responsible for so much in my life. My experience forces upon me, as soon as my critical rethinking is relaxed, a sense that my way of life is inextricably dependent upon others. I seem to wear clothes made by others, to eat food grown by others, to drive a car whose parts are made in many countries by many workers, powered by gas conveyed from well to pump by an international transportation network, requiring an international currency-credit network, just as I seem to learn from books written by others, not one of which seems to be written by a solipsist who thinks all the rest of us are figments of her or his imagination. The thought expressed by "I live in a world with others," though it is a thought about real beings who lie beyond my field-of-experience 'world,' i.e., about beings who, if real, are every bit as 'transcendent' as any divine person(s) worshipped by me or any of those transcendent-to-my-experience human persons, is certainly pragmatically true.

Simone Weil, if she existed, was right: I must resist passion unless it is approved by cool, calculating reason. Even if I can't fool my thoughts' Source, I may fool those others. May. For a time. Till I die. If I do. And then . . . ?

E. Self-Interested or As-If Altruism.

Oh, yes, self-interested altruism. Consider that what follows is an introduction to the climactic next chapter. The difference between as-if altruism and genuine altruism is a matter of inner motives.* Sorting out the tangled concepts involved here has taken a lifetime of thinking and rethinking. (*The first ms of mine to get published was *Essence of Ethics*, where the issues in what follows here are discussed at length.)

The first thing necessary is to distinguish external behavior and internal motives. The difference is pure common sense. Even the biologist, Richard Dawkins, felt obligated to make the distinction in his book, *The Selfish Gene*.

> It is important to realize that the above definitions of altruism and selfishness are *behavioral*, not subjective. I am not concerned here with the psychology of motives. I

am not going to argue about whether people who behave altruistically are 'really' doing it for secret or subconscious selfish motives. Maybe they are, and maybe they aren't, and maybe we can never know. (2006, p.4)

Aristotle erred by not making the distinction a major premise in his famous *Nichomachean Ethics*. The result is a *contradiction* between (i) the idea that everyone's aim *is* to enjoy happiness, the fruit of virtuous activity (as Aquinas teaches), and (ii) the idea that humans' aim *should be* the virtuous activity* itself. In Book Nine, where the idea of motive is central to his ruminations on goodness and on friendship, it is easy to see that Aristotle's ultimate view of the best friendship *is really a matter of self-interest*, viz., how to be happy yourself versus how to make others happy, a view that attempts to identify the two by means of the blatant fiction that "a friend is another self." (*Now frequently translated as "flourishing," that is, behaving after having acquired every faculty-perfecting habit or 'virtue.' How silly. Jesus Christ, a paragon of virtue and certainly flourishing in that sense, became an even more exemplary paragon while dying on a cross. But happy?! Aristotle himself noticed how silly that is when he wrote, vis-à-vis the happiness that 'all people want': "Those who say that the man on the rack or the man who falls into great misfortunes is happy if he is good, are, whether they mean to or not, talking nonsense." See *Nichomachean Ethics*, Bk. VII, ch.13.)

The very title of Dale Carnegie's *How To Win Friends and Influence People* raises the motive question. It is extremely useful and pragmatic—'it works'—to recognize the truth that others like being liked and appreciated, dislike being taken advantage of and merely 'used,' and to speak and act at least outwardly in accordance with that truth.

Machiavellians, too, recognize that, to succeed in 'using' people, it is helpful to at least *pretend* to be honest, fair, and concerned about them. In the language of ethics, it is smart—self-enlightened or prudent—to act AS IF inspired by altruism, regardless of whether the outward appearances are matched by an inner altruistic attitude or not.

How essential it is to sort out our tangled ideas on these issues is essential to assessing Simone Weil's life and what to many seemed (falsely) her fatal anorexia.

Chapter Four

Altruism Without A Hook

Role Model. Called to love. That is what she finally concluded was the one phrase, the essential truth, the fundamental premise that put sense into her life. She was to love. If we step back and look at her life as a whole, we can see that everything points to the truth of her conclusion. Of course, "look at her life as a whole" is a metaphor. Words, words, and more words—plus a handful of photo reproductions—are all I have ever seen, and I've had to reconstruct "her life" in my imagination. Yet the words she left behind as her chief legacy to us are so clear on the matter of her calling that we can feel confident she regarded the divine call to love as the one thing that put the events of her life into perspective.

Clearest of her words on the subject are those that make up or seem to make up a letter she wrote to her sister, Marie. It was sometime in mid-September, 1896, a year before she died. She was looking back over an already long lifetime of just 23 years, 8 1/2 months, explaining how its multitude of adventures finally fell into place and made sense. Here is some of what she wrote:

> [. . .] I seem to have so many other vocations as well!
> I feel as if I were called to be a fighter, a priest, an apostle, a
> doctor, a martyr; as if I could never satisfy the needs of my
> nature without performing . . . every kind of heroic action
> at once. I feel as if I'd got the courage to be a Crusader, a
> Pontifical Zouave, dying on the battle-field in defense of the
> Church. And at the same time I want to be a priest . . .

284

I was still being tormented by this question of unfulfilled longings and it was a real martyrdom in my prayer, when I decided to consult St. Paul's epistles in the hopes of getting an answer . . . I met this comforting phrase: "Prize the best gifts of heaven. Meanwhile I can show you a way which is better than any other."

What was it? The Apostle goes on to explain that all the gifts of heaven, even the most perfect of them, without love, are absolutely nothing; charity is the best way of all, because it leads straight to God. Now I was at peace; when St. Paul was talking about the different members of the Mystical Body I couldn't recognize myself in any of them; or rather I could recognize myself in all of them. But charity—that was the key to my vocation.

Therese Martin was no priest. Her words, though, have made converts of thousands. In that, she was like her mentor, Saul of Tarsus, better known as Saint Paul. Most of his work, too, was stirring souls with his words. Had she been a priest, the meaning of her life might have been less clearly crystalized. But then, just what is a priest? Better, what is love?

A. Habits-I: Habits of Thought.

Truth—the whole truth and nothing but the truth—must be our holy grail. We crave the truth for ourselves. Since there is no time except the present time, really not even that, knowing the truth means knowing what is presently going on. All of us are apt to become nervous if we begin to suspect that part of what is going on is that we don't know what is going on.

We also have an obligation to learn the truth. Or, if not to learn it, to at least *try* to learn it. We must embrace the truth when we recognize it and include as much searching for more of it as we can fit into lives already burdened with responsibilities.

First, we crave the truth for ourselves. We want to know what is going on. We want newscasters to broadcast the truth, newspapers to report the truth, the labels on food packages to list the true ingredients, our teachers to teach what's true, the used car's odometer to indicate the true mileage, drug companies to be honest about their products' safety, witnesses to not-perjure themselves, jury members to reach their verdict without bias, etc. Whoever decides to collect headlines with the word "truth" in them—e.g., "In Search of the Truth," "The Truth About Deficits," "At Last, a Victory for Truth," are samples quickly gleaned from a handful of clippings from *Newsweek*—will soon discover how many there are to choose from. Whoever wants to know whether people crave the truth for themselves is invited to begin noticing the sea of positive evidence that surrounds us.

The case for our craving becomes even clearer when we turn our attention from the positive evidence to its correlative: our dislike for the ocean of lies that also surrounds us. The cleverness of the 10-5-92 cover of *Time*, "Lying . . . Everybody's Doin' It (Honest)," highlights the simple truth that many people lie, then lie about their lying or not telling the truth. The inside story, entitled "Lies, Lies, Lies," begins with the lies and half-truths encountered in recent political campaigns. The writers capture the public's current distrust with the question: "Is anyone around here telling the truth?" The article goes on to explore three common motives for not telling it. There's lying to protect the feelings of others ("I just love your new dress"), lying to protect yourself ("The dog ate my homework"), and lying to cause harm ("Trust me this time"). In the same way that we are taught that every word of God is true, because God "can neither deceive nor be deceived," it is often suggested that no words from a used-car salesman (have you ever heard this use of gender reprimanded?) can be trusted, a lesson reinforced by the photo accompanying *Time's* third-motive headline. (The whole truth would include mention of the fact that the text itself singles out, not used-car salesmen, but Shakespeare's Iago as the model of harm-causing liars.) Whoever hasn't noticed how many are the lies encountered by citizens living in free-speech countries is invited to start noticing what's going on.

Whoever wonders whether we crave the truth for ourselves has only to start asking: Would I like the rival presidential candidates to start saying more of what they really believe or stick to what we want to hear?, Do I wish the history books in school would tell the truth about the American Revolution by colonists against their mother country, Britain, or to perpetuate myths about it?, Do I hope future Red

Cross blood donors will tell the truth or lie when asked those new and intrusive questions about their sexual activities?, etc. And, as they do their answering, to climb alternately into the shoes of Republicans, then Democrats, of Americans, then British, of bed-hopping playpersons, then hemophiliacs. We crave the truth for ourselves, however willing we might be to let others remain a lot or a little in the dark.

Still. We not only crave the truth for ourselves. Seeking it is a moral obligation. That is the reason for beginning this section with the claim that truth *must* be our holy grail. We have a choice about whether or not we will assent to the truth that we have such an obligation. We have a choice about whether or not we will fulfill it. But the obligation will confront us as soon as we begin to wonder "Must I believe what is true?" An inescapable obligation, in fact, as can be recognized by anyone who quietly reflects on the question, "Can I honestly believe it is true that I don't have to honestly believe what is true?", and who reflects on it without changing the meanings of "is true." (In truth, each of the things I believe is something I believe is true. And you? Can you believe it is true that you can believe that something you believe is false is really true?)

The logic behind our obligations relative to truth is easy to understand. They are part of our Creating Parents' more general command and of our correspondingly general obligation to love. Consider the oft-repeated truth that our obligation to be moral can be summed up in the golden rule, "(You, like I, must) do unto others what you would have done unto you." That entails that we who crave truth for ourselves must be ready to do our part in making it available to others. Before we can make it available to others, or rather before we can do our part in the process whereby others learn the truth, it is normally required that *we first find out what the truth is.*

The qualification, "normally," is added in order to cover those times when others misunderstand us or when we lie. If we tell the truth—"telling the truth" means trying to help them learn *what we think* is true, even if it turns out that what we believed was the truth wasn't. If we lie—"lying" means trying to dupe someone else into believing *what we believe* is false—we may help them learn the truth if what we believe to be false is really true. Either way, telling the truth and lying are inextricably connected to knowing the truth, and any obligation we have to tell the truth and not to lie makes sense only within the context of a prior obligation to try and learn it.

Be careful, though. Each of us has an absolute moral obligation to be honest, but not an absolute obligation to tell *everyone* the truth, the whole truth, and nothing but the truth—all of it!—every time we have a moment to speak to them! We'd never have a moment to shut our mouth. That's not our obligation. In fact, it's absurd.

Not even our Creating Parents, the very embodiments of goodness, do it. They do not instantly reveal everything to us at birth. They gradually teach us that there are other beings who can feel joy and suffer agony as much as we do and that our obligation is to be a source of joy, not agony, but they weave such truths into a background tapestry of naive-realist deceptions, that is, making us think it's others that we see, hear, and touch.

Our absolute obligation to try and learn the truth is to be open to the truth, always open to more of it and thus not to ignore intimations that something we believe is false, thereby aiming for nothing but the truth. This is not just wise advice for us if we think it will make us happy ourselves if we learn the truth, that is, not a mere hypothetical, if-then imperative, but a categorical imperative that admits of no if's, and's, or but's—not even if million of others say ignorance is bliss or who say they're too old to think a different way. Unless we learn the truth, we won't be able to pass it on at the appropriate time to other individuals whose mind-shaping environment we are part of.

Absolute truths. Fulfilling our obligations is often pleasant. That is absolutely true. For example, to live, we must eat. As we sit down to a traditional Thanksgiving meal, we give thanks for the food that will make it a pleasure to fulfill that duty. To stay healthy, we need our rest. Who among us complains as we lay our weary head down for a good night's sleep? We must have love for one another. Does anyone think Romeos and Juliets have to force themselves to agree to the other's desire for marriage?

But our obligations are often unpleasant. That, too, is absolutely true. Whoever suffers chronic loss of appetite but feels forced to eat, whoever suffers chronic lying-for-hours-awake insomnia but feels forced to get sleep, and whoever suffers chronic abusiveness but feels forced to turn the other cheek can testify to that.

288

Both same things apply to our obligation vis-à-vis truth.

Learning is enjoyable. That is absolutely true. In the right environment, children spontaneously develop such a taste for 'getting into things' that, were there anti-curiosity pills, some parents would be grateful. Many of the greatest discoverers worked for years on end, often far into the night, because finding the truth became an end in itself for them. The work became their enjoyment. The greatest of the Greek thinkers thought so highly of knowing the truth that they inaugurated the tradition of seeing "knowledge for its own sake" as the highest good of all. In Aristotle's mind, it is so good that the Supreme Being is perfectly content with perfect knowledge and nothing else. Not even wine or ice cream. Just knowledge.

But if discovering the truth can be one of life's greatest pleasures, enjoyed for its own sake, learning the basic truths needed by citizens of advanced societies and relearning them often enough to remember them on a habitual basis can involve sheer drudgery. That, too, is absolutely true. Ignoring the obvious truth that the young and ignorant are initially as ignorant of what is good for them to know as they are of what is good for them to eat and good for them to play with, and as uninterested in or even resistant to learning it, the reverse sides of which are that they do not initially know when what they want to know, to eat, or to play with is bad for them, but are very interested in and desirous of doing it, is an example of the kind of bad, half-truth-for-the-whole-truth thinking that leads to the "Learning should be fun!" educational philosophy, which is a sub-section of the "Life should be pleasant!" half-truth. The person I know best had to write out each next-day's spelling lesson three times as routine homework and—too unclairvoyant to foresee how often he would give thanks for it later on—would, if he could, have gladly avoided the drudgery. That is simply the first generalization-destroying truth that comes to mind.

What generalization should be drawn? That truth is a craving but truth is an obligation, that learning it is enjoyable but that learning it is drudgery? Or a synthesis of the antitheses, viz., that whoever knows enough detailed facts can put that knowledge to the kind of use every follower of Hegel can, viz., can recall a "but" for every generalization and use that negation to show that every whole truth is only one of thousands of partial-truth affirmations? Or are all of these truths absolutely true, though none by itself is the whole truth?

Clearly the last. It is more of the whole truth. Each partial truth, if true, is absolutely true at the moment I think it with my mindset adjusted as it is at the moment, just as each re-becomes absolutely true when I recall it with the appropriate mindset-context. Whoever wants to know my mindset vis-à-vis any single sentence, or every single sentence!, I use to 'express' my thoughts will have to read this entire book, perhaps read some of the other things written before this, and may even have to spend considerable time in the library becoming familiar with works by authors referred to in these and those other pages. This is part of another of the absolute truths that forms the heart and soul of the overall belief-system that these rows and rows of tiny figures are your cues and clues to: the meaning of each complete sentence is the complete thought in the mind of the person meaning to help another understand something, and each moment's complete thought carries that person's entire mindset on its back. Put another way, the context for each writer's particular thought is the writer's overall belief-system.

The problem of communicating with each other—a one-way process here, while you're reading, not a dialogue—is that, whereas we often begin with things we both understand in similar ways because those things are part of our everyday common-sense models, we eventually shift into our differing professed or professional mindsets where our thoughts become miles and miles apart. Until we learn the most important of all reading habits, namely, how to put ourselves in the place of another party and look at things from alternative mindset-contexts, we will remain trapped in part of the truth.

What further generalization should be drawn? That a price is to be paid for the thrill of enjoying the whole truth. Presuppose the existence of billions of individual thinkers, each with an entire mindset-context partly like but partly unlike every other. Even if we ignore the animals, vegetables, and minerals, that is a lot to learn about. What's more, others' minds are changing constantly, so we can never be done having to learn new truths to be added to our collection of present truths about the past. Or about what once was true. Which is perhaps the most difficult part of learning the whole truth: learning how to separate only apparent from genuine contradictions. "She is at the store" may be true now, but if I say it tomorrow, it may be false. Does what is true become false, then? No, we merely have to learn how to find ways to fit the two pieces of the whole puzzle together. By recognizing what we too often forget: we must never pluck a thought from the thinker and from the thinker's mindset-context, as if it is a flower that can live all by itself, suspended in mid-air.

Whenever someone asks "What is love?", the expert-thinker will rephrase the question. Several times. First, as "What does 'love' mean?" Then, as "What does 'love' mean for whom?" Then, as "Now how many things can 'love' mean for me?" But the clincher must always be, "Does love exist?" (Insert. My answer is no. Not as an isolated thing. Persons exist, not love. Only persons who decide lovingly, who feel or experience the emotion named—in English—"love," etc. End of insert.)

Who can best explain love? Poets? Or scientists? Some people have erected a wall in their mind between science and poetry. Or, since science and poetry do not exist, between scientists and poets. Our thoughts—those of some people and mine—are miles and miles apart on this. And that, too, is an absolute truth. Though I expect it is obvious to anyone that, given my meaning/thought of "thought," it is also absolutely false. The same way that Aesop's fables are absolutely true, though they are also absolutely false. At first, this seems like a contradiction in terms. Like patent nonsense. Like out-and-out irrationalism.

To understand such matters, it is essential to understand thought. Thought is perhaps the hardest thing to think clearly about. For instance, to say that Aesop's fables are both true and false seems to be a contradiction. And, to be sure, such a formula in someone else's mouth, from someone else's pen, as a clue to part of someone else's belief-system, might be those things. But not the way it is meant here.

One way to study and learn about thought is by ANALYSING thoughts.

Analysis. Learning how to analyse things, to break them down, is a lesson that cannot be learned overnight, but only through practice, more practice, and ever more practice, till it is second-nature habit. Poets use images. Scientists do, too. Whoever wishes to learn the absolute truth about thinking, that is, to become a scientist on thinking, must become an expert at detecting poetry, imagery, metaphors, analogies, and so on.

For instance, the word "analysis" was born as a metaphor that meant just what "break (them) down" means. Even as a formal-looking, adult, technical term, it remains at its core nothing more than an image.

Its twin, synthesis, is no different. Not in that respect. Though, from another point of view, it is just the opposite, as different from it as night is from day. Both name images. So does "miles and miles apart."

People's thoughts can be miles and miles apart. To find out how that can be true and how it can be false, you have to understand what I mean by "miles and miles apart." I mean one thing when I think of the earth and the moon being miles and miles apart. The image that "miles and miles apart" conjures up is a spatial image of two items separated so far apart that 1760 yardsticks or 5280 one-foot rulers could be laid end to end between them for every single mile making up those miles and miles. (That is called "operational definition.") Usually we think that the only things that can be miles and miles apart are the earth, moon, and other things of that kind. "That kind of things" refers to things mentally lumped together, in this case the ones also labeled "bodies," though it must be added that our imaginations often picture areas, called "places," that stay behind after the bodies are removed, and we often think of these imaginary 'places' as being among the kind of things that can be literally miles and miles apart. Thoughts, however, aren't the kind of things that can be miles and miles apart the way bodies can, so we would describe the opening thought of this paragraph as an absolute truth that is expressed in the garb of a metaphor. The thoughts one person is certain are true may contradict those that another person firmly assents to, and that is a more literal way of saying what is meant by the absolutely-true-if-correctly-understood statement that thoughts can be miles and miles apart. Of course, if we trace "contradict" back to its origins, we discover that it conjured the image of two persons speaking rather than thinking, and speaking against one another.

Which is the way Aesop's absolute truths are expressed, in the garb of analogies or comparisons. After all, who ever heard a fox, after trying fruitlessly (literally) to jump high enough to reach some delicious-looking grapes, walk away muttering "They were probably sour anyway"?! But people often refer to things they've previously craved but never managed to get their hands on with analogous phrases, such as "I'm sure it was a piece of crap anyway." Aesop wasn't thinking only or chiefly of foxes, but of all of us humans who, like foxes we think of as crafty, craftily pour cold water upon our simmering cravings with distractions, even untruths. But wouldn't the truth have been expressed far more exactly by a psychologist writing a dry, technical treatise on the way frustration can often be dissipated if we change the way we are thinking of the irritant, if we turn our attention away, if we immerse ourselves in something else, etc.

More amply. Who can "explicate" or unfold better what "sour grapes" means? A poet? Or someone who has often returned to the phrase (which assumes linguistic capabilities), practiced "free association" (which presumes considerable experience-memory), kept notes on the ensuing "trains" of associations (which assumes writing skills), read a great deal of other people's thoughts about the interplay between thoughts and the emotion of frustration (which presumes reading habits), then done the same in regard to the interplay between thoughts and other emotions (which assumes an ability to notice less specific but more numerous connections), then studied the various theories about thinking (which presumes sustained attention), about the laws that appear to "govern" thoughts in relation to each other, to imagery, to language, to sense-experience, to the physical environment believed to cause sense-experience (laws describable as logic, psychology, linguistics, epistemology, psycho-physics), to the laws that govern the way light radiations, molecular vibrations, pheromones, etc., do that causing (the physiology of sensation), to the source of those laws (theodicy), to the entire universe which appears to be the product of a coordinating intelligence infinitely superior to our own (ontology or metaphysics), even though our own intelligence which can discover such coordinating patterns, author library-fuls of books about them, disagree with other human intelligences about them and about every detail associated with them, is infinitely superior to any alleged animal-intelligence (comparative what's-its-name), etc.? The psychologist, of course. If her/his poetry is right.

> Little flower—but *if* I could understand
> What you are, root and all, and all in all,
> I should know what God and man is.

We think of poets as indulging in imagination and imagery. We do not think of them as scientists concerned with pure truth. Part of the reason is that, like poets who cannot give a scientific explanation of what they do any better than Plato's Ion could long ago, we do not understand the further thoughts beneath the distinction between poet and scientist. We stop our digging before we reach the bottom-line recognition of persons, thoughts, images, truth and error. Whether, like Maya Angelou, some are regarded as poets and others, like Andrei Sakharov, are regarded as scientists, they belong to the same human species, think with images, feel strongly, their thoughts are either true or false, they can all look back over the words that supposedly 'captured' their thoughts to see how well or poorly they have succeeded, and so on. Relatively minor differences in how many images are used, in how consistently one image is sustained, in efforts to relate to concrete facts, in attention to rhyme and rhythm, are appearances that divert our eyes from the realities.

Whoever wishes to discover whether or not to agree with this proposed cold, hard fact about thinking, whether that of poets or scientists, will first have to ANALYSE and understand the full mindset that is the context for its meaning. S/he may have to do what was mentioned above: (re-)read this entire book, perhaps some of the other things, etc. S/he will then have to analyse the meaning of each term they mention or use while defining them or describing their essence or explaining how they are different, including the difference, if any, between defining, describing, explaining, narrating, etc., and to get to the root of all the relevant matters, including how poets and scientists are distinct from flowers (the way animals are distinct from vegetables in the Twenty-Question version of Porphyry's Tree)—including the ones in crannied walls—and from their roots. And we know from the poet, Tennyson, where that is going to take the scientist! And yet, the journey down to the roots of every thing is part of our obligation to learn the truth. Yet again, once the price has been paid, the pleasure that follows is its own reward.

This brief section on poetry and truth is drenched with poetry, metaphors, and so on. It can be viewed either as poetry that is true or as science that makes use of images. Let it serve as an introduction to the work of imagination, imagery, and metaphor in all of science about science, i.e., in all true thinking about thinking and rethinking. ANALYSIS—thought interpretation, exegesis, translation, hermeneutics, all began as poetic imagery, they all mean the same thing here (I know, since I am doing the meaning)—of your own thinking will give you your evidence on these matters. What you see are merely cues and clues to help you notice, and having noticed to attend more. (Note: One person's literal is another's metaphor and vice-versa. Compare Descartes and James on "I", James and Watson on "mind.")

Thought and 'Scientific' Psychology. Throughout this work, the model of human thinkers constructing inner models as scaffoldings for their thoughts has played a major role. The aim is not to create a model—that is poetry—but to help others understand a THEORY about human thinking. Jerome Bruner remarked once that "You can never get a direct test on reality. You must take scraps and test them against your mental model of the world." The thesis here is that Bruner's remark itself proposes a model to explain how we know reality, especially that part of reality that is whatever the "You" is who never gets a direct peek, whatever a "model" is, and how mini-models appear inside the total model.

The theory here is constructed from material copied wholesale from other thinkers' discoveries. One large part of it comes from the ancient Greeks, especially Plato and Aristotle, whose scientific ambitions included a study of the mind. One of the staples of the psychology I learned first was a model that Saint Thomas borrowed from Aristotle, namely, that our thoughts are accompanied by images. And, though Aristotle's observation was only a beginning, it was important, for it brought to the attention of later learners a phenomenon that needed to be further investigated. It was left to the Big Three of British Empiricism to begin exploring the vast, dark continent of imagery. Their heroic efforts spurred the creation of a new school, staffed by "associationists," to rival the old school staffed by "rationalists" whose specialty was the study of reason and logic. Then, during the last century some dissidents decided to break away and create a school for the "scientific" study of the mind. Much of this text's theory is an elaboration of earlier ones made possible by studying the conclusions of these dissidents. The insistence on the entirely different mindsets of "scientific psychologists" results from studying the dissident's history.

"The Great Lock-Out" is a metaphor for the mindset that, by the mid-1900s had come to dominate Anglo-American psychology. G. Humphrey's *Thinking: An Introduction to Its Experimental Psychology* taught us to recognize the revolution by John Watson and the other padlockers as the outcome of an early debate that emerged when, as was inevitable, an effort was made to study the relations between imagery and thought. Not as philosophers study it, but experimentally. It seemed to some that perhaps Aristotle had been wrong to say that it is impossible to think without imagery. (What about inner words, which some think are better imagined as symbols than as images?) Others thought that Aristotle had been right.

It is hard to imagine a better report than Humphrey's on the debate. Recall that Wundt, James, and the other inaugurators of 'empirical' or 'scientific' psychology said that the method for psychology had to be introspection, looking into one's own mind. The outcome of debates about the need for images was a stalemate. Some 'introspecting' psychologists working in Wurzburg were able to think complex thoughts without any images or internal speech accompanying them, but none of the introspectors working under Titchener in Ithaca could do such pure thinking. (The whole truth would require reference to those working under Wundt at Leipzig. See Wann) The stalement created a crisis. No one could think of a scientific method for resolving this debate. No one could think of a scientific method to prove that, apart from images and words, there is any thinking. Given thinking's importance in humans' lives, the controversy suggested that perhaps psychology could not be scientific. That there would be a still-birth.

And then John Watson strode onto the scene. He declared that the sole remedy was for "behaviorists" to seize control of the School of Scientific Psychology and to banish or eliminate all direct or unambiguous reference to any inside conscious experiences researchable only by introspection. Nothing inside—thoughts and images fall under that rubric—would be allowed into the data. Only outer behavior of animals, whether human or infrahuman, that is, what could be proven by direct observation (sic), would be studied. Only what was reported in terms reducible to behavior-actions or operations, e.g., laying yardsticks or rulers between bodies such as the earth and the moon or the nucleus and the electron, would be countenanced as scientifically genuine or as genuine science. "Stay with what is on the 'OUT' side of your skin!" became the rule.

Not till there is a massive uprising of the world against that rule will there be an end to the mounting violence that threatens to erupt in a conflagration that could dwarf even the "world wars" of recent times. Not until those lulled into a zombie-state by the widespread acceptance of Watson's outrageous advice to imagine that we are unconscious, unthinking, unfeeling, unresponsible robotic androids that only outwardly mimic the behavior of human beings, whose mimicry reaches its apex when the body utters aloud or mutters under its breath, wake up and issue a general call to arms, will we be able to collectively throw off the blankets of fiction known as "objective science" that are presently smothering us. Watson's monstrous program, to treat humans as beasts and both as biological automata, was carried into effect—as were other monstrous programs in this century—by zealous brownshirts whose youthful enthusiasm far outreached whatever unstable wisdom they had as yet acquired.

Many will regard such characterization of behaviorist psychologists as prejudicial. What true facts are there to justify such an outburst of extreme sentiment? Such indulgence in imagery? Such rhetoric? Is there any truth to the thought behind it? Critical, rethinking readers will ask that. Few, however, will examine the backdrop of their questions. What is thought? What is truth?

(Note. Some answers were presented in the opening section of the last chapter. Since most of today's violence results, not from the ill-will of some, but from the poor thinking of most, only an end to that poor thinking will make peace possible. The strongest force in the world is what comes in the form of social pressure to shape up, especially when it is reinforced by the power of rhetoric and seemingly good logic. The pressure to avoid poor thinking *habits* will not come into being until each single one of us who contributes to what comes in the form of social pressure to everyone else puts an end to our own poor thinking. A major crisis in today's theories about thinking comes from the difficulty of thinking about the meaning of the "words" we use while we are doing it. That is why this work began with a theory about meaning. This section will amplify what was begun there.)

Let these introductory paragraphs under the title "Truth and Abstraction" serve as a bridge from poetry which is believed to use imagery, via rhetoric which can clothe truth as well as error with images, to that Big Deal called "Science with a capital S" that the whole modern world is in the habit of regarding as the complete opposite of poetry and rhetoric. Its goal is to present just a little less abstractly the thesis that ALL thinking comes clothed in images. Seeing that calls for images, the ones that help us direct our attention in the right direction.

In order to get in the *habit* of thinking correctly about thinking. And having seen, to attend.

Abstraction. One of the best images ever found, first as the scaffold for the pre-Descartes science about thinking, then as a picture of original sin in existentialism's rhetorical war against science, is abstraction. But what does the metaphor "abstraction" mean literally? Or originally? How should the image be used?

To grasp the long history of theories conjured by "abstraction," begin with the picture conjured by "extraction" and "removal." Next, take the nouns that play central roles in the everyday common sense from which 'science' takes off. Every common-sense person learns to distinguish humans, animals, vegetables, and minerals from each other. It was natural that thinkers striving for a grand unifying view would single out such 'general' terms as "human," "animal," "vegetable," "mineral," and so on.

To get an idea of abstraction, consider the question, "What is a human being?" The 'general' answer that Aristotle gave was, "A human is a rational animal." It is quite obvious that we can think the thought conveyed by that sentence without thinking specifically of such individuals as Tom, Dick, or Harry, of Mom, Sis, or Grandma, when we say "a human being." We can also—without thinking of any individual dog named Fido, Tippy, or Trapper, Washoe, Koko, or Nim—say "animal."

More recently, the focus is on general laws, and Newton's laws are the most famous. "Every body keeps standing or moving the same way unless acted upon by another body" can be recited without the slightest idea of Cleopatra's Needle or Halley's comet popping into our minds. And so, scientific thinkers began aiming for universal propositions when trying to think scientifically. QU: How are scientific concepts related to real-life people, places, and things they ignore? AN: The scientific concepts extract from each individual just a tiny bit of what each has 'in common' with all the rest. The extract is an abstract or abstraction.

On this image, the medieval schoolmen built their theory or theories about the mental process or mechanism of the mind involved. "The mind abstracts the form or essence" is the traditional formula. This gives us the Mental Extraction Theory. Concepts are forms or essences extricated either from particular animals, vegetables, and minerals, or

298

excavacated from the phantasms put together by the inner synthesizing sense. Those who adopt this empiricist model, as I did for years, vie with one another to make the image fit a little more closely the various kinds of thoughts they notice being expressed. Here is a list of some of the concepts they created: abstraction of forms, abstraction from matter (from prime matter if forms, from accidents if essences or substances, from both *"materia signata"* and *"materia insignata"*), abstraction of the whole, judgements of separation, etc. Those are but a few of the concepts created to make the initial metaphor applicable to radically differing aspects of human knowledge vis-à-vis its alleged objects. A voluminous literature is available on the topic of abstraction, just the way there is a voluminous literature on every topic 'ABSTRACTLY' or briefly-and-synthetically just listed.

During the 1900's other individuals known as "existentialists" used the term "abstraction," not to convey the image of various mechanisms whereby the mind acquires its concepts from the senses, but as the most powerful metaphor available for describing an illness to which scientists generally fall victim. Scientists are not interested in individuals as such. After an individual has served to 'verify' a generalization, it becomes superfluous to science. Scientists especially have no interest in the full-blood of full-blooded individuals, only in the tiny vial drawn from them. Watson's mental illness, for instance, was abstraction.

In fact, if there is such a thing as a perfect paradigm for abstraction, the closest thing to perfection in the entire history of abstractions is Watson's behaviorology. He was ruthless in excising all psychological experience from his professional theory, ruthless in his tunnel-vision'd attention to external, observable-by-someone-else, physical behavior. Ignore the quagmires of equivocation offered by Watson's waffling successors who began their "General Psychology" textbooks with an unravelling-the-mystery-of-man's-behavior chapter which acknowledged that "Literally, the word psychology means the 'science of the mind,'" but which went on to warn that "Most contemporary psychologists would agree on a definition of psychology as the science of the behavior of organisms," which apologized for the oxymoronic switch in meanings by saying that "psychologists have never been satisfied with [the original] definition because 'mind' is a vague term that defies objective definition," and finally proceeded to compose a rich compendium of facts that were as often about conscious experience as they were about behavior. (Question: Would Watson turn over in his grave or keep snoring—define those as a phenomenalist or idealist would—if he read books on "behavior therapy" that make good sense withIN a common-sense framework that has room for never-observed anxiety and imagery, but perfect nonsense withOUT it?)

(PS Someday, when world history is complete, the Twentieth Century's Great Lock-Out, brought about by two naked emperors, W and W, and their hordes of brownshirted followers, who forbade 'scientific' psychologists to look into their own mind and insisted on sticking to the behavior of others [or mice], will rank first among the Eight Wonders of the World's History.)

The preceding paragraphs are themselves abstractions if they are understood apart from the theory of meaning and definition which was explained in Chapter One, apart from the radically opposite analyses offered as the meaning or definition of "observation" presented in Chapter Two, and apart from the last chapter's explanation that there are no such things, literally, as organisms and their behavior, not even brains and neuronal behavior. Now for a less abstract description of abstraction.

With the assistance of a radical gestalt-shift in our thinking, the metaphor of abstraction and abstract can become a powerful aid for thinking about thoughts. First, recall the context of these pages: the conclusion-premise that nothing at all exists except persons, the thoughts that come to and are understood by them, the sense-data and memory-images directly present to their awareness, and bodies which are no larger than a-toms. Second, since each new thought, sense-datum, and memory-image is thought of as a short-lived thing in itself, that is, since each one is a being utterly separate from the other quintillians, each is a creation unto itself, not a chip from some old block. Not extracted, in other words. Thirdly, abstraction is a reification. No such thing exists. Watson had thoughts. He had feelings. He got into the *habit* of ignoring them, i.e., abstracting (an act) from them, in the interests of science. After systematically ignoring them and making a *habit* of reverting to a professional theory that had no room for them, he became theory-blind to the thoughts and feelings he relied on in his everyday life. Each time he did think about them, he re-refused to believe in them. You do understand the thoughts that just re-came to you, right? The fourth important conclusion-premise is that persons are free to choose and re-choose which understood option to believe.

Still, though there will be abstraction for anyone who reads any part of this work without being aware of its author's mindset, it is better here to recall that all of us begin as students of life who must learn everything, but that, by the time any of us is ready to begin as students of 'Distinct Disciplines,' we already have learned most of life's essentials. Since the gestalt-shift referred to above is most important for refurbishing the psychology that, for nearly a century, has been neglected in favor of the new science of behaviorology, we picture a stage cleared of all 'professional' theory. The Watson-Wittgenstein Wall erected to keep us out of our inside experience is set aside. *Plain common sense is brought on and introduced as the key player for what follows.* This is the same common sense that plays the key role in the everyday mindset our Creating Parents furnish each of us with in our early years. It is what students bring to school, not what they get from it. It is knowledge that is prerequisite for even the most average reader to make sense of passages such as the following.

The following passage offers all that is needed for recognizing how easy it is to turn our attention away from the outward behavior of OTHERS, our clues to what THEY experience, and to what WE think and feel. To OUR OWN thoughts and feelings.

> Back in my room, I walked straight through it onto the balcony, letting the curtains fall behind me to cut off the light. The night was calm, and unexpectedly warm. There was still no sign of fog, but I thought that I could see a paler darkness away in the valley's depths. The damp of spring hung in the air. An owl called below me, down in the woods; called again. Its muted melancholy found too ready an echo in me. I felt tired and depressed. Too much had happened today; and the pleasant things—the morning's encounter with William Blake, my gay little flirtation with Florimond in the salon—had somehow faded back out of my mind and left me with this queerly flattened feeling.
>
> I know what it was, of course. I'd lived with loneliness a long time. That was something which was always there . . . one learns to keep it at bay, there are times when

> one even enjoys it—but there are also times when a desperate
> self-sufficiency doesn't quite suffice, and then the search for
> an anodyne begins . . . the radio, the dog, the shampoo, the
> stocking-to-wash, the tin soldier . . . (*Nine Coaches Waiting*.)

Everyone who is equipped, not with eyes detachable from their
sockets to look back at their vast inner "world," but with a readiness
to *notice* its mute presence "in here" or "back there" (whichever spatial
image helps most should be indulged in), can become aware of what
Mary Stewart, who wrote that, was referring to, and *go from that to a
glimpse of a vast inner "world."* That glimpse will come when it comes,
normally only after efforts to notice at least as much of what is in-here
as of what is out-there, to attend to what seems outside AND to what
seems INside.

Attention to the concreteness of the surroundings—one's room, the
balcony, the scene that extends during daylight as far as the horizon
and as far as the stars on a clear night, the clothes that are readily
detachable, all of which are called surroundings by contrast to one's
self in the center—AND the concreteness of the feelings in one's
breast, of memories of them, of snatches of recalled conversations,
of thoughts of 'other things to do,' all carried with us from inside the
room out to the balcony: such 'concrete' attention to what is on BOTH
sides of the invisible line between what is me-and-mine and what is
not-me-and-not-mine must become a matter of routine, second-nature
habit.

The next stage is getting into the *habit* of noticing what else is
obvious. Others' thoughts and feelings, even their loneliness, are
as much on the "in" side of their skin as one's own are. Theirs must
be guessed at by one's self as much as one's own must be inferred by
them. And yet, how smoothly that guessing can go. So smoothly that
it seems, during intense conversation, that we have immediate access to
others' thoughts. Then getting in the habit of resisting that "Illusion of
Immediacy" by realizing that, as soon as one switches from one's native
language to a poorly-learned foreign one, the "fluency" of the thoughts'
flow is replaced by hard-to-miss internal translating, or by noticing
how easily the thoughts "fly right off the page" when one is reading
familiar material such as Mary Stewart's description in contrast to how

difficult "digging the meaning out of the text" is when one is wrestling with unfamiliar material.

Return now to your here-and-now. You, your mindset, this 'text,' my mindset, me. It takes little imagination to think of books as bridges spanning the space-time distance between human book-readers and book-authors, of the world as a vast network of criss-crossing spans. Rarely do we pay enough attention to notice metaphors, but that is as obvious as the metaphor that this book, right now, is a bridge between two minds. One way to expose a metaphor is by using another as a contrast. So here. Though all the sentences co-exist, laid down, one by one, in nice neat roes, I did not pour them out only in a simultaneous heap, then pull them apart and arrange them neatly. Even more slowly than your row by row swallowing of them, they were spooned, one at a time, onto successive pages. And you take them in, spoonful by spoonful. Each single spoonful is from an ocean. THAT is a key to the best use of all for the abstraction-metaphor.

Each sentence is a spoonful from an ocean.

The metaphor can be turned around. No sentence-spoonful is received into a dry ocean-bottom. On the contrary, each new thought that comes to you upon the occasion of glancing at these catalysts is, if it seems to be understood easily, instantly inserted into the most "natural-for-your-mindset" context. If it seems difficult to understand, it is because of hesitancy about where to put it. If it seems equivocal, there is a narrowing of the choices to one, two, three, whatever. If it seems absurd, it is because it clashes with an important feature of that mindset. Your mindset.

It seems clear that what is noncommonsensically viewed here as the outer half of one's inner "world" is commonsensically viewed as if it *IS*! the outer, objective world. That was Kohler's point. But even if we compare (our ideas of*) the vast universe outside with the meager content anyone can 'put into a single sentence,' the paltry quantity of the latter naturally seems like a tiny amount extracted from that outside reality. Notice how "Kohler's point" actually refers to everything one individual thinker had in mind as he sat by lake's edge to begin a book to present all the ideas we "find" in *Gestalt Psychology*. Recalling that one pair of psychologists took 435 pages for a single day's activities of a single seven-year old, and recalling how many pages Becker estimated it would take James Joyce to record the simple river-crossing by Caesar, helps us understand why every sentence about what someone else believes is an 'abstraction.' Imagine reading a biography of a single individual person, say, John Locke, then reading every word he wrote to get a sample of the billions of thoughts he thought, then studying the history of his times to get some sense of how accurately his thoughts reflected that history. Then look at the brief sentence: "John Locke was a man of his times." Now THAT! is an abstraction. (*That is the key to Descartes' Greatest Thought Experiment.)

Whoever meditates on how easily we can squeeze so much into so little will catch a glimpse of how well Chinua Achebe compressed a great lesson on abstraction into a brief paragraph about a fictitious paragraph. It comes at the end of his brief novel, *Things Fall Apart*, the life-story of a man named Okonkwo:

> In the many years in which he [the Commissioner] had toiled to bring civilization to different parts of Africa he had learned a number of things. One of them was that a District Commissioner must never attend to such undignified details as cutting a hanged man from the tree. Such attention would give the natives a poor opinion of him. In the book which he planned to write he would stress that point. As he walked back to the court he thought about that book. Every day brought him some new material. The story of this man who had killed a messenger and hanged himself would make interesting reading. One could almost write a whole chapter on him. Perhaps not a whole chapter but a reasonable paragraph, at any rate. There was so much else to include, and one must be firm in cutting out detail. He had already chosen the title of the book, after much thought: *The Pacification of the Primitive Tribes of the Lower Niger.*

Whoever grasps what I am trying to convey here can also do it if they notice how "thin," relatively speaking, will be the thoughts of a first-grader asking "What does pacification mean?," "What is a tribe?", "What does primitive mean?", "Where on the map is the Niger River?", in contrast to the massive amount of knowledge the commissioner would "have in mind" whenever he'd pause and savor the full meaning of his book's proposed title.*

Whoever learns the history of what happened when the Europeans came to the Ibo villages in Africa, then reads this story of what went on in the heart and soul of a single man caught up in the clash between old and new ideas, will understand why this story of the life of one fictitious man can be viewed as 'a general concept' of or else as a stark 'symbol' for the real-life-stories of many individual Ibos. S/he could imagine herself or himself in the shoes of Achebe when he made up those final lines of his novel that packed into the ironic choice of "pacification" the contrast between a common blindness to the vast amounts of suffering that occurred because of the UNpacifying of peaceful Ibos by the Europeans, and his own keen sense of that suffering, which the reader is invited to feel as well. Which half-truth must be balanced by the equally important fact that, unlike Okonkwo, many real-life Ibo villagers felt grateful to God for the advent of the Europeans who brought liberation from the bondage of tribal superstitions. How many total mindsets there are. How radically different. The mind of everyone who wants to know the full truth—or to all truths—must open wide enough to embrace as many of them as God's mind does. (*Think of *Why Control Your Imagination?*)

Only the reader who grasps the separate details of the preceding, in one total sweep, will understand what this book is all about: the way the meaning of each and every complete sentence is a thought whose context is the rest of the mindset of the person who understands it. Which is why another's sentence's meaning can only be grasped by a recipient in a degree corresponding to how much or how little the recipient's mindset parallels that of the source's. Ignore for the moment the fact that none of us has any direct access to the thoughts—image-accompanied or not—of anyone else. If these cues and clues are succeeding for you, you will grasp the meaning of Hobbes' psychological observation about how swift and yet how carefully structured thoughts can be:

> [...] in a discourse of our present civil war, what could seem more impertinent than to ask, as one did, what was the value of a Roman penny? Yet the coherence to me was manifest enough. For the thought of the war introduced the thought of the delivering up of the king to his enemies; the

thought of that, brought in the thought of the delivering
up of Christ; and that again the thought of the thirty pence
which was the price of that treason; and thence easily
followed that malicious question, and all this in a moment of
time; for thought is quick.

What Hobbes describes is familiar to everyone who has dissected
scores of thinking experiences in order to abstract the laws that are at
work. He was describing a "train of thoughts" (Hobbes' own phrase, from
the same third chapter of his *Leviathan*) that related to real, historical
events. Had anyone asked Chinua Achebe to say what he had in mind
at the instant "Pacification" flowed from the tip of his pen, he could
have broken his thought down (same metaphor) the same way, even
though his unbroken-down thought related to events that had one foot
in actual history and the other in pure fiction. It takes years upon years
for any learner to build the kind of inner world-model with the massive
amounts of detail and the fantastically intricate criss-crossing strands
of association—and to attach the 'language-hooks' to them by EXTRA
memory-image associations—required for such lightning-swift
thoughts as those just alluded to and to become capable of analysing
them by readily tracing the 'language cues' to their various image and
thought roots. Even more years to build a model of thinking to help
grasp the fact that thinking is always accompanied by imagery. *Even
thinking about thinking is.*

The limitations of the imagery and metaphors we use to understand
thinking constrict our view if they are not recognized. The way to
escape the limitations imposed by the 'abstract(ion)' metaphor is to
strain to notice less the meagreness of what we explicitly abstract and
notice rather the vastness of what we're abstracting from. And to begin
noticing ALL the oceans of meaning distilled into words that evoke an
image-picture worth thousands more. More words. For those familiar
with their meaning-thoughts.

Again. Our words connect with something like an internal
space-time-continuum representation that is a distant echo of God's
flawless recall of the past and perfect knowledge of every single thing
that exists anywhere. What this means cannot be put into words (that
don't exist), but it can be intimated. The following passage, with its

examples of limited! global thinking, provides a jumping-off model or picture for grasping it.

> For instance, a short while after reading *The Decline and Fall of the Roman Empire*, one may be aware of the immense vista of a civilization's history as Gibbon created it. That experience can hardly be conveyed except through the medium of the book itself, and to that extent it is ineffable, and a minor version of James' widened consciousness. Suppose one then read *War and Peace* and acquired Tolstoy's perspective of historical events and their determination by chance factors. Again, this is an experience hard to express without returning to the novel. Now suppose that one could "see" not only each of these world views individually but also their parallel relationships to each other, and the cross connection between the individual conceptual structures. And then suppose that one added to these conceptual strata the biochemical perspective expressed by *The Fitness of the Environment*, a work which deals, among other things, with the unique and vital properties of water molecules. Then the vertical interrelationships of all these extensive schemata might, indeed, be beyond verbal expression, beyond ordinary conceptual capacities—in other words, they would approach the ineffable. (A.J. Deikman, in C. Tart's *Altered States of Consciousness*.)

In that poem, Deikman puts into words all those moments when we feel! how impossible it is to 'put into words' everything we have 'in mind' all at once. The aim of the poem in your hands is to lay down a trail of cues and clues for a model of thinking capable of assisting readers to arrive at a peak of insight where it becomes obvious why we can never, NOT EVEN ONCE, put into words what a normal adult OR FIVE-YEAR OLD has 'in mind' in waking moments. Which insight becomes possible only after having become liberated from the myth of language in order to attend to the thoughts we understand and to notice the jungle of images that accompany that understanding. Usually, our thought is so swift that the imagery is barely subactivated. But, if we 'look back' over our written word-cues, the invisible structure of our image-embodied-thoughts becomes noticeable. As well as the endless variety of thought-illuminating metaphors. For instance.

An endless list of the other images that have been found useful in efforts to 'get at' the unfathomable miracle going on right under our very noses is that evoked by "BOOK." It seems as if part of the "world" you are experiencing right now is this book. It is helpful to think of the entire stream of the sense-data you experience as a book or text upon which you can impose whatever reading you choose. The first reading any of us learns to impose is the naive-realist THEORY that what we experience are the parts of always-there nature, made of persons, animals, and vegetables living on this earth, illumined by the sun by day and the moon and a canopy of stars at night. Then, in the same way that any ordinary book can be viewed as a window into the mind of a human author, nature can be read as a book revealing the mind of God. Still, only someone who can fully understand what is really going on while, it seems, their eyes scan row after row of tiny little ciphers can fully understand how all those "reading" experiences, which seem so different, can be read the same way: they involve a person who understands increasingly-rich thoughts co-presented with or accompanied by imagery and sense-data, whether the sense-data are OF print on the page of a book, OF the subtitles on the movie-screen during the showing of an undubbed movie, OF the smoke formations left behind by a sky-writer, or whether they are OF the face of the man-in-the-moon, OF the belt of Orion in the sky, OF the path of the quark in the bubble-chamber's fluid, OF the spikes of the brain-waves on the strip of paper, the one, same kind of inference that "makes science" is at work.

Structure. Another is the image of "structure." Which is a recent name for "form." Form, as mentioned in Chapter One, is one of the oldest metaphors used for thinking about thinking, one popularized by Pythagoras, Plato, and Aristotle. It has many aliases: format, form, pattern, gestalt (a foreign import), structure, etc. The concept originally refers to something visible: say, to the shape of the statue, the outline that appears when the child equipped with pencil and number-recognition draws lines between the numbered points on the otherwise blank page, the shape or outline or gestalt that gestaltists swear they see even before the lines are drawn between "the three dots with the triangular shape" on the empty page, etc. With the aid of that metaphor—simply abstract what those and thousands of other particulars have in common—we can see things so much more clearly, most importantly the difference between what is observed and what is not. The observable matter, like the unseen form, also has aliases: content, materiel, elements, substance, stuff, etc.

Great advances—or what are called "great advances" by many who are called experts—are made by nothing more than taking a metaphor and noticing how far it can be extended before it finally becomes bedridden. Kant thought the "science" of logic was all done, some now believe it barely got started before the middle of the 1800's. He also thought geometry was fairly complete, but that was before some thinkers discovered how Descartes' approach could be used to broaden it immeasurably. One might have thought that, by his theory about the categories, etc., he had exhausted the application of the "form" metaphor, but it was not till this century that some saw how vast was the matter in which forms can be found. Jean Piaget's brief work entitled *Structuralism* can serve as an excellent introduction to yet more volumes, including H. Gardner's *The Quest for Mind* whose final chapter is entitled "Structuralism as a World-View."

This "book" provides ample material to illustrate the preceeding. A structuralist could note that, in setting out to write this book to explain that there really are no books of any kind in the entire universe, I already had a many-years-old mindful of ideas and needed only a structure or format for them. I pre-planned a five-chapter format. As the work proceeded, it just happened that each of the first three chapters got divided into four segments apiece, that is, each has a four-item form. (I have pre-planned a three-item or triadic pattern for this chapter to break the symmetry.) A structuralist might note also the way the opening sub-section of this "A" section of this chapter is structured similarly to the opening paragraphs of the second sub-section: short ab, longer a, longer b. Or could point out that the combination of this section and the second paragraph of Chapter One can be viewed as "longer-a-&-shorter-a" if content rather than structure is the content of our scope, though from another point of view, this section can be seen as an expansion of one theme (abstracted from many) running through the last chapter which was an expansion of several pages of

Chapter Two. In fact, there is no end to what can be found just in the small non-book you hold in your hands.

Which helps to notice that, like other analogies, this one, too, limps. Pushed to an extreme, it is clearly absurd. Noticing how absurd these extremes are when someone confronts us with a neat "reduction to an *ad infinitum* absurdity" is critically important for anyone who wishes to become a better thinker about thinking. For, in fact, forms and structures are not abstracted from 'matter,' regardless of the aristotelians' and gestaltists' claims to the contrary. The only observable forms are the seen color-fields we normally sense, unless it is the outlines in our faint memory-images of them. Colors are normally shaped and patterned, whether we see them as buildings on Manhattan's skyline, as paints spread over a canvas entitled "Manhattan's Skyline," as tiny dark figures that look like "Manhattan's Skyline" against a white background (these rows and whrohs of ciphers), etc. In each instance, the shaped outline of one color-area is identical with the shaped edges of the abutting color-area(s). One of the most convincing proofs that what we see are not physical bodies out there is the fact that, without any change in those bodies' shapes, the shapes of the color-areas in a myopic's total visual field blur as soon as s/he removes her or his eyeglasses. Interposing a magnifying glass, prism, etc., will reverse the left-right or up-down orientation of the seen shapes.

The number of interesting details discoverable just in visual sense-data as they relate to form, structure, or shape—e.g., the shape of the whole visual field itself seems roundish to me, a circle, less and less distinct toward its outer periphery where it just . . . disappears, with no sharp line between its outer boundary and an abutting nothingness—helps realize how we can use ready-made 'concepts' and apply them if they fit or reject them if they do not. In fact, debates about "What, if anything, do we see?" (to which Chapter Two is a *very* brief introduction) are endless and lend even further support for the claim that we have ready-made 'concepts,' especially the two named by "observed" and "not-observed," and can apply them if we think they fit or reject them if we do not. That is, for the claim that we see what we choose to see and are blind to what we choose not to.

Without a passion for truth, it is easy to miss the importance of the fact that a "True Believer" can go to her/his grave insisting that structuralism is an adequate theory of the universe *with the same ease* with which a "True Disbliever" can die insisting, "That's bosh" (as Skinner and Rogers each died convinced the other's psychology was 'bosh'). That fact—that we can either cling to a theory con-'structed' around the 'struct'-ure metaphor OR we can recognize such a theory as one option among many—allows us to construct a better theory that captures the ultimate significance of the controversies that swirl around any and every topic: *our choices are arbitrary, i.e., free,* but not necessarily irrational, since we can find endless rationales or reasons for those free choices. (But, as in the case of Skinner and Rogers, free choices can create powerful, almost unbreakable structures of thought-habits.)

Re-viewing the preceding—any writer/thinker can re-view what s/he has written in order to make sure it squares with the shape of her/his vast inner theory of everything—shows that the last observation serves to 'integrate' those image-models. It shows how to put the images together, i.e., to synthesize them to construct new syntheses . . .

. . . or how to form larger gestalts from a trio of points about unlike imagery. Point ONE: *everything is partly like and partly unlike everything else.* We can mentally one-ify—into a single class, group, set, category, genus, kind, or species—all of the things that, however clearly distinct and/or discernible from each other they may be, are also like or similar to each other. We can even refer to scattered individual pieces of trash as "a LOT of trash," just as we can say "People's minds are full of trash." Point TWO: when we try to explain this 'one-ness,' the seeming clarity of the traditional answer that "We can do it because they have this (or that) in common" makes us sympathetic to the traditional theory about the mind's ability to extract an essence, nature, or form which they have in common. Point THREE: an alternative approach is to believe that, if we can impose a unifying or one-making form on, i.e., mentally join together, really dissimilar things (e.g., a trio of dissimilar points), the cause is to be sought, not in things but in us, not in their shared something but in our (power of) free thinking or imagining. FOUR: rather than being incompatible, that first trio of considerations fit together if we just expand the third approach. We are free, (i) to adopt tradition and believe that our concepts and categories are gotten FROM grouped things that have in them a foundation for our mind's activity or (ii) to adopt the alternative model that we are free to read INTO things whatever unity we wish because that is the kind of power our mind has. In other words, we can put together whatever we want

311

and then look for a suitable model for it. FIVE: this model applies to every triad—1, I, and one (numbers), mother, father, and child (family), animal, vegetable, and mineral (Twenty-Questions), thought, sense-data, and memory-images (mental representations), yesterday, today, tomorrow, and past, present, future (time)—that we choose to one-ify as a threesome. SIX: the idea is generalizable beyond trinities. Our mind has . . . rather, we have an enormous capacity for imposing different readings on our similar-but-dissimilar life-texts or life-movies or streams of experience or . . .

This 'larger' gestalt helps make sense of that most stunningly obvious fact about human thinking: the fact that even in "The Age of Science" (with a capital S), no one has found a way to make experts agree who choose to believe they are right and others are wrong. Think of Einstein and Bohr, Skinner and Chomsky after them and Darwin and Wallace earlier. Of James and Royce, Freud and Jung, Churchill and Hitler, Stalin and Truman, Ratzinger and Kung. Even when the parties are genuinely committed to the quest for the holy grail, namely, the truth, the whole truth, and nothing but the truth, there are no two persons who think alike about everything. Not even, after a century of trying, about the right psychological theory to explain the seemingly limitless human capacity for inventing new theories, giving old theories new twists, putting new skins around old wine, discovering facts hitherto unknown, noticing what was always right under our nose . . .

. . . Yet, the explanation has been clear all the time. It must be our power of unfettered imagination. Which can disguise the same thought with trio, triad, threesome, trinity, and any number of inventible threes. If the universe contains literally zillions of particulars—something not difficult to imagine—and if we have imaginations capable of inventing ever-more ways to take note of the similarities and differences, it is no wonder that the world's presses, more numerous and efficient than at any time in all of history, cannot keep up with the outpouring of new? old? thoughts. Of course, this explanation assumes that we know what "imagination" means and have evidence for believing it exists. And have evidence that our theories about humans' imaginations are not theories about a figment of our imagination, that they do not need to be analysed further before the bottom-line is reached, before we get to the bottom of everything, before . . .

Do you get the picture? Rather, do you understand those thoughts—which together 'make up' a theory—about thoughts and images, among them the image of models, both global inner models as well as mini-models? Even if you disagree with any or all of them? Which is not reasonable unless you first understand them, of course. You understand that, right? Even if you disagree with it, too. Most people overlook the fact that their vast inner "world" includes, not only a knowledge of all the things they believe, that is, give assent to. It also includes their knowledge of the things they disbelieve, i.e., of the thoughts they dissent from. *Humans understand more than they believe.* Of course, if they believe the thoughts they dissent from are assented to by others, the thought about others' thoughts is one of their thoughts, one they believe, that is, give assent to, as opposed to those other thoughts of theirs that they dissent from or believe are false. In plainer words (sic!), one's vast inner "world" includes memories of every single theory one has ever learned and not forgotten. Any one or any number of the previously rejected thoughts can be recalled and rethought. That is the model proposed now. At some point, it becomes not reasonable to continue not deciding which model-theory is true.

Maps. Years ago, I came across an article referring to experiments suggesting that we use inner maps or images of maps. The first article was accompanied by a drawing showing a shopper in a mall consulting an intersection-map with an arrow indicating "You are here." Like road-maps and wall-maps, mall-maps help us know the way from the place we are at to some other place. Especially if the map is facing the way we are facing, so that its north, east, south, etc., match our north, etc. Think of what happens when walkers-by are asked by drivers-by for directions: instinctively, direct'rs turn and face in the direction of the target-location. That way, they can say their Take-a-right-turn's and Take-a-left-turn's far more quickly and easily than if they tried to give directions to a location somewhere behind them.

Thinking about this common-enough experience gave someone the idea that we carry mental maps or map-images that, like 'real' maps we seem able to hold and look at, are easier to read when turned to face the way we face. Of course, our inner 'body-centered-map' faces the way we face, which means we must 'translate before speaking' if we face away from the target-location. (The different "perceptions" we get from natural and/or doctored photos of faces when they are viewed right-side up and up-side down adds to Kant's perceptive insight into space-perception, and all these things relate to the difference between reading the way you are now and reading from bottom to top, right to left, upside down, back in Chapter Two.)

The link between that and language and inner imagery did not begin taking shape until I came across a second article, some time later, about experiments suggesting that animals, too, create maps to help them get around. It made me rummage through my back issues of *Science News* to retrieve the earlier one by W. Herbert. ("Getting From Here to There," 3/19/83) Eventually, new connections between those scattered ideas and my earlier collection of mental notes *about the use of imagery in thinking* began to "occur." (Notice how much we must take on faith whatever we believe about other people's inner "worlds." Throughout this work, I have cited authors, quoted from their writings, and so on. Much of my overall evidence rests on what I believe about what others think, the way you will have to take it on faith that I am trying to tell the truth about my sources AND that I do not unintentionally misquote. The most critical readers prefer to check sources, which is why an absence of footnotes is often seen as a shortcoming by them. Even if the sources are quoted correctly, this report of how the idea of mental maps gestated for me . . . Well, believe it or not.)

Chief of those earlier notes was the image of higher and lower levels or tiers of knowledge. Ever since Plato suggested that horizontal lines can be drawn to mark off varying levels of knowledge or theory or thought, a suggestion so famous it is often referred to as "The Line" (found at the end of Book Six of his *Republic*), ever since his student, Aristotle, canonized that into his model of three degrees or levels of abstractness, and ever since the most innovative thinkers between then and now have further embellished those giants' views, it has become hard for us successors to resist the powerful influence of that metaphor. I have already mentioned the visceral reality this sense of a scale or ladder or stairway of knowledge—leading upwards from the ground-level of everyday concrete experience of particular people, places, and things to the penthouse where sacred theology was housed—once held for me. And a quick glance at current literature will show that the ancient metaphor lives on . . . cloaked in new skins with "meta-" affixed to their lapels . . . in the entire educationo-curricular runthrough, with its lower and higher grades, lower—and upper-level courses, and so on . . . in metaphors of grandness, implying that grand unifying theories are higher than less-than-grand ones, since the public will or at least should look up more to (see) the proposers they come from.

The ancient theory of concepts*, analogized in Porphyry's famous tree, embodies the higher/lower metaphor for understanding our everyday talk and thought. The idea is that there are several concepts/ branches, and each higher one extends out farther than any single one of the lower ones because it covers or contains, embraces or holds more things than any lower ones. A high-up branch umbrellas all corporeal or bodily beings, both those hanging from the branch of unconscious, non-living bodies and those hanging from the branch of conscious, living ones. The latter divides into one lower branch of living but unconscious organisms and another lower branch of living and conscious ones. This last sub-branches into living, conscious, but not-rational animals, and into living, conscious, rational humans. (*The invention of Venn Diagrams helps to 'picture' what occurs when we reason: we use mental groups. Study modern 'symbolic logic,' which complements the ancient Aristotelian, *'dictum de omni, dictum de nullo'* logic.)

Only a little effort is needed to see the link between our everyday talk and this diagram. "What is in the box is a thing" tells us far less than "What is in the box is some kind of animal," because the concept named by "thing" is vague and has little content, while the concept named by "animal" contains the added information that the thing is alive and conscious. One concept covers, extends to, reaches more beings than the other. Every analogy limps, and endless debates about concepts and their content—e.g., about whether the most general concept, that of being, is richer or poorer than the less general ones (each is half of the whole truth that "You can take it either or both ways"), about whether Kant's claims about which judgments' predicates are contained in their subjects and which are not, is clear—grew out of taking the tree's ramifications seriously.

Thinking of knowledge-levels, of getting to the root of things or reaching the pinnacle of insight, must be demythologized, lest it block our ascent to the peak of insight. Each and every thought is a complete thought. None but the present moment's thoughts exist. Present thoughts may be about earlier thoughts or still-to-come thoughts, but the earlier ones no longer exist and, if the future ones existed, they would not be still to come. Once we stop imagining thoughts as birds to be captured and caged on different stories of a tower—or, worse, imagining that they are some image-kind of thing we can look at—and begin to pay attention to our present thoughts, each of which is the only one we can think at its moment, we will also notice that, try as we will, there is no way to arrange one thought on top of another.

If we convert our thoughts to maps that represent less as well as more territory, it is clear how useful the higher-lower metaphor can be for helping us notice facts about human learning and the knowledge which is its end product. Especially the linkage between words and what they can lead us to expect. Each of us individual learners begins by creating an inner map of just the things in the local area. The relations inside the mapped areas eventually become so definite and so quickly referred to, that if someone blindfolds us, leads us by the hand for a walk, stops and says "You are standing right in front of your house again, facing it," we will instantly know, when the blindfold is removed and we see whatever we see, whether what we see matches what their words 'led' us to expect or whether we see something else.

The map-model and cognitive psychology were made for each other. The most obvious generalization any cognitive psychologist should make is that all humans are LEARNERS, and there are several ways to think of each learner's acquisition of maps. First, as the enlargment of one and the same single map. At first, our inner map's borders enclose little, because we know too little of the cosmos. Eventually, we library-users can expand our provincial map into a cosmopolitan one. The way the map of one area becomes part of a map of a larger area, our neighborhood becomes part of a continent, a solar system, a galaxy, a universe. A second model, the one which Chapter Two proposed, is to imagine that we construct just two maps: our original one, named "our everyday common-sense model," and a second one, named "our profess-ional map." A third way to map or model the learning process is to imagine that we create many distinct, same-size, higher and lower maps that are metaphorically higher and lower because they model larger and smaller areas. The same way, it seems, real—that is, physical—maps with the same size can be metaphorically called "larger" and "smaller," because the territory they represent, as if drawn by a bird looking down from a higher or lower elevation, is larger and smaller.

316

In this chapter, the third map-metaphor will be used most of all. Cognitive psychologists will have several uses for this many-maps-model. Especially after a few more words are added to help make it one of those pictures worth a thousand words. The first use is to notice how it helps to connect apparent behavior—real somatic sense-data describable as "MY doing such-and-such" (it should never be forgotten that so-called 'behavior—or action-therapy' is performed by persons awake enough to *understand* their usually-verbally-administered homework-assignments, *remember* enough of what they have learned to connect the therapist's words, words, words with the appropriate 'behavior/action,' and *experience* the sense-data that normally accompany the so-called brain's neuronal activity, i.e., never forgotten that therapists do not give their instructions while sleep-talking nor do their clients homework them while sleep-walking)—with expected sense experience. Three different maps, say, one of the whole USA, one of the state of Ohio, and one of the city of Akron, will all have areas that correspond to certain parts of the North American continent on the planet earth near one of the stars in the Milky Way, but both the Ohio and the USA map will have marks for things not on the Akron map, and the USA one will represent things not on the Ohio map either. Should someone want to get some idea of the relative distances between Los Angeles and Cleveland and between Cleveland and New York, only one of those three maps will be suitable. A native of Los Angeles, told "Go to the intersection of Burkhardt and Firestone in Akron, Ohio, face north, and you will see a house on the corner exactly like yours," s/he would know what to expect and could, with the assistance of the three maps, go, look around, and confirm or disconfirm those expectations. Quite the way someone who once thought the earth was flat could book passage on a space-ship to the moon and check what they'd see from that vantage-point against predictions by pancake-earth and sphere-earth maps.

Higher education can also be lower. Once we have completed a degree in 'higher' education, we may find we have something like a city-map rather than a cosmic one. Imagine we have pursued a degree in psychology. We enter our 'field' through a door called "General Psychology" which provides us with a map, something like that of the United States. We then take courses that provide us with maps like various state maps. If we later on specialize, say, in the treatment of children—whose parents and/or teachers and/or neighborhood police bring them to us because they are having or causing "trouble"—we may begin to build a city-map with markers for the various types of children we see over a period of time. If we have studied Freud and liked his sketch of what lies hidden inside our clients, we may develop very elaborate mental constellations to represent the inner items we pay attention to—e.g., the id-ego-superego structure, the psycho-dynamic forces, the developmental stages each should be in if intrapsychic processes are unfolding normally, etc. (works like H. Guntrip's *Psychoanalytic Theory, Therapy, and the Self* will provides a window onto the enormous variations there are among those who all profess to be "following Freud")—and their map-markings will correspond to a classification system similar, say, to the one that map-makers use to distinguish four-lane beltways, two-lane streets, unpaved roads, paths, and so on. Selective attention to or preoccupation with a narrow range of phenomena can result in selective inattention to factors other psychologists (socially-oriented ones) attend to when they try to understand children: differences in children's parents, different types of families, the dissimilar racial and ethnic natures of different children's neighborhood communities, the differences in economic class, and so on. Given the limited amount of time we have at our disposal and the amount of new literature in our field that appears every month, this growing tendency to know more and more about less and less, this over-stress on alleged depth of comprehension at the expense of even minimal extension, this increasing immersion in the minutiae of smaller and smaller scale maps is to be expected. The resulting situation poses two opposed temptations: to either shrink our cosmic map so it turns into a tunnel-visioned city-map or to simply declare that we can be experts on one city without having any idea where the city is located in the one great spatio-temporal, cosmic-sized universe.

Or, if we do develop interests in some area outside our meadow of expertise, whatever extra city-maps we create will be kept quite separate. The results can be pictured in two different ways. Either we ignore the connection between the two maps, as when someone has a map of Akron and another of Akron but has no idea of states (Ohio and Georgia) and of which are the sites of the two mapped areas. Or we think of them as two maps for the same area in the same cosmos but as maps showing different features of the area, e.g., those which highlight roads and streets, those that emphasize tourist attractions, those that feature waterways, those that show above-and-below-sea-level elevations. For instance, we may also have an intense passion for amateur astronomy, be familiar with constellations, the kinds of galaxies and stars, the planets and their moons, etc. Unlike astrologers, we amateur astronomers may have no inclination whatever to see any connections between the set of maps used to 'get our bearings' on each new emotionally disturbed child sent to us and the set of maps we use to 'get our bearings' vis-à-vis Taurus, Scorpio, etc., or on the phases of the moon, even though it is commonsensical to think that, if astrologers can see connections, we might also. If we chose to.

Any good cognitive psychologist intent on explaining what "the truth, the whole truth, and nothing but the truth" means would find the map-imagery to be of the greatest imaginable use. If maps really existed, then a single cosmic map of everything would have to be part of the holy grail described as the whole truth and nothing but the truth. It would have to be a map that, when laid over reality, would be found to match it, point for point, down to the last detail, with not a single marker too many or too few. Only that way could we be sure that every individual existent was represented. Saint Thomas maintained that God has no need for universal concepts which furnish such vague knowledge that we cannot tell how many countable individuals they cover and cannot tell from their extracted content how any given individual actually differs from another given one. Or given two. Or given three. Etc. The more we know with a single, less-content-ful universal, the less we know about any ones. The more we zoom in to think about one mapped individual, the less we know about any other individuals . . . except for its closer and closer clones. Only by knowing all, but withOUT universal concepts, could we grasp each creature the way God does, in its full, unique glory.

The key (thought) is expressed by "not a single marker too many or too few." As anyone familiar with Ockham's Razor—or the principle of parsimony or the KISS* Principle, etc.—knows, reductionists insist that non-reductionists believe in too many things, i.e., have too many items in their maps. For instance, Ockhamists claim that whoever believes in any truly-universal AND non-particular realities, as opposed to particular realities that we—if we abstract from or ignore their particularness—can view 'in relation to many,' believes in at least one thing too many. Rather—since universal'ists believe in many of them—in at least one kind of thingS too many. The higher-maps-and-lower-maps metaphor is fantastically useful for connecting our theories of knowledge and truth with Einstein's succinct formula: Keep it simple, silly, but not too simple. (*The less playful version of the same kiss is "Keep it simple, stupid.")

Maps help on the mathematical, quantitative side of learning: on the side of accurate COUNTING. They are also useful on the unifying, qualitative side of learning: on the side of mathematically exact counting of the (mental) classes used in bottom-line CLASSIFYING. Thinking about learning with the assistance of the many-maps image allows us to kill both birds with one stone: both sides of the "COUNT AND CLASSIFY CORRECTLY" ballistic. Getting bottom-line maps that mark off each and every single existing item, not one too many or one too few, or—since that is the impossible dream of quixotic questors for certainty—getting the right upper-most maps: that is the best direction for reaching the peak of insight. Each higher map provides unification for the things on the lower levels and counts as one step further up the ladder. Maps use symbols for unique sites (each individual existent which is partly like but partly unlike every other) as well as symbols to indicate how some individuals (rivers, lakes, highways, county roads, towns, cities, capital cities) are THE "SAME" AS (similar to, like, not-different-from) the other ONES. This makes "maps" useful for *counting* individuals and for *classifying* them by indicating which genera, sets, species, classes, etc., we are categorizing them "as."

B. HABITS-II: CRAVING HABITS.*

Conclusion About Fictions. Finally, in order to bring closure to this opening section (A) of this second-from-last chapter, let me offer another adjustment for your inner model of reality. At least occasionally, it is worthwhile remembering that we can, if we choose, use hypothesis and fiction to name distinct kinds of thought and use construct and figment to name distinct kinds of thought-about objects. "We guess" goes well with a picture of persons with thoughts to which they semi-assent in a situation where they do not yet possess conclusive evidence for the truth of this or that thought. "Guess" names a cluster: a person, an understood thought, tentative assent to the thought's truth. ("Giving assent to its truth" here means the same as "holding the thought as true, i.e., as measuring up to whatever reality-norm it is that true thoughts measure up to and false ones don't.") In such cases, we can call the thought either an *hypothesis* if we wish to indicate it is a thought on whose truth or error (i.e., on whose actual truth or mere AS-IF appearance of being an actual truth) we do not want to make a final commitment (though we may act on it), or we can call the thought a *fiction* if we wish to coindicate that we believe the thought THAT such-and-such is false and that the thing OF which it is a thought is a thing that does not exist out in reality. The content or object which either of those kinds of situated-thoughts are about can be called a *construct* (more often, hypothetical construct) in the case of the hypothesis or a *figment* (of imagination) in the case of the thought whose context we squeeze into "fiction." Only by occasionally pausing and rethinking such distinctions and analyzing other expressions into them can we build up the habit of recalling the distinctions when they are critical for avoiding Expert Thinkers' Blocks. That is, the mental blocks that come, not so much from knowing too little (that is an Infant Thinkers' type of block), but from taking too much of what is known as if it is fact rather than what it truly is, fiction about figments.

Are the "objects of thought" things or facts? Things, such as cats and mats, spruces and hills, Fords and parking lots? Or universal affirmations and negative instances, such as "Every non-non-cat is elsewhere than on a mat" vs "My cat isn't," "Spruces on hills are all colorless" vs "Not the one I'm looking at," "Everyone knows you park Fords in the parking lot" vs "I don't believe cars even exist, so—as Kant would say—there aren't any cars whose essence includes the passive capacity for being parked"? We escape by realizing that we use—or should use!—"fact" to mean "a thought that is true" and "thought" to refer to what is it we assent to because we believe it is true.

When the thought is false, as in "Chapters do not exist," the 'object' of the thought (chapters) is a fiction or figment of our imagination. Debates about "What exists?" go hand-in-hand with debates about "Which thoughts are true?"

*This is where section B should begin and where the above headline ("Craving habits") belongs, IF you are the type who craves a universe whose order must reflect whatever order you have created in your mind and not the type whose one passion is to have the order in your mind reflect whatever pre-existent order exists in the world you hope, by your decisions, to help re-order. That is, this is where the section headline belongs, IF you are the type who believes there must be a thing in the one spatio-temporal universe to match every single thing in your inner map of reality which "map" is 'made up' of at least two real things (thoughts and images). Or two kinds of things. Each of the thoughts you understood while thinking about maps, like each of the images that were their bridesmaids, were individual realities, and you used two mental bins—genera, kinds, species, types, sets, classes, categories, etc.—to pigeonhole or file them into. The mental bins, if thought about as a third type of reality over and beyond thoughts and images, are figments of imagination, that is, they are made by the imagination, that is, they are classes made by the mind, that is, they are class-i-facts or class-i-fictions or class-i-fications. The same way sections and headlines are.

What's the point of the above? Just this. Sections and headlines are fictions and exist nowhere but 'in your mind.' Whoever puts her/himself in the shoes of the emperor's-parade-watching toddler will see only "little black things" (e.g., C r a v i n g), maybe "writing" if s/he is a prodigy, but hardly "a new section"! What's a section? How are they determined? How new can it be if it's existed since the book—or non-book—was printed? You are error-laden-perceiving, projecting your concepts onto these little black things, or seeing things that are-not, if you 'see' sections anywhere but in your mind. If you crave the truth, you absolutely must begin paying attention to and weeding out such bad thought-habits as believing you see anything but visual sense-data or believing that, among the things you do not see, there are anythings except persons, their thoughts, their sensed-givens, their memory-image replicas, and (maybe) a-toms. You must learn how to use Ockham's Razor until you believe no fictions, that is, assent to nothing but the truth. And, if you do not crave the truth that is not only good for you but good for others, then you are obliged to begin trying to cultivate that craving, since it is quite unlikely you will undertake the necessary, hard Rethinking without that craving.

If you are like me and if you have strong objections to the views proposed by these non-pages, then I fully expect that you will not merely contemplate the thoughts that just now passed before you, as part of your stream of consciousness. You will also feel something.

Much the way that people feel something when one of those words that will not—but, if the whole truth be told, also will—hurt is aimed their way, e.g., the word "stupid." Or scan "I'm sure it was a piece of crap anyway." Such feelings are not unconscious, merely unattended-to. We would do better to begin attending to the passions and emotions we feel (which is why they are also named "feelings") in conjunction with thoughts that pass and repass on that non-stage, the "mind," that Hume wrote about. (It is hard to decide which of Freud's blunders is worse, his failure to adopt Leibniz' correction of Descartes and to merely distinguish the contents of our field of experience into things that catch our attention and things that are there but unattended-to or his map of what-is-mental that focussed people's attention on what is neither consciously noticed nor conscious-but-unnoticed but non-existent: that elaborate, highly-structured, and mythical 'unconscious mind.') *Most of the people I know* are far more likely to feel a pleasant sensation if they are asked to "Keep it simple, silly" than if they are told to "Keep it simple, stupid." Silly may amuse, stupid often hurts.

As soon as we begin paying fuller attention, as soon as we begin noticing both thoughts and feelings, so soon do we begin noticing the variety of pairings and triplings, etc., that we know are possible (in the future) because we have so often experienced them (in the past). A variety of feelings can be aroused by the thoughts passing before you as you scan these rows and rows. The passion of curiosity perhaps (to draw you on further), feelings of irritation (at the author's arrogance), a twinge of fear (that you may have to rethink things). There are the passions and feelings that join thoughts compatible with our own (vindication, silent applause, inspiration, enlightenment, eureka-ness) and those we feel re thoughts that oppose ours (irritation, panic, astonishment, scorn). Passions, feelings, or emotions we feel when we become passionate (start emoting) about thoughts are, believe it or not, things that are directly present to us. That adjective, "that are directly present to us," indicates that I am classifying them with colors, sounds, odors, tastes, felt warmth and coolness, "physical" pleasure, "physical" pain, etc., all of which I also classify with things that are not-physical. All of which, when I wish to make you think of them but not other not-physical things (such as thoughts and memory-images), I classify as 'sensed givens' or 'sense-data.' If you 'understand English.'

Of course, most of the *people I do not know* won't feel anything but puzzlement, since English words will not reach into their psyches, conditioned to respond to Chinese, Japanese, Arabic, French, etc. Which people are pleased and which people are hurt by our words becomes an important concern. But we must give equal time to studying our own emotional and passionate reactions to thoughts and theories. Our emotional reactions, scratch-tests for our own mindset, are directly present to us, however bad—i.e., not good—are our habits of attention and inattention. Again, they are sensed, to be mentally class-ified with (non-physical) colors, sounds, odors, "physical" pleasure and pain. Into the same class named "sense-data" belong (non-physical) cravings which we feel, at least so long as we pay attention in thought to the object we crave. (Like anger, etc., craving often vanishes as soon as we can concentrate every ounce of our attention on the feeling and thereby push its object off the stage where our stream of consciousness passes by in review.)

Some who notice all this think the heart has reasons that reason knows not whereof, but they pay too little attention to the fact that the distinction between heart and head is a metaphor-model invented to map out our human experience. It is an invention created by imagination, if imagination exists, and the model's defense is tended to by reason which is often playing slave to an impassioned heart rather than cross-examined by a careful mind attending to the cold facts. Belief that such a distinction is true or measures up to facts must be verified the same way that any psychological theory is. Pascal's poetry is in the same boat with common expressions such as "Follow your heart" or "Go with the flow." It and they call for analysis, not incantation. So, you old fart, do you crave the truth enough to analyse more?

An Interlude. Therese's style rouses a sentiment in some that is described by such names as sentimental, syrupy, saccharine, cloying, too pious, intolerable. It is perfectly alright for people to believe in God, but we feel they ought to keep their intimate *tete a tete*'s with God private. Out of the public forum where praying aloud to God makes us think either of posturing hypocrites or of deluded fools talking to unseen white rabbits named Harvey. Monsignor Ronald Knox, the scholarly translator of the Bible whose last great endeavor was translating her story (he died without being able to correct his translation's proofs) and who had one of the century's best novel-authors as a biographer, seems to have been guided as much by a desire to desyrupize her language as to faithfully render her meaning. Retranslating the work's title from *Story of a Soul* to *Autobiography of a Saint* causes a reverse shock, sentiment-wise, to those fond of the old title. How our cravings differ from the cravings of others!

Even from our own earlier cravings. Had I encountered her words earlier in my life than I did, I probably would have been as put off by them as I once was by the style of Saint Augustine's *Confessions*. My callow youth had begun to end, my tastes were in transition, so I didn't notice the stylistic aesthetics attended to so piously in so many college courses. The miraculous wisdom of this woman who died before reaching her twenty-fifth birthday pierced the soul of still another reader. And caused one more in a lifetime of changes. One of the most important being changes about what's trivia pursuit and what trivia's not. A great deal of the philosophy I had simultaneously begun learning from J.Gredt's two-volume textbook was medieval trivia, but at least it helped me convert my earlier implicit or tacit common-sense assumptions into explicit or profess-ional principles, many of which became and remain bedrock premises for every thought being spooned out here and, I realize in retrospect, made it possible for me to eventually reach the present vantage point that allows me to appreciate the utterly miraculous wisdom found by Therese and permanently available to readers like myself fortunate to encounter her writings. If they are ready to get past her style.

For most of us, her life-style presents a far greater put-off than her writing-style. Her cravings were too extreme. Had she had a normal childhood, married and raised a family, gone into the convent at 72, then died at 81, mourned by a flock of grandchildren and friends, we might not think of nine years spent in the convent as too extreme. Eight-ninths of a normal and productive life might, in our eyes, balance off nine years of self-imposed imprisonment behind cloister walls. But Therese lived only 24 3/4 years. Her nine years, five months, and twenty-one days shut away from "the world" amount to more than a third of the years many of today's college-educated women spend before getting married. A third of a brief life. Wisdom? Why not call a spade "a spade" and say "That's nuts"? What's even more strange, she seems less to have sacrificed the things she craved and more to have looked down her nose at what most people crave. She spent her sixteenth year pleading with her father, her uncle, her bishop, and finally the pope himself, to let her do what she craved above all: enter the cloister immediately and spend the rest of her life there. Even now, a further truth is that I came to find her craving-style too difficult for me, which is why I am no longer 'in a monastery' as I was in 1955.

Her cravings, then, are the big issue. Well, the whole truth in this case is that it is the discomfort we might feel when we compare our cravings with hers. That is, the big issue is our cravings. For instance, our craving to have the truth presented in certain styles and not in styles we are uncomfortable with. She, after all, seems not to have been uncomfortable with hers. In fact, the gushiest part of her story is the long letter which she addressed to her sister but in which she did most of her speaking as-if-to/to Jesus, her Beloved, and she adopted that form because she said it made it easier to express herself. And, typically for her, she shows her extraordinary sensitivity by adding that "It may be that you'll find some of my expressions overstrained; if so, you must make allowances and put it down to my wretched style." She followed her craving but noted others'.

Were ANY of her cravings normal? Dorothy Day, unlike Augustine (the whole truth demands that we add "in his later years"), certainly had nothing against sex, one of normal people's most powerful cravings. Did Therese? The story of her life should prompt us to ask, Did she even notice she had a body, or was she a Gaul who actually fitted Descartes' usual (usual but not uniform) view of us humans as angels using body-taxis to get around in? Could she think of nothing better to do with her body than get it into a cloister and to do it as quickly as possible? Those questions are meant to raise the obvious next question. What reason could there be to hold up an extremist-ascetic, one whose normal cravings were so abnormal, one for whom normal-for-her-age cravings were, it seems, so rare as to be anti-normal, as a role model for anyone vis-à-vis anything? Unless for extremist-sect believers willing to allow their geneological tree to end with them. Unless, of course, Modern Science were to make the *Brave New World* vision of extra-uterine incubation come true the way dreams of cold storage for Overpersons' sperm and ova, test-tube fertilization, surrogate-intra-uterine incubation, etc., have come true. To what end, though, if the offspring are bred for a similar-to-hers lives of discomfort, poverty, chastity, and subservience to authority? Or does all this miss the point? What was wise about her? What about her is so wise?

Only a unifying vision of humans, of the purpose of humans' life, and of the realities behind the ingeniously deceptive appearances we are led by our Creating Parents to mis-take as a physical world, will frame satisfying answers to those questions. She missed much of 'scientific' truth and sacrificed some 'worldly' beauty. Her words are extreme and, like Augustine's "Our hearts are restless till they rest in Thee," often suggest that a single moment spent enjoying anything apart from God is a moment stolen from God. Like every whole truth about a whole human's whole life, the truth about her is complex and encompasses many truths. The miracle of her wisdom was her extraordinary sensitivity to the everyday psychology of everyman and everywoman, one that allowed her to bring the loftiest abstractions of ethics down to the minutest details, the full truth, of each person's here-now.

It would take at least a brief book to begin listing the thoughts that surge into my mind when Therese Martin's name is mentioned. It would take Robert Coles to do it well the way he did in the cases of Dorothy Day and Simone Weil. The most that can be done here is to provide more of the framework which not only shows that her life made complete sense, but which also allows one like me to appreciate the miles and miles that separate us, the bell-curve's majority, from history's greatest hero(in)es. *Cut.*

Cravings and Semantics. Pleasure is what humans' lives are all about. So, Epicurus did get the formula right. What he had wrong was so much of the full meaning he put into it. Only by thoroughly reorganizing our own mindset in such a way that we can put the right meaning into the formula can any of us hope to get to the bottom of what humans' lives are all about. That is, only by grasping what the meaning of "Pleasure is what humans' lives are all about" *ought to be* will anyone reach the pinnacle of insight into the truth, the whole truth, at least in general, and at least not too much of what is not the truth. William James travelled infinitely farther toward Peirce's asymptote of the whole truth than Epicurus. And James' writings are so much better on good craving when we need so much less of war and so much more of its moral equivalents, that it is a crying shame—a sin, too?—that so many experts appear readier to revive Epicurus (and/or Lucretius) than to learn and publicize James.

That is the simplest MODEL: We love pleasure and we hate pain. We crave pleasure and discrave displeasure. We chase pleasure and flee pain. We are pleased by pleasure and pained by pain. We like enjoyment and dislike disenjoyments. We enjoy pleasure and we disenjoy pain. We desire what gives pleasure or pleases, we fear what gives pain or displeases. We want what's good or what is pleasing, whether in the short term or in the long term; we don't want what's bad or what is painful, whether in the short term or in the long term. Best would be having all pleasure, less good (or merely better) is having mostly pleasure, even less good (or merely good) is having relatively little pleasure and mostly pain, and no good at all is having no pleasure at all, not even the pleasing or pleasant prospect that the future will bring a little, then more, then complete pleasure to replace the actual pain or the pain that is the mere absence of all pleasure.

One MODEL, but only one, is that two-pair correlation. A model invented by the imagination to help us put order into the mass of otherwise-impossible-to-synthesize-or-see-in-a-single-God's-eye-view, chaotic, particular facts about particular beings. The vocabulary—the preceding is only a sampling, and only from the English pool—is not the essential thing. The thought is. And whoever learns how to analyse all the 'words, words, words' that constitute, it seems, the avenue by which the bulk of information about higher-level thinking and about others' insides comes to us, will discover that sometimes a three-part diagram is better, that othertimes several layers of maps or diagrams are better than just a single map, and that it is only for purposes of seeing everything most clearly that stillothertimes the simplest, two-item model is preferable. That is, there are many models.

For instance, the three-item DIAGRAM that I just thought about is needed to unravel Epicurus' confusions. The *first* item is named "positive pleasure which is more than the absence of pain," the *second* is named "absence of either positive pleasure or positive pain," the *third* is "positive pain which is more than the absence of pleasure." Inasmuch as these are shorthand reifications for total situations (there must always be an enjoyer or sufferer, sometimes the felt pleasure or pain has nothing to do with thoughts, othertimes the felt pleasure or pain—but which one is that feeling, real and undeniable, that we name "anger"?—is a parasite that withers without the thoughts and/or memories that shock treatment, alcohol, other drugs, time, amnesia, etc., take from us, and so on), it is essential to begin trying to line up the infinite variety of human experiences under the right headings, then to get crystal clear on the obvious fact that, with the slightest shift in our gestalt or point of view (take your choice of metaphors), what was lined up under one heading can be relined by any willing rethinker under another. Since all of this is abstract shorthand generalization for thoughts about various human experiences, the way to be clear for those who are unfamiliar with the connections I make between what I put on paper, it seems, and what is in my mind is to offer egs.

At this moment—it is the morning after the Saturday evening when I watched and became excited by the "The Rascals" episode of Star Trek—the whole truth is mixed. The memory of that excitement even now rekindles a feeling of pleasure in me, as does my anticipation of inserting it into a paragraph I hope to 'put on paper' later in this non-section. Those are positive pleasures. *I am enjoying this*. Accompanied by some positive pains: a sense of dis-satisfaction, because I cannot instantly telepath my memories to you (if you have no recollection of the episode, perhaps—if you have not seen it—not any memory of it), and a sense of un-fulfilledness, because I have to get some other things down before I can fulfill my desire to write that paragraph. *I am not happy*. The fuller truth than either of those half-truths is that I am AND I am not enjoying this. Or that I am enjoying this, tho not completely, AND disenjoying this, tho not completely. Which partial-truth shall I notice? Which part of my "world" shall I attend to in order to invite the correlated feeling to increasingly crowd the other off-stage?

How realistic are those reflections? In years past, I'd often wonder "Am I happy?" I clearly recall the profound impression Aristotle's mis-named ethics had on me when I discovered how much order could be imposed on a lifetime's worth of experience by his simple observation that, beneath all the variations of outward appearances, every one of us has but a single aim: to be happy. "Am I happy?" became the yardstick by which to measure "the way my life was going" each time I recalled it, particularly if it was reinforced by "really," that mother of rethinking. "Am I REALLY happy?" At that stage of my life, before I had found the completely adequate model for integrating my still-juvenile mini-models of 'real pleasure' and 'real pain,' my naive-realist views of the physical world, and my growing-up catechism lessons about moral obligations ("God made me to know, love, and serve Him in this life—by keeping the Ten Thou-shalt and Thou-shalt-not Commandments—and be happy with Him in the next"), the juvenile or inexperienced mini-models of 'real pleasure' and 'real pain' dominated my mindset when I picked up the yardstick to measure the extent of my 'present happiness.' How unclear I still was.

Ask: How many onlookers would judge what I am doing now as "doing something that makes me really happy"? How many would judge the aforementioned, so-easy-to-overlook 'fringe' feelings to be any more than pastels? I am not feeling the feelings most people—probably even I during my careless hours—think of when they hear "pleasure" or "enjoyment," particularly if they are in the bad habit of impaling themselves on the "pleasure or the pleasant vs goodness or the good" dilemma. I am experiencing none of the things most people—probably even I during inadvertent moments—think of when they hear "pain" or "misery," unless they are padlockers in the ungood habit of scorning "pain" as a mere hypothetical construct needed only by those who need more for their spurious cognitive "science" than behavior that meets the padlockers' eye*. For most people, in other words, there must be the REAL pleasure or REAL pain of "Eat, drink, and be merry" fame before they are willing to invoke the names of pleasure or pain. (*Who try to imitate Skinner's inconsistent use of "negatively reinforcing contingency" to refer to what's out-, not in-side, i.e., to translate "pain" into references to what's not pain.)

"Real pleasure" and "real pain", like "happy" and "unhappy," are shorthand, though, and the best way for you to be sure what I mean is if I "unpack" my meaning with egs. I am not at this moment raising an ice-cream-laden spoon to my lips, not sipping wine with finger-lifting elegance, not self-absorbed in plateau-ascending activities referred to as erotic, not experiencing any breathtaking, roller-coaster free-falls, not enjoying present-transcending conversation with a likeminded friend, etc.* Nor is my face being beaten to a pulp by an attacker, my visage being contorted each time my stomach is pummelled by another fist, my mouth issuing groans as cigarette butts are applied to my body. So most people might think from looking at a photo taken of me right now—or even from viewing a videotape of same—that it would be hard to tell whether I am enjoying or toiling, whether I am feeling pleasure or pain, or whether I am *in a third state, a neutral* state best described as the absence of pleasure *and* the absence of pain. Epicurus-students are normally surprised when they realize that he defines "pleasure" in radically different ways: 1-sometimes as the direct presence of something positive, that is, as the real existence in their field of experience of something MORE, ADDITIONAL, EXTRA, OVER and ABOVE the bare, mere experience of possessing one's health, which something-more might incline us to invite friends to share the fun while warning them against the danger of too much of it, and 2-sometimes as the absence of the pain brought on those who did not heed the warning and who, on the morrow, only wished they were dead, that is, as the total experience of having one's health but nothing else. In fact, the commercial suggesting that, when we have our health, we have just about everything, is an update of half of Epicurus. (*Structuralists enjoy looking for pattern-reversing forms.)

That is an excellent illustration of the need to take more than a frozen-time snapshot into account when trying to understand the unbelievably complex constellations of meaning we can pack into a single-word sentence like "Happy?" or "Miserable?" Health is, I mean. Is it not obvious that countless utterly bored, miserable, unhappy people are completely healthy at the same time? We need only think of the number of perfectly healthy—"physically" healthy, we usually add—who commit suicide. How, then, can anyone ever have believed "When you have your health, you have just about everything" made sense except in the unnoticed total-environment context that included the horse the speaker sat on or the smiling spouse s/he was being hugged by, etc.? How? Easily! The claim makes perfect sense if we imagine ourselves at the end of a two-year bout with cancer, a two-week bedride with the flu, a two-hour siege from an excruciating migraine, i.e., if we place ourselves on the border between the two total-experiences—James and Rogers would instantly know the full meaning of "the experiences" here—named "being ill" and "being healthy." No longer worrying about the 'growth' which foretells an end to another-new-day wake-ups, climbing out of bed looking forward to a nice breakfast or a nicer browse in the library, being released from a headache's vise-grip: each spell r-e-l-i-e-f. Why is it that, as soon as we sit down to think professionally about right and wrong, we take our eyes off the incredible varieties of pleasure—and pain-including experiences that give "doing right and not doing wrong" their entire meaning? (Hint: Abstraction.)

Good ethics is as hard as good psychology. Good theory about ethical topics is as difficult as good theory about psychological topics. Good thinking about right and wrong is as demanding as good thinking about people. And, as more than a century of the most concentrated-thinking-ever about people has shown, sure-footed thinking about persons, the thinkers of thoughts, the feelers of cravings, the acquirers of habits of thought and craving, is as demanding as good thinking about good and bad. What has preceded is offered as premise-conclusions for the claim that one major difficulty is posed by "semantics," i.e., by the many-meaning-ness of 'words' whose links to thinkers' thoughts snake thru each one's jungle of memory-image associations.

Solving "the semantic problem" is crucial. Solving it requires that we overcome bad thought habits and replace them with good ones. The worst of today's bad habits is thinking that "language" names an independent being or class of beings, as opposed to the traditional view that *thought* is the only thing that gives natural sounds, ciphers, gestures, etc., the added "conventional" or "instrumental" value of being more than merely things heard, seen, and felt. Their unnatural, that is, extra utility as "signs" or "symbols" is an extrinsic addition created by users who acquire the required (association) habits. Just as a rock with a natural 'pocket' in it—used now as a projectile, now a paperweight, now an ashtray—never itself is anything but a rock, neither are the sounds, etc. When this reifying Myth of Language is combined with today's anti-mentalist delusion that not only thoughts, but even the private images Hume studied so carefully are non-existent, the route to escaping epistemology's age-old knots is effectively barred. Only by reopening our minds to the fullest exploration of the jungle of immediate experience can we begin to notice our incessant use of imagery, to overcome our excessive reliance on limited imagery, and begin the never-excessive exploration of the uses and abuses of every kind of the imagery that forms the missing link in attempts to uncover the correlations between "language" and humans' thoughts.

The time has come when every psychologist, i.e., each one of us who craves to "Know myself" and—since knowing one is knowing all (who are like the one, at least in the respect to which attention is being paid at the one, same moment)—each one of us who also craves to know all who are like my one self, must find the right model(s) to use for the whole truth about good psychology and good ethics, both of which are thinking thoughts and/or theories that use model-metaphors galore. Since we have an obligation to seek the whole truth, and part of it is the truth about thinking, and since "ethics" deals with obligation and "psychology" with thinking, we MUST seek one theory for both.

Generalizations and Details. "THE" model is pluralism for pluralists. This is not a model for psychology—"psychology" names an abstraction, a fiction—but for 'psychologists,' that is, for persons who "do" psychology or SHOULD "do" it, that is, *for all of us*. William James is "**THE**" model of good professional thinking about things human. Good thinking about everything was a passion with him, but most of all good thinking about selves and the varieties of their experiences. Individual human selves were the dead center of his attention, the endless variations in their experiences the flame that he always returned to, no matter where his flights of exploration might temporarily take him. He knew enough of everything—especially everything that affects humans' lives—so that he was no man's fool on anything. But, if ever there was a living exemplar of the thesis that "the proper study of the human is the human," it was William James.

For several reasons, the full extent of his genius has not been generally enough appreciated. For one, the realization that indeterminism reaches into the tiniest regions of space lacked the massive verification that now confronts any smug claim that determinism is the one and only genuinely 'scientific' faith. Too, the dead-endness of materialism and its identical twin, physicalism, had not yet been glaringly demonstrated by a century of futile searching for a 'linguistic' explanation of scientific thought to replace monist idealism. Nor had the electron microscope settled the Golgi-Cajal debate. Most of all, though, James' brilliant-in-practice syntheses of previous traditions are presently obscured by his needless, wavering theory-rejection of Descartes' common sense. As late as 1898, he still wavered:

> Doesn't it seem like the wriggling of a worm on the hook, this attempt to escape the dualism of common sense? And is not the contrast I have been forcibly led to between

the brain terminatively or entitatively considered and the
brain "in the field" (= the brain *represesentatively* considered)
indistinguishable from the common sense contrast between
the objective brain and the brain-thought of? It looks so.
(James, *Manuscript Lectures*, pp.247-48)

Descartes took the decisive step in using Ockham's lasso to begin
regrounding the human imagination which, on a long-ago afternoon
in Athens, took flight toward the highest reaches of UNscientific
abstraction. Its implications have not yet been fully accepted, but in
practice James accepted them and then some. If we imagine that Plato
captured the gist of an actual dialogue between Socrates and Meno,
then we know it was the moment when the human mind was launched
on a journey away from the beings we deal with in daily life—where,
for instance, each person has a unique face, a unique set of fingerprints,
a unique DNA blueprint, and most of all a unique mindset—into the
upper realms of abstractions, where we search for, say, the original
blueprint that makes each and every person human rather than animal,
vegetable, mineral. Plato's *Meno* records Socrates' impatience with
anything less than bee-hood in general, color in general, virtue in
general. In the fourteenth century, Ockham rebutted arguments for the
reality of universals by reminding everyone of the fact that everything
we experience is particular, even your ideas of beehood or anything else
in general, my ideas of beehood or anything else in general . . . (Only
after years of believing in universals and universality in general—J.
Gredt describes several kinds of universals, which logically implies
that, if they have universalhood in common, there's an essence of
universalness common to all universals!—did I discover through a
careful rereading of Aquinas' *De Ente et Essentia*, that he, too, admitted
that only non-universal things exist, that universalhood is, as it were,
created or at least added to particular ideas by abstracting minds.)
As a postscript to Ockham's reminder, Descartes in the seventeenth
century drew attention to one inescapable everyday fact that was still
being escaped by so many professional thinkers two centuries later
when Kierkegaard drew it again, viz., the inescapable fact that the most
important individual that any professional thinker can be certain about
is her or his own self, the being s/he calls "I." If s/he speaks English. If
s/he needs English's nominative case. If there are any s/he's. As you scan

these rows and rows, the most important self you can be certain about is your self that is certain, that is still trying to be certain, or that has decided to give up the quest for certainty, not any other deciding-selves. Do you know for certain whether Socrates, Plato, Ockham, Descartes, James, etc., exist at this very moment? Do YOU know?

It is a monumental switch, this switch FROM thinking of science—take "science" **HERE** to be synonymous with "the best in human knowledge of what is really going on"—as timeless knowledge of timeless realities TO thinking of the general and/or abstract statements proferred by most 'scientists' as shorthand for thoughts that are about individuals or else about nothing (only individuals exist, and what does not exist is not anything or, for short, is nothing), and not about just any thoughts in general, but as shorthand for the thoughts of the particular speaker or writer at the moment s/he is using it. That switch is the very bone and marrow of James' outlook. When he was still a young man, he captured the 'essence' of Ockhamism in this magnificent formula: "No one sees farther into a generalization than his own knowledge of details extends." Because it is the antidote to the myth of universals, it should be highlighted:

No one sees farther into a generalization than his own knowledge of details extends.

Jacques Barzun, whose *A Stroll With William James* brought that formula (from a letter James wrote home from his Amazonian expedition with Louis Agassiz) to my attention, added this perfect comment: "The statement prefigures one of the seminal principles of his later philosophy—the passion for concreteness and the riddling not merely of false but of misused generality."

Einstein said something like "I want to know the mind of God, all else is details." His monotheist ancestors would have replied, "The mind of God does not overlook a single detail, whether it is a falling sparrow or a hair." Some monotheists take the view that God dwells *only* in the details. To which the obvious reply is, "That is a grand generalization that alludes in a most vague way to vast numbers of vastly different details."

For humans whose minds are immeasurably inferior to God's, abstractions and generalizations are necessary tools. They are not, however, quarry to be sought for their own sake, they are tools to be used in cataloguing, classifying, and—in that way—knowing the real quarry, quintillions of individual existents that are all partly like all the others and partly different, both in ways that are all partly like each other and partly different. *Each complete sentence is a tour of classifications,* e.g., "sentence" means I am attending to some things from the aspect of being similar to each other but different from non-sentences and "sign" indicates I am thinking of similar things insofar as they are different from non-signs, etc. As Robert Coles noted in his review of Barzun's *Stroll,* Barzun himself added a phrase James would have applauded: "The ladder of increasing generality is traveled up and down a dozen times an hour without one's noticing it." P.S. AI experts, those who, it seems to them, are trying to get computers to compute the way we computers do, understand that even this understates the truth by a factor of three. Thirty?

James' pluralism serves as an antidote to more Great Thinkers' Blocks than just Plato's. In the same way that Jews, Christians, and Muslims resist Plato's abstraction by simply transferring his Best Forms (Truth, Goodness, and Beauty) into their file on the supreme individual, God, James can be said to have resisted other Sirens trying to lure him from individuals by finding a place for their abstractions in the files of his grand, unifying system. The Sirens are two: the Pantheist Monism of the 1800's and the Social Groupism of the 1900's. The two errors go hand in hand, and there are many INDIVIDUAL THINKERS who merge them into their own professional theorizing. Aristotle begins his *Politics* with a passage that is an excellent illustration of this bad thinking:

> Every state is a community of some kind, and every community is established with a view to some good, for mankind always act in order to obtain that which they think good; but, if all communities aim at some good, the state or political community, which is the highest of all, and which embraces all the rest, aims at good in a greater degree than any other, and at the highest.

Unlike Aristotle, who simply took over his mentor's *Republic* myth that states 'made up of' sub-classes (law-makers, law-enforcers, law-[supposed-to]abiders) are real, James rejects such groupism, especially when it is extended to individuals' psyches:

> We talk of the 'spirit of the age,' and the 'sentiment of the people,' and in various ways we hypostatize 'public opinion.' But we know this to be symbolic speech, and never dream [sic] that the spirit, opinion, sentiment, etc., constitute a consciousness other than, and additional to, that of the several individuals whom the words 'age,' 'people,' or 'public' denote. The private minds do not agglomerate into a higher compound mind. (*Principles of Psychology*, chapter six.)

Though once again millions of Westerners are embracing pantheist models the way millions, following Hegel, did in the last century and the way millions in the East have always done, the more common occurrence in the West is for individuals to embrace a materialist, emergent-whole-ist model. Put enough atoms together and you get molecules, enough molecules create cells . . . , from the "uniting" of many people emerge those higher social organisms with such names as "family," "tribe," "village," "town," "city," "county," etc. Or "Man," "Woman," "the White Race," "the Black Race," "Christianity," "Ireland," "The West," "The East," etc. James—like any good Missouri'an who would ask to see "the Upper Class," and like Ryle's university-watchers who, even after being driven through Beverly Hills, Palm Springs, etc., would persist in asking "Well, when do I get to see the Class?"—would have none of it. Which is surely what we might expect him to reply to the complaint that his *Varieties* turns off those who look for an institution to go with the name "religion." Yes, we all crave fellowship, we want to "belong," and—when the first flush of infatuation wears off—to belong to more than a single spouse, that is, belong to a group. What we experience even in those peak "belonging to a group" experiences, tho, is private.

The fact that we never see groups, however, does not prove they do not exist. Pantheists believe in non-bodily Being. Descartes and Locke believed in physical bodies even though none of us has ever seen one, not others' bodies nor our own, and they believed it for reasons that have seemed perfectly reasonable to thousands of their readers. The same might be true of social bodies. But the important fact in relation to all those unseens is that what is experienced is intrapsychic and private. In Kohler's model, the world is unseen, each of us experiences our "world." Extend that as it should be and each of experiences, not mom and dad, but "mom" and "dad," thought-about "persons" which are part of our reading of our sense-experience. In fact, we cannot even turn around and take a peek at our own self. One's experienced-self is one's own self-concept, another part of one's personal reading of experience. Thought-about "persons" add up only to thought-about "social groups." The way thought-about a-toms add up. Or don't.

Master-psychologist that he was, it is not surprising that James did not overlook the intrapsychic nature of inter-"person"-al relations. The analysand stretched out, it seems, on a couch and talking with the analyst about his continuing battles with his father, now long deceased, is dealing directly with his "analyst" and his "father," not his analyst or father. (It helps to recall that we NEVER see others' thoughts or feelings, not even those of a spouse or lover.) The split between intrapsychic, solipsist models and social-interactional, interpersonal-relations models in the meadow of "personality theory" creates false-dilemmas. Only an **INTRA-PSYCHIC, INTER-"PERSON"-AL** theory will do. Which is what we find in James' treatment of the total self-concept with its four parts: the part corresponding to the thinker (one of the unseen plus's included in the *Varieties'* description of the total field of experience cited in the last chapter), the physical me, the spiritual me, and the social me or social self. "Properly speaking," he wrote, "a man has as many social selves as there are individuals who recognize him" [which is an elision and should read, "as there are individuals he believes recognize him"]. These selves, like the individuals who recognize us, are facets of our total SELF-concept! The interpersonal theorist, H.S. Sullivan reworked James' idea into his roles-model formula, "For all I know, every human being has as many personalities as he has interpersonal relations," and his idea that "Even though only two people are actually in the [therapist's consulting] room the number of more or less imaginary people that get themselves involved in this two-group is sometimes really hair-raising" must be part of any enlightened approach to "doing therapy."

These superb solutions which James found for ancient issues help turn to ashes another old epistemological chestnut. Aristotle asked "Are the essence and the individual one?", and that became the question, "Can the universalizing intellect know singulars?" Only those whose mental eye is mesmerized by verbal surfaces and bad theory (e.g., that human thoughts are built from abstract[ed] concepts) will insist that our word-guiding intellects can never know the singular. Or know it directly. They appeal to words: the boy first calls all men "daddy," so "daddy" must be universal and the child's abstracting mind must be aimed directly at those men's common essence. Hegelian monists reply that this begs the question. A closer look at language shows that reason never reaches the individual: the world's telephone directories show that we use and re-use proper names for totally different people the same way we use the dictionary's (improper?) names for radically different things. The intellect cannot reach as far as the concrete individual, because there aren't any. Oh? There aren't?!

Au contraire! These blunders are caused by having bad models for how we learn. We do not begin by constructing complex images from sensed colors, sounds, etc. We begin building an entire inner model of the individual items in our neighborhood. The various classifications into things that neither grow nor move without a kick, things that grow but aren't conscious, and things that move, yelp or yell if kicked, and maybe bite back if bitten, are not put into words one by one, but signify that we not only associate but must simultaneously discriminate. No one gets a peek at what is in back ("my own self") nor at what is out front ("minerals," "vegetables," "animals," or "other selves"). We must work with nothing but (!) an increasingly rich inner "world-model" populated, not only by daddy, but by Santa Claus, friendly fairy godmothers, wicked spell-casting witches, guardian angels, satanic devils, etc., when we're young, and later on by figures from works of fiction, non-documentary movies, TV soaps, and so on. That is, by representings of things that are not out there. And by MISrepresentings of things that are. Which things are? What??

Each INDIVIDUAL thinker will argue for our own answer. Each can best persuade her—or himself. None can force anyone else, if anyone else exists!, to conform theirs to ours. A final choice of unifying theory is a choice, it remains so only so long as no rival is chosen. James' final choice was, like mine, pluralism. Since only individuals exist, the only existents we can possibly know are individuals. "Naming" cues—proper or class cues—should be imagined as keys to mental files. We construct our spatio-temporal model of the universe, *open a file* on each oft-re-cognized, self-identical existent—the best retrospective *class*-ification of the outstanding feature of such existents is not "mineral," "vegetable," or "animated," but "permanent," hence the popularity among Piagetians of the phrase "object permanence"—to which files on individuals (which we learn *proper* names for) we are constantly adding 'notes' that consist of particular facts. [These "files" must be re-analysed within the context of this book's model as hybrids 'made up of' understood thoughts and memory-images of sense-data.] We further de-fine and de-limit and *not*-proper-ly name each 'file-concept' of each permanent object IN OUR MODEL by reference to those others to which it is more similar and from which it is less different, as well as those to which it is less similar and from which it is more different, thus creating group (species, etc.) files. Think of one particular person, place, thing, etc., and begin describing it. Compare your "description" with these [abstract!] analyses.

Synthesize all of this with the picture of 5.5 billion individual humans and 5.5 billion private mindsets, each one a 'world' unto itself. Then weigh the Solipsist Challenge—WHY do I believe there is anything but my self and my private 'world'—by bringing, not merely the galaxy-surrounded Milky Way Galaxy, into your private 'world,' but all 5,499,999,999 other selves and all 5,499,999,999 of their 'worlds' into it as well. Since, let me repeat, only individuals exist, the only existents you can know are individuals. Think, for instance, of your father, mother, B.F. Skinner, Kelly, etc. Each 'name' you just scanned took you right to the file—your file—named. IF you have one. (If you have several, you'll not know which *I* went to without some further clues.) 'Man' will take you right to your file (also English'ly-labelled "male upright walking featherles biped," etc.), the one that originally had the uni-name "daddy" on it, and when you open it, you will suddenly find yourself—if you are my clone—in the files marked "I myself," "Daddy," "Danny," "Uncle Vince," as well as for *any other* beings that are enough like me, my dad, my brother, my uncle, etc. Still, not even identical twins will have an identical inner model of 'self in the world with other selves.' Each twin's SELF-concept will be far more developed than her or his TWIN-concept, each will remember all the parents' attention given to the other as having been given to the not-self, etc. Hence, the accuracy of the 7-28-87 *N.Y. Times* "Each Sibling Experiences Different Family" report and the 12-7-91 *Science News* "Same Family, Different Lives" follow-up, which only confirm what every observant rethinker has more than enough first-hand evidence for. This intrapsychic inter'person'al aspect is the missing wing that must added to every Kantian 'appearance vs reality'—own-person-(vis-a-vis-other-'persons')-al-'world' vs objective world—model.

This expanded 'representationalism' of James surpasses Hegel's and Heidegger's impersonal models. This total, inter'person'al, 'my self in the world with others,' *self-model* adds yet another dimension to the four types of self-knowledge distinguished by M. Novak in chapter two of his *Belief and Unbelief*. The final implications are enormous. Especially this implication: no two human mind(sets) are identical. James relished the variations. One of his biographers, G.H. Allen, quotes passages from a letter that gives a picture of his mindset vis-à-vis such variety.

> Although I absolutely reject the platonism of [Santayana], I have literally squealed with delight at the imperturbable perfection with which the position is laid down on page after page; and grunted with delight at such a thickening up of our Harvard atmosphere." If their students [Allen paraphrases] could now begin to understand "what Royce means with his voluntaristic-pluralistic monism, what Munsterberg means with his dualistic scientificism and platonism, what Santayana means by his pessimistic platonism . . . , what I mean by my crass pluralism, what you mean by your ethereal idealism, that these are so many religions, ways of fronting life, and worth fighting for, we should have a genuine philosophic universe at Harvard. The best condition of it would be an open conflict and rivalry of diverse systems . . .

That is what is behind the complete sentence underlined earlier, *"Each complete sentence is a tour of classifications."* It means each utterance is a tour of one intersection in ONE person's way of dividing up the world. Since each mind(set) is so diverse—James above refers to only a handful of the most unplain cases of professional divergencies, but in *Pragmatism*'s opening chords he approves Chesterton's view that every plain man has a philosophy, "the most practical and important thing about him"—each 'word' must be viewed as a clue to some part of the unique mind(set) which is that word's source, and the fact that new connections are always being made between the quintillians of items

341

already lodged in the source-person's mindset explains why Chomsky's insight must be part of the whole truth that Skinner's emphasis on mere repetitions of old verbal behaviors is only one part of. That is why careful readers always expect the Humpty Dumpty rule at any given moment, why they will read each book, each article, each poem, as a set of keys to the vast geography of yet another human's reading of a total sensory 'environment,' a little or a lot different from any other already encountered.

This book illustrates what is meant by radically different mind(set)s. Readers who are unfamiliar with Santayana, Royce, Munsterberg, and Palmer ("you"), will have to visit the library for tours of their minds. To forestall the need to lay this book down for a visit to a library at this point, Chapter Two dwelt at some length on two mindsets, Skinner's and Roger's, in order to provide a sample of how patiently we must explore to reach the bottom-line basic assumptions or premises of complex thinkers in order to understand what any snippet of their view really amounts to. Whoever wants graphic examples of what "radically different mindsets" means, needs only to turn back to that chapter for a quick reminder. Though not everyone will have the opportunity for a lot of time-consuming exploration, everyone must become profoundly aware of the meaning of the "EACH PERSON IS A 'WORLD' UNTO HER—OR HIMSELF" principle. That is not all, however. The name of William James has been invoked often throughout these pages, and the portrait of (parts of) a third mindset, that of James, is being presented in this chapter as a framework for thinking about Skinner and Rogers. That is not all, either.

From beginning to end, the book it seems you are reading presents a fourth mindset, for instance, this author's reading of the three of theirs. It, like any far ranging work available in the library, will provide a peek at the complexity of a single mindset, and thus convey a lesson about all. And about your own. You are understanding all four of ours from within the single, unified world of your own belief-system. Your view of the world, if you have been till now unfamiliar with James, Skinner, and Rogers, is enriched by tours of three other mindsets, or rather by this tour of your author's mindset which has files on those three. But you are not literally touring my mindset or my files on them. You are understanding the thoughts which are each taking their turn appearing on the stage of your mindset as, it seems, your eyes scan this line and, now, scan this string of ciphers and, now, these letters and, now . . . The thoughts you are now enjoying in the privacy of your own self's consciousness only seem to be tours of things I am letting you peek at in my mind. (If the thoughts 'match' mine, that is, are true thoughts, then your thoughts are your 'windows' onto mine.) And your mindset, molded by a lifetime of habits, is the basis for the evaluations you pass on the things being presented for your consideration. You know which of the thoughts and which facets of which of the thoughts coming to you in conjunction with your scanning of these rows and rose you assent to, which you dissent from, which you suspend judgment on. And, at each new moment of life, you have some power over the direction your life will take in the future. You can remain firm in your present evaluations. You can rethink them. You can make a decision that will be your first step in changing an old habit. You, the recaller of what you have believed in the past, are the lone arbiter of what you will believe in the future.

Welcome to your mind(set).

The theater for EXPERIENCED disputes is not the yard at Harvard, not the auditoriums where debaters from Harvard and Yale square off, not the halls of Congress. The *immediate theater for every debate is the mindset of someone who understands* the conflicting thoughts being presented to the arbiter-thinker who must be her or his own judge and jury of one. In your case, you. You are not arbitrating now between your vision of reality and my vision of same, but between your view of reality and your view of my view—I might be dead, this could be the work of an unknown imposter, maybe no one but you ever existed and your unconscious is the source of your thoughts ABOUT "my"? thoughts—and you have to decide which to make the container, which the contained. A naive-realist behaviorologist will hold to the personal view that there are no personal views. A neuro-materialist will hold that everyone's views are coded in the nodes of her/his brain. A new-Huxley'an will hold that everyone's views are byproducts of her/his brain. An idealist . . . You just re-viewed several your-views of theaters and views. All alone. In the privacy of your inner "world." Where you decide what YOU will believe. The only voices you hear are those gaining access to the theater of your own mind, as this voice or these voices are doing right now.

James: The Model of an Ethical Re-Thinker. Each of the three parts of this chapter have "habit" in its title. Something James is most famous for is his views on habits: creating habits, the strength of habits, changing habits, and so on. Whoever studies his personality-theory—almost called *The Varieties of Human Experience*—will discover how up-to-date he is on the favorite thesis of so-called cognitive scientist-therapists: thought—and belief-habits. Whoever knows how to plug the "virtue" theory of ethics into James' framework—virtues are good habits, vices are bad ones—will discover what it took me a long time to discover: that James is, above all, a cognitive-moral-pluralist.

First, another word on habits. They are not on my list of what-exists. No one has ever observed one. Even behaviorologists who are honest will have to confess that they rely on memory to recall the beginning of any pattern of behavior they believe they are watching AT THIS MOMENT—just as you have to rely on memory to recall NOW any of the thoughts that came to you as you scanned earlier lines on this page—and on imagination to anticipate NOW the finale of any behavior pattern they are watching AT THIS MOMENT. In the identical way that THIS DAY is always TOday (ex-children recall being amused by "Won't it ever be tomorrow?"), it is always NOW. So "habit" re-names link-chains sequentially "observed" if they sufficiently resemble other (glibly-named "observed") patterns of behavior, or else it names the unseen source of the sequential links in the (glibly-named "observed") pattern of behavior. "Habit," therefore, names a useful fiction—how useful, even indispensable! a fiction it is—that is, a 'higher' mental pigeonhole useful for filing away information about countless DIFFERENT 'patterns of behavior' or their unseen sources inside some agent. ("Disposition," "predisposition," "probability," etc., and similar equivocations re what-appears vs nonappearing-causes must also be unmasked, i.e., analysed.)

All of us who want to become 'scientific'—in the *genuine* sense of the word (a favorite trick for demoting others' theories)—psychologists must study and learn well what Einstein said has become a staple in the "world" of physicists: theoretical fictions. The lesson comes under dozens of labels, among which are "appearance vs reality," "real to the eye only," "saving the appearances," "useful constructs," "hypothetical entities," "paradigms," etc. The lesson is easy. Just as it is possible to be a remarkably skilled car-driver without knowing much, if anything, about how the steering-wheel and foot-pedals (the only things the driver touches) are connected to the four wheels (the only things that touch the ground), scores of those who have tried to fathom the correlations between abstract formulae ("All bodies attract all others with a force . . . ," "Solid bodies are nearly empty space," and so on), sense-data, and the underlying nature of things, have concluded that the underlying nature will forever remain beyond the reach of our minds, even though we are acquiring greater and greater control over whatever it is. So here, the one thing that is clear is that none of us can 'lift the hood' on our minds, as it were, in order to inspect the engine that is responsible for the miraculous feats of co-awareness, remembering, anticipating, understanding, and deciding, that are everyday commonplaces. The important thing, however, is not to view "habit" as naming a single, isolated concept, but as naming only one of an entire tool-kit of fictions useful for 'putting some order' into our thinking about an otherwise unruly jungle of facts or mass of details far too numerous for any but the Divine Mind to keep distinct track of.

The tool-kit has a noble lineage. Begun by Plato, improved by Aristotle, polished by Aquinas, it is re-viewed here as a set of useful, theoretical fictions. Book IV of Plato's *Republic*, one of the texts to which all of us are indebted footnoters, reveals the work of a master analyst as he labors to construct a model of the psyche from which spring the various streamlets continually pouring into each of our great oceans of consciousness. Slowly untangling the threads of experiential fact, he builds a simple, three-part model of the human psyche. Our more contemporary names for them might be: the part that thinks and understands thoughts, the part that craves and cringes, the part that affords the power to side with better thoughts, even against cravings and cringings. (A slight twist further improves the model: WE are in part understanders of thoughts, in part affected by cravings and cringings, in part capable of making decisions that go with our better thinking (either with or against the flow of current passions) or decisions that go with the preferred passion and invite reason to invent suitable rationalizations.) Upon this psyche-model, Plato hung his ethical discussions of virtue and vice, that is, of good and bad habits. Aristotle, in his *On the Soul*, explicitated the context for habit-acquisition. The person or individual engaged in moral striving, is the **AGENT** behind the **ACTS**. We are capable of a variety of act(ivitie)s by virtue of operative **POWERS**, e.g., reason, memory, senses, that we do not lose even when we discontinue the acts for a good night's rest. Cognitive acts especially have **OBJECTS**. Repeated acts vis-à-vis specific kinds of objects will produce specific kinds of **HABITS** which improve or worsen the abilities and, thereby, improve or worsen the faculties' owners. (Among the facts that escape this procrustean-if-stretched too far is the fact that our sense faculties often deteriorate, however noble the things we look at, listen to, reach for, etc.). Chapter One explained how Aquinas' further-refined model "put order into my thinking" for years. And countless other models have been offered by thinkers—from Descartes to Kant—in the years since, so that the library-visitor now has an enormous range of models to choose from.

James himself subscribed in separate places to each part of the model of human learning that has been guiding the composition of the previous paragraphs which have recast his presentation a bit . . . . But he summed up the central cluster-idea AS IT APPLIES TO THE ETHICS OF THOUGHT-HABITS in one brief, stunning passage. True, there are so many passages of sublime beauty in James' works that it would be silly to single out just one and declare it "Best of all!" And yet, were I to indulge my craving to pick the best of James' poems the way I've often indulged my craving to pick my favorite pie (who listened when I later said "I now like BCP best"?), my favorite song (each new one that later made me want to scream when it was replayed on the radio for the 666th time that same week), my favorite symphony (which now I never re-listen to on my own initiative because I overdid it, too), I'd not hesitate for an instant. (Unless my focus changed.) He penned it in a burst of creative intuition while composing what became his *Principles'* chapter on "Association," a topic central to empiricists' analysis of thought and imagery habit-networks:

> Why do we spend years straining after a certain scientific or practical problem, but all in vain—thought refusing to evoke the solution we desire? And why, some day, walking in the street with our attention miles away from that quest, does the answer saunter into our minds as carelessly as if it had never been called for—suggested, possibly, by the flowers on the bonnet of the lady in front of us, or possibly by nothing

that we can discover? If reason can give us relief, why did she not do so earlier?

The truth must be admitted that thought works under conditions imposed *ab extra*. The great law of habit itself—that twenty experiences make us recall a thing better than one, that long indulgence in error makes right thinking almost impossible—seems to have no essential foundation in reason. The business of thought is with truth—the number of experiences ought to have nothing to do with her hold of it; and she ought to be able to hug it all the closer, after years wasted out of its presence. The contrary arrangments seem quite fantastic and arbitrary, but nevertheless are part of the very bone and marrow of our minds. Reason is only one out of a thousand possibilities in the thinking of each of us. Who can count all the silly fancies, the grotesque suppositions, the utterly irrelevant reflections he makes in the course of a day? Who can swear that his prejudices and irrational beliefs constitute a less bulky part of his mental furniture than his clarified opinions? It is true that a presiding arbiter seems to sit aloft in the mind, and emphasize the better suggestions into permanence, while it ends by dropping out and leaving unrecorded the confusion. But this is all the difference. The *mode of genesis* of the worthy and the worthless seems the same. The laws of our actual thinking, of the *cogitatum*, must account alike for the bad and the good materials on which the arbiter has to decide, for wisdom and for folly. The laws of the arbiter, of the *cogitandum*, of what we *ought* to think, are to the former as the laws of ethics are to those of history.

What he thought on the day he penned that can be summed up even more briefly. *Thoughts—often brand new revelation-insights— continually come to you*; if you notice them you can do what you will with them; you *ought* to be on the lookout for them (whoever does not resist the padlockers' invitation to the worst possible habits of inattention imaginable is the most dangerous of today's thinkers); since "the business of thought is with truth," i.e., since this is the moral *cogitandum*, you *must* be on the lookout for true ones and *must* cultivate them. An entire book could be written to unpack James' full meaning. In fact, the rest of his works should be read from that perspective. This book can be viewed as a short commentary, if a few of the themes presented earlier are called back on stage: bad thought-habits, acquired "when we weren't looking," i.e., when we were too young to know anything about controlling our imagination's productions, if imagination exists, can make OUR task of right thinking or of recognizing the truth a near impossibility, however many other folks have already achieved that right thinking or recognized the truth; hence the obligation, by those obliged to seek the whole truth and nothing but the truth, to cultivate that passion for truth that ordinarily makes the rethinking task an easier one. Hence the prior obligation for some to first convert from bad character-habits and to not-shirk life's difficult tasks even before difficulty-easing cravings have replaced bad ones.

Yes, one more emendation. Your present thoughts are continuing your tour, through a few more of the backroads of my mind(set), to suggest ways to re-think what constitutes the back*ground* of yours, but they *will not appear* to be sauntering into your mind. They *will seem rather* to be coming off this page, through your eyes. Pure poetry. Sheer imagination. In this case, bad pure poetry, unsupportable sheer imagination, if taken as any literal part of the literal truth. If you believe otherwise, because long years of naive realism have made the wrong view seem nearly self-evident, this will be a chance to re-consider what the previous chapters have taken great care to present. (Yes, more poetry. "I took the care" is closer. But your thoughts aren't from me. My care is an invitation to THE Thought-Presenters to present these thoughts to you.)

James began his psychology-as-a-natural-science with the warning that this was only provisional science and warned at the end that a science not integrated into the right 'metaphysics' cannot be relied on as a final word on anything. His warning is ignored by the 'experts' today who mutually reinforce one another's habitual belief in the blatant Myth of Distinct Disciplines and thus into the habitual avoidance of the bottom-line theory-question: "Since no one can know what they are talking about unless they know what there IS to talk about, what is YOUR semantic-determining grand, unifying theory: materialism, idealism, or . . . ?" James, as could be expected of "**THE**" giant thinker of the contemporary era, would accept no such peer-approved, one-meadow superficiality.

> When, then, we talk of "psychology as a natural science," we must not assume that means a sort of psychology that stands at last on solid ground. It means just the reverse; it means a psychology particularly fragile, and into which the waters of metaphysical criticism leak at every joint, a psychology all of whose elementary assumptions and data must be reconsidered in wider connections and translated into other terms . . . (*Psychology: Briefer Course*, Epilogue.)

Having thus concluded the shorter version of his "psychology," he—as he usually did—practiced what he had preached and spent the rest of his life reconsidering, reexamining, rethinking. His learning career was a concrete illustration of "the" scientific method so nicely abstracted in M. Novak's *Belief and Unbelief*: after enough sense-experiences have built up a backlog of memory-imagery, thoughts and eventually insights begin to come to us, we begin to exercise critical judgment vis-à-vis those accumulating-into-a-habitual-belief-system thoughts, newer insights come to us, we continue exercising critical judgment on the old thoughts and the new insights, newer insights come, etc. The learning process is a spiral. It spirals upwards toward the light for those who embrace the true and escape the false, it can spiral downwards toward the darkness for those who embrace the false as the overarching framework for their half—and lesser-truths. James kept trying. Near the top of the pyramid of ever-broader generalizations he used for synthesizing his vast accumulation of true particulars, he kept making a few wrong choices (which he'd promptly ignore when he'd promptly redescend the ladder to the particulars). But he kept trying. The last fruits of his lifetime of reconsiderations undertaken in pursuit of the WHOLE truth are in his final lecture series, *A Pluralistic Universe*.

Only in 1989, the fifty-sixth year of MY learning-career, did I begin to plumb the real depth of James' understanding of things. I had already read his *Pragmatism* in the early 1960's, but I was partly put off by his half-wrong analysis of truth and for years often presented it in class as one of the impossible theories to be eliminated on their way to finding the one that, improbable as it might seem, had to be the truth. (The best no-nonsense account of its shortcomings is the second of M. Gardner's *The Whys of a Philosophical Scrivener*, footnote 9 must not be overlooked.) In the early 70's, I began using James' *Psychology: Briefer Course*, later in the 70's introduced *Varieties of Religious Experience* into a course, during the same 70's learned from M. White's *Science and Sentiment in America* how to use James' three approaches to "truth" to read James' on truth, in 1983 felt impelled to look into the larger *Principles of Psychology* and discovered James' thorough grasp of "philosophy," later read J. Barzun's *A Stroll With William James* and 'met' James, the human being. But December 28, 1989, was a turning point in my understanding of James: C.H. Seigfried read to a small audience the long passage from *Varieties* cited in section C of Chapter Three, a passage so completely congruent with my own final synthesis that I finally took *A Pluralist Universe* and the larger, two-volume *Life* by R.B. Perry from the library and learned the full truth behind James' various 'wrong turns.' None of them was taken in ignorance of the classical traditions. Quite the reverse. He shuttled with complete ease from such "trifling" facts as the murderous thought that struck him upon leaving Chautauqua (who else would have set himself the task of understanding what most would call "a single, passing thought"?) to the dialectical pyrotechnics of Hegel and Royce. Whatever credence I had once given to the opinion that the logician Peirce was the "most rigorous" and the educator Dewey the "most influential" of the three American Pragmatists, the truth finally dawned on me that James' breadth and depth were light-years beyond theirs.

For one, in spite of not grasping how the correspondence view of true thoughts fits with his "what happens will BE the true-making meaning of present expectancies" pragmatism, he never got stuck writing about abstract "individualISM" but as a matter of habit flew down to the level of life-shaping individual differences:

> I know that you, ladies and gentlemen, have a philosophy, each and all of you, and that the most interesting and important thing about you is the way in which it determines the perspective in your several worlds . . . [T]he philosophy which is so important in each of us is not a technical matter; it is our more or less dumb sense of what life honestly and deeply means.

Still, he understood the need for shoppers seeking a (w)holist system to have some general guidelines, and—before S. Pepper made the same point—he approved the traditional practices of reducing millions of systems, for convenience, to a handful:

> A philosophy is the expression of a man's intimate character, and all definitions of the universe are but the deliberately shaped reactions of human characters upon it . . . If we take the whole history of philosophy, the systems reduce themselves to a few main types which, under all the technical verbiage in which the ingenious intellect of man envelopes them, are just so many visions, modes of feeling the whole push, and seeing the whole drift of life, forced on one by one's total character and experience, and on the whole *preferred*—there is no other truthful word—as one's best working attitude. (*Pluralistic Universe*, lec. I)

It became his habit to emphasize the connection between unique cognitions, habits, *AND individual, self-initiated moral efforts*:

> But let us now close in a little more closely on this matter of the education of the will. Your task is to build up a *character* in your pupils; and a character, as I have so often said, consists of an organized set of habits of reaction. Now of what do such habits of reaction themselves consist? They consist of tendencies to act characteristically when certain ideas possess us, and to refrain characteristically when possessed by other ideas.
>
> . . . How is it when an alternative is presented to you for choice, and you are uncertain what you ought to do? You first hesitate, and then you deliberate. And in what does your deliberation consist? It consists in trying to apperceive the case successively by a number of different ideas . . . The search for the right conception may take days or weeks.
>
> The proper conception . . . may be hard to attain; or it may be one with which we have contracted no settled habits of action. Or, again, the action to which it would prompt us may be dangerous and difficult; or else inaction may appear deadly cold and negative when our impulsive feeling is hot. In either of those latter cases it is hard to hold the right

idea steadily enough before the attention to let it exert its adequate effects. Whether it be stimulative or inhibitive, it is *too reasonable* for us; and the more instinctive passional propensity then tends to extrude it from our consideration. We shy away from the thought of it. It twinkles and goes out the moment it appears in the margin of our consciousness; and we need a resolute effort of voluntary attention to drag it into the focus of the field, and to keep it there long enough for its associative and motor effects to be exerted. Every one knows only too well how the mind flinches from looking at considerations hostile to the reigning mood of feeling.

Once brought, however, in this way to the centre of the field of consciousness, and held there, the reasonable idea will exert these effects inevitably; for the laws of connection between our consciousness and our nervous system provide for the action then taking place. Our moral effort, properly so called, terminates in our holding fast to the appropriate idea.

If, then, you are asked, "*In what does a moral act consist* when reduced to its simplest and most element-ary form?" you can make only one reply. You can say that *it consists in the effort of attention by which we hold fast to an idea* which but for that effort of attention would be driven out of the mind by other psychological tendencies that are there. *To think*, in short, is the secret of will, just as it is the secret of memory.

This comes out very clearly in the kind of excuse which we most frequently hear from persons who find themselves confronted by the sinfulness or harmfulness of some part of their behavior. "I never *thought*," they say. "I never *thought* how mean the action was, I never *thought of* these abominable consequences." And what do we retort when they say this? We say: "Why *didn't* you think? What were you there for but to think?" (*Talks to Teachers*, Chapter on "The Will.")

Mix these ingredients into a doggedly pluralist picture of the world—with its 5.5 billion humans and their billions of unique habit-shaped mindsets and their billions of shifting attendings to wildly varying facets of billions of here-and-now total fields of experience—and the sum, a greater insight than any of the disconnected, partial insights, comes out in his masterpiece of social-wisdom distilled: "Habit is the flywheel of society."

> Habit is thus the enormous flywheel of society, its most precious conservative agent. It alone is what keeps us all within the bounds of ordinance, and saves the children of fortune from the envious uprisings of the poor. It alone prevents the hardest and most repulsive walks of life from being deserted by those brought up to tread therein. It keeps the fisherman and the deck-hand at sea through the winter; it holds the miner in his darkness, and nails the countryman to his log-cabin and his lonely farm through all the months of snow; it protects us from invasion by the natives of the desert and the frozen zone. It dooms us all to fight out the battle of life upon the lines of our nurture or our early choice, and to make the best of a pursuit that disagrees, because there is no other for which we are fitted, and it is too late to begin again. It keeps different strata from mixing . . .
>
> If the period between twenty and thirty is the critical one in the formation of intellectual and professional habits, the period below twenty is more important still for the fixing of *personal* habits . . . (PP I, chapter IV)

ALL personal habits. Thought habits. Passional—craving and cringing—habits. Habits that can be changed. Contrary to the "No late changes!" message clearly implied by the above words of his, James wrote eloquently of changes in *Varieties'* sections on "The Divided Self" and "Conversion." Where he noted that, like Augustine's, bad habits rarely die instantaneously, all too often they yield to good habits very, very, even v-e-r-y slowly.

But they do. If we don't quit trying. If we don't die first.

C. HABITS-III: HABITS OF FORGIVENESS.

You are the man! Woman? Or are you? Perhaps it's I? Or us?

Who is in need of habit-changing? Those with the mental illness of bad thought-habits. (Where is the treatise on intellectual vices?) And which habits most need to be changed? The bad thought-habits! The habits that underlie our habits of acting without a second thought, the habits that back up our efforts to seriously undertake to improve our habits or our loss of hope that we can ever change, the habits most directly related to our optimism and our pessimism, etc. Most of all, the following.

In 1989, H. Kirschenbaum and V.L. Henderson published *Carl Rogers: Dialogues*, an anthology of exchanges between Rogers and such luminaries as Buber, Tillich, Polanyi, and others. The last entries include an exchange of letters between Rogers and Rollo May. In the "Notes on Rollo May," Rogers tried to pinpoint their biggest disagreement: "I suppose my major difference with Rollo is around the question of the nature of the human individual. He sees the demonic as a basic element in the human makeup, and dwells upon this in his writing." What did Rogers think? "My experience leads me to believe that it is the cultural influences which are the major factor in our evil behaviors. The rough manner of childbirth, the infant's mixed experience with the parents, the constricting, destructive influence of our educational system, the injustice of our distribution of wealth, our cultivated prejudices against other individuals who are different . . ." To which Rollo May replied in "The Problem of Evil: an Open Letter to Carl Rogers." He wrote, in part:

> 2. In your letter you acknowledge the evil surrounding us. You say, "I am very well aware of the incredible amount of destructive, cruel, malevolent behavior in today's world—from the threats of war to the senseless violence in the streets." But you say that you "believe that it is cultural influences which are the major factor in our evil behaviors."
>
> This makes culture the enemy. But who makes up the culture except persons like you and me? You write about "the destructive influence of our educational system, the injustice of our distribution of wealth." But who is responsible for this destructive influence and injustice, except you and me and people like us? The culture is not something made by fate and foisted upon us.

Whoever among us desires the full truth and nothing but the truth must take this rejoinder to heart. Unlike sermon-hearers who cannot wait to get home and pass on the message to the absent folk who "really" need it, we must pause regularly to make certain we are not joining our companion citizens—all with logs stuck in our eyes—and inventing a faceless it which is collectively made up of anonymous they's whom we can criticize to our hearts' content *while we go right on collectively making things worse and worse.* Anthropologist C. Kluckhohn warned us:

> I have said that 'culture channels biological processes.' It is more accurate to say 'the biological functioning of individuals is modified if they have been trained in certain ways and not in others' . . . It is only a helpful shorthand when we say 'The cultural patterns of the Zulu were resistant to Christianiza-tion.' In the directly observable world of course, it was the individual Zulus who resisted. Nevertheless, if we do not forget that we are speaking at a high level of abstraction, it is justifiable to speak of a culture as a cause. One may compare the practice of saying 'Syphilis caused the extinction of the native population of the island.' Was it 'syphilis' or 'syphilis germs' or 'human beings who were carriers of syphilis'? (*Mirror for Man*, ch.2.)

James' systematic pluralism renders S. Weil's fear of collectives and Rogers' condemnation of them unnecessary. It alone provides us with a clear-eyed vision of what must be done to gain control of a world careening toward disaster. For a century, we have heard from systematists that it is, e.g., "the whole economic system" that must be changed. Against the systematists, preachers have been insisting—rightly—that it is individuals who must be converted.

What individuals must first be converted to, however, is the need to stop believing that groups are real. Then they must be converted to the need to rethink their beliefs about culture, political power, economic processes, interpersonal relations, etc., that are based on a belief in groups. But the belief in groups—all "we versus them"—must be the first thing to be rethought. Once our group-fictions have been gotten out of the way so we can see the real-life individuals the group-fictions conceal will we be able to start looking for sll those splinters and logs we call "our blind spots." Starting with our own. Praying. "Oh, wad some Power the giftie gie us, to see oursels as ithers see us!"

355

How symbolic that James' dying act—permit a bit of imaginative dramatization—was to revise (but not perfectly) the essay, "A Pluralistic Mystic," which in effect proved to all abstracting, monist, wholist groupists that James could understand perfectly both their position and his negation of it as well as they could understand his position and their negation of it, by showing that he understood well Paul Blood's conversion from their side to his. His truth undercuts the utterly false dilemma, "*SHOULD WE REFORM 'THE SYSTEM' OR INDIVIDUALS?*" There is no system—not the kind Marxists made millions believe in, not the one so-called capitalists would have more millions believe in, not the one earthologists now want all the millions to believe in—only billions of the individuals who systematically expound on these private, **SIMILAR** myth**S** of theirs. James, who reached the true bottom line that "the brain is a fiction of popular speech," offers better thinkers the true bottom line about the myths popularized by ecclesiologists, by sociologists, by polis-ologists, by pantheists, that is, by groupists of every variety: "group" does not name a reality, but rather a theoretical fiction useful for discussing in shorthand the doings of many, many individual humans whose slow-as-molasses or mercury-quick habit-changes can be tracked, if at all, only with the sophisticated use of those guessing-techniques called "statistical sampling." If ever there was a time in the history of the world when this insight was needed by the experts in charge of education, whether formal ('schools,' etc.) or informal ('popular media,' etc.), it is now as we strain collectively to reach that milestone named "The Twenty First Century." So . . .

Who needs to change perhaps previously-unnoticed, hurting habits? YOU are the man! Oh, woman? Or ARE you? Perhaps it's I? Us?

Interlude. James was a rationalist intent on giving his head reasons to show he had a right to follow his heart, but it is clear that he would only use that right if and when his head told him it was leading him the right way, that is, if and when his head found reasons to believe his heart should be trusted. Such metaphorical talk only conjures 'psyche-anatomical' imagery useful in synthesizing the hard facts: WE understand thoughts; some thoughts correlate with a *sentiment* easily described as "a feeling *that* this is right" and some with an oppositely-described sentiment; most of US, when WE take time to reflect seriously, admit that WE feel there is an important difference between what WE call right and what WE call wrong; most of US are happy to agree when someone praises US for doing what is right and ready to argue in OUR defense if accused of doing wrong; each of US can reexamine yet one more time his or her explanation for such phenomena; and each of US is free to conclude whatever s/he chooses to, either to stick with an old explanation or to exchange it for a new one. There is even a phrase for this: "Humans'—OUR—Search for Meaning."

Therese Martin, though near the end of her life she *felt* as if God might not exist, never felt any "other-minds" doubts about other people or about her calling to love them. "To put it quite simply, charity had found its way into my heart, calling on me to forget myself and try to bring happiness to others; and since then I've been as happy as the day is long . . ." Happy? Well, no and yes. Even though most think of a cloistered convent as only a slight cut above a concentration camp, she voluntarily refused to accept the small creature comforts available even there, lest they make less valuable the sacrifices she undertook to earn divine favors for others. Though three of her sisters lived in the convent, she sought out the company of others, one of them a woman "who has the knack of rubbing me up the wrong way at every turn; her tricks of manner, her tricks of speech, her character, just strike me as unlovable." Determined not to allow natural antipathy to make her treat less well this individual than she allowed family ties to influence her treatment of her three sisters, she said she was . . .

> . . . determined to treat this sister as if she were the person I loved best in the world. Every time I met her, I used to pray for her, offering to God all her virtues and her merits . . . But I didn't confine myself to saying a lot of prayers for her, this sister who made life such a tug-of-war for me; I tried to do her every good turn I possibly could. When I felt tempted to take her down with an unkind retort, I would put on my best smile instead, and try to change the subject; doesn't the *Imitation* tell us that it's better to let other people have their way in an argument, than to go on wrangling over it? We used often to meet, outside recreation-time, over our work; and when the struggle was too much for me, I used to turn tail and run.

Still, it is easy to tell that, like any of us who succeed well in a difficult project, the thought of her triumph brought her a feeling of satisfaction with a job well done:

> She was quite unconscious of what I really felt about her, and never realised why I behaved as I did; to this day, she is persuaded that her personality somehow attracted me. Once at recreation she actually said, beaming all over, something like this: "I wish you would tell me, Sister Therese of the Child Jesus, what it is about me that gets the right side of you? You've always got a smile for me whenever I see you."

Nearly half a century later, a man found himself involuntarily in a real concentration camp, enduring the most severe physical hardship. Yet, as he later reported in *Man's Search for Meaning*, love came into focus for Viktor Frankl as well. It came to him as a sudden (re)revelation on the way to a day of forced labor. It began with thoughts of someone who attracted, then expands:

> As we stumbled on for miles, slipping on icy spots, supporting each other time and again, dragging one another up and onward, nothing was said, but we both knew each of us was thinking of his wife. Occasionally I looked at the sky, where the stars were fading and the pink light of the morning was beginning to spread behind a dark bank of clouds.
>
> A thought transfixed me: for the first time in my life I saw the truth as it is set into song by so many poets, proclaimed as the final wisdom by so many thinkers. The truth—that love is the ultimate and highest goal to which man can aspire. Then I grasped the meaning of the greatest secret that human poetry and human thought and belief have to impart: *The salvation of man is through love and in love.* I understood how a man who has nothing left in this world may still know bliss, be it only for a brief moment, in the contemplation of his beloved. In a position of utter desolation, when man cannot express himself in positive action, when his only achievement may consist in enduring his sufferings in the right way—an honorable way—in such

a position a man can, through loving contemplation of his beloved, achieve fulfillment. For the first time in my life I was able to understand the meaning of the words, "The angels are lost in perpetual contemplation of an infinite glory."

I failed for years to fathom James' words. But then I realized that they testified to a single-minded quest for THE human goal. In his diary, on February 1, 1870, the 28-year old James wrote:

> Today I about touched bottom, and perceive plainly that I must face the choice with open eyes: shall I *frankly* throw the moral business overboard, as one unsuited to my innate aptitudes, or shall I follow it, and it alone, making everything else merely stuff for it? I will give the latter alternative a fair trial. Who knows but that the moral interest may become developed.

Equipped with James' profoundly moral-pluralist vision, we can now revisit the library and glean the gold from the glitter. In some areas, the vein of gold is thicker. For instance, whoever would study 'society' will discover another who carries on, at the Harvard James loved so much, the tradition he championed in all his works. I refer to Robert Coles who has understood, as James did, that nothing moves us so much as the call of stories, of real heroes' actual stories, but also of the merely-possible stories imagined by artists. He—wisely prodded by Jane Hallowell Coles!—has supplied so many otherwise anonymous *they's* with masterfully edited voices that educate, sensitize, amuse, challenge—and all ways enrich—us, their grateful readers, their new acquaintances. Is there any better way to conclude this intermission than by presenting an example of the wisdom that, tragically, will continue going unnoticed until we stop learning about man or humankind and begin learning about and from people? Like this one of the *Women of Crisis—II*.

> I read all those articles and reports, and I wonder what's going on. The Negro is this, and the Negro is that. Who are the Negroes those experts are talking about? . . .
>
> To me, each person is different, and that holds for our colored as well as for the white. When I hear someone

describing us, all of us, as brave and courageous, I'm almost as upset as when I hear us called all the bad names we've been called here in Anniston, and everywhere else in my home state of Alabama. My daddy is a minister, and he says that every person is good and bad, though the percentages of each are different. Now I don't like a lot of the preaching I used to hear from him; he's too kind to the white man, and he's always telling his congregation to be patient, to pray and wait for the Lord's answer. The 'answer' is for us to make our own answer . . .

Unless to add that this black teacher's "philosophy" provides the perfect framework for everyone who wants to fathom "the banality of evil," shorthand for how the small cowardices NOW in each of us are hints of how well [sic] we would do if there, but for the grace of God, we were placed, a framework to help understand why an Eichmann alone does not a Holocaust make, and challenges us to go from one to the next of those 5,499,999,999 other humans' shoes, lest—stubbornly blind to our own sinfulness—we pass unfair judgment on those others. *Now, back to business.*

A Thought-Experiment re God's Plan. If the solution to age-old problems requires that we discover the right model to help us put voluminous details into the right perspective, then such is the case when we are trying to fathom issues about good and evil, about right and wrong. Unleash your imagination, then, and entertain the following simple scenario and its congruence with some of our best ethical and/ or moral 'intuitions.'

This *thought experiment's* starting point must be our early commonsense naive-realism. Descartes based his certainty about the physical world on ethical grounds. For him, the combination of a belief that no physical world exists with a belief that God makes it nearly impossible to overcome the belief that the material world is what we directly sense, and makes it entirely impossible not to fall back into that belief as soon as we relax our attention to the abundant evidence that it is not what we directly sense, was blasphemous: such a lying god did not measure up to his definition of "God." Francis Bacon, however, had already fingered God's justification. Expand a bit now on Descartes' discovery and Bacon's suggestion with the following bit of fiction.

Imagine you yourself to be the Divine Community. Suppose the idea comes to You to create beings like the ones which in these pages are named "human person." Since no-thing but You exists as yet, You will have to be the source of every-thing: of the persons who have sense-data "experiences" and retain memory-images of them (including the facets named "pleasure" and "pain," "cravings" and "cringings"), persons who also understand thoughts (thoughts that are, above all, about persons like themselves), persons who can freely decide (especially decide which of the thoughts You'll present & they'll assent to, etc.). That means that You will also have to create the immaterial objects they'll understand and experience. If You create them and decide to furnish them with "worlds" that make them happy in the ways You are happy because of what You enjoy, and if You do not bring other humans' contributions into the plans You have for each of them individually, they will have no need to relate to each other, but solely to You.

If part of Your enjoyment is Divine Community-ship, however, You can decide to make at least some of what You do for each human dependent upon other persons' decisions vis-a-vis them and vice-versa. You will have to make them experience a world that, besides all of 'nature,' includes other people. That is, even though each will be living alone in a virtual reality of their own, You will make it seem to them that their 'virtual-reality world' has other humans in it along with stars, squirrels, trees, and so on. You will also make it seem to each one that, in one or many ways, he or she depends on those others and vice-versa.

The way to create this seeming inter-dependence is to give them the power to choose from various thought-about options at certain moments and accompany each choice with anticipations of specific pleasure-ful and pain-ful consequences for themselves, as well as pleasure-pain consequences for others. Sometimes there will be pleasure for both, at times pleasure for one and pain for the other, and then there will be situations in which there is pain for both. (Each reader must make an effort to fill such empty abstractions with all the relevant illustrations stored in his or her capacious memories of past experience. One friend buying tickets to take another friend to a movie, someone getting out of bed in the middle of the night to rescue a friend whose car has broken down, or a soldier easing his grief and anger over a buddy's killing by randomly shooting defenseless villagers for revenge, a mother practicing tough love vis-a-vis an erring child, are the type of examples we can all find in our memory bins, the type we must learn to take out, examine from a variety of vantage points, and then use to fill otherwise-empty, general formulas whose sole utility is to help evaluate those examples, those facts, in relation to other examples and facts.) You, Who will offer Your creatures the alternatives for action from which they can choose, will help them remember the choices and their outcomes, later offer them alternative ways of evaluating their decisions, and—as a consequence—enrich their deliberations with more complex alternative-options to ponder and select from.

To safeguard Your creatures' independence, though, You will "stay behind the scenes." You will make everything seem "completely natural." And the most obvious feature of each one's lifetime experience can be captured in one word: LEARNING. Each learner begins with her or his private text: sensed givens or sense-data. For the infant who, it seems, opens her or his eyes onto the world for the first time You will simply add visual sense-data. You will already have provided her/him with what James christened "a stream of consciousness" fed, You will make it seem, by ears, skin, muscles, joints, and viscera. Eventually, to the rich tributaries of colors, sounds, odors, tastes, feels, and body-data You will add those expectancies we call "memory-images" of past sequences of sense-data, which will thicken the individual's private "world" or stream of experiences. Finally, You will provide thoughts with which to understand what is going on: an expanding understanding of her—or himself living in a world with other humans, eventually with an understanding that there are a variety of options available for reading life's text, the sensed "world." All geared to Your goal of providing them with a wide spectrum of enjoyments: instant self-gratifications, enjoyable recollections of a rich personal history, "vicarious experience" of the experiences of dozens, then thousands, even sketchily of millions of others similar to themselves (thus adding "history" to their recollections of their own past) . . . plus a quasi-divine sense of having some control over their own destiny. And, to a degree, some control over the destiny of others who, to a degree, have a reciprocal control over their destiny, via an entire gamut of interactions ranging from what seem to be direct, hands-on behaviors to ocean-crossing ripple effects. In order to combine Your goal of making them feel they've personally *earned* what You freely *give* (that quasi-divine "I did it" feeling that will be one of their greatest enjoyments) with Your goal of making them feel personally *indebted* to others who are *indebted* to them (another of their greatest enjoyments), You will nudge their assenting and dissenting in certain directions by attaching emotion-cues to Your various thought-proposals. Depending upon the individual's position in geo-space and geo-history, You will furnish her or him with clues to what is really going on by means of new thoughts, both about nature and about Your behind-the-nature-scene activities. And, unless they are blind to the tacitly obvious, they will learn that they are learners, that others were here before them and may have a thing or two to teach them, that they have made mistakes before and must constantly be open to finding yet another mistake in their thinking, that clinging stubbornly to errors leaves not just others but THEM in the dark, and so on. Yet, here more than anywhere, You will leave them free. To believe what they choose to believe. As if they are "running the show." Even though they can only do so within the limits of those restrictions of Yours their "scientists" think of as the laws of nature, including the laws of psychology. Which they can try to LEARN. Or not.

That piece of imagining, that hypothetical model to be used in a THOUGHT EXPERIMENT designed to get to the bottom of the traditional Christian answer to that ancient question, "What is my life's purpose?", is sketched very roughly. Completing it is not difficult. Begin by mixing in the details that are referred to on the other pages of this work. The model—which builds on the anthropomorphic premise that the Creating Parents resemble in remarkable ways us humans who are created after Their image and likeness (why think it a mistake to expect that the original of a portrait will be something like the likeness?)—is a God's-eye view of the identical phenomena that the human's-eye view captures from the phenomena's midst. Its justification is exactly like whatever justification we have for such "scientific" theories as Copernicus' heliocentrism (no human ever watched the earth and its neighbors "from outside" them), Newton's absolute space and time (he didn't inspect the whole of space or time from a vantage point "high above" both), Einstein's relativity (Einstein's postulate that light's speed is finite led him to agree with Russell's "Naive realism leads to physics, and physics, if true, shows that naive realism is false"), and for Rutherford's discontinuity-theory (an inspired transference of the "solar-system" model to a second series of appearances still not completely "saved"): it is intended as a theory about the UNobserved "mechanisms" behind the OBserved phenomena.

Which observed phenomena support it most? Attend selectively to the following. First, our sense of obligation. Over and beyond the expectable temporal order (before, together, and after) in the phenomena handily named "the laws of nature," among which is the far more complex, variable order in the phenomena handily named "the great law of habit itself," there is what we'll call the moral sense of human learners. Think of the moral sense as something directly related to our Creators' desire to enrich our existence with a feeling of interconnectedness, which feeling, we may surmise, is part of that enjoyment of Theirs which They wish to 'share' with us. It is the sense of obligation we feel toward each other. We feel obliged to please and not displease the others with whom our experiences are most intimately correlated. As time has gone on, humans have felt obliged to recognize how far the obligation extends, so that today we sense *that* we must care for all people, regardless of race, color, creed, etc.

It is essential to distinguish *the moral sense* that we *should* and should not do certain things from *the ability sense* that we *can* or cannot do certain things. Even children know the difference. Children are known to ask their parents, "Can I?" E.g., "Can I go outside and play?" Smart parents habitually restate the question before answering it, for they know that the child's question shows either an ignorance of a crucial distinction or carelessness about attending to it. That is, there is a huge difference between "*Can* I go out?"—meaning "Am I capable of going out if I decide to do so?"—and "*May* I go out?", meaning "If I decide to go out, will that be alright with you?" If our historical records can be relied upon at all, they indicate that in all the parts of the world some individuals have arrived at the conclusion that, although humans have the power to disobey felt obligations, the obligation to love one's neighbor at least as much as oneself *is felt*, no if's, also's, or but's about it.

It is also essential to distinguish the sense of moral obligation from theories that attempt to justify, explain, or account for it. Some have felt that ours is not to question why, ours is but to do or die. But the world's greatest thinkers have, in effect, replied: Ours may be to do or die, but not until we first ask why. E.g., WHY should I control my imagination? They have sought for a rational justification, explanation, or account for this moral sense, this categorical—Take it!, You'd better not leave it!—obligation. They have asked searching questions: Is it something not logically provable, but intuited, recognizably obvious, or self-evident?, Should it be traced back to feelings or sentiment or to a sixth sense?, And where do such moral intuitions, moral sentiments, and/or a moral sense come from?, From our genes?, From 'society'?, From on high via special revelations given to prophets?, etc. Regardless. The *fact* is that—if centuries' worth of other humans like me have existed and asked "Why (should I) do or not do X?"—it is becausee they sensed that they were under obligation to do certain things and not do others.

There have always been disagreements about specifics, about which things we must do and which we must not do. But, as we can conclude from the reflections of so many thinkers, from Moses (see his *Exodus*) through Plato (see his *Euthyphro*) and Kant (see his categorical imperative) to C.S. Lewis (see his *The Abolition of Man*), only theoretical psychopaths and sociopaths deny the generic fact: normal humans sense they are under obligation.

That last thought—that there is a difference between i) the general 'sense' of right and wrong that every normal human being is endowed with and ii) the specifics that vary from time to time and place to place—is so important that it is worth highlighting:

There is a difference between i) the general 'sense' of right and wrong that every normal human being is endowed with and ii) the specifics that vary from time to time and place to place.

We who are at the climactic end, not of history but of centuries' worth of the gradual or piecemeal revelation-learnings we might mentally assemble under the title "Science," are fortunately in a position to conclude that there's but one categorical obligation: "Love!" Expandable into "Love your neighbor at least as much as you love yourself." Expandable into "Treat every other person the way you would, if you were smart, like them to treat you." Expandable, in the era of international or global communication and trade, into Marx's inspired formula: "Give as much as you are reasonably capable of (that is what we 'instinctively' want to demand from others as our 'rights'), be satisfied to take only as much as you reasonably need." Those are statements of PRINCIPLE. They capture the ideal as it would be realized in a utopia. If we are honest, we will recognize the truth that—inasmuch as the real world is made up of humans like us, each with habits as deep-rooted as our own—there is a gigantic chasm between the way things are and any such future utopian world where the real and the ideal overlap. Still, the idea of the ideal is available for anyone with eyes to see and ears to hear. The ancient notion that we are all sisters and brothers belonging to the one human family—and, if a family, all children of the same Parents—is now distilled into the democratic ideal that I should treat every other human as a person whose dignity is the equal of every other person inhabiting this globe, even equal to mine.

A note. Those familiar with the Nurenberg Trials know that this hypothesis about a God-inspired moral sense *begs the question*, that questions about this part of this grand theory of everything can only be answered by other parts of this same grand unifying theory. But any theory that intends to be perfect—to be a theory worthy of being labeled "scientific"—must, besides being perfectly comprehensive, be *internally consistent*. Any theory about the "first principles" of moral reasoning will be part of epistemology, a truly comprehensive theory's sub-theory which accounts for theories, whether theories about theorizing or theories about normal persons' basic sense of right and wrong, both of which must be part of a perfectly satisfying theory about the human person who is the agent challenged to understand every aspect of her/him-self. Godless theorists must explain the given that, as we say, "Someone or something tells us that some things are wrong," e.g., that dashing the heads of little ones against a rock is wrong (pray-ers have recently dropped the ending of Psalm 137 from their prayers)—however much sadistic onlookers enjoy watching—which is why the godless put faith in some hypothetical gene or in a hypothesized communication-process whereby guilt-producing superego convictions are internalized from significant others. That is, godless theorists have their own circularly-argued views-of-everything, chief of which are those based on evolutionist biology or on folk-sociology and the one which is a shuttle-hybrid (now this, now that) known as "sociobiology." In chapter five, these alternative *causal* explanations (which ones are illogical, wishful thinkings?) will be assessed. For now, the task is to briefly indicate how this proposed hypothesis is congruent with the rest of this theory.

The hypothesis here is not new. We find it written about by old Hebrew sages who envisioned God writing the law in our hearts. We find it more recently in a letter from Thomas Jefferson, one of the major authors of the political constitution still envied by knowledgeable people around the globe, to his son-in-law:

> He who made us would have been a pitiful bungler if he had made the rules of moral conduct a matter of science [learnable only as a part of 'higher education']. For one man of science, there are a thousand who are not. Man was destined for society. His morality therefore was to be formed to this object. He was endowed with a sense of right and wrong merely relative to this. This sense is as much a part of his nature as the sense of hearing, seeing, feeling; it is the true foundation of morality . . . This moral sense, or conscience, is as much a part of man as his leg or arm. It is given to all human beings in a stronger or weaker degree, as force of members is given them in a greater or less degree. It may be strengthened by exercise . . .

The record of humans' history is fully compatible with the grand hypothesis you are now considering as your eyes, it seems, scan these rows and rows. Until I came to understand that "Love and do what you will" is not mere rhetoric, but the best generalized formula for all the more specific moral guidelines found in world literature, I would have disputed that. Where, for instance, is the moral sense among tribes of head-hunters, bands of marauding thieves, Cosa Nostra families, Salem witch-burners, etc.? But closer inspection reveals that head-hunting tribespeople feel a natural bond with their kinspeople, that mafiosi often display admirable loyalty to family members, that there is often a code of honor among thieves, and that, like some grand inquisitors, some witch-burners were motivated by compassion for the innocent likely to be harmed by those judged and found guilty. Jefferson himself, noting that in time of war people who feel hostility toward each other lay aside their differences and fight for one another, remarked that an occasional war might be good for the people. The difference between then and now is not a matter of basics. It is a matter of rethinking specifics or details in order to comply with the basic categorical imperative. It is a matter of replacing parochialism with universalism. Wisely.

All of us must engage in an all-out effort to rethink all those belief-habits acquired when we were too young to question them. Jefferson's notorious failure to fully implement "self-evident" equality (the blacks and the females in his household had no voice in government equal to his), like Ruth Benedict's failure to see that her anti-ethnocentrism ("Our ways are good, yours are bad") contradicted her moral relativism (she did not view her anti-ethnocentrism as a merely different, culturally-based prejudice!), is merely a vivid instance of the inconsistencies so "normal" among us humans, inconsistencies we call "blind spots." How many of the things we outsiders size up as injustices done to the innocent are the result, not of bad-will, but of bad habits, especially bad thought-habits, bad or mistaken 'principles'? How many of our own commissions and omissions, just as accurately sized up as injustices by dispassionate onlookers, are the same? Perhaps none but Divine Parents Who understand our hearts, moment to moment, infinitely better even than Dostoevsky understood them in general can pass judgments that are free of all doubt, but we should not appeal to the "Judge not!" rule until we have done our best to learn how to make 'morally certain' judgments of thoughts and words and (other) deeds. Especially our own. Honestly.

Secondly, the model proposed by this thought-experiment provides an unforced way to integrate two outstanding traditions: the two-thousand-years-old view that all the commandments can be reduced to one, namely, "Love one another!", and the insight underlying Plato's *Republic* claim that justice is desirable both now for its own sake and for other things in the long run, a claim that Aristotle beefed up in his *Nichomachean Ethics* which he built on the premise that what we all want is to be happy, both of which boil down to the claim, made earlier, that ethics is all about pleasure and pain. Like any thought cued by 'words' lifted from the midst of the other thousands that are added as clues to an inner, mindset context, neither of the traditional claims is the whole truth. The whole truth—expressed in a brief formula which is shorthand for all the thousands of more particular, detailed thoughts it is shorthand for—is best expressed when qualified by the addition of one word, "Whose?"

Ethics, like love, is about "**WHOSE** pleasures and pains?"

There is only one rule about our obligations to others, say-able in a great variety of ways. Be concerned about others' pleasure and pain, both now and in the long run, and not just your own. Do unto other persons as you would crave having them do unto you if you knew what was good for you, that is, if you knew what would contribute to the pleasure you get from life and would diminish your pain. Love others' selves; and, if you insist on having an answer for "How much do I have to love them?", the answer is "At least as much as you love your self, i.e., fifty-fifty." That is, be fair. What is fair? Contribute fifty percent of what you are capable of to satisfying the needs of others. If you want to love more, that is perfectly alright, and then the formula will be "From each according to his/her ability, to each according to her/his need, then split whatever is left over." Love, then do whatever else you want, but be smart about it and be clear and distinct about the MANY meanings of "love" . . . About which and whose pleasure is sought by a stud insisting "If you love me . . . ," about which and whose pleasure is sought when she yields, about which pleasures most people love most, which pains most people love least, which pleasures and pains involve persons who are loved and which involve persons not loved, which pleasures come from being loved by the lovable and which come from being loved by the unlovable who learn to be lovable, etc.

Notice that there are two ways to love even oneself, i.e., pursue one's own pleasure: stupidly and smartly. With Epicurus, we note that today's orgies produce tomorrow's hangovers, heroin-highs now often produce AIDS or (and?) enslaving addictions later, cruelty inflicted risks cruelty suffered, honeymoon weddings beget childbearing toils, and so on. So, when Plato set out in his *Republic* to prove that Socrates in prison, lacking everything except virtue, was better off than a freeman who lacked only virtue, he fixed on three good habits (virtues) to which he opposed three bad ones (vices). His model was clean and simple: the three virtues—wisdom, temperance, and disciplined strength—correlate with three features of the psyche, viz., intellect, cravings, and will. "Justice," a fourth name he used, should be viewed as a synonym for the sum, viz., "an orderly psyche" or "mental health." The portrait that emerges from Plato's skillful analyses is a perfect answer to the question, "Why pursue wisdom, temperance, will-power, and mental health?" His answer is best given by another question: "Would YOU prefer to be stupid rather than wise, prefer to be tortured by cravings and anxieties rather than enjoy peace of mind, prefer to be weak-willed rather than be disciplined enough to pursue your long-term goals with unswerving determination?" But . . .

But who uses "mental health" and "moral character" synonymously? Aristotle's enlightening defense of enlightened *self*-interest, which includes *self*-interested altruism toward friends who—to count as friends at all—must return as good as they get (else they are only occasions for aristocratic magnanimity) is chiefly an amplification of Plato's argument, but he at least restored parts of our common sense. Because there's a difference between good storm-troopers, good bank-robbers, and good wine-tasters who are very smart, very temperate, very disciplined, and not at all in need of a psychotherapist, and the people we think of as moral heroes, Aristotle insisted that the new meaning Plato gave to "justice" is not what most people mean when they use "justice." He also insisted on the difference between intellectual and moral virtues, a common-sense distinction blurred by Plato's (Socrates' as well?) view that no one does evil knowingly . . . which view, in essence, means that none of us would choose *our own* present self-gratification and willingly pay the price of *our own* subsequent pain, including the loss of *our own* even-greater pleasure, if s/he REALLY weighed the two dispassionately (or should we say passionately?) and leaves totally unexplained our admiration for a person who lays down her or his life—thus bringing to an end all their *own* earthly pleasure and pain!—for a loved one. (Why is it that we admire Socrates but not the probably more knowledgeable Plato or Aristotle as a moral hero?) Lastly, he insisted, justly, that friendless, ill-reputed, shivering, crust-eating, water-drinking wisdom-lovers ("philosophers") are not to be envied, however lacking in vices they may be, a point that must be kept in mind before we recommend the enjoyment of wisdom or philosophy as the one thing necessary for everyone.

But Aristotle, too, failed to get it right. Aquinas, who thought Aristotle was right so far as human wisdom ("philosophy") goes, restored basic, everyday common sense under the guise of revealed wisdom ("theology"). In addition to the virtues that Aristotle viewed as their own reward, i.e., as enough to make all good-habited persons happy in their own right, Aquinas insisted that the supreme virtue is charity. Love for God, love for others. Charity, as Aquinas interprets it, is not good advice for yuppies but a commanded obligation imposed on everyone. It was left to Kant to realize that, even in the 'natural' realm, Aristotle missed what is obvious to every five-year old: We have a DUTY, not to be happy ourselves, but to do the things that might make us deserving of happiness. A DUTY. No if's, also's, or but's. But who deserves to be happy? It was left to the best of the utilitarians to realize that being principled, obeying commands, and fulfilling duties aren't good when the principles, commands, and duties are wrong, but only when the principles, commands, or duties maximize the best pleasures for everyone, a fact that Kant had tried to "cover" with his maxims and that, to some degree, Plato and Aristotle dealt with in their political, not ethical, theories. "Duty for its own sake" is as empty as "good" and "love" are, when any of those words are seized on as high wisdom rather than abstract shorthand. In short, whoever wants to get it right must integrate Plato, Aristotle, Kant, J.S. Mill, etc. Or the best of wise folks' essential, everyday insights.

Thirdly, by recognizing the utter distinction between knowing the difference between right and wrong (shorthand) and choosing the right rather than the wrong (generalization), and by joining that recognition to a clear-headed insight into the difference between habitually caring most for one's own pleasures and trying to get in the habit of tending to others', we have the perfect framework for understanding why—perhaps more than ever before in humans' history—FORGIVENESS is the single most pressing duty of all for who love others in the most important sense of that easily-abused word. The only other duty that might be more pressing is the duty to seek the truth. Especially the truth about whatever is included in loving one's neighbors, especially by forgiving. Being ready to forgive everyone, but especially those who know not what harm they do, or who know only a bit of it but are blithely ignorant of all the rest (especially when "all the rest" seems to those who suffer the consequences to be synonymous with "most of what they do"), or who know but whose habits of craving and cringing make it especially difficult for them not to.

Why more today than before now? Because, even if women or men have never been islands with no link to others, this is still more so in an age when it is possible to make multi-megaton destructive weapons responsive to a single push-button, when a single command can trigger millions of human chain-reactions to mobilize an entire nation's armed forces, when a CEO's decision can affect millions of jobs, when an error can be instantly broadcast into many millions of homes via radio or television, when a misquotation can be quickly printed onto millions of copies of one day's newspaper, and so on. It makes no difference to the consequent pleasures and pains whether what connects island-humans is an ocean of senseless matter or an omniscient Coordinating Power. The consequences flow 'naturally.' But only if human choosers instigate or cooperate. Both of which can be done in two extreme ways—with an acute awareness of the outcomes or with no awareness of the outcomes—and all of the ways in between. And, now that we have progressed from jungle villages where everyone could, as it were, see the consequences of her or his decision, to a global village where the ignorant perpetrate 'system-atic' inequities on a scale as wholesale as cool calculators do, the need for oceans of forgiveness to dampen blazing passions fanned by talk and more talk of one's own rights—of an ever-expanding menu of mythical rights—is monumental.

The best way to approach "Forgive!" is this: Two wrongs do not make a right. Especially when they are not foreseen by those who intend to not do harm, or when they are committed by those who mistakenly thought they had a right to harm, or when they are perpetrated by those who have a velleity to not harm but who gave in to harm-causing cravings or cringings, or even when they are deliberately and cold-bloodedly inflicted. Two thousand years ago, a cosmopolitan Jew wrote to a group of friends he had made in the great metropolis, Rome:

> To no man render evil for evil, but provide good things
> not only in the sight of God, but also in the sight of all men.
> If it be possible, as far as in you lies, be at peace with all men.
> Do not avenge yourselves.

Saint Paul's message echoed the advice of one of his Hebrew ancestors: "If thy enemy is hungry, give him food; if he is thirsty, give him drink; for by so doing thou wilt heap coals of fire upon his head." In fact, he quoted those words for the Romans and then added, "Be not overcome by evil, but overcome evil with good."

Those words from one tradition merely repeated what Socrates, rethinking-wisdom-pursuers' patron saint, had said to his slow-learning friend, Crito, four and a half centuries earlier:

> One should never do wrong in return, nor injure any
> man, whatever injury one has suffered at his hands. And,
> Crito, see that you do not agree to this, contrary to your belief.
> For I know that only a few people hold this view or will hold
> it, and there is no common ground between those who hold
> this view and those who do not, but they inevitably despise
> each other's views. So then consider very carefully whether
> we have this view in common, and whether you agree, and let
> this be the basis of our deliberation, that neither to do wrong
> or to return a wrong is ever right, not even to injure in return
> for an injury received. Or do you disagree and do not share
> this view as a basis for discussion? I have held it for a long
> time and still hold it now, but if you think otherwise, tell me
> now. If, however, you stick to our former opinion, then listen
> to the next point. (*Crito*, G.M.A. Grube's translation.)

"Let this be the basis of our deliberation." Plato, Socrates'
hero-worshipping pupil who ended the *Phaedo* by praising his hero
as "of all those we have known the best, and also the wisest and the
most upright", composed his *Republic* to explain WHY Socrates'
conclusion-premise was true. Yet, it is in the *Crito* that he best presents
Socrates' own reasons for turning down Crito's urging to escape
prison, Athens, and (awhile) death. Socrates indulges in the rhetoric
of personification and describes how, as he'd flee Athens where older
inhabitants raised and educated him and a large number of the citizens
worked together to make it the best place on earth to live, Athens and its
laws would rise and accuse him of destroying them. With such imagery
he tells why, wronged as he has been by the Athenians responsible for
his imminent death, he will not by his bad example undermine habits
of respect for law and order, thereby make Athens a less good place
to live for the Athenians who will outlive him, and thus diminish the
pleasure of those *others*, his survivors. Instead, by his willingness to lay
down his life for others, even those whom he judged undeserving of
his sacrifice, he has inspired later generations of those who have read
Plato's paean.

Introduction. Less than a page remains for this fourth of five chapters.
If anyone wonders whether there is any good reason why they must do

anything at all or asks "WHY control my imagination?", the answer must be: "Imagine all possible WHYs and select the one that makes the most sense of EVERYthing." A thought just trotted across the stage in that theater Hume would have called your "mind," though he'd have immediately added that your thoughts and mental representations have no walls, ceiling, or floor to box them in. Until you die (if you—as opposed to what you consider your body—ever do) or enter a complete coma or go into a dreamless sleep, new thoughts—like these—will continue to come before you. As James noted, you are the arbiter of your thoughts, deciding which you ought to believe if you have a passion for truth or at least sense a moral obligation to seek it, whatever pain your renewed or revised assents and dissents may cost you. Your present state is this: You are passing to future projects, primed by your past, moving to what is new, guided by what is old, yet free to try and change whatever needs changing. These thoughts introduce you to the rest of your life.

The easiest changes of all are old thought-habits, e.g., the habits conjured by "God." Do you choose a god-ful or a god-less grand unifying theory of everything? Either way, the stream of your sensed data, focus of James' pragmatism, will flow on. Whatever is behind the scenes called, in Kohler's formula, your "world" will remain behind them. Above all, other persons—human or divine—and their inner "worlds" will remain behind them. Even the person you are will remain beyond reach of your looking. The Star-Trek episode named "The Rascals" will provide a movie within your "movie" for understanding the radical difference there is between what appears to be others' bodies and their habit-molded selves. Kaffka's *Metamorphosis* and stories of reincarnation offer additional reflection-material, as does the recent near-death-experience literature. But those are nothing more than rethinking-starters. Only dogged, no-holds-barred, no-"Off-limits"-disciplines-respecting rethinking of the kind that Socrates was famous for and that James has yet to become famous for will suffice for anyone intent on fulfilling her or his obligation to love others. By learning the truth in order to hand on the truth. By facing up to mistakes, lest what is handed on are mistakes. But there are rewards. Not only for others . . .

Another Postscript. Gilbert Chesterton examined the world's great religions and found that all of them have some version of the Golden Rule as part of their moral code. None, however, are so focused on it as much as Jesus and his followers . . . , at least if we judge by what we can read in the Christian Scriptures. Here is a sample.

"This is my commandment, that you love one another as I have loved you."
(Gospel of St. John 15:12)

"You have heard that it was said, 'Thou shalt love thy neighbor and shalt hate thy enemy.' But I say to you, love your enemies, do good to those who hate you."
(Gospel of St. Matthew, 5:43-44)

"Owe no man anything except to love one another, for he who loves his neighbor has fulfilled the Law. For 'Thou shalt not commit adultery. Thou shalt not kill. Thou what not steal. Thou shalt not covet; and if there is any other commandment, it is summed up in this saying. Thou shalt love thy neighbor as thyself. Love does no evil to a neighbor. Love therefore is the fulfilment of the Law."
(Romans 13:8-10)

"Now we, the strong, ought to bear the infirmities of the weak, and not to please ourselves. Let everyone of you please his neighbor by doing good."
(Romans 15:1-2)

"For you have been called to liberty, brethren; only do not use liberty as an occasion for sensuality, but by love serve one another. For the whole Law is fulfilled in one word: Thou shalt love thy neighbor as thyself."
(Galatians 5:13-15)

"Beloved, let us love one another, for love is from God. And everyone who loves is born of God, and knows God. He who does not love does not know God; for God is love . . . .

God is love, and he who abides in love, abides in God, and God in him."

(Epistle 1 of St. John 4:7-8, 16)

"But the end of all things is at hand. Be prudent therefore and watchful in prayer. But above all things have a constant mutual charity among yourselves; for charity covers a multitude of sins."

(Epistle 1 of Peter 4:7-8)

"If I should speak with the tongues of men and of angels, but do not have love, I have become as sounding brass or a tinkling cymbal. And if I have prophecy and know all mysteries and all knowledge, and I have all faith so as to remove mountains, yet do not have charity, I am nothing. And if I distribute all my goods to feed the poor, and I deliver my body to be burned, yet do not have love, it profits me nothing. Love is patient, is kind; love does not envy, is not pretentious, is not self-seeking, is not provoked; thinks no evil, does not rejoice over wickedness, but rejoices with the truth; bears with all things, believes all things, hopes all things, enduring all things. Love never fails, where as prophecies will disappear, and tongues will cease, and knowledge will be destroyed . . . . So there abide faith, hope and love, these three; but the greatest of these is love."

(I Cor, 13:1-10, 13)

CHAPTER FIVE

The Pinnacle

Role Model. Should it be Edith Stein, an intellectual whose pursuit of truth ended, we trust, the way Socrates' did? Or should it be Simon-Peter, whose openness to truth led him to interpret history's most important dream as a sign that God regards God-fearing and upright gentiles as highly as They regard devout, kosher-laws-bound Jews? Or William James himself—not a Jew like Edith Stein or Simon-Peter but a Gentile like Socrates—whose quest for truth was no "cool exercise of reason [but] the quest of a passionate pilgrim"? (Those are his son's words.)

Or all three? Each of them is counted by many of those familiar with their stories as having led a life that is exemplary, worthy of imitation, on a level well above the ordinary. Edith Stein, like Simone Weil intellectually precocious and involved in social concerns, began as a devout Jewess, pursued a university education in psychology and then philosophy as an atheist, was stirred by the example of other intellectuals to re-explore the possible truth of theism, joined a convent as Therese did, and in 1942 died in Auschwitz. Nineteen centuries earlier, Simon-Peter abandoned a career as a fisherman, became one of Jesus' students, was eventually appointed as chief spokesman of those who formed his innermost circle, and ended his life in Rome, executed for spreading what was taught by Jesus who had earlier been executed as a result of teaching his version of the Jewish tradition. Simon-Peter, a Jew who was succeeded in Rome by non-Jews, is revered as a saint by those same non-Jews—but not by the Jews—including the Pole, (Pope) John Paul II. When John Paul in 1987 officially proclaimed Edith

Stein "Blessed"* some Jews and some Catholics debated with each other about whether her fate as a Nazi-victim in Auschwitz, Poland, was attributable to her Jewish ancestry or to her status as a Christian. A debate that her writings indicate she would have deplored. As should we all. However well-intentioned it was. (*Now "Saint Edith Stein.")

And a debate that might never have arisen if those of each party had been encouraged to put on the mindset of William James. And succeeded. Though he professed no allegiance to any sect, large or small, he offered the world the most balanced, i.e., shrewdly critical and yet open-mindedly appreciative, assessment of those facets of humans' experience class(ifi)ed as "religious." Unlike people who remain conditioned to regard such facets as not natural but supernatural, James saw the continuity of all human experiences and was superbly equipped to assess them all. He had a superb sense of what is meant by "moral worth" as well as a superb command of the psychological 'mechanisms' behind beliefs, both "religious" and "scientific." At a time when humans around the world choose to act violently against one another in the name of poorly reasoned "dogmas" which, unreasonably, they believe are beyond reason, James' better-than-theirs insights are sorely needed. As is imitation of his fidelity to his better insights.

What follows will be a series of 'open letters.' They will attempt to summarize the 'lessons' that can be drawn from the preceding chapters. Each will address one facet of your whole self: your self that is reader, learner, (potential) convert, etc.

—I—

Dear Reader-in-General,

Hello. I don't know you. You are known, though. I'm not addressing you, but you are being addressed. Just as I know me, you know your self. And, just as the one who addresses us both knows me better than I know my self, you are being addressed by one who knows you better than you know your self. The one by whom all of us are known and addressed is the one who created all of us. We who understand all of this can do it only because the one who created us also creates the *thoughts* being addressed to us at the very moment of their creation and of our understanding. That one is the same one who creates the living panoramas that constitute our separate 'sensory worlds,' inch for inch, moment by moment, all the moments we are awake. That is also the same one who creates all our separate 'inner worlds' of imagery which are so nearly invisible and intangible that their reality has been denied by some of the best-known 'professional thinkers' during this, the greatest and most promising of centuries, but inner worlds which are as-palpable-almost as those same-located 'outer sensory worlds' that seem so much more real by comparison.

That is the thesis which, I trust, is being presented to you as you read and understand these lines. Or, since all addresses come either from your brain or from God, and since brains do not exist, you should know that

All addresses come from God.

In view of such a thesis, certain gestures are appropriate for those striving to **LEARN** the truth. Even obligatory. Or, at the very least, well-advised. As Sir Francis Bacon, "trumpet" of the new sciences whose nature he badly misconceived, realized.

> Therefore do thou, O Father, who gavest the visible light as the first fruits of creation, and didst breathe into the face of man the intellectual light as the crown and consummation thereof, guard and protect this work, which coming from thy goodness returneth to thy glory. Amen.

These lines are the first part of the prayer given to Sir Francis for the end of "The Plan of the Work" outlining the six parts of his *Great New Beginning* (for human learning) published in 1620. It is chosen from several other "gestures" proposed to me just now, and the reason is easy to explain. What Sir Francis requested in the rest of his prayer—divine assistance to learn what really is going on 'in nature,' so that, once we understand nature's laws, we can by obeying nature command it—has since been fulfilled to such an overwhelming degree that the only thing left for us learners to do is to select the true revelations and to organize them properly by finding shorthand generalizations that will allow us to make out *the forest* from the trees, to see the shape of *Grand-Scale Truth* that makes sense of the partial revelations presented gradually to our ancestors and now available, 'through' what appear to be their words, to us.

A Pictures-Show. Our learning goes hand-in-hand with imagery, and the images or models useful for understanding the above truth are abundant. Let me try to arrange a series of them that will take you from your naive-realist view of things toward the God's-eye pinnacle from which all space and time can be seen.

It makes sense to begin with ISAAC NEWTON, announcer of the model for every GOD'S-EYE perspective: absolute space and time. He spoke of space as God's sensorium, a thing natural for people brought up to believe God is everywhere, and he speculated endlessly on God's role vis-à-vis those magnificent laws revealed to him. Publically, he concentrated on describing bodies and their lawlike movements with mathematically-exact precision. But his private letters and notes on

God and on those movements' *causes* were voluminous. Among them we find these words: "Opposite to godliness is atheism in profession and idolatry in practice. Atheism is so senseless and odious to mankind that it never had many professors."

Using this picture of Newton's, you can think of yourself surrounded by two things: i-bodies, that is, by earthly objects close to you, by the planets and sun of the solar system, the stars of the Milky Way Galaxy, plus billions of other galaxies streaking outward into the infinite, endless night of space, AND ii-God who, as our catechism taught us, is the Supreme Spirit-Being. Even as children, we had a vague understanding of spirits. QU: "What is a spirit?" AN: "A spirit is a being that has understanding and free will but no body, and will never die." See the *Baltimore Catechism*, No.2, 1969 edition.

Almost two thousand years earlier, PLATO had proposed a model useful for thinking of the place where each person builds a model for her/ his God's eye view of things: a cave. At the beginning of the *Republic*'s seventh book, he tells a parable about people growing up as prisoners in a dark cave where the only things they ever see are shadows. He used the parable to say that the 'world' we perceive with our senses isn't as real as we imagine, that the things we sense are only shadows of real things, and that only by developing our mind can we learn about the (other) **TRUE REALITIES** outside the cave. The rest of Plato's parable departs from this scenario, but the "senses afford shadow-appearances only" beginning fits the fact that, when we look up at the star-studded heavens on a clear night (which we don't do much, so Emerson, in *Nature*, draws attention to this instance of familiarity breeding the contempt of neglect by remarking how different things would be if the stars appeared only once every thousand years; or think how much interest there would be in planets if they showed up only once every 76 years!), what we are seeing are like tiny, ceiling projections inside a planetarium. That's better than the suggestion that we see fire peeking through holes in the dome covering a saucer-flat earth (ancients' view) or far-away suns and sun-swarm galaxies (moderns' view). Notice: only WORDS out here, but vast imagery in there.

KANT, two thousand years after Plato but only a short while after Newton, showed how scientifically true Plato's cave-view was. This great thinker who said that one of the things that most inspired him with awe was the starry sky above was much influenced by Newton and especially by the idea of **LAWS**, especially the laws that Newton had discovered. The "world" each of us lives in is a world of appearances in our own private cave. But this "world" appears to be very spacious, appears to stretch out to the most distant stars and beyond. At the center of our private "world" is our own "body," but the only part of our own private world seems to be the thoughts, memories, and feelings inside that body. Kant used this model in order to salvage Newton's laws from the attack of the skeptic, David Hume. Earlier in Newton's century, Descartes had discovered that, if modern physics and physiology, the outcome of two thousand years of efforts to learn the laws of nature, are true, then we don't learn about nature by direct inspection. As Bertrand Russell later on put it, "Naive realism leads to physics, and physics, if true, shows that naive realism is false. Therefore naive realism, if true, is false; therefore it is false." Hume had used this bizarre outcome as a reason to view the quest for certainty as a waste of time, but Kant was confident Newton HAD found the scientific truth about nature and the starry skies above. He went to great lengths to prove it, even though, by the time he was finished, "starry skies above" didn't mean what we grow up thinking it means. Of course, when the meteorologist says "The sun will rise at 5:32 tomorrow," IT doesn't either. Kant's solution was a novel theory: Our minds help to CREATE 'nature.'

> Thus the order and regularity in the appearances [sense-data], which we entitle *nature*, we ourselves introduce. We could never find them in appearances, had not we ourselves, or the nature of our mind, originally set them there . . . However exaggerated and absurd it may sound, to say that the understanding is itself the source of the laws of nature, and so of its formal unity, such an assertion is none the less correct, and is in keeping with the object to which it refers, namely, experience. (*Cr. of Pure Reason*, A125-27.)

The picture is clear. The stream of sense-data is produced in the mind by an outside cause, but—by the time we, or at the same time that we, begin to be conscious of them—they are already *spread out* around us [our "feet" sensations are down, our "scalp" sensations are up, "tree" sensations are out front, though we can have "tilting our head upwards at night when we're outside" sensations followed by "starry sky above" sensations] and *time-ordered* [present ones are constantly turning into mere memories as they are replaced by new ones]. Kant said that when someone like Newton discovers, **i.e., learns!**, a really genuine law of 'nature,' the reason we can have confidence in the law is because we can have confidence that our mind, like every other mind, will continue to impose spread-out and time-ordered lawfulness on the phenomena.

It's a grand, pre-Freudian vision. The mind unconsciously performs the task of organizing the stuff of experience, then the mind consciously learns the truth about what it has been doing! Kant is only one of the writers trying to use vivid pictures to help us learn the truth that is stranger than fiction! Looking closely at his analogy of a mind doing things with the left hand that the right hand has no idea about until long afterwards, we can see that one way to express the strangeness of it all is:

> Truth is stranger than fiction, particularly the truth about the way fiction is essential for learning truth.

Perhaps the most up-to-date picture—until recently!—was the one Karl PEARSON drew for us in his *The Grammar of Science*. It incorporates the important ideas of physics and physiology. First, of physics: every physics textbook has chapters on the properties of sound and light, stimuli for two of our most vital senses (especially for heard and seen WORDS!), particularly on their speed. Sounds travel so fast that only in this century have humans acquired the power to travel at speeds beyond those of sound, but so slow relative to light that light could go around the equator seven times in the one second it takes sound to go eleven hundred feet! And of physiology: before we become aware of things, we must wait for signals from eyes and ears to travel through the afferent nerves and reach the brain. Here is Pearson's analogy:

> We are accustomed to talk of the "external world," of the "reality" outside us. We speak of individual objects having an existence independent of our own . . . How close then can we actually get to this supposed world outside ourselves? Just as near but no nearer than the brain terminals of the sensory nerves. We are like the clerk in the central telephone

exchange who cannot get nearer to his customers than his end of the telephone wires. We are indeed worse off than the clerk, for to carry out the analogy properly, we must suppose him *never to have been outside the telephone exchange, never to have seen a customer or any one like a customer—in short, never, except through the telephone wire, to have come in contact with the outside universe.* Of that "real" universe outside himself he would be able to form no direct impression; the real universe for him would be the aggregate of his constructs from the messages which were caused by the telephone wires in his office. About those messages and the ideas raised in his mind by them he might reason and draw inferences; and his conclusions would be correct—for what? . . . Not a step nearer than those terminals can the ego get to the "outer world," . . . Messages in the form of sense-impressions come flowing in from that "outside world," and these we analyse, classify, store up, and reason about. But of the nature of "things-in-themselves," of what may exist at the outer end of our system of telephone wires, we know nothing at all.

The really-best-NOW picture to help learners learn about their situation was incorporated into a short-story, "A Philosopher's Nightmare," by Jonathan Harrison. It builds around your brain and raises the question Socrates asked at the end of the day-long dialogue he and his friends had on his deathdate in 399 BC (or his birthdate to the next phase of his existence): "Is it the blood by which we think, or air or fire. Or is it none of these, but the BRAIN that provides the senses of hearing and sight and smell, so that from these arise memory and opinion, and from memory and opinion in tranquillity comes knowledge?" Harrison's story is about a baby eventually named Alfred Ludwig Gilbert Robinson*, Ludwig for short, whose magnificent BRAIN is extracted from his soon-to-be-dead deformed body, installed in a high-technology laboratory tank to keep it alive, then hooked up to a computer which feeds each nerve—optic, auditory, gustatory, olfactory, tactile, somasthetic—the identical impulses his BRAIN might be receiving from the outside world via his eyes, ears, tongue, etc. The computer also "reads" the feedback BRAIN waves in order to know what Ludwig is thinking and, especially, wanting to do. If

Ludwig wishes to visit the library and READ WORDS IN BOOKS (like these!), the computer will give him the sensations, even though Ludwig's brain never goes anywhere. Harrison has Ludwig reading science and philosophy books like this and finally deciding, like Hume, that he'll take reality just as it . . . comes? seems? (*The names refer to Alfred J. Ayer, Ludwig Wittgenstein, and Gilbert Ryle, famous 20th century philosophers Harrison mocked because they ignored modern discoveries re the brain and the rest of the central nervous system.)

Your situation. If you put those pictures together, you will learn that they are consistent with the thoughts that have come to you during the time you have spent READING the WORDS of the first four chapters. Naturally, the idea is to help you wonder whether you're Ludwig! The same way it seems you can see, visualize, and think about trees, forest, stars, it will seem that you see these rows and rose of WORDS, conjure imagery galore, and understand the thoughts that come to you, no matter what they are about. If your course of learning proceeded much the same way mine did, you long ago came to believe that when you "pick up books" such as the *Baltimore Catechism* or *Why Control Your Imagination?*, you are picking up THINGS a-that can be left in a room while you and everyone else leaves, b-that will continue to exist while you and everyone else goes to bed and sleeps, and c-that you can go to the next day and find in the same condition you left them in.

But you will also have learned it's not all that it seems. Ever since Thales concluded that no books exist (books are really water congealed to look like paper), that no stars exist (stars are really water congealed to look like stars), that food does not exist (food is really water congealed to look like food), and so on, and ever since Einstein updated that conclusion into the theory that everything is either mass released as energy or energy that is congealed into sub-atomic particles ("Lederman and other physicists are searching for the ultimate building blocks from which all things—the stars, the earth, you, I, and the atom—are made": *National Geographic*, May '85, p.634), the idea that things are not what they seem to the naked eye to be has been available to anyone with access to WORDS from the books in the library or to WORDS from teachers in the classroom.

What is the truth? That becomes the great question. The outcome of modern physics and neurology—that the reality we do have access to is a kind of "virtual reality," while the physical world that SUPPOSEDLY existed before *any* humans arrived on the scene, the physical world that existed before *me* or *you*, and the physical world that *my* body and *your* body are supposedly part of is a world we can never get a direct peek at—is the boomerang question: Then how can we be certain what the world is really like? If this were a "virtual reality" demonstration, the rows and rose you are scanning would be lit-up portions of a video-screen activated by electrons coming from you-can't-see-where. Of course, you'd also be confident you could "get back to true reality" and that you could re-prove to yourself that the source of your strangely-unreal-but-real movie is the computer to which you were hooked up. Here, though, there is no way to check and see whether "nature as it appears to you" is from a brain riding a taxi-body able to take you to a library to read this book or from a brain that never leaves the lab and that depends for its consciousness on the well-being of the computer to which it is attached. Getting out of your real "virtual reality" to see what is really producing it is something that can't literally be done. The physics relied on to build computers proves they'll never be sensed. Such thoughts as these offer us worlds within worlds. Imagine watching "The Mousetrap," the playlet inside the play *Hamlet*, in its movie version, viewed on a video-taped copy of the movie of the playlet within the play. Yet, keeping our thoughts straight turns out to be simple. Three things come to us: sense-data, imagery, and thoughts. Directly from the hands of our Creating Parents. (Do you really believe the thoughts coming to you start here on the page, fly thru your eyes, etc.?!) *The truth is very strange*, indeed!

Truth is available. The question, "IS there truth?", can only be understood by someone who has learned the difference between dreamlike or virtual reality and real reality. Learners have always known this. Over two thousand years ago, the Hebrew psalmist wrote: "How suddenly they [the wicked] are swept away . . . As though they were a dream of one who had awakened" (Ps 73). Aristotle's *Metaphysics* (IV:6) reflects the Greeks' debates about whether the whole world might not be a dream and truth impossible to achieve. Protagoras, for instance, decided that no two people have the same "truth," while Gorgias of Leontini said that (i)nothing exists, (ii)if something does exist, we can't know it, (iii)even if someone does know it, s/he can't put it into words for anyone else. But Socrates', Plato's, and Aristotle's confidence about truth triumphed when, after barbarians overran Europe and ancient learning was forced to retreat to monasteries and church schools, doubts about the existence of truth were replaced by increasingly dogmatic formulations that made truth very exact.

It is usually thought that, between the death of Saint Augustine in 426 and the birth of Descartes in 1596, the pursuit of science was replaced by the study of ancient writings. Some historians view the period as the "Dark Ages," a period when civilization nearly died out in the West. Though Augustine himself (born in 354) explored just about every major belief-system current in his day, his extensive writings which encased some of Plato's views in a rigidly "theological" framework became, with the holy scriptures, the core of what learning there was. The literature and traditions of ancient Greece were almost completely lost and, for centuries, intellectual life consisted chiefly of clerics and monks poring over hand-copied copies of sacred texts and writing commentaries on them. That is one way to view a thousand-years' worth of learning. Or lack of it.

But, as usual, the same cornucopia of historical facts can be RE-sampled in order to show that good things were going on as well. **UNIVERSALS**. Before he was executed, a scholar named Boethius had time while in prison to compose some works. His translation of Porphyry's *Isagoge*, a work on logic and his commentary on the problems it raises about universals inspired a long and fruitful inquiry into the alternative ways of interpreting the doctrine that grew out of Socrates' answer to Meno's question, "Can virtue be taught?" Debates over universals in relation to reality, to the mind, and to language, gave Ockham his inspiration to say "Universals as such do not exist, ONLY *particular* things," and led to Descartes' decisive realization that if anyone ever gets around to wondering WHICH *particular* things exist, the place for the wonderer to begin is with her/him-self, a point Augustine had already noted, but one that Descartes combined with neurology and the re-beginnings of brain science (pretty much abandoned after Socrates, Plato, and Aristotle abandoned the view of Hippocrates that the brain is important). **ONE TRUTH**. But there was still another major achievement of the long period between Augustine and the various renaissances of ancient cultural traditions: a slow growth in the view that we can distinguish human knowledge into two categories. In addition to the things that can only be learned from sacred WORDS handed on from prophets who received the WORD directly from God, there are truths that mere! human reason can, functioning on its own, learn directly from nature. The thousands upon thousands of words left behind by people who explored these questions with an unswerving confidence that the truth can be and is known established the solid foundation upon which what we call "Modern Science," a boldly confident attempt to learn the truth about God's creation, was built. When Siger of Brabant began teaching that the truths found in sacred scripture could diverge from those found in nature, Aquinas vigorously defended the totally commonsensical conviction that, though the truth may come to us either from a person's words (God's WORD) or from a person's deeds (God's CREATION)—two SOURCES of truth—there is only ONE TRUTH.

Immersion in the medieval Aquinas' thinking seeded my mind for Ockham/James and Descartes. First, by taking the notion that forms, essences, or natures are the basis of reality, combining it with the notion that forms exist one way in things outside the mind (they are not universal but "individuated" by matter) and in another way in concepts in the mind (by dematerializing the forms, the mind "universalizes" them), Aquinas concluded that we can be confident our knowledge is true because the forms in our mind match, are exactly like, are in fact the same as, the forms found in things existing outside the mind. The fact that things outside and concepts inside individuals' minds are themselves particular and the fact that there is one God, the distinct creator of all distinct creatures, prepared the ground for James' Ockhamist view that only particulars exist. The fact that there are special areas of reality called "minds" and that each and every person has her or his own where her or his ideas exist, forms the picture behind Descartes' *Meditations*.

Then came the explosive learning about learning we find in Descartes who put so many older and newer learnings together. Copernicus' view that astronomy would be simpler if we assume the earth revolves around the sun prompted questions about learning cosmology from scripture. Galileo's experiments, as well as what he saw through his telescope, overthrew the violent-vs-natural-motions physics and sky-bodies-vs-earth-bodies cosmology found in Aristotle's texts. Descartes' own study of raindrop-lenses, eye-lenses, and the brain helped him learn how each solitary learner is disconnected from the physical world. **MOST OF ALL**, though, Descartes put the best theology available into his Grand Framework. He took over the ancient Hebrew God-Science or theology. God is a purely spiritual Being, under no obligation to any laws God's not responsible for, the all-knowing source of all the laws that creatures, human or otherwise, are subject to, is powerful enough to do anything that is rationally conceivable, and so good that the idea of doing evil doesn't even come up for God.

The thesis here simply takes an idea that Descartes occasionally uses and builds on it. In *Meditation I*, Descartes confronts the skeptics. He poses a clear dilemma: EITHER nothing exists (or if it does no one can know it) OR at least one thing exists (and I, at least, can know it). In the course of his meditating on that—these are things that require enough peace and quiet to begin intense, meditative thinking, not so easy in a world where radios and TVs provide escape from peace and quiet from infancy onward—he asks himself how he can prove that God or some other powerful spirit, e.g., the devil, is not constantly lying to him, putting errors in his mind whenever he tries to learn the truth. It is natural that, as a mathematician, he recalls how often he's made mistakes while working out math problems and asks "How do I know that I am not deceived every time that I add two and three, or count the sides of a square, or judge of things yet simpler, if anything simpler can be imagined!" He goes further and asks "How do I know that He has not brought it to pass that there is no earth, no heaven, no extended body, no magnitude, no place, and that nevertheless [I possess the perceptions of all these things and that] they seem to me to exist just exactly as I now see them?" Descartes directs most of his attention in the first meditation to the fact that he himself makes mistakes by wrongly interpreting his sensations, but for a time he seriously raises the question: "Am I being systematically lied to? By GOD?!"

Then, after making sure the reader has gotten the point (God is the only being with enuf unlimited power to do something like this), he calms the worries of the scrupulous by suggesting that they imagine, not God, but some very powerful spirit (a wicked one like the devil) doing the lying. In the second meditation, this idea of a being telling us lies returns at the very point where he makes up his mind he'll believe he's certain that he exists:

> But is there not some deceiver or other, very powerful and very cunning, who ever employs his ingenuity in deceiving me. Then without doubt I exist also if he deceives me, and let him deceive me as much as he will, he can never cause me to be nothing so long as I think that I am something.

Descartes introduced nothing new here. The idea of the Supreme Being who is the source of all truth and beauty was/is familiar. The notion of GOD ADDRESSING us is as old as the story about Adam and Eve's evening walks with God through paradise's orchards and as recent as stories of end-of-the-world revelations. The idea of supernatural sources of artistic inspiration are as old as Plato's *Ion* and as recent as the inspired version of Mozart's inspiration named *Amadeus*. In fact, the idea of ideas coming to me from unseen sources was nothing new. We learned through the catechism that good thoughts came from a guardian angel trying to offset the bad thoughts put in our minds by the devil. But, however often I read and re-read those passages from Descartes, the thought that my thoughts come from God never 'registered.' Till the spring of 1989. Then, the final puzzles dissolved.

Your situation now. These rows and rose are conjuring thoughts. Via imagery. The thoughts can take you out to the most distant galaxy at the universe's edge. You can imagine yourself taking a god's-eye look at yourself: one of the 5,500,000,000 humans living on a planet near a star in an arm of the Milky Way, one of billions of galaxies. Your thoughts can zoom back to earth, in through your skin, to your brain, then into the mind where sense-data, memory-images, and thoughts (parallel with the events in your brain?) are coming to you. You can think about the a-toms that 'make up' the physical cosmos: they streak, orbit, jump, and dance together according to the choreography described by the laws of physics, chemistry, and biology. Then you can think about the stream of sense-data, memory-images, and thoughts whose presentations to you can be described by the laws of psychology, one of the most important of which is the one James wrote of: "The great law of habit itself—that twenty experiences make us recall a thing better than one, that long indulgence in error makes right thinking almost impossible." Then you can choose which of the thoughts accompanying your scanning of these rows and rose are true. You do understand them, right? (Chapter One.)

I knew I could understand the thoughts. Or at least **THE MEANING OF THE SENTENCES** which 'expressed' the thoughts. The formula, "the meaning of ALL the words," became THE First Principle that I fell back on, no matter what difficult issues remained unclear. As, for a long time, problems involving thoughts' origin, introspection, and the brain's role did.

One other resource became and remained solid and unshaken, viz., the thesis set forth by St. Augustine in *On the Teacher*. In that work, which reinforced a growing realization that "language" is shorthand for many distinct things, none of which is really language-as-such, Augustine took up the issue often referred to as **THE CRITERION OF TRUTH**: "How can we pick out what's true from all the opinions presented to us?" Augustine's answer? "God, by enlightening us from within, points us toward truth."

—II—

June 8, 1993

> Quantum mechanics is certainly imposing, but an inner voice tells me that it is not yet the real thing. The theory says a lot, but does not really bring us any closer to the secret of the 'old one.' I, at any rate, am convinced that *He* is not playing at dice. (A. Einstein, *Letter* to M. Born.)

Why did Einstein, who learned later on how Niels Bohr thought, refuse to give up his earlier-learned way of thinking? Why didn't he admit that LaPlace's determinism had fallen the way so many other physicists did, even though they learned to call the downfall of determinism "the downfall of causality"? What would (should?) James say? Or Oliver Sacks?

Whoever doesn't learn what it is that so many physicists, like Hume and Kant, meant by "causality"—i.e., what they thought of when they used the 'word' while thinking about the laws of physics and biophysics—will not learn to appreciate James' views about the Great Law of Learning, namely, **HABIT**, that is, the 'law' that "twenty experiences make us recall a thing better than one" and "long indulgence in error makes right thinking almost impossible." The most important kinds of human learning, e.g., the kind you are doing now, involve thinking, which is why learning the laws of learning requires learning the laws of thinking, regardless of whether thinking is called "induction," "deduction," "inference," "classifying," "classifying 'thinking' into such species as induction, deduction, inference*, or classifying," etc. (*Or is "inference" a genus, with induction and deduction as species?)

Why, then, did Einstein continue thinking his way rather than Bohr's? That question can be viewed as one particular under a more general question, *"Why does ANY thought follow any OTHER thing: sensation, memory-image, thought, or decision?"* The same query can be directed in general at anyone's next thought that continues an earlier thought-life. For instance, why are each of your current, this-reading thoughts what they are? Or the query can be directed specifically at someone's next thought. For instance, what's YOUR answer to "Why did Einstein not convert?" Determinists like LaPlace, Freud, and Skinner would track your answer to YOUR specific life-history. They'd also have to say that, in spite of appearances, you have no control over whether or not you, like Einstein, will continue thinking your old way rather than some other way. Say, like Descartes or James. (Unless you already think the way they did.) Or Sacks. When I thought of him, I thought of magic and miracles.

> Do you believe in magic? Suppose that you had been born blind. Suppose you had learned braille and could read it quite well. Now, suppose that by virtue of one of those routine miracles of modern surgery, the thick cataracts that had kept you from seeing were removed and you gained your eyesight. Would you be surprised to read here that the great magician, Houdini, learned how to juggle so well that he could keep four balls in the air at once AND READ A BOOK propped up in front of him at the same time *AND* that, after a thirty year lay-off, was still able to juggle three balls and read at the same time? Which would be the greatest feat of magic—miracle?—referred to in this paragraph?

Unfortunately, most who graduate from college these days do not learn much about causality, correlation-'causality,' determinism, quantum physics, or the great law of habit, not even that the minority who do learn about such things are hopelessly at odds over what's really going on.

This ignorance among the supposedly well-educated at this end of the twentieth, greatest and now most dangerous of all centuries (a century ago, TNT was still the Rolls Royce of explosives), is the greatest obstacle to world peace. Why? Because the gap in their understanding of recent history is coupled with a general 'sense'—it makes up much of the atmosphere of 'today's culture'—that science and God are topics that are unconnected. That is, today's learners are likely to learn that a scientist MAY CHANCE TO BE a church-goer (just as s/he MAY BE an avid fan of the opera or be a Jew or be black or be female!), but that there is no link between what s/he knows by "science" and what s/he believes on "faith." The more they DO learn about what the most-published writers on "science" think, the greater the chance they'll believe the quest for truth is doomed, since different people's learned beliefs are the product of—caused by—their different neurons and/or society, neither of which are under their control, which logically implies that none are personally responsible for their own beliefs, i.e., habitual thoughts habitually assented to.

However, those with a smattering of ideas about the history of human knowledge will know how large a role is played by cultural myths or, as Bacon called them, Idols of the Marketplace and (via trickle-down) of the Theater. They will discover that it is only recently that, one, experts began thinking there is a special category of thought(s) named "physics" that is not just one part of a universal category of expert knowledge named "philosophy" and, two, that a completely adequate understanding of the world is quite independent of the question, "Does God exist?" That is, the cultural myth that science, philosophy, and theology are Independent Meadows with solid fences between them is a recent one. And subject to the same query about Einstein: "Why does anyone continue, day after day, believing science, philosophy, and theology are distinct?"

The thesis here—one that pertains to 'scientific' psychology—is that the thought you will understand by the time you finish this sentence is a thought coming to you, not from your brain or society, but directly from God: you are free to try learning the different theories of learning and free to choose which one you will assent to as true, even if it is different from the one you are in the habit of believing. You may have to overcome your tendency to do to the thought you understood a moment ago what I tend to do when my wife accuses me of thinking I am always right. Instead of paying attention to what she goes on to say, I begin getting my reply ready so I can show her why she's wrong and I'm right.

Reading words. One of the most ingenious parts of the Creators' plan is this: They make it seem that truths THEY are offering us are really offered by other humans. Where would you be without words? Without books such as this? Reading leans heavily on learned expectations, e.g., expectations about the words to be used in couth presentations. Expectations that psychologists in general used to call "association" before so many got in the habit of NOT associating "learning" with inner, invisible, conscious experience and in the habit of associating it only with outer behavior. Except when they do not get in the habit of thinking the way Watson did but continue with their common-sense thinking and allow both inner experience and outer behavior to count, even systematic-desensitizing imaging, so long as it is renamed "behavior" in order not to disturb John Watson's ghost which long ago left his machine. Such facts point to the need for the first thing James tackled in Lecture Two of *Pragmatism*: the problem of WORDS' meanings. The title of his lecture was "What Pragmatism Means."

Typically for him, he began with a down-to-earth incident. With an argument among some campers over what "Does the man go round the squirrel or not?" means. Having settled that controversy to the satisfaction of most, he turned his audients' attention to what "pragmatism" means. With much less success*. James' friend Peirce had proposed pragmatism as a theory about meaning, and James used Peirce's proposal to tackle the question, "What does 'true' mean?" The goal here is to broaden their question: How do we learn anything, including how do we learn the meaning of words such as "learn," "meaning," and "words"? Especially, how do we learn to understand the meaning of others' words. Would you ever have learned about Santa Claus if words did not exist? How much of this paragraph or of any book at all could you read if you had no familiarity with words? How do we learn to read words, though? (*A. Lovejoy did a search and found "pragmatism" meant thirteen different things.)

The thesis here is that words as such do not exist. Learning that our INDISPENSABLE concept of words is a "useful fiction" and that words as such do not exist is crucial for getting at the question, "Where do thoughts come from?" What we call "words" are really either sense-data, images, or a-toms. The painting of a pipe by Magritte is helpful. Draw a picture of a pipe-smoker's pipe. Draw four sides (a square frame) around it. Under the frame, write "This is not a pipe." Which it isn't, since it is only a picture of a pipe. Now, erase the picture, and you'll notice that "This is not a pipe" isn't a pipe, either, since it's a sentence. Finally, write "These are not words," and—using the non-words of the first chapters—re-think your beliefs about WORDS. That is one reason why our first learning is not through words. They don't exist.

But they seem to. And one of the most important questions a learner can ponder is, "Whose WORDS am I most influenced by? Whose voice do I tend to listen to with the most respect?" (Is the voice you hear as you read on and on HERE a friendly-sounding one, a threatening one, or what?) Another important question is, "Whose WORDS got to me first?" (Whose voice was most influential at the beginning of your learning career?) A third question puts those together: "Do the people whose opinions carry the most weight with me right now have a world-view similar to the world-view of the people whose opinions carried most weight with me at the beginning of my learning career?" Better perhaps is the question, "Is my present world-view still the same as the earliest world-view I held or have I switched?" By "world-view" I mean what others often use "philosophy," "metaphysics," and so on, for. Everyone who is old enough and normal has one, though not everyone who has one notices the fact. A fact not unlike the one Moliere noticed, namely, that everyone old enough and normal speaks prose, though not everyone who does so notices. (Because they lack the names? Or the clearly distinct ideas? Or both?)

Our "listener-responses" and "reader-responses" to the thoughts seemingly proposed by other humans will depend, as Einstein's did, upon the views and attitudes we have acquired as HABITS. CHANGEABLE habits. A moment's reflection reveals that fact with blinding clarity. Even if other believers are only figments of our imagination, our thoughts about them AND ABOUT OUR DISAGREEMENTS WITH THEM are PROOF that *OTHER habitual views* and attitudes are available to us. And we are free to check the evidence FOR those other views before planning our objections AGAINST them. For instance, are you a victim of the myth that 'scientists as such,' e.g., psychologists, need adopt no position vis-à-vis God whom Einstein called 'the old one'?

First learning is not word-learning and not learned via words. The July 1993 issue of *Life* magazine has a cover story entitled "Babies are SMARTER than you Think." (Thanks, P.) Alright, we think, just one more e.g. of the difference between appearance and reality. (My calendar tells me that it is really Saturday, July 3, rather than Tuesday, June 8. There are aesthetic reasons for keeping the old date, even tho I decided three days ago to reorganize the layout of this final chapter.) But wait, there are more WORDS on the cover: "They can ADD before they can COUNT. They can UNDERSTAND a hundred words before they can SPEAK. And, at three months their powers of MEMORY are far greater than we ever imagined." Do those words arrest your attention? Do they jar your current habits of thinking? If someone leaned over your crib and spoke them, would they have done so?

It is essential to keep in mind that there is only *one learner* whose entire lifetime of learning you have better access to than anyone else has access to: *your self*. It not only makes sense then to begin trying to compare other people's theories about how you learned and your experience/memory of the actual process, but—in view of the fact that, presumably, your life has some purpose besides being a test-case for theories of learning—by learning how you learned your present views about life's purpose, test whether it's time for a change. Jerome Bruner has suggested that paying attention to the stories of our lives is important because—according to an article in the 10-20-87 N.Y. Times—such stories, when they are OUR stories, create "the framework in which [. . . we] live and will live. These life stories reveal what [. . . we] feel is significant now and in the future." (Thanks, A.) The clearer we become on our own life stories, the better we'll be able to examine them in light of William James' theory about the important items in our growth and development, the theory presented in what should be renamed *The Varieties of Human Experience*. The first chapter is about open-mindedness, the second on Rethinking your church affiliation, the third is devoted to recognizing the existence of the unseen, and the next ones take up the question, "Does your world-view have room for ALL of life's experiences?" Then, prior to chapters on living practically-moral lives and peak experience, come pivotal chapters dealing with the 'divided self,' the search for 'unification' [or reunification], and 'conversion.' Human learning, growth and development, are clearly at the core of this, James' personality theory.

How do we begin learning, though? Seventeen years before I learned about J. Bruner's ideas on life-stories, I had learned of a picture he drew that's hard to beat: "You never get a direct test on reality. You must take scraps and test them against your mental model of the world" (11-29-70 *N.Y. Times Magazine*, p.32). This, of course, fits the model of model-building and model-switching used so extensively throughout this work. It fits with the thesis about 'words': Babies cannot distinguish which of the sounds they hear at the outset of life are 'words' and which are 'sounds.' Their first learning is the kind that Romulus and Rema would have done if they really existed and really were raised by wolves whose favorite vocals were howling at the moon. (Would they have thought that the moon was called "ooooooo"? Or that "ooooooo" named the passing clouds that occasionally hid the moon from sight? A critical issue if they tried to verbally identify which was moving.)

First-learning is acquiring sense-expectancies. Sensations last no more than a moment. (How long will you be on this sentence?) *Sensory*-expectancies consist of MEMORY-imagery ('from' previous sensory-sequences) amid present streams of conscious sensations. James, as we might expect, did not overlook these. In fact, his chapter on "habit" is chiefly about sense-related expectancies. It is the source for the Houdini part of the "magic" question. James inserted a long passage from "Carpenter's 'Mental Physiology' (1874)" about Robert Houdin's (not, I just noticed!, the same as H. Houdini) feat of juggling. James mentioned it in connection with something every reflective person (not John Watson, though) will take note of: our ability to think of matters other than the meaning of our words. We can verbally behave AND THINK: sing the national anthem while thinking about other things, recite a prayer while "our mind" is 1000 miles away, recite numbers while paying *selective attention* to f's (count the f's in the first six sentences of this paragraph), and so on. This is the chapter from which I earlier borrowed the passage about our *awareness*, inattentive to be sure, but awareness nevertheless of the sensations we experience while getting out of bed, walking, washing our face, dressing, making a cup of tea for our spouse, driving to an unaccustomed destination (and getting part way to work or to church or to the store before *noticing* that we're going in the wrong direction, so distracted were we by a conversation), and so on.

James calls the memories of previous sensations which are evoked by each moment's new sense-data "sensations to which we are usually inattentive," and he puts his finger on the kind of consideration we must think about in order to notice these usually UNnoticed features of our experience: i-we ARE conscious or aware of them, and ii-we DO notice them *as soon as they GO WRONG!* Examples abound. We go to sit down and a prankster who is too young to know better or else an older fool pulls the chair away. Even before we feel the floor, we realize that an expected sensation hasn't materialized. Someone offers us a glass of lite wine and we gulp a good mouthful, only to cough and sputter because it was cognac instead. We reach out to touch the coins floating atop an "Optigone" or "Optic Mirage," but like Macbeth are surprised not to feel what we see when [the image of] our hand reaches what we see. Magicians excel at studying people's expectancies and at ways of starting a customary sequence, but then interrupting it and producing what seem to be reality-defying, impossible! second-half sequences. The history of astronomy—from i-noticing that the moon's sequences have a regular, predictable pattern to them, through ii-noticing the changes in exactly where the sun comes up over the horizon and how the changes go in one direction half of the year then in the other direction in the other half of the year, to iii-noticing that some of the "stars" wander around—as well as the history of every other science is nothing more than learning what sensations can be expected to follow what sensations. Babies are unwitting scientists, but only in the sense that they are equipped to build up an inner model of their neighborhood and the objects making it up, an inner model that allows them to develop a WORD-less 'sense' for what to expect next and, the flip-side, a WORD-less 'sense' that will be surprised if something different from what is expected is experienced. The "unwitting" means they do not have any self-conscious understanding *that* this is what is going on. Witting requires the next step in learning: WORDS.

> **Conclusions.** First learning is not word-learning. Our sense expectancies, once accompanied by an inner model, constitute a vast, silent, inner 'world.'

Word-learning. Next, we learn "names" for figures, grounds, gestalts, sequences, and so on. If Victor, the so-called Wild Boy of Aveyron, had been a triplet (along with Romulus and Rema), he would have gotten accustomed to how wolves behaved, he would have learned something of the part of the forest he lived in, and so on. But he'd have lacked name-tags for things. H.S. Sullivan used humor to suggest the insider's view of name-learning:

> All children and for that matter, I believe, all the young of all the species on the face of the earth enjoy, whatever that means, playing with their abilities . . . And so, before it is possible for a child to articulate syllables, there is a playing with the phonemal stations which the child has finally been able to hit on in the babbling and cooing business. There follows the picking up of some syllables, and sooner or later every child falls upon the syllable "ma." If there is a slight tendency to perseveration so that it becomes "ma-ma," then truly the child discovers that there is something that he had not previously suspected: namely, magic in this noise-making apparatus of his, because very significant people begin to rally around and do things, and they don't hurt—quite the contrary, they are pleasant. I suppose that that little experience is the beginning of what to most people seems to be a lifelong feeling that there is nothing about them that is as powerful as the noises they make with their mouths. ("The Illusion [sic] of Personal Individuality.")

Once we get a "fix" on the fact that WORD-learners have to figure out **FROM INSIDE** which sounds to associate with which things, we can begin getting rid of myths about human learning and learning the truth about it. Provided, of course, that we first learn all about all that pre-word learning discussed above, which includes what James discusses often in his *Principles*, namely, becoming aware of the samenesses* (the rough shape we'd call "mother's body, especially her face," if we had the concepts to go with the "words" and if they were English) reappearing in our stream of consciousness, which is the top-side of the coin whose underside is becoming aware of differences*: "they" won't get excited if we utter "ma-ma" when dad appears AND when they hold up a rattle AND when we see our reflection in a mirror, etc.! The fact that the word-learning builds on the inner-world—or inner-model-building is usually overlooked, precisely because two things are mis-taken to be the SAME even though the DIFFERENCE between them is radical.

The tradition of forms, essences, natures, and so on, results from our tendency to mis-take SAME-as-similar for SAME-as-one. We grow up believing that what we see when, after breakfast, we pick up the *Baltimore Catechism* and resume our study, IS what we saw last evening when we put IT down and went to bed. That is naive realism. In fact, what we see this morning is LIKE what we saw last evening. THEY are (i)two time-separated sets of visual sense-data AND (ii)distinct from the physical book, if it exists. Even "exactly alike" does not mean "one": identical twins are TWO beings, just as two hundred clones are TWO HUNDRED. When we count, we focus on how many, when we classify we focus on how many are alike enough to belong to one (mental) category-bin or class-file or pigeon-hole that is different from all other categories, classes, and pidgin wholes. (The mental thought's the thing here, not the visible triggers you see. That is, it's what you see, not what you see, that counts, though without what you see, you'd likely not see it's not what counts.) Socrates asked Meno to concentrate on what worker bees, drone bees, queen bees, big bees, little bees, sitting bees, and non-spelling bees have in common—what's the same about them—that makes us call all of them by the same! name "bee." Ditto for color and virtue and all the other forms it's so easy to start "seeing"!

We can change our naming habits, though. Names go with mental classifyings, and rethinkers must be ready to inspect every name to make sure we haven't assumed a THING exists because we have invented a mental class and named it. Entire systems are involved. We did not just classify some bees as different *from other bees*. We had to first pick out all bees *from every other species*, from hives and honey just for starters. This is where rethinkers from Thales to Einstein come in: "Those things, when *I* compare's 'em, ain't that different. They're all water [Thales] or they're all mass or energy [Einstein]." After we discriminate poetry from prose, we can understand even Parmenides: "Well, gang, they ain't all water and they ain't all air or energy or anything so indistinct as the unde-*fin*-able, because 'They' is poetry and the only worthwhile scientific prose is 'It' or 'What-Is'." If we change "What-is" from Greek to "A *be*-ing," we can follow him when he adds that, "Since '*non*-being' can't be the name of anything real—a REAL non-being would be!, hence be a being, hence not non-being—a being is all there can be." Plato thought long and hard about that, which is why he composed *The Sophist* and concentrated on Being, Nonbeing,

The Same, The Different, and so on*. There is only one way any one of us can cut through the Idols of the Mind that all these WORDS generate and it! is the same! way for every one! of us: each of us must aim for the day when we've learned enough about all our options that we can be decisive AND RIGHT when we cut down the number of things on our "real" list and put them over on a "figment" list. (*Just as "similarity" is a thing-ification—it converts "They ARE similar" into "They HAVE a similarity"—so are "sameness" and "difference." None are on the five-item list [reification from list, listed, listing] of existing things. Each of us must [re-]decide what s/he will list on her or his final being-list.)

A Pause. What things might you feel confident enough about already? (1)You already know the difference between being right and being mistaken, that is, between assenting to what's really true as opposed to what's mistaken. Either God exists or God doesn't, and whoever chooses from those two options the one that matches what's really out there is right, the other is wrong. (2)Your thoughts can be divided into two groups: thoughts about things which you think of as "matched" by real things that exist even when you go to sleep and stop thinking and those which are about things that exist only in your imagination and that will stop existing as soon as you go to sleep and stop thinking.* (3) "See" names three different acts: a-being aware of total patterned-color-fields that are directly present, b-visualizing or being aware of memory-images OF them or parts of them, and c-understanding thoughts, e.g., *that* there is a difference between seeing these rows and rose of whatever-they-are and understanding the thoughts co-presented. (4)There is a huge difference between understanding your thought-options and deciding which you will assent to as the ones you're confident 'match reality.' (*This is the most important thing Saint Thomas' writings helped me become clear and confident about. It took a long time to get over the belief that, when I thought of a triangle as a three-sided figure, I was knowing an essence independent of my conscious thought, a view coupled with the idea that, if a real triangle is drawn on a piece of paper, that concrete triangle's essence and its existence are really distinct. That led to questions about the status of such not-existing essences as "the present king of France" or "a solid-gold mountain," and thence to theories about subsistence, intentional existence, inexistence, and so on. There are no essences, existence is a noun-reification of a verb, and whatever does not exist does not exist, period!, even though I, my thought *that* such-and-such may someday exist, and a creator powerful enough to bring into existence things that do not now exist, really exist. Sometimes the meaning of a single passage can collide with an old ideas-intersection, shake them into a new way of seeing, and—if re-adopted often enough—become a HABITUAL new (therefore old) way of looking at things. Saint Thomas' answer to objection 2 of article 5 of *De Potentia*'s 3rd question did that once: ". . . before [a quiddity] has *esse*, it is nothing ("quia antequam esse habeat, nihil est"). He added the qualification, "unless perhaps in the mind of the creator where the creature does not exist but the 'creatrix essentia'." God, God's mind, and God's creative essence are REALLY ONE, Thomas thought.) *End.*

Rethinking reading. Are words really words? Once a young learner has acquired basic inner-model associations, language associations begin. The story from Helen Keller (cited near the end of Chapter One) is a memorable re-telling of how she learned that Annie's non-word-ful hand-motions had purpose behind them. Most of us are so long-practiced at "instant-association-naming" that it takes determined rethinking to weigh the evidence FOR the claim that "There is no such thing as language-as-such," i.e., to try to think of 'spoken words' as sounds, 'writing' as shaped and arranged ink marks, and now* computer 'bytes' as simply electric impulses, bits of magnetized metallic coating, etc. (*MIT's N. Negroponte's sounds like a sober voice in a crowd of enthusiasts excusably intoxicated by the potential of "interactive technology": *Newsweek*'s 5-31-93's cover-story quotes his warning that "Multimedia is the wrong word. Everything has now become digitized. We have created a unimedia, really. **BITS ARE BITS.**")

The literal truth was learned by earlier learners. In 1690 John Locke tore to shreds the idea that anyone receiving a brand new idea from God could literally pass it on to others via 'words.' For instance, if I tell you that I have a leopard in my pocket, do you understand me? What if I tell you I have a blit there? The thoughts I have in mind are ones you'd regard as familiar ones; but, even if I tell you one is true and one false, would you know which is which?

First, Then I say, that no man inspired by God can by any revelation communicate to others any new reflection. For, whatsoever impressions he himself may have from the immediate hand of God, this revelation, if it be of new simple ideas, cannot be conveyed to another, either by words or any other signs. Because WORDS, BY THEIR IMMEDIATE OPERATION ON US, CAUSE NO OTHER IDEAS BUT OF THEIR NATURAL SOUNDS, and it is by the custom [habit] of using them for signs, that they excite and revive in our minds latent ideas; but yet only such ideas as were there before. (*Essay*, IV, xviii, 3; "Of Faith and Reason." EMPHASIS ADDED.)

Locke's "It's memory" is identical with Aristotle's *Posterior Analytics* where he hands on Plato's [Socrates'?] learning-is-remembering theory: "All instruction given or received by way of argument [reasoning using WORDS rather than ESP] proceeds from [the learner's] pre-existent knowledge." But Augustine gave the most careful dissection of our original, common-sense view in his remarkable dialogue, *On the Teacher*. Nothing can substitute for a careful study of it, but his conclusion and Locke's agree:

For it is the truest reasoning and most correctly said that when words are uttered we either know already what they signify or we do not know; if we know, then we remember rather than learn, but if we do not know, then we do not even remember, though perhaps we are prompted to ask.

We DO learn to associate "names" with the landmarks of our inner model of reality (with mama, daddy, kitty, doggy, etc.), and we rapidly expand the links between "names" and expectancies. We add "names" for our nose, our toes, our fingers. We learn cues for whole complexes: "No" means mom will get upset if we keep doing what we're doing. We learn more about "names." We learn *that* "mama" is detachable when we learn our mama isn't the only mama in the world (she, too, has a mama, Grammy Rose, no less), *that* we're not the only daddy's little boy in the world (because daddy's his daddy's, grampa's, too), *that* those are stars way up at the top of the whole world, *that* people who stop waking up and talking get put in boxes and covered over by dirt (some other places they get burned up like dead leaves), or *that* yesterday (that's the day that used to be today) was once a tomorrow (that's the day that's going to be the next today when today's today becomes its yesterday and yesterday gets moved back a day) . . . It's hard to find words for these things, but you will get the idea (if you can get the picture). You have to in order to read the good books (but not the bad ones?) the anti-theorists urge us to replace Plato with, the way Jefferson told his son-in-law to read good books rather than waste time on ethics courses. Jefferson told him to even before the government's role vis-a-vis tea imports became a topic in business ethics. How far did he think the moral sense extended?

To learn the truth about learning is possible only if we apply Ockham's Razor correctly. Rows and rose of these have been crossing the center of your visual field. Worlds of imagery have come to you at the same time. Thoughts that you've understood have been flowing by as well. Many of these sense-data seem like words coming from us and your thoughts seem to come from the words. They aren't and they don't. All come from God. According to laws. Many of which are those probability laws called "habits." Why DID a thought about Sacks follow one about Einstein? Some thoughts just saunter in, some pour in as we stand under the shower, "leopard" meant "a folded photo of a leopard," and "blit" meant "a two-[boy+girl]-couple group."

—III—

June 9, 1993

> "Blessed are you, Lord God of our forefathers, and worthy of praise! Your name is glorified forever . . . We have sinned grievously in everything, and have disobeyed your commands; We have not observed them or done as you commanded us to do, *for our own good.*" (The Song of the Three Children.)

Learning who/what exists and who/what doesn't. To this day, I recall K telling R (who had just come home) what had happened to people I assumed were mutual friends of theirs. Bad things. The kind of things that make friends feel bad for their friends undergoing them. I laughed with disbelief when I learned that the "mutual friends" were soap-opera characters and that those two adults could seriously care about such things. On the other hand, a year or more of late-hour reruns of "St. Elsewhere" left me sad when it all came to an end. Which, now that I think about it, reminds me how thoroughly I had gotten to know Kristin, daughter of Lavrans. And to love her. How readily fond feelings for her resurface:

> Her mother took the empty bowl and put it upon the step. Then suddenly she threw her arms around her daughter, and pressed her tightly to her and kissed her.—Kristin felt that her mother's cheeks were wet and hot:
> "May God and Our Lady guard and shield you from all evil—we have naught else but you, your father and I, that has not been touched by our ill-fortune. Darling, darling—never forget that you are your father's dearest joy."

All it takes is those few WORDS from "The Bridal Wreath" (sec.4) to fetch them back. And yet, however much I wished it were possible to meet her in the hereafter, it never once crossed my mind to *BELIEVE* it so. Kristin Lavransdatter, a creation of Sigrid Undset's imagination, was now a (re)creation of mine as well. That, at least, is one way of fitting a very large snatch of READING experience into an inner model of the reality I can get no direct peek at. Another is more accurate: about-Kristin thoughts, like all my about-things thoughts, is a divine creation proposed to me. At first, when I had no counter-evidence, I (like Spinoza and James) didn't doubt thoughts about any thought-about person, i.e., didn't doubt mama was my mother, daddy was my father, Santa put presents under the Christmas tree, Adam was made out of the earth's dust and Eve out of Adam's rib, my guardian angel was always by my side, the devil would like to take me to hell, and my soul would go to heaven IF I kept God's commandments. Kristin wouldn't. She never existed. I never thought she did, either. I had learned from unlearning about Santa that not everyone (or everything) I understood thoughts about was real.

Such convertible decisions about *existence* and *non-existence* are to be expected in the case of anyone entirely cut off from any direct access to people, in the case of anyone dependent on "scraps of evidence" for testing an unbelievably complex model of literally thousands of radically different INDIVIDUAL persons, ranging from intimates to strangers, including literally thousands upon thousands of distinct facts—parents, physical appearance, talents and handicaps, opinions and beliefs, challenges and life-shaping responses, etc.—about some of them. Each with definite space-wise and time-wise correlations to all the others, that is, all situate-able somewhere on this one planet earth, in this one solar system, in this one galaxy, all date-able at some exact time-period between this planet's formation and now. Let others think we and our planet are insignificant, too infinitesimally small to be seen from even one of the other billions of galaxies and too short-lived to matter in the context of eons. The people who wake up each morning, wash their own face yet one more time, linger perhaps over this latest delicious cup of coffee, meet and converse with this or that unique human being, and—a long eighteen or so hours later—curl up in bed and fall off into a nightful of sleep and dreams, are each of such stature as to be a 'universe' all by her—or himself. Thoughts of such worlds-unto-themselves make up much of my 'universe.' Particular individuals. Individual particulars.

And when I immerse myself again in Undset's *Kristin Lavransdatter*, I enter an entirely new world of individual particulars. As I do when I immerse myself in the world of tempestuous, even fevered thoughts and loves and passions thru *The Insulted and Injured*, enter the dank prison of *Darkness at Noon*, slip into a limbless, sightless, soundless hulk lying in a hospital bed in *Johny Got His Gun*, join the richly detailed life of Okonkwo in *Things Fall Apart*. I do the same when I bury myself in works that tell me about Galileo's life and thoughts, about Kepler's life and thoughts, Descartes', Newton's, Locke's, and Einstein's. Or in works with titles like *The Spiritual Lives of Children* by authors like R. Coles (that's just one of the Coles' books you brought home these past couple of years and stuck under my nose where I couldn't ignore them), in which book I can meander through the slowly-day-by-day-evolving 'worlds' of so many radically different youths. World-fuls of individuals, real and unreal, life-fuls of events, true and imaginary, and mind-fuls of experiences about which—a whole world away from all experiences but this ever-changing, cosmic-sized field of experience I call my own—I can make instant assessments: these people lived but those didn't, these events happened but those didn't, these thoughts were thought, but . . . Surely, Sigrid, Fyodor, Arthur, Dalton, Chinua thought thoughts similar to . . . Not to Kristin's, not to Vanya's, not to Rubashov's, not to Joe's, not to Okonkwo's thoughts, for they no more existed than Hamlet or the players he hired . . . But similar to the thoughts that I once enjoyed during liesurely reading, similar to thoughts I just re-thought-about in rapid review, similar to MY thoughts. Mine? Yes, but where do I store them when I'm not using them? In a non-existent brain? A soul? A memory? What do those names stand for? What thoughts do I have when I use those words? Do thoughts even exist?

Of thoughts, I have no doubt. I understand them. They make all 'worlds' **CONSCIOUSLY** real to me. Without them, I'd be no better than a rock. (Does anyone think rocks sit and think all day?!) Thought-about 'worlds,' real and unreal, make up a vast amount of the thought I am understanding with this fully wakened mindset right now, this brand new thought that will be added to all those others, this brand new thought that I will later rethink with a new thought when, it seems, I re-read this long sentence making up part of this long, opening section of this 3rd letter. Thoughts. What would my learning be without them?

> Where, though, do all these thoughts of mine come from? Which single one of them would I have had if I lived in a world without words? In the jungle with Dumbo's ancestors, in the ocean with Willie's, in the air with Jonathan's? In a world with no Walt Disney and no Mickey, i.e., in a world without words, without word-captioned photos, without word-accompanied movies? But I don't live in a wordless world. Or do I? Words are my magic carpet to those other worlds. Or are they?

There are moments now when I am amazed that the traditional story I learned about the relation of my human intellect to *INDIVIDUALS* and particulars ever made sense to me. But it did.

> If, with Aristotle and St. Thomas, *thing* and *object* are distinguished in this fashion but not separated, and if, while maintaining their unity, allowance is made for what comes from the thing and for what comes from the mind in knowing, then it is clear that from the things which exist outside our mind and constitute what may be called the universe of existence, the mind draws forth a world of objects composed of abstract and universal concepts which we may term the universe of intelligibility or of human knowledge. And that universe is, on the one hand, detached from the universe of existence, in order that it may be known. It is, on the other hand, identified with it, in order that it may itself subsist. Thus, we really do attain the things of the world of existence when we attain the world of intelligibility, but we do not attain them in their singularity nor in the contingency proper to the flux of their singular occurrences. Our senses attain them that way . . . (J. Maritain, *Degrees of Knowledge*, Ch. III, sec.29.)

If it really were nature's law, as so many Thomists claim, that my intellect cannot know INDIVIDUAL things as such and my senses cannot know universal concepts as such, then how did *I* ever learn that they are different? If my intellect didn't know the individuals, how did it know their differences well enough to leave them aside while extracting what they had in common? In *Theatetus*, Plato it this way: if my eyes know color and my ears know sound, but my eyes don't know sound and my ears don't know color, then how do *I* know that color is DIFFERENT from sound? Leopards and photos of them: are they the *same*? Are "They're alike" and "They are the same" and "They're one" *different*? Are A and a the same? Are 10 and ten different? You and your body: are they one or are they the same or are they alike? Is "Or ARE they?" the same or not? The bottom line here is simple. My thoughts are about individual, plural, particular things. Period! They are the only things that exist, the only things to think about. Even when I think about universals or essences, they are individual, particular ones. I may, however, think simultaneously about all of them (mythical as THEY are) with the mental shorthand I call "thinking in general terms about them all." Except when I use other images for the same* thought. (*Same one thought? Another similar one?)

Unlearning such hard-learned false theories, myths!, and replacing them with true ones (often previously-rejected ones) is the kind of rethinking needed today. There are so many truths, and we must temporarily ignore some in order to get clear about others. The challenge is not to gain insight in one area but lose it elsewhere. Often we must grab onto and at least try out bold new models that may be far more roomy than our old ones and, if the evidence says they're true, to simply step beyond old, misleading theories, however many hundreds of hours we've spent on them, however many thousands of hours were spent on them by however many thousands of thinkers who thought they had grabbed onto a coattail or two of eternal truth. We must not expect to find all of our questions answered or all of our doubts quelled instantly, immediately. Those familiar with grand revolutions will tell us, sometimes briefly, sometimes at length, that Newton's great synthesis which astounded the world was bold in outline, brought together many disconnected sub-theories, brought mathematical precision to the description of an unheard of number of natural phenomena, but that his synthesis also had large gaps, trailed off into many loose ends, and even was in conflict with some measurements generally accepted at the time.

For learning how we learn about the real world of real people with real experiences they are really trying to make their real lives out of, the old naive-realist, thoughts-from-our-senses model is an anachronism. It was shown to be outdated three centuries ago. Everything that has been learned since has confirmed that it is outdated. But that was shown to others, it was learned by others. What others know or knew is of no help in our knowing until we're shown what they were shown, until we learn what they learned, for ourselves, so that we—in our turn—can get beyond our naive realism, too. Jerome Bruner's model is infinitely better. It helps us to notice the fact that poses the biggest question of all. How can I—or you!—conceive a universe so complex as ours, with billions of inhabitants with inner 'universes' each as complex as ours, all in one, single thought such as this one that this string of shaped, arranged letters seems to be a vehicle for. A thought that comes to you so effortlessly. So long as you don't turn the book upside down and try to scan the 'words' from left to right, top to bottom.

Dear potential convert to a wholly new way of looking at things, I am not thinking of you individually. I have no idea right now who you are in particular. Especially if I add "in general" to "dear potential convert." Still, in a sense, I am thinking about you. I don't believe I alone inhabit this universe. I believe there are 5.5 billion of us on this planet and that there are roughly 5,499,999,999 you's to whom I am sending this message-in-a-bottle. (On occasion, I do try to directly address specific you's.) If you now find yourself apparently holding and reading a book, then you are being addressed personally. Not by me, though, but by the Ones who created both of us. We may live amid a vast ocean of space through which entire galaxies whirl lazily or speed like torpedos, but we also are held in a divine palm that has everything under control, down to the last detail, whether it is a new follicle beginning to show, a data-packed thought fully understood, a dying sparrow fluttering to earth. How can we explain this incredible 'imagination' we possess, this 'mind' that seemingly lets us see in a glance the entire universe and its entire history, this 'faculty' that allows us to capture vistas so similar to the vistas that the Hebrew prophets said only the God of Abraham, Jacob, and Moses enjoyed? What better way than by imagining that with such image-laden thoughts, we ARE being taken into the Creators' confidence? These are vistas such as we never dreamed about when we were born, vistas unsuspected by those babies featured in *Life*. As we once were, they still are deaf to words. I trust you are not. You do understand these thoughts, am I right? Whatever your present frame of mind, your current intellectual attitude, your LEARNED-SINCE-YOUR-BIRTH profess-ional views may be. How have you learned so much?

> **PROPOSAL**. Dissolve the humanities and the sciences. The theory that there is any distinction in reality to match that distinction in today's myth-ridden 'culture' is scientifically, empirically, testably, verifiably falsifiable. In fact, it's just obviously ridiculous.

C.P. Snow made a stir in 1959 when his "The Two Cultures" lecture was published. Various experts read and reacted to him, and he responded with 1963's "The Two Cultures: and a Second Look." One of the most important things in his book was in the form of a story that packs as much dynamite as the harmless (!) tale about one little kid who told it like it was when all the experts in the society oohh'd and aahh'd about the emperor's new mind, I mean, clothes. Snow's tale could start a revolution in thinking about experts, humanists, experts, scientists, experts, *ad inf.*

> I believe the intellectual life of the whole of western society is increasingly being split into two polar groups. When I say the intellectual life, I mean to include also a large part of our practical life, because I should be the last person to suggest the two can at the deepest level be distinguished . . . . Two polar groups: at one pole we have the literary intellectuals, who incidentally while no one was looking took to referring to themselves as "intellectuals" as though there were no others. I remember G.H. Hardy once remarking to me in the 1930's: "Have you noticed how the word 'intellectual' is used nowadays? There seems to be a new definition which certainly doesn't include Rutherford or Eddington or Dirac or Adrian or me. It does seem rather odd, don't y' know."

The name of G.H. Hardy, combined with the mention of theory vs practice, pure science vs applied science, pure math vs applied math, inevitably makes me think of J. Bronowski's *Science and Human Values*, whose opening scene is a November, 1945, drive through Nagasaki that evoked awe at the destructive force of the single bomb that levelled the city and sparked a flash of insight into the phrase "the power of science for good and for evil." Followed by an imagined debate between the humanities'ists and the science'ists over whose "baby" that bomb was. Bronowski:

> This absurd division reached its *reductio ad absurdum*, I think, when one of my teachers, G.H. Hardy, justified his great life work on the ground that it could do no one the least harm—or the least good. But Hardy was a mathematician; will humanists really let him opt out of the conspiracy of scientists? Or are scientists to forgive Hardy because, protest as he might, most of them learned their indispensable mathematics from his books?

What savannah-roaming 'Neanderthal' ever thought of the distinction between the sciences and the humanities? What jungle-dwelling 'savage' would have understood the cover-story question of the 12-28-92 *Time*: "What Does Science Tell Us About God?" Why does any of us believe we can think about Neaderthals and savages we have never known, can even ask intelligent questions about what they did or did not think about or understand? Why do any of us think that the real question isn't "What Does God Tell Me About Science?" Why do any of us believe there is such a thing as science that we've never observed, that 'it' is superior because 'its method' that there are hundreds of theories about is superior, that its most fanatical devotees know more about the universe and what life is all about than Kristin Lavransdatter would have had she lived and that readers who can understand her story often do? What will it take for us to remove our blinders, things Francis Bacon who believed in God called Idols of the Mind?

READING. The myth that is told and sold in all (many?) introductions to science texts written for ignorant humanities'ist students and then passed on by them to THEIR unwary humanities'ist students, is that science'ists learn in a radically different way from humanities'ists. Science'ists open their eyes and look at nature, whereas humanities'ists do nothing but read books that cite texts from authorities who wrote books so that later students could learn from the books what they'd figured out by opening their eyes. Science'ists learn by getting close to nature, humanities'ists by going around with their noses in books. Allow me to cite a sample from one general psychology text. It begins with the myth that began spreading like a computer virus from book to book a good century ago:

> Psychology did not begin as a science. Rather, it started in primitive mysticism, became a branch of philosophy, and then, after more than 2000 years, finally achieved status as a science. All the other sciences had a similar transition: from mysticism through philosophy to separate development as scientific disciplines. Psychology, the youngest of biological sciences, began its separate development less than 100 years ago. [Long lives they have!]

The next subdivision explains scientifically what science is:

> The essence [oh?!] of science, from the standpoint of the scientist himself, is "a disposition to deal with the facts rather than with what someone has said about them." [A footnote reference to who SAID this and where is inserted at this point.] This means that the scientist must observe for himself and that what he observes is the primary basis of his speculations and conclusions. The importance of observation for science is brought to a focus in the following story from Francis Bacon, a leader (1605) in the history of scientific investigation. [There follows a passage CITED from what someone else, in an intermediate book, SAID Bacon SAID in one of his books.]

Now ask yourself where so many people get their idea that there is a huge difference between science'ists and humanities'ists. Whether they would have gotten that idea had they grown up in a wordless

415

world? Whether they would have gotten that idea had they grown up in a world with thousands of words, but no equal for "sciences" and "humanities"? Ask yourself how many people who use those 'words' will, if asked, write out similar analyses of what they mean. Ask how many have ever wondered where they got the thoughts 'behind' the words "sciences" and "humanities" the same way many have wondered where we get the thoughts behind the word "God." Then READ and ponder the following WORDS:

> What else has cognitive psychology discovered? Well, we have found out how recalcitrant the cognitive activities of everyday life are to experimental study. For example, the fact that we understand so little about reading after years of study is very impressive to me. Many people think we do understand it; there's an awful lot of theory about automa-tic processes, decoding, storing, and so on. It doesn't seem to me, though, that those models are particularly helpful. You can make any number of them, and none seems to help kids learn how to read. (U. Neisser, in B. Baars' *The Cognitive Revolution in Psychology*, 1986, p.282.)

Is there such a thing as a science, even a youthful one, of psychology? One in which words do not count so much as research? Certainly it is not 'scientific' when someone ignores the role of brains, either as indispensable sources of humans' conscious experience, or as an indispensable theoretical fiction needed to predict the Creators' presentation of sense-data, imagery, and thoughts. What does any psychologist know about his or her own brain, though? What do YOU know about YOUR own brain through personal research on it, as opposed to seemingly READING WORDS about brains, upon which you base your faith about your brain? Consider the thought you will understand through the next words:

> You've never seen your brain, so if you believe it exists, that's an act of faith on your part. And if your brain stands between you and the physical world, including all other brains and the bodies they allegedly inhabit, then you've never seen them either, so if you believe they exist, that's an

act of faith on your part. And if your brain and the 'out' sides of their bodies and brains stand between you and their inner experiences, you've never seen them either, so if you believe they exist, that's an act of faith on your part, and if you believe you know what they're like, that too is an act of faith on your part. Do you know what I am thinking right now? Do you know anything I've ever thought? Do you know me? Are you sure I exist at this moment?

Thomas Aquinas, to defend the unschooled wash-woman's simple faith in God (it's like the unwashed monk's contentment with feeling compunction, though unable to define it), pointed to our massive reliance on *other* faiths (here, "faiths" = the thoughts we assent to when evidence is less than conclusive) in our daily lives. When James argued that zealot experimentalists ignore the massive amount of faith behind their naive pontificating, he was relying on far more science and far less faith than they. But even he did not notice quite so acutely the full extent of our reliance on words. Jerome Bruner's *Acts of Meaning* might help dispel our lack of awareness of how much we rely on words and of how disastrous is the consequence of that lack: people who don't realize they don't understand others' words. Or their own.

> I have written at a time when psychology, the science of the human mind as William James once called it, has become fragmented as never before in its history. It has lost its center and risks losing the cohesion needed to assure the internal exchange that might justify a division of labor between its parts. And the parts, each with its own organizational identity, its own theoretical apparatus, and often its own journals, have become specialties whose products become less and less exportable. Too often they seal themselves within their own rhetoric and within their own parish of authorities. This self-sealing risks making each part (and the aggregate that increasingly constitutes psychology's patchquilt whole) ever more remote from other inquiries dedicated to the understanding of mind and the human condition . . . (Harvard Un. Press, 1990, pp. ix-x.)

Quintalism. A Jamesian type of philosophical system,* according to which there are only five kinds of things in existence, possibly (if Berkeley, Mill, and James were right), only four: at least one person (you), your mindset (shorthand for your private sense-data, imagery, and thoughts), and a-toms (bodies, the largest of which seem to be protons, neutrons, electrons, and photons). The name "Quintalism" would be a cousin of quintet, quintuplets, quintessential, etc. (*Some of the other books in which this system is presented at length are *The Wonderful Myth Called 'Science,' James Vs Darwin, Re-Meditations*, all by the author of this text.)

The thoughts that came to you while "reading Bruner" summarize with enviable shorthand the utter shambles in which "scientific psychology" currently finds itself, i.e., the utter disagreements among people who are regarded by other people as the "experts" on what makes people tick. Things are even worse in the "social sciences," where most do not even know that no such things as groups exist, where the actual, concrete facts are hid from view by abstractions as "vicious" as any that the medieval schoolmen* or the nineteenth-century absolute idealists were wedded to. They are even worse in the physical sciences where oriental pantheism is as likely to stand behind an intepretation of quantum theory as naive-realist materialism. And of course no one expects anything but a shambles among the philosophers and humanities'ists who don't care about scientific exactness in the first place. What does it all mean? Only that, if you are right to believe we are out here, you're on your own, trying to make sense of an experienced 'world' where it SEEMS as if we learn from words but don't. (*It makes no difference whether these PLAIN FOLK are called "philosophers" or "theologians.")

STARTING OVER. Let me try to pull together a few pieces of the argument. Each person old enough to have acquired his or her wordless inner model of a spread-out, ever-changing world that has his or her felt-'body' at its center and then to have learned to attach EXTRA sounds ("spoken words") to various parts of it and to have thoughts presented to him or her, has an overall view of things that deserves enough attention to call it "his or her common-sense philosophy." William James, contrary to the popular myth, did not go from psychology into philosophy. Throughout his life, his view was the one he expressed in the beginning of the first of his *Pragmatism* series of lectures: the most interesting thing about each person is her or his philosophy or world-view. That's not all. No one can understand his *Principles*'s and *Briefer Course*'s protestations of *provisional* phenomenalist-positivism (how many today could explain that?) and not know that he went to "psychology" with a "professional philosophy." The majority of people, it is fair to say, cannot read James well because they are still comfortable naive-realists.

Between 1879 and 1880, ten years before *The Principles*, he worked out the main lines of his life-long world-view. The results were published as one of his most famous essays, "The Sentiment of Rationality." The task of the philosopher, he says, is to pursue a grand unifying theory of everything that will "on the whole be more rational than that somewhat chaotic view which every one by nature carries about with him under his hat." How will the rationality be recognized? By a "strong feeling of ease, peace, rest," by a "transition from a state of puzzle and perplexity to rational comprehension," a transition "full of lively relief and pleasure." Newton's physics—which is half a theory, since it covers only whatever bodies, if any, exist—gave him all these "marks" of rationality long before the *Principia* were published, that is, when the theory existed only in Newton's mind. He did not need "society" to make his theories more rational than any previous physics. But he would never have come by them in the Creators' ordinary plan of things if he had not had access to the WORDS of Euclid, Descartes, Ptolemy, Copernicus, Kepler, Galileo and a host of others to bring him from his naive realism to his Pasteur-like preparedness to make that momentous leap from the "pull" exerted on the apple to see that the "pull" reached all the way to the moon and then to begin reweaving the threads in the tapestry of his mindset. James wove the threads of his thinking together to ask: "What is the ultimate question?"

> Let us now turn to the radical question of life—the question whether this be at bottom a moral or an unmoral universe—and see whether the method of faith may legitimately have a place there. It is really the question of materialism.

In 1890, the year of *The Principles'* publication, he outlined his answer in "The Moral Philosopher and the Moral Life":

> It would seem, too—and this is my final conclusion—that the stable and systematic moral universe for which the ethical philosopher asks is fully possible only in a world where there is a divine thinker with all-enveloping demands.

Descartes, two and a half centuries earlier, argued that no one can possibly have *good*, that is, adequate grounds for guessing (inferring) WITH CERTAINTY anything beyond her or his utterly private 'inner world' and her or his conscious awareness of the truths and errors so chaotically mixed together there, until s/he understands the reasons to be confident that the Creator of one's craving-to-know exists. Now that I have finally learned to read James, by switching back and forth between common-sense realism and phenomenalism, it is clear that his views overlap Descartes'.

P.S. In the later sections of *A Leg To Stand On*, Oliver Sacks offers a memorable account of a memorable learning career. I expect from his perceptive "To See and Not See" (5-10-93 *New Yorker*) that he'd say no born-blind, braille-reading person would be able, right after surgery, to instantly read VISIBLE! 'words' about surgery, Houdin, etc. The quantum law of habit-formation normally requires years of repetition or practice to forge the needed millions of sensation-image-thought associations. Such suspension of a law of nature would be genuine *magic*. A *miracle*. James knew, however, that the law of habit is very "loose." Hence his qualification: "Long indulgence in error is ALMOST impossible."

—IV—

Dear Bodiless-Spirit, June 10, 1993

> When I behold your heavens, the work of your fingers,
> the moon and the stars which you set in place—
> What is man that you should be mindful of him,
> or the son of man that you should care for him?
> You have made him little less than the angels,
> and crowned him with glory and honor. (Psalm 8)

Of course, that's not what ALL those poets of ancient Israel felt about us humans who are the apples of Jehovah's or Yahweh's eye:

> Lord, what is man, that you notice him;
> the son of man, that you take thought of him?
> Man is like a breath;
> his days, like a passing shadow. (Psalm 144)

    That's the trouble with believing that every word, even every jot and tittle, of the sacred library is an infallibly true message from God, who can neither fool! nor be fooled: you're left trying to explain why obvious contradictions aren't contradictions. It would all be so much easier if we just said "Oh, can't you tell the difference between prose and poetry? That's poetry, they've been granted poetic licenses, so they can write anything and it's up to you to figure out what it REALLY means." Of course, whoever has eyes to see and ears to hear knows that's what people DO. They just don't want their right hands to know, or admit!, that that's what their left hand is doing. Words! Why couldn't God—who can do anything a fairy godmother can do, and that's just about anything, as anyone who can unlimber their imagination to recall the days of childhood when mice became horses, dogs coachmen, pumpkins coaches, princes frogs (switch to a wicked witch), princesses swans, at the wave of a wand or, more prose-aically? and less poetically, at the utterance of a few words—have skipped words and communicated directly with us?

James is often thought to have condoned sloppy use of words, and at times his words are sloppy enough to be interpreted that way. Still, he BEGAN "What Pragmatism MEANS" (*Pragmatism*, lec. II) with an example of the need to clarify one's MEANING. Still more, tho, his effort to answer the question and to clarify the meaning of HIS answer was not perfectly successful. In fact, after he explained what pragmatism means and that he'd gotten it from his friend, C.S. Peirce, Peirce said "You got mine mixed up with someone else's"* and renamed his "pragmaticism" so no one would ever get confused again (!). And so it goes with James. One minute he's telling us that everyone believes changes in the brain cause changes in consciousness and that his *Principles* will prove that principle is correct, whereas next minute he's saying that "brain" names a fiction of popular speech (literally, brains don't exist), that further explanation of what words really mean will show that idealism is true (the most common meaning of that word is "a denial of matter"), that Berkeley who said apples are ideas in our mind didn't really deny matter but just said what it really is (biting into an apple is biting into ideas**?!). You would expect, wouldn't you, that someone who was so sensitive to words would have been more careful when writing his books and giving his lectures to point out that he didn't really think people had or were bodies, since he explicitly said "The thinker is the present THOUGHT"! That's exactly what Aristotle said God was, thought thinking itself. (*It seems clear that James knew his applications weren't Peirce's. **Berkeley answered this QU.)

Descartes, too, seems to have had a problem with language. On the one hand, he insisted over and over (the dedication, the preface, the outline, etc.) that to understand his *Meditations*, it is absolutely essential to get free of the senses in order to pay attention to thought, but spends most of *Meditation I* talking about the senses, then for five meditations he refers to himself as a partless, dimensionless mind, but ends *Meditation VI* by insisting that he, a mind, and his 3-D body make up only one, single thing and that that's proven by the fact that the pain we feel is not just an idea we contemplate but something that seizes or grabs us! Descartes is almost universally called a dualist (a "two-ist"), but here he insists and gives proof that he's a one-ist. Words, words, words. The vehicles through which we learn, yet so utterly confusing. Is there any way out? Can we unravel the sacred scriptures, James, Descartes, and ourselves? YES!

What Augustine noted—that God 'coaches' us—must be woven into the final picture. God addresses us directly, but normally along with what appear to be OTHERS' words. (These fit that idea, no?) Use pictures, models, maps, in all your counting and classifying, but never mistake such imagery for the thoughts you understand. Do not try to look at things that cannot be looked at, trying to picture things that have no dimensions, particularly when trying to think about thoughts. Thoughts are understood, not looked at. True, we must use pictures of thoughts floating in front of the soul, self, ego, mind, PERSON! doing the act of understanding *to* the thought, but the image and the thought are two, not one.

There is more. *Verbal contradictions are inevitable.* Sometimes they indicate inconsistencies in theory, other times the penalty of having a thought with a silent background that is context for the spoken foreground. The former we work on more, the latter we "explain" by switching out of the 1st picture to assert the thought (using a 2nd picture!). We must commit ourselves with care, avoid a FOOLISH consistency [how unfair I was to have ignored Emerson's qualification for so long!] that lands us on one of the garbage piles of *unrecognized* fiction mistaken for pinnacles of wisdom. E.g., thought-about figments such as Santa and perfect 2-D triangles are not things that exist, we only understand thoughts *about* them and even "thoughts about them" is best avoided and replaced by "we understand the thought *that* Santa and 2-D triangles do not exist," lest we wind up with those figments called forms, essences, natures-considered-in-themselves and dozens of other lures God presents to us as They play the game of wits with us that Francis Bacon noted the sacred author (THE sacred author?, there were dozens and they contradict each other) noted. And, so vast and complex is our web of beliefs, our network of associations, our criss-crossing "lingistic" references, that it takes months, even years, to fully untangle them all on a habitual basis. But it can be done. With the help of the **MOST USEFUL PICTURE EVER REVEALED.**

There are in the history of civilization certain dates which stand out as marking either the boundaries or the culminations of critical epochs . . . Such a date is 1642 of our epoch, the year in which occurred the death of Galileo and the birth of Newton. This date marks the center of that period of about a hundred years during which the scientific intellect of Europe was framing that First Physical Synthesis which has remained down to our own times as the basis of science . . . Galileo represents the assault [on the Aristotelian tradition] and Newton the victory . . . (1923)

A brief, and sufficiently accurate, description of the intellectual life of the European races during the succeeding two centuries and a quarter up to our own times [1925] is that they have been living upon the accumulated capital of ideas provided for them by the genius of the seventeenth century . . . The whole development of thought occupied exactly two generations. It commenced with Galileo and ended with Newton's *Principia* . . . [T]he lives of Descartes and Huygens fall within the period occupied by these great terminal figures. The issue of the combined labours of these four men has some right to be considered as the greatest single intellectual success which mankind has achieved. In estimating its size, we must consider the completeness of its range. It constructs for us a vision of the material universe, and it enables us to calculate the minutest detail of a particular occurrence . . . (1925)

These pieces of rhetoric from the pen of A.N. Whitehead (from "First Physical Synthesis" and *Science and the Modern World*'s ch. III, passim) should be a centerpiece of all modern education. Of course, like Carl Becker, we must be prepared to cut through the rhetoric and say what the literally true facts are. For instance, there are no races, this 'IT' is not a single success, and the truth is that 'single intellectual success' is shorthand for what many separate thinkers, each of whom began as a complete dummy in his crib and each of whom had to learn first-hand every single thing he ever learned. But rhetoric or more-than-usual use of imagery can serve important functions, when millions of minute daily facts, by selective attention, are snapped into an enlightening alternative-angle shape. The reason Whitehead's snippets should be a centerpiece of today's education is clear. *If we are going to stand on the shoulders of giants, we must learn to climb onto them.* In an age of democracy, we must all learn to see for ourselves. In an era when knowledge has given us the power to command nature to make this planet once again uninhabited, we need the truth about ourselves and the moral purpose of life. Though he himself rejected it, Whitehead put his finger right on the most important outcome of the revolution: *it enables us to calculate the minutest detail of a particular occurrence.*

The *minutest detail* means the exact place and time. Aristotle's physics was built on naive realism, with a confidence that if we can hold our hand up to the sun and SEE that it is solid, not just swarming subatomic gnats dancing the unbelievably difficult choreographies twentieth-century researchers are still learning more about, then it IS solid. Our hand is also flesh-colored, warm, motionless when we want it to be, attached to our wrist so seamlessly and to all the other "parts" of the body that, unless a meat cleaver is used, there really aren't SEPARATE "parts" but only the potentiality for the one body to be hacked into actually separate things. Aristotle's biology built on that solidly commonsensical basis: if someone's arm is severed in an accident and lying on a table or if some ghoul rips a person's eye out and puts it on a table, the things on the table are not an arm and not an eye. An arm's only an arm as long as it is an appendage of a body, and now it is an arm-shaped body in its own right; an eye's only an eye so long as it is part of an organism that uses it to see with, so this is only an eye-shaped piece of tissue.

> Decisions on the right or true answers to the question "What IS it?" are critical when policies hinging on the answers are critical. "Is it a baby, a biologically alive organism, a piece of tissue, a part of the woman's body?" Or, "Is it a comatose person, brain-dead living organism, vegetable, assemblage of organs for transplant surgery?" Or, "All life is sacred" . . . Is that every piece of moss, every still-attached tomato, every bacterium, every flea and tick?

If the inspired writers had known their Thales and Aristotle better, they'd not have used such **OXYMORONS** as "The idols of the nations are silver and gold, the handiwork of men. They have mouths but speak not, they have eyes but see not" (psalm 135). Thales said, "Let's call a spade 'a spade': things may look like they are different, like pieces of silver, blocks of ice, slices of tomato, warm flesh, but everything is really one, really the same, really water," which means what the inspired writers had in mind were EITHER idols OR finely carved blocks of silver OR gold, but not THREE things at once. Aristotle would have said, "Those aren't eyes, either!"

What is an oxymoron? A fancy word that people who like to appear smart substitute for the real words which are "A contradiction in terms." Oxymorons are used like crazy at wakes: "The dead man is over there in the box" (it's only a man if it's alive; a dead human-shaped body is literally a cadaver; which is why pumping bullets into a man gets you the chair or life, but not pumping bullets into a cadaver), "Uncle Charlie looks better than he did the last time I visited him in the hospital" (if uncle charlie is still hanging around and hears you say that, he may have a bone to pick with you when you're an angel, too, and join him in heaven), "She looks like she's finally found peace from all her troubles" (ask embalmers what their tricks are and perhaps you can look that way even before you croak and it's no longer you that looks), etc.

A 'sense' that we are contradicting ourselves—when one piece of the puzzle won't fit—is one of God's hints that we should do some rethinking. Metaphors are fine, but sloppy use of words *when precision is called for* reveals poor-quality thinking. In an era of powerfully effective physics, those who call themselves educated must learn physics' lessons. If anything is certain, it is that nothing physical is colored; reference to skin color is useful fiction or else it's an anachronism. If anything is sure even before the Waxahachie Waste is completed, it is that there is no brain or human body at all, so references to brain death or physical death are literally false, however true it is that, as Berkeley noted, God offers present really-existing sense-data as signs of sense-data to come. And, if brains and larger-than-atoms bodies do not exist, then money and national debts and deficits don't either. Anyone who thinks there are dollar bills, colored dollar bills, and numbers on dollar bills, should logically conclude there's a white house and a man there, too. Those who say the meaning of words consists in their proper use betray their lack of ability to use words correctly, and if they define "correctly" as "the way society approves of," let them point out society to us and tell us what "society" says is the correct way to refer to what is growing in a woman's womb. I am here slipping into naive realism to show why Russell was right about it. It contradicts itself. Or would, if there literally was any "it"! You know what I mean. Don't you say that?

The beauty of the revolutionS in the thinking of Galileo, etc., is that they show us how to make our thoughts almost perfectly clear to one another. Again, the key is in the thought cued by "It constructs for us a vision of the material universe, and it enables us to calculate the minutest detail of a particular occurrence." Aristotle's loose naive realism was replaced by mathematically-precise description. "As a rock falls, it speeds up because it's getting closer to home" is the literal meaning of Aristotle's theory of "natural motion." Galileo said: "Let's see exactly how fast it speeds up." "Throwing a rock up in the air is forcing it to do something against its nature" is the literal meaning of Aristotle's theory of "violent motion." Newton said: "It's so natural that we can predict with mathematical precision exactly how it will behave, and the laws are identical for its speeding up when moving 'naturally' and its slowing down when moving 'unnaturally.'" Aristotle said, "Things in the sky are different from those on the ground," but every learner today who believes in bodies at all knows it's been discovered that what goes on inside the sun is the identical process that threatens to make a nuclear hell here on earth. That discovery came about, in part, by learning about photons and how their mathematically exact behavior correlates with nuclear events and how spectrums of seen colors in private visual fields can be used to infer unseen photons' behavior from which further inferences can be made about the unseen nuclear events. Exactness pays. Aristotle was satisfied to know that sound doesn't travel instantly, but today's theorists insist on knowing that it doesn't travel 741.5 miles per second but 741.1 (*N.Y. Times*, 5-27-86). Aristotle was satisfied to think that simply watching a sunrise proved that light travels instantly, but now we know that photons travel so slowly (299,792,458 meters per second) that it takes 8 minutes for one to get just from the sun to the earth and 160,000 years to travel from supernova 1987A to the earth. The seventeenth century reached back and joined hands with Pythagoras this way:

EVERY SINGLE A-TOM IS EXACLY LOCATED.

"A-tom" is a convenient substitute for "an unsplit body," most of which are thought to be protons, neutrons, electrons, & photons. If any exist. Whitehead summarized the revolution by noting that it means that, IF YOU COULD STOP THE WORLD to take inventory, you would discover that every a-tom's location vis-a-vis every other could be described with any desired degree of exactness. A-toms are exactly where God moves them to. God works with absolute, total precision. True, Whitehead himself was not bold enough to adopt their view, and he showed his disapproval by dubbing it "The Fallacy of Misplaced Concreteness." Still, he understood it and praised its clarity. You, too, can understand these thoughts that are coming to you, isn't that true?

Whitehead rejected it because many who defended it ignored human consciousness or made it useless. The French mathematician, Pierre LaPlace, was one. **IF**, he said, a supermind knew the exact whereabouts of every single atom at just one single moment, knew its exact state of rest or motion, and also knew the laws of nature [he meant Newton's laws], that supermind [God!] could predict the future course of history, i.e., of those bodies' meaningless shufflings through dark, empty space, for the rest of time, down to the last second. That view, that gigantic act of faith made by so many of the materialists James had to contend with, is called variously, determinism, mechanism, deterministic mechanism, and those are only English callings. And, because even some of the people who deny they are determinists are, much the way some murderers who deny they are murderers are, it's important to look for the thought or meaning behind the clues, as every reader of Orwell and his talk of doubletalk knows. But, by revealing the fact that They work with mathematic precision, our Creating Parents made it possible to finally crack Their code.

Begin as always by situating **YOURSELF** in the **BIG PICTURE**. First, mentally draw three coordinates: an up-down line thru you from your head to feet, a right-left line thru your chest, and a back-front line intersecting the other two inside your chest. (You may wish to have them intersect inside your cranium.) Then get ready to see that **YOU AND IT ARE REVERSIBLE.** Zoom out to the edge of the universe, look back and tell exactly how far away the Milky Way is and in what direction from you, then describe with exactness where our local star-sun is, go to the carousel earth (stopped till the inventory is done), map the exact location of all 5.5 billion human bodies (for the moment, you can pretend the human-body-shaped-swarming a-toms are solid human bodies) vis-a-vis all others and vis-a-vis every single letter of every single page of print and every single air-molecule whose movement will be counted as part of a sound-wave and, lastly, every single photon. Do not overlook the fact that, if Einstein could imagine riding the crest of a light-wave, a more energetic thinker can imagine zillions of individual crests or photon-lines arranged like military parades (through Red Square) or football bands doing half-time parades (in the Los Angeles Colosseum).

P.S. At the same time, be warned against being intimidated by Einstein's bad use of the discredited Illogical Positivist verifiability principle in his denial that we can meaningfully think about "simultaneity" in this "Stop the World All At Once" thought-experiment. In the 17th edition of *Relativity: the Special and General Theory*, he was still saying "The concept [of 'simultaneity'] does not exist for the physicist until he has the possibility of discovering whether or not it is fulfilled in an actual case" (Ch. VIII). No one has ever seen a photon, let alone seen any hit in front of and behind a train at the same time. Even if you COULD see through your private, nonphysical visual field of colors, do you think you could prove that any two photons hit your retinas at the same time?! We can take an invented concept (Einstein said that even our concepts of numbers are creations of our imagination), use it to imagine unobserved and unobservable bodies (Einstein agreed with Russell's denial of naive realism), and come to understand how trapped Einstein was in the myth of mechanist determinism that James refuted over and over. His "use" of non-euclidean "straight" for common-sense "curved," his faith in non-existent "fields" and "forces," his belief in space-time when not even space or time really exist, were other sources of his considerable confusions. If you can recall being able to understand "at the same time" the two times it was used in this paragraph, you should have evidence that you know what I meant and got thoughts *similar to mine*, even though you'll never be able as a physicist or anything to observe mine. In fact, Einstein's postulate that nothing can travel faster than the speed of light only confirms the complete privacy of each human's experience: no one sees till the photons, if any such exist, reach person-al eyes and send impulses to skull-encased brains. The PICTURE is clear. End.

Now notice that your visual field and your body sensations are never far apart. Hence an ealier correction: you may picture yourself enjoying a visual-field picture of the universe as seen from an outermost galaxy, but YOU, the VIEWER, are wherever your [sense-data OF] your feet, your shoulders, your tongue inside your mouth, your eyelids and eye-muscles around your eyes are. When you check to see where you have been during that imaging, you'll discover your feet have never left the planet earth. Or what, commonsensically, *seems* like the nearest portion of the surface of the continent you're presently occupying. So all of the bodies in the universe are exactly located vis-a-vis you.

Now for the payoff. Once your inner-model or picture is in place (stop and PAY ATTENTION to how natural it FEELS to imagine your self in the midst of a universeful of galaxies, riding on this planet twirling like a top as it circles around a sun-star in an arm of the Milky Way which itself is slowly twisting), it is easy to attach one whole **SENSE-DATUM** package of colors, sounds, odors, tastes, etc., one whole volume of **MEMORY-IMAGERY**, and one total **THOUGHT** (the second most supreme mystery!) to each of the 5.5 billion human **BODIES,** and then to add one separate immaterial, conscious, free-to-choose-what-to-believe **PERSON-BEING** to each of those three-part mindsets ("mindset" is shorthand for each of the sense-data + memory-imagery + thought packages). Now, whenever you think about a thought, make certain you mentally keep track of whose thought it is and where it is located, regardless of how many things or chinese boxes of things (the earlier page's description of plays inside plays inside movies) or how many imagined laws inside laws (recall the passage from Kant) are part of a single, total thought. Most of all, do not lose track of the relativity of "inside" and "outside." With relation to everything OUTSIDE your mind(set), stream of consciousness, experiential-field, total-thought (the thought's the thing!), everything you directly experience is INSIDE. But, until you discover that what you took to be "starry skies above" and "these two hands I see" are AS MUCH INSIDE as the tickles and pains are, it SEEMS that they (the phenomena upon which Kant says your mind imposes spread-outness) are OUTSIDE and the tickles and pains are INSIDE. Thus, what Kohler refers to as "the world as we find it, naively" (the one BEHIND which Galileo, etc., discovered the other, very different one) is the one James says everyone divides in a different place. That is because each of us divides our own! You needn't believe any of this. You do understand, though, don't you?

That brings up the trickiest subject of all, time. This entire subject was dealt with at length in the [unpublished] prequel, *Will You Control Your Imagination?*, to which this is the sequel. So what's in between the before and the after? If the past is time that no longer exists and the future is time that doesn't yet exist, then what's in between them? The present, we say. But there's no present, either, only persons, thoughts, imagery, sense-data, and a-toms which are never in more than one place at a time, and not even that since all places are imaginary. Here, more than any where else, is where we must be like hound-dogs, keeping our nose to the ground of concrete experience, following the scent of good sense, lest we suddenly get yanked up into the clouds of *vicious* abstraction (James used the phrase more freely as he got older and wanted to make sure people HEARD him!). Despite appearances, it is July 6 if it's anything, though that is an arbitrary set of ink-mark notations useful for taking you to an exact location in your world-history record book that, if it exists at all, exists as a combination of memory-sensing-anticipation "in the present." The formula is this: there is no time, only things that were not always what they are and things that will not always remain what they are, though what they are is the only thing they are. And the only things that are are persons, one of whom is you, thoughts, one of which is the one you are understanding, etc.

Our Creating Parents have added one more major trick. To our expanding common-sense model of our neighborhood, they add a mix of "cultural beliefs," that range from those of our "family" (parents), to those of our "neighborhood," our "church," our "nation," etc. At first, **some persons appear as "AUTHORITIES."** At least until we are old enough to know enough to re-think what we originally just take-for-granted are true opinions. Our parents are infallible to us at first. Then we learn they're not. In the course of these pages, I have described who my early UNQUESTIONED authorities were and what considerations led me to switch my allegiance to other authorities. That, too, must not be ignored. What appear to be *the results* of technology convince me that certain theories are to be preferred to, say, parts of my original naive realism, to Aristotle's physics, to Aquinas' view on concepts, etc. The "fit" with other views is a criterion when I decide which thoughts, seemingly from "experts," I will cite in support of my views. I rely on your sense of which theories "fit together" when I present lists of quotes on major issues.

Consider what follows as an Argument from Authority for the Big Picture on which this work is based. Descartes', Berkeley's, Kant's, Kohler's, and Pearson's model is as defensible in 1993 as it was when James was living, the same way that "The earth spins around the sun" is as defensible today as it was at the time of Galileo. P.S. Do not fail to notice how universal is the tendency for each author to speak for all of us at the moment of insisting he is alone. All slip from "I" to "**WE**." It is a God-given tendency to insure that we'll not forget our obligations toward each other. P.S.S. Also notice that the same theories that make it easier to communicate with each other show that we are utterly cut off from any direct contact with them.

> It must be premised, that it is wholly impossible absolutely to prove the presence or absence of consciousness in anything but one's own brain, though, by analogy, we are justified in assuming its existence in other men. (Huxley, in his essay, "Animal Automatism," 1874.)

> To be specific, when Dr. Watson watches rats in mazes, what he knows, apart from difficult inferences, are certain events in himself. The behavior of rats can only be inferred by the help of physics, and is by no means to be accepted as something accurately knowable by direct observation . . . To return to the physiologist observing another man's brain: what the physiologist sees is by no means identical with what happens in the brain he is observing . . . In a strict sense, he cannot observe anything in the other brain, but only the percepts which he himself has when he is suitably related to that brain. (B. Russell, *An Outline of Philosophy*.)

> Some existentialists have held that man is ultimately isolated from his fellow man because all of his contact with other humans is indirect and mediated by the senses. No information from the environment ever reaches the brain without first getting by the sensory receptors and the neural pathways; man never has immediate knowledge of

432

the world's objects, other people, or anything. Psychology has thus come to consider the physical world as *stimulus*, its effects on a person as sensation, and his interpretation of the effects as perceptions. (CRM Books, *Psychology Today: an Introduction*, p.255.)

In the words of V.B. Mountcastle, the dean of living psycho-biologists: "Each of us believes himself to live directly within the world that surrounds him, to sense objects and events precisely, and to live in real and current time. I assert that these are perceptual illusions. Contrarily, each of us confronts the world from a brain linked to what is 'out there' by a few million fragile sensory nerve fibers, our only information channels, our lifelines to reality." (R. Restak, *The Brain: The Last Frontier*, p.426)

Second, we have used "person" as the first argument* of Perceive. In some contexts this argument should be defined more broadly, in others more narrowly. Psychologists who study the perceptual capacities of animals, for example, might wish to interpret this argument as "living organism," and workers in the field of artificial intelligence might wish to extend it even to machines having certain capacities for sensing the environment. On the other hand, given the present state of neurophysiology, the only perceptions to which you have direct access are your own, so in those cases where you wish to stick your neck out very little you might wish to limit this argument to yourself, to "ego." (*Language and Perception*, G.A. Miller and P.N. Johnson-Laird, 1976, p.31; *your 'world' hangs on it!)

Philosophers have questioned 'Other Minds'—consciousness, awareness, or sensation in other people. Since we cannot enter anothers' mind, how can we verify that he has a mind . . . We cannot prove consciousness in others, but neither can we produce effective doubt to challenge what we all believe to be true. So it is rational to accept that other people have 'inner worlds' of experience.

But it is an unanswered question whether 'lower' animals have experience—or experiences at all like ours. (R.L. Gregory, *Eye and Brain*, 1990 edition, p.226.)

"Our only channel of information about the world is the impact of external forces on our sensory surfaces. So says science itself. There is no clairvoyance. How, then, can we have parlayed this meager sensory input into a full-blown theory of the world? This is itself a scientific question." (Quoted from W.V. Quine on the back cover of the 1990 paper-back edition of his *The Roots of Reference*.)

It is evening, I'm tired. To keep going would require too much effort. Painful effort. I'll see you tomorrow. Ciao.

—V—

Dear Must-Be Scientist, June 11, 1993

> At that last crossroad where thought hesitates, many men have arrived and even some of the humblest. They then abdicated what was most precious to them, their life. Others, princes of the mind, abdicated likewise, but they initiated the suicide of the mind, thought in its purest revolt. The real effort is to stay there, rather, in so far as that is possible, and to examine closely the odd vegetation of those distant regions. Tenacity and acumen are privileged spectators of this inhuman show in which absurdity, hope, and death carry on their dialogue. (*The Myth of Sisyphus.*)

Why Control Your Imagination? The question is clearly one of motivation. The short answer to WHY? is "For all three motives: out of love for others, to be happy yourself, and—if neither of those move/motivate you—from a sense of duty."

The answer can be expanded upon. First, control it for the sake of others. In endlessly varied degrees, each of us plays our part as others' environment. Success in their cradle-to-grave dash to outgrow infant-ignorance and learn the truth, all of it!, will be delayed if we fail to propose the truth or, worse, if we propose error in its place. Second, for the sake of your own enjoyment of the truth, all of it! Thirdly, because—even if you will always be left free not to—you are obliged to. You MUST control your imagination if you are ever to learn the truth and thus fulfill your duty to others or add to your enjoyment.

The rest of these pages and the prequel expand a bit more on this question which is like all others insofar as it can be discussed ad inf, i.e., expandable to *ad infinitum*, expandable to from-here-to-eternity, *ad inf.* The reason it can be discussed from here to eternity is simple: each one of us gets one last word, our own. That means others get their own. That often means I will have another of my own. For instance, when I think you have just criticized what you think is an error of mine, I pray I will be motivated to acknowledge it (if it is an error) as honestly as King David did (he, not his brilliant son, is the one most of us regard as the saint) or else that I will hold my peace out of consideration for you, or else, out of consideration for the innocent who may suffer more than they'd profit if I allow your challenge to go unchallenged (grrr!, you just made me realize how poor I am at this), that God will provide yet another of that endless, Chomsky'an supply of last words* so I can effectively rebut your error. I must pray, tho, to have the wisdom to objectively assess your criticism, the wisdom to know whether the error is yours or is mine. I also must pray to have the good sense not to assume I know what you meant by the 'wording' of your criticism, so that I can ask you to clarify if necessary. I could go on and on, but I won't, since I assume you are old enough to now dig into your vast stock of memory-experience to understand what I meant when, on July 8, I chose to stop here and move on. (*Though not here, since I have an auto-imposed limit, the reason I have been doing so much rewriting and rewriting and . . . Familiarity with what appear to be others' objections against the views expressed in these pages, I might go on *ad inf*, had I not decided back at the end of August 1989 to begin imposing pre-set limits on whatever I write and then change my mind only for the most reasonable of reasons.)

Those are the rules that everyone in the world must sooner or later choose to live by. As James noted in his final *Talks to Students*, the two halves of the population—rich and poor—tend to be utterly blind to one another's mindset-worlds, a truth Robert Coles has expanded upon. The poor think the rich are spoiled, insensitive, and mean; and they object when someone points it out to them, as Andrew Carnegie did (by noting that there was a time in history when not even native chieftans enjoyed the conveniences today's "poor" do). The rich think the poor are lazy, clearly just waiting for the government—that is, hard-working folks who are paid by rich taxpayers—to take care of them, too shiftless to keep their neighborhoods clean, proof positive that Freud was right about the correlation between the ability to impose control over the libido and the level of civilization achievable, etc. Karl Marx proved scientifically that both are wrong, that *homo faber* is just a huge caterpillar undergoing another of its periodic, scheduled metamorphoses on its way to butterflydom, that classes aren't wicked, it's an historically determined matter of a socio-economic structure readying for an overhaul. Messiah-expecters have it on divine say-so that all this IS the result of wickedness and that there is only a short time remaining till Armageddon. Some know from Locke's proof about the origin of private property rights that "This land is our land, because our long-dead ancestors worked to make it what it is." Others, again, have Moses' proof that "This land is our land, because God Himself cleared it for our long-dead ancestors." Hence we have wars, skirmishes, embargoes, sieges, gunfights, ostracisms, discriminations, with all of the horrible-to-see emaciation, maiming, wailing, displacement, and other visible signs of private pain that results. *Ad inf.*

Until all learn what James meant by "A Certain Blindness" (e.g., by enough discussions of *To Kill A Mockingbird, Fiddler on the Roof, The Chalk Garden, West Side Story*, and MANY similar values-clarifying, audio-visual fictions), until all bring cataracts-removed vision to the peace table, until all join in trying to find compromises that promise the least pain and most enjoyment, bad results reported by good media can be expected to continue.

WAIT, WAIT, WAIT, WAIT!!!

All of the preceding is supposed to explain why we should control our imaginations in order to discover the truth. We are supposed to want truth because so much pain and suffering is avoidable error. But a gigantic mindshift was sneaked in. To wit . . .

The last couple of pages are posed in *common-sense* terms. In terms of my professed-ly true thinking, God is the source of everyone's thoughts, FALSE as well as true. God is even the source of the thoughts I have when *I* talk to my *self* (do you REALLY believe there are two of you when you talk to your self?), and the "my voice" sound that I *hear* as my vocal cords, whose muscular exertion I *feel* making them, is from God (does one of you hear and your double feel?). **AND GOD TEACHES US OUR TWO BIGGEST ERRORS!**

God is the source of two grand deceptions. There's Grand Deception I, your growing-up naive-realist view that what you see is a book with an independent reality of its own, and G-D II, the illusion that you are getting thoughts from another human, me, as you read this book. If that "voice" of our conscience is God's voice telling us we must learn the truth in order to at least TRY to tell it, then how can God who has always known it be excused? Such thoughts quite clearly crossed Descartes' mind as he wrote his opening Meditation. Clearly, too, he rejected them. But only after devoting a surprising amount of his Meditations to justifying the ways of God to himself. Most people believe he was so wrong about other things that they pay little heed to Descartes effort to remove the contradiction between his own proneness to error and God's supposed all-goodness. So . . .

The claim that faith in God involves an oxymoron—the existence of an all-powerful God ABLE to prevent evil, who is an all-loving God WANTING evil to be prevented, but a God who DOESN'T prevent all evil—has for a long time been the most powerful argument against the existence of God. Atheist after atheist has used the existence of evil as proof positive that God does not exist. So convinced was he of this argument that J.L. Mackie (1917-81) entitled one of his books, *The Miracle of Theism.*

Whoever is ruthlessly thorough about this rethinking business, whoever takes up the challenge passed on by Plato who implies he is only repeating Socrates' own words from his second trial-speech, namely, "The unexamined life is not a worthy sort of life," whoever professes to believe as Galileo, Descartes, Newton and Locke—all anti-naive-realist, matter-spirit "dualists"—that God gave us a mind to put to work, not to play ghetto-defense with, must take Albert Camus' *Myth of Sisyphus* challenge seriously. We must not abdicate the life of reason, must not join the suicide of the mind. Rather must we stay on, go as far as we can into these "far out!" regions, exert our tenacity and acumen. **IF GOD EXISTS**, especially if we have been introduced to the clash of doctrines that Whitehead baptized "an opportunity, not a disaster" and have experienced the cognitive discomfort that is God's way of beckoning us to continue our search, then . . .

The first thing we must do is rip the mask of euphemism from our descriptions of God's doings. God does not "permit" sharp pain, lingering agony, savage torture, broken-hearted anguish, hell-like despair, and so on. It is absurd to think that God stands by, hands off, allowing some sort of "natural forces" do their thing. God does not just create nature, program it with built-in "laws," and let us deal with the results the best way we can. When I was young, I learned that, prior to the Original Sin of Adam and Eve, God had made a special arrangement whereby the laws of nature were suspended in case someone fell from a high branch of an apple tree, fell into a swift-current river without knowing how to swim, accidentally began choking on a fish-bone. The arrangement was named "The Preternatural Gifts" (to set them off from supernatural and natural ones), and it was revoked as a result of Adam and Eve's damned fruit-tasting. We wouldn't even have had to work if those oh-so-nice parents of ours hadn't blown it for all of us. These views are "deist" views. Pure rubbish.

God-believers (e.g., Job) have always wondered . . . St. Augustine quite correctly noted that "evil" is a thing-ification. An act of the will (well, of the person) may be evil, but evil is not some thing, just as nothing is not some thing or something. "So that when I now asked what is iniquity, I realized that it was not a substance but a swerving of the will which is turned toward lower things and away from" God (*Confessions*, VII:xvi). This is the hole-in-the-apple theory, absolutely indispensable for those who do not want to get suck(er)ed into the beautiful book of abstractions Alan Watts called *The Supreme Identity*. Think of an apple, perfect in every way except for a tiny, clean hole bored out by a grub that hatched inside: what's there is all good, our objection is that we ALSO demand to have what's missing. The evil we call "sin" names an all-good act from which CONFORMITY WITH THE MORAL LAW is missing. But pain is an actually sensed thing, a given. Not a hypothesis, no "Doctor, I'd like you to check and see *if* I have a headache." It grips, it seizes, it overwhelms you. Pains are situated, often quite pinpointedly, among the spread-out phenomena Kant and James drew attention to: I don't think of my feet when you speak of stomach aches, nor do I think of my head when I'm reminded of my first tetanus shot (right in the sole of my foot where the rusty nail came back out of after I stepped on it), and heart-ache is aptly named. And God, acutely conscious of what we will feel and ready to see what we'd like as "our reaction," creates those pains and sticks them to us directly. So, though Augustine's "what's missing" analogy is a wonderful antidote to one reification, it can—in the wrong hands—become a denial of concrete experience. Even the good suffer what we're tempted to call "bad": really bad pain!

St. Thomas weighed and rejected the direct-action view presented here. He held a modified deism. God's hand IS right there in every single event in the universe, but only as providing created beings with premoving and conserving force, a supplier of gas to make the car's engine work on its own. He wrote a long defence in *Summa Contra Gentes* against "The view of those who subtract from natural things their proper actions." His theme? The idea of God delegating some power to creatures is more befitting a God than the idea of God keeping all the power, so that must be what God did. (See Bk. III, ch.69-70). Hume's analysis of causality, a beautifully strategized assault on every claim that we learn FROM our senses what "cause" means, is the definitive answer to such "It would be nice" arguments. The question is about *facts*, not about our personal *tastes* in universe-designing, and to find out the facts we have to check experience: how DOES God actually work things? Berkeley's analysis shows, as clearly as it shows any thing that, if there is ANY identifiable cause of our sense-data ("ideas" is no longer a good choice of terms!), including the species named "pain," that cause is God. But, God the torturer?!

Is it any wonder that people who make themselves familiar with William James' life are suspicious of the "conscious" reasons why he, knowing as much as he did of depression, mental illness, human abnormalities, all those horrors he goes to great lengths to catalogue in the *Variety*'s lecture on "The Sick Soul," simply would not give up his belief in God? **BUT WHY?** What motive kept him from becoming an atheist*? In the first *Pluralist* lecture where he said he'd say nothing about materialism, he also said he'd have nothing to say about "old-fashioned dualistic theism," he once wrote he found the Bible "so human a book that I don't see how belief in its divine authorship can survive the reading of it," so why didn't he become an atheist? (*Before I learned to read the "James'ian" language, I wasn't sure he wasn't an atheist. Sometimes I was sure he'd come down on the side of "God exists," but on the next reading I'd decide that he bobbed and weaved so carefully that, like Jung, he only wanted to talk *about* the value of belief in God for OTHER people, but without ever making a personal commitment. Then I discovered that "Absolute" didn't mean what he meant by "God," and that he did believe in God. His final set of lectures, *A Pluralist Universe*, can be read as an effort to focus a lifetime of study onto one single question: What is God like?, and what is the real relation between God and us? He kept trying to LOOK, to PICTURE, and the best parts of his magnificent mindset never gelled, but God was in the wings and made regular stage-appearances.)

One believing dis-believer put the question to believers in God this way: "Just how much evil would it take to get you to admit God does NOT love you?" Some scientists—their tone of voice SEEMS unmistakable—add "And what more proof would it take to get you to admit God does not even exist?" Illogical positivists once claimed the statement "God exists" is meaningless. But why didn't James become an atheist? Or at least an agnostic?

WAIT, WAIT, WAIT, WAIT!!!!

This letter is addressed to you as a scientist, and the question is not about OTHERS' motives, but YOURS. If YOU don't believe in God, why NOT? If YOU DO believe in brains and matter, WHY? The belief-question runs in every direction. Here, it sounds like this: "Just what will it take to get YOU to admit YOU have no evidence apart from strong habit for YOUR **FAITH** in a physical world? And other people? Other people's feelings and thoughts? Even that any of them believe that God loves us all?" The aim is to push the belief question as far as it can be pushed, as far as Descartes pushed it. What good reasons are there for choosing ANY belief at all over ANY other belief, even that there are beliefs, any recognizable difference among beliefs, any choosing of beliefs, anyone to choose beliefs, and so on.

> In short, THE question is not "Why is there something rather than nothing?" THE question is "If you can grasp 'Why isn't there nothing?,' then you understand what 'There is nothing' means, so why don't you believe there is nothing?, Why have you chosen to believe there is something and that you have chosen to believe it?"

The thesis here is that, having read and understood thus far, any claim you may still have to "good-faith ignorance" will end by the time you finish the next sentence, and if you do not read it because you do not want your good faith to end, then it's already too late: when we sense that we have an obligation to learn, eg., whether that is a deer as we'd like to believe or a hunter as we fear, our decision to NOT-FIND-OUT is not excusable if (a)there is no good reason to make a best guess and to act decisively and if (b)harm to others results. You can never again say with honesty that the thought "I have an obligation to rethink these matters as part of my duty to learn WHY, IN THE FACE OF EXPERT TESTIMONY, I BELIEVE IN BRAINS, ETC., so that I can make truth rather than error available to others."

Why is knowing truth important? First, YOUR future depends upon it. The law in THIS universe is clearly "Might makes right." **If there IS a God**, and if it is part of God's plan to hold us to a strict accounting re the Golden Rule IF WE KNOW IT or to whatever other version of "What should be done and what ought not to be done" (what not-severely retarded human never hears that certain things are "wrong"?) then we take our chances that the source of PRESENT pains does not have a long-range plan for balancing the scales of justice. (It is wrong to suspect people of bad faith without justification, but some people who say that God can't possibly be good and allow all this world's suffering, turn around and say God is too good for there to actually be a hell.) And **if there is NO God**, then WHY should I sacrifice my pleasure for poor people who won't get here from the Third World until after I'm dead and why, ABOVE ALL, should *I* care about the NEXT GENERATION of the unborn? That is the final question Camus reached when he re-thought Marxists' infliction of pain and death on INNOCENT individuals of THIS generation in order to make life more pleasurable for LATER ones. Why should one life be sacrificed for another? Why should one single pleasure of mine be sacrificed for that of some one else?

i- Either there IS a good reason why YOU should care about others EXCEPT from self-interest, i.e., so YOUR pleasure can be increased or YOUR pain diminished. (Epicurus said: Never break a law, you can't be sure you'll not talk in your beer or your sleep!, and Don't get married, THAT's a hassle.)

ii- Or else there isn't. And if what you think would be nice, clashes with what someone else thinks would be better, you WILL do whatever you do, WITHOUT any reason that is BETTER than "That's what I felt like doing" or

"That's what I wanted to do" or "That's just what I did,"
ad inf.

If there IS a God and if part of God's plan is to give joy in a measure with God's willingness to give joy, but to withhold joy in a measure with God's willingness to withhold joy, then you may have to (a) satisfy yourself with whatever pleasure YOU think Sisyphus was given by God (pride and stubbornness, "I did it MY way!", do bring a measure of satisfaction, at least FOR NOW) and (b) then sit with Dives outside the gate because you refuse the invitation to join the company of lovers.

That is a second reason why the truth is important. There ARE many people who WANT to do what is right, but who—like the kids featured in the 5-24-93 *Time* cover-story, "Kids, Sex & Values: What's a kid supposed to think?"—are muddled by the stupidities uttered by naked emperors and left in the dark by experts' deafening silence on other things. Frederick Douglass, a one-time slave, said that "When a great truth once gets abroad in the world, no power on earth can imprison it or prescribe its limits or suppress it." Wrong! This century has shown how precarious truth can be. How else explain the update on naive materialism at the end of the twentieth century found in the 4-20-92 *Newsweek* with its "Is The Mind An Illusion?" (follow-up to its "The Brain: Science Opens New Windows on the Mind" cover-story). Subtitle: "Yes, say the philosopher-scientists. The brain is a machine. We have no selves, no souls. How do they know? Well, it's just a matter of faith." Here is where we learn the truth? That those who believe Descartes was right "are obsolete as manual typewriters"?!

Consider the opposite. Since the largest bodies are a-toms, there are no brains or biological organisms. To "make sense" of our sense-data—what would the shapes and colors on the movie-screen be without the Snow-White-plot-THOUGHTS to go with them?—these fictions are needed, but fictions they remain. Understanding the truth about the human makeup clarifies issues relating to IDEAS about sex, affection, love, and moral commitments. i-HE asks HER to prove her love for him by offering what seems to be her body to provide him with pleasure. If she follows the Golden Rule in a stupid manner, she will know that it is HIS pleasure, not hers, that she should consider. She goes to bed with him. Or else she says "But *I* may get pregnant;

you can just walk away. Do you know what that means FOR ME? Prove you love me by taking a cold shower instead." If he follows the Golden Rule, he showers, tho if he's willing to pay, the 6-21-93 *Time* explains that there are women willing to make a *quid pro quo* exchange. (Men are at times reputed to have been the first *customers* in history.) ii-Then, in addition to that **non-physical "physical" pleasure** which is always quite localized in men, though Freudians have argued for a century about which is the true locale in women (it is a grave error to mistake the cause—tastes in causes vary radically—with the localized effect), there is a whole range of **feelings** known as liking, affection, infatuation, etc., that are of an entirely different nature. (Perhaps that semi-fusion of the "genital" pleasure which is in the mind with strong affection or attraction, also in the mind, is a good example of what James wanted to say when he denied that we experience discrete atoms of sensation . . . tho they often exist apart, a fact normally taken as evidence of "real" distinctness.) Last, there is the iii-**unfelt decision** to choose what does not bring pleasure in order not to cause pain, to prefer causing pain to obtain pleasure, to choose what causes and brings short-term pain for the sake of giving long-term pleasure, and so on (see the last two chapters, etc.).

An aside. It took awhile to learn that "Love God with your whole heart" did not mean liking God more than mama and daddy, and I would have been horrified if I'd known the idea some people would get if they heard "Go make love to God." Isn't it comforting to learn through the news media that "the scientific branch of psychology" is about to begin research on "love" and thus take it off the hands of poor benighted philosophers and humanities'ists? End of aside.

Now, applying the Golden Rule wisely, that is, with an awareness that the neighbors we MUST love are ALL other humans will require careful consideration of such issues as: What is best for the training of new generations of young people who must learn that loving means unselfishly attending to the welfare of OTHERS and not seeking chiefly your OWN pleasure, sexual or emotional. There are many kinds of pleasure, and instructions for them—in how-to books, aesthetics courses, and so on—are available. Kierkegaard's descriptions of how to graduate from super-aesthetical to humbly ethical were written long before opera-loving Nazis showed how not to cross the line . . . or, "Why Kierkegaard was right and Nietzsche wrong." P.S. The fate of the Nazis confirmed Hitler's view that might makes right: like many tyrants who play the game of "Keep them divided lest we fall," they over-estimated their ability to beat the combined MIGHT of mostly better people everywhere. P.P.S. The fact is that those with might AND a commitment to the Golden Rule (parents?) often sacrifice themselves to reeducate the selfish and teach them the greater wisdom of self-sacrificing love. Theists understand that God, the source of the Golden Rule, can be trusted to have our good in mind, whatever may happen. Hence the quote that begins Letter III.

BUT WAIT . . . A

The library-evidence available at the end of the twentieth century shows how controversial is every single claim made in these pages. I have been invited by a friend to examine my conscience for traces of hubris: "Isn't it prideful to claim that YOU know *the* Truth?"* I have shamelessly begged every question, invoking as my defense the rule that you need not agree with anything until you first feel confident you understand. Thus, if you were Yul Brynner, *The Double_Man*'s leading character, you could weigh "I am certain I am the real person and that is the imposter" and "I wish I could recall whether I am the real person or the imposter" against the evidence only if you could understand those options. Who, you may ask, authorized me to declare the "Intelligo" to be a rule? (*Thanks to E. Roosevelt for reminding us: "No one can make you feel inferior without your consent.")

NEVER be satisfied to simply quote someone else as an authority for things you can prove for your self. For instance, can you read? If you take the answer on another's authority, will their answer come to you in writing? You'll have to read it. Will it come *viva voce*? You'll have to understand what you hear. How will you know you can read or understand what you hear? How will you know they're telling the truth and not lying? How can you know the difference between true & false?

God HAS put answers within reach. Look at whatever is "off to the right" of the **"BUT WAIT . . ."** at the beginning of this section. What do YOU see? Presuming you're not blind and haven't forgotten the lengthy discussion of Chapter Two, weigh your options against YOUR evidence. What options? I'll start you off, you can choose: a-one word, b-one indefinite article, c-one vowel, d-one shaped ink mark, e-three lines arranged to look like one of the above, f-part of one alphabet, g-part of every similar alphabet, h-a large part of every English text, i-a large part of every French text, j-ink molecules, k-atoms, l-sub-atoms, m-part of a sense-datum.

EXPERIMENT: Stare at whatever it is you see—above—off to the right of "BUT WAIT." That will put **IT** at the center of your visual field. Then *slowly cross your eyes*. That will replace it with **THEM**. If you're like me, that is. If it doesn't do that for you, perhaps you're a Kaffka-esque butterfly living in a human body. Or a dog turned into a coachman by a fairy god-mother who will let you go back to being yourself at midnight. If you'd like God-given clues to how other humans interpreted the private experiences THEY experienced, try: Hume (*Enquiry*, Sec. XII), James (*Principles*, ch. XX; *Briefer Course*, ch. III), Charles Sherrington (*Man on His Nature*, ch. IX), et alii.

If you'd like to get really convinced before getting in the habit of regularly REproving it to yourself, do the experiment using a single candle in a dark place. Or use the moon on a cloudless night. Do you REALLY think you can make things happen **TO THE MOON** up there from the earth down here?!

Saint Augustine, in his incredible *On the Teacher*, made a note on a very important point. We can learn the truth for ourselves from someone *who thinks the truth we learn is an error*!

> Whoever can discern those things which are grasped by the mind is inwardly a pupil of truth and outwardly a judge of the speaker, or rather of his statements. For often he knows what has been said, though the speaker himself does not know; as if, for example, someone who is a follower of Epicurus [or Freud] and so thinks the soul is mortal [or non-existent], should recite the arguments on the soul's immortality expounded by men of greater wisdom. If someone who is versed in spiritual things hears the speaker state the argument for the immortality of the soul, he will judge that true things have been said, but the speaker does not know that they are true." (ch. XIII)

Learn about G.H. Mead, then read:

> According to the traditional assumptions of psychology, the content of experience is entirely individual and not in any measure to be primarily accounted for in social terms, even though its setting or context is a social one. And for a social psychology like Cooley's—which is founded on precisely this same assumption—all social interactions depend upon the imaginations of the individuals involved, and take place in terms of their direct conscious influences upon one another in the processes of social experience. Cooley's social psychology, as found in his *Human Nature and the Social Order*, is hence inevitably introspective, and his psychological method carries with it the implication of complete solipsism: society really has no existence except in the individual's mind, and the concept of the self as in any sense intrinsically social is a product of imagination. Even for Cooley the self presupposes experience, and experience is a process within which selves arise; but since that process is for him primarily internal and individual rather than external and social, he is committed in his psychology to a subjectivistic and idealistic, rather than an objectivistic and naturalistic, metaphysical position.

G.H. Mead showed clearly in this note on page 244 of the A. Strauss edition of his papers, entitled *George Herbert Mead on Social Psychology*, that he grasped clearly the contradiction between his behaviorism and Cooley's view. He understood his options. He simply chose badly.

Changing our mind, especially when it's been made up for years or tens of years, is never easy when the issues are *foundation*-al as these are. John Dewey wrote: "It is easier to wean a miser from his hoard, than a man from his deeper opinions." The friend who sent me that quote also drew my attention to a tiny detail I'd not noticed before: "Maybe I'm egocentric, but I've always referred to my thoughts as exactly that—mine. Yet that's wrong isn't it?"

Why does God do it this way? To increase our enjoyment.

—VI—

Dear Unique Eclectic,   June 12, 1993

> Then Paul, knowing that part of them were Sadducees
> and part of them Pharisees, cried out in the Sanhedrin,
> "Brethren, I am a Pharisee, the son of Pharisees; it is about
> the hope and the resurrection of the dead that I am on trial."
> And when he said that, there arose a dispute between the
> Pharisees and the Sadducees, and the multitude was divided.
> For the Sadducees say that there is no resurrection, and that
> there are no angels or spirits, whereas the Pharisees believe
> in both. So there was a great uproar . . .

QU: What is the secret of poetry, as opposed to science? Pretend that is
THE question of this letter. Pretend, for this letter, that Chapter
Four is set aside and another answer is needed. AN: Poets have
a license for uncontrolled-imagination flights, it's called Poetic
License, it gives them freedom from all laws of censorship, majority
opinion, orthodoxy, and so on*. I have found that, on the subject
of "religion," nothing is so helpful as letting my imagination off
its usual leash. (*Except God's moral law forbidding poets and
scientists to scandalize the young, that is, to pervert them. The
penalty is the Murder-Incorporated Treatment: a millstone around
the neck to hold the guilty under water till they're dead. From
Amos to Jesus, the Hebrew prophets were living embodiments
of James' moral view that human misdeeds are quite serious, the
underside of the coin that our good deeds count. For good! God
forgets NOTHING. P.S. In this century, some countries have
revoked the poets' licenses.)

The first thing I do is pretend religion doesn't exist and that there are only people, all learners at different points in their learning career, rebels who decide what they'll believe and then look for authorities they can praise (or blame) as the sources of their 'faith'. This makes so many other things perfectly clear. Buddhists follow Gautama who kept trying to make it by the old Hindu rules, decided there must be a better way (saying that God gave him a revelation to that effect might offend the Buddhist experts who say it's a godless religion), and launched Protestantism in the East long before the West invented the word. In the West, the best theology is the Jews'. Their version of God explains all revelations made to anyone anywhere, since their God created everything and holds the right to "enter history" any time and any where God thinks "intervention" is called for. About the turn of history from BC to AD, the Jews split up into those who stayed with the older, vague notions of sheol and those who thought the recent idea about a glorious hereafter made better sense. For whatever mysterious reasons, the majority stayed with the old tradition—Jews are nothing if not a people of "The Book"—and many who adopted the newer idea joined Jesus. Soon Gentile joiners outnumbered the Semites. Gentiles are the same as other humans, though, and they eventually created their own protest movements. Some people say "How odd of God to choose the Jews." Even odder, though, Jesus-joiners are usually called Catholic, Orthodox, or Protestant today, rather than Christian or Resurrectionist-Jews. Another thing happens when I unleash my imagination like this. Dozens of mental Berlin-Walls come tumbling down. No more people inside the church (synagogue, mosque, temple, hall, etc.) VS those outside, no more outside the church VS outside the state, no more laity lying down VS clergy sitting on them, no more end to revelation VS beginning of tradition, and so on. A far more clear picture saunters into my mind: of 5,500,000,000 "just plain folk," each of whom stands face-to-face with God, even though God is staying behind the scenes* in order to let each person free to **CHOOSE** the unique mix-and-match set of beliefs s/he wants. Even in tight-knit families, "religion" often isn't brought up because people have their own hotly-held disagreeing views, because religion is supposedly based on faith rather than reason, so it's best to let others reject the true faith (each thinks s/he has THE true view on each dogma) and pray God will have mercy on their soul at judgment time. In other words, all cling tightly to their own views and don't dare apply the rethinking-rule to themselves and their views. Blessed, they say, are those who have not seen but have believed. Even if they're wholly unclear what the true answer to Chapter Two's question, "But what DO you see?!", is. (*A saying passed on to me yesterday replaces the by-now old distinction some drew between religion and spirituality: "Never let your religion stand between you and God.")

Enough of this flight of uncontrolled imagination. Time to get back to business. Though I confess that my uncontrolled imagination does at times intrude into what I write, as if there's a genuine connection or two here that I should be thinking about. I have no idea what it might be. P.S. You probably think I'm lying. You may even point to Chapter One's section on conversion, etc., as proof. Sorry. That was automatic writing. My genes, plus contingencies of reinforcement to which I've been exposed, are entirely responsible for THOSE words. (See the section on B.F. Skinner in Chapter Two). I will admit this much, however: it SEEMED as if those thoughts were mine, from my imagination. But Freud has convinced me they were merely sent up from my unconscious while my hands automatically copied them.

Your thoughts. Your choices of what you'll believe. If your thoughts are your magic carpet to tour the infinite or infinitely creative mind of God, your **belief-decisions** determine where you will "live." This is the central idea of Chapter XXI of James' *Principles*, much like Husserl's idea of "constitution" later on: the epoche´ (a suspension of assent and dissent, a totally willed commitment to not making any commitment) allows us to take tours with the divine real-estate agent before choosing where we'll settle down (unless it's where we're already living). I mention James, because, as he brings out in the passage quoted earlier, each total thought—a Kantian "world-as-it-appears-at-this-moment"—has "tendrils" that we are naturally drawn to track outwards to see where they lead. James, as usual, wriggles free of current jargon, not like Heidegger by inventing a worse jargon, but by plugging directly into our everyday, common-sense talk, as if the "world" of our everyday lives IS what we have to make sure we understand. In *Varieties*, James says our "world" always has **PLUS**'s or **MORE**'s we must think more about. It is . . .

A conscious field *plus* its object as felt or thought of *plus* an attitude towards the object *plus* the sense of a self to whom the attitude belongs—such a concrete bit of personal experience may be a small bit, but it is a solid bit as long as it lasts; not hollow, not a mere abstract element of experience, such as the 'object' when taken all alone. It is a *full* fact, even though it be an insignificant fact; it is of the *kind* to which all realities whatsoever must belong; the motor currents of the world run through the like of it; it is on the line connecting real events with real events. (Lecture XX)

This means that I must ask and answer further questions: What am *I*, back at the paying-attention end of consciousness?, What is **the world**, out at the paid-attention-to end? Nor does James ignore what he'd emphasized in *Principles*, ch. XXI: there's a third MORE!, namely, our **ATTITUDES** vis-a-vis the objects we have thoughts about, i.e., the phenomena that the Serenity Prayer is all about.

VIP NOTE. Be attentive whenever you mindset-switch **FROM (a)** YOUR God's-eye view of all galaxies and all mindsets **TO (b)**YOUR "from down and in here" view of private models of never observed stars and others' mindsets. They're both YOUR views, God wants you to enjoy the one but realize the other. The more often you practice **ATTENDING** and **NOTICING** this switch, the easier will it become. "Habit" is the label we put on that fact or set of phenomena. By learning various God's-eye views, i.e., grand unifying guesses about what's out there, including the possible "There's nothing out here, there's ONLY your mindset," you'll be able to pay more attention to your evidence, ie train your ear to hear the coach's coaching, and thus decide whether your society, your church, your brain, your divine self, or God is doing the coaching. (End of note.)

It's July 11 Sunday, week's first day, just a few pages left. Only because, as an autonomous agent with free will, I imposed on my self an obligation to stop at the bottom of a non-yet-existing page???. I could reject that decision. I live in the USA, people in the USA are totally free, so I'm totally free.

But not totally free. There are some laws I cannot change, namely, the laws of nature. One of the most important here is a law of nature regarding our psychology. Someone or something makes it impossible for me to ALWAYS be gestalt-switched into my profess-ional mindset. It's one of the present laws of (my?) nature that I will fall back, Hume-wise, into my naive-realist mindset as soon as I hear her voice, asking for a cup of tea. (You don't have to remind me that I've said it's not her voice literally; do you think I'm not in the habit of remembering what a gigantic switch I make when I go from a naive-realist view to a Berkeley-James view of my sense-data?!) Then I'll have to remember which kind of tea to use, wait for it to steep, etc. I don't blame her for thinking I'm obsessed whenever my 'automatic habit-pilot' sometimes guides me [?!] to make the wrong tea for her, to put her sugar into my coffee, etc. Habits! Now there's a topic for you!, especially since, not being a sleep-walker, I am wide awake, consciously aware of what I'm experiencing, only just not thinking about it because my thoughts are directed to other things. Like, directed to "What should I focus on in the few remaining pages of THIS relatively brief tour of my mindset?"

QU: What is the most important big idea of all? AN: The idea that certainty in science is a PACKAGE-DEAL where each major decision must be the right one, and the right one must fit with your other major decisions. A good model for decisions of this type is the JUROR. For a guilty verdict that is beyond reasonable doubt, a juror must decide (a)that something criminal happened, (b)that someone was responsible, (c)that things can be explained IF the accused is the one responsible, (d)that there are too many things NOT explained if there was no crime, if no one is responsible, if someone else was responsible, and so on.

QU: What are your God's-Eye, Biggest-Idea options? EASIEST AN: Start with the five kinds of things making up the QUINTALIST view proposed to you while you've been reading these non-pages' rows and rose. DUALISM* or PURE MONISM, the view that there is only one kind of reality. We can IMAGINE monism is a genus, subdivided into as many classes as we wish, has four additional species: a-ATOMIST MATERIALISM (only bodies distinct from each other), b—PHENOMENALISM (only sense-data and imagery), c-ROMANTIC OR GERMAN IDEALISM (only thoughts), d-SPIRITISM (only souls). Some people explicitly combine more than one kind of item in their mix-and-match belief systems. Berkeley, for instance, combined d and b. Others do so unwittingly. James "used" d and b except when he had to deal with the question, "Are there soul-selves?", at which times he would still "use" the idea of soul-selves while apologetically explaining why he'd decline one more time to commit himself to it. (Hume wrote "*I* believe . . ." rather than "All of us percepts believe . . .!) The goal is to be a GOOD ECLECTIC or CRITICAL CHOOSER and to make a bouquet of facts or theories that are logically coherent, that do not contradict each other.

(*Why do people imagine "dualist" can have only one meaning? There is a difference between body-mind dualism [two things make up one person], matter-spirit dualism [suppose all creatures are bodily and that only God is spirit], epistemological dualism [mental representations in our minds are the direct objects of knowledge and everything outside is an indirect object], sense-intellect dualism [basis of empiricism vs rationalism], subject-predicate dualism [essential for understanding the ontological "proof" for God], etc. In a similar way, there is more than one meaning of "nominalism": even though there are radical differences between Hobbes' name-ism, Berkeley's and Hume's image-ism, Ockham's and James' pluralist-individual-ism, Locke's and Kant's conceptualism, they are all called "nominalism" at times.)

QU: What about "consciousness." AN: First, it's an English word. Second, Descartes used the 1600's French and Latin cousins of the English "consciousness" to cover every act of a non-material being, such as being awake, being aware, being confused, being mistaken, being right, being free to affirm or deny any thought, and so on. Third, you can check to SEE whether you understand those act-terms by checking to see whether you remember the three different meanings of "see." Fourth, you can then check to see whether you can REMEMBER anything. Fifth, you can check to see whether you understand the difference between being right when you THINK you remember and being wrong when you

THINK you remember. Sixth, you can check to see whether you are right when you THINK you remember having done a lot of remembering before the most recent time that you woke up or whether you are wrong when you think the same thing*. Seventh, you can check to see whether you can ever remember the SAME thing or whether you can only remember a new thought-about-fact that is SIMILAR to or like the first ONE that it, the second, is supposed to be the same as. Eighth, you can check to see whether any of your later acts of remembering is EXACTLY like any of the earlier acts of memory or whether, on the contrary, there are always slight differences since you are older and each new act of remembering is done with a mindset that has been changed by the addition of at least one more act of remembering, the one just before the latest. Ninth, you can check to see how huge a role the topic of "memory" plays in the Big System of Descartes, in Locke's criticism of theories about the IDENTITY of selves, souls, or persons, in Hume's criticism of Locke's concept of "self," in the theories of Kant, Fichte, Schelling, Hegel, Schopenhauer, about "mind," etc. (*You CAN remember the first half of a sentence while reading the second half, right? Do you remember for sure whether it was you who read the preceding pages here? Was it a clone? Alter-ego?)

Tenth, you can study to see how huge a role the topic of MEMORY plays for William James who, in spite of all his "provisional" talk about brains, brain functions, neural grooves as brain'al equivalents of habits, and localized regions of the brain as the physical counterparts of distinct components of the stream of consciousness, explicitly asserted his belief that brains as such do not exist, explicitly asserted his decision to adopt the phenomenalist (Kantian, positivist, movie, virtual-reality) view of physical things, but did repeatedly emphasize that the present total-thought, field-of-experience, stream-of-consciousness of any individual person normally is swelled to the bursting point by memories of the individual's past, Paul's thought by memories of Paul's past, Peter's by memories of Peter's past. With his flair for imagery, James wrote this about what happens when Peter and Paul wake after a night of forgetful sleep:

As the current of an electrode buried in the ground unerringly finds its way to its own similarly buried mate, across no matter how much intervening earth; so Peter's present instantly finds out Peter's past, and never by mistake knits itself on to that of Paul. (*Principles of Psychology* I:238).

And study to see also how acutely aware he was of identity-problems.

QU: What about dreams? AN: Begin HABITually using the precious moments called "waking up" for one of your two or three most important psychological tests*. Pay close attention to the remarkable difference between an absurdly terrifying (or merely absurd) dream and the experience of re-becoming wide awake; those moments of rewaking are God-given moments *ideal for comparing the two states while still vividly remembering* the dream. You do understand what "remembering the dream" means, as opposed to "dreaming the dream" (or "being still in the dream" or "being still asleep"), don't you? Once you are old enough to *understand* the difference between "There IS a big difference between dreaming you are 'sleeping' (also called 'making love') with your neighbor's wife and 'sleeping' (ditto) with her" and "There is NOT," you can weigh those two options against *experience* and see which is true. Babies, dogs, & chimps don't know the difference. Thanks to midnight lessons—"It's alright, honey, it was only a bad dream; it's alright, mommy's/daddy's right here"—normal five-year old humans learn to understand it. That is their first step toward an accurate (i.e., non-psychoanalytic) map of the various states of consciousness. The early two-item, "awake-vs-asleep" becomes "awake, sleep-dreaming, and dreamless-sleeping." You should also have subdivided your "awake" map into: normal, normal illusory, normal hallucinatory, and so on. One wise six-year old surprised a Ph.D. with "Maybe I'm daydreaming, but I know I'm not nightdreaming!" (*Or read "Always Trying to Escape" in R. Feynman's *"Surely You're Joking, Mr. Feynman!"* and practice ATTENDING and NOTICING what happens when you fall asleep. Since so many call death "sleeping," it's a worth-while exploration.)

QU: So, where do we start this wrap-up? AN: With a reminder that WE aren't starting anything. YOU are. Surely you remember that? You may wonder at this emphasis on memory. But not on memory.

Rather on **YOUR** memory.

If you do not remember that, you are liable to go the way of the so-called romantic idealists who lost the ability they had when they were younger. When they were younger, they knew when they were being wakened, being fed, being praised, being scolded, being put to bed again. When they got older, their identity got fused with everyone else's, they thought every ancestor's thought was their thought, they thought every descendent's enjoyment was their enjoyment. They began to get in the habit of thinking that way because they thought that, since all pre—and post-decessors were part of their thought, and since the total thought belonged to no single individual, therefore all thoughts were the thought of the one thinker of whom they were all parts while appearing to be distinct. If you do not keep your feet on the ground, you will forget who and what you are: the thinker who thinks only one thought at a time, the one that's entirely your own private one. Like the thought you just had while reading that last sentence and like this new thought you are in the middle of as you are reading this sentence. You are starting a new thought, the one that goes with this sentence. Check your evidence right now to see which of the next thoughts is the true one: "I am God and think all the thoughts of all the thinkers of all time" vs "I am not God and can only think the thought I am thinking right now*." Now, check your experience to make sure you haven't forgotten the first option by the time you get around to reading the second. (*Each time you remember [!], you will have to hurry and check the calendar and your watch before the *present* moment is gone and the *future* arrives to make the present one a *past* one!)

No doubt you will want to begin reading more about MEMORY. I mean, more on scientific research on memory. The trouble is that you will have to first remember what the difference is between scientific research and philosophical speculation. Did you ever learn the difference? Was it recently enough for you to rely on memory to recall the difference? Check your memory, to make certain, before you go to the library to find the "science" section that won't be in the "philosophy" section, that you don't go to the wrong one. In fact, before you trust the librarians who choose which books go into which section, you should check up on their credentials and then hope that you do not forget what you learn one day while you're asleep getting your brain rested for what you will learn the next day. In fact, here is a good question for you.

When did you begin to be you? Was it at the moment of conception? Was it at three months? Was it when God created your soul and joined it to the matter that would be called your body? Was it when God created you—period!—since there is no body? Was it centuries ago, at the moment when you began your first of many (re)incarnations? Was it long before your first incarnation which was a punishment for some transgression? Perhaps you only began existing fifteen minutes ago, and God who created the entire universe at that same moment created your brain with all of its current "encoding," the way "synthesized music" (sounds) are created without any original instruments, the same way that Walt Disney movies were made with no original (you don't REALLY believe Snow White was filmed on location?!), the same way video games (and virtual reality) are created without originals, etc. That is, perhaps God has done to you what you'll read God supposedly did to Adam who was created as a young lad and got to skip all those earlier baby years, etc., i.e., created you fifteen minutes ago and tucked into your mind all of what you take to be your memories, even though none of them is true since none of the things you think you remember ever really happened. Except you probably read the last page and think you can remember it. Test yourself: what did it say? Now see if you recall the question this paragraph began with. Right, when did you begin to be you? Then ask how you can prove it!

Pretend you are sitting next to me on a cloudless night, looking at the moon. You cross your eyes and you see two lovely globes. I keep my eyes uncrossed and see one. Question: How many moons are there? One? (The one I see?) Two? (The ones you see.) Three? (1+2=3) You uncross your eyes and insist there's only one. Why choose one answer over the other? Have your forgotten you saw two? Maybe you didn't. Maybe what you SAW no longer exists? (What happens to Snow White when only the wicked queen is on screen? What happens to the billions of things you think you remember but you're not thinking of right now?) How can you ever keep track of all the facts, all the arguments, all the discussions about selves, self-identity, memory, memory-engrams, ideagenous molecules, the holographic-brain model for memory, the "calpain hypothesis," the "competitor theory" mentioned in the same story, the RNA theory, etc.

The trouble with all of today's "scientific" theories about memory is this: they are efforts to explain what is going on in the brain that "explains" memory, but it is first of all necessary to prove that memory exists (have you ever read any research on how to explain pirots?, or why it is that they kerulize elactically?), then it is essential to prove that the proposed explanation is the TRUE explanation, and finally, it is necessary to prove that you can remember all the details you think are the premises for your conclusion by the time you reach the conclusion. (Without looking back, get a pad and pen and write down all you remember of the premises for the thesis being presented here. You haven't forgotten what the thesis was, have you? Right, how many moons can you see?)

Here is a suggestion. The next time you read up on explanations for conscious remembering that refer to your brain which you have never experienced (one of God's cleverest tricks was to make the brain as such insensitive to feeling pain when it's stuck with pins, needles, probes, electrodes, and so on, and to do it with an eye on the day when you would *read* this*), ask yourself this: if your brain is like a multi-volume encyclopedia and has all of your present knowledge code'd, symbol'd, sign'd, represent'd in it, then is any of that knowledge being remembered when you are asleep? What is the difference between what you have experienced—ACTUAL, CONSCIOUS REMEMBERING—and what you only hypothesize is the never-experienced "explanation" for it? Do you think you can remember the preceding flurry of considerations while, as a judge and juror of one, you try to discover the **TRUE** answer? (*You don't really BELIEVE you are now reading engrams stored in your brain's neurons, do you?)

Or have you chosen to believe that there are no true answers? That the most you can hope for is "knowledge that works" as opposed to "assenting to thoughts that are true"? Are you able to remember the relevant considerations you'll need in order to (a)explain the difference between "what works" and "what's true," to (b)defend your chosen answer, namely, that you're unable to know what's true, by reasons that are clear, distinct, in good logical order (maybe even true!), and to (c)do all that without forgetting whether the you who begins the reasoning process is the very you who ends it (as opposed to a slightly older clone)?

Perhaps meditating on these questions will help you understand the thesis that, even though you are unable to remember every one of the details of your unbelievably complex model of a universe you have never and will never observe, you are relying on much of the rest of it as evidence for the part you are remembering and attending to at a given moment. Who is the YOU who is able to take a tour of the vast mindset that becomes a stored, unthought-of-by-anybody record when YOU enter a dreamless sleep? Who is the YOU who is able to get off at some particular juncture in your tour and take a tour, say, of William James' mindset? Or Descartes'? Or Plato's? Or Freud's, Watson's, Skinner's, etc.? Who is the YOU who gets to select what will go into your own unique eclecticism?

Can you discover what's true? There IS a thesis being proposed as true to you even as you continue reading these rows and rose of non-words. The thesis is that the thesis is being presented /to you by God. The way to find the answer is easy: unleash your imagination enuf to learn all your options*, eliminate all the impossible ones, and the one left over, however far-fetched it seemed at first, must be the true one. In the library, you will learn that, at the beginning of this century, there was a great deal of confidence that "science" could deliver certainty. At this end of the century when the atom was split, DNA discovered, humans walked that moon-globe and returned with samples from it, heart transplants became routine, pocket calculators reduced the years Kepler took for his computations to hours, computers with word-processing programs allowed authors to compose books they'd never have been capable of without them, it is easy to find book after book in which "experts" claim scientists know nothing for certain. Protests against that pessimism are beginning to turn up: see, for instance, the Fall-'89 *Skeptical Inquirer*. But . . . (*James, in "The Sentiment of Rationality," written ten years BEFORE the publication of *The Principles*, said the "question of life" reduces to: "This IS a moral universe!" vs "No, it isn't!")

Check and you'll see there's no consensus on the nature of light, the cornerstone of Einstein's relativity theory. (Incidentally, how much light do you see when you look up at the moon? Do you realize the sky is flooded with it? That it's everywhere except in that tunnel-shadow created by the fact that the lit-up side of the earth is stopping all the light that hits it? That that explains why the moon goes dark every once in awhile? Check and you will see there's no consensus on gravity, the cornerstone of Newton's physics. (Remove IT, you still have laws, but NOTHING TO EXPLAIN THEM!) You'll see that there's no consensus on the age of the moon. "We now know that the moon is demonstrably not there when nobody looks" is from a physicist's pen. (Found in *Philosophical Consequences of Quantum Theory*, edited by Cushing and McMullin, p.50.) Yet, according to the evolutionists nobody was looking for most of the moon's alleged lifetime. You'll see there's no consensus on the definition of species, the direction of evolution, or on any CAUSAL link (as opposed to cor-*relation*) between DNA and morphology. Throw in the anti-naive-realist monkey-wrench, and you may understand why a "senior paleontologist" from the British Museum of Natural History announced a few years back that "it struck me that I had been working on this stuff [evolution] for more than twenty years, and there was not one thing I knew about it" (*Harper's*, February 1985, p.50). Whether he'll REMEMBER why he said that is, of course, the issue here.

Do you believe you can back up a single assertion? One that you make in conversation, or in class, or in a published text? The place to begin is with your here-and-now CONSCIOUS remembering, since there is no other kind. That is, the past is gone, the future isn't here yet. We all make mistakes. But in a sense, I take that on faith: how could I PROVE it was *I* who wrote that? If there is no God, *and if there is no past*, then "a true thought is one that matches reality" is silly. If there is no God and no past, who will reveal to us at the end whether non-cladists or cladists or anti-evolutionists were right? If there is no God and no past, who is to say that those who "erase the holocaust" (see 7-11-93's *N.Y. Times Book Review*) are practicing "perverse ingenuity"? How can there be lies that don't last long enough to catch them? Time is swift as quicksilver. Except time isn't.

—VII—

Dear Thought-full Lover,   June 14, 1993

> I am done with great things and big things, great
> institutions and big successes, and I am for those tiny
> invisible molecular moral forces that work from individual to
> individual, creeping through the crannies of the world like
> so many rootlets, or like the capillary oozing of water, yet
> which, if you give them enough time, will rend the hardest
> monuments of man's pride. (William James; edited by *The
> Catholic Worker*.)

June 14, 1993. It's Monday. Back-to-work time*. What's work,
though? Good people fret because they feel their utmost efforts can't
change the world, so it is imperative that we learn to cut through
abstractions, reifications, fictions (e.g., revolutions), and get to the
truth: history's "big movers" do little but think and give directives to
those who do the *other* jobs. Why didn't Nicolae Ceaucescu blush after
saying "In 20 years, Stalin raised Russia from an undeveloped country
to the second most powerful country in the world"? Stalin did that?
No, Stalin himself merely plotted and signed orders for those who
did the sweating and bleeding. Socrates and Jesus didn't write or sign
anything. Revolutions aren't things, big or small. "Revolution" = many
molecular events. (*Should Christians return to Christ's habit, Sunday'd
be back-to-work.)
  Were James alive today, he'd surely agree. Asked about the above
quote, he'd probably look around and point to the PLURALITY of
molecular facts to which his poetry referred. He'd note that, for some,
back-to-work means another day of dressing the kids, getting breakfast
for them, etc. For others, it's off to the construction site down-town

where a tall office-building is going up. Only God could list all the people and all the small, moment-to-moment doings by all those people, but those doings will make up the one-and-only June 14, 1993, of the world's history. At day's end, the doers will curl up in bed for a night of sleep that will prepare them for yet another dayful of small doings tomorrow. These history makers were once the generation of kids being taken care of and had their whole lives ahead of them. Their lives are shorter now. And a hundred years hence, most will have been consigned forever to some silent plot of dirt in a cemetery far removed from the hustle and bustle of life.

Some people get depressed when they notice that time is passing and that each day brings them closer to this life's end. They do their best to DIS-attend to such thoughts. Especially because today's world is different from the one into which Galileo and Newton were born. Just as there are more deniers of God or gods today than ever before, there are also more deniers of any life after "life." The "social environment" of earlier medieval times can be got from Sigrid Unset's novel, *Kristin Lavransdatter*, which is like a door to another world where death seemed temporary, where rejoining loved ones in heaven was expected, where doubts about "the faith" were seen as a special trial sent by God. Here is a sample:

> "For I have seen it more and more with each year I have lived—no worthier work can there be for a human soul that has found grace to conceive somewhat of God's loving-kindness, than to serve Him and watch and pray for those men whose sight is still darkened by the shadow of the things of this world. Yet must I needs say, my Kristin—hard would it be for me to give up for God's sake the life I have lived on my farms and lands, with cares for earthly things and with worldly cheer—with your mother by my side, and with you my children. Therefore must a man suffer in patience, when he has begotten offspring of his body, that it scorch his heart if he lose them or the world go badly with them. God, who gave them souls, owned them, and not I—":
> Kristin's body was still shaken with weeping; and her father began rocking her in his arms like a little child.

"Many things there are that I understood not when I was young. Father held Aasmund dear too, but not so as he loved me. 'Twas for my mother's sake, you see—her he never forgot, though he took Inga because 'twas his father's will. Now would I wish that I could have met my stepmother again in this earthly home and prayed her to forgive that I set no store by her kindness"—

"But you have said often, Father, that your stepmother did you neither good nor evil," said Kristin, through her weeping.

"Aye, God help me—'twas my lack of understanding. Now does it seem a great thing to me that she hated me not, and never gave me an angry word. How would you like it, Kristin, if so it were that you saw a stepson put before your own son, at all times and in all things?"

Kristin was grown somewhat quieter. She lay now with her face turned outwards looking toward the mountain range. A great grey-blue pile of cloud was passing over the sun, darkening the air—some yellow beams stabbed through it, and a sharp glitter was thrown up from the water of the beck. Then her tears broke out anew: "Oh, no—father, my father—should I nevermore see you in this life—"

"God guard you, Kristin, my child, so that we may find each other again on yonder day, all we who were friends in life—and every human soul.—Christ and Mary Virgin and St. Olav and St. Thomas will keep you all your days." He took her face between his hands and kissed her on the mouth. "God be gracious to you—God give you light in this world's light and in the great light hereafter—" (*The Mistress of Husaby*, Book II, sec.7.)

Even during these last days of the 1900's, there are millions for whom a conversation of this sort would not be unusual. In their 'world,' too, such references to another place called heaven and another time called eternity are as normal as references to any place and time. But, except for those who live in a ghetto, *the 'social environment' is radically different*. Since Newton's triumph, the 'atmosphere of faith' inherited from medieval times has progressively thinned to the point that public references to God's role in the daily events of human lives and to the continuation of life beyond the tomb are regarded as unwarranted intrusions into the 'public arena.' The atmosphere today is not even neutral. We live in a world where 'separation of church and state' creates more of our atmosphere than "in God we trust." Public schools condition impressionable children to believe that a few moments of silence to 'think' ('speak silently to God') put unfair psychological pressure on children of atheists and that the only intellectually respectable account of where humans come from is the evolution theory taught in biology courses. Business news centers around the closing Dow Jones average, said to be the result of market forces restrainable only by laws lawyers cannot find loopholes in. The mass media, responsive to us who enjoy news about the fires, fights, and arrests that we don't get to see in our neighborhoods (unlike those unskilled, unlucky, or unambitious enough to move out of theirs) or who want fantasies of seductions, infidelities, and affairs to brighten our more drab reality, pander to our insatiable appetites and continue to merit the 'wasteland' complaint. We live in a 'world' that often seems safer for modern atheism than for western tradition.

Thought—the habits of thought, the comfortable assumptions, the mutually-reinforced convictions—is the chief determinant of such 'worlds.' *Most of our 'worlds' are the 'CREATION' of thought.* Ninety-nine and forty-four hundredths percent of the things we grow up thinking of as the furnishings of our world are things that exist only in our thoughts or, to change the image, in our imagination. Only five things . . . CHANGE THAT! Only things that are conveniently captured by a mental model with five chief pigeon-holes exist as real things independent of your or my thoughts *about* them: persons (divine and non-divine), thoughts, sensed colors, sounds, odors, etc., memory-images of colors, sounds, odors, etc., and a-toms. Everything else that we have thoughts about (e.g., worlds, social environments, medieval times, tombs, church, state, public schools, Dow Jones averages, market forces, etc.) are fictions or figments of our imagination. Figments have no counterparts in reality (easiest seen by beginning with nothingness, empty space, absences, etc.), but they can and do serve as useful, often indispensible, devices for thinking about the real things that do exist. And the revolution that has transformed the medieval 'world' into the 'modern' one is a revolution in people's habits of thought.

Final progress in the revolution will come only when the myth of "science" as knowledge automatically superior to philosophy and theology, equally mythical, is gone. We all—you, I, and all the rest of the "just plain folk" like us—know what we know, are right about what we're right about, and are mistaken about what we're mistaken about. God exists. That is no more a non-scientific object of faith than "The earth, moon, sun, and other 3-D'al bodies exist" is a scientific fact. If God exists, then whoever doesn't believe it is mistaken, whatever title they prefer for their mistake. God does exist, and that is provable. For centuries, that was the western tradition. Descartes was the first to add that "God exists" is more scientifically provable than that bodies exist. The added facts that i-ALL humans' bodies and that ii-OTHER humans' consciousnesses are unobservable to YOU make "God exists" more scientifically certain than that other humans besides you exist. If the last thoughts to cross your mind are true, everyone is mistaken who believes they're not. And they are. Let me explain with two roundups.

Start with what James emphasized: our THOUGHTS must deal with quintillians of varieties. His anti-abstractionist pluralism centered on people: *each and every "just plain person" is a thousand—or million-faceted wonder.* Like sorters of countless songs composed from the same few notes, numberless poems with only twenty-six letters, and millions of books out of the same tens of 1000s of words, statisticians construct 1,000s of bell curves. But persons show more uniquely overlapping combinations of facets (traits, dispositions, i.e., HABITS, etc.) than can ever be trapped or captured by simplistic lists of "types." The approach to human variations that is presented so meticulously in James' works is expanded in the Coles' books* which introduce "just plain folk" in all of their wondrous depth and variety. (*An excellent companion-author is O. Sacks: e.g., his *Migraine* shows how to approach the overlaps in problems faced by people with various "syndromes" [symptom clusters] ranging from only headache to those with no headache and how to treat them accordingly.)

Combine this with the unifying feature of THOUGHT James always stressed. General thoughts bring unification to our knowledge of a universe-ful of plural particulars. Unification also underlies the idea of *system*. The exposition of this non-text 'text' has emphasized that anyone with access to well-stocked library-shelves in these 1990's can shop from a variety of systems. Two in particular play the central role here: our ordinary, everyday common-sense world-view, the naive-realist component of which is in large measure mistaken, and the profession-al view that has no recognized name (quintuplism?). Understanding these pages requires fluency in switching from one to the other of those two systematic text-readings, a recognition that the second retains two-thirds of the first, and a culminating realization that the second accounts for all the others. Now . . .

Recall that the major thesis of this chapter is that for your THOUGHTS you depend directly on God. Not on us. If we exist! Why trust that your thoughts of us are true? Why else than that they fit with the belief that otherwise your belief-system is incomplete? What you experience may partly depend on us, but only if God coordinates what is presented to you with the intentions of us whose hearts God knows best. The claim was made earlier here that it makes no difference whether we are linked by an ocean of deaf and dumb matter or are each held in the palm of a divine hand. That claim goes only so far. "Is it matter or God?" is about the unseen and unfelt outer **CAUSE** of what you experience inside. Since it's through thought that you know or understand anything outside, "**WHAT CAUSES MY THOUGHTS**?" is the ultimate cause-issue, the chief issue James failed to solve. Once a learner learns s/he is like the elevator-rider in Einstein's earlier-cited *Relativity* and cannot see whether the elevator hangs from or rests on anything, s/he's ready to dialogue with Descartes, Berkeley, Hume, Kant, etc., about this ultimate issue: "Are we and what we experience dependent upon and caused by nothing or by something?" If by something, by what?! *All knew that unobservable bodies-in-themselves are as NON-empirical as God.* Descartes decided the only plausible cause for a non-body spirit (his self) or a spirit with an idea of an infinitely perfect being is God. Berkeley said God is the only plausible cause for sense-data. Kant, like Hume, pleaded agnosticism on the cause-issue, but added that, if this is a moral universe, God and immortality are needed to make sense of it. You, alone there and now with your sense-data, imagery, and thoughts, must decide whether to believe that the thoughts that just crossed your mind—of James, Einstein, Descartes, Berkeley, Hume, and Kant, none of whom you've met and all of whom you know only via "word"-evoked thoughts, and of a cause that is also unseen and known to you only via "word"-evoked thoughts—are true or whether to believe those non-word 'words' are addressing you about persons and causes as fictitious as Kristin and one of her co-causes (?), Lavrans. YOUR thoughts are YOUR only bridges to the unseen and unfelt, in short, to the unobserved and the never-experienced things (IF ANY!) which are out here. YOUR thoughts!

But what IS a thought? No 'word,' recall, can be de-fined by itself. It takes the shape of a mindset to determine any word's meaning, and these are only clues to one part of one other person's mindset. In the materialist model (Watson, Skinner, Ryle, etc.), there are no thoughts, only behavior of bodies such as vocal organs or brains, behaviors that can be double-named as "thoughts" by any English-using Humpty Dumpty, just as they can be TRIPLE-named "cogitationes" by a bilingual (English-latin) materialist. The process is the same as that used to **RE**-de-fine "human body" and "brain" when the user is Berkeley, James, or anyone using the phenomenalist reading for BODIES: bodies don't exist, only non-bodily sense-data mentally telescoped under "bodies." Within the context of the framework proposed via/ *along with* these non-word 'words,' the 'cue/word' "thought" is used for something MORE THAN persons, sense-data, imagery, & a-toms, for the most astonishing realities imaginable, best image'd or picture'd as *perfectly transparent media whereby we understand true facts or false fictions* about things that exist or do not. Thoughts are the kind of thing last noticed and least attended to. (See how those last are de-fined in Chapter One.)

To no one, so far as I know, was the full glory of "a thought" more fully revealed (progress in learning is gradually better and fuller revelation) than to James. First, his habit of equating a person with a present thought, within a pluralist model which he used to indicate the fully separate realness of individuals, led him to notice more and more about total, present thoughts. In one of his supreme poems depicting thoughts cited earlier in Chapter Three, section C ("The world of experience consists at all times of two parts, an objective and a subjective part"), James noted the fact that each moment's thought, like a letter, has several tacit, between-lines messages, each beginning with "There is MORE . . ." But to the THINKER/reader, the thought-about OBJECT, and the thinker/reader's ATTITUDE, we must add: "There is also an addresser-**CAUSE**." The "Letters" of this last chapter are a complex tapestry, weaving back and forth the threads of a total "court-case" that **NOTHING BUT** a person-al, supremely brilliant, omnicompetent, unpredictably reliable, wholly fair being could serve as the sought-for cause of a single thought. Or billions!

A mature thought is a truly **MASSIVE THING**. (Chapter Four was a meditation on this massiveness.) Reading this book in order to rethink things is doing self-analysis. Analysis begins with thoughts: they, with their complex OBJECTS and accompanying ATTITUDES, are the main thing lugged into a therapist's office. The thoughts to be analyzed or rethought are your bridge to all the unobserved universe out here. Whatever you understand about us must funnel through your latest, ongoing thought. Besides space there's time. The past which no longer exists and the future which does not yet exist, must also funnel through your latest, ongoing thought, i.e., everything you've ever learned that you're the least bit conscious of, every calculation about the future between now and your death and beyond. Listen to a clock: only the tick or tock you hear actually exists, the rest are present memories of other ticks and tocks. The same is true of thoughts: only the thought you're thinking as your eyes scan now THESE ciphers . . . and now THESE . . . and now THESE is real. Any past thought you think about (remember) is known through the medium of a present thought. God has arranged matters so that, thru our present thoughts, we are offered proposals *that* we thought this or *that* we thought that in the past, and such proposals will be dated vis-a-vis other timed and dated thoughts. As James noted, new thoughts appropriate earlier ones.

Each moment's thought can be analysed into two facets, fringe and focus*. The BACKGROUND or marginal aspect is *relatively* stable: your belief-system or frame-of-reference plus your individual life-story up till now. A thought's FOREGROUND is *restless* and unpredictable. Both facets are included in James' depiction of our stream of consciousness copied back on an earlier page: "Why do we spend years straining after a certain scientific or practical problem, but all in vain—thought refusing to evoke the solution we desire?" During RE—thinking, the foreground is like a zooming-in to explore this or that background area to change it, then a zooming-back-out to size it up when "put into perspective" of more of the whole, even of eternity: "sub specie aeternitatis." (*The duality is image-inary. You have only one total, many-splendored, ever-changing thought at any moment.

God must even give us a third thought to understand how a last one was an analysis of an earlier one.)

The "case" FOR God as the one who is 'addressing' you right this moment, via the thoughts being proposed (should you choose, God will provide you with sense-data of putting this book aside and you'll be offered other thoughts), seemingly via the 'words' you are reading (I presume you just thought about setting this book aside, tho you may have had no such thought as your eyes scanned earlier 'pages'), is part of a larger "case" whose other parts are smaller "cases" AGAINST your brain, AGAINST these non-words (or shaped-and-arranged ink marks), AGAINST me, and AGAINST society as the cause-source of your present sense-data, imagery, and thoughts. James, like non-traditional thinkers after Kant, rejected all attempts to give a knock-down causal **PROOF** for God, which would question-beg "Does everything have a cause?" His answer to "Whence our thoughts?", tho, is hopeless. From the beginning he rejected the LITERAL, i.e., common-sense, naive-realist meaning of "brains cause thoughts." To the end he also persisted in speaking AS IF they do. So . . .

Go back to naive-realism and astronomy. What keeps the heavenly bodies and the earth moving in such lawlike fashion? Aristotle said that the moon, sun, planets, and stars were moved around the earth by bodiless souls or, in Aquinas' terms, angels. Both held further that there was a hierarchy of soul-movers and that all of them were dependent upon a single greatest spirit, God. Descartes threw out this idea and constructed a new physics based on the idea that the visible planets, etc., swim in a vortex of smaller, invisible bits of matter, which means that big bodies are pushed around by and, in turn, push around an ocean of teeny bodies. After most people accepted Newton's physics as having overturned Descartes'—either there is no invisible ocean of tiny bodies to convey "force" from sun to earth, earth to moon, etc., or it is an ocean of ether that is not solid enough to do the job—the door opened for Berkeley's and Hume's devastating critiques which demolished the idea that physicists could do better than Newton had done: predict **HOW** future phenomena will succeed one another but not tell **WHY***. Those familiar with the library sources will understand the significance of the final essay in the 1989 *Philosophical Consequences* . . . (vis-a-vis what was quoted a few pages ago: "We now know that the moon is demonstrably not there when nobody looks") explaining Newton's quandary over "action at a distance." Rutherford's revelation, soon after James' death, showed that the same quandary extends to the "solar-system" atom and its a-toms. The bankruptcy of god-less physics is complete. (*Only after Newton did physicists get in the habit of explicitly excluding God as the final source of causal power in the universe. Were there room for them, I would restore the pages written earlier this summer on the contradictory, often amusing, but ultimately futile contemporary efforts to explain the **LAW** of gravity.)

But there's more. The **LAWS** which govern the only possibly-real bodies (a-toms) are not uniform or iron-clad as determinists *postulate* Newton's are. To the unbiassed, quantum laws clearly bear the mark of an intelligent controller, an idea that fleetingly crossed at least one mind more than 30 years ago:

> The electron must revolve about the nucleus to generate centrifugal force to counterbalance the attraction of the nucleus. But if it moves, it emits radiation and so moves less and less, and the atom collapses. And if it does not move, the atom still collapses. The objection to the perpetual motion of the electron was the same that had been made to Copernicus' motion of the earth. Where was the force to maintain the motion of the earth? Where was the energy to maintain the motion of the negative electron in a positive field? The prime mover could not, surely, be expected to attend individually to all electrons in all atoms. (C. Schneer, *The Evolution of Physical Science*, p.249)

From Thales to Rutherford, each new discovery confirms the fact that this cosmos is such a stupendous show put on by a peerlessly brilliant Mind, that massive thoughts are required to recognize it. These thoughts we humans think are stupendous. What, other than God, could coordinate the co-production of our billions of massive, stupendous thoughts? The 5-23-88 *Time* cover-story on the body's immune system said this: "As they probe the intricate workings of the immune system, scientists are awestruck. 'It is an enormous edifice, like a cathedral,' says Nobel Laureate Baruj Benacerraf, president of Boston's Dana-Farber Cancer Institute. The immune system is compared favorably with the most complex organ of them all, the brain." Except that brains and bodies, like immune systems, are at best useful fictions about the choreography of free-moving a-toms. If physical bodies exist at all out here! Thoughts about them do exist, as you can verify by a second thought each time you have a first thought about whether or not bodies exist at all. (How clever of our Creating Parents to make it necessary to use pictures AND thoughts: e.g., if the past thought is the object pointed to as one of the "PLUSSES" of a present thought, it indicates we need a picture of a single complex thought, some of whose "parts" are other thoughts! This poses the challenge to notice BOTH. You DO understand, right?)

You have two options. One is to reject the massive evidence that your "brain" cannot cause your THOUGHTS because such an aggregate of discontinuous, predictably unpredictable a-toms is, in James' words, "a fiction of popular speech" and to cling tenaciously to the blind faith that it's not a fiction. The other is to assent to the thought that your THOUGHTS, like the rest of your experiential field, come from an Agent adequate to the task. The Turing Test applicable to the rows and rose of sense-data 'words' of this VIIth letter can be applied to your THOUGHTS. Does it make mower cents two beleev your THOWT-OPPSHUNS, lyke the roz, r frum mindless aye-junts holy un'awear uv wot their dooing#, or does it make more sense to regard all of this as coming from an Intelligent Being who understands all the laws/rules and who manipulates them at will to achieve certain pre-selected ends?

It is no credit to me that I have believed in God from earliest youth. God gave me "cultural" beliefs appropriate to my "social environment." Like Descartes and James, I also was later coached into a habit of preferring "evident natural reasons" to "blind faith." Years of rethinking took place before 1989 when I FULLY realized what I was assenting to when I said "There is a God." (# PS to the preceding paragraph. In his 10th *WHY*, Martin Gardner quoted Chesterton as saying, to an atheist, that the universe is "the most exquisite masterpiece ever constructed by nobody.") A God who hand-moves every a-tom according to a holistic choreography of increasingly complex laws, ranging from Newton's basic, rough-view laws to complex neurological ones, is already enough to stagger anyone's mind. Long ago, tho, a Hebrew psalmist noted the even more stunning fact under scrutiny here:

Thou hast searched me and known me, O Lord. Thou knowest when I sit and when I stand. Thou knowest my thoughts from afar. My journeys and my rest you scrutinize, with all my ways you are familiar. Even before a word is on my tongue, behold, O Lord, you know the whole of it. Behind me and before, you hem me in and rest your hand upon me. Such knowledge is too awesome for me; too lofty for me to grasp. (Psalm 139)

5.5 billion (+/—1 or 2 billion) thoughts per second?! Not just shuffled, like inert, pre-existent a-toms, but deliberately and freely **CREATED** with goodwill aforethought. Those words are not incomprehensible. The thought they bring is remarkably comprehensible when I read them. It is BECAUSE I understand the thought that it seems unbelievable. But, despite its unbelievability, I DO believe it.

WHY that effort to break down the Secularist Wall between physics and meta-physics? The question is about my real aim. Let what follows continue the effort to break down the Washington Wall of Separation between both of those and ethics. We cannot return to the days of Kristin Lavransdatter, but till we restore the philosophy upon which "In God We Trust" makes sense, the growing "Each other we distrust" mentality will continue to spread. Mill's politics of liberty works only with citizens who understand why sacrifice that may not SEEM to pay off WILL pay off nevertheless. Even for themselves. Only a world-view that we can be confident is true and is compatible with ALL the evidence will provide the needed incentive to do what is necessary to improve world-peace. Only a total case whose parts can switch-hit as either a premise (inductive or deductive) or conclusion for the other parts can provide such confidence. We need a theory to energize each of us to **WORK** for others at least as much as we do for us, rather than to hog whatever we can seize by force or win by cunning. Only a Grand Unifying Theory that includes God and eternity will work. "Virtue is its own reward NOW" is only a half truth. Often, even less.

Start with the fact that, if the century just ending 'demonstrates' anything to the fair-minded, it is that fair-minded plain folk recognize that the Nazis' idea to hog earth's riches for themselves at the expense of others was wrong and that Marx's program, "From each according to their ability, to each according to their need," is right. What is also clear is that THINKING people in general want reasons for sacrificing their own interest in order to benefit others, and that two reasons that are one are most powerful. First, when the mythical 'Invisible Hand' allowed the Nazis to begin over-running a self-absorbed world, FEARS ABOUT THEIR *OWN* FUTURE woke the latter to the need to cooperate with others in sacrificing 'for the benefit of all.' Second, HOPES ABOUT A *SHARED* FUTURE can motivate thousands, even millions, to sacrifice their PRESENT comfort and security to work for the sake of a Marx's modern updating of the ancient Hebrew vision.

But what is also clear from the most recent events is that motivation for self-sacrifice begins to fizzle when i-the fear of harm to SELF subsides, ii-the hope of fairly-SHARED benefits fades, iii-the opportunity to pursue ONE'S OWN betterment regardless of the consequences for others brightens. The balance between ME-and-MINE and all-of-OURS-together is delicate and easily tipped.

And, like a 'virus' that makes a marvelous computer 'crash,' there is a world-ful of facts that further demolish every claim that atheist materialism is *adequate*. The dream of a utopia to be shared BY ALL may provide a reason for doing some of the hardest things of all: continuing to give **MY** best when **I** see others shirk, foregoing the second of the two wrongs that don't make a right when someone strikes **MY** cheek, giving up **MY** fun now for all **OUR** fun later, etc. So long as **I** retain **MY** hope for either a tolerable today or a BETTER TOMORROW, it may make little difference whether God or matter is the source of the LAWS that link today's deeds with tomorrow's consequences.

But **WHAT SENSE DOES SACRIFICE MAKE IF THERE IS NO TOMORROW?** If it's dumb matter, then, as Lucretius argued, *I*'m dead when *I*'m dead, and for **ME** there is no tomorrow. So, if *I* am willing to GAMBLE losing the dog-eat-dog game for the chance to grab ALL the gusto I can get during **MY** one, brief moment on history's stage, what down-to-earth reason will convince **ME** that *I* MUST not?

Yet two of the most revered figures in western history knowingly risked and suffered death in service to others. If none had a future except on this side of the grave, those who prefer 'evident natural reasons' should admit that Socrates and Jesus unreasonably accepted an early extinction: there is no rational reason for one to become extinct sooner in order for another to become extinct later or for others to better enjoy their pre-extinction. Were the myth of Sisyphus not a myth, Socrates and Jesus would represent the supreme kind of suckers in an absurd scenario.

But the intuitions of the revering masses have been right. The call to service, answered best by such heroes, comes from a person-al God. To what purpose? For what reason? To provide humans the chance to EARN lasting rewards more satisfying than the indulgence of SLOTHS, to DESERVE accolades better than praise they know they've done nothing to win, but mostly to be LOVED permanently by one or ones whose love wells up from appreciation for love extended to them. In short, to offer humans the opportunity to make the choices that result in the habits we call "moral character," the kind of habits that alone make happiness seem *deserved*.

> Thus not only our morality but our religion, so far as the latter is deliberate, depend on the effort which we can make. *"Will you or won't you have it so?"* is the most probing question we are ever asked: we are asked it every hour of the day, and about the largest as well as the smallest, the most theoretical as well as the most practical, things. We answer by *consents or non-consents* and not by words. What wonder that these dumb responses should seem our deepest organs of communication with the nature of things! What wonder if the effort demanded by them is the measure of our worth as men! What wonder if the amount which we accord of it were the one strictly underived and original contribution which we make to the world! (PP II:578-79)

APPENDIX

Further Footnote Weaving

Our hearts are restless till they rest in Thee. (Augustine)

A Question With an Assumption. Why is one person born in 1842 rather than a century later? Why is that person born with the body of a man rather than that of a woman? Why with the body of a white rather than that of a black? Why do plain folk believe they can understand purgatory and reincarnation, while some sophisticates believe they can't? Why does anyone believe anything? Why do you? (A note. James several times added appendices to his works. This appendix is really like an extra chapter, though there really are no such things as chapters. It, namely, these shaped, arranged ink marks are added in order to make even clearer ideas proposed in the previous chapters, especially the difference between our own thoughts and others' thoughts. Being clear about this difference must be balanced by the thought that, among our own thoughts are our own thoughts about others' thoughts. Or, more precisely, our own thought-inferences about others' thoughts. And their sensations, memories, feelings, etc.)

Thoughts are behind questions like "Whence come thoughts?" Understood thoughts. And understanding. Understanding the thought that's an answer, understanding the thought that's a question. From the beginning of our learning career, dim snatches of thought must have come. Those that came again, i.e., were 'remembered,' were woven into our earliest belief-system. To the question, "Why did you ever start believing this or that, e.g., that other people are conscious like you and not mindless robots?", the best answer a child could give would be "It didn't occur to me NOT to." Such gullibility leaves us with a naive-realist core of beliefs and an outer rind of cultural constructs.

The task of **Rethinking** such beliefs is needed because earlier-acquired errors form many of the premises upon which other errors rest. So, when a later thought comes to us and poses an alternative to one we have taken for granted, we must ask the question, "Why do I STILL believe such-and-such?" Our answers can range from "Why shouldn't I?", through "I am not aware of any GOOD reasons why I should change my mind," to "I've weighed all the evidence and I'm completely *certain* such-and-such is *true*." (A belief + a confident feeling about its truth = convinced certainty, though not necessarily a belief that is true.) This raises the VIP question:

Should feelings count as evidence?

Sentiments and Evidence. In one of James' most famous lectures, a late (1895) talk that (thank heaven!) he entitled "The **WILL** to Believe" (rather than "The **RIGHT** to Believe") he directed attention to our 'passional nature.' He noted that W. Clifford consulted HIS passional nature when he assented to "It is wrong always, everywhere, and for every one, to believe anything upon insufficient evidence." James showed that a major **MOTIVE** lying behind Clifford's pronouncement was simply the FEAR of being wrong again. A loss of nerve. Which passion we OUGHT to follow depends on specific cases. It is easy to understand Clifford's impassioned condemnation of an investor's decision to risk his rickety ship's passengers' lives for his own mercenary gain. But James focusses on a radically different case: what can justify condemning a not-certain-to-succeed hope of saving one's life when the only alternative is a quite certain death?

When he broached this "**WHY** do you think THAT?" question, James was particularly adamant in his accusation that those who reject God's existence in the name of "science" do so, not on the basis of hard evidence, but on the basis of an arbitrary faith, much the way 'scientists' do when they freely choose to slosh through semantic swamps to reach free-choice-denying determinism. In a sweet line from "Dilemma of Determinism" he made clear his faith that any postulate that matter is ruled by exceptionless sequential laws is "as much an altar to an unknown god as the one that Saint Paul found at Athens." In *Pragmatism's* first lecture, he notes the link between thinkers holding onto their dear theories and their temperaments, leanings, emotions, etc., all part of his effort to work out a theory that would include sentiment—or emotion or passion or feeling or mood (the name's not important when it's their similarities that are of interest)—among the "concrete test[s] of what is really true," tests he lists and discusses in "The Will to Believe" (Sec. VI). What motivates anyone who freely, deliberately chooses one test over another?

I FEEL that it is fitting to end this lengthy 'total case' re the nature of the invisible, intangible, conscious, superintelligent, omnicompetent Being whose unbelievably ingenious actions spring from a completely generous motivation, the Being whose doings and motives are no more look-at-able than mine, the Being who is the cause'l PLANNER of feelings as well as of everything else . . . , fitting to end it with a reference to one of James' most idiosyncratic habits: urging that feelings ARE on the scales when we are 'weighing the evidence' for rival theories and insisting that some (we usually have MIXED feelings!) BELONG there in the case of **some** decisions. If rights such as a **RIGHT**-to-believe existed (they're fictions, as is the will), we could say we have a RIGHT to consult our heart, IF . . .

IF, but only if we have done all of the hard **rethinking** that James did over the course of his lifetime. The 'sentiment of rationality' that HE had in mind was *not* the feeling of someone who simply says "The Declaration of Independence states that I have an inalienable right to the pursuit of happiness and I know I won't be happy unless I believe that I have a brain and that God does not exist, so I have a right to believe those things, regardless of all the evidence to the contrary*." (The democratic AND MORAL! approach to the 'burden of proof' is quite clear: it rests on ANY juror who decides to believe or not believe ANYthing that has important consequences.) No more serendipitous, i.e., Providential, title for this total case could be chosen than the title Clifford chose when he pontificated on the wickedness of assent-without-conclusive-evidence: "The Ethics of Belief."

One big end-point of such rethinking (which then becomes the starting point for RE-believing) is what Descartes and others eventually learned, viz., (to use James' words) "There is but one indefectibly certain truth, and that is the truth that pyrrhonistic scepticism itself leaves standing,—the truth that *the present phenomenon of consciousness exists.*"

And, what is *the most certain of all the thoughts in that stream of consciousness,* is that the present consciousness any of us experiences is our own. That consciousness belongs to but is not identical with me, my self, and I! As Descartes put it, I'm thinking, therefore the I who am doing it must be existing. This first REASONED leap [backwards, as it were] over the naive-realist wall confronts me, as it confronted Descartes, Kant, James, and—before them—Plato and Augustine, with the task of searching IN HERE for MY evidence for what's OUT THERE.

But does anyone else exist? Representationalism, fully recognized by James, led him to make this common-sense claim, a claim that no evidence can shake:

> The only states of consciousness that we naturally deal with are found in personal consciousnesses, minds, selves, concrete particular I's and you's. Each of these minds keeps its own thoughts to itself. There is no giving or bartering between them. No thought even comes into direct *sight* of a thought in another personal consciousness than its own. Absolute insulation, irreducible pluralism, is the law. It seems as if the elementary psychic fact were not *thought* or *this thought* or *that thought,* but *my thought,* every thought being *owned.* Neither contemporaneity, nor proximity in space, nor similarity of quality and content are able to fuse thoughts together which are sundered by this barrier of belonging to different personal minds. The breaches between such thoughts are the most absolute breaches in nature. (PP I:226)

How do we know anyone else exists, though? Doesn't it seem that what we experience are others' bodies, not their selves and certainly not their inside experience? Bertrand Russell, whose "Naive realism leads to physics, and physics, if true, shows that naive realism is false" is a major theme of these pages, added that "It is extraordinarily difficult to divest ourselves of the belief that the physical world is the world we perceive by sight and touch . . . Only LONG REFLECTION can make a radically new point of view familiar and easy." And only a mass of concrete experience will encourage someone who prefers the evidence of clear reason over blind faith to REPEAT that long reflection often enough for it to become familiar. Which is the motive behind periodic inserts such as the following. If it is possible to cross our eyes and make an IT become THEY, we who live in modern times have an easy way of making THEM become IT. If you get hold of Reel Two (B1572) of the *Famous Cities Series: London* packet, examine IT to make sure it has TWO FLAT slide-transparencies marked "Charles Dickens 'Old Curiosity Shop'-Museum" (14), insert THEM into a View-Master stereopticon, and peer into its TWO lenses at the TWO slides, you'll SEE only **ONE** total visual field with **ONE** shop window, **ONE** passerby on the left and another **ONE** on the right, etc. (Unless you cross your eyes.)

The fulcrum upon which the 'total case' argument for God rests is the challenge that whoever sneaks "we" into her or his answer to "**WHY** do you think **ANY** persons exist?"—AFTER imitating James by recognizing the error of naive realism—with**OUT** bluntly acknowledging that (i)she or he has never seen a body (in the naive-realist sense), not even her/his own, that (ii)she or he does not use X-ray vision to monitor OTHER people's insides, not even their brains, and that (iii)she or he can therefore only infer (fancy for "guess") the NON-phenomena named "THEIR thoughts and motives," is not being fully honest. We can't afford to ignore Maslow's idea:

> The existentialist stress on the ultimate *aloneness* of the individual is a useful reminder for us . . . (It) alone makes more problematic and more fascinating the mystery of communication between alonenesses via, e.g., intuition and empathy, love and altruism, identification with others . . . We take these for granted. It would be better if we regarded them as miracles to be explained. (A. Maslow, on p. 57 of *Existential Psychology*, edited by R. May.)

Perhaps the best evidence that others exist is the experiential fact that, though many have argued that no physical world exists (they have done it, if any 'they' exist!), even Bridgeman who said he was a solipsist argued with Russell about it (if either of them ever existed). There is no doubt whatever that the thesis, "Other persons exist," will work. But is it true? The false thesis that the earth is flat "worked" for the Hebrew prophets, "Earth is the center of the universe" worked for Galileo's opponents, and "The sun rises and sets" works for the evening weather report. Our need is for theses that are true. They work BEST. Seeking truth means weighing evidence, and we have a moral obligation to weigh it.

Our *moral obligation* to others is perhaps our strongest evidence for their existence. After all, if Jefferson is right and "Do unto others as you'd have them do unto you" is the first commandment given by those 'who made us,' there must be at least some others. It is the basic assumption in all of our thinking about any social entity and how we are to act vis-a-vis, not just one, but many 'others.' Such acting is largely what we call "co-operating."

> A social organism of any sort whatever, large or small, is what it is because each member proceeds to his own duty with a trust that the other members will simultaneously do theirs. Wherever a desired result is achieved by the co-operation of many independent persons, its existence as a fact is a pure consequence of the precursive faith in one another of those immediately concerned. A government, an army, a commercial system, a ship, a college, an athletic team, all exist on this condition, without which not only is nothing achieved, but nothing is even attempted . . . (James, "The Will to Believe," section vi)

Willing cooperation works best. The more people are needed to (en)force unwilling compliance with the rules, the fewer there will be to educate, to plant, to build, etc. Each of us who knows there will be no utopia for all, that any set of laws designed for international cooperation to benefit the many will exact a heavy toll from some of us, wants to know if the toll borne by us will be borne in vain. We ARE part of a vast System or Cosmos, but NOT the way determinists say, as cogs which affect and are affected by other cogs' doings in rigid, fate-determined ways describable as 'IRON-CLAD laws,' the way determinists also think the flutter of this butterfly's wings now will affect the later flutter of every atom, even those in all other butterflies' wings (a passional act of faith, as shown by the NOT-well-enough-known "three-body problem"). God is the bridge between us—why would God put the world in the hands of madmen?—and i)God adjusts our sense-data and our thought-options to the willings of others (but torture-victims often pass out, unforeseen escape-routes are proposed, etc.), and ii)we are always free to choose our **ATTITUDE** of willingness or unwillingness. This last is pure James.

We are free agents who—despite OLD habits—have ever NEW chances to make UN-habit-ual responses and thereby begin a psychological and/or moral conversion. ("Mores" = "habits.") Children CAN stop rebelling, parents CAN take advice and see whether this or that different approach will "work," spouses CAN decide to begin practicing better what they preach to their kids, everyone CAN strive to love more, etc. That is, how one of us **FREELY CHOOSES** to respond to stimuli that seem (SEEM!) to come directly from other members of "the system" and, by responding, to be indirectly (REALLY!) responsible for the further stimuli the others will experience, is not the outcome of any other hidden parameters than the combination of the Creator's and our willings. The Golden Rule ought to be our yardstick for making free choices, our quintessentially free choices are our choices of what we WILL believe, and to the extent that our 'action' decisions will depend upon what we believe, we should will to believe what's True. This emphasis on ethics is in the titles of Chapters Three and Four, whose big difference re altruism goes to the core of moral character: **WHOSE PLEASURES AND PAINS do we regard as most important?**

The most basic assumption of this entire book is that both we ourselves and others like us exist. (Did you think of that assumption when you read the opening paragraph of this appendix?) That assumption is basic to the distinction between self-interest and altruism. It is basic to the distinction between MY pleasure and pain and OTHERS' pleasure and pain.

"Self-Interested Altruism" is the thesis of all egoists. Everything that has the appearance of altruism can be construed by an egoist as REALLY, in the FINAL analysis, motivated by self-interest. Egoists believe that what's called "altruism" is surreptitious, maybe unwitting, self-interest.

For example, the college student, still groggy from last evening's activities, crawls out from under the warm covers and trudges off to a course about the ethics of Aristotle: "On the Good Life for **YOU**." Why? Because s/he wants to be there? Asked "If you knew FOR CERTAIN! that, like so many who got up yesterday thinking it would be one more day in a long life, you would be lying in a morgue just twenty-four hours later, would you want to spend any of these precious last moments sitting here listening to me?", they answer with a resounding "NO!" Why, then? In order to pass the course or, in some cases, to get a better grade. Why desire that? In order to graduate. Why that? In order to get a BETTER job (it often takes a moment for them to recall what's obvious: history's majority have had jobs without ever going to college), and the qualifier "better" usually translates into "one that I enjoy more" or "one that pays **ME** more." Why more pay? For better clothes, better home, better car, and so on. Better for whom? We wait in vain for someone to say "So I will have more money to send to Mother Theresa to use for the destitute." Of course, the egoists are ready with answer**S** for THAT appearance of genuine altruism: "Like Mother Theresa, you will be giving the money in order to get that FIF (Funny Inside Feeling) that warms the cockles of a do-gooder's heart, for the prestige that goes with magnanimous philanthropy (far more prestige than widows' pence earn), to avoid feeling guilty for being selfish, etc." On the other hand . . .

"Altruism WithOUT a Hook" is meant to recall the cluster of ideas that the old saying, "humility WITH a hook," is a memory-hook for. The prophet Jeremiah wrote "More tortuous than all else is the human heart" long before Dostoyevsky was born, and it is daunting to think of the life-long effort needed to untangle our thoughts about pride and humility, about vanity and modesty, about what's false and what's true. Still, the ETHICS OF BELIEF constrain the ethical person to learn the twists and turns of the human psyche that wants the truth, the whole truth, and only the truth.

For example, we're taught that pride is a great sin. Boasting is the garden variety of pride. From "Self-praise stinks" we can deduce that boasting's bad. What should we do when someone ELSE boasts FOR us, then? The naive response to a nice compliment, e.g., "You did a nice job," is to not just stifle the impulse to reply "I really did, didn't I!" but to say instead, "Oh, no, you shouldn't say that." Why would anyone say that? Because, as astute observers learn, the latter response is preferable from the standpoint of enlightened self-interest, because the 'someone else' will OFTEN not only repeat the compliment but embellish it. The skilled egoist learns how to toss back the small compliment in order to fish for bigger catch: apparent modesty is the hook on the fishing-line. The honestly modest person, on the other hand, goes on to learn an additional next-lesson, the one embodied in "Humility is the truth," and tries to select the truth from such alternatives as "Thank you," "I had a lot of help," "It wasn't bad, but if you knew how many slip-ups I made . . . ," etc. Altruism-without-a-hook is a phrase meant, like humility-without-a-hook, to evoke the idea of "the real thing, baby" vs the counterfeit of the hypocrite. REAL love has many synonyms, e.g., a gift that has no strings attached.

There is no short-cut to self-knowledge. It is said that a favorite piece of advice among the Greeks was "Know thyself." That's harder than it seems. The Powers from whom we await the gift to see ourselves "as ithers see us" normally make this a lengthy learning process. And normally make it seem as if we begin to learn about ourselves from those others who seem to see us. From parents who offer compliments like "Oh, what a good girl!", "You're mommy's big boy!", or "What a darling you are!" From parents who offer corrections like "Naughty child!", "That wasn't very nice," or "Don't you ever think of other people?", etc. *Compliments and corrections.*

LATER, each of us must apply to our views of our self the same Rethinking we apply to all the rest of our ideas. We must weigh judgments from outside against our inside evidence: e.g., our memory of how much we knew (vs our ignorance), of what we were paying attention to (vs distraction or negligence), of our cravings and cringings (the degree of difficulty), and so on. Our forebears and peers have created a vast library of works to help us **notice our DOMINANT motives and attitudes***. It ranges from Moses' *Genesis* and Homer's *Iliad*, through the fables of Aesop and the parables of Jesus, to 1990's *You Just Don't Understand* by D. Tannen and 1993's *The Call of Service: A Witness to Idealism* by R. Coles. Through their 'words, words, words,' the Powers offer us the "giftie" of a mirror into which we can look to learn the truth about where our stature, UP TILL NOW!, ranks on the ideal scale of human greatness. (*The Psalms, those invocations to God handed on from the Hebrew psalmists, offer raw material for an education in the slow revelations shorthanded as "increasing self-knowledge." Beginning with blanket approval for us, "Thy loved ones," and sly attempts at conning God into bashing those wicked enemies "for the sake of Thy reputation," progressing to the birth of the idea that we pray-ers have peccadillos of our own to answer for, culminating in a silent plea for forgiveness even for the sins we do not notice.)

Why Control Your Imagination? is an all-encompassing "argument" for the conclusion that God exists. Plato's narration of the discussion about teaching that Socrates and Meno had on an Athens street long ago was an important step in God's plan to reveal the fuller truth to us about what is actually going on at every moment of our lives: we are enjoying a virtual-reality movie, complete with depth-vision, stereo-sound, smells, tastes, body-feelings, accompanied by a vast backlog of experience-memories, accompanied by thoughts that 'make a world' from such givens and by conversations that present all sorts of thoughts to us, all of which are, however, created and presented to us directly by God. Augustine picked up the thread of argument from Plato and explained God's role as the Inner Guru's coaching whose decibel-level ranges from dead silence to shouted dis—and re-sonances.

Descartes felt an internal coherence between perfect benevolence and truth-telling when he developed the 'ontological* argument" for a Creator who wouldn't dream of giving us minds that do not work well enough to learn what's really going on. James' argument for God zeroes in on the specifics of that coherence sense. There are two major sentiments for anyone seeking truth: cognitive discomfort, a warning against possible (NB!) error, and the sentiment of rationality, the mark of at least a partial, given-its-premises, truth. (*EVERY reason offered for belief in any 'noumenal' reality out there, beyond the perimeter of private experience, is an 'ontological argument.')

Beliefs, motives, attitudes, feelings. Earlier, reference was made to James' rejection of his option to reject belief in God the way he rejected belief in the Absolute, and to the difficulty I had in becoming familiar with his clear distinction between the complex thoughts he labeled "God" and those he labeled "the Absolute." (The same way I had to gradually learn the difference between praying to Our Father and to Jesus, between the idea of one consciousness per person and the radically contradictory theories about three persons in one conscious god or about one person with two nature-al consciousnesses.) No one will understand James' life-long effort to strengthen his argument for God's existence AND his ever-fluctuating portrait of God's or the gods' nature who has not personally wrestled with these complex issues. And no one can become a respectable pluralist who does not personally recognize that every GOD-ist is a UNIQUE ECLECTIC, in exactly the same way every a-THE-ist is. The truth which is the whole truth will respect the many facets of something as infinitely complex as EACH of a real person's MANY beliefs. We OUGHT to note them, then apply G. Kelly's theory that each and every human 'scientist*'—searching, as V. Frankl noted, for meaning or sense in our lives—construes the world with super-ordinate, just-ordinate, and sub-ordinate conclusion-premises. So, why did James believe what he did? At such different moments as when he'd join a James-family dispute, put out a view to one of his classes, pen a new sentence? (*Or, in the vocabulary of James and Chesterton, a "philosopher.")

Providence played Their role throughout, of course. That's the first and most basic answer presented in these pages. Jehovah entrusted James to just THOSE parents who thought just those things and said just those words at just those plural moments in his life, so that the "laws of nature" made it not-unnatural that his memory would be stocked with a variety of theories associated with "God," including those of Jesus, Hegel, Swedenborg, etc. Rather than to, say, other, less sophisticated, staunchly "Roman" Catholic parents. God inserted James into history at just that time-period rather than any other, so that according to the "laws of sociology" he'd early on confront the atheist evolutionists' atomism rather than the neo-Thomists' holistic emphasis on human-eye-level THINGS, i.e., substances, beings, or existents. And so on. Providence takes EVERY first step. No response of ours is possible without Their initiatives.

How would James himself respond to "Why didn't you CONVERT to being an absolutist, an ordinary Jewish, Christian, or Islamic monotheist, or an atheist?" Not by giving the anthropological psychologists' reply: "Whose answer—the psychodynamicist's, the humanist-existentialist's, or the behaviorist's—do you want?" Those 'scientists' don't give direct answers (Zeus and souls are for philosophers, theologians, and off-duty scientists), only guesses for "Why do OTHER people believe?" Not the SAME answers, either, as D. Wulff's 640-page report, *Psychology of*

Religion (1991), informs us. Some believe belief in God started when curious ancestors tried in prescientific times to figure out the origins of storms, floods, and droughts. Others are content to say it starts when recent newborns are later indoctrinated by descendents of those ancestors. More 'scientific' others believe it starts in abnormalities of the temporal lobes, a biological view that opens onto the myth-bound country of "abnormal psychology," i.e., onto the domain of the *Diagnostic and Statistical Manual* (ed'n III-R), *Behavioral Assessment: A Practical Handbook* (3rd ed), *Synopsis of Psychiatry: Behavioral Sciences and Clinical Psychiatry* (6th ed). Were he to read them, James might simply smile, when he realized that these "experts," even those who know something of history, seem doomed to repeating it. He'd mocked classifiers of his own day; see the final chapter of *William James on Exceptional Mental States*. Or consider what T.D. Moder wrote to *Science News* when it reported the problems involved while experts were planning the DSM-IV: ". . . I would like to propose another addition to the guide to mental disorders. I call it DAD, for Disorder Addiction Disorder, which seems to afflict those compiling mental disorders handbooks." See SN 3-14-92, p.171.

Still, dejection might get the better of him, if he knew how those badly-exploited miracles known as the "mass media" have infected the masses with trickle-down mental illnesses and/or thought disorders: the boiling-cauldron myth that anger will implode if you don't let it out, the 'disease' myth that bad habits are addictive diseases, and the myth that the right cocktail of psychotropic drugs can substitute for self-understanding and moral effort.

Unlike today's 'scientific' psychologists, James would NOT answer us SIMPLY by talking about OTHER people and as a matter of 'professional integrity' ignoring his own inner sentiments! He would never have turned the word "introspection" inside out and said that it is a method whereby psychologists study OTHERS' psyches! In fact, it is precisely by studying his reasons for finally believing in the existence of God that we will discover the genuine clarification his 'pragmatism' brings to learning **THE RATIONALITY OF SENTIMENT**. James returned, over and over, to sentimentS as the ultimate test for deciding whether what links today's experience with tomorrow's is an ocean of dumb matter, period!, or whether there is a person-al deity out there. From "The Sentiment of Rationality," thru his own magnificent personality theory presented in *Varieties*, to Lecture III of *Pragmatism* and beyond, this full-time wisdom-seeker who for a time took a job as teacher of physiology and then as teacher of 'psychology AS IF it were a natural science,' built his case for the MORE-than-nature being he named "God." SentimentS play a role as crucial evidence in his case for God.

To cap this *Why Control Your Imagination?* or "A Scientific Ethics" case for God with James' theory of sentiment as truth-test, it is necessary to distinguish possible verdicts from the weight of evidence. For instance, all common-sense JURORS know, without having to go to school for it, that they will be presented with two quite incompatible verdicts, "Guilty as charged!" (not innocent) and "Innocent" (not guilty), and that their task will be to attend to all the evidence—in the form of murder weapon, blood-stained shirt, footprint casts, forensic testimony, eye-witness accounts, proferred alibis, etc.—and decide whether, for either of those verdicts, the evidence reaches the required mark on an invisible yardstick for "certainty." And, as James pointed out in his inspired paragraph on 'the great law of habit itself,' each of us is an arbiter, a judge and jury of one, charged with deciding which of all our thoughts—proposals of possible truths—we freely choose or will to believe.

An integrating reflection. These paragraphs are 'weavings,' not neat syllogisms. The most important puzzle about truth needing to be solved relates to evidence. As James realized, every psychologist—and all of us are psychologists of sorts—must recognize that all of our own EVIDENCE for any belief about OTHER persons, human or superhuman, will be our own personal, private-to-us stream of conscious experience!

James was superconscious of the challenge this 'scientific fact' poses for those who wish to have a psychological science based on what is regarded as unscientific-because-subjective-and-private evidence. (For a thorough presentation of how James dealt with the challenge, see *William James on the Stream of Consciousness*, Ch. II, sec.4.) Clearly, James had good reason to be concerned about this issue. Like the authors of the works referred to above, James did not present his *Principles of Psychology* or *Varieties of Religious Experience* as if they were autobiographies. He offered them as authoritative accounts of *every* normal human being's conscious life. Yet, he candidly acknowledged the following: he began with a premise he couldn't prove, a premise he therefore had to take on faith, viz., that *every normal person's experience is, in essential respects, similar to his own.*

Anyone who wishes to explain all normal human experience must assume that every normal human's experience is, in essential respects, similar to his or her own. That fundamental truth is one that 'scientific' psychologists since Watson have sought to ignore or even deny. The reason is simple. No one can know what *any* experience, such as thinking, thoughts, remembering, memories, feeling, feelings, sensing, or sensations, is like, who does not *personally* think, remember, feel, or sense, and who does not have a thorough, clear, understanding of his or her own personal, private, subjective experiences and of whatever differences there are between them.

A corollary to that fact is that whoever wishes to understand anything of anyone else's experience must rely on their own personal, subjective observations of what seem to be those others' words or bodily behavior. But, since this is impossible, given the fact that no one experiences anything except private sense-data, namely, the TVFs of color, wrap-around sounds, odors, tastes, etc., in his or her own mind, any person's beliefs about others and others' experience will be inferences, guesses, or hypotheses. Whoever lacks such personal experience of their own, e.g., the blind, deaf, anosmic, etc., will be inferring 'something-I-know-not-what.'

A thought. Try to find a chimp, gorilla, bonobo, walrus, or dolphin—or even a dog or cat—that can have such abstract thoughts about subjective experience that is invisible and intangible. Whoever thinks animals can have thoughts about them must then ask how animals can do it? By observation? By introspection? How?

A thesis applied. James would surely HAVE to approve of the method used here to weave his words into a tapestry whose shape will look somewhat different from the shape he gave them (except i-explicitly in some brief stretches and ii-implicitly in some longer ones). Aristotle wove vast amounts of Plato's thoughts into his synthesis, Aquinas wove similar amounts of Augustine's into his, and James wove Paul Blood's words into a presentation of his own inspired pluralism. (See James' "A Pluralistic Mystic") Just so, vast blocks of James' thought about thought, truth, and proof, can be lifted out whole from his detours and fitted together perfectly.

That *exegetical advice* fits with this hermeneutical idea (two bits of jargon for "suggestions about how you can learn **SOMEONE**'s meaning"): there's no way of getting inside someone else's mind except by diving into the ocean of 'words, words, words' they put out. James made our task easy, because he repeatedly commented on the way this or that view of his MIGHT fit with the old-fashioned dualism, etc., even though his (passional) leanings drew him away. The good advice Einstein gave on a related matter can be adapted here: "Don't get stuck on all the things James wrote; pay attention to his predominant thoughts." What seems vague at first becomes clear and distinct later. Consider these words from *Briefer Course*'s "Stream of Consciousness" chapter:

> What is that first instantaneous glimpse of some one's meaning which we have, when in vulgar phrase we say we 'twig' it? Surely an altogether SPECIFIC affection of our mind. And has the reader never asked himself what kind of a mental fact is his *intention of saying a thing* BEFORE he has said it? It is an entirely DEFINITE intention, DISTINCT from all other intentions, an ABSOLUTELY DISTINCT state of consciousness, therefore . . .
>
> It is, the reader will see, the reinstatement of the VAGUE and INARTICULATE to its proper place in our mental life which I am so anxious to press on the attention . . .

Is he trying to draw our attention to what's DISTINCT or what's VAGUE, to the DEFINITE or the INARTICULATE? The answer is BOTH! Some givens—color, taste, feel, etc.—can be distinct, and in relation to them, much of what James discusses at first seems vague*. Until . . . After a great deal of attentive effort, one begins to NOTICE all the PLUS's and all the MORE's that James not only noticed but took so seriously. PLUS's and MORE's that are vague at first but can become habit-ually DISTINCT for us! (*We must not over-stress the initial vagueness. His great ability to convert abstract jargon into everyday terms made him an extremely popular lecturer and writer for the "plain folk.") End of I.S.

Start again. James rejected naive realism. His chapter on sight, written for *The Briefer Course*, offers all the evidence anyone needs for an **INTERNAL CRITIQUE** showing that parts of naive realism utterly contradict other parts. James lived before this century when illogical positivists and unthoughtful analysts tripped over one another in their eagerness to persuade everyone (themselves first of all?) that doubt about "an external world," i.e., reality beyond my experience, is non-sensical. WE live AFTER a century of efforts to pooh-pooh the inescapable end-point of Russell's Einstein-approved "Naive realism, if true, is false; therefore it is false." By exploring every possible alternative to escape the obvious, they have left our libraries bulging with the record of countless dead-ends and thereby greatly increased our confident FEELING that what we **DO** experience is **NOT** starry skies or fleshy hands. That discovery is an invitation to attend more closely to what we do **NOT** have to **ONLY GUESS ABOUT**. Every fresh-faced college student who raises a hand to challenge the claim that "You think you see me, but WHAT YOU SEE is not me!" is new evidence that others, too, recognize a departure from naive realism. Each vain effort they make to find a loophole in its refutation is added 'proof' that (i)Rorty was right to say, on p.88 of *Philosophy and the Mirror of Nature*, that "Everyone understands everyone else's meaning quite well indeed" (at least on this subject!), that (ii)James misleads us when he says that Berkeley didn't deny matter but only said what "matter" means (Berkeley DID deny that there are trees and quads for them to be in, then gave SUBSTITUTE de-finitions to "trees," "quad," etc.), and that (iii)the behaviorists' efforts to reduce the meaning of "consciousness" to "observable behaviors and/or probabilities of observable behaviors" is a futile revolt against *the brute fact that private judgment rules in science as it does in theology.*

The **BOTTOM-LINE** question is simple: when do we **MEAN** only ONE (type of) thing, regardless of what one, two, three, or more names we give **IT**, when do our names **MEAN** TWO or MORE (types of) **THEM**? (See Chapters One and Three, above.)

Enter James. From in here, I guess what's out there. Are there any other persons? Well, what does "other person" mean? This is where James made one great contribution. Acknowledging that the phenomena which Peirce and other Berkeleyans focus on will be the same for both theists and atheists, James concentrated on those other phenomena we call 'a sense,' 'a feeling,' etc. They relate to this fact above all: we grasp and feel the difference between "There's only **IM**-person-al **MATTER** out there" and "There are other **PERSONS**, human and MORE, out there." Experience, he said, comes with PLUSSES or MORES. What that means in terms of the OBJECT-plus is something we find out when we notice that in *Pragmatism*'s Lecture III James explicitly contradicts Peirce and all who treat the doctrine of Transubstantiation—the teaching that during the Mass or Eucharist, bread and wine are changed into the flesh and blood of Christ—as mumbo-jumbo. Those who adopt Aquinas' adoption of Aristotle's teaching on the senses' proper objects believe that, by God's intervention into the normal norms/laws of nature, the bread's and wine's "accidents" (color, taste, power to nourish or intoxicate) miraculously do not go poof! when the priest pronounces words to change invisible substances into other invisible substance**S** (alleged to be one): bread into a divine person's flesh, wine into his blood. Peirce pontificated:

> Thus our action has exclusive reference to what affects the senses, our habit has the same bearing as our action, our belief the same as our habit, our conception the same as our belief; and we can consequently mean nothing by wine but what has certain effects, direct or indirect, upon our senses; and to talk of something as having all the sensible characters of wine, yet being in reality blood, is senseless jargon. ("How To Make Our Ideas Clear," Pt. II.)

As usual, James was the superior thinker, as his retort to Peirce's shallow abstracting* shows:

> Yet in one case scholasticism has proved the importance of the substance idea by treating it pragmatically. I refer to certain disputes about the mystery of the Eucharist. Substance here would appear to have momentous pragmatic

value. Since the accidents of the wafer don't change in the Lord's supper, and yet it has become the very body of Christ, it must be that the change is in the substance solely. The bread-substance must have been withdrawn, and the divine substance substituted miraculously without altering the immediate sensible properties. But tho these don't alter, a tremendous difference has been made, no less a one than this, that we who take the sacrament, now feed upon the very substance of divinity. The substance-notion breaks into life, then, with tremendous effect, if once you allow that substances can separate from their accidents, and exchange the latter. (*Pragmatism*, Lecture III; *Peirce later realized he'd fallen into Berkeley's nominalism.)

It was sheer inspiration that James began his all-out, *Pragmatism* effort to answer the "radical question of life . . . , whether this be at bottom a moral or an unmoral universe", with this medieval doctrine, for the **GOD**-question is about the NATURE of the MOST basic thing (or reality or being, i.e., substance) lying beyond the reach of my direct inspection. The eucharistic 'bread' is a **SACRAMENT**, a **SACRED SIGN** pointing to a divine person. Berkeley saw all of 'nature' as a sacrament of God's mind, a series of signs signalling me about what sense-data God intends to furnish me with next. (Even human 'bodies' are sacraments of other [human] persons, i.e., of responsible, free agents that are non-appearing realities beyond my life-MOVIE of sensed appearances, beyond what Kant called "nature as it appears [to ME]"). The God-question is a simple one: "Is this Grand Show put on by an IT or ITS, or by a PERSON or PERSONS? Before Buber made the I-IT vs I-THOU distinction famous, James had written that for most of us just plain folk . . .

> . . . religion comes in a still further way that makes a veto on our active faith even more illogical. The more perfect and more eternal aspect of the universe is represented in our religions as having personal form. The universe is no longer a mere *It* to us, but a *Thou*, if we are religious; and any relation that may be possible from person to person might be possible here. ("The Will to Believe"; 1896.)

The FEELING accompanying an I-Thou relation is everywhere visible to the trained eye. We FEEL shock if we look through a key-hole to spy on someone and discover an eye looking at us, but we only mutter if a key obstructs our view. Does anyone not FEEL the difference between taking part on a firing squad and taking target practice on a manikin? Between calling abortion "murder" and calling it "removing some tissue"? True, as Piagetians note, children (like primitives vis-a-vis nature, neurologists vis-a-vis brains, or AI experts vis-a-vis computers) tend to personify inanimate things, yet it's an initially-vague-but-later-distinct **MEANING** that GOOD psychologists—which all of us who can answer "Is it animal, vegetable, or mineral?" and the "Is it a person?" follow-up are called to be—must learn to handle with ease in our later, profess-ional thinking. The real difference between the clinician, Carl Rogers, and the rat-study'r, B.F. Skinner, was that between someone who deepened his early-life sense of "Thou" and someone who theory-wise repressed his. (See Chapter Two.)

Hence, even though James continued on with his *pragmatist* effort to define meaning by reference to *future* experience, what he'd actually done was insist on the different meanings of *present* impersonal MATTER vs a *present* PERSON-al God. He had pinpointed our most obvious (after the Cogito) naive-realist belief: our belief that OTHER PERSONS exist, too. Thousands have followed Berkeley in concluding that material bodies don't exist, but even those who discuss solipsism do so without doubting that they are writing for other people. James later confessed to his error:

> I see here a chance to forestall a criticism which some one may make to Lecture III of my *Pragmatism*, where . . . I said that 'God' and 'Matter' might be regarded as synonymous terms, so long as no differing future consequences were deducible from the two conceptions . . . I had no sooner given the address than I perceived a flaw in that part of it . . . The flaw was evident when, as a case analogous to that of a godless universe, I thought of what I called an 'automatic sweetheart,' meaning a soulless body which should be absolutely indistinguishable from a spiritually animated maiden, laughing, talking, blushing, nursing us, and performing all feminine offices as tactfully and sweetly

as if a soul were in her. Would any one regard her as a full equivalent? Certainly not, and why? Because, framed as we are, our egoism craves above all things inward sympathy and recognition, love and admiration. The outward treatment is valued mainly as an expression, as a manifestation of the accompanying consciousness believed in. Pragmatically, then, belief in the automatic sweetheart would not work, and in point of fact no one treats it as a serious hypothesis. The godless universe would be exactly similar. Even if matter could do every outward thing that God does, the idea of it would not work as satisfactorily, because the chief call for a God on modern men's part is for a being who will inwardly recognize them and judge them sympathetically. Matter disappoints this craving of our ego, so God remains for most men the truer hypothesis, and indeed remains so for definite pragmatic purposes.

Even this does not save James' pragmatist theory of meaning, but this is not the place to explain why. Return now to James' idea that 'passional feelings' are one kind of evidence for true, as opposed to false, thoughts. View this footnote written later for Pt. VIII of *The Meaning of Truth* as only one of countless bits of proof that, on the crucial issue of OTHER persons and a person-al GOD, James wasn't thinking only about FUTURE payoffs, but of PRESENT reality. The Inner Teacher Augustine wrote of leaves us in no doubt as to the difference between two kinds of things: **PERSONS** and **NOT**-person **THINGS**. Different feelings help us to sort out our thoughts and then to select which should stay and which can go. At times, God's kibitzing is especially loud and clear: e.g., when we have our own "I think, therefore I am" insight that the rug may be pulled from all my OTHER beliefs, but one remains unshaken, or our own "love is the key" insight that vast amounts of the history of humans' strivings fit under one 'word,' or our own recognition that "No greater love is there than laying down one's life for a friend" only makes sense if my belief in others is not just a dream. "It's person-al out there" is the premise for the Golden Rule and joins the great insights of both Descartes and Frankl. Bertrand Russell, who joined Stout in criticizing James for extending 'pragmatism' beyond beliefs about physical THINGS (atoms, etc.) to divine and human PERSONS (even misanthropes, Russell noted, need to believe in people if they're to have anyone to hate), understood:

> She [his landlady] seemed cut off from everyone and everything by walls of agony, and the sense of the solitude of each human soul suddenly overwhelmed me. Ever since my marriage, my emotional life had been calm and superficial. I had forgotten all the deeper issues, and had been content with flippant cleverness. Suddenly the ground seemed to give way beneath me, and I found myself in quite another region. Within five minutes I went through some such reflections as the following: the loneliness of the human soul is unendurable; nothing can penetrate it except the highest intensity of the sort that religious teachers have preached; whatever does not spring from this motive is harmful, or at best useless. (*Autobiography: 1872-1914.*)

But, **UNDERSTANDING** two verdicts—"GOD is the Creator of me, my thoughts, my ongoing 'world' of sensed givens" vs "My sensed 'world' is an epiphenomenal froth produced as a byproduct of mindless MATTER"—does not FEEL like **PROOF** as to which one is true. Not, that is, until that FACT is fitted into a Grand Unifying View that gives me FELT satisfaction that these BELIEF-OPTIONS come from God and not from my mindless, unconscious brain. Descartes' realization that it IS proof is captured by a question: "Which theory has room for the **CAUSE** of my thought of an omnicompetent, too-good-to-make-it-impossible-for-me-to-learn-the-truth creator?", the question whose flip-side is, "What rival cause'l accounts are AND FEEL inadequate?" James cultivated an eye for the intrapsychic evidence that proves which of the rival thought/theories are FALSE and the true one TRUE. This is clear from a close reading of "Sentiment of Rationality," the prelude and epilogue to the *Briefer Course*, the *Varieties*, Lec. III of *Pragmatism*, *A Pluralistic Universe*, and the chapters of his just-begun *Some Problems of Philosophy*. But only in the last did he undertake a thorough examination of **CAUSALITY**, even tho it was the very premise of his "psychology as a natural science" which assumed for LIMITED PURPOSES ONLY the epiphenomenalist view that conscious states are **CAUSED** by the brain. In it he noted, as Descartes did (*Meditation*

III), that it is my EVER-NEW subjective experience whose **CAUSE** I need to learn about first:

> It is hard to imagine that 'really' our own subjective experiences are only molecular arrangements, even though the molecules be conceived as beings of a psychic kind. A material fact may be different from what we feel it to be, but what sense is there to saying that a feeling, which has no other nature than to be felt, is not as it *is* felt? . . . Biography is the concrete form in which all that is is immediately given [to me]; the perceptual flux is the authentic stuff of each of our biographies, and yields a perfect effervescence of novelty all the time. (*Some Problems of Philosophy*, Chapter IX.)

The solipsist challenge now plays its role. "We" and "our" must be replaced, HABITUALLY!, with "I" and "my" while I conduct the ultimate test of **MY** Grand Unifying View of Everything. The only effervescingly new biography I have access to is my own, even when it contains new and renewed memories of the past. Why not believe Descartes et al, are figments of imagination the way Santa and Kristin Lavransdatter are? Much the way others, if they exist, believe Eve and Homer are? The way Freud*, if he lived, believed God is? My ultimate CHOICES, since I have access solely to this utterly private 'world of experience,' fit onto a two-sided coin: Why **not** believe I alone am a person? Why believe in ANY other conscious, intelligent beings who understand and care about what's going on? "Divine" vs "human" are shorthand for different degrees of intelligence, etc. (*James, in "The Will to Believe," made the point clear: "When the Cliffords tell us how sinful it is to be Christians on such 'insufficient evidence,' insufficiency is the last thing they have in mind. For them the evidence is absolutely sufficient, only it makes the other way. They believe so completely in an anti-Christian order of the universe that there is no living option: Christianity is a dead hypothesis from the start." How many atheist materialists ever REALLY question never-experienced, hypothesized-only brains and OTHER humans?)

Laws (Chapter One) play a key role as evidence. Your brain, even if it exists, is no person and understands nothing of an unseen world beyond it. It has no interest in offering you alternative theories and insisting you are free to choose what to believe. Weigh your evidence by taking a two-stage Turing Test vis-a-vis the question, "What is going on now as I read?" Does it make more sense to conclude that these rows and rose of ciphers trace back to a planner who knew where he was heading on page one, knew the laws uv gramm er; speling. punkchoo ayeshunand who was constantly deciding which of the inspirations presented to him would best contribute to reaching that goal, OR duz "These are effects produced by a mindless automaton" mayk mower? Does it make more sense that **THE THOUGHTS* WHICH COME TO YOU** while, but not BECAUSE, your eyes are scanning these rows and rose of non-words **COME** off a page of shaped and arranged ink marks, or from electromagnetic waves bombarding your rods and cones, or from billions of UN-connected neurons mailing chemical-grams to one another, or from zillions of tiny a-toms dancing at city-block-like lengths from each other, or . . . (*Plato long ago realized that they are **THE! effects** to explain.)

Enough. It is September 29, time to stop expecting any better inspirations on how to wrap up this lengthy case for Adonai. The core of this wind-up is nothing less than the core of the Design Argument: efforts to make sense of experience lead to the insight that the experience I have access to is experience private to me, further efforts to make sense of it challenge me to decide how to respond to two thoughts that jostle their way to the forefront, viz., *that* the whole show is a hallucinatory product of mindless matter and *that* the whole show is a stunning production by a master of orchestration, and only the latter brings satisfying resolution to the earlier, discordant strains of unanswered questions. The real challenge is to find a proof that there are any persons BESIDES myself and the Divine One(s), other than the 'proof' that THAT is what the Divine One(s) insistently force upon me. I am free to re-decide that the universe is like a gooey egg that has SELF-ORGANIZED into 5.5 billion person-islands that temporarily defy the second law of thermodynamics, but I choose to RE-believe that every new follicle and every falling sparrow and every slit-traversing photon are guided in every detail by a Being Who already has chosen a Grand Finale and Who has a infinity of intermediate contingency-plans known as "possible worlds" to use in adjusting to the choices of free-choosing humans who are, first and foremost, free-thinkers and free-lovers of self AND others.

This is where the remainder of James' contribution plugs in. He plunged into the thicket of sentiments to track down its 'laws.' Long before the Grand Players revealed to Heisenberg that They handle a-toms in a magical, miraculous, predictably-UNpredictable way, James zeroed in on the ultimate 'quantum law' of science, the Great Law of Habit. God varies the **SEQUENCES** between humans' TRYINGS and sought-for PAY-OFFS, whether the pay-offs are musical skills, athletic skills, or intellectual skills. Ofttimes people are given rewards they've done nothing to earn ("reward" should therefore be changed to "gift"), other times try-ers are denied the reward they've sought (there are still outcomes: memories of self-centered striving or selfless effort or criminal plotting, etc.), some othertimes people are given what they've sought, whether for themselves, for others, or for both (whether to call such con-**SEQUENT**ial events "good" or "bad" is a matter for free-thinkers' judgments). Foresight and effort, first and foremost the effort to attend to a selected foresight, are key concepts here. Neither of them, not even the proper evaluation of their con-**SEQUENCES** named "sentiments," were overlooked by James.

The rationality of sentiment. God's-eye thinkers long ago spied SOME patterns and regularities correlating thought/knowledge and feeling. The first two: You can't love what you don't know, and What you don't know won't hurt you. From millenia past, it has been known that rationalized lust often yields to the kind of guilt King David felt and confessed. The tie between Dickens' or Marx's anger and 'social' injustice is easily recognizable. The further facts that plain folk whose natural sentiments have not been perverted by overexposure to jaded literary critics who prefer Nietzsche (who preferred Schopenhauer) to Russell (who sided with Hume) warm to *Christmas Carol, Gift of the Magi,* and *It's a Wonderful Life,* and are appalled by stories of Armenians buried to their necks in a field before galloping horses are turned loose, by photos of emaciated prisoners emerging from Auschwitz, and by TV scenes of gaunt Sudanese whose starvation tracks outward to fanatics deaf to the pleas of reason, are no brute facts. Nor are they the products of a mythical reification named "natural selection." They are signs of God's judgement. If there's a god to make it, that is. Re-enter James. Again.

Grasping James' case for Allah and a moral universe is achieved by taking our eyes away from what James **SAYS he's doing**, namely, focussing ONLY on a thought BECOMING true in the future or—as he put it—on the MEANING of "true belief" having reference to future consequences, and noticing what ELSE he **IS doing**, namely, focussing on the PRESENTLY-FELT difference between two belief-options and their naturally correlated sentiments. The 'natural' outcome of pondering a god-less universe is what Schopenhauer gave his life to glorifying: pessimism. The nature'l outcome of pondering a properly-conceived God-ful world is what inspires utopians: joy. After amassing his evidences, reports of a grand variety of humans' experiences, James concluded *Varieties* with a thought that, characteristically, he credited to someone else, Edmund Gurney: the difference between the unmoral and the moral views is the difference between "a life of which the keynote is resignation and a life of which the keynote is hope." Wisdom, then, will eventually yield . . .

SERENITY-PRODUCING SECURITY.

His model of a total thought connects directly with what he had in mind. For instance, picture your self and your other-self friend sitting atop Sugerloaf Mountain, enjoying the view. Below are fields, roads, towns, a river. Off to the left lie more tree-covered mountains, on the right the river stretches out to where earth and sky meet. The deep blue of the sky is a backdrop for lazily-drifting clouds whose slowly-changing formations are no match for the swiftly-changing thoughts inside as you talk over all that's been going on lately.

What is going on, tho? Focussing solely on the outside organism-environment relation, as we, like the behaviorists, too often do, is utterly inadequate. Come inside. Is this PLEASURE? Of course. Who would not ENJOY drinking in nature's beauties in the company of one who loves you? Well . . . Babies, hyperactive kids, Alzheimer-folk wouldn't. That's just for openers. The answers become endless once we begin to remember, attend, and notice everything. Imagine you've driven rather than hiked to the summit. Your ENJOYMENT is partly dependent upon the COMFORTABLE expectation that your car is still where you parked it, that it will start again when it's time to leave, that the key's in your pocket and not locked in the car. The list of things that could nibble at your SERENITY is long. What if: you learned that your house is being burglarized (or worse, on fire), your boss is drawing up plans to lay you off, you will lose your health insurance as a result, you have a tumor just starting to take hold in your brain . . . or s/he has one, etc. The total experience has arrows pointing out toward the past (memory) and the future (anticipation), but also toward presently unobserved realities. It is the *present*, background assumptions about *what-is-now!* that yield—change that! to "are correlated with"—much or most of our present SERENE SENSE OF SECURITY.

How soon in life (if ever) we learn God's-eye views and begin to feel the NATURAL emotions that NORM-ally accompany such emotion-laden grand-vistas is unpredictable. The calendar-dates are not the automatic outcome of neat "stages" of growth-and-development, as the wise, like Hume, learn from experience. The Old Ones pick the time and place for such revelations. Ultimate pay-offs may be preceded by earlier experiences, even for atheists. A remarkable instance of this can be found in the life of I. Lepp who, later on, defended atheists against intolerant theists in his *Atheism in Our Time*. He told how his first step toward a tolerant theism was taken via an explicit atheism, inspired by M. Gorki's novel, *Mother*. Reading it turned his life upside down.

> Gorki's novel opened before me an entirely new horizon. With some astonishment I learnt that for millions of men and women, the outcasts of the earth, Communism shed a glow of hope over everything. According to him, even before it could change the social order, it would change men—such men, at least, as had made it the one object of their lives. (*From Karl Marx to Jesus Christ.*)

James, who dedicated *Pragmatism* to John Stuart Mill, a leader in social reform movements, knew from Mill's autobiography of the latter's psychological crisis, precipitated when the enthusiasm he'd previously derived from visions of a godless utopia suddenly collapsed. James argued that such visions simply cannot sustain joy and enthusiasm for anyone who refuses to turn a blind eye to the tragedian's facts. In Lecture III, he says: look down the road to the total extinction predicted by the laws of nineteenth-century thermodynamics. All our efforts and all our ideals are doomed to eventual oblivion. The 'whole truth' (if that's what it is) should be EXPECTED to produce **PESSIMISM**! Many recent writers have made attempts to capture the sense James described in his Lecture III. B. Russell gave it a stunning formulation, part of which is this:

> . . . that all the labours of the ages, all the devotion, all the inspiration, all the noonday brightness of human genius, are destined to extinction in the vast death of the solar system, and that the whole temple of Man's achievement must inevitably be buried beneath the debris of a universe in ruins-all these things, if not quite beyond dispute, are yet so nearly certain, that no philosophy which rejects them can hope to stand. (A sample from "A Free Man's Worship.")

This might be true, of course, if earth, sun, and so on, existed. Why does Russell, the modern thinker who constantly repeated the falsity of naive realism, who acknowledged the wisdom of adopting a "useful-fiction" attitude in modern physics where theories are built on imaginative constructs, and who gave as much attention to solipsism as anyone did, here pontificate so naively? Why did he state his unworship in terms of matter no one's ever seen? Why, indeed?! When another, more norm-al alternative is at hand? And one that Yahweh 'nature-ally' inclines us toward? How? By attaching a sentiment of **OPTIMISM**, hope, even joy to it.

It has become customary in presenting the recent chapters in the history of psychology, to distinguish the structuralist approach which describes the ingredients of humans' experience from the functionalist approach which puts them back into a real-lives framework by asking: "What is this or that ingredient's role in a human's life?" Belly-bound folk ask: Do we eat to live or live to eat? A cognitive or Socratic functionalist will ask: Do we know to live or live to know? Is knowing's purpose survival of the fittest or is this life's goal the joy of knowing and loving? If the chapter headings of *The Principles* seem to emphasize the "structuralist" side of James' psychology, the *Varieties* present the true "functionalist" context for them. Once in possession of the latter, it is easy to read *The Principles* again and see how saturated it is with his one, early-chosen, functionalist vision. Equipped with the full sweep of James' thought, we can recognize that it offers the capstone to the history of science, i.e., the search for the True reasons for all True beliefs: WHY we've been created free to choose which beliefs we'll freely live by.

Moral character should be our priority. What psychologist has so completely joined ancient wisdom and modern insight as James? Is there any wise person who would not trade in the entire heap of pages from the pen of Freud for Lecture VIII of James' *Varieties* all by itself? In his despairing *Myth of Sisyphus*, Camus wrote that the deepest desire of our mind, which is to understand, is the desire "above all, to unify," a truth further evidenced by every new reference to some physicist's misguided quest for a mathematical Grand Unifying Formula.

In his *Varieties* Lecture entitled "The Divided Self, and the Process of its Unification," James put this human quest to make sense of life into the broader, moral context. Moral efforts are most likely to succeed when they are guided by an intellectual unification. He knew rethinkings and accompanying habit-changes can range from those that appear to succeed instantaneously, through those that seem to drag on for years, to those that seemingly don't succeed. His tribute to the genius of Augustine who gave "an account of the trouble of having a divided self which has never been surpassed" is a tribute to his own psychological insight. To his conflation of Augustine's account of how he TRIED and TRIED until, finally, he SUCCEEDED (rewarded by God who decided he'd tried enough), he adds a P.S. connecting it to his texts on habits and willing:

> There could be no more perfect description of the divided will, when the higher wishes lack just that last acuteness, that touch of explosive intensity, of dynamogenic quality (to use the slang of the psychologists), that enables them to burst their shell, and make irruption efficaciously into life and quell the lower tendencies forever.

His texts on habits and will (useful fictions)—*The Briefer Course*'s chapter on "Will" ends with the words copied on an earlier page—are masterpieces. They are the antidote to those who attack the OFTEN-simplistic advice to "Just use your will-power!" with equally-simplistic theories that lay the blame for failure, for mental illness*, for addiction—for all human miseries!—on sick societies, bad genes, hormonal imbalances, misfiring neurons, automatic thoughts, predestination, fate, etc. The time has come to boldly attack ALL simplistic thinking the way James did. It is **TIME FOR HARD RETHINKING**. To ask why, as soon as our attention is relaxed, we revert from NON-naivete and a-toms to the naive world of trees, quads, and body-people whose meanings are in their words and feelings in their expressions (so we could EARN pay-off revelations by a QUEST for certainty). And then to explain why laws at the macroscopic level are so rigid and laws at the sub-atomic level so unrigid (so we could CHOOSE determinism or reject it). And then to concentrate on the most important laws of human psychology: the range of linkages between the compulsive's first surrenders and later obsessions, earlier hearings and day-long replayings of a tune in one's imagination, brain-sneezes and altered consciousness, ingestion of newly-discovered medicines and restored normality, ingested ice-cream and tasty pleasure. James' idea of 'habit' is ample enough for all these CORRELATIONS, even as it helps to reconnect today's discoveries with ancient wisdom. It also goes one step further. (*"Physical" illness is mythical as well, though pain isn't.)

This invincible rationalist returned over and over to the links between ONE grand vision and **OPTIMISM** and between a RIVAL grand vision and **DEPRESSION**. His *Varieties*, subtitled "A Study in Human Nature," puts the grand question to every would-be grand-unifier: What do you make of those marvelous experiences described by so many as indescribable . . . , when, i.e., they're not described as **MYSTICAL**, ineffable, beyond reason, super-nature'al, other-worldly, etc. In the last fifth of that "Study," he summarized his answer, the answer he argued for many times over. They are signs that our ideals-pursuing lives are not tiny candles that flicker for an instant in an eternal darkness, but intimations of the rarely-glimpsed ideals-Source. In terms of recent history, Sartre's *Nausea*'ous epiphany is the natural outcome of an effort to make sense of life by postulating that there's no God to hamper our freedom, whereas Frankl's death-camp epiphany is a revelation of the Truth that all the stirrings, the bloomings, and the raptures which "beauty," "truth," and "love" bring to mind are gifts of Person-al Givers often named Beauty, Truth, and Love Itself.

As is our freedom itself. We are free to wreak wholesale chaos or to improve the world by hardly noticeable deeds, free to blast yet another modern city to rubble or to forge agreements on ways to rebuild, free to press on in killing and maiming others or to risk being the first to be killed or maimed in going to the aid of others, free to exploit 'natural resources' for our selfish pleasure or to join in world-wide efforts to share them.

But the fact that we'll be "cut in on eternal rewards," the inconceivable fact that, as athletes pay the price of immediate gratification foregone, effort expended, and pain endured for the prize they willingly strive for, so we can deserve the love of each other if we are willing to pay a similar price, is the mark of Givers who are as much, or even more!, concerned to add to our bliss than to win applause.

The serenity that comes from knowing that no enemy can change the fact that we will never be in any enemy's power but always in God's hands is serenity synonymous with security. Encourage'd by that serenity, we can imitate God whose sun rises and showers fall on just and unjust alike: the love given us is best repaid by giving it to others. Extended to those who love us, love's not so hard. When it's extended to one who wrongs us, it's called "patience" before s/he repents, "forgiveness" afterwards. This love's not so easy. But even then, as James realized, it's easy-ER when we UNDERSTAND the Truth about what's REALLY going on.

Do you understand? Do you? You?!

You!

THE END

Select Bibliography/Further Reading

(The following is a list that offers information about some of the works explicitly named in the text as well as others that supply additional background reading. Many citations by various authors are from Flew's and Ruitenbeek's marvelous anthologies.)

For Chapter One: Intelligo

Further information on the common sense that is everyone's first philosophy can be found in *William James on Common Sense: the Foundation for all Higher Learning.* one of several books, written after *Will You Control Your Imagination*, that I've had published.

Ayer, A.J., *Language, Truth, and Logic*. (One of the clearest and most influential works on logical positivism.

Block, N., ed., *Readings in Philosophical Psychology*, 2 volumes. (1981 collection of classic writings on philosophy of mind, philosophical psychology, plain psychology, etc. Are they really distinct?!)

Brett, G.S., *Brett's History of Psychology*, in a 1963 abridgement revised and updated by R.S. Peters. (A history of 'philosophical' and 'empirical' psychological theories.)

Bruner, J., *In Search of Mind: Essays in Autobiography*. (A first-hand, 'insider' account, by the author of *Acts of Meaning*, of his own experience during the 'revolutions' in the field.)

Bryson, B., *A Short History of Nearly Everything*. (A popular survey of modern discoveries in various fields of 'science.')

Copleston, F., *Aquinas*. (Copleston is the author of several volumes spanning more than twenty centuries of Western philosophy, all written from a reliable, Thomistic vantage point.)

Dawkins, R., *The Magic of Reality: How We Know What's Really True*. (Dawkins' naive-realist view ("we have fossils, and we can see *them* with the naked eye"!) of the need to control our imaginations. Highly recommended as a beautifully written, 2011 rebuttal to *Why Control Your Imagination?* which is a rebuttal of Dawkins' type of philosophy. You get to choose which is true, by learning about and then controlling your imagination.)

Einstein, A., *Ideas and Opinions*. (A collection of essays, brief and not so brief, that provide the core of Einstein's theory of scientific knowledge, according to which Dawkins' idea of observation is a "plebeian illusion." My own *The Wonderful Myth Called 'Science'* elaborates Einstein's theory of knowledge in some detail.)

Hall, C.S. & Lindzey, G., *Theories of Personality*. (A text that explains the chief elements of 'personality' psychologists ranging from Freud & Jung to existentialists. The Murray quote is from the chapter on his personality theory.)

Hunt, M., *The Story of Psychology*. (An outstanding presentation for non-experts of the history—and the philosophical pre-history!—of 'scientific' psychology.)

Maddi, S., *Personality Theories: A Comparative Analysis*. (Unlike Hall-Lindzey, Maddi concentrates on showing the similarities and differences between those same psychologists.)

Maritain, J. *Creative Intuition in Art and Poetry*. (One of Maritain's several efforts to incorporate modern physics, politics, and psychology into the Thomistic synthesis.)

Ruitenbeek, H.M., *Varieties of Personality Theory*. (Copies of this out-of-print paperback, when available, furnish a matchless collection of core original writings that range from Freud's "Clark Lectures" and the ninth chapter of Jung's *Modern Man In Search of a Soul* to Dollard & Miller's behaviorist version of human learning.)

For Chapter Two: Video Aliquid, Ergo Sum

For a brief introduction to the astonishing diversity of opinions among 'professional' philosophers and psychologists regarding what-we-experience, nothing is so accessible and reliable as the following website available from the *Stanford Encyclopedia of Philosophy* entitled "Mental Representation": [plato.stanford.edu/entries/mental-representation/] That, plus several "competing" websites that can be Googled by the word "representationalism."

Further efforts to convey what I regard as the truth about what we experience, explained in 'everyday vocabulary' rather than 'technical jargon,' can be found in the following books: *You Are Human: What's That?*, *William James on the Stream of Consciousness*, *James Vs Darwin*, *Science: God's Hard Gift*, and *The Wonderful Myth Called 'Science.'*

Baars, B., *The Cognitive Revolution in Psychology*. (An irreplaceable collection of interviews with such behaviorists as Skinner and such cognitivists as Neisser. The differences in their own words.)

Bridgman, P., *The Logic of Modern Physics*. (The pioneer operationalist.)", *The Way Things Are*. (By a professed—or tentative?—solipsist!)

Chomsky, N., *Language and Mind*. (Three somewhat revised lectures on the history and future prospects of linguistics, including a critique of behaviorist 'science.')

Coles, R., *Dorothy Day*.

Evans, R., *Carl Rogers: the Man and His Ideas*. (A lengthy interview with Rogers, plus some chapters by Rogers himself.)

Flew, A., ed., *Body, Mind and Death*. (A matchless anthology of writings on those topics by major thinkers from Hippocrates to Putnam.)

Gardner, M., *The Why's of a Philosophical Scrivener*. (A perfect "re-thinking" tour of traditional 'philosophical' questions, beginning with "Why I Am Not a Solipsist.")

Humphrey, G., *Thinking: An Introduction to Its Experimental Psychology*. (A fine presentation of the Wurzburg vs the Ithaca introspecting psychologists.)

Hunt, M., *The Universe Within: a New Science Explores the Human Mind*. (An excellent presentation of cognitive psychology for the non-expert. As well as for the beginning expert!)

Huxley, T., "On the Hypothesis that Animals are Automata and its History"; in Flew.

Kelly, G., "A Summary Statement of a Cognitively-Oriented Comprehensive Theory of Behavior," in J. Mancuso, ed., *Readings for a Cognitive Theory of Personality*. Kelly's alternative to the behaviorists' philosophy.)

Kim, Jaegwon, *Philosophy of Mind*. (A recent, up-to-date introduction to the intricacies of the current 'philosophical' efforts to invent new distinctions in efforts to give a materialist explanation of consciousness. Read the reviews by Will Tanizaki and Peter Bogaerts at Amazon's listing of the book!)

Kirchenbaum, H., & Henderson, V.L., *Carl Rogers: Dialogues*. (A collection of Rogers' conversations and debates with Skinner, May, and others.)

Koch, S., editor, *Psychology: A Study of a Science* (6 volumes of essays by the leading psychologists of the mid-twentieth century, each charged with describing what they regarded as important achievements of that science. Many of the Rogers quotes are from his essay.)

_____ & Leary, D.E., eds., *A Century of Psychology as Science*. (Over 900 pages of essays similar to the preceding; they provide a snapshot of what Bruner described as a science that "has become fragmented as never before in its history.")

Kohler, W., *Gestalt Psychology*, 1947. (Mentor Books., 1959; original 1927)

O'Donnell, J.M., *The Origins of Behaviorism: American Psychology, 1870-1920*. (N.Y., NYU Press, 1985; an excellent, detailed history.)

Robinson, D.N., "Wisdom Through the Ages," in R.J. Sternberg, ed., *Wisdom: Its Nature, Origins, and Development*.

Rogers, C., "A Theory of Therapy, Personality, and Interpersonal Relationships, as Developed in the Client-Centered Framework." (The best overall presentation by Rogers of his philosophy; found in Volume 3 of Koch's *Psychology: A Study of a Science*.)

Rorty, R., *Philosophy and the Mirror of Nature*.

Skinner, B.F., *About Behaviorism*. (Skinner's explanation, not of behaviorism, but of "the philosophy of behaviorism.")

_____ , "Debate with C. Rogers," in Kirchenbaum & Henderson.

Wann, T.W., *Behaviorism and Phenomenology: Contrasting Bases for Modern Psychology.* (Revealing! presentations plus q&a sessions, by S. Koch, R.B. MacLeod, N. Malcolm, C. Rogers, M. Scriven, and B.F. Skinner.)

For Chapter Three: Self-Interested Altruism

A brief but clear introduction to fictions, theoretical constructs, pragmatic concepts will be found in *Logical Fictions: Tools for Learning the Facts.*

Barrett, W., *Death of the Soul: From Descartes to the Computer.* (A sweet history of attempts by psychologists and philosophers to 'banish consciousness' from the modern worldview.)

Coles, R., *Simone Weil.*

Einstein, *Ideas and Opinions (My own The Wonderful Myth Called 'Science'* explains Einstein's epistemology.)

Ellenberger, H., *The Discovery of the Unconscious.* (A monumental history of efforts to find models that take account of the less noticeable features of our consciousness; there literally is no unconscious, unless it would be the brain, were there such a thing.)

Flanagan, O., *The Science of Mind.* (A survey of Descartes body-mind theory and of recent efforts to replace his dualism with a materialist view of human consciousness.)

_____, *Dreaming Souls.* (Typical attempt to explain what is surely subjective experience without any need to have ever had an experience—even a dream—of one's own!)

Hacking, I., *Rewriting the Soul.* (A sober exploration of 'multiple personality' phenomena.)

Herbstrith, W., *Edith Stein: a Biography.*

Kuhn, T., *The Structure of Scientific Revolutions.* (Chicago, UofC Press, 2nd ed., 1970)

McMullin, ed., *Construction and Constraint: the Shaping of Scientific Rationality.* (Notre Dame, In., NDPress, 1988; essays on 'science,' in response to Kuhn's thesis.)

Peele, S., *Diseasing of America.* (Is alcoholism a disease?)

Podvoll, E.M., *The Seduction of Madness*. (A thought-provoking exploration of schizophrenia, presented via actual cases.)

Weil, S., *Waiting for God*. (A collection of her letters and a few essays.)

For Chapter Four: Altruism Without a Hook

(The three chapters of my *William James on the Stream of Consciousness* use James' writings to explain the topics of this chapter in a more 'textbook' style than here. *The Essence of Ethics* offers what could be viewed as a 'philosophical' brief for St. Therese's "Little Way.")

Angelou, M., Opening pages of "That Which Lives After Us," in Woodruff, P., and Wilmer, H.A., *Facing Evil: Light at the Core of Darkness*. (Simply inspiring.)

Doyle, B., *Free Will: the Scandal in Philosophy*. (A nearly exhaustive listing, sampling, and critical review of theories of determinism—Freud's and Skinner's included—that purport to deny free will.)

Guntrip, H., *Psychoanalytic Theory, Therapy, and the Self*.

McMahon, D.M., *Happiness: A History*. (Everyone interested in the theories of all the great Western thinkers re ethics and morality will find this book indispensable.)

Ramachandran, V.S., and Blakeslee, S., *Phantoms in the Brain*. (Recent treatment of phantom limb phenomena. Though the text states that what we experience and think is our biological body is actually a 'phantom body,' the author is basically a materialist!)

Russell, B., *My Philosophical Development*.

Shepard, R.N., and Cooper, L.A., *Mental Images and their Transformations*.

St. Therese of Lisieux, *Story of a Soul*, trans. R. Knox. (Her best-seller autobiography.)

For Chapter Five: The Pinnacle

For a comparison of James' science vs Darwin's philosophy, see *James Vs Darwin: James' Psychology Trumps Darwin's Biology*.

James, W., *Pluralistic Universe.*
_____, *Principles of Psychology.*
_____, *Psychology: Briefer Course.*
_____, *Some Problems of Philosophy.*
_____, *Talks to Students. (Usually with Talks to Teachers.)*
_____, *Varieties of Religious Experience.*

APPENDIX

The answer to the all-important question, "What is the cause or source of your own stream of consciousness?" is "It's either your brain or God." For a brief introduction to the astonishing diversity of opinions among 'professional' philosophers and psychologists regarding cause and/or causation, see the numerous online websites. One that is especially helpful in grasping the difference between correlations (many of which are referred to in this Appendix) and causation is "Correlation and Causation | Experiment-Resources.com". [www. experiment-resources.com]

YOUR INDEX

(No index is included. That is why there is a detailed table of contents. However, you will find it convenient to make a list of some important titles and/or names *and page numbers*, if, while you are reading, you come across an idea that you will want to return to again. That is why the next few pages are left empty, except for some letters at the top.)

A-E

F-J

K-O

P-S

T-Z

Printed in Great Britain
by Amazon.co.uk, Ltd.,
Marston Gate.